ISBN 978-0-282-44282-8
PIBN 10851913

1 MONTH OF
FREE
READING

at
www.ForgottenBooks.com

By purchasing this book you are eligible for one month membership to ForgottenBooks.com, giving you unlimited access to our entire collection of over 1,000,000 titles via our web site and mobile apps.

To claim your free month visit:
www.forgottenbooks.com/free851913

English
Français
Deutsche
Italiano
Español
Português

www.forgottenbooks.com

Mythology Photography **Fiction**
Fishing Christianity **Art** Cooking
Essays Buddhism Freemasonry
Medicine **Biology** Music **Ancient
Egypt** Evolution Carpentry Physics
Dance Geology **Mathematics** Fitness
Shakespeare **Folklore** Yoga Marketing
Confidence Immortality Biographies
Poetry **Psychology** Witchcraft
Electronics Chemistry History **Law**
Accounting **Philosophy** Anthropology
Alchemy Drama Quantum Mechanics
Atheism Sexual Health **Ancient History**
Entrepreneurship Languages Sport
Paleontology Needlework Islam
Metaphysics Investment Archaeology
Parenting Statistics Criminology
Motivational

A PLACE CALLED JACKSON HOLE

The Historic Resource Study of Grand Teton National Park

BY

John Daugherty

WITH CONTRIBUTIONS BY

Stephanie Crockett
William H. Goetzmann
Reynold G. Jackson

GRAND TETON NATIONAL PARK
NATIONAL PARK SERVICE

A PLACE CALLED JACKSON HOLE

The Historic Resource Study of Grand Teton National Park

BY

John Daugherty

WITH CONTRIBUTIONS BY:

Stephanie Crockett
William H. Goetzmann
Reynold G. Jackson

GRAND TETON NATIONAL PARK
NATIONAL PARK SERVICE

To Chuck McCurdy, thanks for the chance.
To my wife, Susan, and my daughters, Laura and Elizabeth,
for their love and support. —*The Author*

Book Design Jennifer and Lee Ballentine
Copyediting Kate James
Full-Service Production Professional Book Center
Cover Images Top left: photo by W.D. Johnston, Dedi-
cation of Grand Teton National Park, July 29, 1929,
courtesy of Grand Teton National Park; top right: Jack
Huyler playing guitar, courtesy of the Jackson Hole
Historical Society and Museum; center: Grand Teton
National Park, Old Jackson Hole Road, courtesy of the
National Park Service; bottom left: Indian with travois,
courtesy of the Jackson Hole Historical Society and
Museum; bottom right: farmer working land that is
now part of the National Elk Refuge, courtesy of
Grand Teton National Park.

1999 Moose, Wyoming Grand Teton National Park
First Edition   9 8 7 6 5 4 3 2 1

Contents

United States Department of the Interior

NATIONAL PARK SERVICE
GRAND TETON NATIONAL PARK
P.O. DRAWER 170
MOOSE, WYOMING 83012

Foreword

". . . to conserve the scenery and the natural and historic objects and the wildlife
therein . . ." *National Park Service Act of 1916*

"WHEREAS the area in the State of Wyoming known as the Jackson Hole country .
. . contains historic landmarks and other objects of historic and scientific interest . .
." *Federal Register of March 18, 1943, establishing Jackson Hole National
Monument*

The beauty of the Tetons' jagged skyline piercing the sky above the flat expanse of Jackson Hole is an
image known worldwide. As Historian William H. Goetzmann notes in Chapter 18, the Tetons ". . . are
among the most familiar landmarks in the American West." Images of the Teton Range appear in
everything from television advertising to Hollywood movies. The Tetons have become a romantic and
idealized image of what all mountains should look like, mountains of the imagination. What can easily be
overlooked in this stunning landscape is the human element. The wild and rugged view we see preserved
today does not easily reveal that people have been living in the shadow of the Tetons for almost 11,000
years.

The *Historic Resource Study of Grand Teton National Park*, as this document is officially called, provides
an understanding of that human experience. This human or "cultural" view fulfills part of the National
Park Service (NPS) mission to protect and interpret all of its resources, including those created by man.
The project began in the 1980s as part of an effort to gain a better understanding of Grand Teton's historic
buildings and structures. Park Historian John Daugherty wrote the study, but the manuscript was left
unpublished after John transferred to another NPS unit in 1991. In 1995, Grand Teton initiated a much
larger survey and evaluation of historic resources, and the value of the *Historic Resource Study* and the
need to share its wealth of information became even more apparent. In 1996, Grand Teton National Park's
Cultural Resource Specialist Michael Johnson applied for and received a NPS grant to complete and
publish the manuscript.

Grand Teton National Park is indebted to two individuals who made the completion of the study possible.
John Daugherty devoted substantial time and effort to editing his manuscript. The second individual who
deserves our thanks is NPS Historian Christine Whitacre who, at the request of the park, acted as editor and
publishing project manager. Under Christine's direction, additional chapters on mountaineering,
prehistoric life, and the artistic portrayal of the Tetons were contracted for and added to complement John's
work.

Most importantly, this study helps us understand the significance of the park's cultural resources, and
provides valuable data for cultural resource management and interpretive planning. The human record is
extensive, from American Indian prehistoric life, to the early Euro-American explorers, and the more recent
settlement period that left a legacy of over 260 historic buildings. Jackson Hole is a very special place.
The sublime scenery, the "old west" flavor, and wildness that ancient Native Americans knew makes Grand
Teton National Park one of America's crown jewels. I hope this presentation of the human story of this
mountain valley enhances your perception and appreciation of "A Place Called Jackson Hole."

Sincerely,

Jack Neckels, Superintendent

A Place Called Jackson Hole

Introduction

As members of society and sharers in the historical process, historians can only expect to be heard if they say what the people around them want to hear—in some degree. They can only be useful if they also tell the people some things they are reluctant to hear—in some degree.

—William H. McNeill, *Mythhistory and Other Essays*, 1986

When Chief Naturalist Chuck McCurdy hired me to fill the park historian position at Grand Teton National Park in 1980, had anyone told me I would work and live there for 11 years, my response would have been "no way." Nor did I envision writing a history of Jackson Hole. Plenty of histories had been written about the valley, so why write another?

Like everything else the federal government does, the answer lies in federal law, in this case a law titled the National Historic Preservation Act of 1966. It created the National Register of Historic Places which, for the first time, recognized sites, districts, buildings, and structures of local, state, and national significance. None of the histories of Jackson Hole evaluated any of these resources systematically or in the depth needed to nominate properties to the National Register. For this reason, I researched and wrote this history.

Officially, this document is a Historic Resource Study (HRS), a National Park Service baseline research report. Its main goals are threefold: (1) prepare a historical overview of the park; (2) collect, evaluate, synthesize, and present results of research concerning the historic resources of Grand Teton National Park; and (3) develop narratives of historic contexts appropriate to the park and its resources.

A context organizes information based on a cultural theme within a geographical and chronological framework. The table of contents is a list of contexts.

In addition, I added two purposes very important to me and, I hope, to the park and public. First, as a park interpreter, I prepared this study to provide baseline information for educational and interpretive purposes. In my experience, too many cultural resources reports do not serve interpretation well, and as a result, go unused, gathering dust on a shelf. Finally, history, in addition to being as accurate as sources allow, is at its best a good story. I hope readers will find this a good story.

There are two things this study does *not* do. Because of limited time and funding, I concentrated my research on gathering information relevant to properties and sites in the park. With few exceptions, I did not conduct detailed research on properties outside park boundaries. Nonetheless, the contexts of the chapters apply to the general history of the valley. Also, I did not write about events well documented in other histories of Jackson Hole, such as the shoot-out at the Cunningham cabin and the so-called "Indian Scare of 1895."

I initiated this project in 1984 by preparing an inventory of more than 400 buildings and structures within Grand Teton National Park. Research and

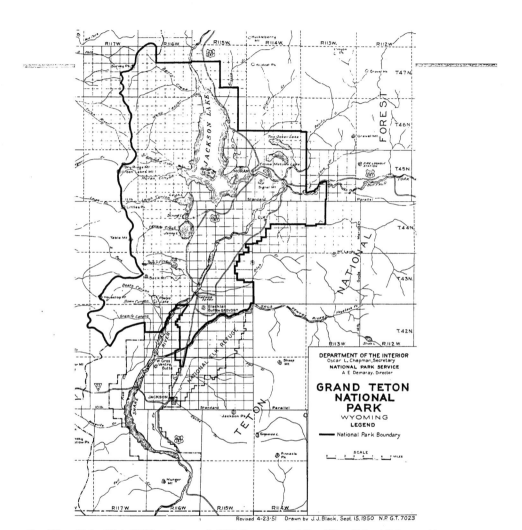

Grand Teton National Park, 1950 boundary map. In 1929, Congress created Grand Teton National Park, comprising most of the mountains west of Jackson Lake and Highway 187. In 1943, President Franklin Roosevelt established Jackson Hole National Monument, which encompassed much of the valley. In 1950, Congress enacted legislation that merged the existing park and monument lands into an expanded Grand Teton National Park. *National Park Service*

writing was done from 1984 to 1986; a first draft was completed in 1987. I revised the manuscript and submitted it for Park Service review and approval in 1990. In 1991, I assumed a new position at St. Croix National Scenic Riverway in Minnesota and Wisconsin. Other reviews were completed in 1994, but it looked like the manuscript would remain a draft until 1997, when Grand Teton National Park secured funding to publish. I edited the document for publication in the winter and spring of 1997–1998. After Grand Teton National Park secured funding, the park asked historian Christine Whitacre of the National Park Service Denver office to manage the publishing of the manuscript. Under Christine's direction, William Goetzmann, Stephanie Crockett, and Reynold Jackson prepared additional contexts for topics that I had neither the expertise nor time to research and write. University of Texas (Austin) professor William H. Goetzmann is the Pulitzer Prize-winning author of *Exploration and Empire: The Explorer and Scientist in the Winning of the West.* Goetzmann, who also wrote *The West of the Imagination*, contributed the chapter on the Teton Range in the mind of Americans. Stephanie Crockett, a contract archeologist from Victor, Idaho, who has done archeological field work in the Grand Teton area, contributed the chapter on the prehistory of the area. Reynold Jackson, the chief climbing ranger of Grand Teton National Park and co-author of *A Climber's Guide to the Teton Range,* wrote the mountaineering history of the park. I thank them for their contributions. Each contributor's conclusions and opinions are, of course, his or her own.

Prior to my arrival at Grand Teton National Park in 1980, Chuck McCurdy sent a lengthy memorandum detailing numerous projects that needed attention. Only recently, have I come to appreciate the significance of his introductory statement, "The Park [the initial 1929 park] has just passed its 50 year mark, thus making it historical. And, so it is significant it is entering its second half of its first century with its first Park Historian." In 11 years at Grand Teton National Park, I witnessed the passing of an era as a generation of people who were born prior to the creation of the 1929 park died, one by one. Among them were Noble Gregory Jr., Stippy Wolff, W. C. "Slim" Lawrence, Homer Richards, Jim

Chambers, Frank Galey, Elizabeth Wied Hayden, Jim Budge, and Eva Topping Briggs.

Several people deserve special mention. I exchanged correspondence and met Dr. Fritiof Fryxell, the park's first naturalist. Known by his friends as "Doc," he was a Renaissance man, holding degrees in geology and English, and a true gentleman. He provided valuable insights on the early administration of the park and personalities of the staff. One has to look no farther than his contributions to *Campfire Tales of Jackson Hole* for evidence of his interest in the history of the area. In 1983, he visited Jackson Hole. The park hosted a surprise open house and presented him with several gifts. Doc wrote, "It was more than I expected. Had I known in advance what was coming, I would almost certainly have cancelled the trip. But now that it is over—and I survived the experience—I look back on the occasion with pleasure and gratitude as one of the highlights of my life." It was the last time he viewed the Teton peaks, some of which he had named.

Dr. Don MacLeod was the country doctor in the valley from the 1930s until his retirement in the 1960s. I know of no one who knew the people of this valley during that period better than MacLeod. He readily shared his knowledge with me, and fortunately his sharp sense of humor. With his death, I lost a friend and an irreplaceable source of information.

Then there was Josephine Fabian, the secretary and later the wife of Harold Fabian, the vice president of the Snake River Land Company. Even in the early 1980s, she remained sensitive to old animosities engendered by the park expansion and land buyouts of the Snake River Land Company. Nevertheless, she was generous with her time and knowledge. Through her, I gained an understanding of the Snake River Land Company and people she knew. I saw her one last time in Salt Lake City. She was gamely fighting a losing battle with Parkinson's disease, which had reduced her voice to a whisper. She died a short time later.

Margaret Murie, called Mardy by her friends, remains an active environmentalist. Kind and gracious to a fault, she is famous for her afternoon tea and cookies. Mardy has always willingly shared her knowledge of Jackson Hole. More than anything else, these people taught me that history, even though it deals with the past and people long gone, is in its essence about living.

I am indebted to many for their assistance in researching and writing this study. First, Christine Whitacre employed extraordinary patience and perseverance in editing and pulling the final document together. Without her, it is doubtful this study would have been published. To Mike Johnson, the cultural resources specialist at Grand Teton National Park, my thanks for helping gather photographs and other materials. Kim Gromer and Lokey Lytjen of the Jackson Hole Historical Society and Museum provided assistance in gathering photographs from their archives. Volunteers Josiah Wagener and Emily Whitacre also helped organize photographs. I am grateful to Mary Risser and Jill Wilson, both former employees at Grand Teton, for typing drafts of this manuscript. At St. Croix, Deb Christensen trained me to use the computer more efficiently for editing.

Several reviewers made important contributions to this study. Former chief historian of the National Park Service, Edwin Bearss, edited this manuscript thoroughly for style and content. His contributions were invaluable to making this a better product. Eunice Fedors, formerly a historian at the regional office in Denver, conducted a complete review, providing pertinent corrections and suggestions. Longtime Jackson Hole resident Virginia Huidekoper provided several pages of useful comments correcting several serious errors. Another resident, Bert Raynes, edited the entire manuscript; his corrections were to the point and helpful. Jack Huyler also reviewed the manuscript and provided several important perspectives on ranching, dude ranching, and tourism. Linda Olson of Grand Teton National Park shared her extensive knowledge of the natural resources to suggest changes to update and correct this chapter. William Goetzmann provided important corrections to the chapters on the fur trade and exploration. Ann Johnson, archeologist at Yellowstone National Park, reviewed and edited Stephanie

Crockett's prehistory chapter. All made important contributions to make this a better study.

Without the blessing and support of decision makers and supervisors, I would not have taken on this study. I thank Jack Neckels, superintendent of Grand Teton National Park, for supporting the publication of this study. St. Croix Riverway Superintendant Tony Andersen generously allowed me time to edit this history. I am grateful to Bill Schenk, former deputy superintendent at Grand Teton, for his support, but especially his encouragement and confidence in me. Bill's successor, Jim Brady, continued to provide that support. I appreciate the time my supervisor, E. Patrick Smith, allowed for the project. Kate Stevenson, formerly of the Rocky Mountain Regional Office, and Rodd L. Wheaton, now assistant regional director for cultural resources and partnerships of the Intermountain Region, deserve special thanks for providing funding for travel to archives to conduct research. Finally, I thank former park biologist Pete Hayden for sharing his insights on the history and character of this valley. He is the son of Dudley Hayden, one of Grand Teton's first park rangers, and Elizabeth Wied Hayden, the author of *From Trapper to Tourist*. Pete has an excellent memory and provided much useful background information about people and incidents from the 1930s to the present.

Finally, librarians and archivists provided critical assistance in facilitating my research. I especially appreciated their courtesy and expertise in seeking files and documents. I owe particular thanks to Thomas Rosenbaum, Harold Oakhill, Jim Shelley, Kathy McDonald, and Dottie Taxter of the Rockefeller Archive Center in North Tarrytown, New York; Lloyd Spring, Sherry Wells, Andrea Joo, and Nancy Sanisteven of the Federal Records Center in Lakewood, Colorado; Jean Brainerd and Paula West Chavoya of the State Archives of the Wyoming Historical Society; Paula McDougal and Robin Tully of the American Heritage Center, University of Wyoming; and Eleanor Gehres and Frederick Yonce of the Denver Public Library.

Prologue, 1927

Nestled in the southern end of a mountain-girthed valley known as Jackson Hole was the town of Jackson, Wyoming, a small frontier village of 500 people. The Jackson Hole valley included a number of communities, of which the town of Jackson was the oldest and largest. In 1921, citizens had voted it the seat of Teton county, a rural county with a population of about 2,000 people, outnumbered by more than 10,000 cattle. New Year's Eve fell on a Friday in 1926. As darkness cast its blanket over the valley, residents prepared to welcome in the New Year, 1927.

Popular entertainment revolved around social gatherings during these years. All-night dances, interrupted only by midnight suppers, were most popular. Others joined friends around a "wireless," as radios were commonly known, to listen to their favorite programs. Avid card players attended parties, perhaps to play poker or "500," a popular variation of rummy. Though these were the years of Prohibition, bootleg whiskey and beer could readily be found in Jackson Hole. Celebrating the New Year with a potent toast would not be frowned on by some residents. Many ranchers and their helpers planned an early bedtime; livestock still had to be fed on New Year's Day. Whatever their plans, the citizens of Jackson Hole could not predict the events that would make 1927 a memorable year.

The *Jackson's Hole Courier*, a small weekly paper, had served the community since 1909. (The newspaper also reflected the valley's original name, which

Dances at the Clubhouse in Jackson were a popular winter activity. The violinist is James H. May of Grovont, the area known as Mormon Row. During the winter, dances would go on all night because it was too dangerous to travel back home through the deep snows and frigid temperatures. *Jackson Hole Historical Society and Museum*

In 1927, the Bureau of Public Roads built a bridge over the Snake River near Menor's Ferry, making the ferry obselete.
Jackson Hole Historical Society and Museum

was soon shortened to Jackson Hole.) The last issue of 1926 reflected the continuity of life in the valley, but also hinted at change.[1] The lead article on the front page dealt with water rights and the Jackson Lake Dam. These issues have been a common thread in the fabric of the valley's history since 1907. Titled "Minidoka Decision on Water Reversed," the article reported a higher court's reversal of an earlier decision concerning a lawsuit over property taxes levied on water rights. In 1925, Teton County assessed taxes on water rights and improvements on Jackson Lake owned by two Idaho irrigation companies. Predictably, they sued the county. The higher court ruled that because the water rights were tied to lands in Idaho, the county could not levy taxes. This was bad news for a revenue-poor county and an economically depressed community.

Community news fed the gossip mills at New Year's Eve parties. Billy Grant, the owner and post-master of a grocery at the Moose Post Office, had purchased Joe Jones's grocery in Jackson. The paper announced the return of the valley's best-known athlete, Mike Yokel. Surprisingly, he was not a rodeo cowboy but a wrestler. Picking up an article from a Salt Lake City newspaper, the *Courier* reported Yokel's return from Australia, where he had completed a successful nine-month tour. A world-class middleweight, he had won 11 of 13 matches, competing before the largest crowds to attend a match in Australian history.

Weather and the condition of Teton-Pass dominated conversations at New Year's Eve parties. Because of severe winters, weather preoccupied valley residents. In December 1926, arctic temperatures froze the water pipes in the courthouse and killed houseplants in homes. Teton Pass served as the valley's main link with the outside world. Mail and most supplies arrived via this route. Situated at the

Jackson Hole's best-known athlete in 1926 was wrestler Mike Yokel. Mike would eventually be employed as a land-buying agent for Rockefeller's Snake River Land Company. *Jackson Hole Historical Society and Museum*

south end of the Teton Range, winter snows made travel over the pass unpredictable and dangerous. "How's the Pass?" was the question on everyone's lips.

Winter was hard on wildlife too. The *Courier* reported a grim discovery on the Snake River near Pacific Creek. Dick Ohl, a U.S. Forest Service ranger, and Fred Deyo, a state game warden, had discovered and removed the carcasses of 46 elk from the river. They surmised that the elk had broken through a thin layer of ice and, unable to climb the banks, drowned in the icy waters. Ever since vigilantes had driven tuskers (poachers who killed elk solely for their eyeteeth) out of the valley around 1900, local residents had maintained a strong proprietary interest in the Jackson Hole elk herd.

Columns in the *Courier* mirrored the valley's composition of small, distinct communities, isolated from each other. "Jackson Happenings," "Wilson News," and "Spread Creek" reported the social news of these communities. The tone of the December 30,

1926, edition reassured readers that life would continue much as before. But, in spite of its isolation, Jackson Hole had always been influenced by national events. Calvin Coolidge was president of the United States. Known as Silent Cal, his most important decision in 1927 may have been his announcement, "I do not choose to run for president in 1928."

More inspirational were the accomplishments of Babe Ruth and Charles Lindbergh. Ruth, the "Sultan of Swat," had set a new standard for baseball by belting 60 home runs, securing him a niche in the pantheon of American heroes. Charles A. Lindbergh reduced human perceptions of distance by completing the first successful transatlantic flight from New York to Paris, a singular feat that catapulted him to fame. These individual heroics overshadowed the ominous failure of diplomats to limit naval armaments at Geneva, Switzerland, in 1927. But then diplomats, like politicians, were not the heroes of the day.

Americans venerated businessmen as much as they did popular sports figures. Henry Ford epitomized the genius and success of American industry. His mass-assembly techniques produced Model T Fords so efficiently that the average American could afford an automobile, revolutionizing American life. In 1927–1928, Ford introduced the Model A, replacing the old Tin Lizzie. Other technological milestones caused profound changes in entertainment. The first talking picture, *The Jazz Singer,* made silent movies obsolete, but 20 years would pass before Americans would feel the impact of the first long-range transmission of television signals.

Perhaps no decade has left more enduring images than those of the "roaring" 1920s: bathtub gin, flappers, F. Scott Fitzgerald. Americans moved to the cities in unprecedented numbers, bought more on credit, consumed more material goods, and generally experienced greater prosperity in the 1920s. But American farmers did not share these good times. World War I had dramatically increased the world's demand for American foodstuffs. Farmers and ranchers purchased additional equipment and land, often on borrowed money, to increase production. But after the end of the war, demand dropped, and the government ended wartime price supports.

In 1925, a massive slide dammed the Gros Ventre River, creating Lower Slide Lake. Two years later, the water breached the natural dam, wiping out the town of Kelly. *Jackson Hole Historical Society and Museum*

Prices plummeted, spelling disaster for American agriculture.

Because cattle ranching dominated the economy of Jackson Hole, virtually everyone in the valley felt the pinch. In 1925, a large group of ranchers and farmers circulated and endorsed a petition support-ing the creation of a "recreation area" in Jackson Hole. The petition stated, "We have tried ranching, stock-raising, and from our experience have become of the firm belief that this region will find its highest use as a playground." Ninety-seven landowners ex-pressed their willingness to sell more than 27,000 acres "at what we consider a fair price" to incorporate into such a preserve or recreation area.[2]

The petition came to be known as the "Jackson Hole Plan," which called for the creation of a pre-serve to maintain the scenic and western character of the valley. Supporters hoped to secure the financial support of a wealthy philanthropist, who could buy up private parcels and donate them to a preserve. Conceived by local citizens, the Jackson Hole Plan was endorsed by Horace Albright, the superintendent of Yellowstone National Park. Albright had advocated adding the Teton Range to the National Park System since his first visit to Jackson Hole in 1916.

In 1926, Albright accompanied John D. Rocke-feller Jr., and his wife on a tour of the valley. The

Rockefellers expressed dismay at the extent of com-mercial developments that marred the landscape. During the visit, Albright explained the Jackson Hole Plan. As a result, Rockefeller decided to fi-nance the purchasing of land. In the pivotal year of 1927, his agents formed the Snake River Land Com-pany to carry out the program. The company pur-chased more than 35,000 acres, of which 32,419 were eventually incorporated into Grand Teton National Park. This donation to the public domain altered the history of this valley forever.[3]

Further, the federal government withdrew re-maining public lands from settlement in 1927. In April, President Coolidge issued an executive order closing 1,280 acres to public entry. This land was to be added to the elk refuge. The following July, Coolidge issued Executive Order 4685, withdrawing a whopping 23,000 acres from public entry. Ostensi-bly to protect elk range, Executive Order 4685 was prompted by a request from Snake River Land Com-pany officials, who sought to prevent rampant land speculation once the company began purchasing land. Other executive orders followed, closing re-maining public lands to settlement. For all practical purposes, the frontier in Jackson Hole ended with the closure of the public domain to homesteading in 1927.[4]

Jackson Hole's best-known athlete in 1926 was wrestler Mike Yokel. Mike would eventually be employed as a land-buying agent for Rockefeller's Snake River Land Company. *Jackson Hole Historical Society and Museum*

south end of the Teton Range, winter snows made travel over the pass unpredictable and dangerous. "How's the Pass?" was the question on everyone's lips.

Winter was hard on wildlife too. The *Courier* reported a grim discovery on the Snake River near Pacific Creek. Dick Ohl, a U.S. Forest Service ranger, and Fred Deyo, a state game warden, had discovered and removed the carcasses of 46 elk from the river. They surmised that the elk had broken through a thin layer of ice and, unable to climb the banks, drowned in the icy waters. Ever since vigilantes had driven tuskers (poachers who killed elk solely for their eyeteeth) out of the valley around 1900, local residents had maintained a strong proprietary interest in the Jackson Hole elk herd.

Columns in the *Courier* mirrored the valley's composition of small, distinct communities, isolated from each other. "Jackson Happenings," "Wilson News," and "Spread Creek" reported the social news of these communities. The tone of the December 30,

1926, edition reassured readers that life would continue much as before. But, in spite of its isolation, Jackson Hole had always been influenced by national events. Calvin Coolidge was president of the United States. Known as Silent Cal, his most important decision in 1927 may have been his announcement, "I do not choose to run for president in 1928."

More inspirational were the accomplishments of Babe Ruth and Charles Lindbergh. Ruth, the "Sultan of Swat," had set a new standard for baseball by belting 60 home runs, securing him a niche in the pantheon of American heroes. Charles A. Lindbergh reduced human perceptions of distance by completing the first successful transatlantic flight from New York to Paris, a singular feat that catapulted him to fame. These individual heroics overshadowed the ominous failure of diplomats to limit naval armaments at Geneva, Switzerland, in 1927. But then diplomats, like politicians, were not the heroes of the day.

Americans venerated businessmen as much as they did popular sports figures. Henry Ford epitomized the genius and success of American industry. His mass-assembly techniques produced Model T Fords so efficiently that the average American could afford an automobile, revolutionizing American life. In 1927–1928, Ford introduced the Model A, replacing the old Tin Lizzie. Other technological milestones caused profound changes in entertainment. The first talking picture, *The Jazz Singer,* made silent movies obsolete, but 20 years would pass before Americans would feel the impact of the first long-range transmission of television signals.

Perhaps no decade has left more enduring images than those of the "roaring" 1920s: bathtub gin, flappers, F. Scott Fitzgerald. Americans moved to the cities in unprecedented numbers, bought more on credit, consumed more material goods, and generally experienced greater prosperity in the 1920s. But American farmers did not share these good times. World War I had dramatically increased the world's demand for American foodstuffs. Farmers and ranchers purchased additional equipment and land, often on borrowed money, to increase production. But after the end of the war, demand dropped, and the government ended wartime price supports.

In 1925, a massive slide dammed the Gros Ventre River, creating Lower Slide Lake. Two years later, the water breached the natural dam, wiping out the town of Kelly. *Jackson Hole Historical Society and Museum*

Prices plummeted, spelling disaster for American agriculture.

Because cattle ranching dominated the economy of Jackson Hole, virtually everyone in the valley felt the pinch. In 1925, a large group of ranchers and farmers circulated and endorsed a petition supporting the creation of a "recreation area" in Jackson Hole. The petition stated, "We have tried ranching, stock-raising, and from our experience have become of the firm belief that this region will find its highest use as a playground." Ninety-seven landowners expressed their willingness to sell more than 27,000 acres "at what we consider a fair price" to incorporate into such a preserve or recreation area.[2]

The petition came to be known as the "Jackson Hole Plan," which called for the creation of a preserve to maintain the scenic and western character of the valley. Supporters hoped to secure the financial support of a wealthy philanthropist, who could buy up private parcels and donate them to a preserve. Conceived by local citizens, the Jackson Hole Plan was endorsed by Horace Albright, the superintendent of Yellowstone National Park. Albright had advocated adding the Teton Range to the National Park System since his first visit to Jackson Hole in 1916.

In 1926, Albright accompanied John D. Rockefeller Jr., and his wife on a tour of the valley. The Rockefellers expressed dismay at the extent of commercial developments that marred the landscape. During the visit, Albright explained the Jackson Hole Plan. As a result, Rockefeller decided to finance the purchasing of land. In the pivotal year of 1927, his agents formed the Snake River Land Company to carry out the program. The company purchased more than 35,000 acres, of which 32,419 were eventually incorporated into Grand Teton National Park. This donation to the public domain altered the history of this valley forever.[3]

Further, the federal government withdrew remaining public lands from settlement in 1927. In April, President Coolidge issued an executive order closing 1,280 acres to public entry. This land was to be added to the elk refuge. The following July, Coolidge issued Executive Order 4685, withdrawing a whopping 23,000 acres from public entry. Ostensibly to protect elk range, Executive Order 4685 was prompted by a request from Snake River Land Company officials, who sought to prevent rampant land speculation once the company began purchasing land. Other executive orders followed, closing remaining public lands to settlement. For all practical purposes, the frontier in Jackson Hole ended with the closure of the public domain to homesteading in 1927.[4]

The Kelly Mercantile Store was obliterated in the flood of 1927. Kelly once was one of the largest communities in Jackson Hole and, a few years prior to the great flood, lost the election to become the county seat by just a few votes. *Jackson Hole Historical Society and Museum*

Concurrently, concerns and disagreements over the health, age distribution, and population of the Jackson Hole elk herd developed. The Elk Commission, a special subcommittee of the President's Commission on Outdoor Recreation, advised the federal Biological Survey to prepare "a comprehensive study of the life history of the elk." In 1927, the bureau appointed a young biologist named Olaus Murie to complete the project. He conducted research for years and eventually published his classic study, *The Elk of North America*, in 1951. By then, Murie had left government service to become codirector of the Wilderness Society. He and his wife, Mardy, continued to reside in Jackson Hole.[5]

In 1925, the most spectacular natural event in the valley's recorded history occurred when a massive block of sedimentary rock sloughed off the north side of Sheep Mountain and blocked the Gros Ventre River, creating Lower Slide Lake. On May 18, 1927, the river breached the natural dam created by the slide. A torrent of water poured down the valley towards the nearby village of Kelly, destroying property and ranches along the Gros Ventre and Snake Rivers. The flood killed six people and caused damage in excess of $100,000. With the exception of the Episcopal Church and rectory and

local school, the flood obliterated Kelly; gone were the hotel, mercantile store, automobile garage, blacksmith shop, livery stable, and homes.[6]

Despite this calamity, people recovered, and most judged 1927 a good year. Tourism continued to expand in Jackson Hole. Dude ranches proliferated, and most were booked full. More facilities were built to cater to automobile travelers. At Taggart Creek, Chester Goss bought 115 acres from Jim Manges and constructed tourist cabins, a store, a baseball diamond, and a large rodeo ground complete with race track, grandstands, and refreshment kiosks. Goss and his partners named it the Elbo Ranch and erected a conspicuous sign proudly proclaiming it "the home of the Hollywood Cowboy."[7] During this period, the Bureau of Public Roads launched road construction projects in Jackson Hole to accommodate increasing car traffic. They built a road from Jackson to Menor's Ferry in 1926. Over the winter, they constructed a steel truss bridge at the ferry, which rendered it obsolete. Maud Noble, the owner of the ferry, abandoned it in 1927.

A few perceived increasing reliance on tourism as a Faustian bargain for Jackson Hole. To Horace Albright, Struthers Burt wrote, "This speedway down here, the El-Bo [sic] Ranch and the south end of Timber Island, not to mention Jenny's Lake, has about sickened me with this neck of the woods."[8] Another dude rancher, Joe Clark of the Double Diamond, complained to National Park Service Director Stephen Mather:

> As you are doubtless aware, there has been a great change in the last four or five years. I remember one evening this summer, standing on the bluff above the Snake River at Menor's Ferry at sundown and looking westward toward the Teton peaks. It was impossible to see anything except the very tops of the mountains by reason of the immense cloud of dust raised by a continuous procession of tourist automobiles going along the new road from the ferry up toward the park.[9]

Pressure from tourist developments, increasing numbers of people, and the increasing diversity of

The Sutton family truck being transported across the Snake River by Menor's Ferry. Before it was "moored to rest at last" the ferry was the only reliable crossing over the Snake River between Wilson and Moran. *Jackson Hole Historical Society and Museum*

recreational demands still constitute an escalating threat to the wilderness and western character of the Teton country.

More than any other event, the beaching of Bill Menor's Ferry in 1927 symbolized the passing of an era in Jackson Hole. Resident Ruth Patterson captured the importance of this event in a poem titled "Passing of the Ferry."

> The old landmarks are vanishing, ·
> One by one they are passing out.
> The tourist with his modern ways
> Has brought this change about . . .
>
> Many things are changing fast;
> Even the Faithful Menor's Ferry
> Has been moored to rest at last.[10]

On New Year's Eve 1926, life went on as people prepared to celebrate the beginning of the year, which altered irrevocably the future of this valley. No one could know that 1927 would be so momentous. Only by looking back does it become apparent.

Notes

1. *Jackson's Hole Courier,* December 30, 1926.

2. U.S. Congress, Senate, "An Investigation of Proposed Enlargement of the Yellowstone and Grand Teton National Parks: Hearing on S. Res. 226," 72d Congress, 2nd Session, 1933, pp. 266–268.

3. Robert Righter, *Crucible for Conservation: The Creation of Grand Teton National Park* (Boulder, CO: Colorado Associated University Press, 1983).·

4. "Hearing on S. Res. 226," 1933, pp. 76–79; and *Jackson's Hole Courier,* August 25, 1927.

5. *Jackson's Hole Courier,* January 6, 1927, and February 3, 1927; and Olaus J. Murie, *The Elk of North America* (Harrisburg, PA: The Stackpole Company, Washington, D.C.: The Wildlife Institute, 1951).

6. *Jackson's Hole Courier,* May 19, 1927.

7. Ibid., May 5, 1927, and July 14, 1927.

8. Struthers Burt to Horace M. Albright, July 18, 1927, Horace M. Albright Papers (hereafter referred to as "HMA Papers"), 1923–1927, Yellowstone National Park.

9. Joe Clark to Stephen T. Mather, September 1927, HMA Papers, 1923–1927.

10. *Jackson's Hole Courier,* September 1, 1949; and poem by Ruth Patterson, ca. 1927.

CHAPTER 1

The Natural Setting

Over these seemingly changeless mountains, in endless succession, move the ephemeral colors of dawn and sunset and of noon and night, the shadows and sunlight, the garlands of clouds with which storms adorn the peaks, the misty rain-curtains of afternoon showers.

—Fritiof Fryxell, *The Tetons: Interpretations of a Mountain Landscape*

Teton Range, late summer. *Michael Johnson*

ritiof Fryxell, a geologist and the park's first naturalist, not only appreciated the beauty of the
Teton Range but also possessed the rare gift of
creating vivid pictures with words. Not all appreciate
the scenery of the mountains and Jackson Hole. One
August morning, I overheard this conversation in the
Moose Visitor Center at Grand Teton National
Park. Walking past the lobby, I heard a brusque voice
demand, "What's there to see in this park?" After
the briefest hesitation, the ranger responded, "Well
sir, along the Teton Park Road you can enjoy some
fine views of the mountains, and . . ." "What mountains?" the voice interrupted. Peeking into the lobby
from the hall entrance, I saw a middle-aged man
staring distrustfully at the nonplussed ranger. Not a
cloud marred the deep blue sky; the Tetons were
hard to miss. The visitor explained that he had left
Yellowstone at sunrise, driving south into Grand
Teton National Park. He had driven his recreational
vehicle down Teton Park Road, which is situated at
the very base of the mountain range. The ranger explained, "Well, sir, the mountains you drove past are
the Teton Range." "That was it!" the man exclaimed.
He turned abruptly and stalked out of the visitor center, muttering to himself. Obviously, he did not share
Fryxell's vision.

Most visitors are awestruck by the remarkable alpine scenery in Jackson Hole, often sharing memo-

ries of their first view of the Teton Range from visits 20, 30, and even 40 years past. The Tetons are one of the most recognizable mountain ranges in the United States. So many descriptions of the peaks exist that the English language seems exhausted. "Jagged ridges," "blue-gray pyramids," "shimmering granite spires," "splendid sentinels" become trite, yet accurate, impressionistic images. Relatively small in area, the Teton Range is about 40 miles long and 10 miles wide. It extends from Teton Pass at the south, to the Berry Creek area near Yellowstone National Park. The mountains rise abruptly almost 7,000 feet above Jackson Hole on their eastern front, then slope more gently west into the Teton Basin in Idaho.

Jackson Hole is the other distinctive geographic feature in the area. (Mountain men coined the term "hole" to describe enclosed mountain valleys such as Jackson's.) This flat valley offers a remarkable contrast to the rugged spires of the Teton Range. Consisting of porous, cobbled soils covered with sagebrush, Jackson Hole is an upland valley surrounded by mountains and highlands. It is one of the largest such valleys in the Rocky Mountains, being 8 to 12 miles wide and 40 miles long.

The geographic position of the Teton Range and Jackson Hole is significant. Both are situated in the heart of the Rocky Mountains, the great chain of peaks dividing the North American continent in a north–south direction from Alaska to Mexico. Classified as one of the major natural regions of the continent, the Rocky Mountain cordillera is subdivided into three physiographic provinces. The Teton Range and Jackson Hole are in the Middle Rocky Mountain Province, characterized as "an assortment of different kinds of mountains with differing trends and semiarid intermontane basins."[1] The Jackson Hole area divides two very different geophysic provinces: the Wyoming Basin to the southeast and the Columbia River Plateau to the west.

The Tetons and Jackson Hole were part of the Wyoming Territory, which was established in 1868. In 1890, Wyoming became the 44th state to enter the Union. Wyoming is an Indian word meaning "large plains." Indeed, the state of Wyoming conjures images of stark buttes framed against an endless blue sky, with a shimmering gray–green sea of

sagebrush in the foreground. Such landscapes are common, but first-time visitors are surprised to find that mountains dominate much of the state, offering a refreshing contrast of mountain and plain, forest and sage. The Laramie, Medicine Bow, Bighorn, Absaroka, and Wind River Ranges cut Wyoming into semiarid basins.[2] In the northeastern part of the state, mountain ranges such as the Teton, Absaroka, Wind River, Wyoming, Salt River, Snake River, Washakie, Gros Ventre, and Hoback dominate the landscape.

The Rocky Mountains appear to be an impassable barrier to travel from east to west. In fact, numerous passes penetrate the mountainous walls. Some provide relatively easy passage. Others are difficult routes. The Marias, Lolo, Lemhi, Union, and Teton Passes are significant breaches in the Rockies from Wyoming through Montana. However, none is more important than South Pass. Located approximately 100 miles southeast of Jackson Hole in the Wyoming Basin, South Pass provided an easy way through the Rocky Mountain barrier to lands west of the Continental Divide. The Oregon Trail crossed South Pass and, just another 50 miles away, the first transcontinental railroad linked the nation in 1869.

Watercourses also served as transportation routes to the western interior. The headwaters of several major river systems originate within a 100-mile radius of the Teton Range. The fabled Three Forks of the Missouri River are northwest of Jackson Hole in Montana. The Yellowstone River begins in the Teton Wilderness northeast of Jackson Hole, just east of the Continental Divide. The river feeds water into Yellowstone Lake, then exits Yellowstone National Park, after passing through the spectacular Grand Canyon of the Yellowstone. The Wind River has its source near Togwotee Pass. It flows southeast into the Wind River Valley where, at its confluence with the Popo-Agie (pronounced Papa-sha) River, it turns north abruptly and becomes the Bighorn River. The Bighorn empties eventually into the Yellowstone which, in turn, joins the Missouri River on the high plains. Across the Continental Divide, the headwaters of the Green River are nestled in the Wind River Mountains from whence it runs south to join the mighty Colorado River. The Snake River, named for the Shoshone or Snake Indians, flows through Jackson Hole. The waters of the Snake join the Columbia River, then empty into the Pacific Ocean.[3]

❦

Jackson Hole appears to be a serene valley anchored by the Teton Range, seemingly immovable and unyielding to the human eye. In terms of geologic time, however, the landscape is dynamic, ever changing. The Tetons are made of some of the oldest and hardest rocks on the earth, consisting of gneiss, schist, and granite. The mountains wage endless war against fierce weathering processes. Hard rocks resist forces such as extreme temperatures, and water and ice, but eventually submit.[4]

Comprehending geology lends understanding of the topography, hydrology, soils, vegetation, wildlife, and human history of Jackson Hole. Two geologic forces shaped the present topography of Jackson Hole and the Tetons: mountain building and glaciation. The Tetons are a classic fault block mountain range, created by the concurrent uplift and downdrop of blocks in the earth's crust. They rise along a series of faults that run in a north-south direction at the base of the range. On the east side of the Teton fault, another block of the earth's crust, Jackson Hole, dropped as the Tetons rose. J. D. Love and John D. Reed offer the best descriptions of the process comparing the vertical movements of the earth along the fault to the movements of giant trap doors:

> They are both tilted blocks of the earth's crust that behaved like two adjoining giant trap doors hinged so that they would swing in opposite directions. The block on the west, which forms the Teton range, was hinged along the Idaho-Wyoming State line; the eastern edge was uplifted along a fault (a fracture along which displacement has occurred). This is why the highest peaks and steepest faces are near the east margin of the range. The hinge line of the eastern block, which forms Jackson Hole, was in the highlands to the east. The western edge of the block is downdropped along the fault at the base of the Teton Range. As a consequence, the floor of Jackson Hole tilts westward toward the Tetons.[5]

Several points are worth noting about the Teton Range. Five to ten million years old, the Tetons are the youngest mountain range in the Rocky Mountains. In contrast, the great chain of the Rockies is 50 to 60 million years old. More important for people today, the Teton fault zone is active and, as a result, the range is still rising while the valley is sinking. Hence, the area is an active earthquake zone. Last, this dramatic rise of mountains explains, in part, the rugged beauty of the mountains today.

Glaciation is the other geologic force that molded the topography of Jackson Hole. Glaciers develop from tremendous accumulations of snow and are nothing more than large bodies of ice, snow, and earth that move by their own weight and gravitational pull. Ten different periods of glaciation have occurred in Jackson Hole over the last million years. Only two have left abundant evidence of their existence. The older of the two, called the Munger Glaciation, entered the valley 140,000 to 160,000 years ago. In this period, a huge glacier filled Jackson Hole with ice up to 4,000 feet thick. The more recent Pinedale Glaciation, which occurred in three phases, began 40,000 to 70,000 years ago and ended 12,000 to 15,000 years ago.[6]

The glaciers' handiwork is apparent in the mountains and valley today. The deep, U-shaped canyons and natural amphitheaters at the heads of canyons, called cirques, resulted from glaciers. Sapphire-colored lakes often form in these bowl-like basins called, logically, cirque lakes. Today, several small glaciers cling to the shaded recesses of the Tetons. These are reentrant glaciers, approximately 1,000 years old. Grinding out of the canyons of the Tetons, glaciers created the prominent terminal and lateral moraines that form the basins and sides of the spectacular piedmont lakes—Jenny, Leigh, Bradley, Taggart, Phelps—along the base of the range. Other prominent moraines, such as Burned Ridge and Timbered Island, were created by glaciers in the valley. These forested ridges contrast sharply against the surrounding sagebrush flats, denoting the different composition of morainal soils. Northeast of Burned Ridge is an area known as the Potholes, a sage-covered plain riddled with crater-like depressions called kettles. These depressions were formed by chunks of

The snow-covered Teton range as seen from Signal Mountain. Signal Mountain offers one of the finest vistas of the entire valley and surrounding mountains and highlands. *National Park Service*

ice left by receding glaciers and buried under the soil. The kettles appeared as the ice melted slowly over time. More important, as the glaciers melted and receded, torrents of water carried millions of quartzite cobbles from other nearby mountain ranges into the valley floor. Today, the sagebrush plant community dominates these glacial outwash plains.

People enjoy spectacular views of the Tetons from almost any location in the valley, but Signal Mountain offers one of the finest vistas of the entire valley and surrounding mountains and highlands. To the south, the Gros Ventre and Snake River Ranges enclose the southern end of the valley. Jackson Peak and Sheep Mountain, summits in the Gros Ventre Range, pierce the horizon. The Mount Leidy Highlands enclose the valley to the east. The Washakie Range and Pinyon Peak Highlands form the remainder of the eastern and northeastern boundary of the valley. From another vantage point, the Pitchstone Plateau, one can see beyond Jackson Lake to the north. The Teton Range to the west completes the encirclement of Jackson Hole.

Jackson Point Overlook is situated less than a mile below the summit of Signal Mountain. At this overlook, a panorama of alpine peaks unfolds before you. Here in 1878, the renowned pioneer photographer, William Henry Jackson, first photographed the Tetons from Jackson Hole. Unfortunately, he took few photographs of the valley or range "because of a smoky haziness that filled the air." Forest fires were responsible for the smoke, and the haze is apparent in his photographs.[7]

Far to the south, Buck Mountain stands out as one of the highest peaks at 11,938 feet. A sharp peak, visitors sometimes mistake it for the Grand Teton. The next peaks are Nez Perce—once called Howling Dog Peak—then Cloudveil Dome and the South Teton. The Grand Teton, Teewinot, and Mount Owen stand out on the horizon. At an elevation of 13,770 feet, the Grand Teton pierces the sky, a sharp alpine peak that anchors the range. From Signal Mountain, Teewinot Mountain and Mount Owen flank either side of the Grand Teton like courtiers. Teewinot is derived from a Shoshone word meaning "many pinnacles." To the right of the Grand Teton, Mount Owen is named for William O. "Billy" Owen, who made the first documented ascent of the Grand Teton in 1898. Mount Owen is the second highest peak in the Teton Range at 12,928 feet and offers one of the most difficult challenges for climbers.[8]

North of this splendid arrangement of peaks is Cascade Canyon, a deep U-shaped gorge yawning over Jenny Lake. A well-developed trail provides access into one of the most popular and beautiful canyons in the park, where a short (2.5 miles) hike rewards visitors with a view of Hidden Falls, a roaring torrent of water spilling over a cliff. Another steep half mile brings hikers to Inspiration Point, which affords a superb view of Jenny Lake and Jackson Hole. From here, sturdy hikers may forge ahead another six miles to Lake Solitude, a serene cirque lake located at the head of Cascade Canyon.

The north wall of Cascade Canyon is the southern side of Mount St. John, named for a geologist employed by the Hayden Surveys. Adjacent is Rockchuck Peak, named for yellow-bellied marmots, common residents of the rocky mountainsides and canyons. At Photographer's Point, Indian Paintbrush Canyon opens between rugged peaks, a textbook example of a glacial canyon. The mouth of Indian Paintbrush merges with Leigh Canyon, which is named for Beaver Dick Leigh, a late-nineteenth-century hunter and trapper who frequented the area. The canyons are separated by a smaller peak called Mount Woodring, named for the first superintendent of Grand Teton National Park.

Perhaps the most distinctive peak except for the Grand Teton, Mount Moran towers over Jackson Lake. The flat-topped mountain was named for Thomas Moran, the prominent landscape artist of the American West who participated in the Hayden Surveys. Skillet Glacier hangs on the east face of the mountain. Moran Canyon, north of the mountain, ends the central portion of the Teton Range. The mountains extend north for another 15 miles, where they merge with the ancient lava hills of Yellowstone. These peaks are less spectacular and, therefore, less well known. Yet, these hills and canyons are prime wilderness, unmarred by developed trails between Leigh and Webb Canyons.

From the summit of Signal Mountain, the Snake River can also be seen winding its way through Jackson Hole, coursing down a cottonwood and spruce-lined channel. Directly east of Signal Mountain is an abandoned channel of the Snake, a mute reminder that the landscape of Jackson Hole is dynamic. The Snake River is the valley's only drainage. It begins as a trickle in the Teton Wilderness, flows north into Yellowstone before looping south into the John D. Rockefeller Jr. Memorial Parkway. Enlarged by the

Lewis River, the Snake flows into Jackson Lake. The river empties out of the lake at the Jackson Lake Dam and travels southwest, cutting the valley in half. It races out of Jackson Hole through the Snake River Canyon and enters the state of Idaho.

Looking at a map, three important tributaries feed the river from the east: Pacific Creek, Buffalo Fork, and the Gros Ventre River. Ditch Creek and the sprawling Spread Creek also enter from the east. Cottonwood Creek flows from Jenny Lake in the west, emptying into the Snake above Moose, Wyoming. South of the park, Flat Creek and Fish Creek are important tributaries, and the Hoback River joins the Snake just before it enters the Snake River Canyon.

Topographic maps show Jackson Hole's other distinctive features, such as Emma Matilda and Two Ocean Lakes, tucked in the hills between Buffalo Fork and Pacific Creek. Several buttes, possible remnants of ancient mountains scoured by glaciers, protrude from the valley floor—including Signal Mountain adjacent to Jackson Lake, Blacktail Butte in the central part of the valley, and East Gros Ventre and West Gros Ventre Buttes in the southern portion of the valley. In the park, Timbered Island and Burned Ridge stand out as prominent stands of lodgepole forest surrounded by gray-green sagebrush flats. The sagebrush flats in the valley seem inconspicuous, yet they are a distinct topographic element. The sage plain east of the Snake and north of Blacktail Butte is Antelope Flats. Baseline Flat is the plain located between the Teton Range and the Snake River. And, of course, the Potholes are situated northeast of Burned Ridge and west of the river.

The piedmont lakes at the base of the Teton Range offer some of the finest scenery in the region. These lakes formed inside the perimeters of glacial moraines. The lakes from south to north are Phelps, Taggart, Bradley, Jenny, String, Leigh, and Jackson. Located at the north end of the valley, Jackson Lake has been made a reservoir. The old Reclamation Service first constructed a log crib dam at the lake's outlet in 1906–1907. After it failed in 1910, the service built the present concrete dam, and added an earthen dike. By 1916, the project was complete. The dam raised the water level 39 feet, and increased the area of the lake from 17,100 to 25,540

Looking across the head of Cascade Canyon. Hiking the narrow Teton Range provides a quick transition from valley floor to treeless alpine zones. *National Park Service*

acres. Its purpose was to provide irrigation water for farms in Idaho. Jackson Lake was added to the park in 1950.

The soils of Jackson Hole and the Teton Range are divided into four primary groups: soils of mountains and foothills; soils of foothills, buttes, and glacial moraines; soils of terraces and alluvial fans; and soils of the floodplains. These four broad classifications can be further broken down into 11 types. In turn, surveyors identified 71 specific soils that are based on "the suitability and potential of a soil for specific uses."[9]

The soils of the mountains and foothills comprise 40 percent of the land surveyed in the 1970s by the Soil Conservation Service. Located at elevations between 6,000 and 13,000 feet, this terrain varies from rolling hills to steep mountains and is characterized by well-drained soils and rubble and rock outcrops. These soils are found in the Teton Range, the northeast portion of the park near Emma Matilda and Two Ocean Lakes, and Mount Reid near Jackson Lake.

Foothills, buttes, and glacial moraines are more limited in elevation, existing between 6,000 and 7,500 feet. These soils comprise 23 percent of the survey area. In the park, they are found in the benches at the base of the Teton Range, on buttes such as Blacktail and Signal Mountain, on glacial

moraines such as Timbered Island, and on highlands in the northeast part of the park.

Alluvial fans and terraces comprise another general soil type and make up 21 percent of the survey area. Found at elevations between 6,000 and 7,000 feet, the terrain is both level and sloping. This zone is identified readily by its plant cover, consisting mostly of grass and sagebrush.

Soils of the floodplain occupy low terraces along major river drainages at elevations between 6,000 and 7,000 feet. The terrain is generally flat and the soils tend to be deep and poorly drained. This grouping comprises about 16 percent of the surveyed area.[10]

To a large degree, soils determine the distribution and variety of vegetation and wildlife, and are no less significant to humans. Today, ecologists recognize a surprising number of distinct zones in the Teton country, where distinct groupings of plants and wildlife can be identified. Known as biotic communities, they are defined as "any organized assemblage of populations of living organisms inhabiting a specific area or physical habitat."[11] In other words, a biotic community is a definable area where specific plants, insects, birds, and mammals will be found with some predictability subject to seasons and the time of day. For example, during the spring and fall, elk can be observed browsing in the sagebrush flats near Timbered Island, especially in the mornings and evenings.

Many biotic communities exist in Jackson Hole and the Teton Range. Most people do not think of lakes, rivers, streams, and ponds as habitat, but these areas make up the aquatic community, a rich mosaic of algae, aquatic plants, insects, fish, birds, and mammals. Bald eagles and ospreys depend on the fish in rivers and lakes for their food, while water is critical for the beaver's survival. The aquatic community comprises ten percent of the park.

The sagebrush community appears stark and barren, yet its look is deceiving. It is the largest biotic community in the park and hosts the most diverse plant communities. No less than 100 species of plants have been inventoried on the sagebrush flats. Meadow communities are dominated by sedges and grasses. Sedge meadows are usually found in low-lying areas, and often flood during the spring. Sedge-grass meadows are situated at higher elevations and are, therefore, drier. A high water table characterizes the shrub-swamp community. Shrubs such as willow, serviceberry, silverberry, and buffaloberry are typical species and important food sources for birds and mammals. Along watercourses, the dominant trees are cottonwood and blue spruce. The willow community is similar to the shrub-swamp, in that both grow where the water table is high and soil drainage poor. The best example of this habitat is Willow Flats, located near the Jackson Lake Dam. Moose are likely to be seen in these areas, since willow is a favorite food source and critical in winter. Groves of aspen cluster on dry hillsides and relatively flat areas, often between grasslands and coniferous forests. In the Rocky Mountains, aspen reproduce through shoots that sprout from the roots of trees.

Coniferous forests comprise three distinct biotic communities: lodgepole pine, Douglas fir, and spruce fir. Lodgepole pine is the most common evergreen in Jackson Hole, growing on the lower mountain slopes in the valley. Many of the lodgepole stands are estimated to be 80 to 100 years old. Mature trees become vulnerable to insect infestations and, predictably, the mountain pine bark beetle has attacked mature lodgepole forests, killing many trees in recent years. Other coniferous trees are limber pine, white

bark pine, Colorado blue spruce, Engelmann spruce, subalpine fir, and Douglas fir.

Few visitors see the alpine tundra, a biotic community that begins at elevations of 9,500 to 10,000 feet and extends to the very summits of peaks. Vegetation is sparse or non-existent. Dwarfed plants cling to the ground in the most extreme climatic conditions. Yet, life exists here, for this is the home of dazzling wildflowers such as moss campion and the alpine forget-me-not, and birds and mammals use this zone during the summer, either migrating or hibernating in winter.

Historically, fire has had a significant impact on the biotic communities in the park. Over the last two decades, research has demonstrated conclusively that fires are an important element in forest succession, influence forest insect populations, and maintain diverse habitats.[12]

The diversity of plant communities explains the rich variety of wildlife in the Teton country. Today, 55 species of mammals inhabit parklands all or part of the year. Three hundred species of birds have been sighted in Jackson Hole. This is remarkable when one considers the impact of 100 years of settlement and development. For example, settlers, particularly cattlemen, exterminated the gray wolf in Jackson Hole after 1900. There were no bison left in Jackson Hole when the first homesteaders came in 1884, but they were reintroduced in the 1940s at the now-defunct Jackson Hole Wildlife Park. In 1968, the herd of 15 animals broke through the fences and, since that time, the herd has been allowed to range freely. More recently, the grizzly bear has returned to historic ranges in the Jackson Hole.[13]

Climate is the final significant element of the environment of Jackson Hole. There are several variations of an old saying that there are two seasons in Jackson Hole—nine months of winter and three months of company. Indeed, the winters are long. The climate of Jackson Hole is classified as "cold-snowy-forest with humid winters." Although it varies from year to year, snowfall covers the ground in the valley from November through April. Most precipitation falls as snow. Moose, Wyoming, averages 23 inches of precipitation annually. During the winter, a mantle of snow 20 to 40 inches deep covers the valley floor. However, precipitation is extremely variable throughout the valley because of elevation and the rain shadow caused by the Teton Range. For example, between 1931 and 1960, Jackson recorded an annual mean snowfall of 76 inches compared to 154 inches at Moose from 1961 to 1981.

Winter is the dominant season. Spring and fall are short seasons, times of transition. Summers are short, with around 60 frost-free days per year. Although temperatures can break 90°F, summer highs seldom exceed the 80s. Summer evenings are cool and crisp, ranging in the 30s and 40s. Although the average minimum temperature at Moose in January and February is 4°F, sub-zero temperatures are common. Thermometers at Moose often dip to −20°F or −30°F.[14]

Jackson Hole represents a mosaic of biotic or plant communities shaped by geography, geologic forces, climate, and fire. The history of Jackson Hole is really the story of human interaction with the environment. That setting was probably much the same approximately 11,000 years ago, when the first humans entered Jackson Hole.

Notes

1. Charles Butler Hunt, *Natural Regions of the United States and Canada* (San Francisco: W.H. Freeman, 1974), p. 6.

2. Fritiof M. Fryxell, *The Tetons, Interpretations of a Mountain Landscape* (Berkeley: University of California Press, 1938), pp. 1–3.

3. Merrill J. Mattes, "Jackson Hole, Crossroads of the Western Fur Trade, 1807–1829," *Pacific Northwest Quar-*terly 37 (1946): 88–89; and Ray Allen Billington, *Westward Expansion: A History of the American Frontier,* with the collaboration of James Blaine Hedges, 4th ed., rev. (New York: MacMillan, 1974), pp. 335–349.

4. Linda L. Olson and Tim Bywater, *A Guide to Exploring Grand Teton National Park* (Salt Lake City: RNM Press, 1991), pp. 24–30.

5. John David Love and John C. Reed Jr., *Creation of the Teton Landscape; The Geologic Story of Grand Teton National Park,* 1st ed., rev. (Moose, WY: Grand Teton Natural History Assn., 1971), p. 9.

6. Ibid., pp. 105–112; and Olson and Bywater, pp. 11–13.

7. Clarence S. Jackson, *Picture Maker of the Old West: William H. Jackson* (New York: Charles Scribner's Sons, 1947), p. 296.

8. Fryxell, *Interpretations of a Mountain Landscape,* pp. 11–12.

9. Jack F. Young, *Soil Survey of Teton County, Wyoming, Grand Teton National Park Area* (U.S. Department of Agriculture: Soil Conservation Service, 1982), pp. 3–11.

10. Ibid.

11. Tim W. Clark, *Ecology of Jackson Hole Wyoming,* A Primer (Salt Lake City, UT: Paragon Press, 1981), p. 40.

12. Ibid., pp. 40–73.

13. Bert and Meg Raynes, *Birds of Jackson Hole, A Checklist* (Moose WY: Grand Teton Natural History Assn., n.d.); *Wildlife of Grand Teton* (Moose, WY: Grand Teton Natural History Assn., n.d.); and William J. Barmore, et al., *Natural Resources Management Plan, Grand Teton National Park* (Moose, WY: National Park Service, 1986), pp. 111–121.

14. Richard A. Dirks and Brooks E. Martner, *The Climate of Yellowstone and Grand Teton National Parks* (U.S. Dept. of the Interior, National Park Service, Occasional Paper No. 6).

The Prehistoric Peoples of Jackson Hole

By Stephanie Crockett

During the 1930s, a Jackson Hole ranch foreman named W. C. "Slim" Lawrence began to collect artifacts along the north shore of Jackson Lake. Over the next 30 years, Lawrence's collection grew to number in the thousands and would help illuminate approximately 11,000 years of human habitation in a place we now call Jackson Hole.[1] The artifacts recovered by Slim Lawrence, combined with subsequent professional archeological research, allow us a glimpse of what life would have been like for the prehistoric inhabitants of Grand Teton National Park and Jackson Hole [see Figure 1].

Professional archeological investigations began with intensity in Jackson Hole during the 1970s. At this time, large-scale investigations were conducted by archeologist Gary Wright and his colleagues from the State University of New York at Albany. Wright and his associates formed an archeological "model" of prehistoric life in Jackson Hole—a hypothesis about the lives of the area's early peoples.[2] This chapter will briefly describe this model and its importance in later research. Using Wright's model as a framework, clues to the general subsistence and travel patterns of Jackson Hole's early populations are explored. Finally, because American Indian peoples do not exist solely within the realm of history,

and tribes—such as the Wind River Shoshone—are still culturally tied to Jackson Hole, a final section of this chapter includes a discussion of these modern cultural ties.

Figure 1. Standing on the east shore of Jackson Lake, rancher and amateur archeologist W. C. "Slim" Lawrence stands near a prehistoric fire hearth, November 1936. At the time Lawrence gathered artifacts, the property on which he collected was privately owned. It is illegal to collect archeological artifacts within Grand Teton National Park. *National Park Service*

An Archeological Model of Prehistoric Life in Jackson Hole

Throughout prehistory, the people of the mountain and foothills environments of northwest Wyoming subsisted as hunter-gatherers. As such, the early people of Jackson Hole most likely resided in the valley on a seasonal basis. Highly mobile, these individuals took advantage of ripening plants and migrating game animals. Prehistoric people also needed an intimate knowledge of the landscape and the behavioral patterns of game animals. However, anthropologists postulate that wild game, although essential to the prehistoric diet, was less predictable and, therefore, of secondary importance. By contrast, the abundance of edible and medicinal plants was critical to the survival of these people. Observation of such plant species on and around archeological sites has led to the development of a predictive archeological model of prehistoric life in and around Jackson Hole.

Basically, archeological models take a general theory and apply it to a limited set of conditions. By observing this limited set, the archeologist can then test his/her hypotheses. Using a model, archeologists can predict where certain types of archeological sites can be found. For example, archeologist Gary Wright and his colleagues formulated a model of "High Country Adaptations."[3] Wright and his colleagues observed the available edible and medicinal plant species within the Jackson Hole region, and then determined where prehistoric peoples may have traveled and settled based on the availability of these plant resources.

Wright's model is based on the theory that the area's earliest humans utilized the valley floor of Jackson Hole in the early spring, then moved to higher elevations during the summer and early fall to follow ripening plants. The first spring plant foods on the valley floor ripened between the third week in April and the middle of May. Early season root crops included spring beauty, bitterroot, Indian potato, biscuit root, and fawnlily, as they are commonly called. All of these plants have fleshy taproots, corms, or bulbs, are available throughout the spring and summer months, and continue to bloom just behind the receding snows at subsequently higher elevations.

Archeologists know that American Indians historically harvested these plants for their roots before or while in bloom, when the nutrient content is high and the plant is readily observable on the ground surface. Thus, according to Wright's model, prehistoric people moved into Jackson Hole by late May or early June, and subsisted predominantly on root crops through the month of June.[4]

According to Wright, the people living in the northern part of Jackson Hole probably spent their early summers at the mouth of the canyons in the northern Tetons. These people established large "base camps" at the head of Jackson Lake, at elevations of less than 7,000 feet above sea level (asl). Archeological evidence supports this theory, as a wide variety of tools, hearths, and roasting pits have been recovered from probable base camp sites, such as the Lawrence Site, on Jackson Lake. The Jackson Lake base camps were apparently used for a variety of activities, such as tool making, food processing, and even fishing, as evidenced by the notched stone artifacts probably used as fishing net weights [Figure 2].[5]

Wright's model also suggests that, as the snow melted, "specialized parties" traveled into Webb, Owl, and Berry Creek Canyons to collect ripening plants. Although Wright had yet to conduct systematic research of high-altitude areas in the park, he theorized that the sites left by these gathering parties would be relatively small and contain specialized "tool kits." Presumably, these sites were occupied for a shorter time by fewer people, all of whom performed the specialized tasks of plant gathering, plant processing, and some game hunting.

During the late summer, the large base camps moved up into the higher valleys of the northern Tetons. These base camps would be at an elevation of approximately 8,000 feet. From here, specialized parties gathered plants as they ripened in the highest mountain meadows. By late summer, the high mountains would have been thoroughly exploited, at which time the entire group moved westward into Idaho for the winter.[6]

A similar but separate model has been formulated for the southern half of Jackson Hole. Here, prehistoric people collected root and herb crops more acclimated to the drier benches and hillsides of

Figure 2. Fishing net weights. Typically, these weights are approximately 4 to 5 inches across. *Jackson Hole Historical Society and Museum*

southern Jackson Hole. These plants included sego lily and arrowleaf balsam root. Prehistoric people in southern Jackson Hole probably also harvested plants along the eastern side of the valley. Having wintered in the Wind River, Green River, or Big-horn Basins in northwest Wyoming, these groups entered the valley from the east, through the Gros Ventre drainage. This is evidenced by the high amounts of Green River cherts that have been found on archeological sites along the southeast end of the valley.[7] As the plants ripened and the season progressed, prehistoric people followed the maturing plants into the Gros Ventre Range to the south. By winter, they had moved into the warmer and dryer inter-montane basins east of Jackson Hole.

During the summer, the prehistoric people in and around Jackson Hole were primarily occupied with gathering plants, but they also hunted. Their travel patterns were in proximity to migrating animals such as mule deer, elk, and big horn sheep.[8] Indeed, bison supplemented the diet of Jackson Hole's prehistoric people. This evidence comes from bison bones recovered from sites within Grand Teton National Park and at the southeast end of the valley.[9]

With this archeological model as a framework for understanding the travel and general subsistence patterns of prehistoric peoples, it is now time to move on to the archeological data, most of which has been recovered since the formation of Wright's model.

The Archeological Record of Jackson Hole and Grand Teton National Park

The earliest human inhabitants of North America probably arrived from Asia, via the Bering Strait Land Bridge. This bridge connected the continents during the last Ice Age, for a period extending from 75,000 to 10,000 years B.P. (Before Present). Archeological evidence from Eastern Siberia suggests that the first humans migrated into the New World no more than 22,000 years ago. Archeologists continue to seek evidence for an earlier arrival, but the current record suggests that by 12,000 years ago humans were living as far east as Maine and as far south as Costa Rica.[10]

The earliest evidence of humans in Jackson Hole dates to approximately 11,000 years ago. By this time, the massive ice sheet that had blanketed much of Jackson Hole had retreated from the valley floor. Through analysis of fossil pollen found at the bottom of area lakes, we know that plant communities consisting of shrubs and herbs had colonized the silt and outwash soils left behind by the receding glaciers by 11,200 years ago. Willows and juniper may have been present during this time period but, in general, the lower elevations of Jackson Hole were probably much like the high alpine meadows of today, with sparse vegetation and a short growing season. It was in this environment that the first humans ventured into Jackson Hole.[11]

So, who were these first intrepid humans to follow the receding glaciers into this high country?

The Paleoindian Period (12,000 to 8,000 B.P.)

The earliest Jackson Hole artifacts made by human hands date to the Paleoindian period. This time period ranges between 12,000 and 8,000 years ago. During this time, the archeological record suggests that humans hunted with finely flaked, lanceolate-shaped, stone spear points. These points were hafted to a large spear that was either hand-thrown or projected by the use of an atlatl.

The atlatl is a simple but ingenious device that greatly enhanced hunting technology during this early period [Figures 3 and 4]. The atlatl is a carved wooden throwing stick, which was used in conjunction with a finely-flaked spear point, hafted to a short wooden dart shaft. The dart was attached to a larger spear that, in turn, was propelled by the atlatl. The atlatl throwing stick was fitted with a thong or socket to steady the butt of the spear, and was generally weighted by a smoothed bannerstone to add force to the throw. The atlatl thus became an extension of the hunter's arm to increase the velocity of

the spear. This hunting technique was used across North America for at least 10,500 years, until the development of the bow and arrow about 2,000 years ago.[12]

The earliest North American people to use the atlatl are referred to as the Clovis and Folsom cultures. These names are from the New Mexico towns where evidence for these earliest Americans was first discovered. The terms also describe the stone spear points used by these early hunters. Archeological evidence suggests that Clovis and Folsom peoples had a diet that relied heavily on large mammals, such as the now extinct species of North American camel, horse, bison and, for the Clovis hunter, the North American elephant known as mammoth. Clovis and Folsom sites have been found throughout the Rocky Mountain West, and as close to Jackson Hole as the Big Horn Basin near Cody, Wyoming. Isolated Clovis and Folsom spear points have also been found in a number of locations in the Green River Basin.[13]

Based on the paucity of artifacts found in Jackson Hole that date from this time period, it is impossible to know how long these populations lived in the area. Part of a Folsom spear point was found at an elevation of 9,000 feet,[14] in the Upper Gros Ventre drainage, which flows into Jackson Hole from the east. A lanceolate spear point was discovered at a site near present-day Astoria Hot Springs at the south end of Jackson Hole, while a spear point resembling the Clovis style was recovered from the Lawrence

Figure 3. The atlatl was used for throwing short spears or darts. *Tracks Through Time: Prehistory and History of the Pinon Canyon Maneuver Site, Southeastern Colorado (National Park Service and U.S. Army)*

Figure 4. Atlatl throwing stick, detail. Fingerloops and weighted bannerstone on lower left. *Stephanie Crockett*

Site on the shores of Jackson Lake. To date, however, no remains of Clovis or Folsom prey have been found in Jackson Hole.[15]

As we move forward in time to approximately 10,000 years ago, the evidence for human occupation begins to increase and the picture of life in Jackson Hole becomes a little clearer. By this time, Englemann spruce and subalpine fir were on the landscape, and the whitebark pine, with its edible seeds, was quickly spreading throughout the region. Archeologists continue to refer to this as the Paleoindian period, yet the spear point styles have changed. Names such as Agate Basin, Hell Gap, and Cody (see time line) are used to describe some of the stone tools used during this time period. Although the styles changed slightly, spear points were still large and probably projected by the atlatl throwing stick.

More durable than bone, wood, and fiber, stone artifacts are often the only evidence that archeologists have to trace cultural and technological changes through time. In addition to stylistic changes, variations in the raw materials used to make stone tools can be an important indicator of cultural change. Throughout the Jackson Hole and Yellowstone region, volcanic activity deposited a valuable stone material that was used frequently by prehistoric people. Millions of years ago, as rapidly cooling lava flowed through underground fissures, a natural semi-translucent glass was formed. Subsequent glacial activity helped expose outcrops of this volcanic glass, known

as obsidian. Obsidian's fine flaking qualities and ability to keep a sharp edge made it a popular raw material for prehistoric toolmakers.

Obsidian affords an added bonus for archeologists in that each volcanic flow has unique chemical elements. Through a technique called x-ray florescence, scientists can identify the exact chemical elements of a particular obsidian artifact. Under this procedure, the obsidian artifact is exposed to high-intensity x-rays. Different elements in the obsidian absorb and release these x-rays at different rates, which can then be measured. When plotted on a graph, the chemical "fingerprint" of an obsidian artifact is revealed. Scientists then compare this fingerprint to obsidian from natural outcrops across the region. A match of chemical components indicates the source for the obsidian in that particular tool.

Several large outcrops of obsidian have been found throughout the region [Figure 5]. These sources include Obsidian Cliff in Yellowstone National Park, Bear Gulch in the Targhee National Forest, the Fish Creek sources in southern Jackson Hole near Wilson (commonly referred to as the Teton Pass sources), Wright Creek near Malad, Idaho, and the Grassy Lake and Conant Pass outcrops at the northern end of the Tetons. Paleoindian obsidian artifacts found in Grand Teton National Park chemically match some of these sources. X-ray fluorescence testing reveals that the most popular obsidian source for early Jackson Hole toolmakers was nearby

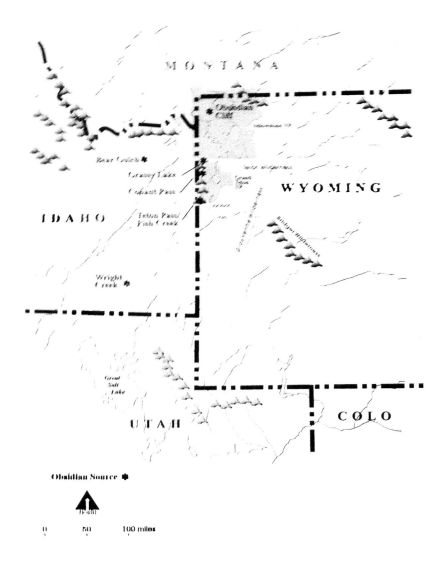

MONTANA

Obsidian
Cliff

IDAHO

WYOMING

Reas Creek

Crescent H

Indian Road
Fish Creek

Bridger Wilderness

Wright
Creek

Great
Salt
Lake

UTAH

COLO

Obsidian Source ✚

0   50   100 miles

Figure 5. Obsidian sources, *National Park Service*

Teton Pass. Obsidian Cliff in Yellowstone, Targhee National Forest and Wright Creek were also used, although to a lesser degree.

Because Teton Pass is the source for the majority of Paleoindian obsidian artifacts in Grand Teton National Park, archeologists believe that humans entered the Jackson Hole valley via the south end, near the pass. However, the fact that the remainder of the artifacts came from a wide variety of regional sources indicates that Paleoindians were a highly mobile people. The distance between Obsidian Cliff, the most northern source, and Wright Creek, the most southern source, is more than 175 miles.[16] The Paleoindian peoples who frequented Jackson Hole apparently had an intimate knowledge of resources available throughout a rather large geographical area.

Bone is rarely preserved in archeological sites. As a result, excavations have revealed little if any evidence to indicate what species of game Paleoindians hunted while in Jackson Hole. Archeological sites just east and northeast of Jackson Hole suggest that around 10,000 years ago two separate cultural groups emerged in the region. One group adapted to the mountain and foothills environment, while the other adapted to the open plains. The groups living in the mountains, such as the Tetons, Wind River, or Gros Ventre Ranges, hunted mountain sheep and some mule deer. Meanwhile, the plains-adapted peoples developed sophisticated, communal bison-hunting techniques.

Traveling in groups, the plains hunters trapped great numbers of bison in arroyos (dry creek beds), sand dunes, or artificial corrals, where they killed them with hand-held spears or atlatls. In the mountains, hunting was done by smaller groups. Archeological evidence from the Absaroka mountains northeast of Jackson Hole, as well as studies of modern-day mountain sheep, indicate that mountain-dwelling hunters used nets to capture big horn sheep. The hunters strung a net, large enough to capture three sheep, across a known migration path. As the sheep became entangled in the net, the hunters killed them with clubs. A Paleoindian trapping net made of juniper bark cordage has been found in the Absaroka mountain range. Mule deer are a less predictable spe-

cies, and were probably hunted individually with the spear and atlatl.[17]

Plant materials have also been recovered from the Paleoindian period. Archeologists have found the remains of plant foods such as seeds, berries, roots, leaves, and bulbs dating to the Paleoindian period in cave sites northeast of Jackson Hole. Paleoindian food cache pits have also been found in the mountains of northwest Wyoming. These contained the remains of sunflower (*Helianthus annus*), prickly pear (*Opuntia polyacantha*), and amaranth (*Amaranthus retroflexus*).[18] Consequently, we can assume that Paleoindians in Jackson Hole ate these plants, and supplemented their diet with mountain sheep and mule deer.

The Archaic Period

Around 8,000 years ago, the warming climate of Jackson Hole reduced the glaciers to mere remnants high in the mountains. Also during this period, lodgepole pine became the dominant conifer in the area, growing in stands with aspen and Douglas fir.[19] During this time, prehistoric populations in the mountains of northwest Wyoming began to eat more small animals and wild plant foods. Changes in spear point styles and food-processing activities signal the beginning of a long period that archeologists refer to as the Archaic.

The Archaic period lasted approximately 6,500 years in this region, and has been divided into three separate periods simply referred to as Early, Middle, and Late Archaic. These divisions are based primarily on changes in spear point styles.

The Early Archaic (8,000 to 5,000 B.P.)

The Early Archaic period took place approximately 5,000 to 8,000 years ago. The oldest buried cultural deposits found in Grand Teton National Park were radiocarbon-dated to around 5,850 years ago, well

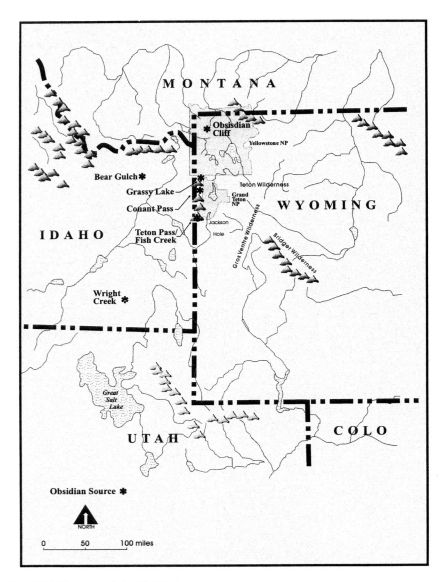

MONTANA

Obsisdian
Cliff

Yellowstone NP

Bear Gulch

Grassy Lake

Conant Pass

Teton Pass/
Fish Creek

Teton Wilderness

Grand
Teton
NP

Jackson
Hole

WYOMING

IDAHO

Gros Ventre Wilderness

Bridger Wilderness

Wright
Creek

Great
Salt
Lake

UTAH

COLO

Obsidian Source

NORTH

0   50   100 miles

Figure 5. Obsidian sources. *National Park Service*

Teton Pass. Obsidian Cliff in Yellowstone, Targhee National Forest and Wright Creek were also used, although to a lesser degree.

Because Teton Pass is the source for the majority of Paleoindian obsidian artifacts in Grand Teton National Park, archeologists believe that humans entered the Jackson Hole valley via the south end, near the pass. However, the fact that the remainder of the artifacts came from a wide variety of regional sources indicates that Paleoindians were a highly mobile people. The distance between Obsidian Cliff, the most northern source, and Wright Creek, the most southern source, is more than 175 miles.[16] The Paleoindian peoples who frequented Jackson Hole apparently had an intimate knowledge of resources available throughout a rather large geographical area.

Bone is rarely preserved in archeological sites. As a result, excavations have revealed little if any evidence to indicate what species of game Paleoindians hunted while in Jackson Hole. Archeological sites just east and northeast of Jackson Hole suggest that around 10,000 years ago two separate cultural groups emerged in the region. One group adapted to the mountain and foothills environment, while the other adapted to the open plains. The groups living in the mountains, such as the Tetons, Wind River, or Gros Ventre Ranges, hunted mountain sheep and some mule deer. Meanwhile, the plains-adapted peoples developed sophisticated, communal bison-hunting techniques.

Traveling in groups, the plains hunters trapped great numbers of bison in arroyos (dry creek beds), sand dunes, or artificial corrals, where they killed them with hand-held spears or atlatls. In the mountains, hunting was done by smaller groups. Archeological evidence from the Absaroka mountains northeast of Jackson Hole, as well as studies of modern-day mountain sheep, indicate that mountain-dwelling hunters used nets to capture big horn sheep. The hunters strung a net, large enough to capture three sheep, across a known migration path. As the sheep became entangled in the net, the hunters killed them with clubs. A Paleoindian trapping net made of juniper bark cordage has been found in the Absaroka mountain range. Mule deer are a less predictable spe-

cies, and were probably hunted individually with the spear and atlatl.[17]

Plant materials have also been recovered from the Paleoindian period. Archeologists have found the remains of plant foods such as seeds, berries, roots, leaves, and bulbs dating to the Paleoindian period in cave sites northeast of Jackson Hole. Paleoindian food cache pits have also been found in the mountains of northwest Wyoming. These contained the remains of sunflower (*Helianthus annus*), prickly pear (*Opuntia polyacantha*), and amaranth (*Amaranthus retroflexus*).[18] Consequently, we can assume that Paleoindians in Jackson Hole ate these plants, and supplemented their diet with mountain sheep and mule deer.

The Archaic Period

Around 8,000 years ago, the warming climate of Jackson Hole reduced the glaciers to mere remnants high in the mountains. Also during this period, lodgepole pine became the dominant conifer in the area, growing in stands with aspen and Douglas fir.[19] During this time, prehistoric populations in the mountains of northwest Wyoming began to eat more small animals and wild plant foods. Changes in spear point styles and food-processing activities signal the beginning of a long period that archeologists refer to as the Archaic.

The Archaic period lasted approximately 6,500 years in this region, and has been divided into three separate periods simply referred to as Early, Middle, and Late Archaic. These divisions are based primarily on changes in spear point styles.

The Early Archaic (8,000 to 5,000 B.P.)

The Early Archaic period took place approximately 5,000 to 8,000 years ago. The oldest buried cultural deposits found in Grand Teton National Park were radiocarbon-dated to around 5,850 years ago, well

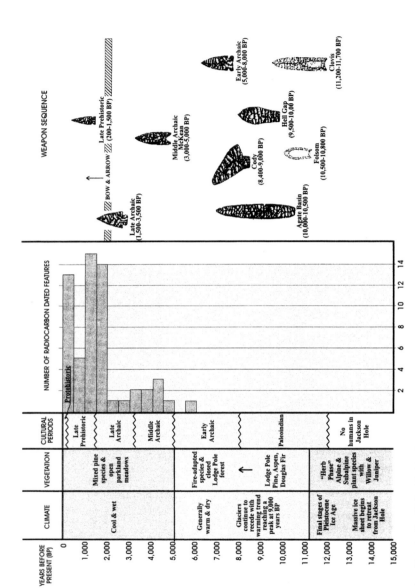

Jackson Hole time line. *National Park Service*

Figure 6. Eroded and deflated roasting pits on shore of Jackson Lake. *Jackson Hole Historical Society and Museum*

within the Early Archaic period.[20] Radiocarbon dating is a technique that measures the amount of Carbon 14 that has decayed from a formerly living organism. All living organisms absorb an equal amount of carbon from the atmosphere. When an organism dies, it no longer absorbs carbon. The Carbon-14 in that organism then starts to convert to Carbon-12 at a known rate. By measuring the ratio of Carbon-14 to Carbon-12 in an artifact such as wood, bone, charcoal, or shell, the relative age of an object can be determined.[21]

In Grand Teton National Park, the earliest radiocarbon-dated deposits are from a large roasting pit found on the north shore of Jackson Lake (Lawrence Site). This pit was probably used for roasting local root plants, and is the earliest evidence for this type of activity in the park [Figure 6]. Early Archaic inhabitants of the Jackson Lake area, as would their successors, filled these pits with quartzite cobbles, which they had probably scoured from nearby hillsides. They would then build a fire on top of the cobbles. When sufficiently heated, the coals would be removed, and the rock-filled pits would serve as ovens. Similar roasting pits were described by the early Jesuit missionary-explorer Father Pierre Jean De Smet during his encounters with tribes in the Pacific Northwest:

They make an excavation in the earth from 12 to 14 inches deep, and of proportional diameter to contain the roots. They cover the bottom with closely-cemented pavement, which they make red-hot by means of fire. After having carefully withdrawn the coals they cover the stones with grass or wet hay: then place a layer of roots, another of wet hay, a third with bark overlain with mold, whereon is kept a glowing fire for 50, 60 and sometimes 70 hours.[22]

Plant remains recovered from more recent roasting pits in Grand Teton National Park indicate that the "wet hay" used to cover the root crops might have been sedge grass or buttercup, which occurs in the wetlands near streams and lakes. The plant remains that were roasted in these pits include a variety of berries, dock, salvia (a leafy sage), ambrosia (a member of the sunflower family), sedgegrass, bistort, and tule or bulrush. These plants require long periods of exposure to moist heat to convert the starches to sugar. Prehistoric people probably also roasted camas roots in these pits, using the same method described by Father De Smet. Camas grows in some of the large meadows on the north end of Grand Teton National Park, near several prehistoric roasting pits.[23]

The records of D. B. Shimkin, the anthropologist who documented much of the Wind River

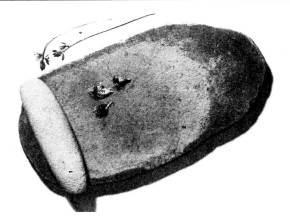

Figure 7. Grinding stones (mano and metate) with blue camas bulbs and flowers. *Jackson Hole Historical Society and Museum*

Shoshone culture during the late 1930s, reveal that these most recent American Indian inhabitants of Jackson Hole traditionally gathered plants for medicine, food, and manufacturing materials. According to Shimkin, individual women or small parties gathered the roots, berries, seeds, pistil, and leaves of a variety of plants. Wild roots, including camas and wild onion, were dug with wooden digging sticks, while currants, rose hips, hawthornes, and gooseberries were picked and then ground with a stone grinding implement. This tool, known as a mano, was usually made of sandstone and used in a back-and-forth rocking motion across another larger flat rock known as a metate [Figure 7]. Berries were also dried and boiled in soup, or mixed with grease and dried meat to form an easily transportable food called pemmican.[24] These food-processing traditions remained unchanged from the Early Archaic period.

In addition to the introduction of plant roasting pits, the stone tools found at Jackson Lake also show a cultural change during the Early Archaic period. Spear points from this time period are large with notches on either side of the base, which were used as a way to haft the point to the spear [Figure 8]. Although the use of chert, a stone material, for spear points increased during the Early Archaic period, obsidian continued to be an important raw material. Obsidian spear points from Jackson Lake show a

continued reliance on the Teton Pass sources. This demonstrates a strong familiarity with, and possible travel route through, the southern end of the valley.

The number of spear points that date to this time period is low when compared to subsequent time periods. To date, the above-mentioned roasting pit is the only feature from the park that is radiocarbon-dated to the Early Archaic. In addition, archeologists have found no Early Archaic residential structures in Jackson Hole. However, in the

Figure 8. Early archaic projectile point, Jackson Lake. *Final Report on the Jackson Lake Archeological Project, Grand Teton National Park (National Park Service, Midwest Archeological Center)*

0		2 in
0		5 cm

nearby basins of Wyoming, Early Archaic people resided in semi-subterranean pithouses. These houses were broad pits dug into the ground and covered with a structure of wood, brush, and hides. An overall paucity of data concerning this time period remains as a gap in the overall understanding of prehistoric life in Jackson Hole.

Middle Archaic Period (5,000 to 3,000 B.P.)

Around 5,000 years ago, prehistoric spear points underwent a notable change. In addition, an increased number of roasting pits date to this era. These changes mark the beginning of the Middle Archaic time period, which extends from 5,000 to 3,000 years ago. The increased density of roasting pits and stone-grinding implements found at Jackson Lake suggests that Middle Archaic people invested more time and energy in processing certain plant foods. The overall increased number of archeological sites across the region also suggests a general population increase, or more frequent travel by these people.

Tipi rings also begin to appear in the archeological record during this time. A tipi ring is a large circle of moderate-sized stones used to anchor a tipi. When the tipi is moved, the stones remain in a circular pattern on the ground. The tipi was made with long poles and covered with animal hides. When the group needed to move, the tipi could be easily dismantled and carried, unlike the more permanent pithouse used in earlier times.

During the Middle Archaic period, a unique type of spear point also appears. Spear points that date to the Middle Archaic do not have side notches, as in earlier times, but have a stemmed base or are lanceolate-shaped [Figure 9]. This new spear point is referred to as McKean, and might represent the influx of a new population into the northwest plains and Jackson Hole. X-ray florescence testing on artifacts from Jackson Lake supports this theory.

Jackson Lake artifacts from the Middle Archaic period show a greater reliance on obsidian for spear points, and a decrease in the use of other stone materials. The most popular obsidian source also changed,

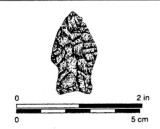

0   2 in

0   5 cm

Figure 9. Middle archaic (McKean) projectile point, Jackson Lake. *Final Report on the Jackson Lake Archeological Project, Grand Teton National Park (National Park Service, Midwest Archeological Center)*

from Teton Pass to Obsidian Cliff, approximately 70 miles north. This suggests that people were now entering the valley from the north, and bringing with them this slightly different style of spear point.[25]

This travel pattern, however, is not supported by artifacts found in archeological sites in the Wind River, Gros Ventre and Teton Wilderness areas of the Bridger-Teton National Forest adjacent to Grand Teton National Park. Obsidian artifacts found in these areas reveal that throughout prehistory no major travel corridor existed between the Yellowstone Plateau and Jackson Hole. In these areas, the primary obsidian sources are continually Teton Pass, Wright Creek, and Bear Gulch on the Targhee National Forest.[26] As to whether the new spear point style was brought to the region by an entirely different culture is still debated.

The landscape in Jackson Hole and the surrounding mountains also changed during the Middle Archaic period. The drought-and-fire-adapted species of lodgepole pine, Douglas fir, and aspen gave way to closed forests of pine spruce and fir. These species reflected a shift to the cooler, relatively moist climate, which we continue to experience today.[27]

Late Archaic Period (3,000 to 1,500 B.P.)

The Late Archaic period is well represented in Grand Teton National Park. The disappearance of

Figure 10. Late archaic projectile point, Jackson Lake.
Final Report on the Jackson Lake Archeological Project, Grand Teton National Park (National Park Service, Midwest Archeological Center)

McKean-style spear points, and the appearance of a point that exhibits distinct notches at the corners generally signal this time period [Figure 10]. The corner-notched spear point came into use around 3,000 years ago, and lasted approximately 2,000 years. During the Late Archaic period, humans continued to hunt large mammals and gather plants. They also continued to use large roasting pits for plant processing. The large number of archeological sites that date to this period in Jackson Hole and in the northwest Plains indicate a population expansion. However, the short growing seasons in these environments probably acted as a controlling mechanism to prevent over population.[28]

X-ray fluorescence testing of obsidian tools dating to the Late Archaic demonstrates a shift back to Teton Pass outcrops as the primary raw material source for Jackson Hole inhabitants. In general, the Late Archaic inhabitants of Jackson Hole used a wider variety of obsidian sources than did any of their predecessors. The travel patterns of this later group, however, closely mirror those of the earliest inhabitants 7,000 years earlier. They had a wide travel range and exploited a variety of obsidian sources ranging from Obsidian Cliff to southeastern Idaho. But, while human use of the valley intensified, the basic lifestyle remained unchanged. Plant gathering and processing, supplemented by hunting, were still the primary activities.

Late Prehistoric Period (1,500 to 500 B.P.)

Around 1,500 years ago, we see the beginning of a period known as the Late Prehistoric, which is signaled by the most dramatic change in subsistence patterns and technology to date. At this time, the bow and arrow replaced the atlatl as the primary hunting weapon. Consequently, projectile points also changed, from large spear points to much smaller arrow points [Figure 11].

The bow and arrow significantly changed hunting techniques. It requires much less body movement to shoot a small arrow from a bow than it does to use an atlatl throwing stick to project a large spear. The pull of the bowstring simply requires use of the arm, and the hunter can be standing, seated, or lying. The atlatl, on the other hand, has to be used in a standing position in a considerably open environment and, most successfully, in a situation where the animal is on a driven course or contained in some way. In contrast, a hunter can draw a bow slowly and deliberately, without violent movement or hindrance by underbrush, which allows him to work individually in a variety of environments.[29]

Another significant innovation in the Late Prehistoric period is the use of steatite or soapstone bowls and clay pottery [Figure 12]. Steatite is a soft stone that outcrops naturally in spots along the Teton and Wind River Ranges. This material is soft enough to be carved by an elk antler or other stone

Figure 11. Late prehistoric projectile point, Jackson Lake.
Final Report on the Jackson Lake Archeological Project, Grand Teton National Park (National Park Service, Midwest Archeological Center)

Figure 12. Steatite bowls. Most
steatite bowls are 10 to 16 inches
high and 8 to 10 inches wide.
*Jackson Hole Historical Society and
Museum*

tool, and can be hardened by fire and exposure to air.
In other areas, such vessels were used for cooking
and storage, which was probably also the case in
Jackson Hole. As before, Late Prehistoric inhabitants
of Jackson Hole also engaged in hunting and plant
processing. The number of roasting pits found in the
park reached its peak during this period.

The travel patterns of Late Prehistoric peoples
changed slightly from that of their recent predecessors. An analysis of obsidian arrow points shows that
the most popular sources for obsidian were Teton
Pass, Obsidian Cliff, and Targhee National Forest.
In general, fewer obsidian sources were used when
compared to earlier times, and the use of obsidian
sources in southeast Idaho was discontinued. This
analysis, coupled with the discovery of the less portable steatite and clay vessels, suggests that the Late
Prehistoric inhabitants of Jackson Hole had a much
tighter range of travel than earlier groups. They did
not range the 175 miles from Obsidian Cliff to
Wright Creek as did some earlier populations.

In general, the archeological record reveals little
cultural change in the period between 10,000 to 500
years ago. The primary meat sources for mountain-
dwelling humans were deer, elk, bighorn sheep, and
some bison—while bison and antelope were staples
for residents of the Great Plains. In both cases, humans relied on hunting and gathering. There is no
evidence to suggest that prehistoric inhabitants of
Jackson Hole practiced agriculture or established permanent settlements, as did populations in the southwest and eastern United States. It is important to remember, though, that from the Paleoindian through
Late Prehistoric periods, the inhabitants of Jackson
Hole and the entire New World were primarily pe-
destrian. It was not until the first Europeans arrived
(around A.D. 1500) that the inhabitants of the New
World acquired the horse. In the Rocky Mountains,
horses were not widely used by tribes until around
A.D. 1700. The arrival of the horse—and the influx
of European trade goods such as beads, metals,
cloth, and guns—brought about profound changes in
the economic and cultural systems of the region.

Protohistoric Period
(A.D. 1700 to 1850)

The presence of European goods in the archeological
record signals the beginning of the Protohistoric period. This period lasted from around A.D. 1700 to
1850, by which time North American Indian tribes
were being relocated to reservations.

Probably the most significant item to be acquired by the tribes was the horse. The introduction

of the horse broadened the territories of mounted Indian peoples. The horse increased the mobility of many tribes and brought together the Great Basin and Plains cultures. According to D. B. Shimkin, the introduction of the horse into the Wind River Shoshone culture upset the economic and social balance. Because horses were initially scarce, the men generally rode in order to be fresh for hunting. As a result, women had to walk, which upset the social equilibrium between the sexes. Individuals and families acquired more movable goods, and hunting, gathering and fishing territories changed. The tribes with horses also became more efficient at communal hunting, which allowed them to provide more food for a larger population. At the same time, however, these tribes lost their intimate knowledge of the smaller game species, such as squirrels and rabbits.[30] In and around Jackson Hole, however, early nineteenth-century trappers encountered mountain-dwelling peoples who appeared to be thriving without horses. Trapper and explorer Osborne Russell described an 1835 encounter with mountain-dwelling people in the Lamar Valley of Yellowstone National Park.

Here we found a few Snake Indians comprising 6 men 7 women and 8 or 10 children who were the only Inhabitants of this lonely and secluded spot. They were all neatly clothed in dressed deer and Sheep skins of the best quality and seemed to be perfectly contented and happy—Their personal property consisted of one old butcher Knife   ly worn to the back two old shattered fusees[31] near which had long since become useless for want of ammunition a Small Stone pot and about 30 dogs on which they carried their skins, clothing, provisions etc on their hunting excursions. They were well armed with bows and arrows pointed with obsidian. The bows were beautifully wrought from Sheep, Buffaloe and Elk horns secured with Deer and Elk sinews and ornamented with porcupine quills and generally about 3 feet long.[32]

These people lived on berries, herbs, roots, small mammals, and larger game animals such as elk, deer and mountain sheep. Their diet also included native trout and whitefish from the mountain lakes.[33]

Other nineteeth-century encounters with American Indian peoples in the region describe them as traveling in small family groups. Large dogs, used as hunting and pack animals, accompanied these groups. Often, these dogs pulled a V-shaped travois, used to carry moderate-sized burdens. The travois was made of two long poles; the front tips were attached to a harness at the dog's shoulders, while the ends were left dragging on the ground. Midway up the poles was a frame used to carry burdens such as wood, food, small children, and the sick or elderly [Figure 13].[34] Therefore, it appears that although the introduction of European trade goods brought about changes in the economic and cultural systems

Figure 13. A travois, shown here being pulled by a horse, was made of two long poles with an attached frame for carrying people and items. *Jackson Hole Historical Society and Museum*

of the plains tribes, the mountain-adapted peoples of Jackson Hole maintained their highly adapted and efficient subsistence strategy.

The Shoshone in Jackson Hole

The first mountain-dwelling peoples encountered by the trappers and early nineteenth-century explorers in Jackson Hole were generally known as the "Sheep-eaters" and were said to have spoken in the "Snake" tongue, which is a reference to the Shoshone.[35] The Shoshone language is part of a large language group known as Uto-Aztecan. Members of this group range from the Northern Plains to the Cascade Mountains and into the southwestern United States to Mexico.[36] It is not certain where the Shoshone got their name, but the earlier-used term "Snake" was likely a misinterpretation of the serpentine hand gesture used to describe the in-and-out motion by which they wove their grass-and-brush shelters.[37]

The term "Sheep-Eaters" described those members of the Eastern Shoshone who subsisted, at least in part, on mountain sheep. The "Tukudika," as they called themselves, remained high in the mountains and were still without horses when they were placed on the Wind River Reservation around 1868.[38] The "Sheep-Eaters" were just one of several specialized groups considered part of the Eastern Shoshone tribe. Other names, such as "Kucundicka" (meaning the "Buffalo Hunters" of the Plains), the "Pa'Iahiadika" or "Elk-Eaters," who hunted the western slopes of the Tetons, and the "Do'yia" or "Mountain Dwellers," who were scattered throughout the mountains of the Yellowstone region, describe members of a single cultural group. Although these groups utilized the mountains and northwest Plains in much different ways, they were all members of one tribe, the Eastern Shoshone.[39]

To the Shoshone, these names did not define a rigid political or cultural division of people. All were one tribe and spoke one language, and their names did not separate individual political or social groups. Instead, they defined ecological niches. For example, the Sheep-Eaters of the Northern Rocky Mountains specialized in hunting mountain sheep, while the

Elk-Eaters hunted primarily elk. These individual group names demonstrate the way American Indian tribes, such as the Shoshone, conveyed important information concerning the ecosystem within which they lived. They also offer a clue to the vast and intimate knowledge that these people had of their homeland and the species within it.[40]

D. B. Shimkin wrote a similar account of Wind River or Eastern Shoshone demographics. According to Shimkin, during the early 1800s the entire Wind River Shoshone tribe was comprised of 2,000 to 3,000 individuals. During the winter and spring, this tribe split into three to five smaller groups called bands. Each band was made up of 100 or 200 people and occupied a different portion of the Shoshone territory. During the summer, each band divided into individual extended family groups. These family groups might have consisted of 10 to 30 closely related individuals, like the group encountered by Osborne Russell in 1835.

With the coming of the autumn months, the individual family groups reunited with the larger tribe for the annual communal bison hunt in the intermontane basins and open plains. This hunt was necessary for obtaining and processing dried meat supplies for the upcoming winter. For the winter, the tribe could again divide into smaller bands, each of which resided in a different part of the vast Shoshone territory.[41]

Archeological remains also offer insight into the spiritual bond that the Shoshone and prehistoric peoples had with Jackson Hole. High in the mountains of both the Teton and Gros Ventre Ranges are semicircular stone enclosures. These enclosures, and many like them in the mountains of northwest Wyoming, offer clues to the spiritual importance of these high mountain peaks.

For the modern Shoshone, who continue to maintain close cultural ties to this region, the majestic and snow-capped peaks of the Tetons hold special significance. In the Shoshone belief system, mountain peaks provide access into the spirit world, where they gain special powers for such things as hunting or healing. On these peaks, referred to as "puhadoya," which is translated as "Power Mountain," individuals enter the spirit world through visions or dreams.[42]

Prehistoric people from the Great Basin, Great Plains, and Northwest traveled to Jackson Hole, and archeologists have identified 11 (A–K) distinct travel routes into and out of the valley. Some of these routes were later used by trappers and survey expeditions.* The map on page 37 illustrates these routes.

Route A. The first route begins at the delta where Owl Creek flows into Jackson Lake from the west. Traveling up Owl Creek, a broad canyon with a low pass could be easily crossed into Berry Creek Canyon to the north. Berry Creek could then be followed to its headwaters, allowing access into the more temperate valleys of Idaho.

Route B. The second route into northern Jackson Hole leads from Yellowstone National Park, down the Lewis River to the north shore of Jackson Lake.

Route C. The third route into northern Jackson Hole connects the Yellowstone Plateau to Jackson Hole through the Pacific Creek drainage. This route begins at the point where the Yellowstone River enters the south end of Yellowstone Lake. It follows up the Yellowstone River through the Thorofare to Atlantic Creek. From Atlantic Creek, the route crosses Two Ocean Pass and follows Pacific Creek into Jackson Hole.

Route D. The final route into the north end of Jackson Hole begins to the east, and follows the Wind River to Togwotee Pass at an elevation of 9,658 feet. From Togwotee Pass, the route drops into Blackrock Creek and follows it to its confluence with the Buffalo Fork, which flows into Jackson Hole from the northeast. Due to the high elevation and often severe weather experienced on Togwotee Pass, this route was probably used only in late summer and early autumn.

Route E. To avoid the heavy snows of Togwotee Pass, prehistoric people may have utilized the Gros Ventre River drainage, which flows into Jackson Hole from the east. Early trappers and explorers are reported to have also used this route, entering Jackson Hole from the Wind River Basin via Union Pass. This route ascends Warm Springs Creek to Union Pass (8,500 feet). From here, it descends the south fork of Fish Creek to the Gros Ventre River.

Route F. Jackson Hole was also reached from the Wind River Basin by traveling from Union Pass down the north fork of Fish Creek, and then into the Gros Ventre River drainage.

Route G. Prehistoric people also entered Jackson Hole from the Green River Basin by traveling up the Green River and over Bacon Ridge and down the Gros Ventre River. This route is known for its plentiful deer and elk populations. Numerous prehistoric sites are located along this route.

Route H. Although arduous due to steep cliff faces, violent river crossings, and steep talus slopes, Jackson Hole could have been reached from the Green River Basin by traveling through the Hoback Canyon. Trappers and American Indians also used this route.

Route I. The Snake River Canyon route connects Jackson Hole to Star Valley, which allowed access to other points to the southwest. The Snake River
Canyon is a steep, walled canyon with fast-moving water, making crossing
difficult to impossible much of the year. Portions of this canyon could have
been avoided by using the trail that connects the Little Greys River to Bailey
Creek, which then enters Star Valley. The early trapper and explorer Osborne
Russell used this route in 1837–1838.

(continued next page)

PREHISTORIC ACCESS ROUTES (continued)

The final two routes (J and K) allowed access, however arduous, to valleys south and west of Jackson Hole. Although trappers reported a well-marked trail over Teton Pass, this ascent to 8,429 feet was steep and heavily forested. Some historians credit John Colter, a member of the Lewis and Clark expedition, with being the first explorer to use the pass in 1807. In 1812, Edward Robinson and Jacob Reznor were familiar enough with this route to lead Wilson Price Hunt and his Overland Astorians westward over Teton Pass. Trappers used this pass extensively between 1820 and 1840. In 1860, Jim Bridger guided Capt. William Raynolds of the Topographical Engineers over Teton Pass and into Pierre's Hole. Teton Pass is also an important source of obsidian. Chemical-sourcing techniques have identified the pass as the source of obsidian for many artifacts recovered in Grand Teton National Park.

Route J. One of the Teton routes follows up Mosquito Creek to the divide at 8,300 feet. This drainage connects lower Jackson Hole to Swan, Star, and Teton Valleys to the south and west. Obsidian pebbles, which may be the result of prehistoric tool making, have been found in the gravel washing out of Mosquito Creek.

Route K. Phillips Pass, the final travel route, lies at an elevation of 8,900 feet, and leads west into Teton Valley, Idaho, through Phillips Canyon along the southern end of the Teton Range.

*These routes were identified by Gary Wright in "A Preliminary Report on the Archaeology of the Jackson Hole Country, Wyoming," and Charles M. Love in "An Archaeological Survey of the Jackson Hole Region, Wyoming." Also see Osborne Russell, *Journal of a Trapper*, ed., Aubrey L. Haines; and Melissa Connor and Raymond Kunselman, "Mobility, Settlement Patterns, and Obsidian Source Variation in Jackson Hole, Wyoming."

According to anthropologist Åke Hultkrantz, who has extensively documented the Shoshone culture, the attainment of power for the ordinary Shoshone individual requires special preparation. Alone and without a weapon, the individual sets out for places known through legend and tradition to be the home of the spirits.

Sometimes he turns his steps towards the hillocks or solitary rocks out on the prairie where the desert *puha* [powers] generally appear. At other times, he travels to the water where the fish *puha* may manifest themselves. But most often, he makes his way to the mountains.[43]

During the vision quest, a person remains on the mountain for at least two, and perhaps as many as five days without food or water. While on the mountain, the person dreams and acquires the full power of those dreams throughout the following year. The stone enclosure serves as a bed in which the vision seeker lies during this quest.[44]

The importance of such sites is difficult to impress on a culture that separates religion from the day-to-day activities of life. For the American Indian tribe that is culturally and spiritually linked to Jackson Hole, this separation does not exist. For the Shoshone, all of life—including religion, politics, daily subsistence, the natural environment and the spiritual world—are interrelated and connected by the life sustaining energy or "puha" that flows through all things.[45]

Summary and Conclusions

Although local residents have long been aware that extensive prehistoric sites and a wealth of artifacts can be found throughout Jackson Hole, it has only been during the last 25 years that archeologists have been able to piece together part of the prehistoric record of this area. This record has revealed that prehistoric people lived in Jackson Hole for much of the last 11,000 years. During the earliest Paleoindian period, human populations were generally small and probably occupied the area sporadically. There is little evidence to suggest that humans were in the valley for anything other than hunting and procuring obsidian for their tools until around 5,800 years ago.

During the Archaic periods, the number of archeological sites increases in Jackson Hole. Roasting pits also appear in the archeological record. These findings suggest an increase in the overall population, or an increasingly mobile population. However, it is difficult to use the size of an archeological site to indicate population size, since people probably used the same campsites time and time again.

Although spear point styles and travel patterns changed, hunting and food-processing techniques remained fairly constant throughout prehistory. Even as hunting technology shifted from the atlatl spear-thrower to the bow and arrow, and the horse was introduced to many tribes, Jackson Hole's people continued a hunter-gatherer form of subsistence and lived in relatively small groups. By the time the early trappers arrived, this area was part of the vast territory of the Shoshone tribe. In general, we know that throughout the time period extending from about 1,500 to 11,000 years ago, plants heavily influenced the travel and subsistence patterns of Jackson Hole's prehistoric people. Sites found at high elevation that date throughout the prehistoric continuum, and which are associated with edible plant species, support this model.[46]

D. B. Shimkin's demographic description of the Wind River Shoshone also supports the original archeological model proposed by Gary Wright. The large base camps found along the shores of Jackson Lake could well represent the locations where a band of individuals camped during the spring and early summer. Smaller sites found in the canyons and higher alpine meadows could represent the individual family camps. Consequently, the overall population residing in Jackson Hole at any given time would have been relatively small and on the band—rather than tribal—level. During the summer months, this group would disperse into family groups throughout the mountains surrounding Jackson Hole. However, recent findings have revealed that obsidian, other raw material sources, topography, and spiritual pursuits also guided the travel patterns of American Indians. These cultural necessities were not addressed in the original predictive archeological model proposed by Gary Wright and his colleagues.

Clearly, there are many unanswered questions about the prehistory of Grand Teton National Park and Jackson Hole. It is still unknown what types of living structures were used within the park through much of early prehistory. There also remain questions about the different adaptive strategies for the northern and southern parts of the valley. Future archeological investigations within the park and surrounding areas will continue to evaluate and reconstruct models of adaptation and, perhaps, lead to new theories and a better understanding of the cultural and spiritual lives of the earliest people of Jackson Hole.

Notes

1. The Lawrence Collection is currently housed in the Jackson Hole Museum and Teton County Historical Society in Jackson, Wyoming.

2. Gary Wright, Susan Bender and Stuart Reeve, "High Country Adaptations," *Plains Anthropologist*, Vol. 25, No. 89, p. 181.

3. Ibid., pp. 181–198.

4. Stuart Reeve, "Lizard Creek Sites (48TE700 and 48TE701): The Prehistoric Root Gathering Economy of Northern Grand Teton National Park, Northwest Wyo-

ming" (Lincoln NE: National Park Service, Midwest Archeological Center 1983).

5. Ibid., 7:122.

6. Gary A. Wright, "The Shoshonean Migration Problem," *Plains Anthropologist,* Vol. 23, 1978, pp. 117–120.

7. Ibid., p. 6.

8. Gary A. Wright, *People of the High Country: Jackson Hole Before the Settlers* (New York: Peter Lang, 1984).

9. Within the boundaries of the National Elk Refuge in Jackson, Wyoming, lies the Goetz site. Although never extensively excavated, this site reveals bison bone in association with prehistoric tools, suggesting that it is a butchering or kill site. The radiocarbon date from this site suggests that the site is 1,480 years old. Older style points are reported to have come from this site as well. Although this site has not been properly recorded and tested to today's archeological standards, it does demonstrate that bison was present in the prehistoric diet of Jackson Hole residents. See Charles Love, "An Archaeological Survey of Jackson Hole Region, Wyoming," M.A. Thesis, Department of Anthropology, University of Wyoming, Laramie, 1972.

10. Christy G. Turner II, "New World Origins," *Ice Age Hunters of the Rockies,* ed., Dennis Stanford and Jane S. Day (Denver, CO: Museum of Natural History Press, 1992), p. 8.

11. Cathy W. Barnowsky, "Late-Quaternary Vegetational and Climatic History of Grand Teton National Park and Vicinity," *Jackson Lake Archeological Project: The 1987 and 1988 Field Work,* Melissa A. Connor, et al. (Lincoln, NE: United States Department of the Interior, National Park Service, Midwest Archeological Center, 1991), p. 26.

12. George Frison, *Prehistoric Hunters of the High Plains,* 2nd edition (New York: Academic Press, 1991), pp. 211–212.

13. Ibid.

14. Charles M. Love, "An Archeological Survey of the Jackson Hole Region," p. 96.

15. Connor, et al., *Jackson Lake Archeological Project.*

16. Melissa A. Connor and Raymond Kunselman, "Mobility, Settlement Patterns, and Obsidian Source Variation in Jackson Hole, Wyoming," unpublished paper presented at the Second Biennial Rocky Mountain Anthropological Conference, Steamboat Springs, Colorado, September 27–30, 1995).

17. George C. Frison, "The Foothills-Mountains and the Open Plains: The Dichotomy in Paleoindian Subsistence Strategies Between Two Ecosystems, *Ice Age Hunters of the Rockies,* ed., Dennis J. Stanford and Jane S. Day (Niwot, CO: University Press of Colorado. 1992), p. 323.

18. Ibid.

19. Ibid., p. 4.

20. Ibid., p. 70

21. Brian M. Fagan, *World Prehistory: A Brief Introduction* (Boston: Little Brown & Co., 1979).

22. Hiram Martin Chittenden, *The Yellowstone National Park Historical and Descriptive,* 5th edition (Cincinnati, OH: Robert Clarke, 1905), p. 387.

23. Stuart Reeve, "Lizard Creek Sites (48TE700 and 48TE701): The Prehistoric Root Gathering Economy of Northern Grand Teton National Park, Northwest Wyoming" (Lincoln, NE: National Park Service, Midwest Archeological Center 1983).

24. D.B. Shimkin, "Wind River Shoshone Ethnogeography," *Anthropological Records,* Vol. 5, No. 4.

25. Ibid., p. 8.

26. James R. Schoen, "High Altitude Site Locations in the Bridger Gros Ventre and Teton Wilderness," paper presented at the Third Biennial Rocky Mountain Anthropological Conference, Bozeman, Montana, September 18–21, 1997.

27. Ibid., p. 4.

28. Ibid., p. 5.

29. Ibid

30. Ibid., p. 24.

31. A term applied to smooth-bored, flintlock guns traded to American Indians primarily by the Hudson's Bay Company. They were usually shortened for ease of handling on horseback. The word is probably a corruption of the French *fusil,* which itself probably comes from the Italian *fucile,* a flint. These guns were vastly inferior to the rifled guns of the trappers in range and accuracy. Osborne Russell, *Journal of a Trapper,* ed., Aubrey L. Haines (Lincoln, NE: University of Nebraska Press, 1965), p. 157, no. 25.

32. Ibid., p. 26.

33. Ibid.

34. Ella Clark, *Indian Legends from the Northern Rockies* (Norman, OK: University of Oklahoma Press, 1966), pp. 11–12.

35. Ibid.

36. Virginia Trenholm and Maurine Carley, *The Shoshonis: Sentinels of the Rockies* (Norman, OK: University of Oklahoma Press, 1964), p. 3.

37. Ibid.

38. Ibid.

39. Åke Hultkrantz, "The Shoshones in the Rocky Mountain Area," *Annals of Wyoming,* Vol. 33, April 1961, 34; and Adamson Hoebel, "Bands and Distributions of the Eastern Shoshone, *American Anthropologist,* Vol. 40, No. 3, 1938, p. 410.

40. Julian Steward, "Some Observations of Shoshonean Distributions," *American Anthropologist,* Vol. 41, 1939, p. 262.

41. Ibid., p. 24.

42. Deward Walker Jr., "Protection of American Indian Sacred Geography," *Handbook of American Indian Religious Freedom,* ed., Christopher Vecsey (New York: Crossroads Publishing, 1993), p. 104.

43. Åke Hultkrantz, *Belief and Worship in Native North America* (Syracuse, NY: Syracuse University Press, 1981), pp. 34–35. Italics original.

44. Julian Steward, "Culture Element Distributions," XXIII Northern Gosiute Shoshoni, *Anthropological Records,* Vol. 4, No. 2 (Berkley, CA: University of California Press, 1945), p. 282.

45. Sherri Deaver, "American Indian Religious Freedom Act (AIRFA) Background Data" (Billings, MT, Bureau of Land Management, 1986), p. 78.

46. Ibid., p. 26.

CHAPTER **33**

The Fur Trappers

We descended the Gros vent fork to "Jacksons hole" about 20 mls. general course West. 28th We followed wis' fork thro the valley crossing several large streams coming in from the East. We then left the valley and followed the river about 5 mls thro. a piece of rough piney country and came to Jackson's. . . . We encamped at the outlet. . . .

—Osborne Russell, *Journal of a Trapper*

"Green River Rendezvous," painted by William Henry Jackson. Rendezvous provided an opportunity for trappers to gather and trade news, stories, pelts, and supplies. The closest rendezvous to Jackson Hole was Pierre's Hole, west of the Teton Range. *Jackson Hole Historical Society and Museum*

Trappers knew the Three Tetons and Jackson Hole well by the time Osborne Russell bivouacked at the outlet of Jackson Lake in 1836.[1] For a decade, mountain men had traversed the high passes into this valley. Almost 30 years had passed since John Colter set out on foot in 1807 from Fort Manuel, a fur-trading post at the junction of the Bighorn and Yellowstone Rivers, to become perhaps the first white person to enter Jackson Hole. The "Astorians" traveled through in 1811 and 1812. Unlike Colter, there is no doubt that Wilson Price Hunt and Robert Stuart led the Astorians through the valley, locating overland trails from St. Louis to the Columbia River. The Astorians, representatives of John Jacob Astor's American Fur Company, had ventured west to locate a trading post on the Columbia, just one step in Astor's grandiose dream to establish a fur trade empire from the Great Lakes to the Pacific

Coast. The War of 1812 thwarted Astor's scheme, his partners at Astoria sold the post to Britian's North West Company before a British warship could take it. For the next ten years, the British went unchallenged in the Pacific Northwest, until Jedediah Smith, the great American explorer, turned up at Flathead Post on the Salmon River in 1824. As part of that same journey, Jed Smith had crossed South Pass from the east, leading American trappers to the rich trapping grounds that lay beyond the Continental Divide. For the next five years, an American company—the Rocky Mountain Fur Company—dominated the fur trade in the West, trapping fine beaver country at the headwaters of several great river systems.

There were four general centers of exploitation in the western fur trade, the British Northwest headquartered on the Columbia River, the South-

Furs had been a valuable commodity in Europe for centuries. In the eighteenth and nineteenth centuries, beaver pelts became particularly popular, and mountain men in America trapped the beaver to near extinction. *Jackson Hole Historical Society and Museum*

west centered at Taos and Santa Fe, the upper Missouri River and, finally, the South Pass area. Beneath the Tetons, trails intersected in Jackson Hole. Mountain men crossed significant passes en route to trapping grounds at the headwaters of the Green, Snake, Yellowstone, Three Forks of the Missouri, and Wind Rivers—all located within 100 air miles of Jackson Hole and the Teton Range. Thus, the Tetons were a major landmark for trappers, and the valley became the crossroads of the fur trade in the northern Rockies.[2]

The fur trappers' frontier spanned four decades in the Trans-Mississippi West, beginning with the explorations of Lewis and Clark in 1804–1806 and ending with the last rendezvous held in 1840. The fur trade was intimately tied to European exploration and expansion in North America. The rise of the fur trade coincided with the rise of capitalism and nation-states in Europe.[3] Furs have been a valuable commodity for much of recorded history, being practical garments in the temperate climate of

Europe. During the Middle Ages, fur clothing represented high fashion and high social status. Excessive trapping and hunting of fur-bearing animals in Western Europe led to serious shortages by the 1400s. Extremely high prices resulted, making fur garments available only to the rich. European merchants sought other sources to meet the demand, and a significant trade developed with Russia and eastern European countries. When Europeans began probing the coast of North America seeking a sea route to Asia, they initially failed to recognize its potential as a source of furs.[4] But, within ten years after Christopher Columbus's first voyage to the New World in 1492, Europeans began to appreciate North America's fur-bearing resources.

The first European fur traders in the New World were Spanish and Portuguese fishermen. They often traded with the Indians they encountered, exchanging manufactured trinkets for furs. Following Spain and Portugal, France and England explored the North American coast, seeking a Northwest Passage as well as gold and silver. In 1534, the French explorer Jacques Cartier traded with the Micmac Indians in what is now Canada, exchanging ironware for furs. After 1598, the fur trade expanded rapidly in North America. Colonization coincided with this development, serving as the vanguard of European expansion. Through trade with Indians and the establishment of trading posts in remote territory, the French and British competed for an empire. Imperial rivalry caused a series of wars that resulted in the expulsion of the French from Canada.[5] By the late eighteenth century, the British Hudson's Bay Company and North West Company had expanded as far west as the Mandan villages on the Missouri River.

Spain claimed the Louisiana Territory in the eighteenth century, although its hold was tenuous at best. Alarmed at the appearance of British traders on the Missouri River, Spain tried to use its fur trade to consolidate its hold on this vast territory. Spanish authorities offered the equivalent of $3,000 to the first trader to reach the Pacific coast. No one succeeded. However, Spain did establish trade with Indians on the central Missouri in the 1790s from the small town of St. Louis, which became the principal outfitting center for the western fur trade. From St. Louis, trappers and traders traveled three major routes: the Missouri River, the Platte River to South Pass (the Oregon Trail), and the Santa Fe Trail.[6]

After France acquired the Louisiana territory from Spain, Napoleon Bonaparte sold Louisiana to the United States in 1803. President Thomas Jefferson selected Meriwether Lewis and William Clark to lead an expedition up the Missouri River to the Pacific coast to explore these newly purchased lands and to locate a water route, if possible. The expedition, which departed from St. Louis in 1804, succeeded in spectacular fashion. Lewis and Clark returned to St. Louis in 1806, reporting a country rich in beaver, friendly Indians, and a transportation route up the Missouri River. This news generated a small stampede in 1807, as entrepreneurs prepared outfits to ascend the Missouri River. A trader named Manuel Lisa led the way.[7]

Leading a party of 42 trappers and voyagers, Lisa and his brigade manhandled a keelboat up the Missouri and Yellowstone Rivers. Lisa constructed a fort where the Bighorn River flows into the Yellowstone. For the next year, Lisa directed trapping and trading operations from Fort Manuel before returning to St. Louis with a fortune in furs and new wisdom. He concluded that only large trading companies could operate efficiently and profitably. Soliciting a group of St. Louis merchants, Lisa formed the Missouri Fur Company in 1809, the first of the large American fur trading companies to work the upper Missouri.[8]

While traveling up the Missouri in 1807, Lisa met John Colter, a veteran of the Lewis and Clark expedition. Colter was the prototypical mountain man. An experienced frontiersman, he honed his skills with the Lewis and Clark expedition. Both officers considered him a reliable man.[9] Colter had been discharged at the Mandan villages in 1806 at his request, after two trappers named Hancock and Dixon persuaded him to return to the Rockies. Hancock, Dixon, and Colter spent the next year trapping the Yellowstone River, perhaps wintering on Clark's Fork of the Yellowstone. Colter broke up the partnership and was canoeing down the Missouri in 1807 when he met Manuel Lisa. Again, the mountains beck-

COLTER'S ROUTE

On his return to St. Louis in 1810, Colter described his journey of 1807-1808 to General William Clark, who added it to the map which accompanied the 1814 edition of his report on the Lewis and Clark Expedition.

A portion of the Lewis and Clark map is reproduced at the right. Below is a modern map on which Colter's route is more clearly indicated.

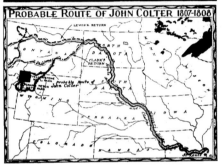

PROBABLE ROUTE OF JOHN COLTER 1807-1808

The precise route of mountain man John Colter's 1807–08 journey through what is now northwestern Wyoming is not known, as he left no written account or map. The most probable route, derived from William Clark's map and contemporary accounts, indicates that he traveled through Jackson Hole and Yellowstone. *National Park Service*

oned, and for the next three years Colter worked for Lisa's Missouri Fur Company.[10]

In the winter of 1807–1808, Lisa persuaded Colter to travel west to locate bands of Crow Indians and inform them of the trading post at the confluence of the Yellowstone and Bighorn Rivers. Colter completed a 500-mile trek in the middle of the winter of 1807–1808, possibly traveling through Jackson Hole. Henry Brackenridge left the only contemporary account, based on information obtained

The head-shaped Colter Stone, which may have been carved by the famous mountain man, was discovered near Tetonia, Idaho, in 1931. One side reads, "John Colter," the other, "1808." The stone was found by a farmer plowing his field; he traded it for a pair of boots. *Grand Teton National Park*

from Manuel Lisa. "He shortly after dispatched Coulter [sic], the hunter before mentioned, to bring some of the Indian nations to trade. This man, with a pack of thirty pounds weight, his gun and some ammunition, went upwards of 500 miles to the Crow nation; gave them information and proceeded from them to several other tribes."[11] Colter must have used snowshoes to make this journey in the winter, but there is no evidence to verify this conclusion. Some believe a Crow Indian accompanied him as a guide but, again, this is conjecture.

In 1810, William Clark produced a map of his route across the West. The map was published in 1814 in Paul Allen's *History of the Expedition Under the Command of Lewis and Clark.* A circular track appears on the map bearing the legend "Colters Route in 1807." The map shows Colter cutting a circular route around Lake Biddle, generally accepted as Jackson Lake, and Lake Eustis, widely believed to be Yellowstone Lake. Colter apparently met with Clark when he returned to St. Louis and gave information

regarding his trip. It is not known whether Colter described the route or drew a rough map for Clark. (No journal or map by Colter is known to exist.) In any event, Clark's map provides the primary evidence that John Colter was the first white to enter Jackson Hole, Teton Basin (Pierre's Hole), and Yellowstone. But the map's topographical inaccuracies and imprecise scale make it impossible to determine Colter's route with absolute certainty.[12]

Other evidence helps establish Colter's route. The Missouri Historical Society possesses a manuscript map drawn by William Clark in 1808. Another Lewis and Clark veteran, George Drouillard, provided information for this map, which shows that Colter definitely reached the boiling springs at present-day Cody, Wyoming. No longer active, these geothermal features were the original Colter's Hell, rather than Yellowstone.[13] Yale University also possesses another map attributed to Clark that documents Colter's route. This manuscript map shows Colter crossing Teton Pass. The map also documents Wilson Price Hunt's Astorians route in 1810–1811, who exited Jackson Hole via Teton Pass.[14]

Artifacts provide other evidence. In 1931, William Beard and his son discovered a curious block of stone while clearing scrub timber from their land, five and one-half miles east of Tetonia, Idaho. The stone—a block of rhyolite lava 13-inches-high, eight-inches-wide, and four-inches-thick—was clearly carved into a crude face. One side bears the inscription "John Colter," the other "1808." Beard placed the stone on his porch, where it remained for two years. When neighbor A. C. Lyon learned of the stone, he traded a used pair of boots for it. In turn, Lyon donated it to Grand Teton National Park in 1934. Geologist Fritiof Fryxell, the park's first naturalist, concluded that the inscriptions had been exposed to weathering consistent with the 1808 date. Further inquiries also established that the Beards were not familiar with John Colter. Thus, Fryxell ruled out a hoax by the Beard family.[15]

Yet doubts about the authenticity of the Colter Stone persist today. In recent years, writer W. C. Lawrence has alleged that A. C. Lyon planted the stone to curry favor with the National Park Service in order to secure the horse concession at Jenny

Lake.[16] But this is an unlikely motive because Lyon acquired that concession in 1929, and the stone was discovered in 1931. (Lyon lost the concession for poor service in 1937.) [17] If the stone is not authentic, the more likely culprits were pranksters with the Hayden Surveys. The Colter Stone is one of six such stones found within a 25–mile radius in Teton basin. Two are obvious frauds; both bear the legend "Clark–1805," although Lewis and Clark did not pass through this area. Other stones were found at the possible site of Henry's Fort. The inscription reads, "GOD CAMP 1818 H.WELLS," "AL THE COOK BUT NOTHING TO COOK," and "FORT HENRY 1811 BY CAP. HUNT." A retired Episcopal minister, J. Neilson Barry, studied this puzzle for years and concluded that "campfire doodlers" with the Hayden Surveys carved the inscription in 1877. Thus, rather than put it to rest, the Colter Stone fueled the controversy over John Colter's route.[18]

Another inscription was found on a tree on Coulter Creek in northern Teton Basin in the 1880s. The initials "JC" were carved under a large "X." Western writer Phillip Ashton Rollins and two guides examined the carvings, and concluded they were about 80 years old. Around 1890, Yellowstone National Park employees cut the tree down and salvaged the portion bearing the initials. The log was to be placed in the park museum, but disappeared. Historian Aubrey Haines, who noted that there was no park museum in 1890, offered the theory that the lost inscriptions were for John Merle Coulter, a botanist with the Hayden Surveys and for whom Coulter Creek is named.[19] Haines also identified one place in Yellowstone where Colter with "reasonable assurance" passed through. This is where the Bannock Trail crosses the Yellowstone River. The Clark Map shows Colter's crossing with a note "Hot Spring Brimestone," where there are clear geothermal features such as tepid springs and fumaroles today. It is the only such crossing for miles in either direction.[20]

Even though the evidence remains inconclusive, the consensus of most historians is that John Colter did pass through Jackson Hole. Stallo Vinton, Colter's first biographer, believed Colter crossed Union Pass, then made his way into Jackson Hole

via the Gros Ventre River. According to Vinton, Colter left Jackson Hole via Teton Pass, traveled north through Pierre's Hole, returned to the northern end of Jackson Hole via Conant Pass, and moved on to Yellowstone. Another theory is that Colter entered the valley and simply traveled north along the eastern shore of Jackson Lake. By contrast, J. Neilson Barry concluded that Colter crossed Two Ocean Pass and traveled northwest into Yellowstone, bypassing Jackson Hole. However, Colter's latest biographer, Burton Harris, believed Colter crossed Togwotee Pass into Jackson Hole, traveled south, and left via Teton Pass. Harris also theorized that Colter may have carved the Colter Stone while holing up to avoid unfriendly Indians, then fled south back across Teton Pass, and then traveled north past Jackson Lake into Yellowstone. David Saylor believed Colter took the Togwotee Pass, Jackson Hole, Teton Pass, Pierre's Hole, Conant Pass route. Aubrey Haines, in his biographical sketch of Colter, concluded that his route beyond Cody, Wyoming, is debatable, and questioned the authenticity of the Colter Stone.[21] Colter's exact route will probably never be determined. Did he enter Jackson Hole and Teton Basin? It remains an intriguing story, but one that will hardly alter the course of American history. John Colter left the West for good in 1810, moving near the present town of Dundee, Missouri. There, he settled down and married. He died of jaundice in 1812.[22]

Whether or not John Colter reached Jackson Hole, other trappers working for the Missouri Fur Company explored and trapped in Jackson Hole. In 1810, Andrew Henry, a partner in the company, led an expedition from Fort Manuel to the Three Forks of the Missouri River, the heart of Blackfeet and Gros Ventre territory. This formidable confederacy drove Henry's brigade out of this beaver-rich land into Pierre's Hole. The trappers retreated to the Henry's Fork of the Snake River, where they established a fort. From Henry's Fort, the rivers and streams of Jackson Hole were trapped for the first time in 1810–1811.[23] In 1811, Henry disbanded the starving company, after a miserable winter at the first American post west of the Continental Divide. Three trappers, John Hoback, Edward Robinson, and Jacob Reznor headed east, crossing Teton Pass into Jackson Hole and exiting the valley via Togwotee Pass.[24] On the Missouri River, the veteran trappers met Wilson Price Hunt's brigade of Astorians bound for the Pacific Coast.

Hunt represented John Jacob Astor's American Fur Company, formed in 1806. Astor planned to establish a chain of forts from the Great Lakes to the mouth of the Columbia River. All furs would be shipped to the headquarters post on the Columbia and thence to the Orient. Astor not only hoped to realize large profits, but sought to drive the rival British Hudson's Bay Company and North West Company from the Pacific Northwest. He envisioned a worldwide commercial empire from St. Louis through the northern Rockies, to the mouth of the Columbia, and across the Pacific to China. In 1810, a group of Astor's traders began a journey by sea through the straits of Magellan to the mouth of the Columbia. There, in 1811, they began the construction of Astoria.

Wilson Price Hunt was one of the "Overland Astorians" who were traveling by land from St. Louis to meet up with their fellow trappers at Astoria. Upon meeting up with Hoback, Robinson, and Reznor, Hunt was impressed with their experience and persuaded them to serve as guides and hunters. Because of reports of hostile Indians on the upper Missouri, Hunt abandoned the river and traveled overland. Hoback and his partners led Hunt's party up the Wind River Valley and over Union Pass in September 1811. "The hunters who served as guides to the party in this part of their route assured Mr. Hunt that, by following up the Wind River, and crossing a single mountain ridge, he would come upon the headwaters of the Columbia." From Union Pass, the Astorians saw the Teton Range for the first time. "Here one of the guides paused, and, after considering the vast landscape attentively, pointed to three mountain peaks glistening with snow, which rose, he said above a fork of the Columbia river. They were hailed by travelers with that joy which a beacon on a seashore is hailed by mariners after a long and dangerous voyage." This is the first reference to the Tetons as the celebrated landmark of fur trappers. Washington Irving noted that by the 1830s

these peaks were known as the Tetons, but "as they had been guiding points for many days to Mr. Hunt, he gave them the name of Pilot Knobs."[25]

The Astorians descended Union Pass to the upper waters of the Green River, then traveled to "a stream about 50 feet in width, which, Hoback, one of their guides, who had trapped about the neighborhood when in the service of Mr. Henry, recognized for one of the headwaters of the Columbia." This was Hoback River. Irving's description of the trail down the Hoback Canyon to the Snake River is unmistakable, it "meandered among rocks and precipices," forcing several dangerous river crossings. "Sometimes the banks advanced so close upon the river, that they were obliged to scramble up and down their tugged promontories, or to skirt along their bases where there was scarce a foothold."[26] Horses scrambled on the slopes, lost their footing, and sometimes fell. One horse rolled 200 feet into the river, load and all, but to everyone's amazement was unhurt.

After two days travel, the Astorians reached the confluence of the Hoback and Snake Rivers, where "their united waters swept off through the valley in one impetuous stream."[27] At what is known as Hoback Junction today, Hunt and his followers debated the possibility of abandoning their horses and traveling down the Snake River by dugout canoes. Hoback, Robinson, and Reznor were unfamiliar with this portion of the Mad River, as the Snake was known in 1811. Hunt dispatched three men down the Snake River Canyon to determine if it was navigable, while the others began constructing dugout canoes. Two Shoshone Indians entered their camp, saw what they were doing, and in sign language informed Hunt that it was not possible to canoe down the river. The scouts returned with a similar discouraging report. Therefore, Hunt decided to continue overland. In early October, the brigade broke camp, forded the Snake River, and trekked over Teton Pass. Guided by Hoback, Robinson, Reznor, and the two Shoshone, the expedition proceeded north through Pierre's Hole to Andrew Henry's abandoned post on the Henry's Fork of the Snake.

Promising trapping grounds interested Hunt nearly as much as locating a route to Oregon. While

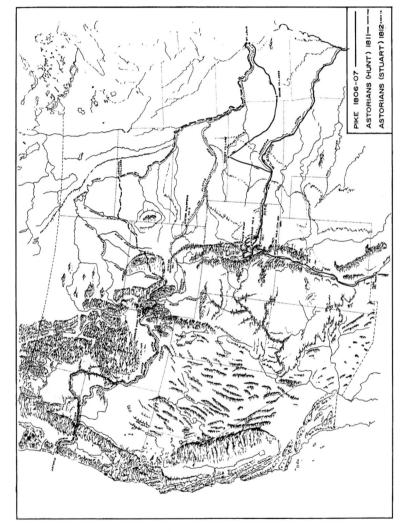

Map showing the route of the Astorians, 1811–1812. *National Park Service (Great Explorers of the West, The National Survey of Historic Sites and Buildings)*

they camped at Hoback Junction, Hunt's party noticed favorable beaver sign in the area. Hunt detached four men to trap the upper waters of the Snake River, Alexander Carson, Louis St. Michel, Pierre Detaye, and Pierre Delaunay. They were to trap a load of pelts and then make their way to Astor's new post on the Columbia. At Henry's Fort, Hoback, Robinson, Reznor, and a man named Cass agreed to stay and trap the waters in the Henry's Fork area. A malcontent named Miller also remained.[28]

Hunt then led the remainder of the brigade to Astor's post on the Columbia. The Overland Astorians were the first Americans to cross the continent since Lewis and Clark. They pioneered a new route of which Union and Teton Passes were important links. Although the Overland Astorians were a commercial venture, their arrival on the Columbia challenged the British for sovereignty in the British Northwest. As such, they were a vanguard of American expansion.

In June 1812, Robert Stuart led a party of seven traders from Astoria to St. Louis carrying dispatches for John Jacob Astor.[29] Stuart's party followed the Port Neuf River from the Snake across a divide to the Bear River. There, they encountered a band of Crow Indians. Friendly trade degenerated into a confrontation when a Crow chief demanded that Stuart trade away his horse and some gunpowder. Stuart refused the first, but made a gift of 20 loads of gunpowder to avert violence.[30] To avoid further contact with the Crow, the Astorians traveled north from the Bear River to more familiar country. They eventually made their way down the Grey's River to its confluence with the Snake. On the morning of September 19, 1812, the same band of Indians rushed Stuart's camp, successfully stampeding and stealing all of the horses. The Crow chief "checked his horse, raised himself in the saddle, and clapping his hand on the most insulting part of his body, uttered some jeering words." Without horses, Stuart understood their vulnerability and refused to allow one of his men, Ben Jones, to fire at "the mark so fair and the insult so foul."[31] This incident occurred on McCoy Creek near present day Alpine Junction, Wyoming.

Now on foot, the returning Astorians constructed a raft and floated down the Snake for 100 miles. They abandoned the raft and crossed the Snake River Range into Pierre's Hole. The eight men stalked south, keeping to the foothills of Pierre's Hole to avoid Blackfeet. They crossed Teton Pass on October 7, 1812:

> We continued on up the right hand Fork for 13 Miles S E by E to the summit of the Pilot Knob Mountain on which we found little or no snow—9 Miles same course brought us to Mad [Snake] River and in 2 more reached the opposite bank having crossed Five channels of from 30 to 60 yards wide each and from 1-1/2 to 3 feet water a very rapid current, and in every other respect of the same character as the part where we descended on the Rafts, with the exception that the valley is here several miles wide, and some of the Bottom upwards of a mile in breadth and thickly timbered with bitter Cottonwood and Pines.[32]

Stuart's party followed Hunt's route up the Hoback Canyon. Finding no food in Jackson Hole and on foot, starvation threatened them. So desperate was their plight, one of the party proposed casting lots, the loser becoming the evening meal. Stuart dissuaded the man with his rifle and restored order. They crossed the river and entered the Green River Valley, where through good fortune they killed an old bull buffalo, possibly saving their lives. Stuart and his comrades crossed South Pass from the west, following the Platte River east. They reached St. Louis in 1813. The Astorians "discovered" South Pass, but there is no evidence in Stuart's journal that he understood the significance of the pass. Also, they had traveled much of the route of the Oregon Trail, with the exception of their diversion into Jackson Hole.[33]

By the time Stuart and the seven members of the party reached St. Louis, Great Britain and the United States were at war. American Fur Company officials at Astoria sold the post to the British North West Company as a British warship was poised to seize it. Astor's grand plan was dashed. The War of 1812, the successful resistance of the Blackfeet to the encroachment of trappers in the Upper Missouri, and government indifference persuaded Americans to abandon the northern Rockies for the next decade. The British were winning the competition for dominion in the Pacific Northwest.[34]

Two licensed British companies competed against each other in western North America prior to 1821, the North West Company and the Hudson's Bay Company. The North West Company was very successful, largely because of its policy of trade with the Indians. This aggressive company established itself first in the Pacific Northwest.[35] In 1818, Donald MacKenzie led a party of North Westers from Fort Nez Perce on the Walla Walla River. A competent bourgeois, MacKenzie led 55 men on a long journey that may have included Jackson Hole. MacKenzie reported his route to Alexander Ross who, in turn, recorded it in his *Fur Hunters of the Far West* (1855). Ross's narrative provides the primary information on MacKenzie's route. Although historian Merrill Mattes recognized that Ross's description was "admittedly vague," he concluded that the available evidence "strongly suggested that MacKenzie did reach Jackson Hole in 1819." MacKenzie described his route as follows:

> From this place [Boise] we advanced, suffering occasionally from alarms for twenty-five days, and then found ourselves in a rich field of beaver, in the country between the great south branch and the spanish waters, . . . I left my people at the end of four months. Then taking a circuitous route along the foot of the Rocky Mountains, a country extremely dreary during a winter voyage, I reached the headwaters of the great south branch. . . .[36]

Contemporary references to the Spanish River are generally understood to be the Green River. The "headwaters of the great south branch" may well be the upper Snake River in Jackson Hole. In his book, Ross described the Jackson Hole area, possibly based on MacKenzie's knowledge:

> The most remarkable heights in any part of the great backbone of America are three elevated insular mountains, or peaks, which are seen at a distance of one hundred and fifty miles: the hunters very aptly desig-

nate them the Pilot Knobs (they are now generally known as the Three Paps or Tetons; and the source of the Great Snake River is in their neighbor-hood). . . .[37]

Also, Ross wrote a fantastic account of boiling springs and hot springs in the Yellowstone area, which could only come from a first-hand account. Mattes further pointed out that, since MacKenzie had been with the Astorians in 1811, he "would hardly miss the opportunity to investigate Upper Jackson Hole."[38] The Tetons and Pierre's Hole may have been named by Iroquois or French-Canadian trappers in MacKenzie's brigade.[39] Finally a tree carving was discovered in Yellowstone in 1880 (yes, another tree carving), which read "JOR Aug 19 1819." Could "JOR" have been a member of MacKenzie's North Westers? Mattes cautioned that no absolute proof of MacKenzie's trip exists, but that he passed through Jackson Hole is a reasonable conclusion.[40]

MacKenzie returned to Fort Nez Perce with a fortune in furs. Encouraged, other British brigades were dispatched to trap the waters of the Columbia and Snake Rivers. In addition to trapping beaver for profit, the British hoped to trap out an arc running roughly from the Snake River drainage through to northern California. They thus hoped to keep Americans out of the Oregon country, reasoning that American trappers, finding a swath of country devoid of beaver, would become discouraged and turn back. In 1821, the North West Company and Hudson's Bay Company merged, ending decades of fierce rivalry that had escalated to murder.

Two years later, in 1823, Finnan McDonald led the Hudson's Bay Company's annual expedition to the Snake River country. McDonald guided his brigade over the Salmon Mountains, then south to the Bear River. Stanley Morgan believed he traveled through Pierre's Hole, where the Three Tetons guided his route south. From the Bear River, McDonald may have crossed the mountains to the "Spanish River" or Green River. McDonald may have led his band of trappers north through the Hoback Canyon into Jackson Hole and on to Henry's Fork of the Snake. The British trappers crossed the Continental Divide again and traveled as far east as Great Falls, Montana.[41]

AMERICA ☞ THE WEST, 1790 TO 1860

While 1,000 trappers at most waded icy streams setting traps, the vast majority of Americans preoccupied themselves with building a new nation. Jackson Hole and the Teton Range were forgotten after the demise of the trappers' frontier. Attention shifted to the Oregon Trail. Tom Fitzpatrick guided the first emigrant wagon train to Oregon in 1841. By 1846, 5,000 Americans had settled in Oregon's Willamette Valley. In 1847, Mormon pioneers located their own trail from Council Bluffs, Iowa, to the Salt Lake Valley. Both trails crossed South Pass. Then in 1848, workers discovered shiny flakes of gold in a millrace at Sutter's Mill in California, precipitating the greatest gold rush in American history. Meanwhile Americans fought a two-year war with Mexico beginning in 1846, wresting the Southwest from their southern neighbor.

Most Americans remained east of the Appalachians, where colonists had won their independence from Great Britain in 1783. They faced a myriad of problems: How far would the reluctant revolution go toward reform? Should there be a national government? If so, how much power would be given the new national government? How much power would individual states possess? How would revenues be raised? Should there be a standing army and navy? What about the vast lands west of the Appalachians? How would they be incorporated into the United States? How could a nation founded on principles of equality and individual rights uphold the institution of slavery? Americans grappled with all of these issues and dealt with them, some more successfully than others.

By 1790, the Constitution had been ratified and a new nation established. The nation grew rapidly from 1790 to 1860. The population increased from 3,929,000 in 1790, to 31,443,000 in 1860. In 1790, the Mississippi River was the western boundary of the United States. By 1860, the United States boundaries stretched from ocean to ocean, its territory more than doubled. Several developments were especially important to the West.

After the War for Independence, the United States controlled vast tracts of public domain between the Appalachian Range and the Mississippi River. Two problems loomed across the Appalachians. Settlers squatted on lands, while speculators hatched grandiose schemes to buy and sell western lands for substantial profits. An orderly way had to be devised to transfer public domain to private ownership. The second problem centered on the ultimate political status of the public domain. American territories were really colonies, and the congress of the Confederation recognized that somehow equal political status must be granted, or they would separate just as the 13 colonies had with Great Britain. Congress enacted two landmark pieces of legislation to address these problems, the Ordinance of 1785, and the Ordinance of 1787.

The Ordinance of 1785 divided federal lands into square townships, an area of 36 square miles. Each township was divided into 36 sections, each totaling one square mile or 640 acres. The government sold land at regularly scheduled auctions for a minimum price of $1 per acre. The government reserved one section to fund schools. Not only did this act provide for an orderly transfer of land from public to private ownership, it brought much needed revenue to the nation's treasury.

The Ordinance of 1787 established a process whereby territories could eventually become states rather than remain colonies. When the population of a territory reached 60,000, citizens could draft a state constitution and apply to Congress for statehood. Between 1791 and 1860, 20 new states entered the Union. Both ordinances set laws that lasted until the public domain closed in the twentieth century.

The United States was an agrarian society, its people tied to the soil. Urbanization and industrialization began and accelerated between 1790 and 1860. Urban centers grew rapidly along the eastern seaboard as the nation's commerce developed. The Industrial Revolution began in the early nineteenth century with Slater's Mill in Rhode Island and the textile mills at Lowell, Massachusetts. New technology and industry had a profound impact on the West. Cities and industry demanded raw materials and foodstuffs; the West could fill some of those needs. Improved transportation in the form of steamships, canals, and later, railroads cut costs and shipping time dramatically, which promoted internal trade. The first settlers in the Old Northwest and Mississippi Valley were isolated and largely self sufficient, producing few exports. By 1860, as a result of improved transportation, American farmers produced most of the world's cotton and production of wheat for export increased substantially.

Some Americans believed that the North American continent was a divine gift. As such, they perceived that Americans had not only the right, but the duty to settle, develop, and expand a continental republic. This belief became known as Manifest Destiny. The doctrine rationalized the growth of a continental empire and the displacement of native peoples. The Louisiana Purchase of 1803 initiated the expansion of the United States. Florida and the Gulf Coast were acquired in 1819. Americans rebelled and established a republic in Texas in 1836. Great Britain and the United Stated ended their joint occupation of Oregon in 1846, settling on the 49th parallel as a boundary. Texas joined the Union in 1845. Mexico ceded the entire Southwest and California as a result of the Mexican War. The Gadsden Purchase added a tract in the Southwest in 1853. The United States seemed blessed.

Behind all of these issues and events loomed slavery. When a Dutch trader sold 20 blacks into slavery at Jamestown in 1619, he planted the seeds of bitterness and bloodshed. Slavery was permitted in all 13 colonies, but ideas generated by the American Revolution had significant implications for slavery. If all men were created equal, how could one human being own another? By 1804, all states north of Maryland had abolished slavery, while in the South, cotton and slavery flourished.

As always, America remained a land of contradictions. Even as a sense of nationalism developed, sectionalism fed on the slavery issue. The question of extending slavery to western territories caused the pot to boil over. Southerners maintained that slavery was a dynamic institution that required expansion. To preserve parity in the Senate; they also knew that new slave-holding states would have to keep pace with new free soil states. The Compromise of 1850 seemed to settle the problem in the West. But, the Kansas-Nebraska Act of 1854, the Dred Scott decision in 1857, and bloody warfare between abolitionists and slavery advocates in Kansas opened unhealable wounds. Increasing emotions on both sides polarized the North and South, fired by John Brown's raid on Harper's Ferry in 1859 and his subsequent execution. In 1860, the American people enjoyed their last year of peace; war was their future.

Such was the character of the nation as the explorers and miners crossed the Mississippi River into the American West.*

*This section is a synthesis of Ray Allen Billington's *Westward Expansion; a History of the American Frontier,* 4th ed; and *The Americans: A Brief History* by Henry F. Bedford and Trevor Colbourn, ed. John Morton Blum (New York: Harcourt Brace Javanovich, ca. 1976).

McDonald was a superb field leader. Not only did he lead his brigade the farthest east of any British bourgeois, challenging Americans on the Missouri River, he thrashed a band of Blackfeet near Lemhi Pass in Montana and returned to Spokane House with nearly 4,500 beaver pelts. It was a very successful season. But, when offered the command of the 1824 expedition to the Snake River, McDonald refused. "I got Safe home from the Snake cuntre . . . and when that Cuntre will see me agane the Beaver will have a Gould Skin."[42]

The appearance of British trappers on the upper Missouri did not go unchallenged. American fur traders prepared to reenter the beaver-rich upper Missouri after abandoning the field for a decade. In 1822, General William Ashley and Missouri Fur Company veteran Maj. Andrew Henry formed a new fur trading company. They recruited "one hundred young men to ascend the Missouri River to its source."[43] The men who enlisted were often little more than boys, and virtually all were *mangeur de lard* or "pork-eaters," a term for newcomers to the West. Yet, some became ideal mountain men. The Ashley-Henry employees list is a "Who's-Who" of the fur trappers frontier. On the list were Jim Bridger, Tom Fitzpatrick, Jed Smith, Etienne Provost, Bill and Milton Sublette, David E. Jackson, and Robert Campbell.[44]

Andrew Henry ascended the Missouri River by keelboat and established a fort at the mouth of the Yellowstone in 1822. Setbacks dogged the company in 1823. First, Henry led a party into Blackfeet country, where four of his men were killed. As in 1810, the Blackfeet confederacy drove Henry from the headwaters of the Missouri. Then, disaster struck on the Missouri. General Ashley led a party of green recruits up the river to join Henry. While camped at the Arikari villages, the Indians attacked Ashley's brigade, killing 13 trappers in a fierce fight. Ashley's brigade retreated down the river.

Taking a gamble, Ashley dispatched a party overland. Led by Jed Smith, the trappers traveled west from Fort Kiowa on the Missouri and wintered among the Crows in the Wind River Valley east of Jackson Hole. From the Crow, Smith learned of plentiful beaver across the mountains. He attempted to cross Union Pass, but snow blocked the way. Smith then followed the Popo-Agie River south and crossed South Pass from the east in February 1824. Smith's feat began a new chapter in the fur trappers' frontier. He reopened the abundant beaver streams west of the Continental Divide to American trappers. Just as important, the British faced their first serious competition since the Astorians in 1811. After trapping the Green River Basin, the brigade divided into four parties. Tom Fitzpatrick returned east with dispatches, rediscovering the Platte River route, which became the Oregon Trail.[45]

Smith traveled north with six companions. Based on Washington Hood's manuscript in the Missouri Historical Society Archives, Merrill Mattes and Harrison Dale believed Smith passed through Jackson Hole:

> After striking the Colorado, or Green River, make up the stream toward its headwaters, as far as Horse creek, one of its tributaries, follow out this last mentioned stream to its source by a westerly course, across the main ridge in order to attain Jackson's Little Hole, at the headwaters of Jackson's fork [Hoback River]. Follow down Jackson's fork to its mouth and decline to the northward along Lewis's fork, passing through Jackson's Big Hole to about twelve miles beyond the Yellowstone pass [sic], crossing on the route a nameless beaver stream. Here the route passes due west over another prong of the ridge, a fraction worse than the former, followed until it has attained the headwaters of Pierre's Hole, crossing the Big Teton, the battleground of the Blacksmith's fork; ford Perre's fork eastward of the butte at its mouth and Lewis fork also, thence pass to the mouth of Lewis fork.[46]

Mattes believed that Smith traveled down the Hoback, called Jackson's Fork in this account, to Jackson's Big Hole and crossed the Teton Range via Conant Pass. The exact route is impossible to determine, because the place names in Hood's manuscript are confusing. Smith could have crossed Teton Pass, but the identity of Yellowstone Pass in the narrative is unknown. It became known as the route from the upper Snake into Yellowstone.[47] Jed Smith's biographer, Stanley Morgan, suggested that Smith did not pass through Jackson Hole at all, but traveled north via the Bear River, crossed the divide to the Blackfoot River, then followed it to the Snake River in present day Idaho.[48] Most historians believe that Jed Smith entered Jackson Hole in 1824, although whether he crossed Teton Pass or Conant Pass is uncertain.[49] At any rate, Smith went on to the Snake River in Idaho, where he met a group of Iroquois trappers employed by the Hudson's Bay Company. He then traveled to Flathead House, much to the discomfort of Alexander Ross, the bourgeois.

Smith's adventure in 1824 is significant for several reasons. A new overland route via the Platte River and South Pass was established, enabling trappers to trespass into Blackfeet country from the south. For the next 15 years, Jackson Hole served as an important crossroads for trappers. Trails intersected in the valley that led to important trapping grounds at the head of several great rivers. Americans challenged the British for control of the Pacific Northwest. Moreover, General William Ashley devised a different strategy for the Ashley-Henry fur-trading operation. He determined to rely on company trappers, rather than trade with Indians to obtain beaver plews. Instead of establishing trading posts, Ashley decided to bring goods and supplies to a predetermined location and gather the year's catch of beaver pelts. These gatherings became the famous "rendezvous." This system allowed trappers to stay in the field year-round, eliminating the need to haul their plews to forts on the Missouri River. The first rendezvous was held on the Henry's Fork of the Green River in 1825.[50]

Historian Merrill Mattes evaluated the evidence and believed four expeditions of the Ashley-Henry company passed through Jackson Hole between 1825 and 1828, but the lack of sound documentation makes it difficult to determine exact routes.[51] In 1825, Jim Bridger and Tom Fitzpatrick returned to the Rockies, after escorting Smith and Ashley to the Missouri River with the first year's catch of the "Rocky Mountain Fur Company." Leading 30 trappers, they may have crossed into Jackson Hole via

Togwotee or Union Passes, then followed the Snake River into Yellowstone. They may have dispersed in Jackson Hole and trapped the valley intensively for the first time. Based on Jim Beckwourth's biography, William Sublette and other trappers traveled from the Blackfeet country to "Lewis' Fork on the Columbia" and "all moved on together for the head of the Green River" in 1826. The Teton Pass-Hoback trail would have been a logical route from the Lewis' Fork (Snake River) to the Green River.[52]

In 1826, a reluctant Daniel Potts probably crossed Conant Pass into Jackson Hole, followed the upper Snake River to Two Ocean Pass, and then traveled along the Yellowstone River into Yellowstone. Potts would have joined brigades headed for other parts, rather than venture into Blackfeet country, but events conspired to make him the first to describe the Yellowstone country in his letter published in the *Niles Register* in 1827.[53]

Meanwhile, General Ashley had made a fortune from furs. He decided to quit the mountains and sold the company to three reliable employees, Jedediah Smith, David E. Jackson, and William Sublette, in 1826.[54] At the Bear Lake rendezvous in 1827, Smith, Jackson, and Sublette agreed to meet at the headwaters of the Snake, or Jackson Hole. Smith, having just returned from his remarkable trek to California, set out again. Sublette assumed the responsibility for transporting pelts to St. Louis and returning with supplies. Davey Jackson commanded the trapping brigades for the next two years. He dispatched trappers to the Green River Basin, the upper Snake, and the Bear River country. Trappers probably entered Jackson Hole in 1827 and 1828, but there are no reliable records to confirm this conclusion.

In 1829, Bill Sublette led a pack train and 60 men from St. Louis to Jackson Hole. A young recruit named Joe Meek accompanied Sublette. Years later, Meek recounted the trip to his biographer, Frances Fuller Victor:

> Sublette led his company up the valley of the Wind River, across the mountains, and onto the very headwaters of the Lewis or Snake River. Here he fell in

with Jackson, in the valley of Lewis Lake, called Jackson's Hole, and remained on the borders of this lake for some time, waiting for Smith. . . .[55]

Based on this description, Sublette undoubtedly crossed Togwotee Pass. When Smith failed to arrive from California, Jackson and Sublette set out to find him. They were reunited in either Pierre's Hole or southwest Montana. The sources are contradictory on this point. This passage may be the source of the story that Sublette named Jackson Hole for Davey Jackson in 1829. But Jackson, through four years of trapping, probably knew this valley well by 1829.[56]

Significant changes occurred after 1829. First, encouraged by Ashley's financial success, other American companies entered the field in the 1830s. Astor's giant enterprise, the American Fur Company, sent a brigade into the Rockies in 1830. Jackson Hole figured prominently in this competition. Second, Smith, Jackson, and Sublette sold the company to their longtime companions Jim Bridger, Tom Fitzpatrick, Milton Sublette, Henry Fraeb (pronounced Frap), and Baptiste Gervais in 1830. The new owners dubbed the partnership the Rocky Mountain Fur Company. After 1829, mountain men entered Jackson Hole regularly. No rendezvous were held in the valley, nor did anyone contemplate building a trading post here, but several important trapper trails converged in the valley. Mattes believed that at least 30 expeditions passed through Jackson Hole between 1830 and 1840.[57]

In contrast to the 1820s, several fine accounts exist describing the fur trade in the 1830s, a decade that encompassed its heyday and precipitous decline. The Teton Range and Jackson Hole are mentioned frequently in many of these descriptions.[58] Osborne Russell 's *Journal of a Trapper* and Warren A. Ferris's *Life in the Rockies* are two excellent memoirs of the Rocky Mountain fur trade. Both authors were well-educated men who became experienced trappers. Both waded icy streams setting traps; both were wounded in skirmishes with the Blackfeet. Owing to a combination of mountain skill and luck, both survived to retire from the mountains. Their journals establish the relationship between the trappers' frontier and Jackson Hole.[59]

The Three Tetons, known today as the South, Middle, and Grand, were among the most significant landmarks in the fur trade era. By the 1820s, the mountains were known as the "Trois Tetons," the Three Paps, or the Three Tetons. Iroquois or French Canadian trappers from the Pacific Northwest may have been responsible for the new name. In 1831, Warren Ferris saw the Three Tetons for the first time from the Gray's River south of Jackson Hole. He described them as "three inaccessible finger-shaped peaks of a lofty mountain overlooking the country to a vast distance. . . . Their appearing [sic] is quite singular, and they form a noted landmark in that region." Osborne Russell saw the Tetons for the first time from Pierre's Hole, where they are most visible and distinct. From Russell's vantage point, the range appeared as "Mountains piled on Mountains and capped with three spiral peaks which pierce the cloud. These peaks bear the name of Tetons or Teats—The Snake Indians called them the hoary headed Fathers."[60]

The Three Tetons guided trappers to passes and trails through the valley. Two passes provided access through the Teton Range, Conant Pass, and Teton Pass. The latter pass was the most important. Other important passes were Togwotee, Union, and Two Ocean. Significant routes through the valley were the Hoback Trail, the Yellowstone, and the Gros Ventre River route. Because Jackson Hole is located between South Pass and the upper Snake River country, it was common for trappers to follow the Hoback or Gros Ventre Rivers from the Green River Basin, then cross Teton Pass. Parties traveling from the Bighorn Mountains in the east followed the Wind River and crossed into Jackson Hole via Union or Togwotee Pass. At Union Pass, trappers could turn south, strike the Green River and head south to other profitable trapping grounds. Mountain men entered or exited the Yellowstone country via the Lewis River (today's South Gate of Yellowstone) or Two Ocean Pass.

In 1832, the experienced bourgeois, William Sublette and Robert Campbell, led a pack train loaded with supplies over the Hoback trail to the rendezvous in Pierre's Hole in 1832. Nathaniel Wyeth and 18 green Yankees accompanied Sublette and Campbell. Wyeth recorded the trip down the Hoback and over Teton Pass.

> We passed along a wooded River and through a very difficult road by its side so steep that one of my Horses loosing his foothold in the path was rooled [sic] down about 100 feet into the river he was recovered but so much injured as we had to leave him shortly after: Made this day 20 miles.[61]

The next day the large caravan entered Jackson Hole. On July 7, 1832, "we proceeded up a small brook coming from a gap of the mountain due south of the Trois Tetons." They crossed Teton Pass "without much difficulty it is a good pass for such a range and fresh animals would have no difficulty in passing through it."[62]

Following the rendezvous of 1832, Warren Ferris recorded the passage of the American Fur Company brigade through Jackson Hole. The trappers, led by Andrew Drips and William H. Vanderburgh, sought the company supply train that had failed to arrive at the rendezvous. After crossing Teton Pass and the Snake River, "we entered a dark defile, and followed a zig-zag trail along the almost perpendicular side of the mountain, scarcely leaving space in many places for the feet of our horses"; the trappers walked and guided their horses over the worst portions of the trail, "but notwithstanding this precaution, three of them lost their footing, and were precipitated sixty or seventy feet into the river below." Miraculously, two of the horses were only slightly injured.[63]

In 1835, two Protestant missionaries, Marcus Whitman and Samuel Parker, accompanied Tom Fitzpatrick to the annual rendezvous in the Green River Basin. Parker continued with Jim Bridger through Jackson Hole en route to establishing a mission among the Flathead Indians in the Northwest. Crossing the divide between the Green River Basin and the Hoback drainage, Bridger and Parker camped in Jackson's Little Hole. On Sunday, August 23, 1835, Parker conducted "public worship with those of the company, who understood English." The next day the brigade passed "through a narrow defile, frequently crossing and recrossing a large stream of water [Hoback] which flows into the

Snake river. . . ."[64] The Hoback River Canyon was a key route in spite of rugged terrain.

The Gros Ventre River drainage provided an alternate route between Jackson Hole and the Green River-South Pass country. Although longer in distance, the Gros Ventre was an easier trail and more versatile route. For example, trappers had access to the Wind River Valley and the Bighorn Mountains to the east via Union Pass. Or, like Wilson Price Hunt, one could cross Union Pass and travel south to the Green River Valley. After the rendezvous of 1832 in Pierre's Hole, William Sublette and Robert Campbell led their pack train back to St. Louis via the Gros Ventre River.

Osborne Russell first visited Jackson Hole in 1835 and, after nearly drowning in the Snake River, exited the valley "up a stream called the "Grosvent fork." As they were trying to get to the Yellowstone country, this choice proved to be a mistake. Their guide got them hopelessly lost.[65] Two Ocean Pass and the Lewis River were the correct routes from Jackson Hole into Yellowstone and the dangerous but profitable trapping grounds in Blackfeet country. Conant Pass was the only other convenient crossing in the Teton Range. (Historian Merrill Mattes believed Jed Smith may have exited the valley through this pass in 1824.) In 1839, Osborne Russell hobbled back to Fort Hall in Idaho via the Lewis River and Conant Pass, after being wounded and robbed by Blackfeet near the outlet of Yellowstone Lake.[66] Togwotee Pass provided a relatively easy way into Jackson Hole from the headwaters of the Wind River, although this did not seem to be a primary route based on limited contemporary records.

The Snake River Canyon, where the mountain man's Lewis River exited Jackson Hole, does not seem to have been used. Wilson Price Hunt not only learned from two Shoshone Indians and three scouts that the river was unnavigable through the canyon, but that it was difficult for horses. Warren Ferris stated that the Snake River left the valley "through a deep cut in the mountains, impassable for pack horses."[67] Indeed, there is only one known account of trappers entering the Snake River Canyon. In June 1837, Osborne Russell and a party of trappers crossed Teton Pass into Jackson Hole. In Russell's

own words, "The next day myself and another trapper left the Camp crossed Lewis fork and travelled
down the valley to the south end The next day we
travelled in a SW direction over high and rugged
spurs of Mountain and encamped on a small stream
running into Gray's river. . . ." Russell and his partner travelled down a portion of the Snake River Canyon to cross into the Gray's River drainage.[68]

In Jackson Hole, the Snake River was an obstacle to travel. According to tradition, the trapper ford
was located near the present Jackson-Wilson Bridge.
Rather than one location, there were probably a series of fords across braided channels of the river east
of Teton Pass. The Snake River could be treacherous.
John B. Wyeth recounted the dramatic fording of
Nathaniel Wyeth's brigade and Sublette and Campbell's pack train in July 1832. The crossing took all
day; "one man unloaded his horse, and swam across
with him leading two loaded ones, and unloading
the two, brought them back, for two more, . . ."
Wyeth himself was thrown from his mule, when it
stumbled on a round cobble. Pitched into the torrent, "the current was so strong, that a bush which I
caught hold of only saved me from drowning."[69]

Osborne Russell ran into similar difficulties on
July 4, 1835. Entering Jackson Hole, Russell and a
party of trappers attempted to cross the Snake in a
bullskin boat. When it sank after one crossing,
Russell and his party constructed a log raft. As soon
as they launched, the river current swept the raft,
laden with ten men and gear, downstream out of control. Abandoning the raft, Russell "would fain have
called for help but at this critical period everyone
had to Shift for himself fortunately I scrambled to
shore among the last swimmers."[70] The group spent
a miserable night along the Snake River, pondering
the loss of their weapons and gear. They were lucky,
for the next day, they discovered the raft lodged on a
gravel bar with all their gear intact.

Several locations in Jackson Hole were regular
bivouacs, as they were conveniently spaced along
well-traveled trails. The junction of the Hoback and
Snake Rivers, fords on the Snake River, and the base
of Teton Pass near Wilson, Wyoming, were all men-

tioned as camping locations. Osborne Russell found
the outlet of Jackson Lake a good site, except for the
innumerable "swarms of horse flies and muske-
toes."[71] In general, documents suggest that stays in
Jackson Hole were limited. Mountain men trapped
the streams and rivers in the valley, but most often
were enroute to other destinations.

Tradition has it that Davey Jackson wintered
along the shores of Jackson Lake. However, this is
unlikely, as there were much better places to spend
the winter, where game and forage for horses and
mules were more reliable. There are no documented
accounts of trappers wintering in Jackson Hole.
Like the Indians who adopted the horse culture,
trappers found Jackson Hole poor country for
spending a winter.

There were few conflicts with Indians in Jackson
Hole. The best documented battle between trappers
and Indians occurred in Pierre's Hole in 1832. A
band of Gros Ventres, implacable enemies of the
mountain men, happened to be returning from a
prolonged stay with the Arapaho on the Arkansas
River. Crossing Teton Pass, they clashed with trappers in Pierre's Hole. The battle resulted in a stand-
off and casualties on both sides. The Gros Ventre
escaped under the cover of night, slipping over Teton
Pass.[72] Several days later, seven men quit Wyeth's
company to return east. Somewhere in southern
Jackson Hole, or perhaps the lower Hoback, they
were attacked by Indians, most likely the Gros
Ventres. Joseph More and a Mr. Foy were killed.
Alfred Stephens was wounded and died several days
later in Pierre's Hole.

Joe Meek recalled a harrowing encounter with
Blackfeet that may have occurred near Teton Pass. In
1839, Meek trapped the Snake River country with a
comrade named Allen. They "finally set their traps
on a little stream that runs out of the pass which
leads to Pierre's Hole." Collecting their traps one
morning, they discovered Blackfeet approaching
them. Meek succeeded in concealing himself in a
thicket of willows, but the Blackfeet spotted Allen,
wounded and captured him. The Blackfeet tortured
and dismembered Allen, nearly driving Meek "in-

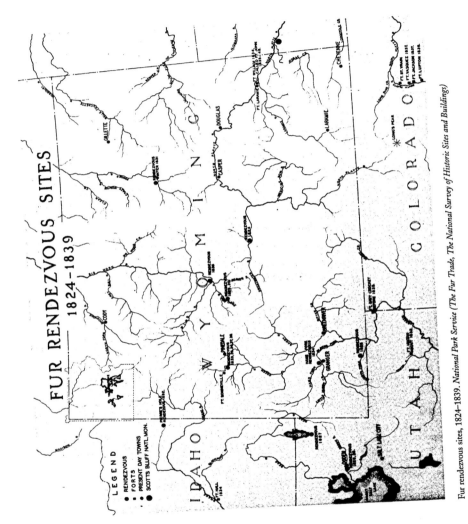

Fur rendezvous sites, 1824–1839. *National Park Service (The Fur Trade, The National Survey of Historic Sites and Buildings)*

sane through sympathy, fear, horror, and suspense as to his own fate."[73]

In the 1830s, emphasis switched from exploration to trapping and trading in Jackson Hole and the surrounding region. Cutthroat competition in the region accelerated the decline of the trappers' frontier.[74] In 1830, the American Fur Company entered the Rockies to compete with the Rocky Mountain Fur Company. Others entered the field, notably Nathaniel Wyeth and Capt. Benjamin L. E. Bonneville, but were not much of a threat compared to Astor's giant company. In 1833, the Rocky Mountain Fur Company and American Fur Company negotiated an accord, dividing the northern Rockies between them. The American Fur Company trapped the Flathead country, the Tetons, and Salt Lake Valley, while the Rocky Mountain Fur Company trappers restricted their trapping forays to the Green River, Yellowstone, and Three Forks of the Missouri. Only a year later, the partners dissolved the Rocky Mountain Fur Company. Three of the partners, Fitzpatrick, Bridger, and Milton Sublette joined the American Fur Company.[75]

In 1841, Osborne Russell travelled to the headwaters of the Port Neuf River in Idaho. Now a seven-year veteran, he observed the ominous changes that had taken place in a few short years:

> In the year 1836 large bands of Buffaloe could be seen in almost every little Valley on the small branches of this Stream at this time the only traces which could be seen of them were the scattered bones of those that had been killed. Their trails which had been made in former years deeply indented in the earth were over grown with grass and weeds. The trappers often remarked to each other as they rode over these lonely plains that it was time for the White man to leave the mountains as Beaver and game had nearly disappeared.[76]

Osborne Russell quit the mountains in 1842. Along with his counterparts, the Rocky Mountain fur trappers left a significant stamp on this country's history. The trappers' frontier was the first of the successive waves of Europeans to sweep across the West. Geographic exploration was the greatest contribution of the mountain men. In their search for lucrative trapping grounds, they discovered the trails and passes and showed others the way west. Although the fur trade was a business, first and foremost, it was the cutting edge in the American-British competition for empire in the Pacific Northwest. Jed Smith's crossing of South Pass from the east in 1824 proved decisive. His old companion, Tom Fitzpatrick, guided the first wagon train of emigrants over the Platte River–South Pass route to Oregon in 1841, and the British lost their bid to secure a border on the Columbia River.

The Indians lost too. Fur traders and mountain men were the first whites to contact the American Indian tribes in the West. Tribes such as the Shoshone and Flathead were renowned for their friendliness. Others, notably the Blackfeet and Gros Ventres, were implacable foes of the mountain man. The Arikari and Crow were unpredictable at best. Mountain men introduced manufactured goods and alcohol, which caused cultural disruption among these tribes. Trappers also brought disease. Smallpox, measles, cholera, and venereal disease swept through the tribes of the West, reducing already small populations. The impact of this contact impaired the ability and will of Native Americans to resist the subsequent encroachment of later frontiersmen.[77]

The Ashley-Henry partnership of 1822 gathered a group of inexperienced young men and boys, who became the ultimate mountain men. They crossed the Continental Divide and stayed in the field year-round. Combining the skills and experience of the American backwoodsman, the British-French trapper, and the Indian, the best of them surpassed all of the former in mountain skills.[78] Jed Smith, Tom Fitzpatrick, Jim Bridger, Kit Carson, Bill Sublette, James Clyman, and Bill Williams represent the image of the mountain man, and the mountain man became a significant figure in American folklore.[79]

Who were these men? There were never very many; estimates vary between 600 to 1,000 in the business at any one time.[80] In the late 1960s and early 1970s, historian Leroy Hafen assembled 292 biographical sketches of trappers and traders. The

This beaver trap, found in the Conant Pass area, is believed to have been used by Richard "Beaver Dick" Leigh. *Jackson Hole Historical Society and Museum*

result was a ten-volume work titled *Mountain Men and the Fur Trade*. Hafen prepared a statistical sketch of mountain men based on these biographies, cognizant that most mountain men left no records.[81]

Most trappers were born between 1793 and 1810. More than 50 percent hailed from Canada, Kentucky, Virginia, and Missouri. The majority left for the mountains between 1825 and 1830. Forty-one percent worked at one time as free trappers, the top of the heap in the trapper's social hierarchy. They worked for themselves, selling their plews to the highest bidder. There are several surprises in Hafen's essay. The majority married white women rather than Indians. Most could read and write, which is contrary to the perception of mountain men as illiterate bumpkins. Finally, most lived to retire from the mountains; only 11 percent were killed by Indians.[82] Most of the subjects of the biographies left the mountains between 1810 and 1850, with 30 percent turning to farming and ranching. Missouri, California, and Oregon were the most popular places of retirement.[83]

Several figures who were known to have passed through Jackson Hole typify the range of personalities and experiences of mountain men. David E. or Davey Jackson remains an enigma. Though a prominent partner of Bill Sublette and Jed Smith, little is known of his life or activities. While Smith explored much of the West and Sublette supplied goods from St. Louis, Jackson directed the trapping operations of the partnership from 1826–1830. He was a capable field leader who was responsible in great part for the partnership's profits. During this period, Jackson Hole acquired its name. Whether this valley was Davey Jackson's favorite haunt is questionable, and the claim that he wintered in Jackson Hole is doubtful, but he used the trails through the enclosed valley to conduct trapping operations. Thus, it is likely that Jackson Hole acquired its name from Jackson, based on his role as a field manager for Ashley, Smith and Sublette.[84]

Robert Campbell was another graduate of the Rocky Mountain Fur Company's "school." Campbell was one of the few to profit from the fur trade. Born in Ulster, Ireland, he accompanied Jed Smith west to improve his health. Well-educated, Campbell served first as a clerk, and by 1832, earned the respect and right to be a bourgeois, leading trapping brigades into the heart of the wilderness. He experienced several close calls with the Blackfeet, proving his courage and sound judgment. Campbell later joined Bill Sublette supplying goods to the Rocky Mountain Fur Company. This provided the basis of his fortune in St. Louis, where he became a wealthy merchant, banker, and landowner. After the battle in Pierre's Hole in 1832, Campbell wrote "to confess the truth, I am heartily sick of it." True to his word, he abandoned the mountains for good in 1833.[85]

If Robert Campbell represented sound judgment seasoned with courage, Mark Head symbolized the image of the mountain man as a hell-raising wildman dressed in buckskin. Mark Head went to the mountains in the trade's later years. He may have accompanied Sublette and Campbell's pack train west in 1832. It was late enough in the trappers' era that Head may have tried to live up to the developing image of a mountain man as a reckless and fearless frontiersman. At any rate, he attracted trouble. One contemporary recalled that his body was covered with scars from injuries and wounds. Mark Head took people literally. In 1834, an Englishman, Sir William Drummond Stewart, stormed about camp when he learned that an Indian named Marshall had stolen his favorite rifle and horse. Stewart rashly offered $500 for Marshall's scalp. Mark Head returned the next day with Stewart's favorite horse, prize rifle, and Marshall's scalp. Stewart appraised Head as "the best and most reckless trapper save one." One contemporary recollected that:

he possessed the most remarkable aptitude for getting into scrapes and out of them in a damaged condition of any man I ever knew. He had gunshot and arrow wounds, had been clawed by bears and horned by a buffalo bull. His endurance and recuperative powers were equalled only by his pluck and misfortune. I saw him once just as he had been brought out of a plum thicket into which he had followed a wounded cinnamon bear. When rescued he looked, to use his own expression, "as if he had been chewed up and spit through a rail fence."

Head drifted to the Southwest and was killed during the Pueblo revolt in 1847. His biographer concluded he "seems to have made an impression by reason of his rash temerity and that alone."[86]

Jedediah Strong Smith was not a typical trapper, but he stood head and shoulders above the rest. Largely forgotten until after 1900, Smith earned praise as one of the most accomplished explorers in American history. Only Lewis and Clark overshadow him. In eight short years, Smith rediscovered South Pass, became the first to reach California overland from the American frontier, was the first Euro-American to cross the Sierra Nevada, and was the first to journey across the Great Basin. Finally, partially owing to good luck, Smith survived three major disasters, the fight with the Arikari in 1823, the Yuma massacre on the Colorado River, and the massacre on the Umpqua in Oregon. More than 40 trappers were killed in these battles.

Smith was unusual for a mountain man. He remained clean-shaven, while his comrades grew beards. He was literate and kept notes, something very few trappers bothered with, assuming they were literate. Unlike most of his contemporaries, Smith did not smoke or use profanity, and he drank only

sparingly. Life in the wilderness did not diminish his strong religious convictions, rather it may have reinforced that faith. Smith's singular appearance, education, and manners were so extraordinary that Alexander Ross, the factor of the British Flathead House, was convinced that his American guest was a spy. Smith's comrades found him different, yet accepted him as a leader. Always to be counted on in a tight fix, he had the "har of the bar" in him, a trapper's phrase for courage and reliability.

Jed Smith sold his interest in the Rocky Mountain Fur Company in 1830 and entered the Santa Fe trade in 1831. While scouting for water on the trail, he disappeared without a trace. The caravan moved on to Santa Fe without him. Only later was his fate learned. At an isolated water hole, he had been attacked by Comanches and killed. It was a lonely and ironic death, given the scrapes he had survived. Jed Smith's accomplishments as an explorer remain one of the great stories in American exploration.[87]

In seeking prime beaver country, mountain men came to know a West that is gone today. This West exists only in our imaginations, inspired by the wonderful artwork of Karl Bodmer, George Catlin, and Alfred Jacob Miller, or scarce contemporary accounts. It was a vast country of diverse and startling landscapes—plain, mountain, and desert—populated with abundant wildlife and occupied by free peoples. Perhaps the mountain man's environment explains in part their stature as American folk heroes.

Yet, the fur trapper began the successive waves of Euro-American frontiers that altered the ecology of the West so drastically. Some of them knew it, too. The lack of beaver and buffalo on the Port Neuf River alarmed Osborne Russell in 1841, a short 17 years since Smith had first crossed South Pass. Once there were an estimated 200,000,000 beaver in North America. Mountain men trapped them to near extinction in many places. Today, the beaver population has recovered to an estimated 2,000,000 animals. There were once an estimated 60,000,000 buffalo in North America. Wild game provided the trapper with virtually all of his food. Buffalo was the favored meat. Bighorn sheep and dog (an Indian favorite) ran a distant second. What the mountain man began, later frontiersmen nearly finished. By 1900, fewer than 600 buffalo were believed to exist.[88]

The mountain man's frontier ended about 1840, the year of the last rendezvous. The trade declined abruptly after its peak in the early 1830s. Prime trapping grounds had been picked clean; beaver were scarce and easy profits a memory. More important, changes in fashion caused the price of beaver plews to plummet from as high as $6 a pound to less than $3 per pound in 1841, after silk hats became the rage in Europe. Moreover, rabbit felt also displaced beaver felt as material for hats. Last, intense competition crippled the trade. A brisk trade in buffalo hides continued after 1840, but the shining times of the 1820s and 1830s were gone. Isolation returned to Jackson Hole for 20 years until civilian and military explorers followed the trappers' tracks across the high passes.

Notes

1. Russell, *Journal of a Trapper*, p. 42.

2. Merrill J. Mattes, "Crossroads, 1807–1829," pp. 87–108, Merril J. Mattes, "Jackson Hole Crossroads of the Western Fur Trade, 1830–1840," *Pacific Northwest Quarterly* 39 (1948): 3–32; and Hiram M. Chittenden, *The American Fur Trade of the Far West: A History of the Pioneer Trading Posts and Early Fur Companies of the Missouri Valley and the Rocky Mountains and of the Overland Commerce with Santa Fe*, 2 vols. (Stanford, CA: Academic Reprints, 1954), 1:306–307.

3. Paul Chrisler Phillips, *The Fur Trade*, with concluding chapters by J.W. Smurr, 2 vols. (Norman: University of Oklahoma Press, 1961), 1:3–14.

4. Ibid.

5. Ibid., 1:15–26.

6. Billington, *Westward Expansion*, pp. 370–371.

7. Ibid., p. 379.

8. Ibid.; and Chittenden, *The American Fur Trade*, 1:126.

9. For biographies of John Colter, see Stallo Vinton, *John Colter: Discoverer of Yellowstone Park* (New York: Edward Eberstadt, 1926); and Burton Harris, *John Colter; His Years in the Rockies* (Wyoming: Big Horn Book Company, 1952, reprint 1977).

10. Harris, *John Colter*, 36; and Mattes, "Crossroads, 1807–1829," p. 91. Dixon is also spelled as Dickson.

11. Harris, *John Colter*, p. 82. Quote from H.M. Brackenridge, *Views from Louisiana Together with a Journal of a Voyage up the Missouri River in 1811* (Pittsburgh, 1814), p. 91.

12. Mattes, "Crossroads, 1807–1829," p. 92.

13. Harris, *John Colter*, p. 91.

14. Ibid., p. 104.

15. Grand Teton National Park, Collections Accession File, "The Colter Stone," Accession File 63, 2 folders, F.M. Fryxell to National Park Service Director Arno Cammerer, May 8, 1934.

16. Paul Lawrence, *John Colter: A New Look at an Old Mystery* (Jackson, WY: Pioneer Press, 1978), pp. 13–14.

17. Department of the Interior, National Park Service, September 4, 1936, October 6, 1936, and June 5, 1937, Grand Teton National Park Files.

19. Harris, *John Colter*, pp. 108–109; and Aubrey Haines, "John Colter," *The Mountain Men and the Fur Trade of the Far West*, ed. LeRoy R. Hafen, 10 vols. (Glendale, CA: The Arthur H. Clark Company, 1965–1972), 8:78–79. This book is hereafter referred to as *Mountain Men*.

20. Haines, "John Colter," *Mountain Men*, 8:79–80.

21. Ibid., 8:76–80; Vinton, *Colter: Discoverer of Yellowstone*, pp. 58–61; Mattes, "Crossroads, 1807–1829," pp. 92–93; Barry Maps, Grand Teton National Park Files; Harris, *John Colter*, pp. 73–114; and David J. Saylor, *Jackson Hole, Wyoming: In the Shadow of the Tetons* (Norman, OK: University of Oklahoma Press, 1970), pp. 8–34.

22. Harris, *John Colter*, pp. 152–165.

23. Mattes, "Crossroads, 1807–1829," p. 93.

24. Ibid. Mattes made a reasonable inference that they crossed Togwotee Pass, based on their knowledge of the area, when they led the Astorians across the Rockies.

25. Washington Irving, *Astoria*, 2 vols. (Philadelphia, PA: Carey, Lea, and Blanchard, 1836; reprint, unabridged ed., Philadelphia, PA: J.B. Lippincott, 1961), 1:222.

26. Ibid., 1:227.

27. Ibid.

28. Ibid., 2:230–234.

29. Mattes, "Crossroads, 1807–1829," pp. 97–98; and Philip Ashton Rollins, ed., *The Discovery of the Oregon Trail: Robert Stuart's Narratives* (New York: Charles Scribner's Sons, 1935), pp. 130–177. Stuart's party lost John Day, who went mad, but were joined later by Miller, who had left Hunt's party at Henry's Fort.

30. Irving, *Astoria,* 2:334; and Rollins, *Discovery Oregon Trail,* pp. 130–131.

31. Irving, *Astoria,* 2:337; and Rollins, *Discovery Oregon Trail,* pp. 134–135.

32. Rollins, *Discovery Oregon Trail,* p. 153.

33. Ibid., pp. 154–186; and Mattes, "Crossroads, 1809–1829," pp. 97–98.

34. Chittenden, *American Fur Trade,* 1:221–223.

35. Billington, *Westward Expansion,* pp. 382–383.

36. Alexander Ross, *The Fur Hunters of the Far West,* ed. Kenneth A. Spaulding, reprint 1855 edition (Norman, OK: University of Oklahoma Press, 1956), p. 135.

37. Ibid., p. 167; and Mattes, "Crossroads, 1807–1829," pp. 99–100.

38. Mattes, "Crossroads, 1807–1829," pp. 99–100.

39. Ibid.

40. Ibid.

41. Edgar Stewart, "Finian McDonald," *Mountain Men,* 5:212–213; and Dale Morgan, *Jedediah Smith and the Opening of the West* (New York: Bobbs-Merrill Company), pp. 124–125.

42. Stewart, "Finian McDonald," *Mountain Men,* 5:213. According to Stewart, McDonald returned with 4,459 pelts, while Morgan cites a lower figure of 4,339 pelts. Either number represents a successful trapping season.

43. Mattes, "Crossroads, 1807–1829," p. 100.

44. Phillips, *Fur Trade,* 2:35; and Chittenden, *American Fur Trade,* 1:246–262.

45. Mattes, "Crossroads, 1807–1829," p. 101. See Dale Morgan's biography of Jed Smith.

46. Harrison Clifford Dale, *The Ashley-Smith Explorations and the Discovery of a Central Route to the Pacific, 1822–1829,* revised ed., (Glendale, CA: Arthur H. Clark Co, 1941), pp. 92–93.

47. Mattes, "Crossroads, 1807–1829," p. 102.

48. Morgan, *Jedediah Smith,* pp. 128–129.

49. Mattes, "Crossroads, 1807–1829," p. 102.

50. Phillips, *Fur Trade,* 2:396.

51. Mattes, "Crossroads, 1807–1829," p. 102.

52. Ibid., pp. 103–105.

53. Ibid.

54. Chittenden, *American Fur Trade,* 1:288–289.

55. Frances Fuller Victor, *The River of the West: Life and Adventure in the Rocky Mountains and Oregon* (Hartford, CT: Columbian Book Col., 1870), p. 58.

56. Mattes, "Crossroads, 1807–1829," pp. 105–108.

57. Mattes, "Crossroads, 1830–1840," pp. 3–4.

58. Ibid.

59. Ibid; Russell, *Journal of a Trapper;* Warren A. Ferris, *Life in the Rockies,* ed. Paul C. Phillips (Denver, CO: Old West Publishing Co., 1940); and Mattes, "Crossroads," 1830–1840," p. 3.

60. Ferris, *Life in the Rockies,* p. 85; ed. F.G. Young, "The Correspondence and Journals of Captain Nathaniel J. Wyeth, 1831–1836," *Sources of the History of Oregon,* Vol. 1, Parts 3–6 (Eugene, OR: University Press, 1899), p. 158; and Russell, *Journal,* p. 15.

61. Young, *Sources of History,* p. 158.

62. Ibid., pp. 158–159.

63. Ferris, *Life in the Rockies,* pp. 156–158.

64. Rev. Samuel Parker, *Journal of an Exploring Tour Beyond the Rocky Mountains,* 4th ed. (New York: 1844), p. 88.

65. Russell, *Journal of a Trapper,* pp. 18–20.

66. Ibid., pp. 99–108; and Mattes, "Crossroads, 1830–1840," p. 29.

67. Ferris, *Life in the Rockies,* p. 156.

68. Russell, *Journal of a Trapper,* p. 90.

69. Mattes, "Crossroads, 1830–1840."

70. Russell, *Journal of a Trapper,* pp. 18–20.

71. Ibid., pp. 42–43.

72. Mattes, "Crossroads, 1830–1840," p. 10; and Washington Irving, *Adventures of Captain Bonneville,* 2 vols (New York: G.P. Putnam's Sons, 1837), 1:76–84.

73. Victor, *River of the West,* pp. 253–255. This incident may well have occurred west of Teton Pass in Idaho.

74. Mattes, "Crossroads, 1830–1840," pp. 3–4.

75. Chittenden, *American Fur Trade,* 1:304–305.

76. Russell, *Journal of a Trapper,* p. 123.

77. Ibid.

78. Bernard DeVoto, *Across the Wide Missouri* (New York: Hougton Mifflin Co., 1947), pp. 158–160.

79. Phillips, *Fur Trade,* 2:574.

80. Chittenden, *American Fur Trade,* 1:7; and Billington, *Westward Expansion,* p. 355.

81. Richard J. Fehrman, "The Mountain Men—A Statistical View," *Mountain Men,* 10:9–15.

82. Ibid.; Chittenden counted 151 trappers killed by Indians between 1820–1831. One source claimed that Blackfeet and Gros Ventres were killing "an average of 50 Americans a year" by the 1830. I believe this is too high, but determining more accurate figures would be difficult, if not impossible. See Thomas F. Schiltz in "The Gros Ventres and the Upper Missouri Fur Trade, 1806–1835," *Annals of Wyoming* 56 (Fall 1984):21–28.

83. Fehrman, "Mountain Men—A Statistical View," *Mountain Men,* 10:9–15.

84. Carl D. Hays, "David E. Jackson," *Mountain Men,* 9:215–244; and Ferris, *Life in Rockies,* p. 157.

85. Harvey L. Carter, "Robert Campbell," *Mountain Men,* 8:49–60.

86. Harvey L. Carter, "Mark Head," *Mountain Men,* 1:287–293.

87. Harvey L. Carter, "Jed Smith," *Mountain Men,* 8:331–348.

88. Stephen H. Jenkins and Peter E. Busher, "North American Beaver," *Mammalian Species* (American Society of Mammalogists, June 8, 1979), No. 120; and Ed Park, *The World of the Bison* (New York: J.B. Lippincott Co., 1969), pp. 37–57.

Explorers and Scientists

He was the slim, bearded, white man who always carried a bag over his shoulder and a little pick in his right hand and who darted from one dry run to another, climbed up buttes and escarpments, picked at the rocks, and then went on. Once, a party of braves had surrounded him and dumped the contents of his bag onto the ground. It had nothing but rocks. So thinking him loco, they had given him a name that meant "man-who-picks-up stones-running" and let him go.

His real name was Ferdinand Vandiveer Hayden, M.D.

—Richard A. Bartlett, *Great Surveys of the American West*

When Meriwether Lewis and William Clark set out on their epic journey in 1804, Americans knew little of the North American continent west of the Mississippi River. President Thomas Jefferson considered the expedition so important that he wrote the orders for the expedition himself, and participated actively in planning the enterprise. Jefferson prescribed objectives that set standards for later government explorers. Lewis and Clark launched 75 years of government surveys that lasted until the late 1870s.[1]

Manifest Destiny became the nation's rallying slogan in the 1840s. Proponents of this doctrine believed that it was the destiny of the United States to expand over the North American continent. No one personified this idea more than John Charles Fremont. A member of the Army's Corps of Topographical Engineers, Fremont led his first expedition to the Rockies in 1842. Mapping a route for emigrants to Oregon, Fremont crossed South Pass into the Green River Basin, then turned north along the Wind River Range. He climbed what he thought was the tallest peak in the range, known today as Fremont Peak. Describing the day as "sunny and bright," Fremont "could just discover the snowy heads of the Trois Tetons" in the distance. He led several more surveys west, but this was as close as he ever came to Jackson Hole.[2]

Later surveys concentrated on locating a route for a transcontinental railroad. The need for such a link was both symbolic and practical. After the Mexican War ended in 1848, the United States spanned the continent from east to west, and hence required a reliable transportation route to secure political and economic ties and to defend the new western empire. Moreover, the transcontinental railroad symbolized the nationalism of the country. Unfortunately, intense sectional rivalries fueled by the issue of slavery tainted rational debate concerning an eastern terminus and route. Protagonists believed that the region securing the eastern terminus would enjoy overwhelming and permanent economic advantages over others. The issue pitted not only North against South, but communities and states against each other. No one seemed to accept the possibility of more than one transcontinental railroad.[3]

In 1853, Congress allocated funding to survey practicable routes to the Pacific Coast, charging the War Department with the task. Isaac I. Stevens, a former army officer, surveyed the northern route between the 47th and 49th parallels. Lieutenant John W. Gunnison led the 38th parallel survey, which covered an area through the Colorado Rockies and central Utah. The 35th parallel survey scouted from Fort Smith, Arkansas, to Santa Fe, then on to California. Lieutenant A. W. Whipple directed this survey. Two survey parties reconnoitered the 32nd parallel, which crossed Texas, New Mexico, and Arizona. The 38th parallel survey explored the general area of the eventual alignment of the first transcontinental railroad from southwestern Wyoming to the Pacific Coast. None of the surveys evaluated a route through Jackson Hole.

Influential citizens in Washington Territory (which included what is now the states of Washington, Idaho, and parts of Montana and Wyoming) supported a railroad over South Pass with branches to San Francisco and Puget Sound. Consequently, they were disappointed with Stevens's recommendation for a northern route through Montana to Puget Sound. As a result, the Washington Territorial Legislature provided funds for the survey of a South Pass route. A civil engineer named Frederick West Lander conducted the survey. Lander surveyed south of the Teton Range and Jackson Hole, essentially following the Oregon Trail.[4] The United States Government published the surveys in a preliminary report in 1855, but Congress failed to agree on a route as the slavery issue inflamed sectional rivalries over the eastern terminus of the railroad. The Union stood on the threshold of dissolution and war when Captain W. F. Raynolds expedition entered Jackson Hole in 1860.

Raynolds's expedition was the first of three military surveys to pass through Jackson Hole. A member of the Army Topographical Engineers, Raynolds was instructed to explore the upper Yellowstone, Gallatin, and Madison Rivers. Like so many military surveys, Raynolds was to "ascertain the numbers, habits and disposition of the Indians inhabiting the country . . . as the army scouted potential opponents."[5] Further, Raynolds was to survey agricultural and mineral resources, climate, and, in particular, potential rail or wagon roads "to meet the wants of military operations or those of emigration through, or settlement in, the country."[6]

After travelling up the Missouri River by steamboat to Fort Pierre, South Dakota, the survey set out overland on June 18, 1859. Raynolds employed none other than Jim Bridger as a guide. Also accompanying the expedition was a young physician who exhibited a passion for geology and paleontology. He was Ferdinand Vandiveer Hayden, the organizer and leader of the post-Civil War Hayden Surveys. The military surveys of this period inventoried the flora, fauna, and geology of the West as a matter of course. Respected institutions such as the Philadelphia Academy of Sciences, the Albany Academy, and the Smithsonian Institution sent scientists with these expeditions. As a result, a new perception of the American West emerged; scientists saw it as a gigantic natural laboratory. The scientist was a frontiersman, as much so as the soldier and mountain man. Yet, he perceived the West's natural resources in a much different light; they were most important for the knowledge that could be gleaned from them. Thus, in the Raynolds's expedition, mountain man, soldier, and scientist merged in the surveyors' frontier.[7]

Jim Bridger guided the party across the badlands of South Dakota, past the Black Hills, and west to the Yellowstone River. Hayden's penchant for wandering off to collect rock and fossil specimens caused Raynolds and Bridger considerable worry. On August 11 or 12, 1859, on Rosebud Creek, Raynolds noted, "Dr. F. V. Hayden, geologist, had departed for Wolf mountains in such a state of scientific obsession as to neglect to obtain permission." Hayden was missing for at least one night. He returned August 13, "happy in having examined the mountains." Always the soldier, Raynolds ordered "that no one should thereafter be absent overnight without express permission."[8] Later, on the Little Bighorn, Hayden asked to examine a nearby bluff, but Raynolds denied the request "as Mr. Bridger was very decided as to the danger of parties going abroad alone while there were evidences of the vicinity of Indians, and as I could not encourage unnecessary work on the Sabbath."[9] As winter approached, the expedition found abandoned cabins along Deer Creek near present day Glenrock, Wyoming, where they holed up until spring. A very religious man,

Raynolds espoused his faith and apparently tried to convert Hayden. Soldier, mountain man, and scientist must have spent a long winter on Deer Creek, broken only by the vivid yarns of Jim Bridger and other mountain men.

Raynolds's party moved out on May 8, 1860. They intended to follow the Wind River to its headwaters and cross a divide to the headwaters of the Yellowstone. In late May, Raynolds tried to cross the Continental Divide. Bridger warned against this, stating that it would be necessary to cross into the Columbia drainage before seeking the headwaters of the Yellowstone. Ignoring his advice, Raynolds found his way blocked by a basaltic ridge, "rising not less than five thousand feet above us." Bridger remarked to Raynolds: "I told you you could not go through. A bird can't fly over that without taking a supply of grub along." They returned to the Wind River, where Bridger determined to guide them over Union Pass.[10]

Thus, terrain and snow forced the Raynolds's survey to seek a route through Jackson Hole. On May 31, they set out. Bridger assured them that they would camp that night on the waters of the Columbia within five miles of the Green River. Steep slopes and deep snow hindered their progress so much that "Bridger for the first time lost heart and declared that it would be impossible to go further." The expedition floundered, but eventually reached the Continental Divide completing this "most laborious" march since leaving Fort Pierre. Raynolds named the divide, Union Pass, and the nearby summit, Union Peak. On June 1, the survey party trekked down the Gros Ventre Fork valley. Snow and deep mud exhausted both men and stock. Here, Jim Bridger lost his bearings. Although he knew the general area well, Bridger's memory for details seems to have failed him. He tried unsuccessfully to find a way through the Mount Leidy Highlands to Togwotee Pass and Two Ocean Pass. The snow and rugged terrain foiled him. Disappointed, Raynolds determined to follow the Gros Ventre west. He recorded, however, that Hayden and his assistants remained busy collecting specimens, despite the ordeal.[11]

"Flower-painted meadows" greeted the expedition when they entered Jackson Hole. The Snake

Ferdinand V. Hayden led some of the most notable surveying expeditions of the Yellowstone and Jackson Hole area. *National Park Service*

River presented another obstacle. It was a roiling torrent, fed by the spring runoff from the surrounding mountains. They traveled south seeking a safe crossing, but tragedy struck when one man drowned while testing a ford. Raynolds then ordered a raft built, which promptly failed a trial run. Meanwhile, Bridger had begun fashioning a bullboat of poles, blankets, and lodge skin. Using the boat, they ferried their gear across three 100-yard channels losing only the wheels to the odometer. They spent three days crossing the river. On June 18, Bridger guided the expedition over Teton Pass into Pierre's Hole.[12]

The survey followed the Madison River, then the Missouri River, back to Fort Pierre. Raynolds failed to locate the upper Yellowstone River. Why Jim Bridger did not follow the Wind River then divert to Togwotee Pass and Two Ocean Pass remains a mystery. Even more puzzling was the decision to cross Teton Pass rather than travel north through

Jackson Hole to Two Ocean Pass. Both routes would have enabled Raynolds to locate the headwaters of the Yellowstone. There are two explanations. Bridger may have felt the snow would be too deep to try either route, or the passing years may have dimmed his memory. It is clear that he became confused in the Upper Gros Ventre River country for Raynolds observed that Bridger seemed "more at a loss than I have ever seen him. . . ."[13]

Nevertheless, the Raynolds survey is significant for several reasons. It was the first government survey to explore Jackson Hole; and for the first time scientists turned their attention to this area and collected specimens. It was also during this survey that Raynolds gave Union Pass its name. The presence of Jim Bridger linked the fur trappers' frontier to the explorer and surveyor's frontier. Finally, Raynolds concluded in his report that the Jackson Hole and Yellowstone country were too mountainous for a railroad.

While Raynolds conducted his surveys, divisions over slavery escalated in the United States. Abraham Lincoln's election to the presidency fractured the Union in 1860, and when the volunteer army of the seceded states opened fire on Fort Sumter in April 1861, they hurled the nation into its bloodiest war. Exploration in the West came to a halt. After the Civil War ended in 1865, military surveyors again looked to the western horizon.

In 1873, Captain William A. Jones, Army Corps of Engineers, was ordered to reconnoiter an area from Fort Bridger, Wyoming, to the Yellowstone country. He sought to locate a military road, linking the Yellowstone and the Montana settlements with the Union Pacific tracks. Jones assembled a party of specialists that included Theodore B. Comstock, geologist; Dr. C. C. Parry, botanist; C. L. Heitzman, surgeon and chemist; and Lt. S. E. Blunt, astronomer.

The Jones expedition set out from Fort Bridger in June 1873. Their route took them through the Green River Valley, over South Pass, up the Wind River, where they crossed the Owl Creek Mountains into the Bighorn Basin. When they reached the Shoshone River (then called the Stinking Water), Jones turned west into Yellowstone Park. The survey made a loop through the Yellowstone country, spending the month of August in the new national park.

South of Yellowstone Lake, their Shoshone guides rebelled, stranding the expedition in the Thorofare country. Jones enticed them to continue with promises of food and new respect. However, all of the Shoshone were lost except for one, and he proved unreliable. The party finally made their way up the Yellowstone River, crossed Two Ocean Pass, traveled down Lava Creek, then up Blackrock Creek to Togwotee Pass. Rediscovering this pass, Jones named it for one of the guides. In his 1875 report, Jones recommended the construction of a wagon road from the Union Pacific line across Togwotee and Two Ocean Passes into Yellowstone Park. However, the road was never built.[14]

In 1876, Lieutenant Gustavus Cheney Doane led a small party of soldiers into Jackson Hole. Doane had been ordered to "make exploration of the Snake River from Yellowstone Lake to Columbia River." Since the geography of the Snake River was reasonably well known, the need for this expedition remains obscure. Doane appears to have ignored the military chain of command, bypassing his immediate superior, Major James S. Brisbin, and proposing the expedition to General Alfred Terry, who issued orders approving the scheme. Doane's personal interest in exploration seems to have been the catalyst for the expedition.[15] He was authorized to take a sergeant and five troopers. The army issued mounts, pack animals, 60 days' rations, camp equipment, and a prefabricated boat that could be assembled and disassembled. Two additional enlisted men, brought along to handle extra mules and a wagon, accompanied the expedition for a portion of the journey.

On October 11, 1876, the expedition set out from Fort Ellis, Montana, optimistic and seemingly well prepared. Doane described their outfit as an "arctic one;" "We had buffalo coats and moccasins, rubber boots and overshoes, heavy underclothing and plenty of robes and blankets." The soldiers brought carbines, while Doane carried his Sharps buffalo rifle. He rejected pistols as being "worthless" in the mountains, adding, "in fact, they are worthless anywhere in the field." Knives, axes, mess and kitchen gear, a tent, and plenty of tobacco and tea were packed. Doane brought a prismatic compass, an aneroid barometer, maximum and minimum temperature thermometers, and a long tape measure. He noted caustically: "None of these were provided by a generous government, but all were purchased by myself as usual in such cases."[16]

They had traveled for two days only, when the wagon cramped and tipped over, crushing a wheel and reducing the box to "kindling wood." This was an omen of things to come. By the time the cavalrymen reached Jackson Hole on November 23, survival, not exploration, was their main concern. Snow and dense vegetation hindered their progress through Yellowstone Park. They had abandoned one horse and eight mules by the time they reached Jackson Lake. Moreover, the boat was proving to be a hindrance; besides the energy expended hauling it over land, it had swamped the day after Doane's men assembled and launched it on Yellowstone Lake. Since then the boat had been repaired three times causing delays of at least four days.[17]

Snow pelted the expedition as Doane led them down the upper Snake River, where they entered the calmer waters of Jackson Lake. They camped in the vicinity of Waterfalls Canyon on the west shore of the lake. Doane's decision to travel along the west shore is inexplicable. The route is much easier along the east shore, especially since a well-known Indian and trapper trail existed here.[18] He recalled that travel was terrible with the pack train "climbing over rocks and through tangled forests of pine, aspen, and other varieties of timber." They abandoned another horse. On November 24, they camped at the north end of Moran Bay. Short of food, they killed and cooked a river otter, but Doane recalled that "[T]he first mouthful went down, but did not remain." The party gave up on otter as a food source. Fortunately, the native cutthroat trout provided an alternative. Doane decided to camp for a day giving the pack animals and the troopers a rest. Doane killed a deer, providing their first fresh meat in some time. On November 26, they continued along the lakeshore. Doane abandoned his horse, leaving them with four horses and one mule. They passed around Elk Island, traveling ten miles before setting up camp in a grassy meadow somewhere on the south shore of Jackson Lake. They journeyed another 15 miles the next day. On November 28, the expedition made only two miles when high winds and heavy snow forced them to bivouac. To make matters worse, diar-

rhea struck the entire party. Doane blamed deer meat gone bad, but his biographers, the Bonneys, believe it may have been caused by drinking water from glacial melt.[19] Most recuperated enough to travel by November 30. They reached the outlet of Jackson Lake in the afternoon, making good time to an area near the present day Snake River Overlook. The next day, December 1, Doane led his party down the Snake River where they camped at Blacktail Butte. The boat carried all the gear at this point, because the remaining animals were too worn to pack equipment. Although the fishing was good, Doane complained "fresh fish is to[o] thin a diet to subsist on alone. We now have no coffee, sugar, tea, bacon, and, worst of all, no tobacco. Nothing but a few beans left. The game is scarce and shy."[20] Even on an empty stomach, Doane left a vivid description of the Teton Range:

A glorious night. Moon in the full, but empty stomachs. We are now far enough away from the lakes to be clear of the clouds of vapor and local snow storms. Our camp is about at a central point with reference to obtaining a view of the Tetons, and at a distance of fifteen miles from the nearest part of the range. The moonlight view was one of unspeakable grandeur. There are twenty-two summits in the line, all of them mighty mountains, with the gleaming spire of Mount Hayden rising in a pinnacle above all.

There are no foothills to the Tetons. They rise suddenly in rugged majesty from the rock strewn plain. Masses of heavy forests appear on the glacial debris and in parks behind the curves of the lower slopes, but the general field of vision is glittering glaciated rock. The soft light floods the great expanse of the valley, the winding silvery river and the resplendent deeply carved mountain walls.[21]

They laid over the next day to hunt. Having no success, they killed and butchered the weakest horse. Even though the soldiers seasoned the meat with gunpowder, Doane recalled that "[T]he flesh tastes exactly as the perspiration of the animal smells."[22]

As they made their way down the Snake River on December 3, all were aware that the expedition had become an exercise in survival. They camped at the mouth of the Gros Ventre River. The boat now

This odometer was used in one of the Hayden Surveys of Yellowstone. The Raynolds Survey of 1860 used a similar odometer in Jackson Hole, until the wheels were lost in a river crossing. *U.S. Geological Survey, William Henry Jackson #1290*

had to be repaired almost daily; troopers poured hot water on leaks that promptly froze over, sealing the boat. On December 7, Sergeant Server encountered an old trapper named John Pierce, who had a crude cabin somewhere in the southern end of Jackson Hole. Pierce visited their camp the next day, bringing a welcome quarter of fat elk.

Doane and his men moved on into the Snake River Canyon, where the boat capsized, "dancing end over end in the swift cold current." On December 18, they reached Keenan City, a mining camp located in the Snake River Range. Doane's weight had dropped from a robust 190 pounds to a mere 126 pounds. The rest were in similar condition. They arrived at Fort Hall, Idaho, on January 3, 1877. Doane planned to secure a new outfit and press on down the Snake River, but his commanding officer ordered him "with his escort to rejoin his proper station Fort Ellis, as soon as practicable."[23]

Doane later reported that his commander, Major Brisbin, had disapproved of the entire project from the outset. The fact that Doane had circumvented Brisbin to secure permission for the expedition may have contributed to his recall.

In retrospect, Doane's expedition exhibited poor planning and timing.[24] The goal of exploring the

Snake River from Yellowstone Lake to the Columbia River was very general. Why the army required such a survey is unknown. Further, making the trip in winter was foolish. Doane recalled that the old trapper, John Pierce, "was evidently completely puzzled as to what motive could have induced us to make such a trip in such a way and at such a season."[25] Doane and his fellow cavalrymen were lucky to survive the trip. He lost his journal when the boat capsized in the Snake River Canyon. He wrote his narrative much later, using Sergeant Server's cryptic journal. Regardless, it remains one of the most interesting records of exploration in Jackson Hole; the foolishness of the trip adds to its appeal.

Expeditions such as Doane's did nothing to promote military surveys, which conflicted increasingly with civilian surveys after 1865. The U.S. Geological Survey of the Territories was formed in 1869. This Interior Department bureau competed with the military and, through this bureau, the civilian scientist replaced the soldier-explorer in western surveys. Ferdinand Vandiveer Hayden, a veteran of Raynolds's 1860 survey, became one of the premier civilian explorers after the Civil War. Hayden had launched new surveys in 1867, eventually reporting directly to the Secretary of the Interior in 1869. As his influence grew, surveys received increased funding from Congress.[26]

In 1871, Congress appropriated $40,000 for a survey of the Yellowstone country, which was very generous for a notably stingy group of solons. Hayden spent the season in Yellowstone accompanied by a party that included William Henry Jackson, the pioneer photographer, and Thomas Moran, the landscape artist. Hayden's flair for publicity, aided by Jackson's photographs and Moran's artwork, contributed to the creation of Yellowstone National Park in 1872.

Hayden returned to the Yellowstone country to explore the sources of the Snake and Missouri Rivers in 1872. This survey was significant for several reasons. Most important, it established Hayden's dominance in the field of exploration for several years, overshadowing both civilian and military competition. Further, as Hayden matured as a survey leader after the Civil War, he recognized the importance of public relations in securing funding. He cultivated conscientiously the support of congressmen, railroad magnates, soldiers, and westerners. As a result, his interest shifted from the purely scientific to general inventories of the West's exploitable resources. His reports remained truthful, but tended to emphasize the positive, which delighted Western boosters.

As a result, Hayden's surveys were well funded for the next few years. The 1872 survey employed the largest field crew yet; 61 men were divided into two divisions. Hayden led one group into Yellowstone, while James Stevenson led the other party into the Snake River country, which included Teton Basin and Jackson Hole. Snake River Division members included the following people: Professor Frank Bradley, chief geologist; Gustavus Bechler, topographer; John Merle Coulter, botanist; C. Hart Merriam, ornithologist; and William H. Jackson, photographer. The Hayden Surveys provided experience and exposure for men who would distinguish themselves in their fields. The 1872 survey was notable also for the number of political appointees included in the expedition; the packers and guides referred to them .as "pilgrims." While some carried their weight, others did not. Hayden, mindful of future funding, cultivated the favor of politicians by accepting these pilgrims.[27]

The Snake River Division left Ogden, Utah, on June 24, 1872, and reached Fort Hall, Idaho, on July 3. From Fort Hall, Stevenson led the division into Teton Basin, formerly called Pierre's Hole. They spent two weeks surveying the basin and mapping the Teton Range. Two notable events occurred: N. P Langford and James Stevenson made the first ascent of the Grand Teton, and William H. Jackson took the first photographs of the Grand, Middle and South Teton. Hayden reported the ascent by Langford and Stevenson in the introduction of his 1872 report, stating "so far as we can ascertain they are the only white men that ever reached its summit." Langford also wrote an account of the climb for *Scribner's Monthly*.[28] Their claim went unchallenged until 1898, when Franklin Spalding, Jack Shive, Frank Petersen, and William O. Owen reached the summit. Owen challenged Langford's claim for reasons discussed in another chapter of this study, launching a controversy that still flares up periodically today.

Ferdinand V. Hayden (left) and William Paris in camp, 1872. *William Henry Jackson Photograph, National Park Service*

Meanwhile, Jackson set out from the camp on Teton Creek to find a suitable vantage point to photograph the Tetons. He recalled that "this side trip to the Tetons was really secondary to the main object of the expedition, but by this time Yellowstone had lost something of its novelty, and the Tetons, never before photographed, now became of the first importance, so far as I was concerned."[29] Jackson was accompanied by his assistant, Charley Campbell, John Merle Coulter, the botanist, P J. Beveridge, and a packer named Aleck. They ascended Table Mountain situated to the west of the three Tetons. The mules carried food and camp gear, while Jackson's mule, "Old Molly," hauled his precious photographic equipment. They set up camp at tree line, spent three days exploring the area, and sought a good vantage point for photographic work. While making their way to the summit of Table Mountain, they found their passage blocked by a wall of rock. "On one side was a sheer precipice, but on the other a ledge supported a bank of hard snow, 'which offered a passage around the wall.'" The snowbank formed a dangerous angle, hanging over a sheer drop of several hundred feet. Deciding the risk was worth the view, they first packed a trail on the snow, then carefully guided their saddle and pack animals across the snowbank. Jackson spent most of the day making 8 × 10-inch, 11 × 14-inch, and stereoscopic negatives. One exposure shows young Jackson kneeling beside his dark

Photographing in High Places by
William Henry Jackson, 1872.
Jackson and an assistant ascended
Table Mountain to photograph
the surrounding area during the
Hayden survey of 1872. His photo-
graphs were the first ever made of
the Tetons. *U.S. Geological Survey,
William Henry Jackson #172*

tent near an abrupt precipice with the Teton peaks
looming on the horizon. He arranged the photograph, while Aleck the packer made the exposure.
Jackson's photographs of the Grand Teton are among
the most famous of his thousands of remarkable images of the American West. The Grand Teton was
revealed to Americans for the first time. After ten
days on their own, Jackson's party returned to the
main camp.[30]

The Snake River Division made their way north
toward Yellowstone, meeting Hayden's division in
Yellowstone in mid-August. A portion of Stevenson's
division set out to explore the headwaters of the
Snake River and Jackson Hole in early September.
They surveyed about 40 small streams that make up
the headwaters of the Snake, then moved down the

river into Jackson Hole. W. H. Jackson did not accompany Stevenson on this portion of the survey,
thus no photographs were taken of the Teton Range
from the east.[31]

On September 19, the division reached the inlet
of Jackson Lake, flanked by trees cloaked in the yel-
lows and pale reds of autumn. Geologist Frank
Bradley described the scene: "The Teton Range had
been before us for many days as a prominent feature
of the landscape, but now its peaks stood up as the
features of main interest, bounding the valley on the
west with a series of roof-like ridges and pointed
peaks, well besprinkled with patches of snow."[32] At
their camp, less than a mile above the inlet of the
lake, Beaver Dick Leigh, the popular guide, rejoined
them. One member of the party, Robert Adams,

took the first soundings on Jackson Lake, securing a reading of 258 feet in depth before a driving squall forced him off the lake. Adams's canoe trip was the first record of boating on Jackson Lake.

On September 21, the Snake River Division moved south along the eastern shore of the lake, camping at a location possibly east of Sargent's Bay. The next day they reached the outlet of Jackson Lake and followed the course of the Snake River to the Oxbow Bend area. They camped here for two days.

Topographer Gustavus Bechler followed the Buffalo Fork nearly to its headwaters. Meanwhile, Frank Bradley possibly ascended Lozier Hill rather than Signal Mountain for he described Jackson Hole "from the top of the butte at the mouth of the lake." From the summit, Bradley observed that the Snake River had abandoned its southern channel for its present course in the remote past. His description suggests Signal Mountain, but the map of his route through Jackson Hole indicates Lozier Hill. On September 24, Stevenson's division forded the Snake River below Oxbow Bend. Here the party split up, one group following the river along its west bank, while the other group traveled in a southwesterly course to the glacial lakes at the base of the Teton Range. At String Lake, they camped from September 25 to 28.[33]

In his report, Frank Bradley left a record of a landscape that remains remarkably unchanged today. The survey team traveled over broad sagebrush-cov-

"Beaver Dick" Leigh and his family at Blackfoot, Idaho. Leigh was the guide for the 1872 Hayden Survey; Jenny Lake was named for Leigh's wife. *Jackson Hole Historical Society and Museum*

ered plains, interspersed with isolated ponds. They crossed a narrow belt of spruces, then descended into the old channel of the Snake River. Bradley described clearly the Potholes and Burned Ridge, a forest-mantled glacial moraine. Rudolph Hering, an assistant topographer, prepared the first cross-section of the valley, based on elevation statistics. Bradley's narrative is the first scientific description of Jackson Hole. The survey team named the lakes in honor of their guide, Beaver Dick Leigh, and his wife Jenny, hence the names Leigh and Jenny Lakes. This constituted a refreshing departure from the Hayden prece-

	Snake River Division Camps in Jackson Hole	
Dates	Site	Location
Sept. 19–22, 1872	Inlet of Jackson's Hole	Possibly Lizard Creek
Sept. 21–22, 1872	Jackson's Lake	Unknown
Sept. 22–25, 1872	Outlet of Jackson's Hole	Oxbow Bend area
Sept. 25–28, 1872	Eastern foot of Mount Hayden between glacier lakes	String Lake
Sept. 28–30, 1872	Snake River, at junction with creek from glacier lakes	Cottonwood Creek
Sept. 30–Oct. 1, 1872	Snake River, below mouth of Gros Ventre Creek	Opposite north end of West Gros Ventre Butte
Oct. 1–2, 1872	East end Teton Pass	

dent of naming features for themselves or congressional supporters. William Taggart, Bradley's assistant, hiked up Cascade Canyon for a short distance, where he "found a cluster of falls and rapids about 250 feet high with lofty precipitous walls on either hand."[34] Taggart had visited Hidden Falls, one of the most beautiful places in the park. Predicting lakes at the mouths of other canyons, Bradley and Taggart located two, which they named Taggart and Phelps Lakes. (Beaver Dick Leigh informed them that a hunter named George Phelps had first seen and reported the southern lake; they named it in his honor.) Bradley Lake appears on the map, but it is not mentioned in Bradley's report.

On September 28, they followed Cottonwood Creek to its junction with the Snake River, just above present-day Moose, Wyoming. They camped in this area until September 30. While here, Gustavus Bechler forded the river and ascended "a high rocky butte" which they named Upper Gros Ventre Butte. This conspicuous summit is Blacktail Butte. Based on Bechler's field notes, an illustrator produced an excellent drawing of the Teton Range from Blacktail Butte. This may be the first artistic illustration of the Teton Range.[35] Bradley wrote that this area consisted of a series of terraces dominated by sagebrush. They saw antelope in Jackson Hole for the first time. Noticing the effects of fire, Bradley wrote that around Blacktail Butte, "large areas of the sage had been burned off, and the grasses had grown up densely, forming fine pasturage."

The Snake River Division moved south along the west side of the river on September 30, camping about a mile below the mouth of the Gros Ventre River, across from the South Gros Ventre Buttes. The next day they camped at the foot of Teton Pass. On October 2, the Snake River Division split, one party crossing Teton Pass, while the other group followed the course of the Snake River into Idaho. Stevenson's Snake River Division ended their season's work at Fort Hall on October 11, 1872.[36]

The Hayden Surveys returned to Jackson Hole in 1877 and 1878, but neither proved historically as significant as the 1872 survey. Later surveys examined the area to develop a detailed map and a systematic geological survey of Idaho, Montana, and Wyoming.[37] Gustavus Bechler led the Teton Division in 1877. Hayden directed Bechler to map the sources of the Snake River. Bechler managed to survey approximately 6,000 square miles before Chief Joseph's retreating Nez Perces forced his division to suspend work in the fall.[38]

Orestes St. John accompanied the Teton Division as staff geologist, entering the valley in August 1877. St. John noted in his letter of transmittal that his fieldwork supplemented the work of Bradley and Taggart. But, in doing so, he added more detailed information about the Teton Range and Jackson Hole. St. John examined the central Teton Range confirming the granitic and metamorphic composition of the peaks. He investigated the vast morainal deposits in Jackson Hole and speculated that while glaciation explained the canyons scoring the Tetons and moraines at their base, the "potency of simple-acting atmospheric influences" was the cause of water-worn debris in the valley.[39]

Making more general observations, St. John found the soil in the valley fertile and that there was plenty of water, but concluded that latitude, altitude, and a short growing season would prohibit the development of agriculture. He believed the valley was more suited to grazing. Further, the variety and abundance of wildlife impressed him; noting that "at seasons the woods are stocked with game; elk, deer, antelope, and bears abound, while in the forest two or three kinds of grouse are found, and the streams afford abundance of large delicious trout."[40] In the 1880s and 1890s, Jackson Hole would become famous for its hunting and fishing. Finally, while investigating the mountains in the vicinity of Togwotee Pass, St. John reported "immense columns of smoke from forest conflagrations rose high in the air, in places blotting out the view of distant mountains."[41]

In 1878, the last Hayden Survey took the field, continuing the work of 1877. Hayden broke the survey into four divisions. F. A. Clark led the Wind River Division, which completed the topographical work that included areas adjacent to Jackson Hole. A. D. Wilson completed the primary triangulations of the entire survey area, begun in 1877. The Upper Saddle of the Grand Teton was an important station. William H. Jackson rejoined Hayden after an absence of two years, leading a photographic division through Jackson Hole.[42]

Wilson came to Pierre's Hole in 1878, after water-swollen rivers had prevented entry in 1877. With Jackson's team, they detrained at Point of Rocks, Wyoming, and set out for the Wind River Mountains. W. H. Holmes, a topographer with an aptitude for drawing accurate sketches of the landscape, traveled with Jackson's party. Hayden himself accompanied the group. They traveled to the head of the Hoback River, then followed the trapper-Indian trail into Jackson Hole. Jackson found the Hoback's scenery attractive, "but it had some serious problems in the long steep slides that crossed it frequently. These made precarious footing for riding and pack animals." One mule stumbled and rolled some 200 feet down a slope, but escaped unhurt. At Little Gros Ventre Creek (Flat Creek) Wilson and Jackson parted company. Wilson's party crossed Teton Pass into Pierre's Hole, while Jackson's division followed the course of the Snake River into Yellowstone Park.

Wilson intended to use the Grand Teton as a primary triangulation station, which required an ascent of that peak. The survey team followed Teton Creek into the gentler western portion of the range, where they set up a base camp. Accompanied by his assistant, A. C. Ladd and his guide, Harry Yount, Wilson set out to climb the Grand Teton in August. The small party made their way up the plateau (Table Mountain) west of the Tetons, a single line of three men on horse trailed by one pack mule. They reached the plateau with no trouble, but found their path to the Grand Teton blocked "by a deep and very abrupt canon [sic]," the South Fork of Cascade Canyon. Even though it was August, heavy snowbanks blocked their passage down the steep slopes into the canyon. Wilson and his companions descended from tree to a basin with enough grass and timber to set up camp. Heavy rain and snow forced them to camp for two or three days. Since they had only brought food for three of four days, Wilson became concerned about the weather.[44]

While waiting for the weather to improve, Wilson climbed a ridge southeast of camp to scout the approaches to the Grand Teton. It was here that he spotted four grizzly bears on a snowbank below the ridge, "playing 'hide and go seek' among the crevasses." Wilson stole into a hidden position in the rocks, apparently undetected by the bears. Then he "fired three or four shots at them, killing two of them; but finding that I had but one cartridge left and two bears, I thought discretion the better part of valor, and . . . 'lit out' for camp!" There is no record that Wilson returned to assure himself that the bears were dead or collect any part of the carcasses for scientific purposes.[44]

On August 20, the weather cleared, allowing Wilson, Ladd, and Yount to try an ascent. They first crossed a pass in the light of a full moon, possibly Hurricane Pass, into the South Fork of Cascade Canyon. They picked their way over a spur, before beginning their climb of the Grand. Scrambling up a slide of loose rock on the southwest side of the mountain, they finally reached the Lower Saddle between the Grand and Middle Teton after an hour's hard work. The group reached the Upper Saddle after a rugged climb. At this point, he could see no way to scale the last several hundred feet to the summit. Wilson expressed his disappointment, recalling "for the first time, after climbing hundreds of peaks during my twelve years of experience, I was compelled to give up reaching the summit." He noted the same circular enclosure discovered by Langford and Stevenson in 1872, along with a pile of rocks supporting an upright stick presumably built by a white man.[45] Wilson and Ladd set up their instruments and recorded their measurements from the Upper Saddle. They returned to the main camp and set out for Yellowstone on the next day. The work of Wilson's primary triangulation survey covered 28,000 square miles. His survey established relative locations between prominent topographical features that were critical to accurate mapping.

Meanwhile, the photographic team traveled north through Jackson Hole. Hayden reported that Jackson photographed "several magnificent views" of the Teton Range from the Jackson Lake area.[46] These are the first known photographs taken from Jackson Hole. Jackson was not so ebullient as Hayden. In his memoirs, he recalled that few negatives were made in the valley, because of "a smoky haziness that filled the air." From a highpoint on Signal Mountain, he made a very credible negative of the Teton Range, framing the Grand Teton on the left and Mount Moran on the right. The haze of smoke

Artist Thomas Moran sketched this early view of Mount Hayden (the Grand Teton) and Mount Moran from Pierre's Hole in 1879. Moran never actually visited Jackson Hole. *Jackson Hole Historical Society and Museum*

from forest fires is clearly visible, looming over Jackson Lake and the valley. In his autobiography, Jackson does not mention photographing the Tetons, writing only that they passed through "the beautiful basin that has the distressing name of Jackson's Hole."[47]

The photographic survey rode north into Yellowstone. Jackson made 45 8 × 10-inch negatives and 110 negatives of 5 × 8 inches, forsaking quantity to produce a selection of quality prints. In September, the party traveled along the Upper Yellowstone River, crossing Two Ocean Pass into the Buffalo Fork drainage. From the vicinity of Togwotee Pass area, Jackson photographed the Teton Range for the first time, although he did not consider the photo-

graphs especially significant. While on the Upper Yellowstone, he stalked and killed a "large silvertip" grizzly bear, which he believed a high point of the trip.[48]

The 1878 survey was the last directed by Hayden, for in 1879, Congress created the U.S. Geological Survey, which dissolved the three civilian surveys then in existence. This included Hayden's Geological Survey of the Territories. He had fallen victim to the intense rivalries between explorers and bureaucracies. The last Hayden Survey ended nearly a century of discovery in the American West. In 1803, the land west of the Mississippi River was a great void on maps. The interior beyond the Spanish settlements in New Mexico and California and west of the frontier on the Mississippi River was unknown to transplanted Europeans. By 1878, explorers, scientists, and surveyors had changed that; they had explored, mapped, and described the American West. The age of discovery was over.

This frontier is significant for several reasons. First, using the knowledge of the fur trapper, explorers opened the West for settlement by mapping and surveying transportation routes. Second, surveyors had prepared accurate and detailed maps by the end of the 1870s. Third, these frontiersmen had produced voluminous reports covering a wide range of topics. Fourth, early explorers such as Fremont guaranteed a United States that would span the continent from coast to coast. Fifth, surveyors and scientists identified many of the problems in administering vast public lands. For example, surveyors argued convincingly, though not with much success, for the systematic classification of western lands. John Wesley Powell believed that political entities in the West should be based on hydrological features or river drainages. Sixth, these frontiersmen explored for the sake of knowledge itself. Scientists and surveyors saw the West as a vast natural laboratory. Resources of the West were exploited, but for their secrets rather than financial gain. Significant discoveries were made in the fields of geology, botany, zoology, paleontology, and ethnology-archeology. It became a golden era in the history of science. Seventh, because of this frontier, science and land management became institutionalized in new federal agencies and new specialties in science. Finally, explorers, surveyors, and scientists revealed the West to Americans through their reports, maps, and illustrations. And in revealing that wondrous land, they helped shape the self-image of Americans. If Americans had no great architectural monuments or long cultural traditions, they could take pride in a vast and splendid empire of deserts and forests and plains and mountains, filled with plants, animals, and natives.[49]

Six surveys associated with this frontier visited Jackson Hole. Capt. W. F. Raynolds came first in 1860. Through this expedition, the frontier of the mountain man, explorer, and scientist merged. Jim Bridger passed on his knowledge of the West to Raynolds and F V. Hayden. For the first time, specimens were collected, as Hayden studied the geology

of the Gros Ventre-southern Jackson Hole area through the eyes of a scientist. Further, Raynolds concluded in his report that the country around the Teton Range was too rugged for a railroad. Finally, Raynolds gave Union Pass its name. It was 13 years before the next survey party entered Jackson Hole, led by Capt. William A. Jones of the Army Corps of Engineers. Capt. Jones's "discovery" and naming of Togwotee Pass may be this expedition's most significant legacy to Jackson Hole.

Surveys, although important sources for historians, did not always prove fruitful. Lt. Gustavus Doane's trip in 1876 accomplished very little. Only the courage and campaign experience of Doane and his cavalrymen, aided by a generous pinch of luck, averted a disaster. Yet, Doane's narrative is arguably the most entertaining of the survey records. Near today's park headquarters at Moose, Wyoming, Doane and his troopers choked down horseflesh that tasted like a saddle blanket smells. Yet, Doane was irrepressible. Even after the ordeal in Jackson Hole, he was ready to press on down the Snake River from Fort Hall, when his superior recalled him to Fort Ellis. Doane's folly points out that exploration was an adventure as much as it was measuring elevations and collecting rock and plant specimens.

The 1872, 1877, and 1878 Hayden Surveys, particularly the 1872 expedition, were the most significant to the history of Jackson Hole, especially the 1872 survey. The 1872 survey produced a generally accurate map of the Teton Range and surrounding region though flawed in detail. Langford and Stevenson claimed the first successful ascent of the Grand Teton, while Jackson took the first photographs of the Grand Teton and Teton Range. In Jackson Hole, scientists evaluated the natural resources in detail for the first time. Frank Bradley and W. R. Taggart reconnoitered the geologic features of the valley, building on Hayden's work in 1860 and beginning a fine tradition of geologic study that goes on today. John Merle Coulter, the prominent botanist, accompanied Jackson on his excursion up Table Mountain, where he undoubtedly examined and collected alpine plants. Coulter collected around 1,200 plant specimens; the list in the report totals 34 pages, a significant number being found in the Snake River Valley and Teton Range. C. Hart Merriam collected a significant number of bird skins, nests, animal skins, and skulls. A representative number came from the "Snake River, Wyo." He collected one specimen of rabbit that he thought was a new species. Called Baird's rabbit, it was actually a snowshoe hare. Frank Bradley, impressed by the scenery in Teton Basin, predicted a bright future for tourism when railroads reached the area. Robert Hering reported a feasible railroad route from the Central Pacific line in Utah through Idaho and over Targhee Pass to Montana. He also located a possible wagon or rail grade north of the Teton Range through the Falls River-Beulah Lake country.[50]

But perhaps the most significant legacy of the Hayden Surveys is the place names of topographic features in the valley. The Snake River Division named a number of peaks and lakes in 1872. Some failed to survive such as North Gros Ventre Butte, known as Blacktail Butte today. They renamed the Grand Teton as Mount Hayden, in honor of their mentor, but it failed to stick. They gave Mount Moran, the prominent peak west of Jackson Lake, and Mount Leidy, east of the valley, their names even though Moran never visited Jackson Hole. In 1879, Thomas Moran visited Teton Basin and saw the peak named for him from the west side of the range.[51] The surveyors named the glacial lakes at the base of the range; Phelps, Taggart, Bradley, Jenny, and Leigh Lakes.[52] Mount St. John was named later in honor of Oreste St. John, the field geologist with the surveys in 1877 and 1878.

Other surveys would follow, but their significance was less important. By the time, President Chester A. Arthur traveled through Jackson Hole in 1883 with a large entourage of guides, Indians, cavalrymen, packers, and political cronies, the avowed purpose was recreation rather than exploration. A year after Arthur's tour, the first settlers entered Jackson Hole, marking a new era in the valley's history.[53]

Notes

1. Meriwether Lewis, *The Expedition of Lewis and Clark*, ed. William H. Goetzmann and Archibald Hanna, 1814 edition, unabridged in 3 vols. (Philadelphia: J.B. Lippincott Co., 1961), 1:xix–xxvi; and William H.

Goetzmann, *Exploration and Empire: the Explorer and Scientist in the Winning of the West* (New York: Alfred A. Knopf, 1966; New York: Vintage Books, 1972), pp. 3–8.

2. Goetzmann, *Exploration and Empire*, pp. 242–244 and 249; and John Charles Fremont, *The Expeditions of John Charles Fremont*, Donald Jackson and Mary Lee Spence, ed., 2 vols. (Urbana, IL: University of Illinois Press, 1970), 1:271.

3. Billington, *Westward Expansion*, pp. 553–556; and Goetzmann, *Exploration and Empire*, pp. 265–266.

4. Goetzmann, *Exploration and Empire*, pp. 265–302.

5. David J. Saylor, *Jackson Hole*, pp. 97–99; and Goetzmann, *Exploration and Empire*, p. 328.

6. Saylor, *Jackson Hole*, p. 97.

7. Goetzmann, *Exploration and Empire*, p. 303.

8. J. Cecil Alter, *James Bridger, Trapper, Frontiersman, Scout and Guide, a Historical Narrative* (Salt Lake City, UT: Shepard Book Company, 1925), p. 337. This material is taken from Capt. W.F. Raynolds's journal.

9. Ibid., p. 344.

10. Ibid., pp. 360–361.

11. Ibid., pp. 361–367.

12. Ibid., pp. 368–369.

13. Ibid., p. 362; and Saylor, *Jackson Hole*, p. 97.

14. Goetzmann, *Exploration and Empire*, pp. 409–412 (Goetzmann believes the accomplishments of the Jones survey have been underrated); Saylor, *Jackson Hole*, p. 109; and Aubrey L. Haines, *The Yellowstone Story: A History of our First National Park*, 2 vols. (Yellowstone National Park, WY: Yellowstone Library and Museum Association in cooperation with Colorado Associated University Press, 1977), 1:201–203.

15. G.C. Doane, "Expedition of 1876–1877," unpublished manuscript typed from original, Grand Teton National Park Library, pp. 1–7; and Orrin H. and Lorraine J. Bonney, *Battledrums and Geysers; the Life and Journals of Lt. Gustavus Cheney Doan* (Chicago: Sage Books, 1970).

16. Doane, "Expedition," pp. 1–7.

17. Ibid., pp. 1–21.

18. Ibid., p. 21.

19. Ibid., p. 23; and Bonney, *Battledrums and Geysers*, p. 516.

20. Doane, "Expedition," p. 24.

21. Ibid., p. 25.

22. Ibid.

23. Ibid., p. 39.

24. Saylor, *Jackson Hole*, p. 110; Bonney, *Battledrums and Geysers*; and Merlin K. Potts, "The Doane Expedition of 1876–1877," *Campfire Tales of Jackson Hole* (Moose, WY:

Grand Teton Natural History Association, 1970), pp. 20–37.

25. Doane, "Expedition," p. 27.

26. Goetzmann, *Exploration and Empire*, pp. 489–490.

27. Richard A. Bartlett, *Great Surveys of the American West* (Norman: University of Oklahoma Press, 1962), pp. 59–73; Goetzmann, *Exploration and Empire*, pp. 511–515; and F.V. Hayden to Secretary of the Interior, C. Delano, March 10, 1873, *Sixth Annual Report of the U.S. Geological Survey of the Territories . . . for 1872* (Washington, D.C.: Government Printing Office, 1873), pp. 1–10.

28. Hayden to Secretary of the Interior, March 10, 1873, *Sixth Annual Report*, p. 2; and N. P. Langford, "The Ascent of Mount Hayden," *Scribner's Monthly* 4 (June 1873):129–137.

29. William H. Jackson, *The Pioneer Photographer: Rocky Mountain Adventures with a Camera*, in collaboration with Howard R. Driggs (Yonkers-on-Hudson, NY: World Book Co., 1929), p. 123.

30. Ibid., pp. 126–127.

31. Frank H. Bradley, "Report," *Sixth Annual Report*, pp. 250–267. Camps of the Snake River Division are listed on p. 814.

32. Ibid., p. 260.

33. Signal Mountain is closer to the outlet of Jackson Lake than Lozier Hill, but the latter hill is shown on the map "Sources of the Snake River." Signal Mountain does not appear on the map.

34. Bradley, "Report," p. 264.

35. Ibid., pp. 261–262, Figure 50.

36. Hayden to Secretary of the Interior, March 10, 1873, *Sixth Annual Report*, pp. 1–10; and Bradley, "Report," pp. 265–271.

37. Bartlett, *Great Surveys*, pp. 72–73.

38. F V. Hayden to Secretary of the Interior, December 1, 1878, *Eleventh Annual Report of the United States Geological and Geographical Survey . . . for the Year 1877* (Washington, D.C.: Government Printing Office, 1879), pp. ix–xvi.

39. St. John, "Report of Orestes St. John," *Eleventh Annual Report*, pp. 411–413 and 443–448.

40. Ibid., p. 446.

41. Ibid., p. 443.

42. F. V. Hayden to Secretary of the Interior, January 1, 1879, *Twelfth Annual Report of the United States Geological and Geographical Survey . . . for the Year 1878*, 2 vols. (Washington, D.C.: Government Printing Office, 1883), 1:xiii–xviii.

43. Jackson, *Pioneer Photographer*, pp. 292–305; and A. D. Wilson, "Report on the Primary Triangulation of 1877 and 1878," *Eleventh Annual Report*, pp. 651–660. There is some confusion as to whether Hayden accompanied Jackson.

44. A. D. Wilson, "Report," *Eleventh Annual Report*, p. 657.

45. Ibid., pp. 656–658.

46. Hayden to Secretary of the Interior, January 1, 1879, *Twelfth Annual Report*, 1:xvi.

47. Jackson, *Pioneer Photographer*, p. 296; and William Henry Jackson, *Time Exposure: the Autobiography of William Henry Jackson* (New York: G.P. Putnam's Sons, 1940), p. 248.

48. Jackson, *Pioneer Photographer*, pp. 299–300; and Jackson, *Time Exposure*, pp. 249–250.

49. Goetzmann, *Exploration and Empire*, pp. 312, 527, 580, and 599–601; and Bartlett, *Great Surveys*.

50. Bartlett, *Great Surveys*, p. 73; Goetzmann, *Exploration and Empire*, pp. 511–515; Bradley, "Report," p. 223; and R. Hering to F. V. Hayden, *Sixth Annual Report*, pp. 92–95.

51. Thomas Moran Diary, 1878, Acc. #114 Cat. #1753, Grand Teton National Park Diary.

52. Goetzmann, *Exploration and Empire*, p. 512.

53. Saylor, *Jackson Hole*, pp. 113–116.

Prospectors and Miners

... "Uncle Jack" Davis, a colorful character, devoted himself to prospecting in the Snake River Canyon, where he had a crude cabin near Bailey Creek. When he died in 1911, his valuables consisted of $12 in cash and about the same amount in gold amalgam. Not much return for at least 20 years worth of prospecting. ...

"Uncle Jack" Davis listed his occupation as "gold miner" in the 1900 census. Davis prospected in the Snake River Canyon, where he had a crude cabin near Bailey Creek. *National Park Service*

The California gold rush occurred in 1849, triggered by the discovery at Sutter's Mill. By the end of the year, California's population had expanded to 100,000 people, most of them Anglo-Americans bitten by the gold bug. At first, pickings were easy. Individuals or small groups engaged in placer mining, a relatively simple process that required only a shovel, pan, and strong back. As the rivers and streams played out, companies displaced individualistic prospectors; large amounts of capital were required to excavate mines and construct mills to extract gold from tough quartz.[1] Prospecting became a way of life to these displaced frontiersmen. Perennial optimists, they dispersed throughout the Rocky Mountain West and discovered gold in Colorado, Nevada, and British Columbia in 1858. In 1862, prospectors located gold in Montana, precipitating the rush to Bannock City and Virginia City in

1863. From southwest Montana, ever-hopeful prospectors made their way into Jackson Hole.

In 1863, Walter W. DeLacy joined a party of prospectors intent on seeking gold "on the south branch of Snake River to its head." DeLacy produced a map in 1865, and published an account of the trip in 1876. Hence, the expedition is remembered for its accomplishments in exploration rather than striking it rich. They failed to find the mother load of gold.[2] DeLacy considered himself "pretty well fixed for such a trip," having "two good horses," provisions for about 40 days, weapons, and $10 in gold dust. He did not mention them, but he also must have brought the miner's traditional tools, a pick, shovel, and washing pan. He joined the band on the Beaverhead River in Montana and was elected captain of the expedition, even though few of the miners knew him. He attributed his election to the fact that "it is frequently a great point in your favor that no one knows anything about you."[3]

DeLacy set out on August 7, 1863, leading 26 prospectors. Since most of them had arrived only recently from the gold fields of Colorado and Montana, none had first-hand knowledge of the Jackson Hole country. Only one, a prospector named Hillerman, had prospected a portion of the south Snake; hence he served as a guide. Another party joined them, increasing their number to 42. The miners' frontier attracted more than its share of disreputable characters, and this expedition was no exception in DeLacy's judgment. He recalled that vigilantes, presumably in Montana, had banished Hillerman for complicity in a murder. Another prospector, named Gallagher, tried to raise a party to attack and steal horses from a band of Shoshone camped adjacent to one of their bivouacks. Fortunately, "respectable" members of the party dissuaded him. Some time later, vigilantes executed Gallagher.

DeLacy established and supervised a routine. The group marched once per day, camping early so men could prospect until nightfall. Pickets were posted to guard against Indians. On August 19, they came to the confluence of the Salt and Snake Rivers, where smoke from forest fires obscured the surrounding mountains. The next day, DeLacy's band entered the Snake River Canyon, negotiating a trail "about one hundred feet above the river, which was very narrow and difficult, and had apparently been very little used for a number of years." Travel was slow and dangerous; a pack animal and horse tripped and tumbled down the steep slopes. DeLacy's band made about 12 miles and camped in a very poor location. This camp is difficult to locate, as DeLacy's descriptions and mileage estimates are imprecise. They traveled ten miles the next day and camped in a small bottom along the cottonwood-lined river. DeLacy noted that the geographic formations had changed from limestone to sandstone. On August 22, the miners crossed to the left bank of the river (the north or west bank) after traveling three miles. Another five or six miles over comparatively open country brought them to the mouth of the Hoback River, where they set up camp.

For the first time, prospectors dipped their pans in the waters of Jackson Hole, hoping to find pay

dirt. DeLacy noted that their guide, Hillerman, had never been this far up the Snake River. (Hillerman and a partner apparently had entered the Snake River Canyon in 1862.)[4] They camped an extra day at Hoback Junction, dispersing to prospect the Snake, Hoback, and nearby tributaries, where everyone found plenty of "color," but none in profitable quantities.

On August 24, they moved up the Snake River 11 miles, camping on a stream "coming in from the northeast." Based on mileage traveled and DeLacy's description, this is possibly Spring Creek. Small groups ventured out to prospect and hunt, but no one experienced success. DeLacy observed that "up to this time and for a long time after we saw nothing larger than rabbits." On August 25, they continued north passing between two buttes, obviously traveling up Spring Gulch between East and West Gros Ventre Buttes. DeLacy described the valley as a large and extensive one. "It is one of the most picturesque basins in the mountains. It is covered with fine grass; the soil is deep in many places and it is capable of settlement, and will, in the future, be covered with bands of cattle and sheep." They crossed the Gros Ventre River and stopped to pan for gold. The miners found plenty of "color," but pressed on across flats, "part of which was covered by the largest and thickest sagebrush that I have ever seen." Based on DeLacy's description, they camped on the east bank of the Snake, opposite Cottonwood Creek. The next day, the prospectors followed the Snake River north, skirting around the Snake River Overlook and camping, somewhere west of where the Cunningham Cabin is located today.

On August 27, they crossed the Buffalo Fork. There, they agreed to move on to Pacific Creek, where they would set up a base camp and explore the surrounding country. At Pacific Creek, the band of 42 built a corral, then participated in a meeting. They agreed to break up into four parties; one group would serve as camp guards while the others prospected. To prevent anarchy in case a discovery was made, the assembly agreed that each individual would be considered a discoverer. Every member would be entitled to five claims of 200 feet each. The prospecting parties left on August 28 and returned the 31st. The exact areas explored are un-

Miners Frank Coffin, Don Graham, and Jim Webb gave up this mine on Pilgrim Creek, claiming that "the gold couldn't be retrieved." *Jackson Hole Historical Society and Museum*

known. One group traveled about 20 miles up the Buffalo Fork, but like the others, had little success. One party did report a stratum of coal along one of the streams.

Discouraged, the expedition broke up, one party returning south, DeLacy and 27 others set out on September 2, following the Snake River to Jackson Lake. They traveled north, about 18 miles from Pacific Creek, striking a trail that ran northwest and camped at the inlet of Jackson Lake. With some apprehension, DeLacy recalled that the mountains to the north appeared to be on fire. They also found fresh horse tracks, which they presumed to be Indian signs, but they never saw Indians in Jackson Hole. From here, they moved on to the Yellowstone country.

DeLacy's narrative is significant for the information it provides about Jackson Hole between the end of the fur trade in 1840 and the arrival of settlers in the 1880s. It is the first record of frontiersmen seeking valuable minerals in Jackson Hole. More important, these miners did not hit pay dirt or the mother lode. The landscape of this valley would look much different today had there been a strike. Hundreds of miners would have stampeded into the valley and boomtowns would have sprung up. The adjacent forests would have been denuded to provide lumber for buildings, millraces for placer mining, and timbers for shoring up shafts and tunnels. Given the boom-

and-bust character of mining, the mines and towns would have been abandoned, leaving eroded hillsides, small mountains of tailings, and hillsides scarred by hydraulic mining. This pattern occurred in California, Nevada, Colorado, and Montana.

DeLacy's account strongly suggests that Jackson Hole was unoccupied. He found no trapper cabins or isolated homesteads in the valley. Although he was concerned about encountering Indians, DeLacy reported only fresh horse tracks, which he took to be an Indian sign. He reported no camps or, for that matter, signs of Indian villages in the valley. There were distinct Indian and trapper trails in the area. The "little used" trail through the Snake River Canyon reinforces the contention that it was not a major route into Jackson Hole. The trail DeLacy's party struck east of Jackson Lake was a major trail through the valley. Finally, his observations concerning forest fires, the lack of wildlife, and the vegetation are useful in reconstructing the ecology of the region prior to settlement.

Although the DeLacy expedition was unsuccessful, prospectors did not give up on Jackson Hole. In 1864, the George Phelps—John C. Davis party entered Jackson Hole from the Green River valley. The miners crossed Two Ocean Pass and traveled into the Yellowstone country.[5] Between 1864 and 1877, miners conducted more extensive operations. Traveling across the sagebrush flats east of the Snake River in

Though gold mining in Jackson Hole was never profitable, some miners were successful retrieving other minerals. This man and his dog are working a talc mine on Owl Creek. *Jackson Hole Historical Society and Museum*

1878, Orestes St. John found prospect pits and the remains of a ditch north of the Gros Ventre River. St. John was told that prospectors constructed it about 1870 or 1871.[6] The ditch ran from near the Teton Science School to Schwabacher's Landing on the Snake River. Ditch Creek derived its name from this early water diversion, which is still known as Mining Ditch.[7]

Very little information is known to exist concerning these mining ventures. Possibly, prospectors entered Jackson Hole about 1870 from the small mining camps of South Pass City, Atlantic City, and Miners Delight. Misled by exaggerated reports of gold strikes, some 2,000 prospectors had descended on the southern end of the Wind River Range in 1868 and 1869. They were disappointed. Although several profitable holes were found, the yields were never great and by 1870 the "boom" was over. Disappointed stragglers may well have tried their luck in Jackson Hole.[8]

Perhaps the most lasting legacy of the miner's frontier in Jackson Hole is a lurid tale of murder, known as "the Story of Deadman's Bar." The incident occurred in the summer of 1886, just a short two years after the first settlers arrived in Jackson Hole. Four prospectors from Montana—Henry Welter, T. H. Tiggerman, August Kellenberger, and John Tonnar—came to the valley to set up placer mines

on the Snake River. Lured to Jackson Hole by stories of gold-rich gravels, they located a claim along the Snake River near Snake River Overlook, set up camp, and began work. Later that summer, a boating and fishing party found the bodies of Welter, Tiggerman, and Kellenberger weighted down by rocks at the edge of the river. A sheriff's posse arrested Tonnar in Teton Basin at the ranch of Emile Wolff, who later moved to Jackson Hole. Tonnar was tried for the murder in Evanston, Wyoming. He claimed self-defense and, since there were no eyewitnesses, the jury acquitted him. The site of the murders has since been known as Deadman's Bar.[9]

One mining company attempted to locate gold in Jackson Hole in the 1880s. Harris-Dunn and Company was formed in 1889, after a man known only as Captain Harris visited the valley and located a mine on Whetstone Creek in the present Teton Wilderness. Harris and a man named Dunn formed a joint stock company. The company built cabins, sluices, and a sawmill, and began operating a placer mine. The sluice box consisted of four-inch-thick planks pitted with holes drilled by a two-inch auger. The gold was supposed to settle in the holes, but in practice they filled with gravel. In 1895 or 1896, James M. Conrad constructed a ferry near Oxbow Bend to transport supplies to the mine, then owned by the Whetstone Mining Company. Whether

Harris and Dunn sold out or changed the name of their company is unknown. By 1897, the mining operation had shut down.[10]

The presence of "color" in the Snake River drainage continued to entice speculators. Around 1900, 160-acre placer claims were filed up and down the Snake River, from Jackson Lake to Menor's Ferry. But, the prospectors failed to locate the elusive bonanza of gold and the claims lapsed. Shadowy prospectors dug small tunnels in Avalanche and Death Canyons; the foundation of a prospector's cabin still exists in upper Death Canyon. Perhaps they were the work of John Condit and Andrew Davis, who listed their occupations as gold miners in the 1900 census. "Uncle Jack" Davis, a colorful character, devoted himself to prospecting in the Snake River Canyon, where he had a crude cabin near Bailey Creek. When he died in 1911, his valuables consisted of $12 in cash and about the same amount in gold amalgam. Not much return for at least 20 years worth of prospecting. About 1905, E. C. "Doc" Steele and several partners located placer claims on the Snake. They excavated the Steele Ditch from Spread Creek. Settlers used it later to irrigate hayfields.[11]

There was plenty of "color" in the rivers of Jackson Hole, but in concentrations so small that placer mining was not feasible. No one ever found the mother lode—that is, the source of gold. DeLacy tried and failed, and all that followed him tasted failure too. After homesteaders populated the valley, some earned a little extra cash through placer mining. No fortunes were ever made, however, and the mining frontier had little impact on the history of Jackson Hole.

Notes

1. Ray Allen Billington, *Westward Expansion*, pp. 529–530.

2. Walter W. DeLacy, "A Trip up the South Snake River in 1863," *Contributions to the Historical Society of Montana*, 1(1876):113–118, transcript in the Grand Teton National Park Library.

3. Ibid.

4. Ibid. Hillerman informed DeLacy that his partner had shot himself accidentally, then died of the wound.

5. Haines, *The Yellowstone Story*, 1:68.

6. St. John, "Report of Orestes St. John," *Eleventh Annual Report*, p. 445.

7. Elizabeth Wied Hayden, *From Trapper to Tourist in Jackson Hole*, 4th ed., with revisions (Moose, WY: Grand Teton Natural History Association, 1981), pp. 29–30.

8. T. A. Larson, *History of Wyoming* (Lincoln, NE: University of Nebraska Press, 1965), pp. 112–113.

9. Fritiof Fryxell, "The Story of Deadman's Bar," *Campfire Tales of Jackson Hole*, pp. 38–42. Fryxell's story of this incident remains the most reliable account, as it was based on an interview with Emile Wolff, who had firsthand knowledge of the incident.

10. Hayden, *Trapper to Tourist*, p. 30; Noley Mumey, *The Teton Mountains: Their History and Tradition* (Denver: Artcraft Press, 1947), pp. 359–361; and National Archives, Record Group 49, "Records of the Bureau of Land Management," Homestead Certificate 373, Lander, J. Conrad, 1902.

11. Census of the United States, 1900, Wyoming, Uinta County, Enumeration District 65, Jackson Precinct, Elec. Dist. 15, Schedule 1, Population, 9 sheets; and Fritiof Fryxell, "Prospector of Jackson Hole," *Campfire Tales*, pp. 47–51.

The Pioneers:
Homesteading in Jackson Hole, 1884–1900

One 4 room log house one log store house 24 × 6 feet. one log barn 40 × 20 feet. one log granary 20 × 20 feet. another store house 24 × 20 feet. Hen house 16 × 20, one cellar 16 × 16 feet. Total Value. $5,000.00

—Homestead Entry, Final Proof Testimony of Claimant,
Norman Smith, April 8, 1918

In 1908, Norman Smith staked out this land claim, located on the northwest side of Blacktail Butte. This 1912 photograph shows a substantial residence and cultivated fields, part of the improvements that are necessary to "prove-up" and receive a patent on the parcel. *Jackson Hole Historical Society and Museum*

When Norman Smith filed papers to secure title to his homestead, he repeated an act performed by millions of hopeful settlers in the West. Through the Homestead Act of 1862, American citizens 21 years or older, could obtain up to 160 acres of public land. Foreigners could secure land so long as they intended to apply for American citizenship. To acquire title, the law required that settlers reside on and cultivate the land for five continuous years. Then the individual making the entry had only to file final proof papers and pay a $15 fee to own 160 acres free and clear. Smith must have felt a keen sense of satisfaction as he completed the required paperwork. Bureaucratic forms could hardly daunt someone who had spent years developing a claim. Smith's patent was approved on September 27, 1919. He, his wife, and eight children now owned their land and home.[1]

Accident stranded the Smith family in Jackson Hole. In 1907, they pulled up stakes and left Cody, Wyoming, setting out with a small caravan consisting of two covered wagons, a small herd of cattle, horses, and children. Bound for Colorado, Smith was not a young man starting out in life, full of dreams, but middle-aged, about 44 years old. They entered Jackson Hole via Yellowstone Park, probably crossing the Snake River over Ben Sheffield's bridge at Moran. Somewhere between Moran and Menor's Ferry one of the horses died. Then, one daughter grew ill. The family crossed the Snake on Bill Menor's ferry and set up camp on the east side of the river near Blacktail Butte to rest and consider their predicament. Camped on a homestead entry of a man named Pembril, they decided to stay and purchased the rights to the property.

Slowly, the Smiths began proving up their new homestead, clearing ten acres for cultivation. For the first three years, Kitty Smith and the children wintered at Kelly, so the latter could attend school. The father endured the winters at their ranch. Aside from caring for the livestock, Smith's first task was to build a house. Winter was a good time to cut trees, for if snow conditions were right, a man and a good horse team could pack a trail into the forest and easily skid logs out. Smith may have cut his own house logs during the winter of 1908. By April 1909, the house was complete.[2]

In 1909, the family cleared sagebrush and cobbles on ten more acres and planted ten acres of oats, harvesting ten tons of oat hay. In 1910, with tremendous effort, another 100 acres were cleared, plowed, and seeded. Smith cultivated 120 acres of oats, barley, and wheat and harvested 983 bushels of grain for livestock feed. From 1912 through 1918, the Smith's cultivated 126 acres, raising oats, barley, wheat, and alfalfa. They harvested 1,000 to 2,000 bushels of grain and 25 to 50 tons of hay annually, depending on weather, rodent damage, or livestock damage. Kitty Smith raised a large vegetable garden that produced ten tons of potatoes per year. A small creek provided water to the farmstead. By 1918, most of the property was enclosed with 1,120 rods of buck-and-pole fence constructed of lodgepole pine. Smith gradually enlarged the log home to four rooms. In 1914, a neighbor named John Rutherford (nicknamed Johnny Highpockets) helped add a room for the large family. Outbuildings included a storehouse, a large barn, a granary, another storehouse, a hen house, and a cellar.[3]

Smith and his family did not get rich, but earned a living on one of the more productive farms in the area. After 1910, a wave of homesteaders joined them. Agriculture boomed as the First World War drove up prices. Then, a one-two punch set farming and ranching back. Agriculture prices plummeted with the end of the war in 1918. To add to their woes, a drought devastated fields in 1919; many farmers and ranchers alike reported total crop losses. American agriculture suffered from a depression a full decade before the economic collapse of 1929. By 1931, Smith was 67 years old, very likely tired of farming. He followed the lead of many oth-

ers and sold out for $4,000 to the Snake River Land Company—the Rockefeller-financed company formed for the express purpose of purchasing private lands for a public preserve.[4]

The experience of Norm and Kitty Lou Smith was similar to that of several hundred other homesteaders in Jackson Hole. After the end of the Civil War in 1865, thousands of Americans and foreigners moved onto the Great Plains and into the Rocky Mountains and intermountain West. Between 1870 and 1900, people settled 430,000,000 acres and cultivated 225,000,000 acres of virgin land. By 1890, settlement of the trans-Mississippi West had progressed so rapidly that the director of the census concluded that the "unsettled area had been so broken into by isolated bodies of settlement that there can hardly be said to be a frontier line."[5] This conclusion gave birth to the belief that an American frontier no longer existed.

Jackson Hole and other remote areas were settled and developed in the late nineteenth century. Geographic isolation, altitude, and climate discouraged earlier settlement. Perhaps more important, lands better suited to agriculture were available elsewhere. John Holland, John Carnes, and Millie Sorelle, his wife, were the first to homestead in Jackson Hole in 1884.[6] Both men had trapped in Jackson Hole previously. They entered the valley from the Green River Basin via the Bacon Creek-Gros Ventre River route. Over this trail, Holland and Carnes hauled dismantled farm equipment with pack animals. One source credits them as the first to bring a wagon into Jackson Hole using the Gros Ventre route.[7]

In 1885, others followed. Robert E. Miller crossed Teton Pass, bringing the first wagon into the valley via this route. A shrewd businessman, Miller became the valley's most prosperous settler through cattle ranching, real estate investments and, most important, banking. Even today, he is remembered as "Old Twelve Percent." J. P. Cunningham may have migrated to Jackson Hole in the same year, although other sources suggest that he came in 1888. A man named Frank Wood arrived in 1886.[8] In 1887 and 1888, the following pioneers settled in Jackson Hole: Fred White, Adolf Miller, Emile Wolff, Joe Infanger, John Pierce, William Crawford, John Cherry,

John Holland (left) and John Carnes (right) were among the first settlers in the valley; both homesteaded in 1884. *Jackson Hole Historical Society and Museum*

Stephen N. Leek, Nick Gass, John (or Jack) Hicks, Dick Turpin, Andy Madson, Mike Detweiler, and Martin "Slough Grass" Nelson, his wife, Elizabeth, and four-year-old daughter, Cora. By 1888, Jackson Hole had a population of 20 men, two women, and one child.

Jackson Hole pioneers included a number of veterans. Emigrating to the United States in 1870, Emile Wolff enlisted in the army. He was stationed at Fort Hall, Idaho, and settled in the valley after his discharge. Jack Shive joined the army in New York City. He served with the 1st Cavalry Regiment at the Crow Agency and Fort Yellowstone until his discharge in 1889. He settled on the Buffalo Fork in 1891. Felix Buchenroth was a German immigrant, who served at Yellowstone after 1900. Placed in charge of Yellowstone's South Entrance, Sergeant Buchenroth first toured Jackson Hole on cross-country skis in winter. He later met Robert E. Miller, who persuaded him to locate in Jackson Hole after completing his enlistment. (In 1935, Buchenroth succeeded Miller as president of the Jackson State Bank.)[9]

In 1888, two eastern dudes, unnamed in the source, toured the valley and left a record of settlement. At Jackson Lake, they met a hunting party guided by Beaver Dick Leigh. Traveling south, they encountered three men named Arizona George, John, and Bob "who had built a cabin two miles away," presumably in the Arizona Creek area, named for Arizona George, a shadowy figure who was reputedly a prospector. The two dudes then encountered settlements just south of the Gros Ventre River. From north to south, they described homesteads in the Flat Creek area. First came John Cherry's cabin on the flat south of the river, then Mike Detweiler's cabin. John and Millie Carnes boasted a cabin with three adjoining rooms. John Holland lived nearby in a two-room cabin. Joe Infanger and Adolf Miller shared a small cabin nearby. Other settlers on Flat Creek were William Crawford and Martin and Betty Nelson. Farther south, R. E. Miller and Emile Wolff had homesteaded on the "outlaw" place at Miller Butte.[10]

In 1889, the first Mormons migrated to Jackson Hole. Several families left their drought-stricken lands in Utah, intent on settling in the Snake River Valley in Idaho. Sylvester Wilson had sold his farm and invested in livestock but, upon his arrival in St. Anthony, Idaho, learned that there was no winter feed available for his horses and cattle. He was in a quandary when his brother Elijah N. Wilson, known as "Uncle Nick," returned from Jackson Hole with a glowing report of abundant native hay and water.[11] The family determined to pull up stakes once more and risk everything on a new start in Jackson Hole.

In 1889, Elijah "Uncle Nick" Wilson persuaded his family to move to Jackson Hole, beginning a large migration of Mormons into the area. Wilson, who claimed he was raised by Indians, led a colorful life that included a brief stint as a pony express rider. *Jackson Hole Historical Society and Museum*

The party consisted of five families: Sylvester and Mary Wilson and their children; their son Ervin Wilson along with his wife and child; their son-in-law, Selar Cheney, his wife, and children; "Uncle Nick" Wilson, his wife Matilda and daughter; and Nick Wilson's married daughter Louise Smith and two sons. They set up a base camp on the west side of the Teton Range, then the men entered Jackson Hole to cut native grasses for winter feed. By late fall, the Wilson-Cheney clan was ready to cross the pass. They shuttled six wagons over the steep Teton Pass two at a time; three teams of horses pulled each wagon over the steep divide. It took them two weeks.[12]

Much has been made of the six covered wagons as the first wagon train into Jackson Hole.[13] In reality, the significance of the wagon train is symbolic and important to local history; the great trains that snaked their way over the Oregon Trail belonged to another period. The arrival of the Wilson-Cheney clan was significant for other reasons. They were the first to bring wagons over Teton Pass since R. E. Miller manhandled a wagon over it in 1885. As a

result, the Wilson-Cheney caravan confirmed Teton Pass as a viable, if difficult, route. The Teton Pass Road became the valley's main communication and transportation artery. Second, their migration began a trend. Between 1890 and 1900, the highest percentage of Jackson Hole settlers came from Utah and Idaho, the majority of them embracing the Mormon faith. Third, and perhaps most important, the arrival of the Wilsons and Cheneys had a civilizing influence, in that five families comprising women and children broke into a bachelor community. Prior to their arrival, only two women, Millie Carnes and Elizabeth Nelson, and one child lived in the valley.[14] As more families settled in Jackson Hole and some of the bachelors married, residents demanded schools, law enforcement, churches, regular mail deliveries, proper medical care, and commercial services. Nevertheless, Jackson Hole remained a bachelor society into the 1890s, its residents described by Thomas E. Crawford as a "homeless, reckless, straight-shooting and hard drinking set."[15] Some homesteaders brought brides to the valley. Lucy Nesbitt met and married Jack Shive in Montana in 1892 before coming to Jackson Hole. Emile Wolff returned to Luxembourg in 1887 for a visit and quite likely to find a wife. He succeeded, bringing his bride, Marie, to his homestead north of Spread Creek in 1892. By 1890, the valley's population had more than doubled in two years to more than 60 people and the task of converting a rough frontier community had begun.[16]

In 1892 and 1893, William O. Owen conducted the first surveys in Jackson Hole, setting township lines and running section lines within townships in some cases. Settlement concentrated in several areas. The earliest homesteaders located in the Flat Creek area, then spread west toward Teton Pass and south into South Park. Owen surveyed the township encompassing the present town of Jackson and a portion of the National Elk Refuge. He recorded 11 homesteads and cabins on the township map. Several were identified: Giltner, Webster LaPlante, Turpin, Miller, Hicks, and Carnes, listed mistakenly as Cane. John Cherry's homestead was recorded as Berry Warm Spring. Owen mapped the Petersen cabin south and east of the present park boundary.

Petersen, who became a prominent settler in the elk refuge area, first came to the valley on a hunting excursion in 1889, then returned to homestead the next year. The Fred White homestead, or the Marysvale Post Office, was located north of the Petersen ranch, about three-quarters of a mile east of U.S. 89 and one mile south of the Gros Ventre River.[17]

Because Owen surveyed only section lines for several townships, no information exists for certain areas regarding settlement in the 1890s. Most of the townships that Owen subdivided into 640-acre sections remained pristine wilderness. Homesteaders settled the Spread Creek-Buffalo Fork area in the late 1880s and early 1890s, but subdivisions for these areas were not completed until 1901 and 1902.[18] Though settlement continued to center around the Flat Creek, South Park, Spring Gulch, and Wilson areas, isolated homesteads began to blossom north of the Gros Ventre River in the 1890s. Homesteaders tended to concentrate along the Gros Ventre and the area north of Spread Creek into the Buffalo Fork Valley and the outlet of Jackson Lake.

John Cherry was the first to settle on the flat between the Gros Ventre River and today's south boundary in 1887. His derelict cabin is situated in a hay meadow just outside the park boundary. In his final entry papers, Cherry reported that he irrigated and harvested 100 acres of hay, which was most likely native grass in those years. Josiah Deyo settled along the south bank of the Gros Ventre in 1894. Harvey Glidden filed a desert land entry in 1897 and a homestead entry south and west of the river and the present highway. Newton Nickell homesteaded 160 acres in 1898 just east of the Cherry place.

Glidden described himself as a 37-year-old rancher from Kentucky when he filed his desert entry in 1897. The next year, he filed a homestead entry on 167 acres. Glidden proved up on the desert entry, cutting the two-mile Glidden Ditch and irrigating the land. Although he had cleared 13 acres, none was cultivated. On his homestead, Glidden built a two-room log cabin and a storehouse. He cultivated only seven acres of grain on this entry. He was dead by 1906, and his wife inherited the ranch.[19]

North of the Gros Ventre River east of today's U.S. Highway 89, ten settlers took up homesteads in the 1890s. They were James I. May in 1896; James Budge, Thomas Hanshaw, Nels Hoagland, and Albert Nelson in 1897; William S. Kissenger and Frank McBride in 1898; Frank Sebastian, Fred Lovejoy, Martin Henrie, and Joe Henrie in 1899. Budge and May were the first to settle south and east of Blacktail Butte. Their homesteads anchored a series of ranches and farms that became known as Mormon Row.[20]

Encouraged by the report of Charles Allen, who had visited Jackson Hole in 1895, four families left Rockland, Idaho, in 1897 bound for the valley. The party included Charles and Maria Allen and their three sons, James and Elizabeth May with their children, Mary Ann Budge, and Roy and Maggie McBride. Maggie McBride kept a journal of their trip, leaving a rare glimpse of homesteading in Jackson Hole.[21]

The McBrides set out with the Budges and Allens after a round of farewell visits and a family dinner. Rather than endure a jolting ride in the wagon, Maggie McBride rode a saddle horse, outfitting herself in a bloomer riding suit and creating quite a sensation by wearing it while visiting friends in Idaho Falls. Outside of Idaho Falls, the Mays joined them. By the end of June, they had arrived in Teton Basin with their wagons and cattle, where they saw the Teton peaks in the distance. While camped on the Teton River, she noticed considerable traffic headed for Jackson Hole.

On July 3, the caravan reached Driggs, where Charlie Allen had his wagon fixed for a second time. They were invited to a Fourth of July dance, but declined as "most of them [the men] were drunk." They moved on, reaching the western base of Teton Pass on July 4. The party began the trek over Teton Pass on July 6; they hitched two teams each to three wagons, but had to triple team to get the wagons over the last stretch to the summit of the pass. Here, they set up camp while the men returned for the rest of the wagons.

On July 9, they reached Menor's Ferry after following the west side of the Snake River from Teton Pass.

Martin "Slough Grass" Nelson, seen here with his children, homesteaded in Jackson Hole in 1887–88. *Jackson Hole Historical Society and Museum*

Took a long time to get our outfit across. The loose horses swam the river. We tried to jew Mr. Menor down on the ferry bill, but nothing doing, even tried to pay him in flour and cured pork, but after we got across and paid him in cash then he wanted some bacon but we didn't let it go, kept it four [sic] our winter supply.[22]

The next day they set up a permanent camp on the north bank of the Gros Ventre River to inspect land available for settlement. After spending the winter with settlers on Flat Creek, the Budges, Allens, McBrides, and Mays dispersed to take up their own homesteads.

Beginning with 45 cattle, Jim May staked out a homestead east of Blacktail Butte in July 1896. By the time he submitted his final proof in 1901, the family lived in a comfortable five-room house. The ranch included stables, corrals, and fencing. After four years, May had cultivated 150 acres of hay. In 1897, he filed a desert land entry for an additional 160 acres. To prove up on the entry, May cut a three-mile ditch to divert water from the Gros Ventre River. He cultivated 40 acres of hay and grain on the tract. Jim and Mary Ann Budge homesteaded a small cattle ranch. Over five years, they cleared and cultivated 70 acres of land, raising hay and grain for

cattle. Like May, Jim Budge filed for a desert land entry in 1901, doubling the size of his ranch.[23]

Albert Nelson was another early pioneer who settled in the Kelly area in 1897. His experience typified that of a large number of foreign citizens who settled in Jackson Hole. Born in Sweden in 1861, Nelson emigrated to the United States in 1883. He spent his first year working in the Nebraska hayfields, then moved on to Rock Springs, Wyoming, to work in the coal mines and ranches in the area. Later, he drifted to South Pass City and Atlantic City, Wyoming, where he worked in the gold mines. While there, Nelson met Uncle Billy Bierer, a trapper and prospector. The two men traveled to Montana to prospect, but having no success returned to South Pass City. In 1895, Nelson and Bierer decided to prospect in Jackson Hole. Both determined to settle in the valley, in spite of arriving amidst the "Indian Scare of 1895." Nelson homesteaded at Kelly in 1897, building up a small ranch, while Bierer located on the Gros Ventre at Slide Lake. While at South Pass City, Nelson learned taxidermy, which together with the growing hunting and guiding industry in Jackson Hole, allowed him to pursue it as an occupation.[24]

The land north of the homesteads strung along the Gros Ventre River remained unoccupied. Two cabins appear on the Antelope Flats area of T. M. Bannon's U.S. Geological Survey map of the Jackson Hole—Teton Range, which was surveyed in 1899. One cabin appears on a tract occupied by the Teton Science School today. This cabin may have belonged to Grant Shinkle, who squatted on the homestead around 1900 and later relinquished his claim. The other cabin was located at Antelope Spring at the western base of Shadow Mountain. T. E. Crawford provides a clue to this cabin in his recollections. When Crawford came to Jackson Hole, he built a cabin at Antelope Spring after abandoning a log dugout on Crystal Creek, a tributary of the Gros Ventre River. This occurred between 1888 and 1895.[25]

In the late 1890s, homesteaders worked their way up the west side of the Snake River from Wilson. Robert Pemble took up a 160-acre homestead along the Snake River, about one-quarter mile east of today's Moose-Wilson Road. For unknown reasons, Pemble delayed taking up residence until October 1900. When he submitted final proof in 1905, the homestead had a log house, corrals, stables, sheds, and fencing. Pemble testified only that he was cultivating land. The Forest Service named one of their earliest trails in this area for Pemble. To the west of Pemble's homestead, John F. Miller settled on 160 acres that straddles today's Moose-Wilson Road at the south boundary of the park. In his final proof papers, Miller testified that 40 acres were under cultivation. In 1903, Emma Edwards submitted final proof to a 373-acre desert land entry as the assignee of Bill Scott. The latter had filed the entry in 1899, then relinquished the claim to Edwards. Located west of the Miller place, she irrigated 50 acres with water from Granite Creek and planted timothy. In 1902, four acres of oats were planted, but produced a disappointing half ton of grain hay per acre. Since the law required only that desert lands be cultivated and irrigated, Edwards did not record any other improvements such as a cabin or fences.[26]

Menor's Ferry was the only homestead west of the Snake River in central Jackson Hole during the 1890s. Acting on the advice of Jack Shive and John Cherry, William D. Menor decided to operate a ferry at present-day Moose, Wyoming. He took up residence on the west bank of the Snake in July 1894. There he constructed a cabin, which he en-

John Pierce Cunningham came to Jackson Hole from New York in 1885. *National Park Service*

larged to five rooms by 1904. Other buildings included a barn, a shed, a storeroom, a shop, an icehouse, and corrals. He fenced the entire 148-acre tract, constructed an irrigation system, cutting a ditch from Cottonwood Creek to his homestead. At one time he drew water from the Snake River with a waterwheel. He cultivated 12 acres in 1895, but cut back to five acres in succeeding years. Menor cultivated a truck garden, raising a variety of vegetables along with currants and raspberries. But most important, his ferry became one of three significant crossings on the Snake River.[27]

In the northern end of Jackson Hole, settlers concentrated at the outlet of Jackson Lake, in the Buffalo Fork Valley and Spread Creek areas. A pioneer settler in this area was J. Pierce Cunningham, who came to Jackson Hole from New York as early as 1885. He was about 20 years old. He reputedly spent his first years trapping. Either in 1888 or 1890, he took up a homestead south of Spread Creek, selecting land with a meadow of native grass. With his bride, Margaret, he established a small cattle ranch, cultivating 100 acres of hay each year for winter feed. In 1897, he filed a desert land entry, irrigating 140 acres for grazing and hay. The Cunninghams produced 75 tons of hay for winter feed. At this time, the Cunninghams owned eight horses and 100 cattle. Cunningham was destined to become one of the most prominent and respected of the valley's early citizens. His homestead cabin marks the site of his ranch today, and is one of the best and few remaining early homestead cabins in the valley.[28] In 1892, his brother, W. Frederick Cunningham, and family settled nearby.

Another settler in this area was Emile Wolff, who abandoned an earlier homestead on Flat Creek before returning to Europe to find a bride. He returned with a young wife and took up a new homestead north of Spread Creek in 1895. In 1897, James and Lydia Uhl filed on a homestead at the base of a hill that bears their name today. All established small cattle ranches and added acreage through the Desert Land Act of 1877. Over a period of seven years, the Uhls increased their acreage under cultivation from 20 acres to 120 acres.[29]

The Buffalo Fork Valley attracted homesteaders before 1900. In 1891, Jack Shive took up a homestead at the Hatchet Ranch, east of the park boundary. Noble Gregory homesteaded on the Buffalo Fork in 1898. Gregory came to Jackson Hole in 1897, accompanied by his father, Samuel Gregory. Traveling by wagon over South Pass to Idaho, they lost their map at Lander's Cut-off. The Gregorys made a wrong turn and journeyed north along the west front of the Wind River Range. They eventually found themselves at the Bacon Creek Divide, which led them to the Gros Ventre River and Jackson Hole. Once in the valley, both men decided to stay, taking up homesteads in the Buffalo Fork in 1898. Over a six-year period, Noble Gregory cleared and cultivated 90 acres, growing hay and grazing cattle.[30]

Between the outlet of Jackson Lake and the junction of the Snake River and Pacific Creek, several homesteads sprang up in the 1890s. James M. Conrad filed a claim on 157 acres east of Oxbow Bend. With his son, Ernest, the elder Conrad proved up the homestead, constructing a modest 16×18-foot cabin and a barn. They raised 20 acres of hay. Whether by intent or accident, Conrad had settled on a section of the Snake River, which was an ideal site for a ferry. In 1897, the Conrads began operating a ferry for the Whetstone Mining Company, which developed a placer mining operation up Pacific Creek. Conrad abandoned the homestead by the end of 1900, relinquishing his rights to a buyer.[31]

Other settlers were the Allens, Lovells, and Ed "Cap" and Clara Smith. Each attempted to raise cattle, relying on the meadows of native grass for winter feed. The Allens and Smiths soon came to depend on travelers using the military road to Yellowstone or the Marysville Road to Idaho. The Allens built the Elkhorn Hotel, which included a roadhouse, store, and post office. "Cap" Smith constructed a large two-story log hotel, which apparently housed a saloon.[32]

The last homestead in this area, and the one located farthest north in Jackson Hole, belonged to John Dudley Sargent. One of the more mysterious characters to settle in the valley, Sargent was a remittance man—distinctive western figures paid to go west because they were real or perceived embarrassments to wealthy families. Anything from a physical disability to alcohol abuse could result in exile in the West. Sargent, the scion of a wealthy Maine family, was paid a remittance to stay away from his family. The reason for his banishment is unknown, but his neighbors knew him to be mentally unstable. Sargent, Ray Hamilton, and John Dodge were the most well known remittance men in Jackson Hole. Their impact in frontier communities has been exaggerated because of their appeal as eccentrics and fodder for local gossip. In Sargent's case, the attention may be justified as he may well have murdered his first wife and did commit suicide some years later.

Sargent drifted into Jackson Hole with his wife and five children and took up a homestead along the eastern shore of Jackson Lake. In his final proof papers, Sargent classified his property as best suited for grazing and farming. Accordingly, he started a small cattle ranch, turning his six milk cows loose on the public domain and raising a family garden. Sargent constructed a log lodge (22×70 feet), consisting of ten rooms called Merymere. Sargent soon began boarding and housing travelers as Merymere became known as a roadhouse.[33]

Other squatters lived along Jackson Lake, but none secured title to land. Several cabins appear marked on Bannon's map. Lakeview Ranch was located at the mouth of Arizona Creek on the east shore of Jackson Lake. George H. "Herb" Whiteman, and Cora and Edgar Heigho began developing the property in 1896. According to local tradition, they intended to start a dude ranch, but a roadhouse

John Dudley Sargent, the scion of a wealthy Maine family, had a homestead on the eastern shore of Jackson Lake, where he constructed a ten-room lodge called Merymere. *Jackson Hole Historical Society and Museum*

is a better description. Cora Heigho was listed as the postmaster of the short-lived Antler Post Office from March 3, 1899, to December 15, 1899. Antler may have been located at the Lakeview Ranch, although a book on Wyoming post offices locates it at the outlet of Jackson Lake. By 1900, Whiteman lived in the Moran area, Cora Heigho had become Mrs. Frank Sebastian, and Edgar Heigho had left the valley. Sim Edwards developed a ranch at the mouth of Lizard Creek in the 1890s. It became a prominent stop on the Ashton-Moran freight road between 1900 and 1920. However, like the Heighos and Whiteman, Edwards never secured title to the entry.[34]

Over time, settlers established small cattle ranches, combining farming and ranching practices. Ranchers grazed small herds of cattle on public lands and cultivated native grasses for winter feed. The availability of winter feed limited the size of herds. Although cattle may have grazed in the valley as early as 1883, Sylvester Wilson brought the first sizable herd of 80 cattle in 1889. Cattle herds generally ranged around 100 head or less; Pierce Cunningham owned more than 100 head in the late 1890s, while Emile Wolff owned 75 head. At first, the ranchers irrigated and raised native grass, but introduced domestic grasses such as timothy, alfalfa, and brome grass in the 1890s.[35]

One hundred sixty acres proved too small for a viable cattle ranch, so most settlers filed an additional 160 acres through desert land entries. Even a 320-acre ranch permitted only a small family operation. Indeed, mountain valley ranching in Jackson Hole would have been impossible without the public domain, which provided thousands of acres for grazing. In general, homesteaders preempted lands with convenient access to water and soils that supported grassy meadows. The sagebrush flats remained unoccupied. Thus, settlement concentrated in the Flat Creek area, along the Gros Ventre, the Snake and the Buffalo Fork-Spread Creek area.

In the early years, most homesteaders lived at a subsistence level. Cash often came from guiding dudes on hunts or from trapping on a small scale. As in the days of trappers, wildlife became an important commodity. Pioneers in Jackson Hole depended on supply centers in Idaho linked to railroads. They imported virtually all necessities and any luxuries. For example, in 1888 Robert Miller and Emile Wolff purchased $646 worth of supplies from the Durrans Winter Mercantile Company in Rexburg, Idaho, illustrating the importance of reliable transportation routes as a prerequisite to the successful settlement of Jackson Hole.[36]

To alleviate isolation, Jackson Hole settlers began agitating for a post office by the late 1880s. Mail delivery was sporadic, as individuals traveling to Rexburg on business would return with the mail. The people first sent a petition to the Postal Service requesting a mail route via Teton Pass from Rexburg. However, the Postal Service required the valley residents to carry the mail themselves for one year to prove that regular mail runs could be made over the pass. They succeeded, and Marysvale became the valley's first post office in 1892. It closed in 1894, replaced by the Jackson Post Office, located at the Bill and Maggie Simpson ranch. By 1900, there were five post offices serving Jackson Hole: Elk, Grovont, South Park, Wilson, and Jackson.[37]

In 1899, Charles "Pap" Deloney opened the first general mercantile store in the valley. Deloney shipped groceries, hardware, dry goods, building materials, and farm machinery into the valley. Shipping costs increased prices, but the convenience of a store appealed to many. The store became a social and financial center in the valley. Because the valley had no bank, Deloney allowed ranchers to secure their checks in his safe. Deloney's store, the post office, and a recreation hall called the Clubhouse (1897) formed the nucleus of the town of Jackson.[38]

Other signs of civilization appeared in the 1890s. As more families settled in the valley, educating their children became a concern. In South Park, Ervin Wilson donated a room in his cabin for use as a schoolroom in 1894. Two years later, South Park built the first schoolhouse, which became known as Cheney. In 1899, a second schoolhouse was built in the Flat Creek area.[39]

Civilization requires a legal code and effective enforcement to settle disputes between people or groups. Jackson Hole was no exception. The killings in 1886 at Deadman's Bar pointed out this need. The nearest court and sheriff's office was located in Evanston, Wyoming, leaving settlers with little protection. Consequently, they took turns serving as justices of the peace and constables to deal with minor offenses. For example, John Holland served as the first justice of the peace and tried the valley's first case in 1892. Dick Turpin was charged with felonious assault and acquitted. Citizen's committees, a polite term for vigilantes, formed to handle emergencies or overt threats to law and order. Citizens'

committees dealt with horse rustlers at the Cunningham ranch in 1893, the Indian Scare of 1895, and elk poachers after 1900.[40]

On the eve of the new century, more than 600 people called Jackson Hole home. Civilization made inroads in the valley, but it remained in essence a frontier community.

Notes

1. National Archives, Record Group 49, "Records of the Bureau of Land Management," Homestead Patents, Patent 708783, Norman Smith, 1918. The Norm Smith family's experience was fairly representative of the homesteaders' frontier; the Smith homestead was located near the northwest corner of Blacktail Butte.

2. *Jackson Hole Guide,* October 12, 1972; and Homestead Patent 708783, N. Smith, 1918.

3. *Jackson's Hole Courier,* May 7, 1914; and Patent 708783, N. Smith, 1918.

4. Rockefeller Archive Center, Harold P. Fabian Papers, IV3A7, Box 23, File 252, Norman Smith Tract.

5. Billington, *Westward Expansion,* p. 613.

6. A few sources date the arrival of Holland and Carnes as early as 1883.

7. Hayden, *From Trapper to Tourist in Jackson Hole,* pp. 37–38; *Jackson's Hole Courier,* January 28, 1909, reprinted in *Jackson's Hole Courier,* January 29, 1948; Agnes Spring Wright, "Early Settlement in Jackson Hole," File W994jk, n.d.; University of Wyoming Archives, American Heritage Center; and Jackson's Hole Courier, July 14, 1932.

8. *Jackson's Hole Courier,* April 19, 1934; Hayden, *Trapper to Tourist,* p. 38; "An Investigation of Proposed Enlargement of the Yellowstone and Grand Teton National Parks: Hearing on S. Res. 226," 73rd Congress, 1934, pp. 266–268; and Homestead Patent HC 1181, Evanston, J. Pierce Cunningham, 1904.

9. *Jackson's Hole Courier,* November 8, 1928, and January 5, 1950; and *Jackson Hole Guide,* December 9, 1965.

10. Nellie Van Derveer, "An Old Time Christmas in Jackson Hole," WPA Subject File 1321, State of Wyoming, Archives, Museums, and Historical Department. I am not comfortable with the accuracy of this report, but the descriptions of homesteads and locations seem generally consistent with other available sources. The Cherry cabin is still standing on the north end of East Gros Ventre Butte, adjacent to the park.

11. Uncle Nick Wilson recorded his life on the frontier in E.N. Wilson, with Howard R. Driggs, *The White Indian Boy: The Story of Uncle Nick Among the Shoshones*, rev. ed. (Yonkers-on-Hudson, NY: World Book Co., 1919).

12. Hayden, *Trapper to Tourist*, 38; Saylor, *Jackson Hole*, p. 118; and *Jackson's Hole Courier*, April 12, 1945.

13. Saylor, *Jackson Hole*, p. 118.

14. Margaret Cunningham may have arrived in the valley around 1890, but there is no convincing evidence to place her here. Many local sources list Mrs. Martin (Elizabeth) Nelson as the first woman to reside in Jackson Hole. Others list her as the first "white" woman, a backhanded acknowledgement to Millie Sorelle Carnes, the Shoshone wife of John Carnes, who was the valley's first female resident.

15. Jeff C. Dyke, *The West of the Texas Kid, 1881–1910: The Recollections of Thomas E. Crawford* (Norman: University of Oklahoma Press, 1962).

16. *Jackson's Hole Courier*, December 8, 1932, January 5, 1950, and December 30, 1954;and Census of the United States, 1900, Jackson Precinct.

17. William O. Owen, T41N, R116W, 6th P.M., October 6-16, 1892, and T42N, R116W, 6th P.M., June 1–5, 1893, Jackson Hole Platbook, Harold and Josephine Fabian Collection, Grand Teton National Park.

18. Ibid.

19. Homestead Patents: HC 1245, Evanston, M. Kiskadden-H. Glidden, 1906; HC 315, Lander, J. Cherry, 1901; DLE 187, Lander, H. Glidden, 1901; and HC 1113, Lander, N. Nickell, 1905.

20. Homestead Patents: HC 334, Lander, J. May, 1901; HC 1006, Evanston, J. Budge, 1904; HC 532, Lander, J. Henrie, 1904; HC 1049, Evanston, A. Nelson, 1904; HC 469, Lander, N. Hoagland, 1903; HC 528, Lander, T. Hanshaw, 1904; HC 526, Lander, W. Kissenger, 1904; HC 529, Lander, F. Lovejoy, 1904; HC 1055, Evanston, F Sebastian, 1905; and HC 1036, Evanston, F. McBride, 1905.

21. *Jackson's Hole Courier*, July 13, 1950; *Jackson Hole Guide*, May 2, 1974 and November 27, 1969; and Maggie McBride, "My Diary," 1896, Jackson Hole Historical Society and Museum Files; also printed in *Jackson's Hole Courier*, July 27, 1950.

22. McBride, "My Diary."

23. Homestead Patents: HC 334, Lander, J. May, 1901; HC 1006, Evanston, J. Budge, 1904; DLE 152, Lander, J. May, 1901; and DLE 752, Evanston, J. Budge, 1904. Desert land entries required a fee of $1.25 per acre, in addition to irrigation of the land.

24. *Jackson Hole Guide*, March 21, 1957; Homestead Patents, Evanston, A. Nelson, 1904; and Census of the United States, 1900, Jackson Precinct.

25. Dyke, *Recollections*, p. 51; and U.S. Geological Survey, "Grand Teton Quadrangle," 1901.

26. Homestead Patents: HC 1175, Evanston, J. Miller, 1905; HC 1170, Evanston, R. Pemble, 1905; and DLE 232, Lander, E. Edwards, 1903.

27. Homestead Patent HC 503, Lander, W. D. Menor, 1904. According to local tradition, Menor came to Jackson Hole in 1892 or 1893. Menor's own testimony in his final proof papers is the most reliable source. See also Frances Judge, "Mountain River Men," *Campfire Tales of Jackson Hole*, pp. 52–58.

28. Homestead Patents HC 1181, Evanston, J. P. Cunningham, 1904, and 36433, J. P. Cunningham, 1908; and "Hearings on S. Res. 226," 1933, p. 267.

29. Homestead Patents: NC 1168, Evanston, W. F Cunningham, 1904; HC 1020, Evanston, E. Wolff, 1904; 30855, J. Uhl, 1904; and 252376, E. Wolff, 1911.

30. Homestead Patent NC 1025, Evanston, N. Gregory, 1904.

31. Homestead Patent NC 373, Lander, J. Conrad, 1902.

32. Homestead Patents: NC 473, Lander, F. Lovell, 1903; and NC 173, Lander, C. J. Allen, 1901; and Lenore Diem, *The Research Station's Place in History* (Laramie, WY: University of Wyoming Research Center, 1978); pp. 4–5.

33. Homestead Patent NC 1024, Evanston, Sargent, 1905; Robert B. Betts, *Along the Ramparts of the Tetons: The Saga of Jackson Hole, Wyoming* (Boulder: Colorado Associated University Press, 1978), pp. 150–154; and Struthers Burt, *The Diary of a Dude Wranger* (New York: Charles Scriber's Sons, 1924), pp. 266–277.

34. USGS, "Grand Teton Quadrangle," 1901; Census of the United States, 1900, Jackson Precinct; and Elliot H. Paul, *Desperate Scenery* (New York: Random House, 1954), pp. 171–174.

35. Hayden, *Trapper to Tourist*, p. 54.

36. *Jackson Hole News*, April 12, 1973.

37. "Alphabetical List of Jackson Hole Post Offices," K. C. Allan Collection, 736, University of Wyoming Archives, 3 pages; and Mae Tuttle to Mrs. Cora Barber, September 5, 1951, Jackson Hole Historical Society and Museum Files, also reprinted in *Jackson Hole Guide*, December 5, 1974.

38. *Jackson Hole Guide*, December 2, 1965.

39. Roland W. Brown Jr., ed., *A Souvenir History of Jackson Hole* (Salt Lake City, 1924), pp. 33–35; and Hayden, *Trapper to Tourist*, pp. 38–39.

40. *Jackson's Hole Courier*, February 19, 1931.

The Census of 1900:
Profile of a Frontier Community

. . . When the McBride wagon train of 1896 camped on the Gros Ventre River, two young bachelors, Jim Lanigan and Jim Simpson, called on them. Not to be fooled, Maggie McBride recorded in her diary ". . . of course they were interested in the girls . . ." referring to the single Allen daughters. . . .

Cutting hay for the long winter. Although most Jackson Hole settlers considered themselves ranchers, they were listed as farmers in the 1900 census. *Grand Teton National Park*

On June 1, 1900, Daniel C. Nowlin initiated the census of the Jackson Hole Election Precinct. The district encompassed Jackson Hole from Hoback Junction to the north end of the valley.[1] Nowlin started with himself and his family, listing names, their relationships to the head of the house, race, sex, date of birth, marital status, number of years married, and the number of children born and living to his wife, Laura. Nowlin, age 42, was born in 1857 in Texas. Laura Nowlin, age 30, was born in 1869 in Missouri. They had been married 12 years. Luckier than many parents, all five of their children were living, three sons and two daughters ranging from nine months to ten years. Nowlin recorded place of birth of each, plus the birthplace of their parents. Since the Nowlins were born in the United States, he left the citizenship column blank. Nowlin entered "farmer" as his occupation, but entered no occupation for his wife. Three of the children attended school for four months per year. He answered "yes" to each question; can read, can write, can speak English.

Nowlin completed the census on June 27. Although it reduces people to statistics, the census sheets reveal much about the people and character of Jackson Hole in 1900. Officially, 638 people resided in the valley in June 1900. Even though the population had increased tenfold over 1890 estimates, this mountain valley remained a sparsely populated backwater. Mae Tuttle recalled "old man Atherton's" remark that people were getting "too darn numerous," when a dozen people turned out for a Fourth of July picnic at Jenny Lake in the 1890s. Atherton soon abandoned his cabin on Flat Creek in favor of a more remote location on the Gros Ventre River.[2]

101

Like most frontier communities, Jackson Hole remained a male-dominated society in 1900. A total of 239 males, age 18 and over, lived in the valley, compared to 118 women, age 18 and over. Of 191 separate households, 91 (less than 50 percent) comprised married couples. Bachelors, widowers, or married men living apart from spouses totaled 68 households. Some were confirmed bachelors, such as Bill Menor, Johnny Counts, Dick Turpin, and Bill Blackburn. Others were widowers in their 50s and 60s, and at least one had left his wife. However, bachelors in their 20s and 30s comprised most of them. In addition, about 80 bachelors lived as boarders or with parents.

It is no coincidence that the plot in Owen Wister's *The Virginian* developed the romance between a cowpuncher and a schoolteacher.[3] Losing teachers to marriage was common in Jackson Hole. People seemed to expect that young female teachers would migrate to the valley, teach for a year or two at most, then give up their careers to marry and have children. Indeed, new teachers provided fodder for entertaining gossip regarding their longevity as teachers, potential suitors, and choice of grooms. Young women drew plenty of attention. When the McBride wagon train of 1896 camped on the Gros Ventre River, two young bachelors, Jim Lanigan and Jim Simpson, called on them. Not to be fooled, Maggie McBride recorded in her diary ". . . of course they were interested in the girls . . ." referring to the single Allen daughters.[4]

The remaining 281 people were children, age 17 and under. The first families to bring children into the valley were the Nelsons in 1888, followed by the Cheneys and Wilsons in 1889. By 1900, children lived in 88 of the 191 households. Although Jackson Hole was predominantly a male society, families with children made up the largest segment of the 191 households, chipping away the rough edges of this frontier valley.

Eleven women listed themselves as heads of households. Mary Anderson supported herself and three children by serving as the postmaster of the Jackson Post Office and running a hotel and boarding house. Unlike others, she was separated from her husband, John Anderson, who continued to live in the valley. Divorces, if less common in 1900, did occur. In 1897, Jack Shive married Lucy Wadsworth Nesbitt, then brought her and a stepdaughter to his ranch on the Buffalo Fork. This was her third marriage. She had been married to a much older man as a teenager and, later, a professional photographer too fond of the bottle. She divorced both men. Her marriage to Jack Shive proved happier.[5]

Other women were widows. Margaret Adams, widowed by age 29, shouldered the responsibility of managing a homestead. Another, Nancy Tanner, and her six children boarded at the Adams homestead. Mrs. Tanner worked as a housekeeper, while two older sons worked as day laborers, undoubtedly at the Adams's homestead part of the time. Mary Wilson, the widow of pioneer Sylvester Wilson, continued to work the family ranch with the help of her son and teenage daughter. In addition, her son, Ervin Wilson, had died, leaving her daughter-in-law responsible for five young children. Ervin Wilson's brother-in-law, Nate Davis, worked at the homestead, listing his occupation as farm laborer. Fifty-five-year-old widow Mary Mangum rented a home with her 17-year-old son, listing her occupation as a day laborer. Seven other women headed households, although they listed their status as married. Six lived on their own homesteads. A Mrs. Holden described herself as a sawmill operator for eight months of the year, while the others listed farming as their occupations. Mrs. Ann Pratt cared for seven children, including twin girls, aged two months, and performed routine male chores in addition to her household work.

The census sheets provide another interesting statistic; each married woman listed the number of children born and the number living as of June 1900. Of 436 children born, 354 survived, representing an 18 percent mortality rate. Although a few died as adults, it is safe to assume that the overwhelming majority died in childhood or infancy. This statistic fits the general pattern of mortality in these years. Parents dreaded the thought of losing a child, yet came to expect it. Families tended to be larger, and the families in Jackson Hole were no exception. Some were lucky, such as the Van Winkles, with eight sons and daughters, all living, but most families had lost at least one child.

Too often, adults died in their prime, causing more family instability than is recognized today. Relatives or stepparents often raised children. Childbirth became all too often a life-threatening ordeal for mother and baby Nels Hoagland was a 41-year-old widower with a one-year-old son. James Hall was a 31-year-old widower with three small children, the youngest a one-year-old boy. It is likely that their wives died in childbirth. Americans in 1900 could not take life for granted. The lack of knowledge concerning preventive medicine and bacteriology caused a much higher mortality rate than today.

Jackson Hole Residents, Place of Birth— The 1900 Census

The Mountain States
Utah: 174
Wyoming: 84
Idaho: 57
Colorado: 20
Montana: 12

The Midwestern Heartland
Iowa: 38
Illinois: 26
Ohio: 13
Indiana: 12
Wisconsin: 9
Minnesota: 5
Michigan: 4

The Southwest
Arizona: 1

The Old Border States
Missouri: 19
Kentucky: 5

The Pacific Coast
California: 9
Oregon: 1
Washington: 1

The South
Virginia: 5
North Carolina: 2
South Carolina 1
Tennessee: 1

The Plains
Nebraska: 20
Kansas: 7
Dakotas: 1
Indian Territory: 1

Texas-Arkansas
Texas: 3
Arkansas: 1

The Mid-Atlantic
Pennsylvania: 19
New York: 17

New England
Massachusetts: 3
Rhode Island: 1
Vermont: 1

Regarding nativity, census-taker Nowlin recorded the birthplace of each person, along with the birthplace of their parents. American citizens listed their native state, while foreign immigrants recorded their nationality. The results reinforce the notion that Americans were a restless people quick to pull up stakes and move on to new country.[6]

Mormons dominated settlement from 1890 to 1900. More than 25 percent of the population, or 174 settlers, claimed Utah as their birthplace. Fifty-seven of their children were listed as being born in Idaho, leaving a record of the migration of Mormon pioneers to Idaho and Wyoming.[7]

It was often true of the frontier experience that settlers moved to vacant lands from adjacent areas since distance was not so great an obstacle. A homesteader from Colorado did not have to contend with as much distance as a settler from Pennsylvania. Moreover, pioneers living in adjacent areas were more likely to be familiar with the unoccupied area. Thus, no less than 283 of the valley's residents were born in Utah, Idaho, Colorado, Montana, or Nebraska. Those born in Wyoming comprised 13 percent, or 84 settlers. Virtually all were children under the age of 18, representing the first and second generation of Wyoming "natives." Only four people over the age of 18 listed Wyoming as their place of birth with James Lanigan the oldest at 36.

A significant number (107) hailed from the Midwestern heartland of the United States. No less than 64 settlers came from the states of Iowa and Illinois. Missouri (19), the gateway to the West, and Pennsylvania (19) and New York (17) were well represented in the valley. Few settlers came from the Pacific Coast, the Southwest, the South, and New England.

Foreign Born Settlers
Sweden: 15
England: 10
Canada (English): 8
Germany: 7
Austria: 4
Denmark: 4
Scotland: 4
Switzerland: 3
Holland: 2
Norway: 2
Wales: 2
France: 1
Ireland: 1

Foreign immigrants comprised a large segment of homesteaders in the American West. Europeans were drawn to the United States by "the most effective advertising campaign ever to influence world migrations."[8] Steamship companies and state immigration bureaus launched ambitious advertising and recruiting efforts to lure European immigrants. They portrayed the West in glowing terms. Kind critics described these representations as overstatements, while harsher ones called them lies. The lure of free land and burgeoning markets for agricultural products provided compelling reasons for many European farmers to risk leaving their land-poor countries.[9] Sixty-three foreigners comprised nearly ten percent of the population of Jackson Hole. Unlike some areas of the West, no foreign colonies were established in Jackson Hole. Although citizens from the United Kingdom and Canada made up the largest segment of the foreign population, 15 Swedes and seven Germans marked the beginning of a wave of immigrants from Scandinavia and central Europe.

The adult population mirrored the history of frontier expansion. Their parents were often born on the frontiers of a previous generation, in particular the Old Northwest and the Mississippi Valley, especially Missouri. The Mormon migrations from Illinois and Missouri, trying to escape prejudice and violence, can be traced on 15 census sheets compiled by D. C. Nowlin. The influx of immigrants, primarily from Scotland, Ireland, and England, is also reflected in the enumeration sheets. Thirty-four parents of Utah homesteaders were English immigrants, probably the result of Latter Day Saint's missionary work in Great Britain.

However, the records of nativity are limited to the extent that the whereabouts of individuals are unknown between their place of birth and their arrival in Jackson Hole. For example, Bill Menor was born in Ohio in 1857 and took up his homestead in 1894, yet it is known that he worked as a cowpuncher on the Kansas cattle trails and served one of the railroads as a buffalo hunter. By the time he arrived in Jackson Hole, Menor was well-traveled. "Uncle Jack" Davis worked the Montana goldfields, before drifting to Jackson Hole in the 1880s. According to local tradition, he was running from legal trouble.[10]

One of the most common questions asked about homesteaders is, "What did they do here?" The 1900 enumeration sheets provide some insight. Of 191 households, Nowlin counted 121 farms owned by their occupants. For some reason he failed to count 16 additional farms, eight of which were rented. Thus, there were 145 separate farms in Jackson Hole in 1900. Assuming a minimum of 160 acres for each homestead, settlers had preempted at least 23,200 acres. Nowlin listed all as free of any mortgage, which is difficult to believe given that most settlers were cash-poor. Mortgaging land was the best way to raise funds.[11]

Occupations—Census of 1900
Farmers: 148
Farm laborers: 48
Day laborers: 41
School teachers: 6
Housekeepers: 6
Carpenters: 4

Blacksmiths: 4
House servants: 2
Lawyers: 2
Miners gold: 2
Taxidermists: 2
Butcher: 1
Capitalist: 1
Commercial traveler: 1
Engineer, locomotive: 1
Engineer, stationary: 1
Harness maker: 1
Horse trainer: 1
House painter: 1
Merchant retailer: 1
Music teacher: 1
Operator sawmill: 1
Physician: 1
Postmaster: 1
Stonemason: 1

❀ Unemployment ❀

Number	Months	Unemployed
Day Labor	29	124 months
Farm labor	18	63 months
Carpenters	3	19 months
Blacksmiths	3	17 months
Taxidermist	2	12 months
Schoolteacher	5	18 months
Stonemason	1	10 months
Horse trainer	1	5 months
Engineer, locomotive	1	12 months
Salesman, grocery	1	6 months
Operator, sawmill	1	4 months
Butcher	1	12 months
Harness maker	1	4 months
Commercial traveler	1	12 months

Most adults listed their occupations. Farmers dominated the list with 148. This is curious terminology, for though they needed farming skills to cultivate hay, most considered themselves ranchers. There seems to be no explanation, except that they might not have qualified as stockgrowers under the census criteria. Moreover, the list of occupations fails to illuminate the variety of work these people undertook to survive. Many guided well-heeled dudes on hunting excursions, trapped, hauled freight, and a few panned for flour gold in the valley's icy rivers, all to raise just enough cash to lay in a winter's supplies and, with luck, provide a few luxuries for their families.[12]

There were 48 farm laborers and 41 day laborers. The distinction between the two occupations is unclear and probably not that significant. Day laborers may have engaged in a wider variety of tasks. Undoubtedly many considered themselves cowboys, although this work included a wide range of tasks at small mountain valley ranches. All but one were men. Most were youngsters from 14 through their 20s, or middle-aged bachelors in their 40s and 50s. Most were family members or boarders where they were employed. While it was generally true that chronic labor shortages plagued the West, this might

not have been a problem in Jackson Hole. Ranchers counted the passage of the years by the annual cycle of tasks such as calving, plowing and sowing hayfields, spring roundups, branding, fence mending, irrigating, haying season, and the fall roundup. Farm and day laborers had plenty of work from spring to fall, but winters could be cold, lean months. Twenty-nine day laborers spent 124 months unemployed or a little over four idle months per individual. Eighteen farm laborers reported being unemployed for 63 months during the previous year, or three and one half months each.

Other occupations indicate the variety and extent of economic activities in the valley. Commerce was underdeveloped with a very limited market. Settlers relied on commercial centers in Idaho for their supplies. Charles Deloney, a merchant retailer, had just opened a general mercantile store in 1899. A commercial traveler (traveling salesman) and a grocery salesman also lived in the valley at this time. The commercial traveler had been unemployed for the last year, and the grocery salesman had been unemployed for six months.

There was a need for food and lodging in these years. In addition to her duties as a postmaster, Mary Anderson ran what may have been the first boarding

The first general mercantile store in Jackson opened in 1899. Deloney's General Merchandise carried groceries, hardware, dry goods, farm machinery, and other commodities. The building now houses the Jackson Hole Historical Society Museum. *Jackson Hole Historical Society and Museum*

house or hotel in Jackson Hole. Cap Smith, the Charles J. Allens, and Herb Whiteman operated roadhouses or hotels, although they did not list them as occupations. John Sargent, the owner of Merymere, was not listed in the census.

Other trades served the agricultural community. There were four blacksmiths. A horse trainer and a harness maker worked in the north end of the valley. Several settlers worked in construction trades. There were four carpenters, a sawmill operator, a housepainter, and stonemason, and two tinsmiths.

The census also confirms the presence of professional occupations. There were two lawyers in the valley, William Simpson and Leslie Allen. One wonders how lucrative their practice could have been. There has always been debate over the first doctor in Jackson Hole. Dr. Luther F. Palmer resided in Jackson Hole in 1900 and did practice in the valley.[13]

The only hint of the importance of the hunting guide industry was the presence of two part-time taxidermists, Albert Nelson and George McKean. Two men, John Condit and Andrew Davis, were perpetual optimists, their occupations being gold miners. Uncle Jack Davis and Johnny Counts were also

prospectors, but listed their occupations as day laborers. Nelson and his old partner, Billy Bierer, had given up prospecting for ranching, and in Nelson's case, taxidermy. A few occupations were unusual. Hattie Green, R. E. Miller's sister-in-law, listed "capitalist" as her occupation. Whether she loaned money to homesteaders in Jackson Hole is unknown. Hugh "Cap" McDermott was clearly in the wrong place if he intended to pursue his career as a locomotive engineer.[14]

Educating children was always a major concern in frontier communities. In 1900, the people of Jackson Hole had to provide for 154 children between the ages of six and 17. There were six teachers in the valley at the time. No fewer than 124 children attended school for a total of 356 months, or nearly three months per child. Although school terms appear to have run from four to six months, a number of school-age children did not attend school at all. Living in remote locations made it difficult for some, while parental indifference may explain the absence or erratic attendance of other children. In these years, the eighth grade was the highest level taught in the valley.

According to the census sheets, school ended for virtually all boys beyond the age of 15. In 1900, 20 boys between the ages of 12 and 17 had entered the labor force, most as farm laborers. School was out for them. Only three teenage boys attended school beyond the age of 14, for a total of 20 months. Perhaps they showed an unusual aptitude, or their parents placed a high value on education. Males were valuable sources of labor, and once they learned to read and write, it was time to begin their apprenticeship as farmers and ranchers. Most were probably eager to leave the schoolroom and begin the rituals of manhood.

Teenage girls appeared to have more opportunities for continuing their education. Of 13 girls between the ages of 15 and 17, 12 attended school for a total of 52 months, or a little over four months per student. Only one girl and her 14-year-old sister had entered the labor force as housekeepers. One 19-year-old attended school for six months. Perceptions of work roles based on gender seem to offer the best explanation. While boys were expected to enter the workforce at the age of 15, females had some additional time until they reached a marriageable age. School was considered a useful activity, and if a family had the means and the daughter showed promise and interest, she might go on to become a schoolteacher.

Although Jackson Hole settlers may have considered advanced schooling a frill, they did value education. According to the census enumeration sheets, all but ten school age children and adults could read, write, and speak English. Of the ten who admitted their illiteracy, six were European immigrants. This is probably a deceptive statistic for the literacy rate seems high. No doubt, a few lied. Like most Americans, the people of Jackson Hole supported education and respected educated people such as doctors and lawyers; being able to read and write was important, but a grammar school education was considered sufficient.

In 1900, Jackson Hole was in its essence a sparsely populated frontier valley, increasingly settled by families. People of all ages lived here, from Charles Wort, less than one month old, to Manuel Bowlsby at 85 years of age. Most took up mountain valley ranching, hoping to prosper. It was a rough life, and some gave up, driven out by the winters and isolation. Many of the names are not familiar to us today. Others stuck it out, and if they did not prosper, they did make a living. The list bears the names of pioneer families whose descendants live in the valley today: Wilson, Cheney, Budge, Ferrin, Lucas, Henrie. The bulk of homesteading occurred after 1900, but the pre-1900 pioneer proved it could be done and led the others. Along with 76,000,000 other Americans, Jackson Hole residents entered the 20th century.

Notes

1. Census of the United States, 1900, Jackson Precinct. I was unable to locate a map or an explicit description of the Jackson precinct. It is unclear whether the upper Gros Ventre valley, the Hoback River, or the area north of Moran were included in the district. The census sheets are microfilm copies.

2. Mae Tuttle to Mrs. Cora Barber, September 5, 1951, acc. 65, Jackson Hole Historical Society and Museum Files.

3. Owen Wister, *The Virginian: A Horseman of the Plains* (New York: MacMillan Company, 1902).

4. McBride, "My Diary."

5. Frances Judge, "Vital Laughter," *Atlantic Monthly,* July 1954, pp. 47–52.

6. Billington, *Westward Expansion,* p. 54.

7. Religious denomination was not a subject of inquiry in the census sheets. I inferred this migration based on knowledge of early Mormon families in Jackson Hole.

8. Billington, *Westward Expansion,* p. 614.

9. Ibid., pp. 614–617.

10. Struthers Burt, *Diary,* pp. 99–101; Frances Judge, "Mountain River Men," pp. 52–58; and Fritiof Fryxell, "Prospector of Jackson Hole," *Campfire Tales,* pp. 47–51.

11. This estimate of preempted acreage does not include desert land entries, which could add several thousand acres of homestead lands.

12. Pierce Cunningham and Emile Wolff were listed as farmers in the census, when more precisely they were cattle ranchers. It is clear that Jackson Hole settlers thought of themselves as ranchers, even though they practiced farming.

13. *Jackson's Hole Courier,* January 28, 1909.

14. McDermott worked for the Reclamation Service during the construction of the Jackson Lake Dam. He served as the pilot of the *Titanic,* a small steamboat used on the project.

The Homesteaders: Post-1900

. . . J. D. "Si" Ferrin was camped on String Lake when he learned of the newly opened lands. Knowing that he had his eye on a benchland of meadow south of the Buffalo Fork, his wife had dispatched a rider to tell him the news. Ferrin saddled his horse and made a beeline east across the Potholes to the Snake River, where he forded at a dangerous crossing. By the time his partner reached the benchland, Ferrin had already driven stakes on his claim. . . .

The Winegar family were among the many settlers who poured into the valley between 1900 and 1920. This photograph, although poor in quality, shows the collection of wagons, possessions, and stock that homesteaders transported to their new home. *Jackson Hole Historical Society and Museum*

The most intense period of homesteading in Jackson Hole occurred after 1900. Settlement peaked between 1908 and 1919, then declined as depressed agricultural prices and natural events such as the drought of 1919 discouraged further settlement. For all practical purposes, the homesteader's frontier ended in 1927, with a presidential executive order withdrawing virtually all public lands in Jackson Hole from settlement.[1] Only a few entrants received patents for land after this year.

Several characteristics distinguish homesteading in the valley after 1900 from the previous century. First, more homesteaders tried to farm the land exclusively, rather than devote their efforts to cattle ranching. Second, as the valley filled up, people settled more marginal lands. For example, after settlers acquired the best land in the Mormon Row area east of Blacktail Butte, others ventured north onto the sagebrush-covered land on Antelope Flats in 1910.[2] Third, after 1910, people filed preemption notices on lands that clearly were ill-suited for agriculture.

Close scrutiny of specific cases reveals that the claimants took up homesteads to establish dude ranches, tourist facilities, residences, or quite simply to engage in real estate speculation.

Finally, government policies toward public lands altered dramatically after 1900. In the frontier West, the role of government was to transfer land and resources to private ownership in an orderly but expeditious way. The rise of the conservation movement in the late nineteenth century altered government policy and, consequently, government functions. New federal bureaus such as the Forest Service regulated and reserved lands and resources. The people of Jackson Hole felt this impact dramatically after 1900, when permits were required for timbering and grazing in the Teton National Forest. Resources remained available for use, but a new figure, the forest ranger, enforced limits, reducing the free-for-all on the public domain that characterized the previous century.[3]

The intensity of settlement transformed the valley after 1900. By 1909, the population of Jackson Hole had increased to an estimated 1,500 people according to the editor of the *Jackson's Hole Courier*. The United States Land Commissioner reported more than 150 "recent" entries in this period. The number of homesteads located on today's park lands more than doubled, supporting the general accuracy of statements in the *Courier*.

By the time the homesteaders' frontier ended in the 1920s, at least 5,280 acres in the area that now comprises the park had been plowed and cultivated. This figure represents the acreage cultivated while ranchers and farmers were proving up their properties. They no doubt continued to clear and plow new land, so 5,000 acres is very conservative. Cultivated land in the park may have approached 10,000 acres eventually, but there is no way to determine this figure accurately. Also, this acreage does not include land used for grazing.[4]

Homesteading in the park concentrated in three zones. Settlers preferred: (1) The valley east of the Snake River and north of the Gros Ventre River to Antelope Flats and (2) The Spread Creek Valley-Buffalo Fork area. The third zone—the valley west of the Snake River—was also homesteaded after 1900, though less intensely than the lands east of the river, and for different reasons.

Within the first zone, settlement advanced north from the Flat Creek area and Spring Gulch toward the Gros Ventre River. South of the river, near Grand Teton National Park's present south boundary, the Nickell family and Harvey Glidden's widow owned much of the acreage along the highway to the Gros Ventre. William Smith filed an entry as late as 1922. He tried to farm land on today's Elk Refuge, but failed in spectacular fashion.[5] Most land north of the Gros Ventre River to Menor's Ferry was preempted after 1901. Settlers primarily filed under the Homestead Act of 1862, which required five years of continuous residence and cultivation. Also, no less than 11 desert entries were filed in this area. The Desert Land Act was different from the 1862 law in two ways; there was no residential requirement and claimants paid $1.25 per acre. Since many could not spare the cash for a desert entry, they generally filed preemption papers under the 1862 law.

Some of the people who settled in this area were Norm Smith, Charles Beagle, Birch Hopson, Frank Connell, John Coon, Marion Coon, Floyd Wilson, Roy Nipper, Frank Newbold, John Braddock, and Nephi Moulton. In addition, a surprising number of women filed preemption papers for tracts in this area, including Alma Moulton, Nellie Burton, Nora Bush, Elizabeth McCabe, Fannie Forrester, and Mary and Ann Lingenfelter.

Settlers filed for available parcels along the Gros Ventre River to Kelly, then moved north along the flats east of Blacktail Butte. Fred Lovejoy, who located a ranch on the north bank of the Gros Ventre River in 1899, added to his 320-acre ranch when his bride, Mary Lovejoy, filed a desert entry for 160 acres in 1908. Likewise, Cora Heigho Sebastian claimed a relinquishment, adding 160 acres to the Sebastian Ranch. A few others settled in this area before 1910, but the Sebastians and Lovejoys took up much of the floodplain along the north bank of the river.

In the Kelly area near the Gros Ventre, and along the foothills on the east side of Jackson Hole, homesteads blossomed. Virtually all of the homesteaders were married men with families, or single men aged 30 or over. Joseph Greenough was 70 years old when he filed final papers in 1912. Only James Williams, who homesteaded what is known today as the Hunter Hereford Ranch, was under 30. He had just turned 23 years old when he established his residence in May 1909. Only five settlers added acreage under the Desert Land Act, notably Bill and Sophie Kelly, who each filed a desert entry along the Gros Ventre. Kelly was a rancher and cattle buyer. Some of these homesteads were devoted to farming rather than ranching. Many were not very successful. William Binkley settled at what is now Kelly and part of the Teton Valley Ranch with his wife and four children in 1901. In five years, he managed to irrigate six acres. But Binkley was known more for his tusking and poaching than his green thumb.[6]

Jim Budge, James May, and Joe Henrie had settled southeast of Blacktail Butte prior to 1900. As more settlers moved into the area, homesteads concentrated east of Blacktail Butte. On July 1, 1908, President Theodore Roosevelt issued an executive order abolishing the Yellowstone National Forest and

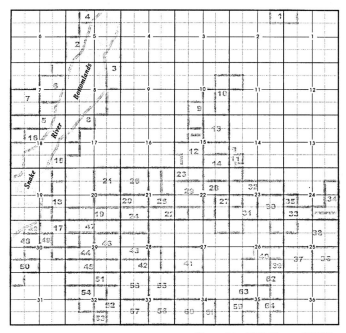

Township 43 N, Range 115 W

1. Talmadge S. Holland	23. John W. Nixon, 1919	45. Joseph Eggleston, 1916
2. Irving Corse, 1926	24. Dick Vander Brock, 1918	46. T. A. Moulton, 1916
3. Geo. M. Ferrel, 1920	25. John Riniker, 1921	47. John A. Moulton, 1916
4. Joe LePage	26. Joe Pfeifer, 1915	48. Holiday Menor, 1919
5. M.S. Burt, 1916	27. James R. Smith, 1917	49. Henry Gunther, 1926
6. M.S. Burt, 1917	28. John M. Young, 1917	50. Norman Smith, 1919
7. Horace Carncross, 1917	29. John C. Rutherford, 1916	51. Jacob Johnson, 1915
8. Karl Kent, 1921	30. James S. Williams, 1915	52. James H. May, 1915
9. John L. Kneedy, 1921	31. Albert Z. Smith, 1914	53. James I. May, 1902
10. Milton Kneedy, 1918	32. Thos. H. Baxter, 1917	54. John J. Hoagland, 1928
11. Esther Hoagland, 1918	33. Ransom Adams, 1916	55. John W. Woodward, 1919
12. Edward Steele, 1916	34. William D. Jump, 1916	56. Albert Gunther, 1916
13. George E. Carpenter	35. James S.Williams, 1918	57. George H. Riniker, 1917
14. Heirs of John Rutherford, 1918	36. Charles Davis, 1919	58. Hannes Harthoorn, 1919
15. William A. Budge, 1927	37. Luther Taylor, 1927	59. William C. Shinkle, 1915
16. Horace Carncross, 1917	38. Gerrit Hardeman, 1930	60. Ray M. Shinkle, 1918
17. Henry Gunther, 1917	39. Wm. R. Taylor, 1916	61. Charles M. Shinkle, 1919
18. Frank Shawback, 1918	40. John H. Taylor, 1916	62. Howard D. Erwin, 1916
19. Thos. Murphy, 1915	41. Tillman V. Holland, 1920	63. Leslie A. Kafferlin, 1916
20. Arthur Mahan, 1916	42. Thos. W. Perry, 1917	64. John E. Erwin, 1916
21. Edward Geck, 1915	43. Andrew H. Chambers, 1916	
22. Wm. Ireton, 1918	44. J. Wallace Moulton, 1916	

Township 43 North, Range 115 West, 6th P.M. The earliest homesteaders claimed the best agricultural lands in the valley. One of the first "zones" of settlement was east of the Snake River, and north of the Gros Ventre River to Antelope Flats. This includes "Mormon Row." Once part of a much larger settlement, "Mormon Row" is today a small cluster of farms along the road that divides Sections 28 and 29. (Note: Patent dates denote when homesteaders actually received their patents, by which time they had already lived on the land for a number of years.) *National Park Service*

In 1908, President Theodore Roosevelt opened up the area northeast of Blacktail Butte to homesteading. The May homestead was one of the first built in this area. *Grand Teton National Park*

expanding the Teton National Forest. This executive order opened lands in the valley previously closed to homesteading. In September 1908, John and T. A. Moulton located homesteads northeast of Blacktail Butte, after the release of the land from the forest reserve. Through December, others preempted the best lands in this segment of the valley. They were Thomas Murphy, Albert Gunther, Joseph Eggleston, George Riniker, and Henry May. One settler, Jake Johnson, may have anticipated the boundary change, for he filed his preemption papers nearly two months before Roosevelt's executive order. Holiday Menor homesteaded on the east bank of the Snake, opposite his brother's ferry. Eight others took up homesteads between 1909 and 1920. Since the majority of the settlers were Mormon, the area acquired the name Mormon Row sometime after 1910.

The land east of Blacktail Butte is comprised of an alluvial fan that provides very deep topsoil suitable for agriculture. Farmers and ranchers coveted land in this area, even though the lack of water for irrigation posed problems.[7] In 1910, as Mormon Row became settled, homesteaders expanded into more marginal lands on Antelope Flats. John Rutherford, Doc Steele, and Joe Pfeifer were the first to move into the sagebrush flats northeast of Blacktail Butte.

Others filed preemption papers for lands along the floodplains and terraces east of the Snake River. Henry Gunther filed papers in 1914 and George Ferrel in 1915.[8]

The Buffalo Fork Valley-Spread Creek area experienced extensive settlement after 1900. A handful of homesteaders, such as Pierce Cunningham and

In 1912, Thomas A. Moulton built this homestead northeast of Blacktail Butte. Several Mormon families homesteaded in the area, which became known as "Mormon Row." *Grand Teton National Park*

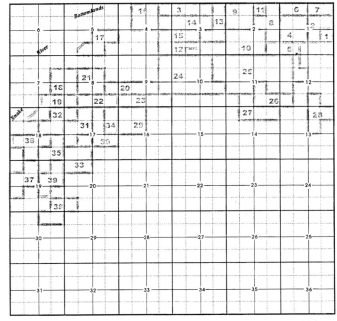

Township 44 N, Range 114 W

1. Lydia Uhl, 1916	14. Josiah D. Ferrin, 1913	27. Gottfried Feuz, 1917
2. James Uhl, 1908	15. Emile Wolff, 1906	28. H.L. Eynon, 1923
3. Nancy A. Thompson, 1910	16. Jos. B. Heniger, 1913	29. George Greenwood, 1917
4. Emile Wolff, 1912	17. Mary C. Coffin, 1915	30. W.F. Cunningham, 1906
5. Will H. Fuger, 1917	18. Rudy Harold, 1916	31. J.P. Cunningham, 1906
6. James M. Graham, 1929	19. Orin Seaton, 1915	32. J.P. Cunningham, 1909
7. Cyrus R. Ferrin, 1929	20. Anton Grosser, 1916	33. John P. Nelson, 1915
8. Marius Kristensen, 1916	21. Fred J. Topping, 1917	34. W.F. Cunningham, 1909
9. Wm. Stilson, 1919	22. Eva G. Sanford Topping, 1931	35. John Fee, Jr., 1915
10. Heirs of Curtis Ferrin, 1923	23. Jos. Bettendorf, 1915	36. Jesse Chambers, 1931
11. Jude Allen	24. James Foster McInelly, 1925	37. Charlie Hedrick, 1915
12. Carl B. Roice, 1917	25. Leonard J. Ferrin, 1925	38. Erving Farrow, 1915
13. Richard L. Thornton, 1918	26. John Dietz, 1915	39. William G. Jump, 1925

Township 44 North, Range 114 West, 6th P.M. Another major zone of settlement was the Buffalo Fork-Spread Creek area, located northeast of Antelope Flats. The Emile Wolff Ranch (No. 15) was patented in 1906. The Cunningham Cabin in Section 17 is all that remains of the Pierce Cunningham homestead claims (Nos. 31 and 32). *National Park Service*

Charlie and Delilah Hedrick homesteaded about three miles south of Spread Creek in 1908. Hedrick Pond marks the site of their homestead. *National Park Service*

Emile Wolff, had established cattle ranches in this area prior to 1900. However, the area remained isolated and largely unoccupied until 1908, when Roosevelt's proclamation altering national forest boundaries opened land. The proclamation generated a small-scale land rush. J. D. "Si" Ferrin was camped on String Lake when he learned of the newly opened lands. Knowing that he had his eye on a benchland of meadow south of the Buffalo Fork, his wife had dispatched a rider to tell him the news. Ferrin saddled his horse and made a beeline east across the Potholes to the Snake River, where he forded at a dangerous crossing. By the time his partner reached the benchland, Ferrin had already driven stakes on his claim.[9] Others who took up homesteads in this area in 1908 were Charlie Hedrick, Rudy Harold, John Dietz, and Joseph Bettendorf. In 1909, Bill Jump, J. B. Heniger, Anton Grosser, Otto Kusche, Jack Fee, Frank Coffin, and Orin Seaton homesteaded here. After 1910, nearly 20 other settlers located on the Spread Creek-Buffalo Fork country.

Although Cunningham, Wolff, and Uhl had added desert entries to their ranches, few newcomers filed papers under the Desert Land Act after 1900.

Two reasons for this may have been a lack of money and available land. Few settlers arrived with a "start," or sufficient capital, to purchase desert lands even at $1.25 per acre. Further, the cost and time involved in constructing an irrigation system was prohibitive for some. Also, after 1908, homesteaders preempted much of the available acreage in the land rush, leaving little to add to a 160-acre parcel.[10]

In 1916, Congress passed and President Woodrow Wilson approved the Stock-Raising Homestead Act, which allowed individuals to preempt up to 640 acres of land considered suitable only for grazing. The law required no cultivation, only range improvements, whatever those might be. Two of Si Ferrin's sons took advantage of the act, filing stock-raising entries in 1920 and 1923 respectively. James McInelly filed for a 520-acre parcel in 1920. He secured a patent in 1925, grazing 260 cattle and horses on the ranch. In contrast, John MacDonald Graham staked out a stock-raising entry on Uhl Hill in 1928. Graham testified that he had not grazed any livestock on the entry and, as a result, a General Land Office inspector recommended denial of Graham's final proof papers. The recommendation was not followed, and Graham received a patent to the property in 1929.[11]

Settlement followed identical patterns along the Buffalo Fork River. Roosevelt's proclamation of 1908 released lands in the Buffalo Valley for occupation. Between 1909 and 1916, homesteaders claimed most of the land along the Buffalo Fork, in and adjacent to today's park boundaries. Only three desert entries were claimed and approved, probably for the same reasons that limited desert entries in the Spread Creek area.

Continuing northward, the terraces and floodplains along the Snake River between Pacific Creek and the original outlet of Jackson Lake provided a smaller area of concentration of homesteads.[12] There was little homesteading activity in this area until 1911, when a number of preemption papers were filed. Some homesteaders had worked on the construction of the Jackson Lake Dam in 1910–1911 and decided to stay. Joe Markham was a Reclamation Service employee who filed on a relinquishment in the Oxbow Bend area in 1914. Others were Herb Whiteman, who filed a gerrymandered claim on the flats north of Moran in 1915, and Charlie Christian, who took up 160 acres at Christian Pond in 1916.[13]

Much of the land north and east of the Moran area remained national forest land, therefore withdrawn from settlement. John Sargent's place on Jackson Lake was the only homestead patented in the north. Whiteman and the Heighos had abandoned the Lakeview Ranch by 1900, while Sim Edwards never received a patent to his ranch on Lizard Creek.[14] Peter Mulligan had a homestead in the Jackson Lake area, but he must have squatted on the property, for no patent exists and its location remains obscure. On the terraces along Pacific Creek, a few scattered homesteaders proved up small ranches after 1910; they were Elmer Arthur in 1913, Harold McKinstry in 1916, Frank Bramen in 1917, and William Snell in 1918. William Thompson filed preemption papers on 160 acres located at the outlet of Two Ocean Lake in 1914. On Pilgrim Creek, Samuel R. Wilson homesteaded a tract in 1916, attempting to establish a small ranch. David Ferrin also filed papers on an isolated parcel on Pacific Creek near the present park boundary. Agricultural uses were limited mostly to cattle grazing on forest lands, alloted by the Forest Service through a permit system.[15]

Although less concentrated than the other two homesteading zones, settlement also increased in the valley west of the Snake River after 1900. Small ranchers and homesteaders moved north from Wilson into this area. Between 1901 and 1910, August Nikolaison, Charles Carlson, Frank Waterman, Charles Ilse, and Paul Lyon preempted 160-acre tracts along the narrow stretch between the timbered benches and the Snake River. William Grant took up 160 acres below the Sawmill Ponds in 1914, which later became the first Moose Post Office. The area is comprised of old stream channels and alluvium consisting of sandy and gravelly loams.[16]

Others filed entries to establish the first dude ranches in the valley. Louis Joy took over Dave Spalding's relinquishment to establish the JY Ranch at the base of Phelps Lake in 1907, which Struthers Burt described as "absolutely useless for ranching purposes."[17] Harold Hammond and Tucker Bispham, an eastern dude, each took up 160-acre parcels and formed a partnership. Originally intend-

ing to go into the cattle business, they decided to switch to dude ranching after the First World War in 1919. This became the White Grass. Harry Clissold started the Trail Ranch in 1916, when he filed on 160 acres north of the White Grass. Cliff Ward took up 160 adjacent acres in 1922, which were incorporated into the Trail Ranch.[18] Several homesteaders filed for 640-acre tracts in the 1920s under the Stock-Raising Act of 1916. Henry Stewart added 637 acres to the JY through this act in 1925. Two dude wranglers and cowboys, Lewis Fleming and Shadwick Hobbs, filed stock-raising entries in 1926 near the JY. Their patents were approved in 1929.[19]

Two land entries may well have been motivated by real estate speculation. Geraldine Lucas purchased just over 38 acres on Phelps Lake under the Homestead Act of 1820. Since she had homesteaded several miles north on Cottonwood Creek, there seems to be no other explanation for this entry. In 1925, Hannah Porter filed and received title to 160 acres of timberland west of the JY through the Timber and Stone Act of 1878. This legislation provided a way for private interests to purchase timber lands. Land unfit for any sort of cultivation could be purchased through a negotiated sale with the government. Porter purchased the acreage for $1,260.[20]

Another group of homesteaders preempted lands along Cottonwood Creek from Menor's Ferry to Jenny Lake. For more than a decade, Bill Menor had the west side of the Snake River to himself, until James Manges filed preemption papers on a 160-acre tract near the confluence of Taggart and Cottonwood Creeks in 1911. Manges had set out from Colorado for Oregon. He arrived in Jackson Hole in the fall of 1910, hoping to make a side trip through Yellowstone. Too late, he learned that Yellowstone's roads had shut down because of snow. He wintered with the Worts in South Park, then followed Wort's advice to homestead on Taggart Creek.

A year later, Struthers Burt and Horace Carncross each filed on 160 acres located on the west bank of the Snake River, north of Cottonwood Creek. They also added 160-acre desert entries; the 640-acre ranch formed the headquarters of the Bar BC, a prominent dude ranch in Jackson Hole. Dudes and employees of the Bar BC often then became homesteaders themselves, including Tucker

Township 43N, Range 116

1. Geraldine Lucas, 1922	14. Harry Clissold, 1923	27. Tucker Bispham, 1923
2. N.R. Colwell, 1922	15. Clifford Ward, 1926	28. Harold Hammond, 1921
3. Geraldine Lucas, 1921	16. Lee Manges	29. Charles Ilse, 1918
4. James Manges, 1918	17. Bryant Mears	30. W.J. Grant, 1920
5. H.F. Sensenbach, 1921	18. Jack Canfield, 1922	31. Buster Estes, 1928
6. Alfred G.E. Bessette, 1921	19. W.D. Menor, 1908	32. Earle W. Harris, 1920
7. Emma Williams, 1927	20. Alice Bladon, 1922	33. Elizabeth McCabe, 1928
8. Chester Goss, 1928	21. H.H. Menor, 1919	
9. Roger Carlson, 1924	22. L. Altenreid, 1923	*Small parcels of land
10. Ivan Basye, 1928	23. E. Dornan	surveyed as lots.
11. May Horel, 1921	24. Norman Smith	
12. Frank Bessette, 1921	25. Harold Brown, 1929	
13. Peter Karppi, 1930	26. Frederick Sandell, 1924	

Township 43 North, Range 116 West, 6th P.M. The area west of the Snake River was settled later, and less intensely. This map depicts the homestead patents in Township 43 North, Range 116 West, which is directly west of the township shown in the map on page 111. William Menor had the first homestead (No. 19) in this area, which he selected for its suitability as a ferry crossing rather than its agricultural potential. *National Park Service*

Manges Cabin. When Jim Manges homesteaded at Taggart Creek, Bill Menor was the only settler on the west side of the Snake River in this area. More settlers soon followed, most starting dude ranches. Manges eventually built tourist cabins on his property. *National Park Service*

Bispham, who moved to the White Grass. Struthers Burt persuaded Alfred and Frank Bessette from Princeton, New Jersey, to work as chefs at the Bar BC. Both took up homesteads in 1914 and 1915 near the Manges place. Bryant Mears, a Bar BC dude, took up residence on a relinquishment above Menor's Ferry, apparently attempting to set himself up as a gentleman rancher at his Sun Star Ranch, now known as the 4 Lazy F Ranch. Others who attempted to set up small ranches were Jack Canfield in 1914, Norm Bladon in 1914, Harry Sensenbach in 1914, and May Horel in 1915.[21]

Farther up Cottonwood Creek, Geraldine Lucas preempted a homestead in 1913. Although she cultivated some acreage, her intent was to build a retirement home. She added 80 acres through a desert entry. A friend of Lucas's, Naomi Brewster Colwell, filed papers on an adjacent parcel around 1916. Moritz Locher was the first to homestead at Jenny Lake, taking over a relinquishment at Lupine Meadows in 1915.[22]

After Burt and Carncross established the Bar BC, individuals preempted lands for the express purpose of starting dude ranches. Buster Estes filed on a 76-acre tract on the west bank of the Snake River in July 1922, which became the STS. Peter Karppi

preempted 160 acres of terrace and benchland on Cottonwood Creek in 1922, starting the Half Moon Dude Ranch. At Jenny Lake, Tony Grace filed an entry in October 1922 on property that became the Danny Ranch.[23] Karppi and Grace had acquired lands that had been withheld from settlement by a withdrawal of nearly 20,000 acres in Jackson Hole under the Carey Irrigation Act of 1894. This law enabled the Secretary of the Interior to donate up to 1,000,000 acres to specific arid states, on the condition that the states sponsor the settlement, irrigation, and reclamation of desert lands. Most states chose to contract with private companies to develop irrigation systems. Several companies took advantage of the law to secure water rights in Jackson Hole. In 1916, the state of Wyoming applied for a withdrawal of land and water rights on Jenny and Leigh Lakes. Called the Jenny's and Leigh's Lakes Project, the application withdrew 19,378 acres of land from settlement, which included virtually all public lands between township line 43 north all the way to township line 46 north, just south of Two Ocean Lake. Ostensibly, the company would irrigate the withdrawn lands, then sell acreage to prospective farmers and ranchers. In effect, however, this application shut down homesteading in Jackson Hole north

of Blacktail Butte. Valley residents smoldered with
anger and resentment as no progress was made to
solve the issue for several years. No ditches were constructed, and it became clear that three companies,
the Teton Irrigation Company, the Osgood Land
and Livestock Company, and the Utah-Idaho Sugar
Company, intended to secure water rights and sell
the water to users in other areas such as Idaho.[24]

In 1921, the Secretary of the Interior rejected
the state's application for the land withdrawal. Com-
plications delayed the release of these lands for several months but, finally, over 19,000 acres were reopened for settlement, effective March 29, 1922.[25]
This initiated a new flurry of homesteading. Hoping
to duplicate the success of the Bar BC, Buster Estes,
Peter Karppi, and Tony Grace preempted lands in
1922. Roger Carlson and Ivan Bayse filed entries
along the Snake River north of Cottonwood Creek
in 1922. Lee Manges took up land at Windy Point
in 1925. They homesteaded for agricultural purposes.
Along the Snake, Joe LePage, the head wrangler and
a partner of the Bar BC, purchased a relinquishment
on a 640-acre stock-raising entry from Slim Armstrong in 1924. Ed K. Smith, nicknamed "Roan
Horse," homesteaded a 160-acre ranch at Lupine
Meadows in 1921, a relinquishment with a cabin
already on site.[26]

Speculators also used homestead laws to establish tourist facilities in the area. Homer Richards
filed an entry on 160 acres southeast of Jenny Lake.
He grazed livestock on 18 acres, but wrote in his final proof papers that his homestead included a gas
station, barbershop, and rental cabins. Harrison
Crandall filed a stock-raising entry on 120 acres
north of Jenny Lake Lodge in 1924. To comply with
the law's requirements, he grazed about 40 head of
horses on the land each summer and seeded about
25 acres to brome grass. He began a photography
business, and constructed the studio that is presently
located at the south end of Jenny Lake. Albert W.
Gabbey filed two stock-raising entries east of Crandall's, one in 1924 and the other in 1927. Gabbey secured a patent to the first entry in 1932. His second
preemption was denied by the General Land Office
and became the subject of controversy when the decision was linked to park extension and Rockefeller's
Snake River Land Company. The Secretary of the

Interior ordered the issuance of a patent in 1940.
Gabbey established the Square G Dude Ranch.[27]

East of Jenny Lake, H. C. Ericcson filed a homestead entry on floodplain and terrace lands on the
west side of the Snake River near Deadman's Bar in
1926. He added a 442-acre stock-raising entry in
1929, establishing a cattle ranch. Ericsson was an attorney from Lawrence, Kansas, who sought and purchased property in the valley for the purpose of real
estate speculation.[28]

General Land Office inspectors investigated the
homestead application of Evelyn Dornan, who filed
on a small 20-acre tract east of the Snake River
across from Menor's Ferry in 1922. This was a small
lot that had been passed over by earlier settlers. Mrs.
Dornan, a widow from Pennsylvania, learned about
the parcel from Holiday Menor. With her teenage
son, Mrs. Dornan established residence in 1923 and
cultivated a one-acre truck garden, harvesting 500
pounds of potatoes and 500 pounds of cabbage.
However, the small acreage attracted the attention of
land office inspectors when she submitted final papers in 1925. The next year, C. S. Dietz inspected
her homestead. He found that Mrs. Dornan had
complied with residency and cultivation requirements, even though the acreage was too small to provide a sufficient income from farming. Dietz recommended the issuance of a patent, concluding that
Evelyn Dornan had acted in good faith.[29]

Many Jackson Hole homesteaders were mature
adults with families, who had moved several times in
search of a new beginning. Charlie Hedrick was
born in Illinois and raised in Colorado, before he
came to Jackson Hole in 1904. John Woodward followed the old Oregon Trail from Nebraska to Oregon in a covered wagon in 1898. He returned to
Wyoming in 1902, crossing Teton Pass, and lived in
Lander, Dubois, and Riverton before homesteading
near Kelly, Wyoming, in 1912. John Simpson settled
in 1892 on what became the town site of Jackson, after following the miner's frontier to Colorado in the
1850s and Deadwood, Dakota Territory, in the
1870s. William Lafferty, a Civil War veteran, settled
in Nebraska, South Dakota, and Cody, Wyoming, before locating a ranch far up the Gros Ventre in 1900.
Frank Lasho, who settled on the east bank of the
Snake River near Moose, was 39 years old and had

Spring Gulch ranch kids traveled to school in this makeshift "wagon-bus." Carl George is the driver. *Jackson Hole Historical Society and Museum*

a wife and child when he relocated in the valley. Illness prevented Will Steingraber from residing on or improving his homestead entry near "Fort Pier" or Pierre, South Dakota. So at age 32, he and his family started over, filing an entry near the Buffalo Fork in 1914. Milton H. Kneedy came to Jackson Hole in 1910 after losing a flour mill in Kansas, when his partner, reputedly a Baptist minister, absconded with his money.[30]

A significant segment of Jackson Hole's settlers were foreign immigrants. Frederick Sandell and Norm Bladon were Englishmen who homesteaded in the Menor's Ferry area. Gerrit Hardeman and Hannes Harthoorn left the Netherlands after 1900, drawn to Jackson Hole by the promise of land. Hardeman built up one of the finest ranches in the valley. Joe LePage was a top-notch wrangler from Canada, who worked his way from employee to partner at Burt and Carncross's Bar BC. He started his own ranch, but died a premature death in 1927. Otto Kusche, who listed his nationality as "foreign" on his final proof papers, homesteaded what became the headquarters of the Elk Ranch. He was probably German, as were his neighbors, Anton Grosser and John Dietz. John P "Pete" Nelson, born in Denmark, and Gottfried Feuz, a Swiss national, homesteaded in the Spread Creek area in 1911. Both raised large

families whose descendants live in the valley today. To many immigrants, who left land-poor countries, the risks of homesteading in the American West were trivial when compared to realizing the dream of owning a farm or ranch.[31]

Overall, nearly 400 homestead entries were filed and approved for lands within today's park boundary, totaling thousands of acres. Water, soil types, and the homesteader's intentions influenced the patterns of settlement in the valley. The first settlers, who were essentially ranchers, claimed the best lands along rivers and creeks. They cultivated and irrigated hayfields to grow the necessary winter feed for their cattle. The Gros Ventre, Buffalo Fork, Snake, and Spread, Ditch, and Cottonwood Creeks were important water sources. Lands comprised of loamy soils of floodplains, terraces, and alluvial fans were settled first and most intensely.

Understanding the motives of homesteaders is critical to comprehending the settlement patterns in Jackson Hole. Most established small cattle ranches of which farming was a significant element. After 1900, some optimists devoted their energy to farming alone. Some homesteaded to provide a residence, while they earned their livings in other ways. Bill Menor took up his homestead to use the single channel of the Snake River for a ferry operation. Beginning with Louis Joy and the JY in 1907, entrepreneurs preempted lands for the purpose of dude ranching. Homesteaders in the Jenny Lake area during the 1920s also took advantage of the growing tourist trade. But, as much as any of these factors, federal land policy, mandated by congressional laws, impacted homesteading in the valley.

Prior to 1890, there were few restrictions on the public domain. Virtually all resources and lands were available for the taking. The Forest Reserve Act of 1891 was one of the most significant pieces of legislation in conservation history. The law allowed the president to set aside forest reserves by executive order. President Benjamin Harrison created the Yellowstone Park Timber Reserve in March 1891. The 1,239,040-acre reserve included the northern end of Jackson Hole, closing the area to settlement. John Sargent managed to secure a patent in the northern end of the valley only because he filed his preemption papers in July 1890, less than a year before the creation of the reserve.

In 1897, President Grover Cleveland issued a proclamation setting aside 829,440 acres under the Teton Forest Reserve. The reserve included much of the public domain in Jackson Hole. Land north of township line 42 north was closed to settlement. Then, on July 1, 1908, President Theodore Roosevelt signed a proclamation establishing Teton National Forest, comprising 1,991,200 acres. The proclamation reopened settlement lands in the valley, but reserved the Teton Range and most of the highlands surrounding the valley. From Washington, D.C., Roosevelt could hardly have known that he generated a small-scale land rush in this isolated mountain valley.[32]

Water development projects influenced settlement in the valley, particularly lands reserved by authority of the Carey Irrigation Act of 1894. The Teton Irrigation Company tied up lands for several years; the water appropriated to irrigate farms and ranches in the valley was sold to irrigation companies in Idaho. In 1916, the State of Wyoming applied for a withdrawal of 19,378 acres for Jenny's and Leigh's Lakes, also known as the "Jennies and Lees Lake Segregation." The Interior Department denied the application in 1921, and most of the land

was reopened for settlement in 1922. But for five years, the project withheld considerable acreage from settlement.[33]

Five years later, President Calvin Coolidge issued a series of executive orders that closed the public domain in Jackson Hole to settlement. Executive Order 4631 closed several hundred acres to entry "pending determination as to the advisability of reserving the lands for elk-refuge purposes." Most of this acreage was located in the area of today's elk refuge. Then, on July 7, 1927, Coolidge signed Executive Order 4685, which closed thousands of acres to homesteading. Three subsequent closures were issued between 1928 and 1930. The purposes of the later withdrawals were not specific and, as a result, stirred up considerable controversy. Valley residents learned several years later that the July 1927 withdrawal was connected to the purchase program of John D. Rockefeller Jr.'s Snake River Land Company. But, that is another story.[34]

Notes

1. "Hearing on S. Res. 226," 1934, pp. 76–79.

2. Homestead Patents: 615005, John M. Rutherford, 1910; 521820, E.C. Steele, 1910; and 485599, Joe Pfeifer, 1910.

3. Samuel P. Hays, *Conservation and the Gospel of Efficiency: The Progressive Conservation Movement, 1890–1920* (Cambridge Harvard University Press, 1959; reprint ed., New York: Atheneum Press, 1975).

4. I added up the acreages that homesteaders claimed to cultivate in their testimony in the final proof papers.

5. Homestead Patent 995670, William Smith, 1925.

6. Homestead Patent HC 1246, Evanson, Binkley, 1906.

7. Esther B. Allan, "History of Teton National Forest," unpublished manuscript, 1973, 143.

8. Homestead Patents: 615005, J. Rutherford, 1910; 521820, E.C. Steele, 1910, and 485599, J. Pfeifer, 1910.

9. Marion V. Allen, *Early Jackson Hole* (Redding, CA: Press Room Printing, 1981), pp. 208–209; and *Jackson Hole Guide*, September 27, 1973.

10. Only Lydia Lozier and J.V. Allen filed desert entries in this area after 1908.

11. Homestead Patents: 958787, Leonard Ferrin, 1924; 1028708, Cyrus Ray Ferrin, 1928; 958788, James McInelly, 1924; and 1028284, John MacDonald Graham, 1928.

12. Jack F. Young, *Soil Survey of Teton County, Wyoming: Grand Teton National Park* (Soil Conservation Service, 1982).

13. Homestead Patents: 796556, Joe Markham, 1918; 707968, George H. Whiteman, 1918; and 804576, Charlie Christian, 1920.

14. U.S. Geological Survey, "Grand Teton Quadrangle," 1901, Grand Teton National Park.

15. Homestead Patents: 587701, Elmer Arthur, 1916; 843343, Frank Bramen, 1921; 842747, S.R. Wilson, 1920; 645202, William C. Thompson, 1917; 863222, William Snell, 1921; and 752972, David Ferrin, 1919.

16. Homestead Patents: HC 1359, Evanston, August Nicolaison, 1907; 174451, Charles Carlson, 1910; 62608, Francis Waterman, 1911; 615962, Charles Ilse, 1917; 641991, Paul Lyon, 1917; and 737603, William J. Grant, 1919.

17. Struthers Burt, *Diary*, p. 42.

18. Homestead Patents: 799046, Harold Hammond, 1920; 902573, George T. Bispham, 1922; 908182, Harry Clissold, 1922; and 977162, Clifford Ward, 1925.

19. Homestead Patents: 970306, Henry S.A. Stewart, 1925; 1037175, Shadwick Hobbs, 1929; and 1038450, George Fleming, 1929.

20. Homestead Patent 985646, Hannah Porter, 1925.

21. *Jackson Hole Guide*, October 13, 1955, October 12, 1972; interview with Noble Gregory by Jo Anne Byrd, #13, "Last of Old West Series;" and Homestead Patents: 639818, James Manges, 1917; 578666, Maxwell S. Burt, 1916; 577944, Horace Carncross, 1916; 584624, M.S. Burt, 1916; 584625, H. Carncross, 1916; 799048, Frank P. Bessette, 1920; 824385, Alfred G. E. Bessette, 1921; 805788, Bryant F. Mears, 1920; 848729, Jack Canfield, 1920; 888052, Heirs of Norman Bladon, 1919; 801007, Harry F. Sensenbach, 1920; and 824386, May P. Horel, 1920.

22. Homestead Patents: 868566, Geraldine Lucas, 1921; 999054, G. Lucas, 1926; and 959955, Heirs of Moritz Locher, 1924.

23. Homestead Patents: 1014042, Buster Estes, 1927; 1037758, Peter Karppi, Jr., 1928; and 1010872, Tony S. Grace, 1927.

24. Roy M. Robbins, *Our Landed Heritage: The Public Domain* (Lincoln NE: University of Nebraska Press, 1962), pp. 328–330; Righter, *Crucible for Conservation*, pp. 10–11; and *Jackson's Hole Courier*, September 1, 1921.

25. *Jackson's Hole Courier*, September 1, 1921, and March 9, 1922.

26. Homestead Patents: 1023026, Lee Manges, 1928; 1016405, Ivan Bayse, 1927; 931323, Roger F Carlson, 1923; 1035908, Joseph Le Page, 1928; and 981691, Ed K. Smith, 1926.

27. Homestead Patents: 1021747, Homer Richards, 1928; 1023025, Harrison Crandall, 1928; 1109105, AW. Gabbey, 1927; and 1057117, S.W. Gabbey, 1931; and "Hearing on S. Res. 226," 1933, pp. 300–330.

28. Homestead patents.

29. Homestead Patent 999739, Evelyn Dornan, 1925; and Inspector C. S. Deitz to Commissioner, General Land Office, November 24, 1926, in Patent File 999739.

30. *Jackson's Hole Courier*, January 1, 1953; Allan Collection, 7637, Charlie Hedrick transcript, Box 3, University of Wyoming Archives, American Heritage Center; Homestead Patents: 707967, Will Steingraber, 1918; and Homestead Cert., 1447, Lander, Frank, Lasho, 1908.

31. Homestead records; I examined the final proof papers for 395 homesteads situated in or adjacent to the present boundaries of Grand Teton National Park.

32. Allan, "History of Teton National Forest," pp. 107–108 and 143.

33. Margaret and Olaus Murie, *Wapiti Wilderness* (New York: Alfred A. Knopf, 1966), pp. 117–118.

34. "Hearing on S. Res. 226," 1933, pp. 76–79.

CHAPTER

Life on the Homestead

Charles Shinkle filed preemption papers on a 160-acre parcel north of Kelly in 1910. His final testimony of proof for Homestead Patent 715943 (1918) documented his setbacks:

1911	2 acres veg. cattle got it.
1912	3 acres 1/2 acre veg. 1 ton.
1913	No crop
1914	No crop too dry.
1915	3 acres cattle got it.
1916	3 acres 1 a.veg. 1/4 ton veg.

The Cunningham cabin was a typical Jackson Hole homestead. The "dogtrot-style" log cabin has a sod roof *National Park Service*

Anyone who has enjoyed or endured—depending on one's viewpoint—a winter in Jackson Hole might wonder what possessed settlers to believe they could cultivate crops in this valley. Nevertheless, homesteaders believed it—and grew crops here. The overwhelming majority adopted mountain-valley ranching, which dominated the economy of Jackson Hole until the tourist industry gained predominance after the Second World War.[1] Few contemporary accounts of settlement in Jackson Hole exist, and available sources shed little light on the homesteaders' frontier. Reminiscences are found in oral history tapes, newspaper accounts, or memoirs. However, care must be exercised in using these sources, for hand-down stories become embellished and memories are notoriously inaccurate. But, coupled with records such as homestead patent files and knowledge of the homesteaders' frontier in America, reasonable inferences can be made about settlement in Jackson Hole.

For much of the nineteenth century, Americans shared a general perception of the plains west of the Mississippi River as a barren desert. The myth of the Great America Desert persisted through the Civil War. But in 1847, Mormons emigrated to the Great Basin, successfully farming land that appeared impossible to cultivate, and proved the feasibility of agriculture in the arid West. In addition, after the Civil War, open-range cattle ranching prospered on the native grasses of the Great Plains.[2]

These events made two things clear. First, the hunter-woodsmen-farmers of the Old Northwest and Mississippi Valley would have to adapt their agricultural lore and experience to a very different environment. Second, technology could be applied to manipulate the environment, such as the Mormons' construction of an impressive system of canals. After the Civil War, technological improvements enabled homesteaders to cultivate lands where once the possibilities seemed remote. Barbed wire, patented in 1874, provided the practical material for fencing fields on the Great Plains. Also, rapid improvements in farm machinery answered the demand for ways to cultivate the larger acreages needed to earn a living in the West. For example, the plow, which evolved rapidly after 1865, enabled farmers to turn over prairie soils more efficiently. By 1873, manufacturers produced no fewer than 16 effective plows in the United States.[3] Acreage was another consideration. East of the Mississippi River, 80 acres were more than enough to support a family adequately. This was not the case in the West, where less rainfall required 300 or more acres for family farms in most instances. Ranches required thousands of acres, both for grazing and cultivating winter feed. In exceptional cases, a family could earn a good living off 40–60 acres of well-irrigated land in some areas of the West.[4]

The farmer's frontier slowly penetrated the Great Plains in the 1870s and 1880s, creeping toward the Rockies from the east. From the Salt Lake Valley, Mormon settlers expanded into adjacent areas such as Idaho. Homesteaders first settled in the Teton Basin in Idaho in 1882. In 1887, a drought parched much of the West. The dry weather cycle hit the Great Plains especially hard, as homesteaders faced ruin as crop after crop failed. To compound the problem, the Midwest and foreign countries produced bumper crops, which kept farm product prices drastically low. This resulted in a decade of serious economic and social disruption. Farmers in western Kansas, Nebraska, South Dakota, and Colorado suffered the most; it is estimated that an astonishing one-third to one-half went bankrupt. In western Kansas and Nebraska, 100,000 people left their homes. Ghost towns, forlorn and empty, dotted the stark landscape of the high plains. Economic depression, beginning with the Panic of 1893, gripped the nation for five years, complicating the farmers' dilemma. The Populist movement swept the agrarian West in these years as leaders such as Mary Elizabeth Lease urged farmers to "raise less corn and more hell." This was the backdrop of events when settlers breached the mountains to homestead in Jackson Hole.[5]

Shelter was the primary concern of the arriving settlers and, like the earliest colonists, people on the frontier used the materials provided by nature. On the Great Plains, where wood was scarce, the sod house symbolized the homesteader's frontier. In Jackson Hole, abundant lodgepole pines provided convenient materials for log cabins, the predominant shelter in Jackson Hole, even after the first sawmills appeared in the valley. Most people started out with

small one and two-room cabins, which seldom exceeded 18 × 24 feet in dimensions. The dogtrot was a common type, consisting of two cabins joined by a covered breezeway or porch. The Cunningham cabin is a good example of this construction. Builders joined the corners with saddle notches, or squared corners fastened with spikes. Cracks between the logs were daubed with a dirt mortar often reinforced along the bottom with willow wands. Roofs consisted of sapling poles covered with dirt. At first, floors were packed dirt, but settlers installed rough board floors as soon as logs could be sawed by hand, or when the first sawmills provided a ready supply of lumber.

The Budge cabin, built southeast of Blacktail Butte in 1897, was a one-room sod-roofed cabin with one door and one window. The younger Jim Budge recalled water and mud leaking through the roof during rainstorms. To keep the children dry, Mrs. Budge placed them under the kitchen table and covered it with oilcloth.[6] Frances Judge described the small homestead cabin constructed shortly after the turn of the century for her grandmother, Mary Wadams. Judge remembered the cabin as a small sod-roofed dwelling with a "brushed earth floor that had been dampened and swept until it was as hard as cement." Mrs. Wadams tacked white muslin cloth on the ceiling to reflect more light in the cabin and catch dirt from the roof. The interior walls were insulated with pages from old magazines. Rodents were a persistent problem, because there were so many entries. Judge recalled how common it was to see the moving depression of a mouse scurry across the muslin ceiling. Her grandmother prepared a flour paste laced with strychnine to control the rodents.[7] Joe Jones filed on a relinquishment south of Blacktail Butte in 1907, which included a cabin abandoned by the first occupant. When the Jones family arrived, they found that cattle had entered the structure, causing considerable damage to the floor. Joe Jones simply pulled up the boards and turned them over.[8]

As time passed and families grew, homesteaders added on to the original cabin or constructed more elaborate residences. Typical was the whitewashed cabin at Menor's Ferry, which had two distinct additions. By 1904, Jim Budge had added two rooms to his cabin to accommodate a growing family. In 1914,

Norm Smith built an addition to provide room for his very large family. The Jim Williams cabin at the Hunter Hereford Ranch has two large wings added in later years.[9] An old photograph of the James and Lydia Uhl residence shows a large cabin with multiple rooms. The R. E. Miller residence, which is extant on the elk refuge, was built after 1892, but prior to 1900. (The W. O. Owen Survey Map of 1892 shows the first Miller cabin located north of the present building.) J. E. Stimson captured the interior of the Miller house; the image shows an affluence not common in Jackson Hole. Pierce Cunningham built a larger house after 1900 north of his first cabin. In 1914, Cunningham's neighbor, Emile Wolff, cut logs for a new and larger home. Bertha Moulton recalled that she and her husband John lived in a small log cabin for the first 17 years of their marriage. They built a pink stucco residence around 1934.[10]

Sawmills provided much-needed lumber for floors, roof, sheathing, and window and door frames. Stephen Leek is credited as the first to introduce a sawmill. He hauled a water-powered mill into the valley from Market Lake, Idaho, in 1893 and set it up on Mill Creek near Wilson, Wyoming. Other sources claim the Whetstone Mining Company hauled a mill into the north end of Jackson Hole around 1889. It is possible that Leek acquired this mill after the failure of the mine.[11]

At any rate, there was at least one sawmill in the valley by 1900, operated by Bonnie Holden for eight months of the year. By 1909, no fewer than three sawmills existed at the south end of the valley. Struthers Burt recalled two active sawmills in Jackson Hole when he and Carncross began constructing the Bar BC in 1912–1913. He recorded the disparaging complaint of one resident, who described the area as "a country where a 12-inch board shrunk an inch a year for 15 years." Lumber could be ordered in advance, but it did not matter much as you took what was delivered and "thanked God for it." Burt called some of the lumber "wanie-edged," a description for boards cut so close to the edge of the log that the bark showed and the board tapered off at one end. Sometimes the edge of a board measured two inches at one end and gradually narrowed to nothing at the other end. The frame addition on the Menor Cabin, built before 1900, suggests that lum-

ber was available. Since, so far as is known, the original roofing on the cabin was board, it implies that lumber was sawn commercially in the valley by 1894, possibly at Leek's water-powered mill. After 1900, frame structures became more common on ranches and farms. In 1919, J. D. "Si" Ferrin set up a water-powered mill to saw lumber for large frame buildings at the Elk Ranch.[12]

Contrary to popular perceptions of sturdy pioneers who secured all they needed from the land, homesteaders in Jackson Hole imported building materials—notably nails, glass, door frames, window frames, and roofing paper. At first, settlers freighted these supplies into the valley from distant communities such as Market Lake and Rexburg, Idaho, but building materials and hardware became available locally when Pap Deloney opened his general mercantile store in 1899.[13]

Thus, using local materials, such as lodgepole pine, and imported hardware and building supplies, settlers developed their farms and ranches. What did a typical homestead look like? The final proof papers of entrants offer some clues, although the detail of descriptions in records varies considerably. Furthermore, desert land entries did not require occupancy, therefore structures were not listed on desert entry papers.

The earliest settlers on Mormon Row and the Gros Ventre established small cattle ranches. At the present Kelly townsite, Albert Nelson constructed an 18 × 24-foot log house with a shingle roof, a log storehouse, a log living room, a shed, and stables by 1904. North of the Nelson place at Kelly Warm Springs, William Kissenger constructed a 16 × 20-foot log house with three rooms, a log stable, and a log shed.[14]

Southeast of Blacktail Butte at Mormon Row, Jim May had completed a five-room cabin and stables by the time he filed final proof papers in 1901. T. A. Moulton completed a new frame house in 1915. Other structures included a cabin, a granary, a stable, and a hoghouse. The granary suggests he cultivated grain, possibly 90-day oats. Jake Johnson settled on his land in 1909 and built a three-room frame house, two log stables, a storehouse, a root cellar, a hen house, and a granary. Andy Chambers homesteaded a tract in 1912; by 1916, the farmstead

Albert Nelson settled in the Kelly area in 1904. His homestead included a log house, shed, storehouse, stables and other improvements. *National Park Service*

consisted of an 18 × 20-foot log house, a 16 × 16-foot stable, and one new dwelling, partially built. The Woodward house was a substantial 20 × 32-foot, one-and-a-half-story log house, consisting of five rooms. It had a stone foundation and a shingle roof. The Harthoorn place consisted of a one-room log house, one incomplete seven-room log house, two log granaries, a large two-story log barn, a hen house, two cellars, and a log machine shed, which became more common with mechanization of farming.[15]

On Antelope Flats, Joe Pfeifer took up a homestead in November 1910 and proved it up with a two-room log home, a barn, and other outbuildings. East of Pfeifer's place and north of Ditch Creek is a hill known as Aspen Ridge. James R. Smith homesteaded the Aspen Ridge Ranch in 1911; by 1916, he had constructed a three-room log dwelling, a log hen house, a cellar, a log barn, and a frame granary.

One-half mile east, James Williams homesteaded the Hunter Hereford Ranch, building a square-shaped log cabin and a small horse stable. Just south of Ditch Creek, Ransom "Mickey" Adams took up a relinquishment in 1911 that is the present Teton Science School. Adams built a four-room house, a large two-story barn (18 × 56 feet), a storehouse, a large cattle shed, a shed, a chicken house, a granary, an icehouse, and a spring house. One building at the school may date from this period.[16]

On the west side of the Snake River, James Manges built a cellar, smokehouse, barn, stable, and woodshed by 1917. He also built an unusual one-and-one-half story log cabin with four rooms. (This building exists today, although modified.) In this area, homestead structures were similar to those near Blacktail Butte, except that none had granaries, indicating that cultivation was restricted to growing hay.

South of Menor's Ferry, homesteaders tried to establish farms and ranches along the narrow strip of land between the Snake River and the moraines and benches at the foot of the Teton Range. Charles Ilse homesteaded the meadow flat just north of Stewart Draw in 1910. His buildings included a two-room log and frame residence and a root cellar. In 1914, William Grant filed an entry next to Ilse. He constructed a seven-room log-and-frame house, a barn, and a chicken house. In the late 1920s, wranglers Shadwick Hobbs and Lewis Fleming filed stock-raising entries south of the JY Ranch. Although they were never developed into full-scale working ranches, their homestead cabins still exist. The Fleming cabin is now the Lower Granite Canyon patrol cabin, while Hobbs's "Starvation" cabin is located on Granite Creek, south of the Granite Canyon Trail. Neither homestead appears to have been developed. Lewis Fleming died in 1926, while Hobbs never established a working ranch headquarters at his cabin.[17]

In the Spread Creek-Buffalo Fork area, more homesteads were devoted to cattle ranching. In 1904, the Uhl ranch consisted of a house, storehouse, shop, spring house, wagon house, smokehouse, stables, and sheds. Pierce Cunningham had built a house, stables, and sheds by 1904. Later homesteads in this area were very similar. Otto Kusche homesteaded what later became the head-

Andy Chambers homesteaded a tract on Mormon Row in 1912. By 1916, the farmstead included this 18 × 20-foot log house.
Arnold Thallheimer

quarters of the Elk Ranch; he built a house, barn, storeroom, and cellar. None of the present structures at Elk Ranch are associated with Kusche's homestead. Si Ferrin began the nucleus of his short-lived ranching empire in 1908; with his wife and ten children, he constructed a residence, barns, and other outbuildings. In 1911, Gottfried Feuz settled on 160 acres with his wife and seven children. By 1917, his homestead consisted of a log house (18 × 36 feet), storehouse, stable, cattle shed, two hen houses, and cellar.[18]

Based on records, the typical homestead in Jackson Hole consisted of a two-room house, usually built of logs. Frame dwellings were more common after 1900. Barns, stables, and storehouses were common outbuildings at both ranches and farms. Granaries and cellars suggested an emphasis on farming, rather than cattle ranching. Everyone tried to live with a relative degree of self-sufficiency. A number of settlers built smokehouses to cure wild game, especially elk. Hen houses indicate the importance of poultry. Hoghouses were much less common, but some settlers kept pigs for personal consumption and, perhaps, sale.

Along with remmant cabins, the buck-rail fence has come to symbolize the homesteaders' frontier in Jackson Hole. Also referred to as a buck-and-pole, buck-and-rail, or four-pole leaning fence, it was the dominant fencing in the first years of settlement, simply because lodgepole pine provided a ready supply of material. The myth prevails that settlers used

this type of fence because it requires no post hole, resting instead on the crossed bucks at each end of the panel. Pioneers reputedly preferred this fence because digging holes in the cobble-laden soils of Jackson Hole was back-breaking work. This is not true. Digging post holes is hard work, but so is cutting and hauling lodgepole pine. A buck-rail fence represented a considerable investment of time and labor. After 1900, barbed wire was introduced in the valley and became the dominant type of fence. If settlers described fences in their proof papers, as often as not they installed "post and 3 wire fence." Homesteaders who continued to construct buck-rail fencing may not have possessed the capital to purchase barbed wire. John Moulton's homestead was typical of many. He constructed a buck-rail fence around his residence, but closed off most of his farm with barbed wire. He recalled that some neighbors objected to the barbed wire, fearing it would injure livestock. If there was concern, it was short-lived, for most of the homesteaders on Mormon Row installed barbed-wire fences.

Occasionally, variations appeared such as a two-pole two-wire buck fence, a modified buck-rail fence that used barbed wire. Post-and-wire fences were sometimes topped with a pole spiked into the posts. These are good fences to use in wildlife migratory routes, for ungulates such as elk and deer can jump them easily without much danger of entangling themselves in the barbed wire. By the 1920s, steel fence posts made their appearance.[19] The buck-rail fence appears frequently in scenic photographs of the park, and their rustic appeal is apparent. However, a post-and-wire fence was more practical for farmers and ranchers. They cost less, took less time to put up, and required less maintenance. The buck-rail fence regained popularity in the 1920s because of its aesthetic appeal, as dude ranches and tourist facilities became more predominant.

Residing for five years on a 160-acre tract was one major requirement of the Homestead Act of 1862; the law also required the entrant to cultivate the land. Most settlers established small cattle ranches and cultivated hay for winter feed. Farmers grew grain crops, primarily 90-day oats that were suitable for areas like Mormon Row. Elevation and climate combined to restrict the growing season for crops. The valley has an average of 60 frost-free days per year. Cyclic weather patterns such as severe winters or occasional droughts prove even more disastrous in a country with such a short growing season.

According to local tradition, John Carnes was the first settler to farm in the valley. He packed dismantled farm machinery to his Flat Creek homestead and probably cultivated native hay. Stephen Leek planted the first domestic grain in the valley at his South Park ranch after 1885. Prior to becoming a rancher, J. D. "Si" Ferrin homesteaded on Twin Creek in the present elk refuge in 1900, where he reportedly proved that oats, wheat, and barley could be raised in the valley. This is a questionable claim, as several homesteaders testified to having planted oats prior to 1900. For instance, Frank Sebastian reported growing 20 acres of oats in 1899. Ferrin may have been the first to raise wheat and barley in the valley. One source claims that Ferrin harvested the first oats as grain in 1902, producing 5,000 bushels. This may be true, as ranchers often harvested oats as hay, rather than risk losing the crop in an attempt to allow the oats to mature.[20]

People raised hay and grain to feed livestock. They cultivated brome grass, timothy, alfalfa, and alsike (a European perennial) clover for hay, and raised barley and oats for both grain and hay. Farmers grew wheat later, but the climate, as well as the lack of a mill, prevented wheat from becoming a dominant crop.[21] Striving to be self-sufficient, most settlers grew garden crops for personal consumption. Potatoes, carrots, turnips, cabbage, rutabagas, onions, peas, beets, radishes, lettuce, and some berries were popular crops. A few settlers raised enough potatoes to sell locally.

After providing a shelter, clearing land became the most important task. Clearing sagebrush was one of the most reviled but necessary chores confronting settlers. If possible, savvy homesteaders filed on land with convenient access to water, and then cut a ditch to the field in order to flood it. Flooding killed the sagebrush and made it easier to clear. Fire was also used to clear fields, but this had to be employed with care. The *Courier* reported farmers busily backfiring grasses in the Aspen Ridge area in 1914, presumably to clear land. There is little available information to determine the extent to which these methods were employed. Grubbing sagebrush—pulling it by hand—was the most common practice. Settlers plowed the soil to loosen roots, grubbed the sagebrush, then stacked and burned it.

Otto Kusche of the Elk Ranch testified that "each year I have grubbed and cleared land which I have need for pasturing my own stock." Between June 1909 and October 1915, Kusche managed to clear a meager 13 acres and seed it to alfalfa. A neighbor, Anton Grosser, cleared ten acres, complaining that his 160-acre tract was "practically covered with willows and aspen brush and is hard to clear." In five years devoted to proving up homesteads, it was common to clear and plow three to seven acres the first season, and perhaps expand to 35 or 40 acres by the fifth year. Other environmental factors hindered the clearing of fields. The soils of Jackson Hole are predominantly glacial deposits and, consequently, the valley floor is covered with quartzite cobbles, commonly the size of large potatoes. Parthenia Stinnett, the daughter of P C. and Sylvia Hansen, recalled clearing cobbles from fields as one of her childhood chores—and not with much fondness. In isolated cases, environmental changes, perhaps natural or induced by man's activities, damaged fields. Martin "Slough Grass" Nelson sold his homestead to Mose Giltner in 1898 because his land on Flat Creek had become so swampy. Sixteen years later, Giltner attempted to drain the swamp by using a dredge.[22]

Jim Chambers stacking hay, 1956. Hay and oats for livestock feed were among the most commonly cultivated crops in the valley. Most farmers practiced alpine valley ranching, grazing their small herds on public lands in the summer, and feeding them hay in the winter. *Jackson Hole Historical Society and Museum*

As stated in an earlier chapter, settlers turned over at least 5,200 acres of land in and adjacent to today's park. This figure is based on claimants' testimonies for nearly 300 homesteads. They undoubtedly cultivated more acreage later, but it is important to understand that very few were lucky enough to locate a 160-acre tract on which all acreage could be farmed. Terrain, access to water, and vegetation were limiting factors. For example, Will Steingraber estimated that only 100 acres of his 160-acre parcel on the Buffalo Fork were suitable for agriculture. Norm Smith was fortunate, because he could cultivate fully 135 acres of his 159-acre homestead. Johnny "Highpockets" Rutherford believed he could cultivate his entire 160 acres on Antelope Flats, even though he managed to break only 16 acres in five years. Jim May, on Mormon Row, found only 65 acres of his land to be cultivable. Along the upper Snake River near Moran, Roy Lozier believed he could farm 150 of 160 acres, even though he claimed 12 acres of timber on the land.[23]

Virtually all settlers cut irrigation ditches to their land and secured water rights approved by the State of Wyoming. These rights were attached to most farms and ranches. Homesteaders constructed ditches with hand labor, sometimes individually, but most often in partnership with one or several neighbors. James I. May cut a ditch, three miles long, from Ditch Creek to his homestead using a plow and team of horses. May and Jim Budge diverted water from the Gros Ventre to their desert entries, cutting another three-mile ditch. In most instances, farmers and ranchers needed irrigation systems to raise crops on their land. Moreover, the Desert Land Act required that desert entries be irrigated to secure title to the land.[24]

After clearing the land and providing water, what did settlers cultivate? Fred Lovejoy located a 160-acre homestead along the Gros Ventre in 1899, where the campground is located today. In five years, he irrigated a ten-acre meadow and cultivated 12 acres in three seasons, presumably hay. He also raised a small vegetable garden. After 1900, Lovejoy added a 160-acre desert entry, cutting a main ditch and one lateral that irrigated 25 acres. He raised oat hay and timothy. In 1903, his 25 acres of oats produced a

mere one-quarter ton of hay per acre, the kind of season that bankrupts farmers. Lovejoy explained that
he "would have produced more but it was destroyed
by gophers and sqirrells [sic]." Presumably, he referred to pocket gophers and Uinta ground squirrels.
His wife, Mary Lovejoy, added a desert entry in
1908, irrigating 45 acres with water diverted from
the Gros Ventre via a three-and-one-half-mile ditch.
Her share of the water amounted to four cubic feet
per second. By 1913 she had planted 45 acres of
wheat and oats, expecting to thresh 1,000 bushels of
grain in the fall. The Lovejoys owned a 640 acre
ranch by 1916, suggesting that even well-irrigated
homesteads of 160 acres were insufficient to provide
a decent living in Jackson Hole.[25]

Just west of today's Kelly, Nels Hoagland, a widower, struggled to start a farm. Filing on a regular
homestead entry and a desert entry in 1897, Hoagland testified that he had raised no crops on his
homestead until 1903, when he managed to complete a ditch. Likewise, it took four years to divert
water from the Gros Ventre via a two-and-one-half-
mile ditch to his desert entry and no crop had been
planted as of 1901. This is a long time to go without
producing crops, and may well have wiped out Hoagland's savings, if he had any. At the Kelly townsite
Bill and Sophie Kelly established a cattle ranch of
40 acres in 1910. Kelly added a 120-acre desert entry
in 1911. He then cut a ditch from the Gros Ventre,
cultivating 20 acres of wheat on the property. In
1917, Sophie Kelly filed a 320-acre desert entry
south of the Gros Ventre in today's elk refuge. Although she failed to bring water to the tract, she
grazed livestock on it for five years and the General
Land Office approved her patent.[26]

Ransom "Mickey" Adams homesteaded a 160-
acre tract that encompasses the present Teton Science School. In five seasons, he cultivated the following crops: 1912: 20 acres, barley and alfalfa; 1913:
45 acres, oats and barley, which produced 30 tons
of hay; 1914: 40 acres, oats and barley; and 1915:
48 acres, oats, barley and alfalfa. His neighbor to the
north, Jim Williams, excavated a ditch that irrigated
100 acres. In five seasons he cleared from 8 to 17
acres, planting oats, barley, and alfalfa.[27]

East of Blacktail Butte, farmers rushed to claim
homesteads after the presidential proclamation of

1908 opened lands to settlement. Farming, rather
than large-scale cattle ranching, dominated this area.
In five seasons, Jacob Johnson cleared and cultivated
110 acres, raising oats and potatoes and 30 head of
livestock. In 1912, John Woodward preempted 160
acres in the Mormon Row area, hoping to provide a
living for his wife and nine children. In the first season, the family raised a garden on one-and-one-half
acres. Between 1913 and 1918, Woodward increased
cultivation from 11-and-one-half acres to 35 acres,
raising oats, hay, and vegetables. A ditch is not mentioned, but one runs through the homestead site. For
domestic use, Woodward excavated a well, digging
98 feet to hit water. This was typical on Mormon
Row, where most wells were dug to a minimum
depth of 90 feet. In contrast, settlers could hit water
at depths as little as 12 feet near rivers. Andy Chambers expanded his fields from 11 acres to 40 acres between 1914 and 1916, producing 1,260 bushels of
grain in 1916. Chambers may have dry farmed his
land, because he did not list a ditch among his improvements.[28]

On Antelope Flats, homesteaders also tried to
establish farms. Between 1911 and 1914, Joe Pfeifer
cleared and cultivated 20 acres, raising barley, oats,
wheat, and a garden. In 1915, he dug a well to a
depth of 104 feet, but it was so dry that he had to
use a sprinkler to settle the dust. Pfeifer gave up on
the well, deciding to use it for a root cellar. He
hauled water for domestic use from Ditch Creek. On
the bench where the Blacktail Ponds Overlook is located today, a young man named Henry Gunther
took up a relinquished homestead in 1914. He cultivated 66 acres of oats and hay by 1917. The Mining
Ditch encountered by Frank Bradley of the Hayden
Survey in 1872 ran across Antelope Flats. Settlers repaired and expanded the ditch to provide water for
their farms.[29]

Similar patterns were followed on the flats south
and west of Blacktail Butte and the Snake River. If
at all possible, farmers and ranchers diverted water
from the Gros Ventre or Snake Rivers or Ditch
Creek to irrigate their fields. Richard Mayers filed a
desert entry in 1902, adding 166 acres to a homestead entry at the present Gros Ventre Junction. He
irrigated five acres with a ditch and four laterals, but
the river flooded the area, inundating his fields for

The winters in Jackson Hole were, and still are, harsh. This 4-horse team and wagon
served as the mail stage on Antelope Flats. *Jackson Hole Historical Society and Museum*

three months. By 1906, he had cleared 22 acres,
planting alfalfa and barley. Roy Nipper filed on a relinquishment in May 1915, west of Blacktail Butte.
He irrigated the land with a six-mile ditch, cultivating 70 acres of oats, barley, and alfalfa by 1919.[30]

Across from the Bill Menor homestead, Holiday
Menor homesteaded 160 acres on the east bank of
the Snake River in 1908. In the first season, he cultivated 20 acres of wheat and barley, harvesting 25
tons of grain hay. The next year, he expanded his
field to 40 acres, raising wheat and barley that he
threshed, producing 350 bushels of grain. He cleared
more acreage until 1912, when he cultivated 80 acres
of wheat and barley, and threshed 1,200 bushels of
grain. From 1912 to 1918, Holiday Menor raised
wheat, barley, and alfalfa on his farm, producing an
average yield of 900 bushels of grain and 35 tons of
hay. Since Menor did not list a ditch among his improvements, and because there is no ditch on his
land, he probably dry farmed.[31]

Agriculture was less important west of the Snake
River. Jimmy Manges cleared 42 acres between
1911 and 1917, raising barley, timothy, and wheat.
By the time Manges sold most of his acreage to
Chester Goss and the Elbo Ranch partnership in

1926, he had little to show for 15 years of work. He
sold 115 acres to Goss for $6,325, more money than
he had ever seen in his life.[32] Charles Ilse and William J. Grant irrigated and cultivated their homestead south of Sawmill Ponds on the Moose-Wilson
Road. Ilse grew 12 acres of timothy, which produced
a mere one and one-half tons per acre. Billy Grant
raised a two-acre garden and 20 acres of clover, timothy, and grain hay. He irrigated 94 acres.[33]

Moritz Locher filed an entry on a relinquishment just south of Jenny Lake in 1915. In two years
he managed to plow only 18 acres, when he perished
in a freak accident. Skiing across the flats north of
Timbered Island, Locher broke his ankle and, unable
to move, died of exposure. After his starved dog
turned up at the Bar BC, rescuers searched for him,
but snowstorms had obliterated his tracks and covered his body. The spring thaw revealed his corpse.
His heirs plowed and planted 22 acres of wheat in
1922 and cut a quarter-mile ditch, but "harvested
nothing." In 1921, Ed K. Smith homesteaded another relinquishment adjacent to the Locher property. Nicknamed "Roan Horse" or "Roany" Smith, he
intended to breed and raise horses. However, since
he was 54 years old at the time, it was more likely a

retirement home. Smith testified before the 1933 Senate Subcommittee hearing in Jackson Hole. When asked what he did for a living on his homestead, Roany Smith replied, "We worked for the Forest Service when we felt like it, fished when we felt like it, and worked on the homestead when we felt like it."[34]

In the Buffalo Fork-Spread Creek area, settlers tended to raise hay and cattle. With the aid of irrigation, Charlie Hedrick cultivated 40–50 acres of hay on his homestead. Hedrick's neighbor, Rudy Harold, broke 40 acres between 1910 and 1915, raising timothy. He dug a well, and struck water at 18 feet, a sharp contrast to the 100-foot-deep wells on Mormon Row. At two homesteads which became the Triangle X, John Fee Jr., and William Jump filed entries in 1909. Fee irrigated and raised 30 acres of native hay, producing one and a quarter tons per acre. Jump cultivated much less, a trifling seven acres of oats for about 13 years. Orin Seaton built a home in 1909 and moved his wife and three children to the ranch in 1910. By the time he filed his final proof papers in 1913, he had fenced and irrigated 82 acres, raising hay.[35]

Along the Buffalo Fork in 1909, Walt Germann irrigated his land, cultivating six acres of barley the first season, and expanding to 20 acres of clover, alfalfa, and oats two seasons later. East of Germann, John Smejkal, a Bohemian immigrant, homesteaded in 1911. Clearing ten acres in 1912, he gradually expanded his fields to 75 acres in 1918, trying a variety of crops such as native hay, barley, clover, oat hay and timothy.[36]

In the old Moran area, Joe Markham claimed a relinquishment in 1914 for 160 acres east of Oxbow Bend. By 1918, he had raised 65 acres of barley. On Willow Flats, George H. "Herb" Whiteman homesteaded in 1914, taking up residence in 1915. While working at Sheffield's camp or on the Jackson Lake Dam, he proved up his irregularly-shaped homestead. In 1915, Whiteman reported clearing 15 acres of sagebrush and cutting 45 tons of native grass. The next year he seeded 50 acres to timothy and winter wheat, harvesting more than 50 tons of hay. In 1917, the same acreage produced 62 tons of wild hay and wheat hay.[37]

North and east of Moran, there were a few scattered homesteads. At the outlet of Two Ocean Lake, William C. Thompson filed an entry in 1914. Four years later he planted 20 acres of barley and oats. On Pilgrim Creek, Samuel R. Wilson took up a homestead in 1916. Between 1917 and 1920, he cleared 21 acres, cultivating timothy, alfalfa, and barley one year, trying clover and millet another year. In 1920, he planted oats. Wilson irrigated his field with a three-quarter mile ditch that diverted water from Pilgrim Creek.[38]

After 1900, new advances in dry farming helped farmers cultivate arid lands. On the Great Plains, farmers reclaimed thousands of acres abandoned during the drought of the 1880s and 1890s. Although settlers in Jackson Hole preferred to irrigate their fields, dry farming provided a way to cultivate lands without irrigation. Based on available information, dry farming may have been more important in Jackson Hole than has been recognized.

Dry farming represented, from a farmer's viewpoint, man's victory over nature—a way to grow crops with a minimum of water. Two practices were critical: using drought-resistant grains, and conserving moisture in the soil, particularly the subsoil. Wheats became the most important crop in the West, because some varieties are especially drought-resistant. Winter wheat, which is very drought-resistant, can also survive extremely cold temperatures. Winter wheat is planted in the fall, when rains help the seeds germinate. Spring wheat, which is grown primarily on the northern plains, can survive even harsher winters. Farmers plant it in the spring, and it matures in late summer. Spring wheat is the most suitable variety for Jackson Hole. To accomplish this, farmers leave land fallow on alternate years, which requires double the acreage. On the Great Plains, strip farming was employed to reduce wind erosion. Weed control was also important, as they compete with grain for the limited moisture.[39]

Settlers practiced dry farming in Jackson Hole, but to what extent is not known. A number of claimants failed to list ditches among their improvements, which would not have been omitted in final proof papers. This omission suggests that they dry farmed. As noted earlier, Holiday Menor listed no ditches.

In 1912, Earle Harris, who homesteaded south of Menor, raised 30 acres of barley and wheat, which produced 18 tons of hay. Two clues suggest Harris dry farmed his land; barley and wheat are both drought-resistant crops and the 18-ton yield is consistent with dry farm production. On Antelope Flats and Mormon Row, a number of settlers such as John Kneedy, Talmadge Holland, John Nixon, Henry Gunther, and George Riniker raised crops, but did not list ditches as improvements. Talmadge Holland planted fall wheat (winter wheat) in 1918, but the severe winter killed the crop. John and T. A. Moulton dry farmed grain until the state built ditches to their properties in the late 1920s. Clark Moulton, T. A. Moulton's son, dry farmed a 160-acre parcel for a number of years, until he sold out to the National Park Service in 1971. Nevertheless, irrigating lands remained the dominant practice in the valley.[40]

Rapid improvements in farm machinery also impacted agriculture in Jackson Hole. Horse-powered machinery cut the time required to plow, plant, and harvest—and partially solved the problem of labor shortages. The Wilson-Cheney party cut native grass by hand in the fall of 1889 to provide winter feed for their livestock. But these were temporary methods for most settlers. By 1900, ranchers and farmers cut hay with horse-drawn mowers. Settlers rented or borrowed machinery if they could not afford equipment. In the spring of 1914, residents of the Flat Creek area heard a mysterious chugging noise echoing through the valley. The noise came from the new steam-powered tractor owned by the J. P Ranch Company. Farmers on Mormon Row used a steam-powered threshing machine to harvest oats and wheat, which provided a more efficient—although not particularly labor-saving—method of threshing grain. It took no fewer than half a dozen people to feed stalks of grain into the machine. The steam-powered tractor also failed to displace the horse as a means of power, because the former was expensive and not especially efficient on smaller farms. The gasoline-powered tractor, first developed by Henry Ford and Henry G. Ferguson during World War I, eventually displaced the horse on the farm.[41]

Several valley residents made limited use of other machinery. The windmill, a common innova-

tion used to draw water from wells in the American West, apparently was not commonly adopted in Jackson Hole. No such windmills are known to exist on the park's few remaining farmsteads, and only one settler, Leslie Kafferlin, reported constructing one in his final proof papers. The Chambers family used one to generate electric power. At least one windmill is extant at a Spring Gulch ranch, south of today's park. William C. Thompson installed a hydraulic crane to pump water from the outlet of Two Ocean Lake. Bill Menor used a waterwheel to draw water from the Snake to his truck garden north of his cabin, but neither of these were common.[42]

As settlers preempted more land in the valley, conflicts with wildlife occurred. During especially severe winters, the elk raided the haystacks of the settlers. In response, homesteaders tried fences, guarded the haystacks themselves or with dogs, and fired guns to scare the elk—or, in some cases, shot them. None of these methods were completely successful. Elsewhere, frontiersmen solved the problem by exterminating the elk, but this was not an option in Jackson Hole. As noted elsewhere, many settlers earned a significant portion of their livelihood guiding wealthy dudes on elk hunts to secure trophy animals. Elk hides, antlers, heads, eyeteeth, meat, and even live elk became significant exports. Instead of killing off the elk, other solutions were adopted—such as controlled hunting, payments for damaged crops, and reserved lands. In contrast, ranchers had no reservations about eliminating the gray wolf in Jackson Hole. Stockmen's associations, such as the Fish Creek Wolf Association, were formed to exterminate wolves.[43] Rodents caused serious damage to crops. Fred Lovejoy produced a meager six tons of oat hay on his desert entry because gophers and squirrels destroyed the bulk of the crop. North of the Lovejoy ranch, Jim Budge experienced similar problems, when Uinta ground squirrels ruined most of a ten-acre crop in 1904.[44]

Severe weather, such as a prolonged drought or a 15-minute hailstorm, could destroy fields. Jim Chambers raised a prime crop of wheat on Poverty Flats (Mormon Row), only to have it wiped out by a sudden devastating hailstorm. He decided to raise hay and cattle in the future. Hail pummeled Geraldine

Lucas's entire 20 acres of wheat in 1914; she raised timothy and alfalfa in succeeding years. Frost or freezing temperatures killed crops, and the hopes of some homesteaders. Talmadge Holland planted fall wheat at his farm on Antelope Flats in 1918, only to lose it to sub-zero temperatures. In 1916, Rufus Smith reported the loss of five acres of oats to frost and roaming cattle at his homestead on the Buffalo Fork. Along the Snake River above Pacific Creek, John R. Brown lost ten acres of oats to freezing temperatures in the same year. In a country that looked so green and appeared to have abundant water in snow-fed rivers and streams, drought seemed a remote possibility, yet settlers learned differently. William C. Thompson intended to plant wheat at his homestead straddling Two Ocean Creek in 1916, but the ground was too dry for a crop. At his farm north of Kelly, Charles Davis plowed 35 acres in 1917, but found the soil too dry for a crop.[45]

Even livestock could destroy crops, if homesteaders failed to install or maintain fences properly. J. R. Brown lost his first three-acre crop of oats to cattle in 1915. On Pacific Creek, Elmer Arthur planted 22 acres of clover in 1916; cattle ruined the entire crop before he could harvest it. In a few cases, homesteaders failed to harvest crops with no explanation. Roland Hunter raised a one-half-acre truck garden on his Buffalo Fork homestead around 1916, but harvested none of it. Joseph Chapline cultivated more than 14 acres of oats in 1920, yet simply let livestock grab it off.[46]

Some claimants were victimized by incredibly bad luck, or their own lack of initiative. In 1919, John G. Brown (not the John R. Brown mentioned above) homesteaded along the Buffalo Fork, but did not take up actual residence "as the snow was so deep that I could not get onto my claim any sooner." He managed to plant a small garden but harvested very little of it.[47] Charles Shinkle filed preemption papers on a 160-acre parcel north of Kelly in 1910. His final proof papers documented his setbacks:

1911	2 acres veg. cattle got it.
1912	3 acres 1/2 acre veg. 1 ton.
1913	No crop
1914	No crop too dry.
1915	3 acres cattle got it.
1916	3 acres 1 a.veg. 1/4 ton veg.

In 1922, William Smith filed an entry on 159 acres near the south entrance of the park. He plowed 15 acres the first season, then added five acres in 1923, planting 20 acres of oats, but "on account of drought and ground rodunts [sic] . . . crop wasn't worth harvesting." The next year he tried again, but experienced the same results. He filed final proof papers in 1928, confessing "I got discouraged with former results and did not again plant a crop. . . ."[48]

Many settlers relinquished their claims prior to securing a patent or title to the land. A significant number of people, forgotten in local history, tried homesteading in the valley, but gave up and left. Some sold their relinquishments, while others simply abandoned their claims. Norm Smith purchased the rights to his farm at Blacktail Butte from a man named Pembril in 1907. On Antelope Flats, several homesteaders acquired relinquishments after 1910. T. H. Baxter took over the abandoned property of Andy Bathgate, who returned to Sugar City, Idaho, in the fall of 1914. A man named Al Sellars relinquished his tract to John Kneedy in 1917. John Nixon took over the John Winkler claim in 1915. According to local tradition, Grant Shinkle homesteaded at the site of the present Teton Science School prior to Mickey Adams arrival in 1911. At Jenny Lake, both Moritz Locher and Ed Smith filed on entries that already had cabins on site, suggesting that others had given up the tracts. Tillman Holland reported a cabin on his entry when he took up residence in 1917. Joe LePage's 640-acre stockraising entry along the west bank of the Snake River had been claimed by Sinclair "Slim" Armstrong in 1922. He relinquished title to LePage in 1927. Joe Markham filed on an entry east of Oxbow Bend in 1914, after Steve Mahoney, the original claimant, was killed in an engine room accident at the Jackson Lake Dam. Dave Spalding homesteaded the JY, before relinquishing rights to Louis Joy around 1907. Even though no records explain why people abandoned their land, hard winters, isolation, lack of a "start" or capital, and the back-breaking work required to build cabins, clear fields, and dig ditches probably discouraged them.[49]

One major limitation, and a critical one for many homesteaders, was the lack of a "start," or sufficient money to devote all of their time to ranching and farming. Families had to be fed and clothed, while equipment, building materials, tools, planting seed, and breeding stock had to be purchased. Few possessed the cash to pay for these items. Furthermore, any kind of bad luck—such as an illness in the family, a barn destroyed by fire, a failed hay crop, or a dead draft horse—could prove disastrous. Thus, most settlers raised cash by working at other occupations or mortgaging their homesteads; sometimes they did both.

Floyd Wilson took up a homestead on the sagebrush flats near today's airport, intending to start a small ranch with a pair of horses and four cattle. Joe Jones started with four horses and four cows and leased acreage to Nephi Moulton for grazing. Neither had much of a start for cattle ranching. The Jump family homesteaded on Ditch Creek in the eastern side of the valley. Ethel Jump recalled that her family could not make a living on the homestead, so they hauled freight, guided dudes, trapped, hunted, and mined coal along Ditch Creek to sell locally. J. D. "Si" Ferrin farmed land on Flat Creek before becoming the largest rancher in Jackson Hole by 1920. In addition to being a farmer and rancher, Ferrin hauled freight, cut and hauled timber, and operated a sawmill. He also served as a state game warden for 14 years, earning a reputation as one of the most effective wardens in the valley. Many settlers became jacks-of-all-trades, taking advantage of any opportunity to earn hard cash.[50]

Besides farming land and grazing livestock, homesteaders used natural resources to earn a living. Trapping is generally associated with the mountain man's frontier, which ended around 1840. Yet itinerant trappers worked the valley during the years prior to settlement, as trapping and hunting continued to be an important economic enterprise in the West throughout the nineteenth century. Pierce Cunningham trapped for a living when he first came to the valley. Pioneer S. N. Leek also trapped to provide an income. After homesteading in the Flat Creek area in 1904, Jim Chambers spent the first winter trapping. He earned $200, enough to purchase a cow, chickens, and two small pigs. Coyotes, beaver, and members of the weasel family, such as pine marten, mink, and muskrat, were the primary targets of trappers. Andy Chambers trapped on the Snake River

from 1918 to 1928. Many were not very scrupulous when it came to trapping illegally. Indeed, poaching added some excitement to the otherwise routine task of running traplines every few days.[51]

As noted earlier, the eyeteeth of elk were valuable commodities, used primarily as watch charms by members of the Benevolent and Protective Order of Elks. Settlers removed the teeth from winter-killed elk and garnered as much $10 to $100 a pair, which was a considerable sum. The high prices eventually caused serious trouble. Rather than content themselves with winter-killed elk, a new kind of poacher—the tusker—began shooting elk for their eyeteeth alone. Tusking reached epidemic proportions before vigilantes acted to curb the problem.[52]

Cutting and hauling timber for fencing and construction materials provided another source of income for settlers. For example, D. C. Nowlin contracted with Jim Chambers to cut lodgepole fencing for the elk refuge. In 1914, Mickey Adams and Luther Hoagland hauled timber for Jim May, possibly for the construction of a church. Others invested in sawmills, such as S. N. Leek, J. D. Ferrin, and the Schofield brothers. Gold was panned from rivers and streams, if not in commercially viable amounts, in enough quantities to provide a little extra cash. Noble and Samuel Gregory earned enough from small-scale placer mining to pay for their annual stock of supplies. Settlers filed a large number of placer claims and some lode claims, hopeful of striking it rich. Early pioneers such as Uncle Jack Davis and Johnny Counts washed tons of river gravel and silt, but never found a profitable claim. One source estimated that Uncle Jack Davis washed 100 rocker boxes of dirt per day and retrieved about a penny's worth of gold for each box load. He did not get rich on a dollar a day.[53]

Many homesteaders worked for wages to live and provide capital for proving up their homesteads. John Rutherford testified that he left his homestead from June 1910 to April 1911 "to earn money to live on and to improve the land." He and his wife were absent from the land from Christmas Eve 1913 to April 1914; while the Rutherfords awaited the birth of their second child, and John Rutherford fed cattle to support his family. Herb Whiteman worked either for the Reclamation Service or Ben Sheffield "to

Settlers cut blocks of ice in the winter; the ice would be stored in well-insulated ice houses to provide refrigeration throughout the summer. *Grand Teton National Park*

earn money to pay bills to improve my entry." Whiteman's neighbor, Charlie Christian, left his homestead from December 1919 to the end of April 1920 to work in the coal mines at Superior, Wyoming.[54] James Manges did not support himself at his Taggart Creek homestead, but worked as a carpenter at the Bar BC in 1913. S. N. Leek hired the Estes brothers to thrash grain at his South Park ranch in 1909. Providing their own team and working for two days, they earned $5. E. B. Ferrin hired out to saw wood for $1 per cord in 1915.[55]

The emergence of dude ranches after 1907 created jobs in the valley. At the Bar BC in the early 1920s, Struthers Burt and Horace Carncross hired "two cooks, a dishwasher, two waitresses, two cabin-girls, a housekeeper, two laundresses, a rastabout [sic], a carpenter, a rastabout's [sic] helper, two horse wranglers, a teamster, a foreman, two young dude wranglers, a truck driver and two guides, two camp horse-wranglers, and two camp cooks." Counting the owners and their wives, the ranch needed 29 people to care for 52 dudes. The same year he submitted his final proof papers, Charles Ilse worked at the Bar BC filling in for wrangler Lewis Fleming. Jimmy Manges worked for a number of dude ranches over his lifetime. In 1924, he returned from Leigh Canyon with a pack outfit from the JY, only to start work as caretaker for the Double Diamond Dude

Ranch. Although he ranched in South Park, Frank Tanner worked as a wrangler at the JY, the Bar BC, and the Half Moon after 1918. A few worked for dude ranches so long that their names became as synonymous with the ranch as the owners. Frank Giles was a cowpuncher who became a wrangler at the Bar BC, and later the caretaker and foreman of Burt's Three Rivers Ranch. Frank Coffin homesteaded on the Buffalo Fork, but worked for Dad Turner at the Triangle X for most of his life until his death in 1951. Dude ranches provided employment not only for men, but for their wives and daughters.[56]

Others built facilities to cater to hunters. Stephen Leek became one of the first to guide eastern dudes in Jackson Hole, one of the most prominent being George Eastman. Prior to 1900, Leek constructed a hunting lodge at the north end of Leigh Lake; the establishment was known as Leek's "clubhouse." He later established Leek's Camp on the east side of Jackson Lake. Ben Sheffield was the largest early outfitter, establishing a lodge and headquarters at Moran. Leek and Sheffield devoted more time to the guide business than most settlers.

Since hunting season took place in the fall, farmers and ranchers reserved this period for guiding dudes. For example, Frank Price filed preemption papers on 160 acres on the north side of the Gros Ventre River in 1901. In 1906, he testified that he was absent for two months every year guiding "tourists." A remarkable number of Jackson Hole settlers were involved in the guide and outfitters business on a part-time basis. Roy Lozier, who homesteaded near Moran, guided hunters for almost 35 years and was considered one of the best in the valley. Abe Ward of Wilson not only ran a hotel, but worked as a tour guide for years; he guided George Eastman for nine seasons. John Cherry, one of the valley's first ranchers, guided dudes until he left the valley around 1917. He was so proficient at "spinning long yarns" that one of his dudes based a book on Cherry, titled *The Life and Lies of John Cherry*. Outfitters hired local help. In 1914, Rudy Harold guided a party of Los Angeles attorneys into the backcountry to hunt elk and bighorn sheep. Charlie Hedrick and J. P "Pete" Nelson accompanied Harold as guides. The J. P Nelson photograph collection records the hunting expeditions of Moser and Trexler; some of the packers and guides included ranchers Frank Sebastian, Frank Petersen, and Guy Germann. The list of guides is long: George Ross, Cal Carrington, Louie Fleming, Milt Young, Jim Budge, James Manges, George "Herb" Whiteman, Jack Eynon, Joe Jones, Dick Winger, and the Wort family, to name a few.[57]

Freighters also assumed special importance in this remote mountain valley. J. D. "Si" Ferrin freighted supplies from Idaho over Teton Pass and throughout the valley. A number of homesteaders hauled freight over the Ashton-Moran freight road for the Reclamation Service and private individuals.[58] Contracts to carry mail were coveted, even though the hours were long and bad weather made the work miserable. The job could be dangerous, too. River fords, skittish horses, and avalanches in winter were hazards that went with the job. Until the 1930s, mail was delivered to Jackson Hole via the Oregon Short Line through Idaho, then by wagon, sled, or skis over rugged Teton Pass. Jack Eynon, who migrated to Jackson Hole from Victor, Idaho, packed mail over the pass on snowshoes for several winters. Early pioneers such as rancher Noble Gregory and Mart Henrie also carried mail in the valley. Henrie hauled mail from Jackson to Moran from 1902 to 1910, while proving up his homestead in the

Kelly area. During hard economic times, mail contracts could make a real difference. Andy Chambers had the Jackson-Moran mail contract from 1932 to 1940. At the same time, he raised hay and cattle on his Mormon Row homestead.[59] Operating post offices provided another source of income, and it was common for women to be the designated postmasters. Of 13 postmasters at Elk between 1897 and 1968, ten were women. All were wives of local ranchers, or were homesteaders themselves, such as Eva Topping.[60]

Mail contracts and postal appointments were two of the numerous jobs classified "government" work. A common perception exists that Jackson Hole settlers were rugged individualists who tamed the land with sheer grit and initiative. Government was an obstacle and hindrance that people could do fine without—a common perception in the West even today. In truth, many Jackson Hole pioneers worked for the county, state, or federal government either through contracts or direct employment. The arrival of the Forest Service, National Park Service, Reclamation Service, Biological Survey, and the State Game and Fish Department marked a new age after 1900. These bureaus regulated, and often restricted, resource uses so common on the nineteenth-century frontier. As the State of Wyoming established laws regulating hunting, fishing, and trapping, local citizens were hired as game wardens, both part-time and full-time. Albert Nelson and D. C. Nowlin were the first game wardens in the valley. Ranchers J. D. Ferrin and Roy McBride also worked as game wardens. Road construction and maintenance provided a very important source of cash in the valley. County, state, and federal governments allocated funds for a succession of road improvements in the years after 1900. For example, Luther Hoagland hired out himself and a team of horses to work on road improvements in Yellowstone in 1914. The construction of the dams at Jackson Lake in 1907 and 1910 generated an economic boom in the valley. Many homesteaders worked at the dam for wages, among them P C. Hansen, Joe Pfeifer, and Herb Whiteman. These construction projects brought new settlers to Jackson Hole. Harold Hammond first came to the valley in 1910 to work for the Reclamation Service as a wrangler. In 1913, he filed entry papers on the White Grass Ranch.

The creation of the Teton Forest Reserve in 1897 brought a new frontier character to Jackson Hole. R. E. Miller, one of the valley's first homesteaders, was the supervisor from 1902 to 1918, earning a salary of $2,000 per year. Unable to make a living as Jackson's first dentist, C. D. Horel received an appointment as a forest ranger. His wife, May Horel, homesteaded along Cottonwood Creek near Moose. Albert Gunther and his brother, Henry, had been raised by the Infangers on Flat Creek. In his early 20s, Albert Gunther homesteaded on Mormon Row in 1908. When times got tough, he worked for the Forest Service at Kelly for 13 years.[61]

Rather than try to earn a living year-round and endure the long winters, a few settlers left the valley each fall and returned after the snowmelt. Andrew Newbold returned to his "Lone Tree" Ranch in April 1914 after leaving for the winter. William Ireton, who homesteaded on Antelope Flats, spent the winter of 1917–1918 in Chicago. May Horel returned to her ranch on Cottonwood Creek in 1917 after wintering in Oregon with her three children. Ellen Dornan left her small tract in 1922, wintering in Pennsylvania. The Sensenbachs, who homesteaded the Highlands Ranch, also spent the winter of 1927–1928 in Pennsylvania. H. C. Ericcson, an attorney from Kansas, was a "suitcase" rancher and land speculator, who spent each winter in Kansas between 1923 and 1931. One entrant, Anton Grosser, left his homestead for more than a year in 1914 for unknown reasons. He failed to acknowledge this absence in his final proof papers, submitted in 1916, a clear instance of false testimony to secure a patent.[62]

Jackson Hole settlers remained mobile after moving to the valley. Mose Giltner owned a ranch just south of Spring Gulch in 1892. Six years later, he purchased the "Slough Grass" Nelson property on Flat Creek, even though it had serious drainage problems. Nelson moved to the Zenith area near the confluence of the Snake and Gros Ventre Rivers. Joe Heniger lived on three ranches or homesteads over his lifetime. Heniger came to Jackson Hole in 1900 and purchased the John Emery place in the Flat

Creek area. Around 1909, he sold this property and filed preemption papers on 160 acres in the north end of the valley, not far from the Wolff ranch. Heniger then sold this property and moved to Utah around 1920, only to return later and purchase the Thomas Murphy place on Mormon Row. Si Ferrin farmed on Flat Creek in 1900, but sold this property and located a homestead south of the Buffalo Fork in 1908. Pierce Cunningham, tired of ranching, sold his 320-acre property to J. P Nelson for $6,000 in 1909. Other sources claim the Cunninghams traded the ranch for the Jackson Hotel. Five years later, the Nelsons sold the ranch to Maggie Cunningham for $6,500. The Cunninghams sold the hotel to Jack Eynon, who relocated in the valley from Victor, Idaho. Occasionally, people staked out a homestead only to find it unsuitable for a farm or ranch. Tom Jump located a good tract of land along the Snake River near Moose after 1900. The first winter he found the snowdrifts to be impassible and abandoned the property for a place on Ditch Creek. Ranchers and farmers leased their properties on occasion, although the records do not indicate if this was a common practice. In 1917, for example, Don Miller leased the Carpenter, Ireton, and Geck homesteads on Antelope Flats. Miller later purchased the Adams ranch on Ditch Creek and leased it to the Kent family.[63]

Like most frontiers, whether the miners' or the farmers', the people who made the most money were merchants or professionals who supplied goods and services. Some homesteaders left their land after a number of years, or worked at an occupation from their farms or ranches. Albert Nelson worked as a taxidermist for about six months of the year at his Savage Ranch at Kelly. His neighbor, William J. Kelly, established a cattle ranch, but made his living as a cattle broker, buying and selling cattle for export. Frank Lasho, homesteading along the Snake River near today's airport, listed his trade as "smithy." Mart Henrie homesteaded in the Kelly area from 1899 to 1910, when he moved to Jackson and opened a boot and harness shop. Norm and Alice Bladon homesteaded west of Menor's Ferry in 1914, while living and working in Jackson to earn money to prove up their land. Bladon was a taxidermist. Joe

Jones left his homestead south of Blacktail Butte and moved to Jackson in 1912. He established the Elk Store, a pool hall and tobacco parlor. Jones later started a grocery, which he ran for ten years. Dick Winger migrated to Jackson Hole in 1912, filing papers on land he had never seen. Winger had been in the valley only a short time when he purchased the *Jackson's Hole Courier* in 1913, which he published and edited for the next six years. Winger later worked as a realtor and contractor on road projects. William Grant eventually opened a grocery on his homestead along the present Moose-Wilson Road, which also became the first Moose Post Office in 1923.[64]

Many of Jackson Hole's settlers left the valley to retire. They left for a number of reasons, such as poor health or to escape the bone-chilling winters. Jackson Hole's first permanent settlers, John Holland and John Carnes, were gone by 1900. Holland left for Oregon, while Carnes located much closer at Ft. Hall, Idaho. Idaho became a popular retirement location because the cost of living was cheaper and the climate milder than Jackson Hole, yet it was close to friends and relatives. Jack Shive retired to Idaho Falls after selling out in 1919.[65] Pierce Cunningham moved to Victor, Idaho, after selling out to the Snake River Land Company in 1928. In 1918, James I. May retired to Honeyville, Utah, another popular location. James and Lydia Uhl moved to Utah in 1918, selling their 240-acre ranch to the Cunninghams. In 1917, John Cherry and "Pap" Nickell sold their acreage at Warms Springs to A. J. Whidden and Dr. W. R. Gillespie. Having nothing to do but rest and fish, Cherry retired to Salmon, Idaho, returning to Jackson Hole in the summers. Nickell retired in southern Missouri. Billy Bierer sold his homestead on the Gros Ventre to Guil Huff and moved to his daughter's home in Pennsylvania, where he died in 1923.[66]

California became perhaps the most popular retirement location, obviously because of its desirable climate. Tired of contending with the vagaries of the Snake River made worse by the regulated water flow from the Jackson Lake Dam, as well as the extreme weather conditions in the valley, Bill Menor sold his ferry and homestead to Maud Noble in 1918 and re-

tired to San Diego, California. Holiday Menor sold out in 1928 and joined his brother. Harry Smith had homesteaded only a very short time along the Gros Ventre before selling his ranch to P C. Hansen. He moved to San Bernadino, California, and became a citrus grower. Others who moved to California were Jude Allen, Karl Kent, Doc Steele, and James Uhl, who left Utah after his wife's death. So many Jackson Hole residents retired to California that they were able to hold reunions, such as a picnic in 1939 attended by nearly 70 former residents.[67]

Poor health forced some to leave the valley. Burdened with a bad heart, John G. Brown sold his homestead on the Buffalo Fork and relocated to Oregon in 1918. Mickey Adams moved to Grass Valley, California, because of a heart condition. The Uhls moved because of Lydia Uhl's poor health. Fred Cunningham left Jackson Hole in 1920, seriously ill with cancer. Despondent over poor health, he committed suicide later that year.[68]

Many of Jackson Hole's pioneers retired during the economically depressed years following World War I. The armistice of November 11, 1918, ended the war, as well as the high demand—and high prices—for American farm products. Prices plummeted in 1919, beginning two decades of depression in American agriculture. In addition, a severe drought parched much of the American West in 1919, delivering another blow to farmers and ranchers. In Jackson Hole, settlers watched helplessly as crops shriveled and cured under the relentless sun. Settler after settler testified to the completeness of the disaster in their final proof papers. On Antelope Flats, Talmadge Holland planted oats and barley but, on account of drought, produced no crops. Neighbor Ray C. Kent, who homesteaded the Lost Creek Ranch, reported "no harvest on account of drouth." West of Blacktail Butte, Sam Smith wrote "dry weather, no farm." John Kneedy, east of the Snake River, lost his crop. West of Menor's Ferry, the recently widowed Alice Bladon produced one ton of potatoes, "but no oats hay, It was too dry." Horace Eynon did not grow a crop on his Spread Creek homestead as it was "too dry." The drought lasted 100 days before an afternoon rainshower settled dust in the valley.

However, as the *Courier* reported, it was too late for most crops.[69]

One bad year does not spell doom for farmers and ranchers. But bad years tend to accumulate and carry over into succeeding years. Frank Bramen lost his crop on his Pacific Creek homestead in 1919, but planted no crop the next year because of the loss of his workhorses. Horace Eynon did not cultivate any crop in 1920 because of a "lack of feed for his stock." The 1919 drought had ruined his crop the previous year.[70] The *Jackson's Hole Courier* listed 34 foreclosures on farms and ranches in Teton County between 1923 and 1932 and a handful of tax sales. It began with the foreclosure of the Tillman and Mattie Holland place near Kelly in 1923. The Hollands were unable to pay off $500 borrowed from Ellen Hanshaw in 1920. In addition, they owed $153.32 in interest and $75 in attorney's fees. As a result, Holland, his wife, and six children lost their land. Most ranchers and farmers scrabbled to make ends meet. Judging from the county records, most got by, for relatively few mortgages were taken out in the 1920s.[71] Still, as the years passed, the lists of property owners owing back taxes increased until they took up a full page in 1926. The roll included some of Teton County's most prominent citizens.

Dude rancher Struthers Burt believed the valley's economic problems originated with the unfortunate propensity of the American to try "to suit the country to himself," rather than "suit himself to the country." According to Burt, cattle ranching was the only suitable agricultural use for the valley. The farmers who came to Jackson Hole preempted grazing range and, in Burt's opinion, were unable to make a living on the land. In his *The Diary of a Dude Wrangler*, published in 1924, Burt wrote "the first farmers came into my valley about ten years ago and today they are broken and ruined men."[72]

A series of executive orders in 1926 and 1927 withdrew public lands in Jackson Hole from settlement, effectively closing the homesteader's frontier. In 1928, the Snake River Land Company began purchasing most of the private lands in Jackson Hole north of the Gros Ventre River. The company, financed by John D. Rockefeller Jr., purchased more than 32,000 acres over a six-year period. The land, which would eventually become part of Grand Teton National Park, included many of the former farms and ranches of Jackson Hole's pioneers.

Notes

1. Census of the United States, 1900, Jackson Precinct.

2. Billington, *Westward Expansion*, pp. 335–337; and Frederick Merk, *History of the Western Movement*, (New York: Alfred A Knopf, 1978), pp. 330–346.

3. Billington, *Westward Expansion*, pp. 599–606.

4. Ibid., p. 607.

5. Merk, *History of West*, p. 474; and Driggs, *History of Teton Valley*, pp. 151–156.

6. Interview with Jim Budge by Jo Anne Byrd, #5, "Last of Old West Series;"

7. Frances Judge, "Second Life," *Atlantic Monthly* (July 1954):58.

8. Interview with Ellen Dornan, #10.

9. Homestead Patents, Homestead Cert. 1006, Lander, James Budge, 1904; and *Jackson's Hole Courier*, May 7, 1914.

10. J. E. Stimson Collection, "Interior of R. Miller's Home, Jackson Hole, Wyoming," D102, Photograph, Wyoming State Archives; Owen, T41N, R116W, 6th P.M.; Harold and Josephine Fabian Collection, Grand Teton National Park; *Jackson's Hole Courier*, September 3, 1914; and *Jackson Hole Guide*, May 24, 1974.

11. Brown, *Souvenir History of Jackson Hole*, p. 12; and Hayden, *Trapper to Tourist*, p. 30. Accounts are contradictory regarding the first sawmill in Jackson Hole and how it arrived here. Leek was the first resident to operate a sawmill in the valley.

12. *Jackson's Hole Courier* January 28, 1909, reprinted in *Jackson's Hole Courier*, January 29, 1948; Census of the United States, 1900, Jackson Precinct; and Struthers Burt, *Diary*, pp. 131–132.

13. Struthers Burt, *Diary*, p. 13; and *Jackson Hole Guide*, October 14, 1965.

14. Homestead Patents: Homestead Cert. 1049, Evanston, Albert Nelson, 1904; and Homestead Cert. 526, Lander, William Kissenger, 1904.

15. Homestead Patents: Homestead Cert. 334, Lander, James May, 1901; Homestead Cert. 1006, Evanston, James Budge, 1904; 496735, Jacob Johnson, 1914; 534689, T. A. Moulton, 1915; 542215, Andrew Chambers, 1916;

and 705531, John W. Woodward, 1918; and *Jackson's Hole Courier*, May 8, 1916.

16. Homestead Patents: 486627, James Williams, 1915; 517650, Ransom Adams, 1915; and 587696, J. R. Smith, 1916.

17. Homestead Patents: 639818, James Manges, 1917; 615962, Charles Ilse, 1917; 737603, William Grant, 1919; 1037175, Shadwick Hobbs, 1929; and 1038450, Lewis Fleming, 1929. I have never found a satisfactory explanation as to why the Hobbs cabin is referred to as "starvation" cabin, an intriguing description.

18. Homestead Patents: Homestead Cert. 1181, Evanston, J. P. Cunningham, 1904; Homestead Cert. 1152, Evanston, James Uhl, 1904; 323588, J. D. Ferrin, 1912; 522255, Otto Kusche, 1915, and 601314, Gottfried Feuz, 1917.

19. *Jackson Hole Guide*, May 20, 1976; and Homestead Patent 1037175, Hobbs, 1929.

20. *Jackson's Hole Courier*, July 16, 1931, and March 25, 1943; *Jackson Hole Guide*, December 2, 1965; and Nellie Van DerVeer, "Teton County-Pioneer Stories," WPA Subject File 1328, Wyoming State Archives.

21. M. H. Kneedy operated a flour mill at Kelly for a time.

22. *Jackson's Hole Courier*, September 3, 1914, and August 17, 1916; Homestead Patents: 522255, Kusche, 1915; and 531858, Anton Grosser, 1916; interview with Parthenia Stinnett by Jo Anne Byrd, "Last of the Old West Series;" and *Jackson Hole Guide*, April 7, 1966.

23. Homestead Patents: 707967, Steingraber, 1918; 708783, Norman Smith, 1918; 516805, John Rutherford, 1910; 504029, James H. May, 1908; and 733997, Roy Lover, 1915.

24. Interview with Clark Moulton by Jo Anne Byrd, #27, "Last of the Old West Series;" and Homestead Patents: Desert Land Entry 152, Lander, James I. May, 1901; and Desert Land Entry 768, Evanston, James Budge, 1901.

25. Homestead Patents: Homestead Cert. 529, Lander, Fred Lovejoy, 1904; Desert Land Entry 233, Lander, Lovejoy, 1903; and 511897, Mary Lovejoy, 1913.

26. Homestead Patents: Homestead Cert. 469, Lander, Nels Hoagland, 1903; Desert Land Entry 169, Lander, Hoagland, 1901; 338393, William J. Kelly, 1913; 831413, Kelly, 1914; and 903929, Sophie S. Kelly, 1922.

27. Homestead Patents: 486627, Williams, 1915; and 517650, Adams, 1915.

28. Homestead Patents: Johnson, 1914; 542215, A. Chambers, 1916; and 705531, J. Woodward, 1918.

29. *Jackson's Hole Courier*, April 15, 1915; Orrin and Lorraine J. Bonney, *Bonney's Guide to Grand Teton National Park and Jackson's Hole* (Houston, TX: by author, 1961, 1972), p. 131; and Homestead Patents: 485599, Joseph Pfeifer, 1914; and 598873, Henry Gunther, 1917.

30. Homestead Patents: Desert Land Entry 767, Evanston, Richard H. Meyers, 1906; and 732049, Roy Nipper, 1919.

31. Homestead Patent 685989, H. H. Menor, 1918.

32. Homestead Patent 639818, James H. Manges, 1917; and Office of the Teton County Clerk and Recorder, Misc. Records Book 1, p. 280, James Manges to C. A. Goss, Agreement for Deed, April 1, 1926; and Deed Record Book 4, p. 114, James Manges to C. A. Goss, Warranty Deed, August 7, 1929.

33. Homestead Patents 615962, Ilse, 1917; and 737603.

34. Homestead Patents: 959955, Heirs of M. Locher, 1924; and 981691, Ed K. Smith, 1926; and "Hearing on S. Res. 226," 1933, p. 271.

35. Homestead Patents: 486340, Charles Hedrick, 1915; 486342, John Fee Jr., 1915; 486346, Orin Seaton, 1913; 516802, Rudolph Harold, 1915; and 899898, William Jump, 1922.

36. Homestead Patents: 396790, Walter J. Germann, 1913, and 769868, John Smejkal, 1918.

37. Homestead Patents: 707968, George H. Whiteman, 1918; and 796556, Joe Markham, 1918.

38. Homestead Patent 645202, William C. Thompson.

39. Merk, *History of West*, pp. 484–494; and Larson, *History of Wyoming*, pp. 359–365.

40. Interview with Clark Moulton, #27; and Homestead Patents: 519467, John Moulton, 1915; 534689, T. A. Moulton, 1915; 563869, George H. Riniker, 1916; 598873, Henry Gunther, 1917; 674905, John Nixon, 1918; 730043, Earle W. Harris, 1918; 802555, John L. Kneedy, 1920; and 813101, Talmadge S. Holland, 1918.

41. *Jackson's Hole Courier*, April 30, 1914; Merk, *History of West*, pp. 591–592; photograph of threshing machine, Book 5, p. 24, Jackson Hole Historical Society and Museum, and *Jackson Hole News*, August 30, 1973.

42. Homestead Patents: 645202, W. C. Thompson, 1917; and 517646, Leslie Kafferlin, 1917.

43. *Jackson's Hole Courier*, July 19, 1914.

44. Homestead Patents: Desert Land Entry 233, Lander, F. Lovejoy, 1903; and Desert Land Entry 768, Evanston, James Budge, 1905.

45. Bertha Chambers Gillette, *Homesteading with the Elk: A Story of Frontier Life in Jackson Hole,* Wyoming (Idaho Falls, ID: Mer-Jons Pub. Co., 1967), pp. 138–141; Homestead Patents: 868566, Geraldine Lucas, 1921;

813101, Talmadge S. Holland, 1918; 645202, W.C. Thompson, 1917; and 710289, Charles Davis, 1918.

46. Homestead Patents: 804575, John R. Brown, 1920; 587701, Elmer Arthur, 1916; 701008, Roland P. Hunter, 1918; and 817079, Joseph Chapline, 1920.

47. Homestead Patent 804575, J. R. Brown, 1920.

48. Homestead Patents: 715943, Charles Shinkle, 1918; and 995670, William Smith, 1925.

49. Billington, *Westward Expansion*, pp. 654–655; *Jackson Hole Guide*, October 12, 1972; interview with Ellen Dornan by Jo Anne Byrd, #10, "Last of Old West Series; U.S. Geological Survey, Grand Teton Quadrangle, surveyed in 1899; *Jackson's Hole Courier*, April 16, 1914, July 12, 1917, December 5, 1919, October 12, 1922; A. N. Davis, G. L. O. Commissioner, Homestead Entry Ledger, p. 98, courtesy of Noble Gregory, Jr.; and Homestead Patents: 674905, Nixon, 1918; 606336, T. H. Baxter, 1916; 802555, J. L. Kneedy, 1920; 796556, Markham, 1918; 788386, Tillman Holland, 1920; 959955, Heirs of M. Locher, 1924; and 981691, Ed K. Smith, 1926.

50. Homestead Patents: 243672, Floyd Wilson, 1911; and 323593, Jones, 1913; interview with Ethel Jump, February 19, 1966, transcript, Jackson Hole Historical Society and Museum; and *Jackson Hole Guide*, December 2, 1965.

51. *Jackson's Hole Courier*, April 19, 1934, March 25, 1943, and November 8, 1945; *Jackson Hole Guide*, February 8, 1968; and Gillette, *Homesteading with Elk*, p. 15.

52. Gillette, *Homesteading with Elk*, pp. 4 and 156; Hayden, *Trapper to Tourist*, p. 53; and *Jackson Hole Guide*, October 6, 1955.

53. Gillette, *Homesteading with Elk*, pp. 4–15; *Jackson's Hole Courier*, April 16, 1914; and *Jackson Hole Guide*, October 6, 1955.

54. Homestead Patents: 516805, John Rutherford, 1915; 707968, Whiteman, 1918; and 804576, Charles Christian, 1920.

55. *Jackson Hole Guide*, July 2, 1964 (this article contained a number of errors); S. N. Leek Collection, 3138, Box 3, Ledger Book; and *Jackson's Hole Courier*, February 4, 1915.

56. Struthers Burt, *Diary*, p. 181; *Jackson's Hole Courier*, May 10, 1917, September 18, 1924, January 24, 1952, and November 15, 1951; and interview with Bill Tanner by Jo Anne Byrd, #39, "Last of Old West Series."

57. Homestead Patent, Homestead Cert. 1252, Evanston, Frank Price, 1906; *Jackson's Hole Courier*, March 25, 1943, August 31, 1933, February 10, 1926, May 14, 1931, September 3, 1914, September 6, 1917, August 30, 1917, October 14, 1943, September 7, 1933, and May 22, 1947; *Jackson Hole Guide*, May 30, 1974; interview with Almer

Nelson by Jo Anne Byrd, #30, "Last of Old West Series;" and interview with Charlie Peterson by Jo Anne Byrd, #31, "Last of Old West Series." I was never able to locate a copy of the Cherry book or confirm its existence.

58. *Jackson Hole Guide*, December 2, 1965, and January 27, 1966.

59. Interview with Joella Taylor by Jo Anne Byrd, #40, "Last of Old West Series;" *Jackson Hole Guide*, October 6, 1955; *Jackson's Hole Courier*, February 14, 1946, and November 8, 1945; Homestead Patent, Homestead Cert. 1127, Evanston, Martin Henrie, 1905; and *Jackson's Hole Courier*, August 18, 1932.

60. K. C. Allan Collection, 7636, "Alphabetical Listing of Post Offices in Jackson Hole," University of Wyoming Archives.

61. *Jackson Hole Guide*, December 2, 1965; Esther B. Allan, "History of Teton National Forest," unpublished manuscript, U.S. Forest Service, 1973, p. 111; *Jackson's Hole Courier*, July 9, 1914, August 18, 1924, and September 9, 1943.

62. *Jackson's Hole Courier*, April 23, 1914, May 2, 1918, October 26, 1922, October 27, 1927, September 17, 1931, May 17, 1917; and Homestead Patent: 531858, Anton Grosser, 1916.

63. *Jackson's Hole Courier*, April 7, 1916, December 19, 1946, May 21, 1914, and May 17, 1917; *Jackson Hole Guide*, December 2, 1965; Homestead Patent 345271, Joseph Heniger, 1913; Teton County Records, Deed Record Book 1, p. 120, J. P. and Maggie Cunningham to John P. Nelson, Warranty Deed, March 18, 1909; Deed Record Book A, p. 327, John and Katrina Nelson to Maggie Cunningham, Warranty Deed, May 18, 1914; Jump Interview, 1966, Jackson Hole Historical Society and Museum; and John Daugherty, "Historical Overview of the Teton Science School," 1983, Grand Teton National Park.

64. *Jackson's Hole Courier*, April 26, 1917, February 14, 1946, January 16, 1936; *Jackson Hole Guide*, July 28, 1966; and Allan Collection, "Post Offices," University of Wyoming Archives.

65. *Jackson's Hole Courier*, April 19, 1934.

66. *Jackson's Hole Courier*, March 31, 1938, May 2, 1918, May 3, 1917, June 21, 1923, November 19, 1925, March 8, 1923; and Teton County Records, Deed Record Book A, 97, James H. and Lydia Uhl to J. P. Cunningham, Warranty Deed, October 2, 1917.

67. Frances Judge, "Mountain River Men," pp. 57–58; and *Jackson's Hole Courier*, January 4, 1933, June 8, 1933, February 26, 1928, June 12, 1924, November 8, 1945, August 16, 1923, and March 16, 1929.

68. *Jackson's Hole Courier,* September 5, 1918, January 1, 1920, and March 4, 1920.

69. Homestead Patents: 755267, Sam Smith, 1920; 802555, J.L. Kneedy, 1920; 813101, Talmadge Holland, 1920; 872259, Ray C. Kent, 1922; 888052, Alice Bladon, 1919; and 898062, Horace Eynon, 1922; and *Jackson's Hole Courier,* July 24, 1919.

70. Homestead Patents: 898062, H. Eynon, 1922; and 843343, Frank Braman, 1921.

71. Teton County Records; and *Jackson's Hole Courier,* December 20, 1923, and June 24, 1926.

72. Struthers Burt, *Diary,* pp. 114–116.

CHAPTER

Cattle Ranchers

If this ground is as valuable as they say it is, there's no way that I can see that our kids are going to stay here and keep ranching. I hope they are not that dumb. Us old fellows . . . we'll probably ride it out, but the kids aren't going to do it. I mean they're going to put her in the bank and go on down the road.

—Earl Hardeman *Jackson Hole Guide,* July 10, 1986

Cattle ranching shaped the character of the western states. From the late nineteenth century through the early twentieth century, ranching was the primary occupation of most Jackson Hole residents. *Jackson Hole Historical Society and Museum*

The open range cattle industry brought other frontiersmen to the American West, the rancher and cowboy. Like those before them—trapper, explorer, miner, soldier—the rancher played an important role in the development of the West, even though the years of the open range cattle industry were short-lived, lasting only from 1866 to 1887. This frontier gave birth to the cowboy, the most popular and enduring of this nation's folk heroes. It also pioneered modern ranching, which dominates the economies of several western states today.

Four important elements contributed to the development of ranching. First, native grasses carpeted the Great Plains, providing grazing for livestock. The establishment of cattle ranches represented an adaptation of farmer and hunter-woodsman to the Great Plains environment. In turn, ranchers manipulated the environment by introducing cattle. Second, the removal of native peoples and the extermination of native animals, such as the buffalo, created a vacuum that cattle and cowpunchers filled rapidly. Third, the Spanish had introduced cattle in northern Mexico and Texas in the eighteenth century, which provided a livestock source. In the Nueces River area, Mexican ranchers learned to raise cattle on the plains, developing the open-range cattle industry. Anglo-Americans learned the techniques of this system from the Mexicans. By 1865, an estimated 5,000,000 cattle roamed the Texas plains, providing an ample supply. Fourth, the Civil War depleted cattle supplies in the Mississippi Valley, creating a need for cattle in eastern markets.

Beginning in 1865, entrepreneurs collected un-branded cattle in Texas and, in the spring of 1866, outfits of six to 12 cowboys began driving herds of 1,000 to 2,500 cattle to a railhead at Sedalia, Missouri. An estimated 260,000 cattle were gathered in 1866 alone. Few reached Sedalia for a number of reasons, but the legendary long drives had been launched. Cattle trails developed from Texas to rail towns in Kansas, such as Abilene, Ellsworth, and Dodge City. If prices were good, the herds were sold for fattening on the Midwest corn belt. If prices were low, drovers moved the cattle to Wyoming, Montana, and the Dakotas.[1]

By 1869, the cattle industry had entered a "golden era." From the great drives, cattlemen settled the northern plains and stocked the range. Ranchers built up empires, preempting choice lands having water, and grazed their herds on the public domain free. The first to graze the range established first rights; it was an extralegal custom, but one that ranchers enforced with guns. Cattle "barons" emerged, such as John Wesley Iliff of Colorado and Conrad Kohrs of Montana. The King Ranch in Texas consisted of more than 1,000,000 acres. To regulate ownership of drifting cattle, control rustlers, eradicate predators such as wolves, and improve breeds of cattle, ranchers formed livestock associations. These groups controlled roundups in given localities where owners separated their cattle. At the spring roundup, they branded calves, castrated male calves (steers), and branded mavericks. Ranchers held fall roundups to gather steers for market.

Several characteristics typified the open range cattle industry in the 1870s and 1880s. To control the range, ranchers took advantage of homestead laws, especially the Desert Land Act of 1877 and the Timber Culture Act of 1873, to preempt prime acreage on the plains. Fraud typified many of the entries. One source estimated that up to 95 percent of desert land entries were fraudulent claims made for corporations.[2] Rather than bothering to secure legal title to land, cattle barons began fencing public land grazed by their herds. Though they had no legal right to do this, no one attacked the practice until the 1880s. To improve the rangy Texas longhorn, ranchers imported English Herefords and Scottish Black Angus. Cattlemen had to adapt to the northern plains where

the winters were much worse than on the southern plains. In Texas, a cow could produce 12 offspring over a lifetime; on the northern plains, a cow could only be expected to deliver six calves. By the 1880s, some ranchers were cultivating hay for winter feed and putting up winter shelters to protect their cattle.[3]

The cattle industry boomed as wealthy investors from the East and Great Britain poured capital into giant cattle ranches in the West. By 1880, profits and propaganda ignited a predictable rush as hundreds of green young men from eastern farms and cities overran the West to join the new western aristocracy, the cattlemen. In 1860, no cattle were reported in the Dakotas, Montana, Wyoming, and Colorado; by 1880, the census listed a figure of 1,881,769 cattle in these states and territories.[4]

In Wyoming, traders had brought cattle to the southeastern part of the state by the 1850s, while Mormons may have introduced cattle in the southwestern part of the state during the same period. John Wesley Iliff, a Colorado rancher, introduced the first large herd into the Cheyenne area in 1868. In 1870, the Wyoming Territorial tax assessment rolls listed 8,143 cattle in Wyoming; in 1880, the U.S. census listed 521,213 cattle in Wyoming Territory. By 1885, there were an estimated 1,500,000 cattle in Wyoming. The Scottish-owned-and-financed Swan Land and Cattle Company was the largest "outfit" in Wyoming, owning 123,460 head in 1885. The majority of cattle in Wyoming were Texas cattle. Cattle similar to longhorns came from the Midwest, Oregon, Washington, and Utah. A. H. Swan and J. M. Carey introduced the first Hereford cattle in 1878, and members of the Wyoming Hereford Association imported 400 head of Hereford bulls and cows in 1883.

In the 1880s, cattlemen dominated the politics and economy of the Wyoming Territory. Cattle accounted for more than three-quarters of the territory's wealth, while the Wyoming Stock Growers Association emerged as the single most powerful organization, wielding tremendous political influence. "Cattle Kings," along with merchants, comprised the social elite in the territorial capital in Cheyenne.[5]

The promise of tremendous profits led to an overstocked range. Experienced ranchers watched in alarm as prime grasslands shrunk and deteriorated under the onslaught of thousands of cattle. Further-more, the increased supply of beef caused prices to decline. Adverse weather busted the industry, begin-ning with a hard winter in 1885–1886. Drought gripped the land during the summer of 1886. Con-cerned about the weakened condition of their herds, some ranchers dumped their cattle; as a result, the price of a steer plummeted from $30 per head in 1885 to no more than $10 each in 1886. Those who sold and took crippling losses may have been lucky.

The winter of 1886–1887 was one of the worst in recorded history and ended the days of free-rang-ing cattle on the Great Plains. The spring thaw re-vealed the extent of the disaster; cowboys spent a life-time trying to forget the horror of thousands of dead cattle, piled up in ravines and along fence lines. Ac-curate numbers are difficult to determine, but it is es-timated that winter losses totaled 40 to 50 percent of the cattle on the plains.[6]

Ranchers in Wyoming suffered less, as losses were believed to be no more than 15 percent of the herds. But this figure is deceptive; the assessed value of cattle in the territory dropped 30 percent, surviv-ing cattle were in poor shape, and the year's calf numbers were small. Low prices continued as ranch-ers dumped cattle on the market. Bankruptcy be-came the only solution for many, sparing neither small ranchers nor cattle barons. When the Swan Land and Cattle Company went bankrupt in May 1887, shock waves emanated through the industry.[7]

Other developments limited the future of the open range cattle industry. In the 1870s, farmers be-gan settling the plains, preempting grazing range and water used by ranchers. Then, in the 1880s, the wool market boomed and sheep were introduced on the range, causing serious competition for grass and sub-sequent range wars between sheepherders and cattle-men. The collapse of open-range cattle grazing pointed out the fundamental inefficiency of the sys-tem; free-ranging cattle were easy prey for rustlers and predators such as wolves, while overgrazing proved wasteful and depleted the overall quality of rangelands.[8]

The open-range days were nearing their end when the first cattle were reported in Jackson Hole. As cattle ranged throughout the West, ranchers intro-duced herds adjacent to Jackson Hole, primarily in

the Green River Basin and southeast Idaho. By 1880, there were approximately 30,000 cattle in southeast Idaho, and perhaps as many as 50,000 in the Green River Basin.[9] In the company of a posse in pursuit of horse thieves, William Simpson entered the valley in 1883 and reported the presence of 100 legally-owned cattle. Most references speculate that the cattle belonged to John Holland, John Carnes, and Mike Detweiler. Since Carnes and Holland came from the Green River country, the cattle may have been driven into the valley over the divide sepa-rating the Green and Gros Ventre Rivers. However, this conflicts with most accounts that cite 1884 as the date of Holland and Carnes arrival. The cattle may have been trailed into the valley to graze for the season.[10]

Jackson Hole's environment prohibited the year-round grazing of cattle on range lands as practiced on the Great Plains. After the disaster of 1887, cat-tlemen adopted mountain valley ranching, called range ranching on the Great Plains. Rather than let cattle range freely in winter, ranchers cultivated hay and fed their herds during the winter months. Cattle were released on the open range during the summer and autumn only. Winter shelters were also built to protect the animals from the worst storms. Thus, the cowboy rapidly became an agricultural laborer, cut-ting and stacking hay and digging postholes for fences.[11]

Long winters, with 30 to 40 inches of snow cov-ering the ground, and limited range made this area unattractive to large companies or cattle kings. Small ranches developed in the valley during the 1890s; the cattle herds were typically small, limited by the amount of winter feed cultivated. They were often in-distinguishable from a farm. Some settlers began with such small herds that they raised hay or grain to sell on the local market, and thus should be. classi-fied as farms rather than ranches. Others switched from one to the other as circumstances dictated. For example, Jim Chambers raised cattle and hay after a hailstorm flattened 40 acres of wheat on his Poverty Flats farm. Lacking water, Andy Chambers dry farmed his land on Mormon Row, raising grains such as oats and wheat until 1927, when he con-structed an irrigation system and switched to raising cattle and hay.[12]

Cattle ranching became the economic mainstay of Jackson Hole. Virtually all homesteaders prior to 1900 started cattle ranches. Pierce Cunningham, Emile Wolff, James Uhl, Jim Budge, Jim May, Frank Sebastian, Frank McBride, and Fred Lovejoy were ranchers in today's park prior to 1900.[13] Four factors circumscribed the size of the ranches. First, the availability of winter feed dictated the number of cattle kept through the winter. In turn, the cultivable acreage of the home ranch determined the tonnage of hay produced each year. For example, according to the tax rolls of Uinta County, Pierce Cunningham owned 27 cattle in 1899. Ranchers planned to feed their cattle for about six months per year. Each cow consumed an average of 20 pounds of hay per day, or 4,000 pounds per season. If we assume that Cunningham fed his cattle for 180 days, he would have needed 54 tons of hay for his herd. In addition, hay would be needed for saddle and draft horses, which required about 5,000 pounds of hay per season. In the final proof papers for both his desert and homestead entries, Cunningham testified that he cultivated hay on 100 acres at his homestead, plus 75 tons on his desert entry. The production of hay can vary greatly in Jackson Hole, depending on soils, weather, and irrigation. If we assume that Cunningham produced an average of two tons per acre on 100 acres, he would have had 275 tons of hay available each year. In 1900, he should have had a large surplus of hay. According to his final proof papers, Cunningham raised 100 cattle and eight horses in 1897, which would have required 220 tons for the winter, providing a small surplus of hay.[14]

Federal homestead laws—which failed to allow sufficient acreage for a cattle ranch in the West—also determined the size of ranches. In 1878, John Wesley Powell of the U.S. Geological Survey issued his famous report which, among other things, recommended that homesteaders be allowed to preempt a minimum of 2,560 acres for stock-raising purposes. In Jackson Hole, early ranchers tried to raise cattle on a 160-acre claim under the Homestead Act of 1862, and an additional 160 acres allowed under the amended Desert Land Act of 1891. Some tried to ranch a 160-acre parcel, which was too small to be successful. Congress passed the Stock-Raising Act in 1916, which allowed settlers to preempt up to 640

acres of land suitable only for grazing. Theoretically, cultivable lands were excluded from this law.

Third, as homesteading accelerated in the valley after 1910, newcomers claimed more accessible grazing lands in the valley, forcing ranchers to drive their cattle to more remote range. This reduced the grazing acreage available and drove up operating costs.[15] Finally, after 1900, the Forest Service began to restrict grazing on public lands through a permit system. Like their predecessors on the Great Plains, Jackson Hole ranchers grazed livestock on the public domain, free and unchecked. The creation of the Yellowstone Timber Preserve in 1891 through the Forest Reserve Act served notice that conservation was a function of government. The service intended to prevent rangeland damage by restricting grazing to specific areas and limiting livestock numbers.

Establishing the grazing permit system became one of the most difficult and persistent problems faced by the Forest Service in its early years, mainly because of public resistance. At first, ranchers balked at any kind of compliance, perceiving grazing permits as an infringement of individual freedom. They also feared that large cattle ranches and companies would secure most of the permits and squeeze out the smaller ranches of Jackson Hole. The Johnson County War of 1892 remained fresh in the memories of local ranchers. This confrontation demonstrated the antagonism that existed between the cattle kings and small ranchers. Eventually, ranchers accepted the permit system, grudgingly in some cases, for several reasons. Cattlemen saw grazing permits on the national forest as a tool to prevent sheep from entering cattle range. Furthermore, their fears of losing public grazing rights to large cattlemen never materialized. And, finally, a few ranchers recognized that unregulated grazing would destroy grasslands over time and, in turn, the cattle business. The acceptance of grazing restrictions represented a victory of conservation values over a 300-year tradition of exploitation. According to Forest Service records, Martin Henrie obtained the first permit to graze cattle and horses in the Teton Forest Reserve, reserving rights to land in the Ditch and Turpin Creeks' drainages in 1902. By 1906, officials of the reserve had issued 56 permits for 4,072 cattle and horses.[16]

Robert E. Miller owned 126 cattle in 1895, and at one time had the largest herd in Jackson Hole. The Miller Ranch was on what is now the Elk Refuge. *Jackson Hole Historical Society and Museum*

The cattle population is difficult to determine but, in general, ranching experienced growth in the valley through the 1930s. Elizabeth Wied Hayden conducted extensive research on this topic, gathering statistics from numerous sources. As stated earlier, William Simpson reported 100 cattle in Jackson Hole in 1883. Sylvester Wilson brought in 80 cattle in 1889, but no reliable figures exist until 1895, when numbers were reported by the Wyoming Stock Growers Association. Twenty Jackson Hole cattlemen, owning 736 cattle, were members of the association. Only two ranchers owned 100 or more cattle: Brig Adams and his brother owned 100, while R. E. Miller owned 126. Other ranchers were: John Cherry, 13 cattle; John Carnes, 51 cattle; Bill Crawford, 59 cattle; Pierce and Fred Cunningham, 30 cattle; Selar Cheney, 10 cattle; Mose Giltner, 45 cattle; "Slough Grass" Nelson, 52 cattle; Ham Wort, 23 cattle; Sylvester Wilson, 41 cattle. The list may have included only association members, as some ranchers are conspicuously absent from the rolls such as Stephen Leek, Emile Wolff, and Jack Shive. In 1896, the Wyoming Stock Growers Association listed 15 ranchers and 546 cattle in Jackson Hole. Mose Giltner, who became one of the valley's largest ranchers, expanded his herd from 45 to 120 animals. By 1899, the local membership in the association grew to 28 members, owning 882 cattle.[17]

The Uinta County tax rolls for the Jackson Hole area in 1899 listed 72 cattle owners and 1,339 cattle, valued at $21,281. This figure indicates that the Wyoming Stock Growers Association included only members on their rolls; thus the numbers are low. The total number of owners is also deceptive. Very few could be called cattle ranchers compared to the scale practiced on the Great Plains. No less than 12 of the 72 owned only one cow, which may have been the family milk cow. Fourteen settlers struggled to establish a ranch with a "starter" herd of two cattle; among them were Jim Budge, John Barker, Joe Henrie, and Frank Petersen. The tax rolls suggest that few homesteaders seriously engaged in cattle ranching, as only 19 owned more than 20 cattle. The largest ranchers were Mose Giltner with 152, R. E. Miller with 198, Bill Crawford with 99 bearing his Bar over C brand, and Mary Wilson with 86 cattle. The following list is a breakdown of cattle ownership by numbers:[18]

Number of Cattle	Owners	Percent of 72 Owners
1–10	41	57%
11–20	12	17%
21–50	14	19%
51– 99	3	4%
100 or more	2	3%

BRANDS   ᴗ̄   ꟻ   ꟼ   ꟼN

Livestock brands can cause serious confusion, because they are essentially property that can be transferred from owner to owner, along with livestock and a ranch. Branding was a practice developed to identify the ownership of livestock. Because cattle invariably wandered on the open range, ranchers needed a way to identify their livestock and deter theft.

The brands used by Pierce and Maggie Cunningham illustrate the confusion that can surround cattle brands. Over the years, people have questioned the origin and accuracy of the Bar Flying U brand— ᴗ̄ —routed on the overhead sign at the Cunningham Cabin in Grand Teton National Park. The first Cunningham brand was the JP— ꟼ —for the first and middle initials of John Pierce Cunningham. However, the Cunninghams sold this brand, along with their ranch and cattle, to J. P "Pete" Nelson in 1909. The Cunninghams bought back the ranch and brand in 1914. Four years later, the Cunninghams acquired the Bar Flying U brand, when they bought the ranch and cattle of James Uhl. Cunningham decided to drop his old JP brand in favor of the Bar Flying U, because the former was too similar to Pete Nelson's PN— ꟼN —brand and J. D. "Si" Ferrin's JF— ꟻ —brand.

In addition, ranch brands and names may be associated with more than one ranch, generating more confusion for researchers. For example, the Elbo Ranch was a tourist facility located on Cottonwood and Taggart Creeks in the late 1920s. The National Park Service leased the Elbo to concessioners until 1955, when it transferred the operation to the old Ramshorn Ranch located on the east side of the valley on Ditch Creek. The concessioner, Katie Starratt, took the name to the new facility, and the Ramshorn became the Elbo.

Several inferences can be made about cattle ranching in Jackson Hole at the turn of the century. First, by 1900 the cattle population topped 1,000. Second, ownership was concentrated in the hands of a few. For example, the five largest ranchers owned 590 cattle, or 44 percent of 1,339 head; in contrast, almost three-quarters of the 72 ranchers owned less than one-quarter—304 cattle. Third, none of the Jackson Hole cattlemen, even the largest owners, could be considered cattle kings, in the sense of barons such as John Iliff or Conrad Kohrs. Last, no cattle barons established themselves in Jackson Hole.

Between 1901 and 1910, cattle numbers increased dramatically. In 1901, the Wyoming Stock Growers Association listed 29 members in Jackson Hole and 1,540 cattle; by 1910 there were 61 ranchers and 10,919 head. (These figures are low since non-members were not included on the list.) Grazing records for the Teton Forest Reserve provide different figures. For example, 39 Jackson Hole ranchers owned 3,257 head of cattle in 1906; Forest Service records issued 56 grazing permits for 4,072 cattle. Not all permittees were Jackson Hole ranchers. Forest Service grazing records listed only 4,905 cattle in the Teton National Forest in 1910, compared to the Stock Growers Association count of 10,919 head. This is a significant difference, reinforcing the difficulty in securing accurate numbers. At any rate, individual ranchers prospered over this decade. Mose Giltner doubled the size of his herd to 301 head; Joseph Henrie had increased his numbers from two to 31 animals; likewise, his neighbor, Jim

Budge, had a herd numbering 35; near Spread Creek, Pierce Cunningham claimed 132 cattle in 1910 compared to 32 head in 1901.[19]

Prices increased steadily through the First World War. In 1916, no fewer than 159 cattle brands were registered in Jackson Hole. Not all of the brands represented full-fledged cattle ranches, since the list included dude ranches, gentlemen's retreats, or homesteads that were never known as working cattle ranches. The Manges place is one example. To promote the return of stray livestock, stockmen advertised their brands in the *Jackson's Hole Courier*. In 1918, 26 cattlemen or companies published their brands in the local paper. These lists included most of the larger ranches in the valley.[20]

Since cattle were Jackson Hole's sole export, access to markets became critical. Ranchers drove their cattle over Teton Pass or over the old Marysville Road north of Jackson Lake to railroad lines in Idaho. By 1910, the Oregon Short Line, a branch of the Union Pacific, had reached Ashton, Idaho, and by 1912, extended south to Driggs and Victor. Even Rexburg or Idaho Falls, Idaho, proved a shorter drive than the nearest railroads in Wyoming. The Union Pacific tracks passed through Rock Springs in 1868, but this was nearly 200 miles from Jackson Hole. In 1906, the Chicago & Northwestern extended tracks to Lander, Wyoming, but this was about 150 miles from Jackson Hole. Marion Allen recalled participating in a cattle drive to Hudson, Wyoming, a town on the Lander Line in 1920, where D. E. Skinner and other Blackrock grazers hoped to secure better prices. But the trails over Teton Pass and the Ashton-Marysville roads remained the primary routes. For example, in 1917, 42 carloads of cattle were driven over Teton Pass to Victor in early October, most of them owned by Preston Redmond and Roy McBride. Jim Francis, a prominent cattleman in Spring Gulch, drove his cattle to Victor every year from 1913 through 1944.[21]

Cattle ranching thrived in the valley as prices increased between 1900 and 1919. A chart listing the price of calves per hundredweight records steady increases between 1910 and 1919. Although the accuracy of cattle counts are suspect, they indicate that ranching and grazing increased significantly in these years. Cattle grazing on the Teton National Forest

tripled from 5,229 head in 1908 to 15,284 in 1917. According to these records, the number of cattle broke 10,000 first in 1916, when 12,591 cattle grazed in the forest. During this period calf prices increased from $7.30 per hundredweight in October 1910, to $10.20 in October 1916, and $12 in October 1917. Figures from October or November were used, because most ranchers sold their stock after the fall round-up. Ranchers lived and died by market prices and were quick to complain about declines. In November 1917, the *Courier* described the prices of cows and steers as meager, despite the fact that prices were good during this period.

After the end of World War I in 1918, the prices for agricultural products plummeted as demand declined and the federal government dropped price supports. In Jackson Hole, the drought of 1919 ruined crops, crippling both ranchers and farmers. In 1918, a rancher who sold calves in October received $12.10 per hundredweight; in 1919, he received $10.60 per hundredweight, a difference of $1.50. The next year brought even worse news as calves sold for $10.00 per hundredweight in October and $9.60 in November. Despite falling prices, cattle broker W. J. Kelly described a top market at Omaha, and passed on compliments concerning the quality of Jackson Hole cattle. In 1921, Kelly reported a slow market, partially caused by the availability of corn-fed beef from the Midwest. Calf prices plummeted to $7.50 per hundredweight in October, and $7.40 per hundredweight in November.[22]

From 1921 through 1926, cattle prices remained poor. By 1924, only 16 ranches advertised brands in the *Courier*, down from 26 in 1918. Within the national forest, cattle grazing declined from 15,284 head in 1917, to 6,594 cattle in the Teton County section of the forest in 1926. Although the last figure does not include all cattle grazing on forest-lands, it suggests the severity of cattle ranching's slide. Furthermore, a 1925 petition signed by 97 landowners, many of them cattlemen, was prompted in large part by the agricultural depression of the 1920s. This petition supported the creation of a preserve or recreation area in Jackson Hole and the Teton Range, and the willingness of the signers to sell their lands.[23]

Prices increased between 1927 and 1929 with prices per hundredweight topping $10 for the first time since 1920. Struthers Burt wrote to Horace Albright that "the cattlemen, for the first time in years, expected to make money." More important, Burt noted that the "dejected state of mind" that had gripped the valley for several years was gone.[24] In August 1928, the *Courier* reported that the cattle market had improved, and some stockgrowers held their herds hoping to build up higher prices "to clear up past obligations," a euphemism for debts. By early October, Jackson Hole ranchers had shipped 100 carloads of cattle from Victor, while another 37 carloads of cattle were being trailed over Teton Pass. In that month, calf prices were $12.40 per hundredweight. The next year, the October price reached a high of $12.50 on the 15th. On October 24, 1929, stock market prices collapsed, and the day, known as Black Thursday, marked the beginning of the worst depression in the nation's history.[25]

Calf prices plummeted from $12.60 in 1929 to $8.30 per hundredweight in October 1930. The bottom fell out as prices nosedived to figures unheard of since the turn of the century. The prices per hundredweight were as follows:

	October	November
1931	6.00	5.70
1932	4.60	4.50
1933	4.10	4.55
1934	4.60	4.10

The Great Depression hit Americans hard; but unlike most of the nation, ranchers and farmers had contended with an economic depression since the 1920s.[26] Cattle ranching declined in the 1930s, not only because of the depression, but the land acquisition program of the Snake River Land Company. The company purchased more than 30,000 acres between 1928 and 1933, much of it belonging to prominent ranchers. Cattle populations remained relatively stable in Teton County, because even though there were fewer ranchers, they owned larger cattle herds to survive lean years and prosper in good

years. The cattle population of Teton County remained stable from 1936 through 1942: 1936, 10,838; 1937, 12,307; 1938, 10,604; 1939, 10,906; 1940, 12,337; 1941, 12,129; and 1942, 12,580.[27]

The advent of World War II brought hell to earth for eight years, but for American agriculture it brought prosperity as worldwide demand for foodstuffs escalated. War began with the Japanese invasion of China in July 1937, followed by the German invasion of Poland on September 1, 1939. By the end of 1941, the war had boosted cattle prices; in September, calves per hundredweight fetched $10 for the first time since 1930. The cattle industry thrived for the next two decades.[28] Like ranching in the American West, world events and economic conditions influenced the cattle business in Jackson Hole as much as local factors.

Cattle ranching in Jackson Hole followed patterns that occurred elsewhere in the West, including stock improvement. Cattlemen imported improved breeds by the 1870s. Wyoming cattlemen introduced English Herefords in 1878. No record was found of the first breed of cattle brought to Jackson Hole, but ranchers were undoubtedly influenced by the trend of improving the quality of herds through selective breeding. Elizabeth Hayden determined that the Wilson brothers introduced the first purebred Hereford bulls in Jackson Hole in 1901. Hereford and Black Angus became the predominant breeds in the valley. In 1914, Bill Kelly purchased a Durham bull for Harold Hammond of the White Grass, who intended to establish a cattle ranch. Gerrit Hardeman, a Dutch immigrant, bought the Charles E. Davis homestead in 1919 for $2,500 and established one of the finest herds of Hereford cattle in the region.[29]

Cattlemen's associations were also important to ranchers in Jackson Hole. These associations represented the cooperative spirit of the westering experience. In the 1890s, a number of Jackson Hole ranchers belonged to the Wyoming Stock Growers' Association, an organization formed to promote industry interests. Membership of Jackson Hole cattlemen in this state organization expanded from 19 in 1895 to 35 by 1910. In practical terms, local associations were more important. Ranchers formed these organizations based on common grazing allotments

Cattlemen's associations were formed in Jackson Hole to address specific problems, such as predators. This photo shows a group of early Spring Gulch ranchers. Left to right: Bert Charter, Harry Harrision, Jim Boyle and Jim Francis. *Jackson Hole Historical Society and Museum*

such as the Gros Ventre River or Blackrock Creek areas. Communal roundups and drives to and from grazing ranges required cooperative efforts. Groups of ranchers pooled money to hire line riders to watch cattle on summer range. At least one line shack, built to house hands, is extant in the Sportsman's Ridge area in Teton National Forest.[30]

Protecting cattle from predators, in particular the gray wolf, seems to have been the major motive for creating livestock associations in the valley's early years. On May 21, 1914, the *Courier* reported that 15 wolves had killed a cow and four yearlings being trailed to summer range on the Gros Ventre. The cattle belonged to Preston Redmond. The next week Roy McBride and Redmond herded their cattle together to protect them from wolves and hired Jess Buchanan to watch the cattle at night. While at Crystal Creek, Buchanan reported that wolves would harass cattle on one side, while he patrolled the opposite side. Cowpunchers also stated that wolves pursued a "favorite pastime" of biting off the tails of calves. Wolves may have tried this as an alternative to hamstringing the animals, that is, bringing prey down by their hindquarters. In June, Roy McBride set out to hunt down the wolf packs. In July, ranchers formed the Fish Creek Wolf Association specifically to eradicate the wolf population on the Gros

Ventre River. They hired Walter Dallas to hunt them, paying him $22 per month. In addition, they agreed to pay a bounty: $62 for a "she-dog," $52 for dogs (males), and $22 for pups. The association offered a $1.50 bounty for coyotes. To pay Dallas's wage and bounties, the association assessed each member 12 cents per head of cattle. This program eliminated the gray wolf in the area by the early 1920s.[31]

Jackson Hole cattle associations also formed to promote ranching interests. In 1921, valley residents created the Jackson Hole Cattle and Horse Association, which remains active today, though hindered by dwindling membership. Early in 1925, several ranchers announced the formation of a new group called the Jackson Hole Cattle and Game Association. To recruit new members, the association guaranteed that the group would not promote the Yellowstone extension, nor serve as a tool for political purposes. Organizers adopted the following goals: oppose opening new areas in Teton National Forest to sheep; oppose further unnecessary grazing restrictions; and oppose destruction of game and commercialization of forests, lakes, and streams.[32]

Stories of range wars between sheepherders and cattlemen are entrenched firmly as a violent chapter in western lore. Tales of Jackson Hole cattlemen

Stephen Leek, cattle rancher, conservationist and entrepreneur. *Jackson Hole Historical Society and Museum*

banding together to drive "woolies" out of the valley date from the turn of the century. One story has it that a sheepherder was murdered at the upper end of Death Canyon, the source of its name. No evidence has been found to confirm this story. Sheepherding increased in the American West in the late 1890s, causing competition and conflicts over grazing range. Confrontations became so violent in Wyoming that historian T. A. Larson rated the range wars between cattlemen and sheep ranchers as "a major theme of the state's history." Between 1897 and 1909, 16 people were killed and possibly 10,000 sheep destroyed in Wyoming. But, like many violent incidents in history, the stories grew bloodier with time, obscuring an accurate record of events.[33]

As ranchers introduced sheep—or cattlemen switched to raising them—Jackson Hole ranchers became concerned. Sheep appeared in adjacent areas such as Star Valley, Teton Basin, and the Green River country. In 1897, local ranchers reportedly published a notice in a newspaper warning that "no sheep will be allowed to pass through Jackson's Hole . . . under any circumstances." S. N. Leek recalled

that ranchers posted signs along the approaches to the valley warning sheep drovers to stay out.

SHEEPMEN, WARNING
We will not permit
sheep to graze upon
the elk ranges on
Jackson Hole. Govern
yourselves accordingly
Signed:
The Settlers of Jackson's Hole

Settlers in the valley followed the general pattern of range conflicts elsewhere in the West; they warned sheepmen that certain areas, in this case Jackson Hole, were off limits, then set boundaries that sheep were not to cross. Confrontation was the most serious phase. S. N. Leek and Lee Lucas remembered that several herds of sheep crossed Teton Pass, but were turned back by well-armed cattlemen at the Snake River. Sheep that had already crossed the river were escorted out of the valley over the Gros Ventre. Specific dates and participants are not known. A. A. Anderson, the first supervisor of the Yellowstone Timber Reserve, drew the rancor of sheepmen when he restricted their grazing rights and drove them off rangelands, where they had no permits. Because Jackson Hole is an enclosed valley, keeping sheep out was relatively easy.[34]

No violent confrontations between sheepherders and ranchers occurred in Jackson Hole. In the upper Green River Valley, cattle ranchers faced off against sheepherders around the turn of the century; they killed a large number of sheep around 1902. Esther Allan reported that 2,000 sheep were killed in one case and 800 in another. Whether these were the same incidents and conflicting figures, or represent separate incidents, is unknown. Another confrontation occurred when A. A. Anderson received information from Washington, D.C., that 60,000 sheep had been turned loose in the Teton Division of the Forest Reserve. The sheep belonged to four owners—and were reportedly guarded by 40 armed herders. Anderson gathered and deputized 65 well-armed men at a place called "Horse-creek" near Jackson Hole and moved out to confront them.

They found 1,500 sheep and several herders and escorted them across the eastern boundary of the reserve. There is no evidence that the sheep entered Jackson Hole.[35]

Sheep were introduced in Jackson Hole later without violence, possibly because of two factors. In 1909, a group of masked men attacked a sheep camp near Tensleep in the Bighorn Basin, murdering two wealthy sheep ranchers and a herder. Woolgrowers associations put up reward money, while the county sheriff and prosecutor aggressively investigated the case. The sheriff arrested seven men; two provided state's evidence which resulted in the conviction of the other five, who received sentences ranging from three years to life in prison. The Tensleep incident served notice to cattlemen that protecting grazing lands with a gun, a holdover from the free-for-all days of the open range, would no longer be tolerated. Second, after 1919, raising sheep became more attractive to stockmen; sheep provided two crops per year, wool and meat, an attractive prospect during a depression.[36]

In June 1923, the *Jackson's Hole Courier* reported sheep in the valley, introduced by J. G. Imeson in South Park. The article stated that sheep might be important in the future, because the sheep market was good while cattle prices remained depressed. In 1926, Lewis Fleming, ostensibly a cowpuncher, reported grazing 450 sheep on his 640-acre stock-raising entry south of the JY. By the 1930s, in the heart of the Great Depression, several Mormon Row farmers and ranchers had introduced sheep, notably Joe May, Clifton May, and Hannes Harthoorn. They grazed sheep on Blacktail Butte and on their own land. Sheep trails to summer ranges also crossed the valley and the Teton Range. In September 1929, Sam T. Woodring, the superintendent of Grand Teton National Park, encountered 1,742 sheep being herded from Fox Creek over Fox Creek Pass to the head of Teton Creek. Since the trail crossed Death Canyon Shelf in the park, Woodring gave the owner, a man named Taylor, permission to pass through park lands, stipulating only that no stops be made. The 1929 enabling legislation for the park grandfathered in existing livestock drifts and grazing.[37]

Some resented the presence of sheep in the valley, but limited their hostility to verbal barbs and letters. Joe R. Jones complained to the editor of the *Courier* that sheep destroyed valuable elk and cattle range and introduced ticks in the valley. Gladys May Kent recalled some prejudice against sheep; as a schoolgirl, during the course of an assignment to write poetry, Mrs. Kent recalled a rhyme dedicated to her: "There's a freckle face girl who lives over the way, her dad's a sheep herder, her last name's May." She also remembered a dog killing sheep on Mormon Row, but could not confirm if it was deliberate on the part of the dog's owner.[38] In 1932, Dick Winger, the field manager for the Snake River Land Company, reported sheep loose on company lands:

> I went to the Kafferlin place above Kelly in my car today, where I served in the capacity of sheep herder. Our good friend, Hannes Harthoorn, has run out of feed and turned his sheep out along the warm springs ditch. I am now trying to prepare proper notices for the sheep owners in that section, which will induce them to keep the "range maggots" off of our property—and still like me.[39]

While residents raised sheep in Jackson Hole, they never replaced cattle, nor were their numbers very large. For example, in 1950, four ranchers owned 815 sheep; by 1954 the number had dwindled to 104.[40]

Larger land and cattle companies eventually dominated ranching in Jackson Hole, another common pattern in the West. As America moved into the twentieth century, the size of cattle ranches grew as the bigger ranchers bought out smaller stockmen. Two dudes named Moser and Trexler bought a ranch near Wilson around 1900. Moser wanted to buy up land in the valley, believing he would eventually make a killing in real estate rather than cattle. He died around 1914 before he could implement the plan. Consolidation began in World War I and accelerated during the hard decades of the 1920s and 1930s. Around 1900, a rancher could get by on 320 acres and about 100 cattle. By the 1920s, ranchers increased the size of their outfit to perhaps 640 acres,

Feeding elk at the Hansen Ranch in Spring Gulch, ca. 1911. Ranchers usually tried to keep the elk from eating their hay, but fed the wildlife during the harsh winters. *Jackson Hole Historical Society and Museum*

plus a sizable grazing allotment on the national forest, and 450 to 500 cattle. Lee Lucas came to Jackson Hole in 1896 and gradually built up a premier ranch in Spring Gulch. By the 1930s, he owned 640 acres and maintained a herd of 450 Herefords and 50 horses. James Boyle bought a large ranch in South Park around 1917, purchasing 1,214 acres for $17,000. P C. Hansen bought the Fisk place in Spring Gulch after 1900. Over the years, the Hansen family built up their ranch, until they owned more than 3,500 acres in Spring Gulch by the 1940s.[41]

Outside entrepreneurs tried to establish two large cattle ranches after 1910 on lands that presently comprise the park. D. E. Skinner, a Seattle shipbuilder, bought land in the Buffalo Fork area, which formed the nucleus of the Elk Ranch. Chester Pederson, related to the Remington firearms family, established the JP Ranch in the lower Gros Ventre River area.

Skinner came to Jackson Hole around 1912 to hunt. Guided by Jim Budge, he was impressed with the valley's potential for cattle ranching. In 1916, he bought the 320-acre Otto Kusche ranch for $14,000; in 1919, he bought Jack Shive's Hatchet Ranch on the Buffalo Fork, about 750 acres for $20,000.

Skinner formed a partnership with Val Allen and purchased his property west of Uhl Hill in 1917 for $6,500. Allen managed the would-be cattle empire for two or three years, then broke off with Skinner. Another settler, Tom Tracy, took over as foreman of the ranch and managed Skinner's sawmill. The Elk Ranch Company started with 450 cattle around 1915, and built up the herd to more than 2,000 cattle by 1919. In 1920, Skinner sold the Elk Ranch to J. D. "Si" Ferrin, with the exception of the Hatchet Ranch formerly owned by Jack Shive.[42]

Meanwhile, Ferrin had begun to build his cattle empire on a homestead west of Uhl Hill. Settling the property around October 1908, Ferrin and his family cleared 50 acres, raised timothy for hay, and built a house, corrals, barns, and other outbuildings. Ferrin valued the improvements at $5,000. In 1914, he secured a lucrative contract to supply beef to the Reclamation Service at the Jackson Lake Dam. Ferrin purchased other homesteads in the vicinity of his ranch, buying the Thompson homestead in 1911, Joe Heniger's place in 1914, Marius Kristensen's property in 1918, the Elk Ranch in 1920, the McInelly's 520 acres in 1927, and the old Thornton homestead in 1928.[43]

The Ferrins prospered during these years. A large family, Si and Emmeline Heniger Ferrin had five sons before she died in 1904. Ferrin married Edith McInelly in 1905, and they had nine more children, four sons and five daughters. As the sons came of age, they took up homesteads, adding to the Ferrin empire. Curtis Ferrin filed a 160-acre entry in October 1917, just before he enlisted in the army. He later died of influenza in Europe. Leonard Ferrin filed a 640-acre stock-raising entry in 1920, grazing 400 cattle on the tract for two months per year. Cyrus Ray Ferrin filed a stock-raising homestead in 1923, grazing 200 head of cattle and horses on the property each summer.[44]

After he bought out Skinner, Ferrin purchased 800 yearlings and 1,100 calves. During the 1920s, the Ferrins owned between 1,200 and 2,000 head of cattle. The Elk Ranch was the largest outfit in Jackson Hole during these years. Despite or perhaps because of depressed cattle prices, Ferrin mortgaged his property for a total of $205,362 to finance his operation. According to county records, he paid off the loan, except for $15,000. At the old Kusche homestead, Ferrin installed a water-powered sawmill and constructed frame buildings that included a house, barns, machine sheds, and shops. According to Ferrin's daughter, Ada Clark, the house burned.[45] Three frame buildings and a concrete spring house remain at the site today. By the time the family sold their holdings to the Snake River Land Company in 1928 and 1929, Si Ferrin owned 1,708.74 acres, Ray Ferrin had 643.57 acres, Leonard Ferrin had 640 acres, and the family owned another 640 acres, for a total of 3,629.09 acres. The company paid them $114,662.12 for their land and improvements.[46]

Ferrin divided the money among his family and invested in cattle, starting a feedlot operation in Sugar City, Idaho. From 1929 through 1933, his son Merritt Ferrin ran the feedlot. Si Ferrin went bankrupt during the depression. According to Ada Clark, he lost everything in the stock market collapse of 1929. Other sources suggest that Ferrin went bankrupt in the early 1930s. Calf prices dropped to $6 per hundredweight in October 1931, then to $4.06 the next year. Ferrin never quite recovered from the

Elk Ranch, headquarters, ca. 1940s. Si Ferrin built up the Elk ranch to be one of the biggest in the valley by the 1920s. By the time the Ferrin family sold the ranch in 1928, they owned 3,629 acres. *Grand Teton National Park.*

blow and this, along with poor health and accidents, "caused Cy [sic] to cease all active pursuits."[47]

In his last years Ferrin worked for his brother-in-law, Ben Goe, at the Cowboy Bar in Jackson as a night watchman, and a shill at the gaming tables. According to one popular story, one morning he mistook his reflection in the mirror behind the bar for an intruder, drew his sidearm, and shot out the mirror. However, Ferrin should be remembered for his success as a farmer, a game warden and, for a time, as a cattleman. If Jackson Hole ever had a cattle baron, Si Ferrin perhaps fit the role as well as any other rancher in the valley.[48]

The Snake River Land Company fenced their holdings in this area and continued to raise hay. Thus, the Elk Ranch of the 1930s and 1940s encompassed the Ferrins' land and other ranches as well. In the 1940s, the Jackson Hole Preserve leased the property for cattle ranching to support of the war effort. Today, the National Park Service leases much of the Elk Ranch for grazing, as part of a land exchange made in the 1950s.

J. D. "Ted" and Chester Pederson began consolidating ranches in the Gros Ventre River area in 1909, forming the JP Ranch Company. Ted Pederson's interest in Remington Arms kept him in the

Branding at the Elk Ranch. By 1918, 26 cattlemen had published their brands in the *Jackson's Hole Courier*. *Jackson Hole Historical Society and Museum*

East for most of the year; nevertheless, his family formed the JP Ranch Company and initiated an ambitious land acquisition and development program. Beginning with the Joe LaPlante homestead in November 1909, J. D. Pederson began purchasing homesteads south of the Gros Ventre River. The next year, Maggie Adams sold her 320-acre tract to the JP Ranch. "Chess" Pederson received a patent to a homestead entry on Botcher Hill. In 1920 they added the Agnes Geisendorfer and August Romey homesteads farther up the Gros Ventre River. By then, the JP Ranch consisted of more than 1,600 acres south of the Gros Ventre River.[49]

The JP Ranch also invested considerable sums of money into their operations. Early in 1914, they purchased a new oil tractor for the spring planting season. This machine was responsible for the mysterious noises that echoed throughout the upper Flat Creek area, arousing both fear and curiosity among the homesteaders. In 1920, the *Courier* reported that the JP Ranch had launched an extensive improvement program. Carpenters built a bunkhouse, tool shed, barns, and remodeled several houses. To improve the irrigation system, five wells were drilled, and ditches were dug to bring water to 1,500 acres of land. Also, the Pedersons constructed

a large two-story log home, one of the finest in the valley.[50]

The family soon got into financial trouble. First, the slump in cattle prices in the 1920s cut the potential income of the ranch. Second, they overextended themselves, buying too much land and investing too much money into improvements. The Pedersons mortgaged their lands in the 1920s, and in 1929, Mr. C. Bakker, a citizen of the Netherlands, initiated foreclosure proceedings for failure to pay a $15,000 mortgage taken out in 1917. The Snake River Land Company purchased the outstanding mortgages, paid off liens on the JP lands, and secured quitclaim deeds from the family and outside parties with financial claims. The company spent a minimum of $17,887.75 in securing the JP Ranch. They certainly spent more, but company records of this transaction are incomplete. By 1927, the Pedersons gave up on the ranch and moved to Idaho Falls, Idaho. The rise of the JP Ranch Company between 1910 and 1920 was significant. The Pedersons could have developed one of the largest ranches in the valley, but their financial collapse was the most notable bankruptcy in Jackson Hole during the 1920s.[51]

While the JP Ranch failed, there were success stories as well. Gerrit Hardeman immigrated to the

United States in 1910 at the age of 19. Born in Teerseen, Netherlands, in 1891, Hardeman was the youngest of ten children. After working in Iowa for a year or two, he came to Jackson Hole in 1911 or 1912. He worked at a variety of jobs for R. E. Miller and others as a farm laborer, teamster, and timber cutter, saving as much of his wages as possible. In 1919, Hardeman had saved enough to buy the 160-acre dryland farm of Charles and Helena Davis for $2,500.

In 1915, the Davises had homesteaded a quarter section in the eastern portion of today's park, about one mile south of Ditch Creek. Davis filed final proof papers in 1918; his improvements included a one-room log cabin (14 × 16 feet), a stable (18 × 24 feet), a potato cellar (10 × 12 feet), 35 acres cultivated for oat hay, and a three-wire post fence and a three-pole, one-wire, buck fence. Hardeman continued to work at other jobs while he cultivated crops on his farm. He planted a crop each spring, then hauled freight for customers, among them the Reclamation Service, the Sheffields at Moran, Jimmy Simpson, who owned the Kelly Store, and the Kneedys, who established the valley's only flour mill at Kelly. In 1922, Hardeman married Alta Lamar Crandall, the daughter of the Crandalls who owned the old Lee Roadhouse on the Teton Pass Road.

Moving onto the Davis homestead, the Hardemans made the place as self-sufficient as possible. They raised chickens, kept a cow to provide milk and butter, raised a large garden, and canned up to 300 quarts of peaches, and 100 quarts of elk meat per year. Gerrit Hardeman suffered several setbacks in the early years. The drought of 1919 wiped out his first crop. This disaster forced Hardeman to cut native grass from the meadowlands near Moran to provide feed for his teams. In the 1920s, the newlyweds started raising cattle. When they shipped their first steers to Omaha, they expected to realize a tidy return. Instead, Hardeman received much less than he had anticipated and suspected that the commission men contracted to sell the cattle had taken advantage of him. In June 1924, a fire swept through the homestead. A spark from the cookstove chimney ignited a pile of straw and quickly

spread out of control. The fire destroyed the barn, storehouse, and granary; in addition, they lost their chickens and $1,000 worth of grain. Gerrit and Lamar Hardeman could have given up, but they rebuilt the ranch.

In June 1926, Hardeman filed papers on a 280-acre relinquishment located in Section 25, adjacent to his homestead. From 1927 through 1929, he cleared and cultivated 45 acres, raising grass clover for livestock. The improvements consisted of a one-room log cabin (18 × 20 feet) built by the previous occupant, a barn (12 × 16 feet), a corral, and a three-pole, one-wire buck fence. The General Land Office issued a patent for the acreage on June 4, 1930. The Hardemans added to their holdings in 1943, when they purchased the Luther Taylor homestead for $2,600, plus added another 40 acres owned by William Taylor. On their 640-acre ranch, the Hardemans and their sons built up one of the finest cattle ranches in Jackson Hole. Determined never to be dependent on cattle brokers again, Hardeman decided to raise purebred Hereford cattle and sell them locally to ranchers who sought to improve the quality of their stock. The family built a solid reputation in the regional cattle industry for the quality of their Herefords. In 1948, experts from the University of Wyoming proclaimed their cattle among the best in Wyoming.

In 1955, the Hardemans sold their ranch to the National Park Service for $100,000 and moved their outfit to a ranch at Wilson, Wyoming. Their sons, Earl and Howdy Hardeman, continued to operate one of the few remaining ranches in Jackson Hole into the 1990s. They have since retired, selling some of the ranch for subdivisions and renting the remainder of the ranch. Much has been written about the thousands of immigrants who settled the West only to be broken by an unpredictable environment, economic conditions, and growing corporate control of the land and resources. Gerrit and Alta Lamar Hardeman's experience tells another story. A 19-year-old native of the Netherlands came to the United States and through hard work, thrift, and sound management established one of the best ranches in Jackson Hole. Others who developed ranches through individual efforts that were known for the quality of their livestock were Walter and Ed Feuz, James Boyle, Peter Hansen and later Clifford Hansen, Rod and Phil Lucas, Bruce Porter, Amasa James, Boyd Charter, and Jim Imeson.[52]

The emergence of "gentlemen ranchers" began in the 1930s. These were people who had made fortunes in other enterprises, bought up cattle ranches and other lands for a variety of reasons—but did not depend on cattle ranching for their livelihood. Many had been introduced to the valley as guests at dude ranches. Stanley Resor made a fortune as president of one of the world's most prominent advertising agencies, the J. Walter Thompson Company. In the 1920s and 1930s, he bought up ranches north and south of Wilson, Wyoming, establishing one of the valley's largest ranches. In the north end of the valley along the Buffalo Fork, the Cockrell family, who earned a fortune in the oil business, bought the Noble Gregory Ranch in 1942 and continued to raise cattle.

Bill and Eileen Hunter purchased the old Jim Williams ranch from Ida Redmond in 1946. The Hunters retired from the retail auto sales business in 1950 and moved from Kemmerer, Wyoming, to their ranch, "where they planned to spend the rest of their lives enjoying a well-earned vacation." As a hobby, they decided to raise Herefords and purchased some from Gerrit Hardeman. Most of the present buildings were designed by a Salt Lake City architect and constructed in the late 1940s. Bill Hunter died in 1951, scarcely a year after retirement. Mrs. Hunter sold out to the National Park Service and spent summers on the ranch until her death in 1985.[53]

Cattle ranching has declined in Jackson Hole over the last 30 years. Land values skyrocketed as the town of Jackson developed a tourism-based economy and the community has pushed to expand the tourist season from three months to year round. In particular, the construction of Teton Village in the 1960s accelerated this trend. Coupled with difficult economic times for agriculture, escalating land prices have proven irresistible to ranchers, who have sold all or portions of their ranches for resorts or residential subdivisions.

Over the long term, the future of cattle ranching is bleak in Jackson Hole. Earl Hardeman summed up the current state of the cattle business succinctly. He believed that Jackson Hole ranchers raised "cattle as good as you'll find anyplace in the world . . ." but cited the high overhead of ranching caused by the need to feed cattle six months per year as a cause for the decline. Further, as ranchers sold out, mutual support declined. Hardeman believed this made it more difficult for ranchers as "you kind of need to be in a place where there are all cow people. You know, it's just better if you all have the same kind of problems. Now, we're ranching in a subdivision really, and it creates a lot of problems." Moreover, ranches no longer are as self-sufficient as in the past. "We once had more ways of really trying to make it. We had the garden, we had the milk cow, we had the pigs. Now we go to the supermarket," Hardeman observed.

> If this ground is as valuable as they say it is, there's no way that I can see that our kids are going to stay here and keep ranching. I hope they are not that dumb. Us old fellows . . . we'll probably ride it out, but the kids aren't going to do it. I mean they're going to put her in the bank and go on down the road.

In 1986, Hardeman predicted that "in 20 to 25 years, there won't be another mother cow raised in Jackson Hole."[54]

Ranching also had a significant impact on the ecology of Jackson Hole. Cattle ranching represented an adaptation to the land west of the 100th meridian, as ranchers introduced techniques such as irrigation and dry farming, as well as domestic livestock and plants. Grazing affected the native vegetation, while overgrazing depleted range land. Settlers displaced or eradicated wildlife. Wolves were exterminated systematically to extinction. Settlers plowed and fenced lands that served as migratory routes and winter range for elk and pronghorn. Today, the Jackson Hole elk herd survives on one-quarter of its historic winter range, and must be fed during the severest winter days at the refuge. Up to 1906, settlers reported an annual migration of pronghorn, more commonly known as antelope, into the valley. W. C. Deloney recalled that hundreds of antelope migrated into Jackson Hole from the Green River Valley via the Hoback. At Granite Creek, the herd split. One group crossed the divide into the Cache Creek drainage; the other herd followed the Hoback into Jackson Hole. Deloney described the migration as a string consisting of thousands of animals that took several days to pass his store at the Jackson townsite. Although accepting his estimate of numbers takes some credulity, other accounts confirm Deloney's story, with the exception of his estimates. The antelope failed to return in 1907. Only strict protective regulations restored the antelope to Jackson Hole in the 1950s. In 1906, the Wyoming pronghorn population was 2,000; in 1952, it numbered 100,000. In 1958, the Grand Teton National Park Superintendent's Report for June confirmed antelope sightings in the Antelope Flats area and near the Jenny Lake Store.[55]

Cattle ranching is most important to the valley's history because it anchored early settlement in the valley, providing an economic base and the stability needed to establish viable communities. Ranching became and remained the economic mainstay through the World War II, when the tourist industry displaced it. The rancher and cowpuncher left a tradition that continues to be an important element of Jackson Hole's self-image.

Notes

1. Billington, *Westward Expansion*, pp. 457–466.

2. Merk, *History of the Western Movement*, p. 464.

3. Billington, *Westward Expansion*, pp. 582–590; and Merk, *History of the Western Movement*, pp. 457–466.

4. Billington, *Westward Expansion*, p. 590.

5. Ibid; and Larson, *History of Wyoming*, pp. 163–194.

6. Billington, *Westward Expansion*, pp. 596–597; and Merk, *History of the Western Movement*, p. 463.

7. Larson, *History of Wyoming*, pp. 190–192.

8. Merk, *History of the Western Movement*, pp. 464–466.

9. Ibid., p. 461.

10. Hayden, *From Trapper to Tourist in Jackson Hole*, p. 54.

11. Larson, *History of Wyoming*, p. 193; and Merk, *History of the Western Movement*, p. 464.

12. Gillette, *Homesteading with the Elk*, pp. 135–141; and *Jackson's Hole Courier*, November 8, 1945.

13. Homestead Patents, Homestead Certificate 529, Lander, Fred Lovejoy, 1904.

14. Homestead Patents: 36433, J.P. Cunningham, 1908; Homestead Cert. 1181, Evanston, J.P. Cunningham, 1904. Estimates of hay consumption by cattle were corrected, based on information provided by Virginia Huidekoper, Earl Hardeman, and Jack Huyler.

15. Struthers Burt, *Diary*, p. 116.

16. Allan, "History of the Teton National Forest," pp. 125, 154; *Jackson's Hole Courier*, February 17, 1949; and Larson, *History of Wyoming*, pp. 268–284.

17. Elizabeth Wied Hayden Collection, Subject File #5, Cattle, Jackson Hole Historical Society and Museum.

18. Ibid.

19. Ibid., Allan, "History of Teton National Forest," p. 158.

20. "Jackson Hole, Wyoming Cattle Brands," File B, Brands, acc. no. 481, Jackson Hole Historical Society and Museum; *Jackson's Hole Courier*, October 18, 1917, and February 7, 1918.

21. John Markham, "Cattle Drives," unpublished manuscript (Ms 167G), Wyoming State Archives Museums and Historical Department; Driggs, *History of Teton Valley*, p. 184; Allen, Early Jackson Hole, pp. 117–154; and *Jackson's Hole Courier*, October 11, 1917.

22. Allan, "History of Teton National Forest," p. 158; "Calves Prices," File MM, Jackson Hole Historical Society and Museum; and *Jackson's Hole Courier*, November 1, 1917, October 28, 1920, and August 25, 1921.

23. "Calves Prices," File MM, Jackson Hole Historical Society and Museum; *Jackson's Hole Courier*, May 22, 1924, and January 27, 1927; and Allan, "History of Teton National Forest," p. 158.

24. "Calves Prices," File MM, Jackson Hole Historical Society and Museum; and Struthers Burt to Horace Albright, October 14, 1927, Horace Albright Papers, 1923–1927, Yellowstone National Park Archives.

25. *Jackson's Hole Courier*, August 16, 1928, and October 11, 1928.

26. "Calves Prices," File MM, Jackson Hole Historical Society and Museum.

27. "Hearings on H.R. 2241,"1943, 383.

28. "Calves Prices," File MM, Jackson Hole Historical Society and Museum.

29. Larson, *History of Wyoming*, p. 167; Hayden Collection, Subject File #5, Ranching Jackson Hole Historical Society and Museum; and Office of the Teton County Clerk and Recorder, Deed Record Book 2, p. 15, Charles and Helena Davis to Gerrit Hardeman, Warranty Deed, April 16, 1919.

30. Larson, *History of Wyoming*, pp. 168–171; and Hayden Collection, Subject File #5, Ranching, Jackson Hole Historical Society and Museum.

31. *Jackson's Hole Courier*, May 21, 1914, May 28, 1914, June 11, 1914, and July 9, 1914. The actual level of predation by wolves is a sore subject, particularly between livestock interests and environmental groups. While reports of mortality may well have been exaggerated or mistaken for predation, they should not be discounted out of hand either. It is doubtful that ranchers would have put up so much bounty money had they not experienced losses.

32. Hayden Collection, Subject File #5, Cattle, Jackson Hole Historical Society and Museum; *Jackson's Hole Courier*, March 19, 1925.

33. Larson, *History of Wyoming*, pp. 369–372.

34. Ibid; and Hayden Collection, Subject File #5, Sheep, Jackson Hole Historical Society and Museum.

35. Allan, "History of Teton National Forest," pp. 125–131.

36. Larson, *History of Wyoming*, pp. 371–372; and interview with Don and Gladys Kent by Jo Anne Byrd, #18, in "Last of Old West Series."

37. *Jackson's Hole Courier*, June 7, 1923; Homestead Patents: 1038450, Lewis Fleming, 1929; interview with Don and Gladys Kent, #18; and Superintendent's Monthly Report, September 1929, Grand Teton National Park.

38. *Jackson's Hole Courier*, June 7, 1923; and interview with Don and Gladys Kent, #18.

39. Rockefeller Archive Center, Harold P. Fabian Papers, IV3A7, Box 6, File 35, Richard Winger to Josephine Cunningham, April 24, 1932.

40. Hayden Collection, Subject File #5, Cattle Ranching, Jackson Hole Historical Society and Museum.

41. Nellie Van Derveer, "Teton County-Agriculture and Industry," WPA File 1327, Wyoming State Archives; interview with Phylis Brown by Jo Anne Byrd, #4, "Last of Old West Series;" and Jackson Hole Platbook, Snake River Land Company, Harold and Josephine Fabian Collection, Grand Teton National Park.

42. *Jackson's Hole Courier*, January 4, 1934; Teton County Records, Deed Record Book 3, 189, Jude Allen to Elk Ranch Company, Warranty Deed, December 18, 1917;

Deed Record Book 3, p. 137, John S. Shive to D. E. Skinner, Warranty Deed, March 26, 1919; Deed Record Book 3, 446, p. Otto Kusche to D. E. Skinner, Warranty Deed, September 1, 1916; John Markham, "The Hatchet and Elk Ranches" (ms. 167F, H70–135/4), Wyoming State Archives; and Deed Record Book 2, 124, Frank S. Coffin to J. D. Ferrin, Warranty Deed, December 4, 1915.

43. Homestead Patent 323588, J. D. Ferrin, 1912; Teton County Records, Deed Record Book 1, p. 302, W. A. Thompson to J. D. Ferrin, Warranty Deed, July 17, 1911; Deed Record Book 3, p. 212, J. D. Ferrin, Warranty Deed, January 3, 1914; Deed Record Book 2, p. 218, J. D. Uhl to J. D. Ferrin, Warranty Deed, April 26, 1918; Deed Record Book 2, p. 409, James and Opal McInelly to J. D. Ferrin, Warranty Deed, October 13, 1927; Deed Record Book 2, p. 293, D. E. Skinner to Leonard J. Ray, and Robert L. Ferrin, Warranty Deed, December 9, 1920; and *Jackson's Hole Courier*, September 3, 1914.

44. Interview with Ada Clark by Jo Anne Byrd, #8, "Last of Old West Series;" *Jackson's Hole Courier*, April 13, 1944; and Homestead Patents: 895259, Heirs of Curtis Ferrin, 1922; 958787, Leonard Ferrin, 1924; and 1028708, Cyrus Ray Ferrin, 1928.

45. Teton County Records, Index Book, T. 44 N., R. 114 W., 6th P.M.; interview with Ada Clark, #8. According to Ada Clark, her father and family owned as many as 5,000 cattle at one point.

46. Teton County Records; Fabian Papers, RAC, Box 21, Files 217, 218, 220, 221, all Ferrin parcels; Deed Record Book 2, p. 461, J. D. and Edith Ferrin to the Snake River Land Company, Warranty Deed, March 22, 1928.

47. *Jackson's Hole Courier*, April 13, 1944; *Jackson Hole Guide*, December 2, 1965; Markham, "The Hatchet and Elk Ranches," Wyoming State Archives; Merritt Ferrin, "The Elk Ranch," transcript, acc. #1455, Jackson Hole Historical Society and Museum; and interview with Ada Clark, #8.

48. Orin and Lorraine Bonney, "Shootout at the Cowboy Bar," *Teton* 14 (1981):12–13.

49. *Jackson's Hole Courier*, October 9, 1919.

50. *Jackson's Hole Courier*, April 16, 1914, and May 13, 1920.

51. Jackson Hole Platbook, Fabian Collection, Grand Teton National Park; *Jackson's Hole Courier*, August 1, 1929; Fabian Papers, RAC, Box 18, File 179, J. P. Ranch 1928–1930; Box 19, Files 180–181, J. P. Ranch 1930–1936; and *Jackson's Hole Courier*, October 27, 1927.

52. Homestead Patents: 710289, Charles Davis, 1918; and 1037836, Gerrit Hardeman, 1929; Teton County Records, Deed Record Book 2, p. 15, Charles and Helen

Davis to Gerrit Hardeman, Warranty Deed, April 16, 1919; Deed Record Book 7, p. 275, Luther and L. M. Taylor to Gerrit and Alta L. Hardeman, Warranty Deed, April 26, 1943; interview with Lamar Crandall Hardeman by Jo Anne Byrd, #15, "Last of Old West Series;" *Jackson's Hole Courier,* June 26, 1924; and *Jackson Hole News,* December 21, 1972, and September 22, 1977.

53. *Jackson's Hole Courier,* August 23, 1951; and Jackson Hole Guide, November 1, 1973.

54. *Jackson Hole Guide,* July 10, 1986.

55. *Jackson's Hole Courier,* December 12, 1948; Superintendent's Monthly Report, June 1958, Grand Teton National Park, Box 743799, Federal Records Center, Denver, CO; Ethel Jump interview, transcript, Jackson Hole Historical Society and Museum; Struthers Burt, *Diary,* p. 41, and *Natural Resources Management Plan, Grand Teton National Park,* pp. 131–133.

, crib dam at the mouth of Jackson Lake failed in 1910,
leted in 1916 The town of Moran is in the background.

arceling out and lands conforming to irrigation dis-
ricts rather than according to rectangular sections
nd townships. Moreover, Powell believed that politi
cal entities should be formed around river drainages.[1]
Because of their experience in eastern states,
precipitation provided adequate water for
American farmers were slow to adopt irriga-
historic people had irrigated lands in the
in and the Southwest long before the first
came to North America, and the Spanish
farmlands in California in the eight-
The Mormons were the first Anglo
te western lands successfully, when
ms and communities in the Great
-organized religious communi-
an impressive mosaic of irriga-
the Salt Lake Valley. De-
ther settlers adopted

Reclamation and Irrigation

We live in Wyoming and have seen and experienced the results of the damming of Jackson's [sic] and using the Snake River for a ditch.

—Editorial, *Jackson's Hole Courier,* January 13, 1921

Construction of Jackson Lake Dam, 1915. After the original log crib dam at the mouth of Jackson Lake failed in 1910, the Reclamation Service built a concrete dam, which was completed in 1916. The town of Moran is in the background. *Jackson Hole Historical Society and Museum*

Major John Wesley Powell received much popular acclaim for being the first to successfully navigate the Colorado River in 1869. This extraordinary feat launched the "Major,' as his friends called him, on a successful career; he became the second director of the U.S. Geological Survey and the founder and first director of the Bureau of Ethnology. Most remember him for these achievements. Powell is less well known for his astute, if somewhat visionary, ideas regarding land reform in the American West.

The Major recognized that much of the United States consisted of arid lands that required irrigation. This ran contrary to popular notions of the American West as a bountiful land wanting only stout settlers to make it blossom. A moist climatic cycle in the 1860s and 1870s reinforced this false perception. In his *Report on the Lands of the Arid Region of the United States* published in 1879, Powell advocated parceling out arid lands conforming to irrigation districts rather than according to rectangular sections and townships. Moreover, Powell believed that political entities should be formed around river drainages.[1]

Because of their experience in eastern states, where precipitation provided adequate water for crops, American farmers were slow to adopt irrigation. Prehistoric people had irrigated lands in the Great Basin and the Southwest long before the first Europeans came to North America, and the Spanish had irrigated farmlands in California in the eighteenth century. The Mormons were the first Anglo farmers to irrigate western lands successfully, when they developed farms and communities in the Great Basin. Through well-organized religious communities, they constructed an impressive mosaic of irrigation canals and ditches in the Salt Lake Valley. Despite Mormon successes, other settlers adopted irrigation slowly.[2]

Irrigation ditch on the
Thomas Murphy homestead
on Mormon Row. Virtually
all of the irrigation projects
in Jackson Hole were the
products of individual or
group efforts.
Arnie Thallheimer

In Wyoming, irrigation made slow inroads. Ranchers and farmers constructed small ditches along rivers and streams in the 1880s, but there were no large-scale projects. The Carey Act of 1894 and the Reclamation Act of 1902 spawned a flurry of activity as various interests sought water rights. Under the Carey Act, the federal government could donate up to 1,000,000 acres of land to designated desert-land states, provided that state governments would promote irrigation, settlement, and cultivation of those lands. Wyoming was the first state to apply for these lands, seeking 457,500 acres. However, the application proved a dismal failure, as only 11,321 acres were patented. Indeed, critics of the Carey Act charged that companies applied to the state for water not to develop land, but to secure water rights to sell for use elsewhere.[3] Furthermore, private irrigation companies often avoided bidding on reclamation projects, because cost overruns caused them to lose money in most cases.

· By 1897, Wyoming had approved eight projects, all initiated by private companies. The state charged

homesteaders 50 cents per acre, while the companies were authorized to charge them $20 or more for perpetual water rights. Only two companies, Big Horn Basin Development Company and Buffalo Bill Cody's Shoshone Land and Irrigation Company, became more than grandiose schemes and even these failed.[4]

The Reclamation Act, passed by Congress and signed into law by President Theodore Roosevelt in 1902, authorized the federal government to reclaim land through water projects. The law allowed provisional withdrawals of land from settlement to prevent speculation. As the new Reclamation Service completed projects, settlers could preempt the withdrawn lands, paying for the irrigation systems through assessments based on acreage owned. In Wyoming, the Reclamation Service initiated three projects before 1910. The Service issued contracts for the construction of the Shoshone Dam near Cody, Wyoming, in 1904. The dam was completed in 1910. A permit in 1905 authorized the construction of the Pathfinder

Dam on the North Platte River, which was completed in 1911. The Reclamation Service built a log crib dam at the outlet of Jackson Lake in 1906–1907. When the dam failed in 1910, they constructed the present concrete dam and earthen dike, completing the project in 1916.[5]

In the judgement of historian T. A. Larson, the Carey Act and Reclamation Act turned water reclamation into a "three-ring circus." "Before 1894 the whole show had been concentrated in one ring, where unalloyed private enterprise prevailed."[6] Under the Carey Act, states became involved in reclamation; and the federal government entered the field with the creation of a new bureau in 1902. The result was competition for water rights—and considerable confusion. All three players brought the "circus" to Jackson Hole.

In the private sector, there were four types of irrigation enterprises: individual and partnership projects; cooperative associations; irrigation districts (which were semi-public organizations); and commercial companies. Of these, individual and partnership activities dominated irrigation. For example, in 1919, this group accounted for more than one-third of all irrigated acreage in the West, followed closely by cooperative associations.[7] This was also the pattern in Jackson Hole, as individuals, partnerships, and groups accounted for all of the irrigation ditches in the valley.

In Jackson Hole, the Teton Irrigation Company tied up water rights and land in 1909 and 1912. The company conducted surveys and filed paperwork, investing nothing in development. The Jackson Lake Dam represents lands irrigated by Reclamation Service projects. To this day, the water rights to the Jackson Lake Dam remain attached to farm lands in Idaho.

Under the federal system of government, individual states control water rights. After achieving statehood in 1890, the Wyoming legislature adopted a constitution that declared all water within its boundaries to be property of the state. The legislature also established a state board of control to supervise the "appropriation, distribution, and diversion" of water, and created a state engineer position to administer waters under its jurisdiction. Wyoming law attached water use to the land for which it was appropriated, whether for irrigation or other purposes. "Water rights for the direct use of the natural unstored flow cannot be detached from the lands, place, or purpose for which they are acquired." Thus, Wyoming water rights cannot be separated from the lands, as can be done in some states.[8] The standard allowance of water for irrigation purposes is one cubic foot per 70 acres, the amount of water that flows through one cubic foot of space per second.[9]

Wyoming adopted the Prior Appropriation System of Water Rights, which basically means "first in time, first in right." Settlers possessing the first claims to water secured priority rights over later appropriators. This system becomes important in times of shortages, because available water is parceled out

⊕ Acres Irrigated ⊕		
Types of Enterprise in United States	1919	1929
Individual and partnership enterprises	6,848,807	6,410,571
Cooperative associations	6,581,400	6,771,334
Irrigation districts	1,822,887	3,452,275
Commercial companies	1,822,001	1,230,763
Carey Act	537,929	86,772
U.S. Bureau of Reclamation	1,254,569	1,485,028
U.S. Bureau of Indian Affairs	284,551	331,840
State	5,620	11,489
City and other	47,952	267,462
Total	19,191,716	19,547,544

Source: Merk, *History of the Western Movement.*

Settlers digging an irrigation ditch from Flat Creek. *Jackson Hole Historical Society and Museum*

to appropriators based on the dates of their claims. A claim takes effect on the date it is filed with the state engineer. The state established the following procedures to secure water permits.[10]

1. File a petition for a permit with the state engineer.
2. The state board of control approves the petition or application, which allows the filer to start construction. The project must be completed in five years from start-up time.
3. The filer must accomplish the following:
   a. Send notice of commencement of work to the state engineer.
   b. Send notice of completion of work to state engineer.
   c. Send notice of application of water for beneficial use to state engineer.
4. To secure final proof, the filer must notify the local superintendent of the water division. The state board of control reviews the application and issues a "Certificate of Appropriation," which conveys a water right to the filer.

A Certificate of Appropriation constituted an adjudicated water right. In his study of water rights in Grand Teton National Park, William L. Mekeel inventoried 258 appropriations now owned by the National Park Service. He also found 19 unadjudicated water rights, or those for which final proof papers were not completed. In addition, he identified 68 alien water rights, of which eight remained unadjudi-

cated. Mekeel defined this classification as "those in which the irrigated land or place of domestic water use and/or the point of diversion and/or the means of conveyance are located with the park boundary." These numbers demonstrate the importance of irrigation to agriculture in Jackson Hole.[11]

Virtually all irrigation projects in Jackson Hole were the products of individual or group efforts. None of the ditches were engineering marvels, but nevertheless represented many hours of labor. According to the *Tabulation of Adjudicated Water Rights* for Water Division Number Four, D. H. Goe secured water rights to 2.28 cubic feet of water from South Twin or Twin Creek dating from June 10, 1883. Water was diverted through Holland Ditch Number 1 to a 160-acre parcel in the Flat Creek area. This water right may have belonged originally to John Holland, who secured the first water rights in Jackson Hole in 1883, according to another source. It was common for ditches to be named for their owners. The date of 1883 is inconsistent with popular tradition, which places the arrival of Holland and Carnes as 1884.[12]

Within the boundaries of the present Grand Teton National Park, homesteaders diverted water from several major tributaries of the Snake River; Pacific Creek, Spread Creek, Cottonwood Creek, Ditch Creek, Gros Ventre River, and the lower Snake River, which encompasses the areas in the park south of Moose, Wyoming.[13] The first ditch known to be excavated in Jackson Hole was the old Mining Ditch on Antelope Flats. As the name implies, unknown prospectors excavated a ditch to conduct placer mining on the Snake River. Orestes St. John, the geologist with the Hayden Surveys, described the ditch in his report of the 1877 survey. W. O. Owen plotted the course of the ditch on his survey map of Township 43 North, Range 115 West, 6th Principal Meridian in 1893. Owen's map shows a ditch approximately three and one-half miles in length, which diverted water from Ditch Creek at a point downstream from the present Teton Science School and ran a northwest course to Schwabacher's Landing on the Snake River.[14]

In 1896, James I. May and William Kissenger dug the first ditches for agricultural purposes in land comprising today's Grand Teton National Park. May excavated the Trail Ditch using a horse-drawn plow and hand tools. He used the water to irrigate 35 acres at the base of Blacktail Butte. Kissenger constructed a four-mile ditch to his homestead at Kelly Warm Springs. Homesteaders utilized water from the Gros Ventre and Ditch Creek to irrigate fields in the Mormon Row-Kelly area and on Antelope Flats.[15]

The first ditches taking water from the Gros Ventre were located in the Spring Gulch area. The earliest water right belonged to P C. Hansen, whose priority dated from June 8, 1894. In 1898, five ranches secured rights to the Spring Gulch Ditch, which diverted water into the gulch. In the park, Nels Hoagland homesteaded west of Kelly with his four children. Filing for water rights in 1898, it took him at least four years to complete the Cedar Tree Ditch. Because of a lack of water, Hoagland was unable to plant a crop until 1903.[16] Plans to divert water from the Gros Ventre began in earnest in 1899, when Fred Lovejoy and George Kissenger filed for water rights to be diverted through the Midland Ditch. On July 31st of that year, Jim Budge, James May, Mart Henrie, and Joe Henrie secured water rights to 9.26 cubic feet of water, and constructed the Hot Springs Ditch above Kelly to divert water to 650 acres of land near Blacktail Butte. Other early ditches along the Gros Ventre were the Hobo, the Wild Cherry, the Sebastian, the Mesa, the Ideal, and the Savage. Rights to water coursing through these ditches date from 1899 and 1902.

Ditch Creek provided the other major waterway for irrigating lands in this area. James I. May tapped this creek with a headgate for the Trail Ditch while William Kissenger constructed a ditch to irrigate 65 acres at Kelly Warm Springs. Except for these two ditches, Ditch Creek remained untapped until 1907 or later, when settlers preempted lands around the creek. Several homesteaders rehabilitated and modified the old Mining Ditch, beginning with James Williams in 1908, O. H. Bark in 1909, E. C. "Doc" Steele in 1911, George Carpenter in 1912, and T. H. Baxter in 1914. The *Courier* reported that A. Z. Smith, J. R. Smith, Carpenter, and Baxter were digging a ditch to their properties in 1914.[17] Between 1908 and 1930, 17 ditches were developed along Ditch Creek. Sometimes springs provided a water source. For example, Norm Smith obtained water from Pemble Spring on Blacktail Butte enabling him to irrigate 20 acres of his homestead.

In May 1927, water breached the natural dam at Lower Slide Lake on the Gros Ventre River causing the catastrophic Kelly flood. Irrigation works on the river were seriously damaged or destroyed. At that time, a group of farmers on Mormon Row had been excavating a canal from the Gros Ventre, each devoting several hours of work per week. They hoped to convert land being dry farmed for wheat and oats to irrigated hayfields. The flood ruined their work. But, for uncertain reasons, Mud Springs (today's Kelly Warm Springs) began producing more water after the Kelly flood. Settlers cut the Mormon Row Ditch to the springs and began irrigating dry lands. John Moulton, T. A. Moulton, Andy Chambers, J. Wallace Moulton, and Joe Heniger owned rights to nine cubic feet per second dating from 1929. To add even more water, settlers diverted water from Savage Ditch, cutting a channel to Mud Springs in the 1930s. The enlarged Savage Ditch added eight users to the system. As a result, Andy Chambers switched from dry farming to ranching, raising hay and cattle.[18]

West of the Snake River below Menor's Ferry, homesteaders began filing water rights around the turn of the century. Farmers and ranchers tapped water from Granite and Lake Creeks. P C. Hansen and Albert Mangum secured rights to 3.49 cubic feet of water diverted from Granite Creek through

Diversion dams served several farms and ranches, and were usually operated by a cooperating association. This dam, typical of many in Jackson Hole, is on Spread Creek. *Grand Teton National Park*

the Granite Ditch. The priorities dated from 1898. Other early ditches irrigating lands were the Chicago, the John Miller, the Brown, the Kaufman, the Pemble Lake Creek, and the Nikolaison. Most of these ditches conveyed water to land located south of the park.

In 1907, Bill Menor was the first to secure rights to water from Cottonwood Creek for his homestead on the west bank of the Snake. Struthers Burt and Horace Carncross secured rights to 7.05 cubic feet of water effective December 6, 1912, when they submitted an application to construct the Bar BC Ditch, a diversion of approximately five miles. Between 1914 through the 1920s, claimants filed for 25 permits to secure water from Cottonwood Creek and its tributaries, Bradley and Taggart Creeks.

Because of concentrated agricultural activity in the Spread Creek area, this watercourse and nearby tributaries became an important source of water. The first water rights dated from 1897, when five applicants sought to divert 8.29 cubic feet of water from Spread Creek through the Wolff Ditch. The owners of the rights were Marie Wolff, J. D. Ferrin, Emile Wolff, Otto Kusche, and J. H. Uhl. Since Ferrin and Kusche homesteaded after 1900, they may have taken over rights from previous claimants. In 1910, Wolff and Fred Cunningham constructed their own

ditches; Wolff built the Elk Ditch, and Cunningham built the Antler.

After the creation of Teton National Forest in 1908, new lands were opened to settlement. In 1909, five settlers filed for water rights in the enlarged Wolff Ditch, then created an association of ten people. Other important ditches were the Jude V. Allen Ditch, and the J. P Nelson Ditch. Because of the availability of water from sources such as springs and creeks, and the braided channels of Spread Creek, more settlers constructed their own ditches rather than form partnerships or cooperative groups. Twenty individual ditches were excavated in the Spread Creek drainage area. One ditch was constructed for placer mining in 1905, during a flurry of speculation in placer claims along the Snake River. The ditch was named for E. C. "Doc" Steele, a member of a loose partnership speculating in placer claims. Lydia Lozier secured a water right utilizing this abandoned ditch to carry the water to 128 acres at a later date.

On the Buffalo Fork and its tributaries there was less irrigation activity; none of the ditches or irrigated lands are in the park. Emil Feuz secured a priority to 1.76 cubic feet from the Buffalo Fork, effective 1913. Jack Shive obtained the first water right in this drainage in 1900, diverting water from Blackrock Creek. Noble Gregory secured a water right to almost two cubic feet of water from Lava Creek, effective 1902.

Limited irrigation took place in the Pacific Creek drainage near Moran. Charles J. Allen had the first adjudicated priority effective in 1899 for 2.28 cubic feet of water from Meadow Creek near Oxbow Bend. Joe Markham, Roy Lozier, and O. W. Snell constructed a ditch from Emma Matilda Creek to Markham's homestead on the east side of the Oxbow. Their priorities dated from 1919.

In 1928, the Snake River Land Company, the Rockefeller-sponsored Utah corporation formed in 1927, began buying homesteads in the valley, which included appurtenant water rights. The company intended to donate the lands to the National Park Service for incorporation into an expanded Grand Teton National Park. The prolonged controversy over park extension posed a problem for company officials. Wyoming state law specifies ". . . if the owner or owners of a ditch, canal or reservoir shall fail to use the water therefrom for irrigation or other beneficial use during any five successive years, they shall be considered as having abandoned the same and shall forfeit all water rights. . . ." Other claimants can then apply for the abandoned rights. To prevent loss of these rights, the Snake River Land Company maintained and altered irrigation systems in the park and leased some lands for grazing, cultivation, or dude ranching.[19]

The company first spent money on ditches when local agent Dick Winger persuaded them to repair ditches on the Gros Ventre River destroyed by the Kelly flood in 1927. In 1936 and 1937, the company spent "several thousand dollars" constructing five miles of canal to irrigate 2,800 acres of land. Civil engineer John Simpson drew up plans to rehabilitate irrigation ditches south of Blacktail Butte. The project involved rehabilitating four and one-half miles of ditch and changing the diversion points and means of conveyance for the Enlarged Midland Ditch, the Enlarged Sebastian Ditch, the Enlarged Mesa Ditch, and part of the Enlarged Ideal Ditch. The company also improved the Newbold Canal and the Enlarged Sebastian Ditch.[20]

Using the old Elk Ranch holdings above Spread Creek as a nucleus, the Snake River Land Company fenced every purchased homestead between Spread Creek and the Buffalo Fork to raise hay for "wild game" and livestock. Cultivating hay required maintenance and improvements to existing ditches. In 1940, the company applied for a permit to reserve 423.3 acre feet of water to be stored in a reservoir to be located south of Uhl Hill. The company also modified the old Wolff Ditch to supply water from Spread Creek. In addition, it changed the diversion points and means of conveyance of the Jude V. Allen Ditch and Steele Ditch. In the early 1940s, the company built the Uhl Reservoir, an earthen fill dam 800 feet in length. The National Park Service took over several of the systems after 1950 and continues to maintain many of them in conjunction with extant grazing permits in the park.[21]

While Rockefeller's company represented corporate-backed irrigation, the Jackson Lake Dam epitomized federal involvement in reclamation efforts. Shortly after the passage of enabling legislation creating the Reclamation Service in 1902, surveyors entered Jackson Hole in September to conduct surveys of Jackson, Emma Matilda, Two Ocean, and Jenny Lakes. They evaluated the suitability of each for reservoirs. In 1907, the Reclamation Service completed a log crib dam at the outlet of Jackson Lake. The dam failed in 1910. The service launched an ambitious construction program, working through the winter of 1910–1911 to build a concrete gravity dam. It added an earthen dike on the north wing and rebuilt the dam, completing work in 1916. The dam raised the water level 39 feet and increased the area of the lake by one-third. The dam was part of the Minidoka Project, an ambitious reclamation program in the Upper Snake River valley.[22]

The dam's construction over the winter of 1910–1911 was a significant accomplishment, given the time frame, logistical problems, and severe weather. Frank Crowe, a prominent Reclamation Service engineer, directed the reconstruction in 1910, while Frank Banks supervised the remainder of the work from 1913 to 1916.[23] The dam impounded 847,000 acre feet of water to irrigate farmlands in Idaho. None was used for irrigation in Jackson Hole. Nevertheless, the project influenced development in the valley in a number of ways. It was the first major

The construction of the Jackson Lake dam was one of the largest government projects in Jackson Hole, providing employment and lucrative freight contracts for valley residents. *National Park Service*

development project, private or public, in the valley and, as such, boosted the early economy significantly. The Reclamation Service employed numerous residents such as P C. Hansen and others. In one of its social columns, the *Jackson's Hole Courier* reported that local settlers Aktor Nelson, Fred Topping, George Greenwood, and Samuel R. Wilson were employed by the Reclamation Service.[24]

Others contracted to haul freight, shipping virtually all supplies for the project. Walt Germann, Gerrit Hardeman, Ben Taylor, Ray Shinkle, and Fred Shinkle freighted supplies over the Ashton-Moran Road. Si Ferrin received a windfall when he secured the contract to supply beef in 1914. According to Eliot Paul in *Desperate Scenery*, Ben Sheffield was not especially happy with the project, but certainly benefited financially from the workers' patronage of his store, restaurant, and guest accommodations at Moran. The economic impact rippled south to Jackson. Traffic between Moran and Jackson increased to such an extent that James I. May and his family operated a roadhouse out of their home on Mormon Row. In a few cases, entrepreneurs failed. E. C. "Doc' Steele opened a saloon near Moran around 1911, but abandoned it by the next year, after work slowed on the dam.[25]

Second, the project at Jackson Lake required more labor than the valley could provide, so the Reclamation Service brought in workers. A number of these men stayed in the area. Joe Pfeifer may have come to work at the new dam rather than to home-

stead. Dude rancher Harold Hammond hired on as stable boss to wrangle Reclamation Service horses. The service hired Joe Markham to serve as head timekeeper for the project. All three of these men homesteaded in the valley. Charlie Fesler was a cook for the service, who stayed on at Moran to run a small grocery.[26]

Third, the sheer scale of the 1910 construction project posed logistical challenges as well as engineering problems. Frank Crowe recognized the need to improve the crude wagon road between Ashton and Moran before starting construction. He chose to link up with Ashton, because the Oregon Short Line served this community, and the three-day wagon trip was shorter than the Teton Pass route. For the next 17 years, this road served as an important supply corridor to the upper end of the valley.[27]

If there was any opposition to the construction of the dam it was not apparent. The reclamation effort represented unabashed western boosterism as a triumph of man over nature. Eliot Paul's autobiographical novel *Desperate Scenery* reflected the "can do" spirit that characterized attitudes about the project. Contrast this with Owen Wister's opinion of the dam; "And here let me pause to lay my ineffectual but heartfelt curse upon the commercial vandals who desecrated the outlet of Jackson's Lake with an ugly dam to irrigate some desert land away off in Idaho."[28]

The Jackson Lake Dam played a part, albeit indirectly, in generating opposition to other reclamation projects in Jackson Hole and Yellowstone. Struthers

Burt described Jackson Lake as "an example so good that it is constantly being used as an object-lesson by the enemies of stupid spoilation." In particular, a significant number of valley residents opposed a plan put forth by Frank Emerson, state engineer and later Governor of Wyoming, to construct a dam at the outlet of Jenny Lake. Opponents used Jackson Lake's fate as an "object lesson" in spoiled mountain scenery; the Reclamation Service failed to cut and clear thousands of predominantly lodgepole pine trees that were killed when inundated by raising water levels. The result was an unsightly tangle of dead trees around the shore of Jackson Lake. The Civilian Conservation Corps cleaned up 8,000 acres of shoreline in the 1930s.[29]

In another instance an editorial appeared in the *Jackson's Hole Courier* in 1921 titled "Remember Jackson's Lake" that opposed a proposed dam on the Fall River in Yellowstone National Park. This was a significant departure for a paper that opposed the proposed Yellowstone Extension into the Teton Country. The editorial stated "we live in Wyoming and have seen and experienced the results of the damming of Jackson's [sic] and using the Snake River for a ditch."

Property damage, inconvenience, and resentment over other states benefiting from Wyoming dams mobilized sentiment against reclamation projects. The *Courier* editorial complained that the Reclamation Service had allowed excessive amounts of water out of Jackson Lake, washing away private land and causing "thousands of dollars in damage." The Ferrins, the Bar BC, and the Cadwalader Ranch suffered the most damage. In 1917, when high water on the Snake washed away the approaches to the new steel truss bridge between Jackson and Wilson, local residents blamed the Reclamation Service for releasing too much water from Jackson Lake. In turn, the service blamed local officials for not riprapping the approaches properly. Teamsters were forced to transport mail and supplies 20 miles north to Menor's Ferry and back again causing considerable delays in mail and freight service. Whether the dam at Jackson Lake caused thousands of dollars of damage is questionable, but the point is that some valley residents perceived reclamation projects as bad.[30] The approaches to the Wilson bridge were moved down-

stream a short distance, and the bridge repaired in 1922 with county, state, and private funds. This time, workers constructed an adequate system of levies and riprap. Despite beliefs of local citizens, the Reclamation Service appears not to have been responsible, for it was never taken to court nor ordered to pay for damages.

Another controversy developed over the dam in 1921 when Teton County, authorized by the state legislature, tried to assess property taxes for reserved water rights on Jackson Lake. Early in 1924, the Twin Falls Canal Company and the North Side Canal Company, both Idaho corporations, filed an injunction in the U.S. District Court in Cheyenne, Wyoming, seeking to prevent the assessment of $12,000 in taxes. In September 1925, Judge Blake Kennedy ruled that the water rights on Jackson Lake were taxable. Company attorneys appealed the decision. An appeals court reversed Kennedy's decision in 1926. The court held that since the water rights were appurtenant or attached to lands in Idaho, Teton County had no right to tax them.[31]

Entrepreneurs and state officials proposed other water reclamation projects in Jackson Hole, but none ever progressed past the planning stage except for headgates installed at Emma Matilda and Two Ocean Lakes. The first proposal was grandiose, initiated under the auspices of the Carey Act of 1894. As explained earlier, this law encouraged the reclamation of arid lands by conveying title of newly-irrigated acreage to states. In turn, states generally contracted with private companies to construct irrigation facilities. In 1909, Charles C. Carlisle and H. G. Porak proposed the Buffalo Fork Canal, a major diversion intended to irrigate 29,078.5 acres east of the Snake River from the Buffalo Fork to the Gros Ventre. They estimated that it would cost $60,000 to construct a 20-mile canal, 36-feet-wide at the top and 26-feet-wide at the bottom, capable of holding five feet of water in depth. The state engineer approved the proposal on May 7, 1909. The Teton Irrigation Company, as Carlisle referred to it, had one year to commence work, five years from commencement to finish work, and ten years to complete proof of beneficial use.

In 1912, Carlisle submitted a modified proposal for a canal system to divert water from Spread Creek south to the Gros Ventre River. The proposed Spread Creek Canal was 12½ miles long, 20 feet wide at the top, 12 feet at the bottom, capable of carrying water four feet deep. Although this plan was more modest, proposing to irrigate 6,413.32 acres, it would feed a large network of canals, the Enlarged Spread Creek, the North Ditch Creek, the South Ditch Creek, and the Gros Ventre. Carlisle estimated the cost to be $35,000. As far as is known, the company never so much as lifted a shovel. Indeed, in 1914, settlers became restless over the company's tied-up water rights and land, complaining "they have done nothing in two years." The General Land Office opened the lands to settlement in 1922, after the company failed to develop an irrigation system.[32] Carlisle's scheme has been clouded by charges of fraud. Struthers Burt was convinced that such projects were never intended to irrigate lands in Jackson Hole, but to divert water to Idaho for a healthy profit.[33]

In 1918 and 1919, homesteaders in the Pacific Creek area began filing for water rights to Emma Matilda and Two Ocean Lakes and their creeks. H. C. McKinstry, William C. Thompson, Joe Markham, Roy Lozier, and O. W. Snell applied for seven permits. Markham, Lozier, and Snell diverted 5.52 cubic feet of water from Emma Matilda Creek through the Markham Ditch to their homesteads along the Snake River. McKinstry and Thompson diverted water from Two Ocean Creek to their properties. The three men were prevented from securing rights-of-way by the presidential executive order of 1918 prohibiting all forms of entry on more than 600,000 acres situated within the Teton National Forest, pending resolution of the Yellowstone Extension. The executive order allowed the National Park Service to veto any undesirable developments. However, Superintendent Horace Albright of Yellowstone interceded on their behalf and the rights-of-way for ditches were granted.[34]

In addition, McKinstry reserved 512 acre feet of water from Two Ocean Lake with a priority date of May 1, 1918, and Markham filed for 1,710 acre feet of water on Emma Matilda Lake on August 18, 1919. A year later, the *Courier* reported that a group of Idaho ranchers of the Osgood Land and Livestock Company purchased the W. S. Thompson

Ranch below Two Ocean Lake along with the water rights of six ranches in the Pacific Creek area. The editor of the *Courier* used this development to rail against the Reclamation Service for using the Snake as a ditch and destroying the Wilson bridge, then criticized "Cheyenne interests," meaning Charles Carlisle, for closing up land to settlement. Actually, neither the Reclamation Service nor the Teton Irrigation Company had any connection with the Idaho company. To complicate matters, Carlisle filed a proposal to construct the Twin Lakes dams at the two lakes in 1919. State Engineer Frank Emerson approved the proposal, but like Carlisle's other schemes, it came to nothing.[35] The Osgood Land and Livestock Company constructed headgates at both Emma Matilda and Two Ocean Lakes in the early 1920s and began diverting water to Idaho. In 1921, the Utah-Idaho Sugar Company purchased the water rights.[36]

Beginning in 1928, the Snake River Land Company began purchasing homesteads. Between 1928 and 1931, they bought the Markham, Lozier, Snell, McKinstry, and Thompson homesteads. This set the stage for litigation. In 1935, company attorneys and agents began putting together legal briefs and reports to challenge the Utah-Idaho Sugar Company's water claims. The Snake River Land Company argued that they had purchased the same water rights since they were appurtenant to the lands. They based their case on Wyoming state law, which stated that "water rights for the direct use of the natural unstored flow of any stream cannot be detached from the lands, place or purpose of which they are acquired." In other words, the company challenged the legality of the earlier sale of water rights. The suit began with a hearing before the state engineer in 1938 and went through the Wyoming State Supreme Court in 1942. Each appeal affirmed that water rights could not be separated from the lands to which they were appurtenant. The Utah-Idaho Sugar Company lost all appeals and, consequently, their claims to water rights, and the case set an important precedent confirming the validity of Wyoming water laws. The dams at Emma Matilda and Two Ocean Lakes were removed in the early 1950s.[37]

The second scheme emerged in 1919; State Engineer Frank Emerson proposed a dam at the outlet of Jenny Lake for irrigation purposes in the wake of the 1919 drought that devastated much of the American West. The proposed dam would have raised the water level of Jenny Lake 20 feet and the level of Leigh Lake ten feet. A small but vocal group of Jackson Hole residents were aghast and sought to block the project. Struthers Burt wrote, "they were going to dam one of the near-by lakes—incidentally ruining the lake, a lake which is as beautiful as any in the world. . . ." Opponents found the Forest Service no ally, for while the service did not support the project, neither did it oppose it. The National Park Service employed the 1918 executive order to prevent a dam at the outlet of Jenny Lake. This controversy mobilized support for conservation among a small group of valley residents. More important, these people began to perceive the National Park Service as an ally in their effort to protect Teton country from commercial exploitation.[38]

Aside from the Jackson Lake Dam, large-scale irrigation projects proved to be failures. The Carey Act of 1894 generated no successful reclamation projects in Jackson Hole. Indeed, critics such as Struthers Burt and Dick Winger believed that entrepreneurs had no intention of reclaiming Jackson Hole lands, but in reality sought water rights to sell to the highest bidder. The history of irrigation in Jackson Hole fits the pattern that occurred elsewhere in the American West. Individual, partnership, and group efforts accounted for virtually all irrigation systems in Jackson Hole. Homesteaders constructed the ditches in the park between 1896 and 1927, and it is probable that they used hand tools and horses to build them. These systems were small-scale. Even the largest ditches seldom exceeded ten appropriated users, and most ditches were no more than three miles in length.

Notes

1. Goetzmann, *Exploration and Empire*, pp. 541–551 and 582.

2. Merk, *History of the Western Movement*, pp. 507–508.

3. Larson, *History of Wyoming*, pp. 301–304 and 347–348; and Struthers Burt, *Diary*, pp. 111–125.

4. Larson, *History of Wyoming*, pp. 303–304.

5. Larson, *History of Wyoming*, pp. 355–357; and Merk, *History of the Western Movement*, p. 509.

6. Larson, *History of Wyoming*, p. 348.

7. Merk, *History of the Western Movement*, p. 508.

8. William L. McKeel, "An Interdisciplinary Overview of the Water Resources of Grand Teton National Park," unpublished ms. (Laramie, WY: University of Wyoming. 1972), pp. 77–85.

9. Ibid., p. 82.

10. William McKeel, "Water Rights in Grand Teton National Park," unpublished ms., n.d., Grand Teton National Park, pp. 7–8.

11. Ibid., pp. 2–3.

12. *Jackson Hole Guide,* April 20, 1967, and October 24, 1968; and McKeel, "Water Rights," see Tabulation of Adjudicated Water Rights. This source is used for the remaining narrative unless otherwise noted.

13. McKeel, "Water Rights."

14. St. John, "Report of Orestes St John," *Eleventh Annual Report*, p. 445; William O. Owen, T43N, R115W, 6th P.M., 1893, Jackson Hole Plat Book, Harold and Josephine Fabian Collection, Grand Teton National Park.

15. Interview with Clark Moulton by Jo Anne Byrd, #27, in "Last of Old West Series."

16. Homestead Patent, Homestead Cert. 469, Lander, Nels Hoagland, 1903.

17. *Jackson's Hole Courier,* May 17, 1914.

18. Interview with Clark Moulton, #27; *Jackson's Hole Courier,* November 8, 1945; *Jackson Hole Guide,* May 20, 1976.

19. McKeel, "Water Rights," and transcript of testimony, Snake River Land Co. vs. Utah-Idaho Sugar Co., June 1, 1938, Rockefeller Archive Center, Harold P. Fabian Papers, IV3A7, Box 15, File 110.

20. U.S. Congress, Senate, Subcommittee of Committee on Public Lands and Surveys, "A Resolution to Investigate the Questions of Enlarging Grand Teton National Park in Wyoming; Hearing on S. Res. 250," 75th Cong., 3rd sess., 1938, p. 217; and Newbold Canal, Plat #3, Jackson Hole Plat Book, Fabian Collection, Grand Teton National Park.

21. Uhl Reservoir, Plat #12, Uhl Supply Ditch, Plat #13, Jackson Hole Plat Book, Fabian Collection, Grand Teton National Park.

22. "Reconnaissance Books," Vols. 2–4, Reclamation Service, 1902, Grand Teton National Park; John Markham, "The Temporary Jackson Lake Dam" MSS167B, H70–114, Wyoming State Archives, Museums and Historical Departments; and "Jackson Lake Dam," Determi-

nation of Eligibility, Wyoming State Historic Preservation Office.

23. Markham, "The Temporary Jackson Lake Dam."

24. Ibid., and *Jackson's Hole Courier,* August 13, 1914.

25. Markham, "The Temporary Jackson Lake Dam;" John Markham, "Biography of Mr. Joseph James Markham," biographical files, Wyoming State Archives, Museums and Historical Department; Paul, *Desperate Scenery;* interview with Clark Moulton, #27; and Allen, *Early Jackson Hole,* p. 66.

26. *Jackson Hole News,* November 22, 1972; and Markham, "Biography of Joe Markham."

27. John Markham, "The Ashton-Moran Freight Road, 1910–1927," Pamphlet File, Grand Teton National Park Library.

28. Paul, *Desperate Scenery; Jackson Hole News,* November 16, 1972, November 22, 1972; and *Jackson Hole Guide,* September 19, 1973.

29. Righter, *Crucible for Conservation;* and Struthers Burt, *Diary,* p. 121.

30. *Jackson's Hole Courier,* January 6, 1921, and January 13, 1921.

31. *Jackson's Hole Courier,* April 10, 1924, October 1, 1925, and December 30, 1926.

32. "Buffalo Fork Canal Application for a Permit to Divert and Appropriate Water in the State of Wyoming," May 7, 1909; "Spread Creek Canal Application for a Permit to Divert and Appropriate Water in the State of Wyoming," December 23, 1912; C. C. Carlisle, "Map of Teton Irrigation Project," June 23–July 6, 1912, October 29, 1912-November 4, 1912, Grand Teton National Park; and *Jackson's Hole Courier,* April 16, 1914, and March 10, 1927.

33. Struthers Burt, *Diary,* pp. 111–125; and Murie, *Wapiti Wilderness,* pp. 117–118.

34. McKeel, "Water Rights;" "Hearings on S. Res. 250," 1938, p. 283; Righter, *Crucible for Conservation,* p. 32; and *Jackson's Hole Courier,* October 19, 1919.

35. *Jackson Hole's Courier,* April 22, 1920; and Docket II, Twin Lakes Reservoir and Supply Ditch, Grand Teton National Park.

36. Fabian Papers, Rockefeller Archive Center, Box 15, File 110, Transcript of Hearing, Snake River Land Company vs. Utah-Idaho Sugar Company, June 1, 1938.

37. Docket 9, Snake River Land Company, Protestant vs. Utah-Idaho Sugar Co., Water Rights Files, Grand Teton National Park.

38. Struthers Burt, *Diary,* pp. 118–119; and Righter, *Crucible for Conservation,* p. 32.

The Transportation Frontier

Mr. and Mrs. J. P. Nelson were down from Elk last Saturday, Mrs. Nelson stating that it was her first trip to Jackson in about four years.

—*Jackson's Hole Courier*, January 13, 1918

Strange how a dominating physical feature moulds the character of a country. The Pass—it is always spoken of as The Pass—is never very far away from the thoughts of the inhabitants of the valley.

—Struthers Burt, *The Diary of a Dude Wrangler*

Heavy snow often closed Teton
Pass, and community residents
had to endure long periods of isolation. Workers struggled to get
the gasoline truck through the
cleared path on Teton Pass, which
was often hand dug each spring.
*Jackson Hole Historical Society and
Museum*

Geographic isolation, more than any other factor,
binds the history of Jackson Hole. Getting supplies and mail over the divides preoccupied valley
residents as much as any other activity. Severe winters compounded their problems. Indeed, poor transportation links retarded development in this valley
well into the twentieth century.

After the United States acquired a continental
empire from coast to coast, finding a way to link this
land drew national attention. Only the great issues of
slavery and sectionalism overshadowed this problem;
in fact, the controversy over a transcontinental railroad route became enmeshed in the politics of slavery. Gold rushes in California in 1849 and Colorado
in 1858 made Americans conscious of the transportation problem. These migrations did not typify frontier expansion; rather than emanating from civilized
centers east to west, the miners' frontier skipped
from the Mississippi Valley and eastern United

States to the Pacific Coast, then headed east to the
Rockies.

The Oregon Trail was the primary overland
route to California and Oregon. This trail bypassed
Jackson Hole, utilizing South Pass about 100 miles
to the southeast. The Oregon Trail was so arduous
that many people preferred travel by ship, either to
Panama and the short overland trip across the isth-
mus or around Cape Horn at the southern tip of
South America. In the 1850s, the army conducted
several surveys to evaluate and recommend a route
for a transcontinental railroad. None of four proposed alignments passed through Jackson Hole.

Meanwhile, western pressure increased to develop reliable mail service between California and
the East. Responding to political agitation, Congress
authorized the postmaster general to let a contract
for semi-weekly or weekly mail service to California.
The Butterfield Overland Mail Company received

the contract and established mail and passenger service between Tipton, Missouri, and San Francisco. The Butterfield route was a tortuous track that skirted southwest and then west through Arkansas, the Indian Territories, Texas, New Mexico, and Arizona, a distance of 2,812 miles. The Butterfield Company contracted with the Abbott-Downing Company of Concord, New Hampshire, to produce a suitable vehicle. The New England company manufactured the Concord stagecoach, which revolutionized travel in the West. These coaches sported special adaptations to western conditions—heavy, broad, iron-rimmed tires that would not sink in sand, wide axles to prevent tip-overs, and leather thoroughbraces to absorb shocks.[1]

In 1860, entrepreneurs established the Pony Express in another effort to link the continent. They set up a route between St. Joseph, Missouri, and San Francisco. Relays of dashing horsemen each rode 70 miles to cover the entire route in just over ten days. The Pony Express never showed a profit and was doomed by new technology, the electric telegraph. In 1861, the federal government subsidized the construction of the first transcontinental telegraph, which construction crews completed in just under four months.[2]

The Civil War delayed construction of the transcontinental railroad until 1866, when the Central Pacific and Union Pacific began laying track across the continental expanse in earnest. The two companies raced over the rugged landscape. The Union Pacific laid track across southern Wyoming in 1867 and 1868. The two companies met at Promontory Point in Utah in May 1869. The completion of a transcontinental railroad was perhaps one of the most significant feats in American history, for it bound the nation together both in symbolic and practical terms. The Union Pacific line, 150 miles south of Jackson Hole, provided access to supplies and mail, and facilitated settlement in the region of northwest Wyoming and southeast Idaho.[3]

Early routes into Jackson Hole were nothing more than the old trapper and Indian trails. The first settlers, John Holland and John Carnes, entered Jackson Hole from the Green River Valley via the Gros Ventre River. The so-called Bacon Ridge Trail was the most used route into the valley at first. The U.S. Geological Survey Mount Leidy Quadrangle, 1902,

and the Gros Ventre Quadrangle, 1910, show the wagon road following the west bank of the upper Green River to Bacon Ridge. At the south end of the ridge, the road splits, one traversing the Kinky Creek Divide, the other the Bacon Creek Divide. The roads rejoined near the confluence of the Gros Ventre River and Fish Creek and followed the Gros Ventre into Jackson Hole.[4] In 1883, President Chester A. Arthur led a large entourage into Jackson Hole from Fort Washakie. Crossing Lincoln or Sheridan Pass, they cut a trail down the Gros Ventre into the valley, then followed the Snake River north into Yellowstone. W. O. Owen's map of Township 42 North, Range 115 West shows a broken four-mile trail along the north side of the Gros Ventre River near the Kelly townsite, dubbed the Sheridan Trail.[5]

The Hoback River route followed the old trapper trail to Hoback Junction, a tortuous trail clinging to canyon walls in places. In 1878, William Henry Jackson traveled this trail, describing it as scenic but difficult because of long steep slides. "One of the mules took a roll of about 200 feet into the stream below, but fortunately with no serious harm to itself."[6]

The Snake River Canyon route was not used much because it remained a rugged horse trail over steep-pitched canyon sides. Further, Jackson Hole settlers had little reason to use it since better routes to supply sources existed. About 1906, Fred White, a local justice of the peace, used this route to take funds obtained from elk licenses to Evanston, Wyoming. After he failed to return, search parties scoured the canyon. They found his body and determined that he had been murdered. Since the money was gone, robbery was the probable motive.[7]

The trail over Teton Pass became the primary route into Jackson Hole, for it provided the closest access to supplies and mail, first to the train station at Market Lake, then later to Rexburg, Idaho. By the late 1880s, a crude wagon track had been cleared over the high mountain pass. According to one reference, R. E. Miller, John Cherry, and Jack Hicks brought the first wagons over Teton Pass in 1888. The three teamsters hauled the baggage with pack animals and drove the wagons empty over the divide. The Wilson-Cheney party brought six covered wagons into the valley in the fall of 1889. It took them two weeks to complete the trip, taking two wagons at a time, each pulled by three teams of horses. Getting to the summit was one thing, but easing the wagons down either side of the summit proved even more difficult. Travelers employed several techniques, either separately or in combination, such as placing the larger rear wheels on the front of the wagon, which helped stabilize it. Some rough-locked the rear wheels, fastening a log across them with a chain, in essence creating a brake. Travelers also dragged a log behind wagons to serve as another brake, which was called "putting on a dowser." Drivers even used this last method to control the descent of early automobiles down the divide. Thus, wagon traffic became commonplace over the pass in the 1890s.[8]

In 1901, Otho Williams surveyed the first formal road over Teton Pass, using a surveying instrument made of a walnut table leaf. The road grade followed the old trapper trail. Peter Karns, the local road commissioner, released $500 for improvements. The source of this money is unknown, but it may have been raised from property taxes in Uinta County.[9]

As the valley's link with the outside world, the condition of the "Pass" preoccupied citizens most of the year, especially during winter. "How's the Pass?" was the question asked most often. Struthers Burt even titled a chapter in his *The Diary of a Dude Wrangler,* "The Pass." He wrote that it was "strange how a dominating physical feature moulds the character of a country. The Pass—it is always spoken of as The Pass—is never very far away from the thoughts of the inhabitants of the valley."[10]

Every resident who crossed the Pass had at least one hair-raising episode to recall—and if they did not, probably made one up. Burt recalled seeing a man thrown around 20 feet from the seat of a sleigh when a runner hit a buried stump. He plunged head-first into the snow "and for a moment nothing was visible but absurdly kicking heels." Burt's son, Nathaniel, recalled a truck turning a corner in too wide an arc, putting a rear wheel over the edge of the narrow road. Other incidents were more serious, such as the massive snowslide that swept down Crater Lake in 1932, killing a teenage boy.[11]

The Marysville (Idaho) Road and the Ashton-Moran freight road were the other significant roads

to towns in Idaho. Residents occasionally used other routes over the Teton Range, but none were especially practical. Parthenia Stinnett recollected that people traveled over Fox Creek Pass at the head of Death Canyon during the late summer, but difficult terrain prevented it from becoming a viable route. In the early years, pioneers crossed Conant or Jackass Passes via the Berry Creek Trail. Carrie Nesbitt Dunn moved to Jackson Hole with her mother, Lucy Nesbitt Shive and her stepfather, Jack Shive, via this route. The Ashton-Moran freight road and the Marysville Road followed river and creek drainages between the north end of the Teton Range and Pitchstone Plateau in Yellowstone. Willis L. Winegar, who later lived in Jackson Hole, claimed to have driven the first wagon over this trail in 1883 enroute to Yellowstone, probably over the Marysville Road route. In 1910, the Reclamation Service constructed the Ashton-Moran freight road to provide a supply line to the dam project on Jackson Lake. This freight road became a significant supply line for people in the north end of Jackson Hole.[12]

The federal government constructed a military road from Fort Washakie to Fort Yellowstone via Togwotee Pass around 1900. Senator Francis E. Warren introduced a bill to construct this road in 1896 as a result of the Indian scare in 1895. A 1902 map of Township 45 North, Range 113 West, 6th Principal Meridian shows a track labeled the Military Road along the north side of the Buffalo Fork. This road joined the trail that skirted the east shore of Jackson Lake.[13]

None of these routes surpassed the Teton Pass Road as the main link with the outside world. Teton Pass, followed by the Ashton-Moran Road, provided the best access to railroad towns in Idaho. In 1882, the Union Pacific began constructing the Oregon Short Line, a trunk road connecting eastern Idaho with the main Union Pacific line at Granger, Wyoming. The Oregon Short Line reached Rexburg, Idaho, in 1899 and St. Anthony by 1902. In 1912, workers laid tracks to Driggs and Victor, the terminus of the branch line.[14]

Memories of the trek into Jackson Hole are common in the few extant personal accounts of early life in the hole. Maggie McBride's journal of the migration of the Budge, Allen, May, and McBride families is one the few and best accounts of a journey to Jackson Hole prior to 1900. Leaving home in Rockland, Idaho, it took them two weeks to make the trip to Jackson Hole. Rather than travel by covered wagon as the McBride caravan did, many settlers traveled by rail. In 1902, J. P Nelson and his family moved to Jackson Hole. They rode the Oregon Short Line to its terminus at St. Anthony, Idaho, then purchased a team of horses and a wagon for the remaining trip through Teton Valley to Jackson Hole via Teton Pass. In 1912, Dick Winger filed on a homestead in the valley that he had never seen. He traveled to Driggs, Idaho, in a boxcar stuffed with farm machinery, furniture, and six cattle. He then arranged to have it all shipped over Teton Pass.[15]

Linda McKinstry wrote an undated memoir about her 1915 trip to Jackson Hole. H. C. McKinstry, her husband, paid for an immigrant car, which was a boxcar available to homesteaders at special rates. In it, they loaded furniture, books, household articles, two mares, water, and hay. They had also purchased "considerable farm machinery," which included a Studebaker wagon, a sulky plow, a mower, and a hayrake. In addition, McKinstry obtained the necessary tools for constructing a log cabin—a crosscut saw, an axe, log chains, a peavey, and a drawknife. Mrs. McKinstry insisted that a Majestic kitchen range be added to the load. McKinstry rode ahead in the boxcar, unloading at Victor. He hauled the most needed goods over Teton Pass and stored the remainder of the freight in Victor.

Linda McKinstry followed on another train from Fargo, North Dakota, to Butte, Montana, where she and her brother-in-law switched to a train bound for Idaho Falls, the entire trip taking three days and two nights on "dirty, dusty trains." The next day they took a train to St. Anthony, a two-hour ride, then switched trains for a four-hour trip to Victor, where she rejoined her husband. They spent the night at the little frame hotel at Victor, which she described as lacking conveniences available in Idaho Falls.

The next day, Mrs. McKinstry persuaded her husband to rent saddle horses for the final leg of the journey over Teton Pass. It turned out to be a terrible mistake. Unused to long horseback trips, they plodded through melting snow on the upper eleva-

tions. "Not only was this hard on the horse, but also on the rider, and a novice would receive a terrific jolt." She arrived in Jackson "lame, sore, and very tired" and "simply fell off of the horse when I was helped down." The McKinstry narrative illustrates the importance of the Idaho railroad system to settlement and development in Jackson Hole. Immigrant boxcars allowed settlers to bring in a much greater quantity of supplies and materials than their predecessors, who had only pack animals or covered wagons. Even so, the McKinstry's trek over Teton Pass indicates the difficulty of getting mail, supplies, and people into this alpine valley. When Struthers Burt first came to Jackson Hole in 1907, the railroad terminus was in St. Anthony, "a 105 miles away a two days' journey if you were lucky and the weather was good, a three to five days' journey if you were unlucky and the weather was bad."[16]

In Jackson Hole, the first roads were primitive wagon trails. The township maps of William O. Owen, surveyed in 1892 and 1893, and the U.S. Geological Survey Grand Teton Quadrangle of 1899 document the early road system. Owen's 1892 map of Township 41 North, Range 116 West, shows an extensive network of wagon tracks in today's town of Jackson and the Elk Refuge area. Roads existed in Spring Gulch and along East Gros Ventre Butte up Botcher Hill. On Township 42 North, Range 116 West, which covered lands north of the confluence of the Gros Ventre and Snake Rivers, Owen mapped a road on the west side of the Snake that conforms in places to the present Moose-Wilson Road. No road is shown crossing the Gros Ventre River. Since Owen did not survey the Jenny Lake–Timbered Island area, no record exists of roads in this area during the early 1890s. In surveying the quadrangle encompassing the Antelope Flats area, Owen plotted the "Old Road," a trail that began southeast of Blacktail Butte and went up Antelope Flats, where it ran north to the Buffalo Fork then bore east up the Buffalo Valley. Owen's survey map of Township 44 North, Range 115 West shows portions of road along the west shore of the Snake River into the Potholes. His map of the next township, Township 45 North, Range 114 West, records a road across the Buffalo Fork near its mouth that follows the general grade of the current highway. Although not labeled as such, this may have been the Sheridan Trail. Owen's township surveys indicate the existence of primitive wagon roads in the park by 1893.[17] The Grand Teton Quadrangle, surveyed by T. M. Bannon in 1899, reveals the road system in the park. Settlers could travel from one end of the valley to the other via roads on both sides of the Snake. Fords and other major river crossings are shown on the map.[18]

Despite more or less reliable access to railroad towns in Idaho and the construction of wagon roads in the valley itself, travel remained a time-consuming and difficult activity. Settlers did not just hitch up the team to the wagon and drive the family to the town of Jackson on a whim. As a result, trips to Jackson were limited for many homesteaders, occurring only once or twice a year. Consequently, Jackson Hole developed as a cluster of several small communities centered around post offices and small villages. Marion Allen recalled that up to 1918, the valley consisted of "three or four parts" centered on Moran and Elk in the upper valley, Grovont and Kelly in the middle, and Jackson and Wilson in the lower end. In October 1918, the *Courier* reported the arrival of Mr. and Mrs. J. P Nelson in Jackson from their Spread Creek ranch. This was Mrs. Nelson's first visit to Jackson in nearly four years, a trip of approximately 30 miles.[19]

The geographic isolation of the Teton country increased the cost and scarcity of supplies, especially during the winter months. Prior to 1900, settlers freighted all of their supplies into the valley, but as businesses developed in Jackson, Wilson, and Kelly, they relied increasingly on local sources. For years, the standard charge for hauling freight was a penny per pound. Freighting added to the cost of living as these charges were added to retail costs. Don Hough recalled, in his tongue-in-cheek *The Cocktail Hour in Jackson Hole,* that a ten-cent box of corn flakes cost a quarter in Joe Jones's grocery. The grocer's "business slogan" was "it's all got to be brought over the Hill." While Hough needs to be taken with a grain of salt, other evidence reinforces the high cost of transport. For example, in 1937, the superintendent of Grand Teton National Park purchased a quantity of supplies at Kemmerer, Wyoming, and Pocatello, Idaho, saving the government 30 percent in costs, much of it due to freight charges.[20]

Isolation caused scarcity, particularly in the wake of a severe winter. Struthers Burt described the frustration he and his partner, Horace Carncross, experienced in securing needed supplies to construct their new dude ranch. A severe winter and abominable conditions on Teton Pass left store shelves empty. Building materials such as nails and roofing paper failed to arrive on time or at all, and the only foods available were canned fruits, coffee, beans, and carrots. Burt complained that not even flour, sugar, or canned milk were available. "Eventually it became difficult to look a canned peach or a bean or a carrot in the face. And the fact that canned peaches are ordinarily the most expensive of luxuries did not increase the doctor's or my appetite for them. We suffered both internally and externally."[21]

Two other factors hindered travel in the valley, severe winters and rivers. Jackson Hole winters are known for their length and the amount of snow that blankets the ground. The Snake River and its tributaries were transportation barriers. In the spring and early summer, watercourses swollen with snowmelt became treacherous. Winter imposed serious constraints on travel, as well as other aspects of life in the valley. Snow can cover the ground for as long as six months per year. At Moose, Wyoming, an average of 196 inches of snow fell annually between 1959 and 1970. This amounts to 30 to 40 inches of snow on the ground during the worst part of winter. Snow depths increase with elevation, which choke the passes into Jackson Hole. Frigid temperatures typify winters, particularly in the months of December, January, and February. The highest daily temperatures seldom exceed the freezing mark and lows frequently dip below zero. In December 1924, the town of Jackson recorded a low of −60° Fahrenheit, while the Elk Refuge recorded a low of −54° Fahrenheit. In 1933, the thermometer plunged to −63° Fahrenheit at Moran. Snowfall comes in uneven amounts, often during severe winter storms. For example, Moose, Wyoming, recorded 21 inches of snowfall in one day in January 1962, while Moran recorded 15 inches in the same storm.[22]

Historically, severe winter storms cut off transportation routes to Jackson Hole. The closure of Teton Pass delayed the publication of the first edition of the *Jackson's Hole Courier* for three weeks in

Game warden Al Austin, ca. 1910.
During the long Jackson Hole
winters, skis were a necessity.
Early skis were homemade; the
single long pole was used for balance and to propel the skier.
Grand Teton National Park

1909. Several years later, in 1916, the *Courier* reported that heavy snows had buried eastern Idaho,
blocking train traffic for more than a week. A year
later, heavy snow and avalanches left the people of
Jackson Hole snowbound for 28 days. To make matters even worse, snow blocked the rails to Victor for
52 days, isolating not only the valley but the upper
end of the Teton Valley in Idaho. In 1927, a series
of blizzards pummeled northwestern Wyoming; on
January 20, the *Courier* reported that just about
every slide on Teton Pass had run, and that there
were snowdrifts up to 15 feet deep. Even in the
1930s, links with the outside world remained unreliable during the winter months as the Pass could be
closed for several days at a time.[23]

Winter was also the time of avalanches, a deadly
threat feared by travelers. Slide runs on the Teton
Pass Road posed significant hazards. Between 1911
and 1913, avalanches killed two mail carriers, Owen
Curtis and Frankie Parsons, both on the west side of
the pass. In 1932, a slide swept down the mountain-
side in the Crater Lake area burying Harry Swanson, 14 years old, in 30 to 40 feet of snow. His body
was not recovered until the following spring.
Stephen Leek described his experience in surviving a
snow slide on the pass. Hearing a booming noise signaling a slide, Leek wrapped his arms around a tree
and hung on for perhaps 30 seconds of sheer terror.
As the slide passed by, he described the mist as suffo-
cating, the noise deafening. Hechtman Lake is

named for Fred Hechtman, who was killed in an avalanche in the Berry Creek area in 1914.[24]

To get around during the winter, settlers used
Nordic skis (also called snowshoes). By today's standards, pioneer skis were cumbersome, heavy wooden
boards sometimes as much as 12 feet long. Skiers
used one large pole made of a sapling rather than
the two lightweight poles used today. The first skis
were home-crafted with native materials. A homesteader on Flat Creek named Big John Emery reputedly made the best skis out of "red fir," also known
as Douglas fir. He cut down a tree two to three feet
thick, quartered it, then let the wood cure. After the
wood dried, he worked skis out of the quartered sections; the tips were soaked in water and lye, then
bent around a tree and fastened in place to fashion a
curve at the tips. The housings could be heavy shoes
or boots attached to the skis, or primitive wooden
bindings. Canvas or seamless sacks served as leg-
gings or gaiters. Settlers improvised waxes—applying
beeswax, elk tallow, and pine pitch to ski bottoms.
There were probably even more wax substitutes that
have not been recorded. To climb steep hills,
Stephen Leek recalled wrapping rope around the
skis to provide good traction. The first manufactured
skis were introduced in the 1920s. Mike O'Neil, a
Forest Service employee, may have been the first to
use manufactured skis in 1925–1926. Valley pioneers
also used snowshoes, constructing frames of sapling
poles and using rawhide strips for webbing.

The Ed Chambers family, who lived west of Blacktail Butte, used several forms of winter transportation: skies, snowshoes, and dog sleds. *Jackson Hole Historical Society and Museum*

Immigrants to the valley, not used to such deep snow, usually had to learn how to ski. Charlie Hedrick swore that big heavy skis were the only way to travel in winter. Others were not so sure. Butch Robinson homesteaded far up the Gros Ventre River, a wonderful but even more isolated country than Jackson Hole. Robinson's brother, Eddie, joined him at the homestead. With the onset of winter, Butch decided his brother would have to learn to ski. So they plodded up an open hill, blinding white in the winter sun. Only a single tree broke the snow-laden slope. Butch explained the rudiments of controlling a descent and, with the instructions fresh in his ear, Eddie took off down the slope. He gained speed rapidly and lost control. Trying to avoid the lone tree, Eddie headed straight for it. Butch yelled, "Ride your pole! Ride your pole!" This technique involved straddling the pole and squatting on it to control speed. Despite his brother's instructions, Eddie Robinson crashed headlong into the tree, knocking himself out. Butch rushed to aid him. When Eddie came to his senses, Butch asked, "Why didn't you ride your pole?" His stunned brother replied, "In the first place, I was going faster than the sound of your voice, and in the second place I was riding my pole but the rear end was on top of one of the skis."[25]

Horse-drawn sleighs were the chief mode of travel in winter and were used well into the 1930s and 1940s. Only when state and county governments began keeping roads open year-round did their use decline. Old photographs show that settlers used a variety of sleighs for travel. The Jackson stage in 1909 was a small cutter, which appears to be nothing more than a platform with runners attached to it. Sometimes people covered the sleds with canvas tops to provide some shelter from severe weather conditions. Others went so far as to install wood stoves in covered sleighs. Al Austin built one for the National Park Service in 1930–1931, which the superintendent referred to as a "Jackson Hole Special." Not only were sleighs used to carry mail and supplies, but they also served an important social function as they enabled groups of people to gather for dances and celebrations, a welcome break from isolated winters. The *Jackson's Hole Couriers* are full of references to people traveling by sleigh to parties and dances. For example, in December 1927, two sleigh loads of neighbors surprised the Woodmans at the Flying V for an impromptu party that lasted all night.[26]

Rivers in Jackson Hole hindered travel, therefore bridges, ferries, and reliable fords became important points in the valley's transportation network. And, like travel in winter, the valley's rivers and streams posed significant dangers. For example, John Sargent's partner, Ray Hamilton, drowned while fording the Snake River prior to 1900. A search party lit a bonfire on the summit of a hill south of Jackson Lake when they found his body—hence the name, Signal Mountain. In 1917, Lorin Loomis disappeared in the Moran area. Search parties dragged the river presuming he had drowned, but failed to locate his body. People speculated about Loomis's fate until

Rebuilding the Kelly bridge after
the original washed out in the
1927 flood. *Jackson Hole Historical
Society and Museum*

memory of him faded. In 1923, the elder John Smejkal disappeared while hunting. A year later, his body
was found in the Snake River at the Harrison Ranch
below Menor's Ferry. Tragedy struck on the Hoback
River in 1928, when the Davis family tried to cross
the river at the old Granite Creek ford while on a
fishing holiday. The wagon tipped over, throwing the
family into the river. Huldah Budge Davis and her
two-year-old son, James, drowned in the accident.[27]

T. M. Bannon's survey of 1899 provides the best
record of river crossings above the town of Jackson
prior to 1900. The map shows fords across the
Snake and Gros Ventre Rivers at their confluence.
Three fords existed on the lower portion of the Gros
Ventre, over the next six miles from its mouth. The
next crossing was near the present town site of Kelly,
which was either a bridge or a ford. A photograph in
the Harold Fabian Collection shows workers rebuilding a log truss bridge over the Gros Ventre River
around 1902. On the Snake River, one ford existed .
between its junction with the Gros Ventre River and
Menor's Ferry. Between Menor's Ferry and Conrad's
Ferry east of the Oxbow, no fords are indicated on
the map. Two crossings are shown near the mouths
of both the Buffalo Fork and Pacific Creek.[28] Three
crossings on the Snake were especially important
transportation links: the Wilson crossing, Menor's
Ferry, and the Moran area.

The first settlers forded the braided channels of
the Snake east of Teton Pass, just as trappers and explorers had done before them. The emergence of a

community around the Jackson Post Office and Deloney's Store, along with concentrated homesteading
in South Park and the Flat Creek area, magnified
the importance of this crossing. High water not only
made fording dangerous, but altered channels and
scoured huge holes in the river bottom, sometimes at
fording points. Residents operated a ferryboat for
some years at the location, but shifting gravel bars
and snags hampered the operation. They may have
installed a winter bridge during the cold season, as-
sembling and taking it down each year. The Jackson-
Wilson ferry ran until 1915 when it was replaced by
a steel truss bridge. Workers completed the bridge in
1915 at a cost of $26,000, leaving $10,000 for riprap
to protect the approaches to the bridge.

The riprap failed in 1917. Swollen with snow
melt, the Snake River washed away the approaches
to the bridge. A report in the *Courier* laid the blame
on the Reclamation Service, charging that they released too much water from the dam. Reclamation
Service officials refused to accept responsibility, as-
serting that no excess water had been released from
the dam in July 1917. They countered that the wash-
out had occurred because Lincoln County had not
properly repaired the cribbing that protected the approaches. Citizens and officials representing county,
state, and federal government wrangled over responsibility and ultimately who should pay for new approaches to the bridge. In September 1918, an engineer representing the Bureau of Public Roads
opposed allocating federal funds for the repairs.

While the haggling went on, the citizens of Jackson Hole had a more immediate problem—no bridge. The 650-foot, five-span bridge, once the longest in Wyoming, protruded across the Snake, a useless monument for five years.

Meanwhile, to cross the river, valley residents strung a primitive cable car across the Snake River at the bridge. In April 1918, County Commissioner James Budge hired William Crawford, a pioneer rancher, to build a ferry until the bridge could be repaired. The ferry was less than three months old when floodwaters washed away a deadman and tripod, causing the ferry to break loose and drift downstream. Even after the ferry was repaired, the washed-out approaches caused delays and inconvenience for freighters, mail carriers, and travelers. Rather than attempt a crossing at the Wilson Bridge, travelers often diverted north nearly 20 miles to Menor's Ferry in order to cross the Snake. Finally, in 1921 and 1922, contractors rebuilt the approaches and modified the existing bridge. Lincoln County provided $20,000, supplemented by state and federal funds, while citizens raised an additional $14,000 to ensure completion of the work. A worker drove the last spike on February 2, 1922; to celebrate, local citizens organized an informal program, setting off 25 sticks of dynamite.[29]

Approximately 15 miles above the Jackson-Wilson Bridge, the Snake River contracts into a single channel for about one mile. Not an ideal ford, it is a superb site for a bridge or a ferry. On July 17, 1894, William D. Menor took up a homestead with that in mind. Moreover, the banks were low, allowing relatively easy access to the river. Because the channel was narrow, the water was deeper than in the braided channels above and below this point. Menor had spent ten days with Jack Shive and John Cherry at their homesteads on the Buffalo Fork, who advised him to pick a location along the Snake River. By 1903, Menor had built improvements valued at $2,500. The most important improvement was his ferry.[30]

Menor's Ferry became the most important river crossing in Jackson Hole, with the exception of the Jackson-Wilson Bridge. Maggie McBride left the earliest record of crossing the ferry. On July 9, 1896, the party reached Menor's Ferry:

Took a long time to get our outfit across. The loose horses swam the river. We tried to jew Mr. Menor down on the ferry bill, but nothing doing, even tried to pay him in flour and cured pork, but after we got across and paid him in cash, then he wanted some bacon, but we didn't let it go, kept it four [sic] our winter supply.

Mrs. McBride's description is generally in keeping with other accounts of Bill Menor. But most important, her narrative stresses the point that Menor built the ferry to make a living; public service was secondary.

Menor operated the ferry during periods of high water. With the aid of neighbors, he assembled a bridge during periods of low water, such as winter. Occasionally, he used a small platform suspended from the cable to get passengers across the river. During periods of high water, valley residents seemed to prefer Menor's Ferry over less reliable fords. For example, in May 1914, the *Courier* reported that teamsters were hauling supplies into Jackson via Menor's Ferry because of high water. After the 1917 flood wiped out the approaches to the Wilson bridge, the ferry assumed greater importance as freighters and mail carriers often traveled the extra 30 miles from Teton Pass to the ferry then back to Jackson.[31]

However, Menor's Ferry was not always reliable. Shifting gravel bars and uprooted trees, called "snags," posed serious hazards. When the river was "in spate," that is, overflowing its banks, Menor refused to risk himself or the ferry. On at least one occasion, a snag struck the ferry with such force that the ropes securing it to the steel cable parted, and the river swept it downstream. The ferry went a short distance, when it struck a gravel bar. While neighbors gathered and considered the best way to rescue Bill Menor, "he stood on the ferry violently cursing the rescue crew and acting, in general, as though they alone were to blame." Struthers Burt recalled that the ferry "went out" in the spring of 1912, "cutting us off completely for a while from the town." It could not have happened at a worse time for Burt and Carncross, who were frantically constructing cabins at the Bar BC to house their first dudes.[32]

Menor's Ferry was an ingenious contraption, consisting of a platform set on two pontoons. The ferry was attached by a rope to a steel cable suspended across the river by cableworks and deadmen, which were logs buried in the ground. The rope was secured to a pulley system on the cable and pulleys and a pilot wheel on the ferry. The current powered the ferry across the river. By turning the pilot wheel, the operator manipulated the angle of the pontoons and steered the ferry to either bank. Menor rebuilt the ferry at least once around 1910.

As Maggie McBride's memory indicates, Bill Menor did not intend the ferry to be a charitable operation. Many early river crossings were built by private individuals, and whether bridges or ferries, they charged a toll. There is some discrepancy regarding Menor's rates. According to Frances Judge, he charged 50 cents for a team and 25 cents for a horse and rider. Yet, an illustration in her article shows a sign bearing the following prices:

Foot Backers	25 cents
Horse Backers	50 cents
2 HORSE TEAM AND WAGON	$1.00
4 HORSE TEAM AND WAGON	$2.00

Stan Boyle, the son of a teamster named Sam Boyle, accompanied his father on several freighting runs into Jackson Hole around 1915. He recollected the rugged trip over Teton Pass to Wilson, which then followed the wagon track to Menor's Ferry. Taking into account that he was a young boy at the time, Boyle remembered prices being 50 to 75 cents for a wagon or team, and 25 cents for an individual on horseback. Thus, only approximate prices can be established.[33]

In 1918, Bill Menor decided to sell out, tired of "high water and low water" and "fog, rain, wind, snow, and sunshine on the Snake." In late July, he concluded negotiations with Maud Noble, Frederick Sandell, and Mrs. May Lee and sold out. Menor retired to California where he died in 1933.[34] Noble and Sandell bought out Mrs. Lee and operated the ferry until 1927. Menor's Ferry remained a major crossing after the advent of the automobile. Noble and Sandell doubled the fare, taking advantage of the increasing tourist traffic of the 1920s. The sharp

price increase angered residents. In one instance, a man became so angry upon discovering the price increase that he leapt into the river and swam across the channel, while "the pilot stood on the ferry cursing the swimmer and yelling that he hoped he would drown."[35]

Cars took America by storm in the 1920s as manufacturers produced affordable vehicles. Americans took to the roads, but found that many of these roads were little more than wagon tracks. Automobile owners pressured governments to improve the nation's road network. Thus, in 1924, the Bureau of Public Roads announced plans to build a 13-mile road between Jackson and Menor's Ferry. In 1926, a construction crew began work on the steel bridge at the ferry. The work did not progress smoothly, however. Si Ferrin provided lumber for the bridge, cutting it at his Elk Ranch mill. He transported one of the first loads down the river on a raft. Above the Bar BC, the raft jammed against a snag and sank, stranding Frank Petersen and a crew of three. After rescuers saved the crew, the tree was dynamited to free the raft, which drifted to a gravel bar just above the ferry. Despite such difficulties, the bridge was completed and operational by 1927, ending the monopoly of Noble and Sandell on the river.[36]

In the northern end of Jackson Hole, important crossings were located on the Snake River between the outlet of Jackson Lake and Pacific Creek. Mystery surrounds Conrad's Ferry because so little information is available. According to Nolie Mumey, Harris-Dunn & Company constructed the ferry in 1895 to transport equipment and supplies to their placer mine on Whetstone Creek. They freighted supplies over Teton Pass and up the west side of the river. They hired the Conrads to operate the ferry. James M. Conrad homesteaded 157.76 acres east of Oxbow Bend in June 1896. Conrad was a disabled Civil War veteran and widower. Aided by his son, Conrad constructed a 16-by-18-foot log cabin and a barn. It is likely that the elder Conrad operated the ferry, rather than Ernest Conrad who was 11 years old in 1896. No photographs of the ferry are known to exist, but Moran resident Herb Whiteman described the ferry as nothing more than a square barge with no side rails. A winch and the current powered it across the river. According to Mumey, a herd of cattle stampeded on the ferry in 1897, causing it to "upset" with considerable damage. Conrad rebuilt the ferry and continued to operate it. The T. M. Bannon survey of 1899 shows Conrad's Ferry, suggesting that it operated until the turn of the century. Because of poor health, Conrad left the homestead in 1900 and relinquished his claim to the homestead to Homer Guerry in 1902. By this time, Conrad was residing in a soldiers' home in Cheyenne, Wyoming, and was "compelled to remain quiet because of his disabled physical condition."[37]

In 1903, Ben Sheffield bought up property at Moran to serve as headquarters for his hunting and fishing camp. Around this time, he built a toll bridge just below the outlet of Jackson Lake that served travelers until 1910, when the Reclamation Service's log crib dam gave out, destroying the bridge. The new concrete dam served as a bridge.[38]

Establishing reliable mail service was one of the first and primary concerns of Jackson Hole pioneers. Mrs. Mae Tuttle, who was the former Mrs. Fred White and first postmaster in Jackson Hole, recalled vividly the erratic mail service and isolation prior to 1900. To Cora Nelson Barber, she wrote:

> Don't you remember how we saw or spoke to a neighbor only once or twice a year and we never got word or mail from the outside from snowfall to spring thaw unless some hardy individual took it into his head to ski across the mountain and bring everybody's mail, and as soon as we heard about it how we all made ski tracks to that man's cabin, pronto.[39]

Around 1891, residents of Jackson Hole and some living in the southern part of Teton Valley petitioned the Postal Service for a mail route from St. Anthony and for a post office in Jackson Hole. Before granting the request, the Postal Department stipulated that local residents carry the mail for a year to prove the feasibility of regular mail service over such a difficult route. Settlers accepted the challenge and took turns carrying mail for the year. On March 25, 1892, a post office was established at Marysville near Botcher Hill, and a mail carrier was paid to make the run between Rexburg and Jackson Hole. S. N. Leek described the rugged mail run in an unpublished memoir. Traveling on homemade

Nordic skis, Leek packed provisions, elk tallow for ski wax, and outgoing mail. He recalled that carriers stripped from the waist down to ford the ice-cold Snake, wading across the river laden with pack, skis, pole and a bundle of clothes. Once on the west bank, the mail carriers hand-rubbed themselves dry, dressed, then set out for the trail over Teton Pass. One carrier was not so lucky as Leek. In February 1896, the *Wyoming Tribune* reported that a mail carrier had lost his boat, toboggan, and snowshoes while trying to cross the Snake River. He managed to save the two most important things—his life and the mail.

Snowslides were always a problem. If a mail carrier happened to be buried in a slide, his chances of survival were slim. The trip to Rexburg took the better part of six days; Leek recollected the trip required one snow camp and four nights at isolated cabins. Mae Tuttle skied over Teton Pass at a later date. The trek to the summit was arduous, making the lunch break at the mail carrier's small snow cabin or "igloo" all the more welcome. Although her description is vague, the shelter seems to have been a snow cave. "The snow was so deep over it that there was just a little hole in the snow down which we had to slide yards and yards till we got to the entrance and then when we made a fire in the corner chimney to boil our coffee, the melted snow began to drip down on us." Leek hauled around 100 letters per trip from Rexburg to homesteaders in Teton Basin and Jackson Hole.[40]

Regular mail service brought immediate changes, as pioneers were no longer quite so isolated. Further, in a land of scarcity, people could take advantage of mail order retailers to order both necessities and luxuries, rather than wait for the annual trip to Rexburg to purchase them. Mae Tuttle remembered "then we really did feel important. We could order things from the mail order houses and get them without waiting for six months." She once ordered a pair of slippers from Montgomery Ward; the company sent a pair of wooden shoes that weighed nearly ten pounds. Mrs. Tuttle shipped them back the next day. As the mail carrier plodded over the pass on skis carrying "that awful parcel," she could well imagine that "what he said about wooden shoes and my bright mind probably melted some snow."[41]

Daily mail service to Jackson began around 1900. According to one newspaper article, James Riggan, 14 years old, began transporting mail in saddle bags over Teton Pass in 1897. Another source stated that daily mail service began in 1902. The census of 1900 listed a Thomas Patten as a mail carrier. By 1900, there were five post offices in Jackson Hole: Jackson, Elk, Grovont, Wilson, and the short-lived South Park, which opened in 1899 and shut down in 1902.[42] In 1909, nine post offices existed in the valley, with mail service six days per week at two of them: Jackson and Wilson.[43]

The United States Postal Service issued mail run contracts, which attracted many local residents because of the reliable income. For example, Si Ferrin secured the Jackson-to-Moran mail run in 1914 at $3,000 per year for service three times per week. Many Jackson Hole pioneers carried mail at one time or another; among them Jack Eynon, Fred Topping, Andy Chambers, and Mart Henrie. William Manning made news in 1930 when he secured a contract to carry mail. He was 94 years old at the time.[44] Although the contracts provided a reliable source of income, the work could be dangerous. Avalanches were a serious hazard, as the deaths of mail carriers Gwen Curtis and Frankie Parsons proved. River crossings could be hazardous, too. Mail carrier George Kissenger drowned while fording the Gros Ventre around 1910.[45]

Mail service was amazingly reliable considering severe weather and distances from rail service. Pioneers did not complain much about mail service, having to cope with difficult travel conditions themselves. There were exceptions, however. At the end of 1918, the *Jackson's Hole Courier* reported that valley residents were "thoroughly disgusted" with mail service between Jackson and the rail terminus at Victor. The contractor, D. B. Brinton of Victor, let parcel post pile up in Victor and failed sometimes to meet schedules. "Getting on in years," Brinton acknowledged his inability to·perform the job and eventually sublet the mail contract to Wallace Ricks.[46]

Around 1918, gasoline-powered trucks replaced horse-drawn vehicles, at least during the warmer months. With the onset of winter, trucks were replaced by sleighs. In 1919, Jack Eynon used a truck to deliver mail in the valley. Trucks cut time and,

therefore, costs. In 1921, Fred Topping went to Salt Lake City to pick up a one-ton White truck to be used to carry mail between Jackson and Moran during the summer. Topping planned to leave Jackson at 7:00 A.M. and return by 6:30 P.M., allowing him to make daily deliveries on his own, and avoiding the cost of another driver and team. But even gasoline engines could be unreliable. In June 1919, the *Courier* reported that Jack Eynon's mail truck had broken down near Kelly, delaying mail service.[47]

As governmental agencies improved roads to accommodate increased automobile traffic, mail routes shifted in the 1930s. For example, in 1931, residents in the northern end of Jackson Hole found it more convenient to route mail through Lander, Wyoming, during the summer. A year later, the *Courier* reported that the Rock Springs postal inspector was reviewing the idea of having Jackson Hole mail routed to and from Rock Springs rather than the Oregon Short Line route to Victor, Idaho. According to the report, the Rock Springs route would save one day on the delivery of eastern mail over the Victor route. In addition, Rock Springs would provide access to air mail. In 1934, the Postal Service switched the mail route to Rock Springs.[48]

Transporting freight and passengers was another concern. Stage service was established by 1909. The first edition of the *Jackson's Hole Courier* reported "in connection with the mail service there is a stage between St. Anthony and Jackson, by Wilson, making the trip of 88 miles in 18 hours of actual travel, the passenger stopping over one night on the road." A postcard printed in Germany shows the Jackson stage on March 1, 1909. Drawn by a pair of draft horses, the "stage" is a small cutter consisting of a platform set on two runners. The service predated 1909 in all probability, but these are the first good references to it.[49]

The extension of the Oregon Short Line tracks to Victor reduced time of travel considerably. But stage trips from Jackson to Victor still took one day, until automobiles and improved roads reduced travel time. Several teamsters achieved a measure of fame for their skill and exploits. Most well known were Clay "Old Rawhide" Seaton, Amasa James, and Henry Scott. They carried mail, freight, and passengers over Teton Pass at all times of the year, over

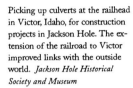

Picking up culverts at the railhead in Victor, Idaho, for construction projects in Jackson Hole. The extension of the railroad to Victor improved links with the outside world. *Jackson Hole Historical Society and Museum*

roads turned to a muddy paste by spring rains and runoff, or on a snow-choked pass in winter. The drivers also kept the winter road packed and usable. The teamsters cleared snow and packed the track with a wye, also called a go-devil. This was a simple W-shaped device made of planks used to grade both dirt and snow-covered roads. James and Scott converted to trucks, probably in the 1920s, but continued to use sleds in winter months through the 1930s.[50]

The Ashton-Moran freight road, also known as the Reclamation Road, was established in 1910 to transport supplies from the Oregon Short Line terminus at Ashton to Moran, the construction site of the Jackson Lake Dam. On July 5, 1910, the log crib dam gave way in its center portion, releasing a torrent of water down the Snake River. The Reclamation Service prepared to construct a new dam, selecting engineer Frank T. Crowe as project supervisor. Crowe recognized immediately that the remote location of Jackson Lake posed a notable obstacle that could delay, or even prevent, the completion of a new dam. He established a supply center at Ashton and constructed a freight road to Jackson Lake. From the Snake River crossing north of Jackson Lake to Grassy Lakes, the freight road followed the alignment of the old Marysville wagon road, which dated from circa 1888. At Grassy Lakes, the new freight road diverted west, while the Marysville Road cut northwest into Yellowstone. The Reclamation Road turned southwest near Loon Lake, before

running a course to Squirrel Meadows and Indian Lake. From this point, the road ran west to Ashton. At the Snake River, the road joined the military road connecting Yellowstone with Fort Washakie.[51]

To supervise the important freighting operation, Crowe hired Joseph "Hold" Egbert. The Service contracted the work to local settlers both in Jackson Hole and the Teton Basin, who welcomed the chance to earn ready cash. Each teamster completed about ten trips per season, the 150-mile round trip taking a minimum of six days. To be as self-sufficient as possible, freighters carried horseshoeing equipment, emergency food, clothing, tools, and extra hay and grain in the winter. The Reclamation Service built or set up roadhouses along the route at Squirrel Meadows, Cascade Creek, Dime Creek, and the Edward's Ranch on Lizard Creek.[52]

Sleighs were used from November through April, and wagons during the remaining months. The Studebaker was the standard freight wagon, being 24-feet-long (probably from tongue to rear) by 3-feet-8 inches wide. Most often, an outfit consisted of two wagons coupled together, pulled by teams of six to eight horses. As a rule of thumb, each horse could generally account for 1,000 to 1,500 pounds of freight; thus a double-wagon outfit could transport up to 12,000 pounds. Four thousand barrels or 850 tons of cement mix for the concrete dam constituted most of the loads in 1910 and 1922. By 1914, teamsters had hauled an estimated 300,000 tons of supplies and equipment over the Ashton-Moran Road.

After the completion of the dam in 1916, people continued to use the freight road to bring supplies into the northern end of the valley. According to one account, freight wagons last traveled over the road in October 1927, when teamsters George Osborne Jr., and Charles Myers brought supplies into Jackson Hole. The Ashton-Moran freight road may have been the last such route used by wagons in the United States.[53]

Not only freighters, but tourists and other travelers created demand for food and lodging. At first, pioneer families extended their hospitality to these people, either free or for a small charge. As demand grew, a few started roadhouses or small hotels. By 1900, there were four hostelries in Jackson Hole: Mrs. John Anderson's boarding house, located at the wye near the future community of Jackson, the hotel at the base of Teton Pass built by Abraham Ward, and at Moran, Edward "Cap" Smith's hotel and Charles J. and Maria Allen's Elkhorn Hotel. Sources suggest that fire destroyed Smith's hotel after 1900. Hoping to profit from tourist traffic to Yellowstone, a few offered lodging and food to travelers bound for the south gate of Yellowstone. John Sargent catered to travelers at his homestead on Jackson Lake. Several miles north of Sargent's place, Cora Heigho and Herb Whiteman built several cabins about 1896 with the same intentions. Neither were particularly successful. The Heighos and Whiteman gave up around 1900. Several roadhouses were built on the Teton Pass Road: the Lee Roadhouse west of Wilson, a lodge on the summit of the pass operated by Mrs. Harry Scott, and Bircher's on the west side of the range. Owen Wister's daughter, Fanny Kemble Wister, recalled a tedious three-day journey to Jackson Hole over Teton Pass in 1912. She remembered the roadhouses as miserable affairs—guests sat on uncomfortable benches at tables, dining off tin plates and cups in dirty surroundings.[54]

The telephone, which revolutionized communication, made its debut in Jackson Hole in 1905, when Fred Lovejoy established the Jackson Telephone Exchange. He connected the first lines between the Jackson Hotel and Mose Giltner's ranch, three miles west of Jackson. The federal government contributed significantly to expanding telephone service throughout the valley. In 1907, the Forest Service built tele-phone lines all the way from the Hoback to the Buffalo Fork and Yellowstone. By January 1909, the first issue of the *Jackson's Hole Courier* reported that the valley had its own system operated by the Jackson Valley Telephone Company. "Its lines, supplemented by those of the Forest Service, extend from one end of the valley to the other, and connect with the Bell System at Victor, Idaho," bringing "the scattered localities of the valley . . . near to one another and to the outside world."[55]

After 1909, telephone communications improved and extended steadily. The Reclamation Service strung a telephone cable from Moran to Ashton along the Reclamation Road. In South Park, J. G. Imeson operated a separate telephone system. In 1918, Fred Lovejoy took over the South Park System, absorbing it into the Jackson Valley Telephone Company. This small company, owned by local residents, was sold to Mountain States Telephone in 1932.[56]

Early car travel in Jackson Hole after 1900 augured great changes. A party of tourists drove the first automobile into the valley in 1908. Traveling over Togwotee Pass from Fort Washakie, a very rough road, they drove along Jackson Lake to the Snake River Station at Yellowstone National Park. Too late, they learned that the army prohibited automobile travel through the park. Superintendent S. B. M. Young would not let them tow the car through the park with a horse team, but let them haul it to the west entrance on a freight wagon.[57]

In either 1910 or 1911, William Dunn drove a Cadillac via the Ashton Road to Jackson Hole. A trained mechanic, Al Austin accompanied Dunn to "mend tires." According to a captioned photograph in the *Jackson's Hole Courier,* Dan Hudson, a state game warden, drove the first car, a "White Steamer," into the valley under its own power in 1910. The route is unknown. After 1910, Mrs. John Moulton, a 14-year-old girl at the time, accompanied her uncle over Teton Pass in his EMF. They required a tow from a tandem of horses to make it over the divide. Mrs. Moulton believed her uncle's EMF was the first auto over Teton Pass. An unreliable vehicle, she recalled a common joke that EMF stood for "Every Morning Fix-it." In 1914, Mr. and Mrs. Ed Burton of Pocatello, Idaho, managed to drive a Hupmobile over the pass without assistance. According to a contemporary account, the Burtons' car was the second to come over Teton Pass, but the first to make it on its own power. In August 1916, attorney Payson W. Spaulding drove over the Hoback Road from Pinedale in the company of another party. Although the journey was rugged, Spaulding found the drive scenic.[58]

Automobiles gained acceptance rapidly among valley residents. Perhaps it was an omen of the new era when a colt turned from its mother and followed Dunn's Cadillac as it chugged through the sleepy town of Jackson. The truth of this story is doubtful, but it suggests that valley residents recognized the changes the gasoline engines would bring. In November 1916, pioneer rancher Mose Giltner purchased a 1917 Buick Four and brought it proudly over the pass. By the end of World War I, trucks were used to haul freight and mail. The 1920s saw a dramatic change as people switched from horse-drawn vehicles to automobiles, although they continued to use sleighs in the winter. Even Jimmy Manges, a homesteader on Taggart Creek, gave in and bought a new car in 1926. The *Courier* reported that he was "enjoying the sensation of driving his new Dodge Sedan himself lately."[59]

Switching from horses to gasoline engines created demand for cars, and several residents established sales outlets. In 1915, Charles Wort and Dick Winger started the first dealership, bringing in three Ford Model Ts. In the same year, Spicer and Lloyd branched out from their saloon business, announcing their intentions to establish a car dealership for Mitchells, Dodges, and Buicks. Even the village of Kelly boasted an automobile dealership in 1919, where Spicer and Curtis sold Fords.[60]

Gas stations—the most familiar of roadside institutions—became conspicuous in the valley by the mid-1920s. In the early years, car owners stored gasoline in barrels at their residences or businesses. Entrepreneurs, such as A. J. Carter of Driggs, Idaho, operated mobile filling stations, delivering gasoline to individuals. In 1921, Carter brought his tanker over Teton Pass twice a week to fill barrels on order. A year later, Chester Simpson installed a pump in front of his hardware store in Jackson and began selling gas. In May 1924, Mike Yokel opened a gas station in Wilson.[61]

The automobile introduced another phenomena, one that has become too familiar, the car accident. In 1917, a Salt Lake City salesman named Carl Gessel lost control of his Oldsmobile Eight while trying to avoid a mud hole and drove off the Teton Pass Road. The car rolled four times, tumbling 60 feet before lodging against a tree. Astonishingly, Gessel was not hurt and even more miraculously, he drove the Oldsmobile back to Salt Lake after replacing a wheel. In August of that year, an accident occurred at Menor's Ferry when George Wilson lost control of his car and it plunged into the Snake River. Wilson managed to rescue his wife, but his 13-year-old daughter clung to a wheel of the car as the current swept it downstream. The car washed against a gravel bar, probably saving the teenager's life. Bill Menor rescued the girl with his boat. As motor cars became more common, conflicts with horse-drawn vehicles occurred. For example, in the fall of 1918, an auto spooked Emile Wolff's team, causing the wagon to spill and throwing Wolff's family and Mrs. Hoagland and her son from it. Again, there were no injuries, but the wagon was damaged.[62]

Poor roads contributed to at least one of the preceding accidents, which reinforced the need for dramatic improvement of the nation's roads. By 1925, three highways served Jackson Hole: the Teton Pass Road, the Hoback Road, and the Togwotee Pass Road. Major highways were constructed over each of these routes because they provided access to the railroad communities of Victor, Idaho, and Rock Springs and Lander, Wyoming. Both the Ashton-Moran freight road, and the Gros Ventre Road fell into disuse in the 1920s. The state and federal government abandoned the Gros Ventre Road into the upper Green River Basin in favor of the Hoback Road, possibly because the former was more difficult to maintain and keep open. The Gros Ventre River drainage was notorious for the number of landslides that occur in the area.[63]

A lack of funding limited road improvements, but ways were found to raise money. For example, in 1921, the voters of Teton County supported a state road bond by a whopping majority of 336 *yeas* to 26 *nays*. Boosters favored almost universally highway construction projects and regarded opposition equivalent to heresy. County, state, and federal agencies assumed responsibility for road maintenance and improvements. In 1925 alone, the *Jackson's Hole Courier* announced that the Bureau of Public Roads, the Forest Service, and the Wyoming State Highway Department planned to work in Jackson Hole during the coming season. In particular, the Forest Service contributed to road improvements in the valley.[64]

Local surveyor Otho Williams laid out the Teton Pass Road in 1900. It still remained no more than a wagon road with a seemingly endless repetition of switchbacks. In 1918, the Bureau of Public Roads completed a new road over the pass. For the most part, it followed the alignment of the old wagon road. Several years later, in 1925, the Forest Service allocated $12,000 to surface the Teton Pass Road. In 1932, the Bureau of Public Roads initiated a major upgrade of the road. They widened the road from eight to 18 feet, surfaced it, and reduced some grades three to four percent over the same alignment. The road was oiled in 1940. The next major roadwork occurred in the early 1970s, when the Teton Pass route was overhauled to include major realignments of the route to improve safety and reduce the impact of snowslides.[65]

The old Indian and trapper trail over the Hoback was adequate for horses and pack animals, but could not handle wagon traffic. Precise information on just when a wagon trail was built in the Hoback Canyon is unavailable, but the U.S.G.S. Gros Ventre Quadrangle, surveyed in 1907, shows a wagon road crossing the Rim and passing through the upper Hoback drainage at Bondurant to the narrows of the canyon. A photograph dated around 1912 records a road crew on the Hoback taking a break. Thus, by 1907, the Hoback Road accommodated wagon traffic. In 1916, Payson W. Spaulding, accompanied by another party, drove two automobiles from Jackson to Pinedale via the Hoback Road. In 1918, the Forest Service proposed to construct a major road through the Hoback. Construction crews began work after 1918 and completed the project by the summer of 1922. The new road tied Jackson to Rock Springs and the famous Lincoln Highway, passing through the communities of Kemmerer and Big Piney. Local dignitaries held official opening ceremonies on July 10, 1922. The production crew filming *The Cowboy and the Lady* recorded the cere-

mony for possible use in the movie. The road proved to be a maintenance nightmare; severe weather and rockslides cut off and damaged the road all too frequently. In 1918, the *Courier* reported that a drenching cloudburst washed out six to seven miles of road. Two years after the completion of the new highway, the Bureau of Public Roads had to rework six miles of it. The new highway continued to deteriorate. In 1932, the *Courier* described the road as a "disgrace" from the Vı Bar Vı Ranch to Little Granite Creek. Nonetheless, it emerged as a major artery into Jackson Hole in the 1930s, as automobiles replaced trains as the primary mode of transportation.[66]

Around 1900, the federal government had financed the construction of a military road over Togwotee Pass to link Fort Yellowstone and Fort Washakie. From Togwotee Pass, the road entered the Buffalo Fork valley and possibly joined the Sheridan Trail alignment at Jackson Lake. In 1917, the *Courier* announced that the road from Lander, Wyoming, to the south entrance of Yellowstone was open to automobiles. The Secretary of the Interior's decision to allow motor vehicles in Yellowstone in 1915 probably generated more traffic through Jackson Hole. About 1919, construction began to provide a major highway. The road opened in 1921 and was graveled in 1922. In that year, the *Denver Post* reported the completion of the highway between Lander and Yellowstone. A private company initiated bus service from Lander in that year, running until snowfall forced the closure of the road.[67]

From an engineering viewpoint, constructing a highway through the Snake River Canyon was the most significant accomplishment. The idea of a road through the canyon had been proposed prior to 1920, but never had been taken seriously. In 1923, the Forest Service sought a federal appropriation to construct a 19-mile road through the canyon. The bureau justified the road for two reasons; they hoped to eliminate the Teton Pass route and claimed the new road would shorten the traveling distance from Jackson Hole to Salt Lake City. Local communities, such as Jackson and those in Star Valley, supported the proposal. However, the plan remained a pipe dream until the Great Depression, when the federal government pumped millions of dollars into such

Civilian Conservation Corps crews built or improved many of the roads in and around the park during the 1930s. *Grand Teton National Park*

projects as a part of an economic recovery effort. In the summer of 1931, an 18-man crew began surveying a road through the canyon, moving the highway one step closer to reality. Nothing happened until 1933, when the State of Wyoming applied for and received $600,000 to build the road. Construction began in 1934. The Civilian Conservation Corps provided workers for labor-intensive activities such as rockwork. By 1939, less than 4,000 feet of preliminary work remained, and only one-and-a-half miles were left to grade and widen. The Snake River Canyon road opened to traffic in 1939, completing "one of the largest" such projects in the West.[68] Other roads received no funding. One was a proposed access road from Ashton to the Yellowstone south entrance. The House Appropriations Committee eliminated $100,000 for this project in 1932. It is unclear whether this road was to follow the old Reclamation Road or another alignment.[69]

The 1920s witnessed tremendous improvements in the valley's road network. Depending on the responsibility, funding for maintenance and administration came from county, state, and federal governments. In 1924, the Bureau of Public Roads completed a project on the Wilson-Jackson Road. To overcome budgetary limits, other methods were employed. For example, the state sponsored "Good Roads Day," which encouraged citizens to come out for one day and patch damaged roads.[70]

The existing roads after World War I were made for horse-drawn vehicles. In some instances, alignments were suited to automobiles. Local officials had to decide whether to commit funds to existing alignments or survey and construct new roads. In 1919 local residents disputed, hotly at times, the route of the Jackson-Kelly Road. Some considered the existing road through Dry Hollow too dangerous for automobile traffic. They eventually settled on routing the main road along the east base of East Gros Ventre Butte. Traditional river crossings were fords or, at best, crude bridges. In this period, permanent bridges were built at most fords. During the summer of 1917, crews constructed a bridge across the deep draw near the mouth of Ditch Creek as part of a new road from Menor's Ferry to the Grovont Post Office, located east of Blacktail Butte. Farther up Ditch Creek, materials had been delivered for another new bridge. To the north, Spread Creek's multiple channels dispersed over a cobbled alluvial fan, posing significant problems for travelers. In 1924, the *Courier* reported that people in the north were determined to have a permanent bridge across the creek, their patience worn out with existing conditions.[71]

In most cases, roads continued to follow the old wagon tracks. The road from Wilson to Menor's Ferry followed for the most part the old alignment when it was improved in 1927. The most significant development in the 1920s was the construction of a state highway from Jackson to Menor's Ferry. The road continued north along the base of the Teton Range past Jenny Lake to Moran, where it linked up with the Yellowstone-Lander highway. In addition to the steel truss bridge erected at Menor's Ferry, the Bureau of Public Roads built a steel truss bridge across the Gros Ventre River near today's highway. The basic highway and county road system was established by the late 1920s, and remained intact until the 1950s.[72]

A proposal surfaced after World War II to construct a new highway from the south boundary of the Jackson Hole National Monument to the Buffalo Fork River. In 1948, National Park Service Director Newton P Drury, responding to a letter from Charles Moore, the president of the Dude Ranchers' Association, clarified the Park Service position. The service was not delaying the proposed project, but rather had some concerns about the alignment of the road and impacts on wildlife habitat. Drury stated that the service favored a highway diverting from the existing road at Blacktail Butte and running north across Antelope Flats to Deadman's Bar, then across Spread Creek and the Buffalo Fork to join the Yellowstone-Dubois-Lander highway. The Public Roads Administration constructed the current highway between 1955 through 1957, just as Drury described in his 1948 letter.[73]

Today, the main highway is kept open year-round, except when severe storms force closure. Prior to World War II, the state and county governments made no attempt to keep roads plowed because of high costs, primitive snowplows, and the lack of public pressure to maintain plowed roads. With the first heavy snows, Jackson Hole residents stored their Model T's, Hupmobiles, and White trucks, placing them on blocks and draining the engines and cooling systems. Oversnow vehicles, sleds, sleighs, and cutters, drawn by the reliable horse, became the principal form of transportation in the winter. Foot travelers strapped on Nordic skis or snowshoes.

In the 1930s, as the technology became available to remove snow, the public came to expect plowed roads. The variability of winter weather made road conditions difficult to predict. Anticipating the costs of snow removal was difficult as mild winters left

tidy surpluses, while severe winters depleted budgets. In December 1929, the park superintendent reported that despite three snowstorms in November, the valley's roads and Teton Pass remained open to automobiles, unusual for that time of year. The winter of 1930–1931 was one of the mildest on record. Only a year later, one of the worst blizzards in several years pummeled the region. Conditions were so bad that heavy snows stranded a snowplow and closed the Hoback Road. No less than 11 feet of snow choked Teton Pass. Harry Scott and Amasa James worked to cut a snow road over the pass. Likewise, in 1936, the monthly Superintendent's Report described terrible weather conditions. Valley residents worked together, committing time and horse teams to keep the roads packed and open. The Hoback Road had been closed most of the month of February, while 50 head of horses were used to clear 65 miles of road to Moran. The storm delayed regular mail deliveries for two weeks.[74]

To combat the isolation enforced by winter, state and local governments began investing in improved snow removal equipment. By 1932, rotary plows were being used to clear snow from highways. On June 16 of that year, the *Courier* reported that rotary plows had opened Togwotee Pass and were pushing on to the south entrance of Yellowstone, which remained blocked by snow. In the winter of 1930–1931, the Hoback Road remained open for the first time in its history, attributable for the most part to a mild winter. The next year the Wyoming State Highway Department announced its intention to keep the highway open as much as possible.[75]

They did not succeed. In March 1933, the *Courier* reported that the Hoback Road would be cleared of snow and open in April after a winter closure. Pressure built to keep the Hoback highway open as this route assumed more importance as a supply link, and the Postal Service began routing Teton County's mail from Rock Springs. The Jackson Lions Club contacted the governor in March 1934, urging him to order the opening of the road from the wye near Daniel, Wyoming, as supplies were getting a little short and some residents were "caught out," while other wanted to "get out." Public pressure had no influence on the weather, however. In January 1936, snow-laden mountainsides shed their loads, causing the heaviest slides in years. The Hoback was completely blocked; 50 volunteers, Forest Service employees, and Game and Fish employees used shovels to try to open the road.[76]

State highway crews kept the Teton Pass Road cleared for the first time in 1937, giving up in January 1938. The following September, the highway department revealed plans to keep the pass open to automobile traffic. To accomplish this, the department allocated a five-ton truck with a push plow. In early December, they received a new 15-ton rotary plow, a huge machine being 25 feet long and 11 feet wide. A 175-horsepower engine propelled the rotor blades. In spite of the new equipment, the highway department gave up on the Teton Pass Road after New Years Day 1940, in the face of severe blizzards. Two hundred angry citizens commandeered two plows from the state highway garages and opened the road. In addition, they protested the local supervisor's decision to the governor. Responding to the pressure from Teton County residents, Governor Nels Smith ordered the department to keep the Teton Pass Road open, ending further civil disobedience. The road was generally kept open until World War II, when gasoline and rubber shortages forced the highway department to reduce plowing, which resulted in closures. Some remember the pass as being generally kept open through the war. By that time, the Snake River Canyon highway provided alternate access to Idaho. Since the war, the pass has been kept open, except for sporadic closures caused by blizzards or snowslides.[77]

In the valley, the roads north of Jackson were not plowed through the 1930s. Plows kept the road to Moran open until January to accommodate the influx of hunters. The highway and county road to Moran were unplowed from January to March or April each year, depending on the snow cover. On January 12, 1939, irate residents of Moran petitioned to have the road plowed through the winter and sought help from the Jackson Hole Commercial Club. By the 1940s, major roads in the valley were kept open, and access in and out of the valley was possible via the Togwotee Pass highway, the Hoback Road, and the Snake River Canyon road.[78]

Auto and train travel, although most common, were not the only modes of transportation. When H. H. Barker and I. G. Winton landed their biplane at the Jackson rodeo grounds during the Frontier Days celebration on August 19, 1920, they raised quite a stir among the crowd. Excited bystanders gathered about the airplane. Leaving Blackfoot, Idaho, at 4:30 P.M., Barker piloted the craft over the Teton Range and landed in Jackson at 5:45 P.M., making the 120-mile trip in one hour and 15 minutes. Barker and Winton offered rides to fairgoers and had 59 riders. It was probably the first airplane some of the passengers had ever seen. The appearance of Barker's biplane above the horizon suggested new possibilities for transportation in and out of the valley.[79]

In February 1926, the *Courier* reported that an Idaho aviator named Tommy Thompson intended to begin air service from Idaho Falls to Jackson Hole, charging $40 for round-trip fare. The flight would cut travel time considerably, when one considered that it took three days to reach the valley by train. There is no evidence that Thompson established the service. In 1930, the superintendent of Grand Teton National Park reported that an airplane had been seen traveling north on two occasions in March. An investigation revealed that a pilot from Idaho Falls had spent some time in Jackson Hole, making plans to establish mail and passenger service from Idaho Falls to Moran. He had invested heavily in the projected service, buying a new Wright plane for the route. But, again, no information exists to show the service became a reality.[80]

Local interest in developing an airport and commercial service evolved in the 1930s. Dr. Charles W. Huff, the valley's physician, led the effort. At the end of 1933, the *Wyoming Tribune Leader* reported that air service might be established from Rock Springs to Jackson with stops in communities in the Green River valley. Promoters of the air service saw a rosy future for winter sports in the valley and believed air service would facilitate development. Dr. Huff sought Civil Works Administration funding to construct an airfield. In 1934, three potential airport sites emerged: the old Frank McBride place north of the Gros Ventre bridge; a tract east of Flat Creek and four miles north of Jackson; and former JP Ranch lands located east of the highway and south of the Gros Ventre River. In early January, Huff toured the valley with aviator A. A. Bennett, seeking suitable sites. In March, Dr. Huff telephoned Harold Fabian, vice president of the Snake River Land Company, to request a five-year lease to the JP site from the company. Rockefeller agent Kenneth Chorley expressed serious reservations about the compatibility of an airport with the Snake River Land Company's plan. Huff dropped the request, when a company called Air Transport Lines built a 200 by 1,000-foot airstrip across from the rodeo grounds in Jackson. This field served the community as a "small, unimproved"·airport through the 1930s.[81]

In 1940, the Jackson town government, individuals, and citizen groups began lobbying for a new airport and commercial service. In early March, the mayor of Jackson, Harry Clissold, led a delegation to Salt Lake City to meet with Harold Fabian, who also served on the board of directors of Western Air Express. Clissold and other supporters proposed locating the airport southwest of Blacktail Butte and east of the Snake River, where the airport is situated today. Located on federal lands and on Snake River Land Company property, the town of Jackson needed to secure leases from both the company and the Interior Department. In addition, Western Air Express had to seek review and approval of a route from Salt Lake City to Jackson from the Civil Aeronautics Authority. The paperwork took time. Moreover, there were other concerns that delayed the construction of the airport; some questioned the need for a commercial airport, and once a consensus formed supporting it, a suitable location became the subject of debate.

Fabian supported the plan probably for two reasons. First, he believed that the market could support commercial air service and, in turn, the service was needed. Second, yet just as important, Fabian perceived the airport as a way to gain acquiescence, if not support, among Jackson Hole residents for the proposed park extension. John D. Rockefeller Jr., Laurence Rockefeller, Vanderbilt Webb, and Kenneth Chorley agreed "that the Snake River Land Company should not take the position of opposing in any way the establishment of a proper airport." However, they expressed concern about the scenic intrusion of an airport located between the highway and the Teton Range. There was not a consensus of opinion. Horace Albright questioned the need for an airport, writing to Chorley that "they are definitely an intrusion into wilderness areas." Chorley responded that even though the need for an airport and personal choice to fly was a matter of opinion, "I am inclined to think that Jackson Hole would be better off without an airport." In a letter to Vanderbilt Webb in May 1941, Fabian wrote "I understood the Park Service does not favor airline service into Jackson Hole; that both the traffic and operating officials of Western Air Lines prefer not to land there [and] that the Snake River Land Company does not favor airline service there nor the construction of an airport between the highway and the mountains."[82]

Nevertheless, the Interior Department and company agreed to give the town a lease. The site remained the only issue. Webb, in his March 27 letter to Fabian, suggested locating the airport in the Kelly-Mormon Row area. All interested parties supported a site on Antelope Flats, but the chief operations officer of Western rejected this location, because of unpredictable winds diverted by Blacktail Butte. They did find a location north of Timbered Island, about one mile east of Jenny Lake. The National Park Service objected to this site. Acting Director Arthur Demaray stated that it "would be inimical to the best interests of the park and local community." To add to the confusion, Moran residents supported an airport south of Signal Mountain, and even scraped out a small airstrip in the sagebrush flats. Then, Mayor Clissold, irate over the Timbered Island proposal, announced his intention to apply for a lease at the original location southwest of Blacktail Butte.[83]

Sometime between 1941 and 1943, local residents cleared an airstrip at the present location, commandeering county equipment according to local tradition. The town of Jackson secured a lease from the Interior Department on June 16, 1942, and from the Jackson Hole Preserve, formerly the Snake River Land Company, in November 1943. Western Air Express initiated commercial service in 1946. Today, the airport operates under a 50-year lease within Grand Teton National Park.[84]

Local tradition has it that a small airstrip existed at the current airport in the 1930s. Documents in the Harold Fabian Papers and Kenneth Chorley Papers in the Rockefeller Archive Center do not mention an airfield in this area in 1940. Had there been one, it seems reasonable that it would have been mentioned in correspondence. Further, the *Jackson's Hole Couriers* during the 1930s refer to the airfield being near the fairgrounds in Jackson. However, no mention of a landing field southwest of Blacktail Butte was found. Finally, a photograph taken from Blacktail Butte of the airport area, dated August 13, 1937, shows that an airstrip did not exist prior to that date at that location. Today, thousands of travelers use the Jackson Hole Airport.

The first permanent occupants of Jackson Hole settled in a remote mountain valley. Mail was irregular and getting supplies into the valley proved difficult and time consuming. Trips to Jackson were made once or twice a year, while excursions outside Jackson Hole were unheard of for most settlers. Railroads facilitated settlement, providing access to supplies and a way for homesteaders to get their only export, cattle, to market. Roads improved gradually until 1918, when the automobile revolutionized life in the United States, not to mention Jackson Hole. Government organizations improved the road system dramatically in the 1920s. Motor vehicles replaced the horse. Rotary plows and blade plows began keeping most roads open by the 1940s. In 1920, the first airplane landed in the valley; 22 years later an airport was established.

Today, a modern highway system is in place with four major routes kept open year-round. Virtually all goods such as food, clothing, and gasoline are hauled by truck over the highways into Jackson Hole. Most of the 2,500,000 visitors who travel to Jackson Hole each year arrive in air-conditioned vehicles, keeping time to music played on tape decks through stereo speakers. Our society cannot conceive the difficulties travel posed for people scarcely a century ago.

Notes

1. Billington, *Westward Expansion*, pp. 547–562.
2. Ibid., p. 551.
3. Ibid., pp. 555–558; and Larson, *History of Wyoming*, p. 3.
4. Nellie Van Derveer, "Teton County Agriculture and Industry," WPA Subject File 1327, Wyoming State Archives, Museums and Historical Department.
5. Owen, T42 N, R115W, 6th P.M.; and Harold P. and Josephine Fabian Collection, Grand Teton National Park.
6. Jackson, *Pioneer Photographer*, p. 26.
7. Interview with Almer Nelson by Jo Anne Byrd, #30, "Last of Old West Series."
8. Mumey, *The Teton Mountains*, p. 205; and Hayden, *From Trapper to Tourist*, p. 38.
9. Nellie Van Derveer, "Teton County-Historical Lore," WPA Subject File 1321, Wyoming State Archives, Museums, and Historical Department; and *Jackson's Hole Courier*, March 9, 1939.
10. Struthers Burt, *Diary*, pp. 32–35.
11. Ibid., Nathaniel Burt, *Jackson Hole Journal*, (Norman, OK: University of Oklahoma Press, 1983), pp. 10–11; and *Jackson's Hole Courier*, February 18, 1932.
12. Interview with Parthenia Stinnett by Jo Anne Byrd, #38, "Last of the Old West;" *Jackson's Hole Courier*, September 10, 1942; Markham, "The Ashton-Moran Freight Road;" U. S. Geological Survey, Shoshone Quadrangle, 1907 reprint 1911; and Frances Judge, "Carrie and the Tetons," *Montana* (Summer 1968):46.
13. Elizabeth Wied Hayden Collection, Subject File #5, "Roads," Jackson Hole Historical Society and Museum, Blount and Artist, T46N, R113W, 6th P.M., July 21–August 20, 1902; Jackson Hole Plat Book; Harold and Josephine Fabian Collection, Grand Teton National Park; and U.S. Geological Survey, Mount Leidy Quadrangle, 1902.
14. Driggs, *History of Teton Valley*, p. 184; *Jackson's Hole Courier*, January 28, 1909, and January 29, 1948; David Crowder, *Rexburg, Idaho* (Caldwell, ID: Carton Printers, 1983), pp. 82–85; and Almer Nelson Interview, #30.
15. Almer Nelson Interview, #30; and *Jackson Hole Guide*, July 28, 1966.
16. Linda McKinstry, untitled memoir, Subject File, Wyoming-Jackson Hole (W994-JH), University of Wyoming Archives, American Heritage Center; and Struthers Burt, *Diary*, p. 33.
17. Owen, T41N, R116W, 6th P.M.; T42N; R115W, 6th P.M.; T42N, R116W, 6th P.M.; T44N, R115W, 6th P.M.; and T45N, R114W, 6th P.M.
18. U.S. Geological Survey, Grand Teton Quadrangle, 1899.
19. Allen, *Early Jackson Hole*, p. 1; and *Jackson's Hole Courier*, October 31, 1918.
20. Donald Hough, *The Cocktail Hour in Jackson Hole* (New York: W.W. Norton and Company, 1951), pp. 157–158; and Superintendent's Monthly Report, March 1937, Grand Teton National Park.
21. Struthers Burt, *Diary*, p. 131.

22. *Jackson's Hole Courier*, December 25, 1924; and Richard A. Dirks and Brooks E. Martner, *The Climate of Yellowstone and Grand Teton National Parks* (Washington, D.C.: Government Printing Office, 1982).

23. *Jackson's Hole Courier*, January 28, 1909, February 13, 1916, February 23, 1933, January 20, 1927, and February 9, 1933.

24. *Jackson Hole Guide*, November 18, 1965; *Jackson's Hole Courier*, February 18, 1932, and April 16, 1914; and Hayden Collection, Subject File #5, Jackson Hole Historical Society and Museum.

25. *Jackson's Hole Courier*, February 19, 1948; and *Jackson Hole Guide*, December 16, 1965.

26. Bicentennial Photograph Collection, Teton County Library and Jackson Hole Historical Society and Museum; Superintendent's Monthly Report, January 1931; and *Jackson's Hole Courier*, December 15, 1927.

27. *Jackson's Hole Courier*, November 6, 1924, June 28, 1928, and July 26, 1928; and Allen, *Early Jackson Hole*, pp. 218–222.

28. U.S.Geological Survey, Grand Teton Quadrangle, 1901.

29. Brown, *Souvenir History*, p. 17; *Jackson's Hole Courier*, August 20, 1914, March 11, 1915, July 19, 1917, April 11, 1918, May 30, 1918, September 12, 1918, June 13, 1918, May 20, 1920, January 5, 1922, and February 23, 1922; and "Ferry near Wilson, 1914," Bicentennial Collection, #311.

30. Homestead Patent, Homestead Cert. 503, Lander, W. D. Menor, 1904; and Judge, "Mountain River Men," pp. 52–58.

31. McBride, "My Diary;" Menor's Ferry Collection, Fabian Collection, Grand Teton National Park; and *Jackson's Hole Courier*, May 10, 1917, May 14, 1914, January 13, 1921, and July 27, 1950.

32. Judge, "Mountain River Men," pp. 52–58.

33. Ibid.; and interview with Stan Boyle by Charles Convis, June 26, 1979, typed transcript, Grand Teton National Park.

34. *Jackson's Hole Courier*, July 25, 1918; Office of the Teton County Clerk and Recorder, Deed Record Book 3, p. 200, W.D. Menor to Maud Noble, Frederick Sandell and May Lee, Warranty Deed, August 1, 1918.

35. Judge, "Mountain River Men," p. 57.

36. *Jackson's Hole Courier*, January 14, 1926,and June 10, 1926.

37. Mumey, *Teton Mountains*, pp. 359–61; Homestead Patent, Homestead Cert. 373, Lander, James Conrad to Homer Guerry, 1902; and Census of the United States, 1900, Jackson Precinct.

38. Mumey, *Teton Mountains*, p. 358.

39. Mae Tuttle to Cora N. Barber, September 6, 1951, Jackson Hole Historical Society and Museum, reprinted in *Jackson Hole Guide*, December 5, 1974.

40. Ibid., K. C. Allan Collection, 7636, "Post Offices of Jackson Hole," University of Wyoming Archives; Hayden Collection, Subject File 5, Leek Memoir, Jackson Hole Historical Society and Museum; Mae Tuttle letter, September 5, 1951, Jackson Hole Historical Society and Museum; *Wyoming Tribune*, February 8, 1896; *Jackson's Hole Courier*, February 4, 1932; and *Jackson Hole Guide*, November 18, 1965.

41. Mae Tuttle letter, September 5, 1951, Jackson Hole Historical Society and Museum.

42. Census of the United States, 1900, Jackson Precinct; *Jackson Hole Guide*, November 18, 1965; Hayden Collection, File 21, Jackson Hole Historical Society and Museum; and Allan Collection, "Post Offices of Jackson Hole," University of Wyoming Archives.

43. *Jackson's Hole Courier*, January 28, 1909.

44. *Jackson's Hole Courier*, July 30, 1914, June 27, 1918, and August 18, 1932.

45. Hayden Collection, Subject File 5, Leek Memoir, Jackson Hole Historical Society and Museum; and *Jackson Hole Guide*, November 18, 1965.

46. *Jackson's Hole Courier*, November 7, 1918.

47. *Jackson's Hole Courier*, June 5, 1919, and May 12, 1921.

48. *Jackson's Hole Courier*, July 12, 1931, and February 4, 1932; and *Jackson Hole Guide*, November 19, 1965.

49. "Jackson Stage-March 1, 1909" photograph, Jackson Hole Historical Society and Museum; and *Jackson's Hole Courier*, January 28, 1909.,

50. *Jackson's Hole Courier*, August 31, 1950, and May 21, 1953.

51. Markham, "The Ashton-Moran Freight Road," U.S. Geological Survey, Shoshone Quadrangle, 1884–1885, 1911 edition.

52. Markham, "The Ashton-Moran Freight Road."

53. Ibid., John Markham, "The Temporary Jackson Lake Dam," unpublished manuscript, Grand Teton National Park Library.

54. Diem, *Research Station*; Census of the United States, 1900, Jackson Precinct; Allen, *Early Jackson Hole*, p. 304; *Jackson Hole Guide*, September 9, 1978; *Jackson's Hole Courier*, August 31, 1950; and Nellie Van Derveer, "Teton County-Towns," WPA Subject file 1322, Wyoming State Archives.

55. Brown, *Souvenir History*, p. 12; and *Jackson's Hole Courier*, February 17, 1949, and January 28, 1909.

56. Markham, "Ashton-Moran Freight Road;" and *Jackson's Hole Courier*, June 27, 1918, and July 7, 1932.

57. Haines, *The Yellowstone Story*, 2:265–266.

58. Brown, *Souvenir History*, p. 11; Hayden, *Trapper to Tourist*, p. 52; *Jackson's Hole Courier*, May 16, 1940, and July 23, 1914; Hayden Collection, Subject File #5, Automobiles, Jackson Hole Historical Society and Museum. "EMF" stands for Everitt, Metzger and Flanders, a partnership that built electric and gasoline powered cars until 1911.

59. Hayden, *Trapper to Tourist*, pp. 52–53; *Jackson's Hole Courier*, November 23, 1916, June 5, 1919, and June 16, 1926; and *Jackson Hole Guide*, April 25, 1974.

60. Hayden, *Trapper to Tourist*, p. 53; and *Jackson's Hole Courier*, September 30, 1915, and December 18, 1919.

61. Virginia Huidekoper, *The Early Days in Jackson Hole*, (Boulder, CO: Colorado Associated University Press, 1978), p. 78; and *Jackson's Hole Courier*, May 29, 1924, and August 25, 1921.

62. *Jackson's Hole Courier*, July 19, 1917, August 2, 1917, and October 3, 1918.

63. *Jackson's Hole Courier*, June 11, 1925; and Nellie Van Derveer, "Teton County General," WPA Subject File 1336, Wyoming State Archives.

64. *Jackson's Hole Courier*, May 12, 1921, and February 5, 1925.

65. *Jackson's Hole Courier*, June 6, 1918, July 25, 1918, February 5, 1925, July 20, 1933, and February 17, 1941.

66. *Jackson's Hole Guide*, November 5, 1970; U.S. Geological Survey, Gros Ventre Quadrangle, 1910 edition, reprinted 1949; *Jackson's Hole Courier*, August 17, 1916, June 6, 1918, June 23, 1921, July 20, 1922, July 25, 1918, May 5, 1932, and February 5, 1925; and Hayden Collection, Subject File 5, Hoback Road, Jackson Hole Historical Society and Museum.

67. *Jackson's Hole Courier*, August 2, 1917; John Markham Papers, 934, Jackson Hole Historical Society and Museum; Hayden Collection, Subject File 5, Roads, Jackson Hole Historical Society and Museum; *The Denver Post*, July 16, 1922; and Haines, *The Yellowstone Story*, 2:267.

68. *Jackson's Hole Courier*, May 17, 1923, August 13, 1931, September 7, 1933, and March 30, 1939; and Superintendent's Monthly Report, February 1936, Grand Teton National Park.

69. *Jackson's Hole Courier*, February 4, 1932.

70. *Jackson's Hole Courier*, June 17, 1920, and April 17, 1924.

71. *Jackson's Hole Courier*, July 3, 1919, July 12, 1917, and March 13, 1924.

72. *Jackson's Hole Courier*, July 7, 1927, September 8, 1927, June 19, 1924, and August 4, 1927.

73. Newton B. Drury to C.M. Moore, February 13, 1948, File 630, Roads, Jackson Hole N.M., Grand Teton National Park.

74. Superintendent's Monthly Reports, November 1929, February 1931, January 1932, and February 1936, Grand Teton National Park; and *Jackson's Hole Courier*.

75. *Jackson's Hole Courier*, December 16, 1931, and June 16, 1932; and Superintendent's Monthly Report, February 1931, Grand Teton National Park.

76. *Jackson's Hole Courier*, March 23, 1933, March 6, 1934, and January 16, 1936.

77. *Jackson's Hole Courier*, January 13, 1938, September 8, 1938, and January 11, 1940; and *Jackson Hole Guide*, April 25, 1974.

78. *Jackson's Hole Courier*, January 4, 1934, March 27, 1934, April 23, 1936, March 30, 1939, and January 12, 1939.

79. *Jackson's Hole Courier*, August 20, 1920; Brown, *Souvenir History*, p. 17; and Huidekoper, *Early Days*, p. 49.

80. *Jackson's Hole Courier*, February 11, 1926; and Superintendent's Monthly Report, March 1930, Grand Teton National Park.

81. *Jackson's Hole Courier*, December 28, 1933, January 4, 1934, January 11, 1934, February 8, 1934, March 22, 1934, and January 28, 1937; and Kenneth Chorley Papers, IV3A3, Box 13, File 109, Harold Fabian to Kenneth Chorley, March 24, 1934, telegram, Kenneth Chorley to Harold Fabian, March 26, 1934; and Harold Fabian to Kenneth Chorley, March 26, 1934, Rockefeller Archive Center.

82. *Jackson's Hole Courier*, March 7, 1940; and Harold Fabian Collection, IV3A7, Box 8, File 66, Jackson Airport, 1940–1941, Correspondence; and Chorley Papers, Box 2, File 16, Jackson Hole Airport, Harold Fabian to Vanderbilt Webb, May 14, 1941, Rockefeller Archive Center.

83. Fabian Papers, Box 8, File 66, Jackson Hole Airport, Vanderbilt Webb to Harold Fabian, March 27, 1940; Harold Fabian to Kenneth Chorley, August 2, 1940; Arthur DeMaray to Harold Fabian, September 25, 1940; Harold Fabian to Kenneth Chorley, September 21, 1940, Rockefeller Archive Center; and *Jackson's Hole Courier*, November 28, 1940.

84. Chorley Papers, Box 2, File 16, Jackson Hole Airport, Arthur DeMaray to Kenneth Chorley, July 13, 1942; and Vanderbilt Webb to Harold Fabian, October 5, 1943, Rockefeller Archive Center.

CHAPTER **13**

The Communities of Jackson Hole

A mass meeting is called for two o'clock Tuesday afternoon at the Jackson Club House to further discuss the subject of incorporating Jackson. . . . Ladies, as well as men, are requested to be present at this meeting let noone [sic] stay away.

—*Jackson's Hole Courier*, May 7, 1914

Death and destruction came down the Gros Ventre River yesterday morning in a great wall of water that snuffed out six lives, wiped the town of Kelly off the map. . . .

—*Jackson's Hole Courier*, May 19, 1927

Town of Jackson, 1907. *William Trester, Jackson Hole Historical Society and Museum*

etween 1850 and 1900, thousands of small towns developed west of the Mississippi River, playing an essential role in westward expansion. Economics drove people to develop communities. Entrepreneurs built businesses such as inns or blacksmith shops along transportation routes to cater to traffic. Townspeople also formed communities around stores and post offices to provide goods and services to farmers, ranchers, and miners. Finally, towns resulted from pure speculation. Federal laws, notably the Townsite Act of 1844 and its more restrictive successor of 1867, gave promoters the means to secure land, luring hordes of speculators west.[1]

Small western towns, particularly agricultural communities, shared a sameness noticed by most observers. Surveyors laid out townsites in the familiar block pattern, making minimal concessions to topographic reality. Architectural patterns were also similar. The false front store became the dominant archi-

tectural style for main street buildings. Residences varied according to income. Modest homes followed standard patterns, while prefabricated homes could be ordered through mail order houses such as Montgomery Wards. Affluent people built substantial homes that reflected their economic status. These houses are popularly known as "Victorian," a general architectural term for styles that flourished between 1860 and 1915. Multiple stories, elaborate ornamentation, and a variety of colors and surface textures characterized Victorian residential architecture. Their sameness reflected the quest of migrants to create the familiar in an unfamiliar, sometimes hostile environment.[2]

Western communities also shared several common institutions. Indeed, towns buffeted by the boom-and-bust cycles of mining and agriculture depended on these institutions for survival. Local newspapers were key, for they helped define the self-image of a community and "created the illusion of a homogenous society." Just as important, town newspapers promoted unabashedly the communities they served, often with little regard for truth. A second institution was the general mercantile store, the main source of supplies. Not only could patrons buy staple items such as flour, salt, sugar, and coffee, they could obtain luxury items such as gold watch chains or china dolls. The general store served as a social center where people congregated to share news and gossip. They also assumed the role of banks, extending credit and, if the store had a safe, securing checks and other valuables of customers.

A hotel was another important component of a frontier town. However crude the accommodations, a hotel boosted the self-esteem of a community. Saloons were an important place for entertainment and socializing. Alcohol provided a cure, however false, for the isolation and boredom that typified so much of life on the frontier. Education assumed more importance as westward expansion progressed through the nineteenth century. Westward migration weakened traditional institutions such as the family, church, apprentice system, and folk traditions.[3] Frontier schools helped fill that void. Spiritual life remained important, and as communities matured, devout citizens built churches. As towns developed, townspeople also established specialized businesses such as drugstores, restaurants, and hardware stores. The blacksmith was the most needed craftsman, shoeing horses and performing essential repairs on tools, machinery, and vehicles.

In Jackson Hole, towns and villages evolved slowly with the gradual increase in population. The first communities were rural post offices, sometimes augmented by country schools, churches, or perhaps a small boarding house. Jackson Hole was able to support only three towns: Jackson, Wilson, and Kelly—four, if Moran is counted. Towns were a twentieth-century development in the valley. Prior to 1900, it remained a sparsely populated backwater, a mosaic of isolated homesteads clustered in the Flat Creek area, South Park, and the Buffalo Fork. As more post offices and schools emerged after 1900, settlers developed a sense of loyalty or identity to their locality rather than the town of Jackson or Jack-

son Hole. One settler recalled that "the valley was divided into three or four parts. There was Moran and Elk in the upper end, Grovont and Kelly in the middle, then in the lower part there was Jackson and Wilson, with Zenith and Cheney scattered around."[4]

Potential towns such as Marysvale and Grand Teton never progressed beyond wishful thinking. On March 25, 1892, the Postal Service authorized the valley's first post office, Marysvale. Located at the Fred White homestead north of Botcher Hill, the post office was named for White's wife, Mary. The Whites managed the post office until 1894, when they abandoned the "swamp ranch" for a more attractive homestead along the Snake River. William and Maggie Simpson took over the post office, which was renamed Jackson. In 1896, the *Wyoming Tribune* reported that promoters were staking out the city of Grand Teton, anticipating a population boom in the coming summer. The proposed townsite was located at the north end of Spring Gulch, one-half mile from the hot springs near East Gros Ventre Butte. The city of Grand Teton existed only in the newspaper article and imaginations of its promoters, for no lands were preempted nor a townsite staked out by surveyors.[5]

A small village evolved around the Jackson Post Office. Charles "Pap" Deloney opened a general store on the Simpson ranch, the first retail store of any kind in Jackson Hole. Deloney's consisted of the store, a barn for building materials, and a small storage cabin. Like most general mercantile stores, Deloney sold an amazing variety of goods; half of the store housed groceries and hardware while the other half displayed dry goods such as clothing and sewing machines. Glass, window and door frames, lumber, and farm machinery were kept in the barn. Around 1897, members of the Jackson Hole Gun Club built the Clubhouse, Jackson's first community building. A two-story, rectangular frame building with a hipped roof, it served as a dance hall, courtroom, men's smoking room, gymnasium, and commercial building. Prior to 1900, Mary Anderson established what may have been the first hotel or boarding house in the valley near Antelope Gap or the wye. Mrs. Anderson became the postmaster of Jackson in 1900. The hotel was moved to the townsite of Jack-

The Jackson Hole Gun Club was built in 1897. Known as the "Clubhouse," the gun club was the town's first community building and was used for a variety of social functions. Although modified, the building still stands on the Jackson Town Square. *Jackson Hole Historical Society and Museum*

son in 1901, where it became known as the Jackson Hotel. The seeds of the community were sown when Bill Simpson laid out the first town plat for Jackson in 1901.[6]

Between 1901 and 1914, Jackson established itself as the valley's primary community. Citizens started the first town school in the Clubhouse in 1903, then built a log school in 1905. In the same year, Mormons constructed the town's first church, a brick building situated on the western fringe of the village. The bricks were manufactured at a kiln located near the wye, owned by two men named Parker and Mullen. Workers enclosed the Jackson Hotel in brick and added a two-story brick wing to the rear of the building. In 1906, Frank and Roy Van Vleck rolled into Jackson driving a wagon loaded with either potatoes or apples, depending upon which account is read. A sick horse prevented them from going on to Oregon. The brothers opened the Jackson Mercantile, selling their load of produce to raise capital.[7]

William Trester took the earliest known photograph of Jackson in 1907. From the east slope of East Gros Ventre Butte, his camera captured a sleepy frontier village on a sunny spring afternoon. The photograph shows a collection of buildings spread across the sagebrush flat. Recognizable structures include the Mormon Church, the Clubhouse, and the

Jackson Hotel. Less recognizable are Tuttle and Lloyd's Saloon, Deloney's store, and Wort's livery barn. Willows reveal the course of Cache Creek east of the village. Before the Clubhouse is a large sagebrush swale, rutted by two sets of wagon tracks. This eventually became the town square.[8]

Following the pattern of other frontier towns, more entrepreneurs started specialized businesses. Sometime after Trester's photograph, Dr. Luther F. Palmer constructed a two-story frame building on the southeast corner of the square, intending to use it as a residence and sanitarium. Convalescent homes were not uncommon in the West, as people with asthma and tuberculosis often relocated to the West for the dry desert air or mountain climate. In 1908, Palmer sold the building to Claude and Maud Reed, who converted it to Jackson's second hotel. Ma Reed's, later the Crabtree Inn, became a local landmark until 1952 when the Crabtrees sold it.[9]

In 1909, Jackson reached another milestone, when Douglas Rodeback published the first edition of the *Jackson's Hole Courier*. The paper gave the village an important voice in promotion, and articulated and helped define the community's self-image.[10] By this time, Jackson claimed a population of 200 people and had established itself as the commercial center of Jackson Hole. E. C. "Doc" Steele opened a drugstore, L. H. Zimmerman started a

The Rube Tuttle saloon was a popular gathering place in Jackson. Lined up at the bar are (left to right): S. L. Spicer, Rube Tuttle, Willard Miner Sr., T. Lloyd (behind bar), Walt Spicer, Frank La Shaw, Jack Grey, and Alva Simpson. *Jackson Hole Historical Society and Museum*

butcher shop in 1914, and Fred Lovejoy brought a touch of modernity by building a telephone exchange in 1905.[11]

In 1912, the Episcopal Church established a mission in Jackson. Members built a rest house in 1912–1913, which eventually included a gymnasium, library, and reading room. The Jackson school district built a two-story brick schoolhouse, which opened in 1914. A year later, on December 10, 1915, fire destroyed both the new brick school and the first log schoolhouse. The valley's first bank opened in August 1914. Located in a small brick building south of the Jackson Hotel, the Jackson State Bank marshaled $10,000 in capital, providing a local source of funding for community development.[12] In the spring of 1914, the citizens of Jackson began considering filing articles of incorporation for town government. Talk became reality, and the townspeople elected a mayor and town council in November 1914.[13]

In retrospect, it is apparent that Jackson enjoyed an advantage over its early potential rivals Wilson and Moran. Because of its central location between clusters of homesteads in South Park and the Flat Creek area, Jackson possessed a geographic advantage and established a more solid economic base than either Wilson or Moran. Most homesteads were situated east of the Snake River, which negated

Wilson's prime location on the road over Teton Pass. At the north end of the valley, Moran was far too isolated, even after the Reclamation Service developed the Ashton-Moran Road in 1910. Struthers Burt recalled that "as winter draws down in a frontier country the principal town becomes the focus of the community." To enable children to attend school, families often relocated to town from isolated ranches, joining unemployed ranch hands holed up in hotels and boarding houses.[14]

Between 1915 and the depression of 1929, Jackson experienced prosperity fueled by high prices for agricultural products and a population increase. More businesses located in the community, and modern conveniences transformed the village to a twentieth-century town. In 1918, the Kemmerer *Camera* portrayed Jackson as a bustling little community consisting of a bank, a telephone exchange, a drugstore, the Elk Cigar Store, a billiard parlor, two hotels, and two general mercantile stores.[15]

Important modern improvements included the installation of electric power and water and sewer systems. In 1920, E. C. Benson constructed a water-powered plant at the mouth of the canyon on Flat Creek, north of Jackson. In the last week of January 1921, electricity from the plant illuminated Jackson for the first time. At least one resident expressed skepticism about the project. Bill Blackburn informed Benson that the electric plant would never work, since "there wasn't a hole in the wire for the electricity to run through." After Benson's plant illuminated the town, Blackburn was chagrined, but undaunted. He decided that if the electric company could make electricity go through solid wire, he could do it too. Blackburn bought cheap wire, secured a 12-volt auto light, and wired his cabin. He threw loose wire over a 120-volt power line tying wires together. The next day, Blackburn confronted Benson with a consumer complaint: "Your juice is no good. It is too hot. It set my house on fire." By 1919, the town government had installed water and sewer lines. In 1916, St. John's Hospital was built with private subscriptions and Episcopal mission funds.[16]

The first edition of the *Courier* in 1921 listed the following businesses and services: the Jackson Mercantile—furniture and hardware; the Jackson Drug Company; Vincent the Tailor—Clothing; R. E. Miller's bank; the J. R. Jones Grocery; William Mercill's Grocery; Harry Wagner—Insurance; the Jackson Valley Telephone Company; the Jackson Billiard Hall; Fuller and Kent's Billiard Hall; the Picture Show, a movie theatre; the Jackson Laundry; the Jackson Leather Shop; Brown and Woods Blacksmith Shop; the two hotels; and the Spicer and Curtis Garage. A June issue listed additional businesses: Deloney's General Store; Charles Fox—Lumber; George Blair's taxidermy shop; the Jackson Meat Market; two barber shops, Mulherns and Fullers; and Wort's livery barn.[17]

Doctors were significant members of any community. In the absence of doctors, settlers relied on their own knowledge to treat injuries and sickness. Several pioneer women were midwives and known for their "doctoring" skills. They included Mary Wilson, Matilda Wilson, Mrs. H. M. Ely, Mrs. C. J. Allen, and Mrs. Sam Osborne. The valley may have had a physician prior to 1900. According to local tradition, a Dr. Woodburn practiced medicine in the valley in 1894, living in the Carnes cabin on Flat Creek. Others remembered a doctor named Reece or Reese. Dr. Luther F Palmer was the first physician known to reside and practice medicine in the valley. Listed in the census of 1900, Palmer treated people during a diphtheria epidemic in 1902, and the first

Courier reported that a Dr. Louis [sic] Palmer treated a patient for blood poisoning in January 1909. At Moran, the Reclamation Service employed several physicians during the construction of the Jackson Lake Dam. Horace Carncross served as resident physician at the JY Dude Ranch and later at the Bar BC. When present in the valley, he also treated residents.[18]

In January 1913, a 24-year old doctor named Charles W. Huff set up a practice in Jackson. Huff had developed symptoms of tuberculosis and had been advised to locate in a mountain climate; he also learned that Jackson had no doctor at the time. He practiced medicine until his premature death in 1937, giving Jackson Hole people over 20 years of stable medical care. Aware of preventive medical techniques, Huff lobbied actively for water and sewer systems and was a driving force behind the construction of Jackson's first hospital in 1916. After his death, Dr. Don MacLeod replaced him.[19]

In 1915, Dr. C. S. Horel set up the first known dental practice in the valley. Initially he set up office in front of the local taxidermy shop, but later thought better of it and moved the office to his residence. Horel practiced part time. He homesteaded near Menor's Ferry, then later secured a job as a ranger with the Forest Service. At the end of 1914, A. C. McKahan set up a veterinary practice, working out of Wort's livery barn.[20]

In 1920, a local political caucus nominated an all-women's ticket to run for mayor and four town council seats. The editor of the *Courier* wrote "if elected this next Tuesday this capable women's ticket will place the city of Jackson in the limelight." On May 11, the voters elected the entire ticket, and they took office on June 7.

Election Results

Mayor

Grace Miller	56
Fred Lovejoy	28

Town Council—2 year term

Rose Crabtree	50
Mae Deloney	49
William Mercill	34
Henry Crabtree	31

In 1920, the Town of Jackson elected the first all-female government in the country. Left to right: Councilwoman Mae Deloney, Councilwoman Rose Crabtree, Mayor Grace Miller, Councilwoman Faustina Haight, and Councilwoman Genevieve Van Vleck. *Jackson Hole Historical Society and Museum*

Town Council—1 year term

Genevieve Van Vleck	53
Faustina Haight	51
Maurice Williams	31
J. H. Baxter	28

Jackson voters made history by electing the first all-female civic government in the United States. In addition, schoolteacher Pearl Williams served as town marshal for a year. In 1921, Mayor Grace Miller and one-year incumbents, Genevieve Van Vleck and Faustina Haight, were reelected.[21]

Public parks and events reflected civic pride and a sense of community. Several Jackson Hole pioneers conceived the idea of a rodeo in Jackson. Frontier Days, as it was named, became the valley's first local celebration. Sponsors built a grandstand in a field southwest of Jackson and held the event in 1912. Bell Flanders, a sister of the Worts, owned the land. She donated 45 acres to the town for Frontier Park in 1920. However, the most notable landmark in Jackson is Town Square, a picturesque park of cottonwoods, post-and-pole fence, boardwalks, monuments, and distinctive elk antler arches on each corner. In the beginning, the square was nothing more than a sagebrush-covered depression surrounded by dirt roads and buildings. In 1924, the town govern-

ment planned to improve the square and fill material was to be hauled in to level the site. But not until 1931 did a citizens group improve the square. To commemorate the 200th anniversary of George Washington's birth, citizens raised money for nursery plants and landscaping and named the improved square Washington Memorial Park. In 1941, the town announced plans to pave the streets around the square, eliminating the dust and mud problems.[22]

The automobile and the growth of tourism changed Jackson from a frontier community to a modern town. Like other American communities, the dogma of progress conflicted with the urge to preserve the familiar or "keep things the way they are." In 1931, for example, Fred Lovejoy constructed a log building, a "real frontier cabin" more compatible with the image the town sought to cultivate. In reality, frame and brick buildings dominated the town. One year later, Bruce Porter installed a neon sign at the Jackson Drug, the first in the valley. In September 1941, Jess and John Wort opened a new hotel, described as Jackson's first fully modern hotel. The Wort has since become a local landmark.[23]

By the early 1920s, Jackson had consolidated its position as the economic and social center of the valley. After the creation of Teton County and the reso-

False-front buildings, such as the Wilson General Store, were a common architectural style in Jackson Hole. *Jackson Hole Historical Society and Museum*

lution of prolonged litigation over its establishment, Jackson became the new county seat by a surprisingly close vote. As the county seat, Jackson became the political center of Jackson Hole.[24]

One community that might have rivaled Jackson was Wilson. Named for pioneer Uncle Nick Wilson and his family, Wilson straddled the eastern end of the Teton Pass road at Fish Creek. The village had its beginning when Nick Wilson homesteaded at the eastern base of Teton Pass in 1889. The Wilsons were in a good position to provide food and lodging to travelers, situated on the main route into Jackson Hole. Wilson and his son-in-law Abe Ward built a hotel, store, and saloon in 1898. Further, the Postal Service established the Wilson Post Office on January 10, 1898. Matilda Wilson served as the first postmaster until 1899; her husband, Nick Wilson, worked as postmaster from 1899 through 1902. The first school in Wilson was held in one room of the Nick Wilson residence in 1898. By 1900, residents had formed a school district. The January 28, 1909, issue of the *Courier* listed several businesses at or near Wilson: the Wilson Hotel; a feed and livery; Roy B. Anderson, General Merchandise—Clothing and Groceries; and three sawmills, the Johnson Brothers Lumber, Kaufman and Barker, and Schofield and Van Winkle. The *Courier* published

a Wilson news column. Nevertheless, Walt Callahan, as a boy in 1917, recalled Wilson as "just a wide place in the road." By 1918, Robert Lundy operated a store, which became an important institution in the community. In 1925, Wilson consisted of a general store, a garage, a blacksmith shop, and a livery stable and had a population of 50 people.

Wilson never competed seriously with Jackson, even though it had more direct access to supply and communication links with Idaho. Because of its location, Wilson was not conveniently situated as a commercial center for homesteaders; most lived east of the Snake River. The river posed another problem as Wilson was and remains vulnerable to flooding. The flood of 1915 and the Kelly flood of 1927 inundated the village. Finally, Wilson residents did not seem to promote their community as aggressively as the citizens of Jackson, who secured a newspaper and a bank, and incorporated in 1914.[25]

One man was most responsible for the emergence of Moran—Ben D. Sheffield. In 1903, Sheffield bought the property of two homesteaders—Frank Lovell and Ed "Cap" Smith—and built the headquarters for a hunting and outfitting business at the outlet of Jackson Lake. In creating the Teton Lodge Resort, Sheffield and his wife had formed a partnership with Marion Lambert, a wealthy

Kent's Korner store in Kelly.
Jackson Hole Historical Society and Museum

Easterner. Situated in a prime location, Moran captured the business of travelers to Yellowstone, Jackson, Ashton, or Lander. Moran also became the first "tourist town" in Jackson Hole, in that catering to travelers and hunters formed the economic foundation of the village.

Prior to Sheffield's arrival, Cap and Clara Smith had constructed the large log hotel described in previous chapters. The hotel probably burned sometime after November 1900. Near the Smith Hotel, C. J. and Maria Allen homesteaded land west of Oxbow Bend in 1897. After the Smith Hotel burned, the Allens built the Elkhorn Hotel. The log hotel included a dining room, saloon, and livery stable. Nearby, W. C. Deloney opened a general store. Either Frank Lovell or Sheffield built a toll bridge at Moran, which became an important transportation link in the valley. Moran had received its name when Maria Allen opened the post office in 1902. In 1907, Sheffield took over the Moran Post Office, which he operated until 1919. Moran became the valley's only government town during the construction of the Jackson Lake Dam from 1910 to 1916. The Reclamation Service built an entire camp replete with barracks, mess hall, a commissary, offices, warehouses, and a hospital in the flats north of Sheffield's.[26]

By the late 1920s, Sheffield's Teton Lodge consisted of a large central lodge surrounded by log guest cottages, capable of accommodating 125 guests. The Sheffields sold out to the Snake River Land Company in 1929. This company turned the complex over to the Teton Investment Company, which operated the lodge. The main lodge burned in 1935. A 1946 site map shows an extensive complex consisting of 113 structures. In the 1950s, the Grand Teton Lodge Company and the National Park Service phased out the operation, and the buildings were removed by 1959. Many cabins were moved to Colter Bay.[27]

The town of Kelly developed later than Moran or Wilson, but emerged as a bustling community that appeared for a time to rival Jackson politically and commercially. Prior to its designation as a post office, settlers referred to the Kelly area as the "Bridge." Around the turn of the century, local residents had constructed a timber bridge across the Gros Ventre River which became an important crossing. By 1909, a school had also been built in the vicinity. Norman Smith's wife and children spent three winters at Kelly so his youngsters could attend school, while he remained at his homestead at Blacktail Butte. In April 1914, the *Courier* reported that the Smith family had returned to their homestead

In 1917, Milton Kneedy hauled flour mill equipment over Teton Pass, and installed it in his mill in Kelly. However, the flour mill was not a success, and the mill house burned in 1921. The man holding the reins in this photograph is Gerrit Hardeman; John Kneedy is standing next to the wagon.
Jackson Hole Historical Society and Museum

after spending the winter at the "Bridge." The following September, local farmers and ranchers had built four new houses on the W. J. Kelly property, so their children could also attend school. In addition, a new school was being built in the emerging town.[28]

By 1914, several entrepreneurs had located businesses in the Kelly area. Among them were the Grovont Mercantile, the Riverside Hotel, and a blacksmith shop. In October, the Postal Service authorized a post office at Kelly. Ben F. Goe was the first postmaster. For a time, the community had a sawmill until it was purchased and the machinery removed in 1918. By 1921, pioneer Albert Nelson owned a feed stable and livery service at Kelly. At one time, the community also possessed a dance hall, which burned at an unknown date.[29]

Milton K. Kneedy constructed the most unique business in Jackson Hole in 1917–1919, a flour mill. A miller by trade, Kneedy determined to open a flour mill after testing wheat grown in Jackson Hole for suitability as flour. In March 1917, Kneedy purchased a 20-barrel-capacity flour mill, manufactured by the Midget Marvel Milling Company, along with a gristmill for producing livestock feed. In the fall, surveyor Otho Williams staked out a site for the mill, but the Kneedy Flour Mill did not produce flour until July 1919. In October, 1921, fire destroyed Kneedy's mill, as well as tons of flour and wheat, ending Jackson Hole's experiment in flour production.[30]

Kelly competed with Jackson for designation as the seat of Teton County in 1921. Unexpectedly, proponents of Kelly garnered considerable support throughout the valley. Editorials in the *Jackson's Hole Courier* reveal a split in the community, characterized by a surprising level of acrimony. The editor of the *Courier* was caught in the middle as a booster of both valley and town. As the June election approached, rhetoric heated up in editorials and letters to the editor. Introducing more controversy, a small but influential minority opposed the creation of Teton County. In May, voters approved a county road bond by a vote of 326 to 26. However, 16 of the negative votes came from the Kelly district. A *Courier* editorial jabbed Kelly residents: "In view of the fact that Kelly is representing herself to be an up-to-date little village, and is bidding for the county seat, we are both surprised and disappointed at the 45–16 Kelly vote." Then, just prior to the election, the local newspaper published an editorial titled "Twelve Reasons Why County Seat Should be at Jackson," presenting both cogent and specious arguments for locating the seat in Jackson. Support for the creation of Teton County won by an overwhelming majority, but the county seat vote was surprisingly close. Jackson beat Kelly by 424 to 402. The vote indicated a distinct split among valley residents and some resentment toward the town of Jackson. The Kelly, Wilson, and Teton precincts formed a substantial anti-Jackson block. The solid Jackson and Cheney vote, as well as the split vote at Elk, made the difference. Adding to the confusion and controversy, 19 Alpine residents cast votes, even though this district was not part of the new county. Opponents in the Kelly area filed suit, seeking to block the creation of a new county, and the issue was only resolved in 1923 with new state legislation and a state supreme court decision affirming the creation of Teton County.[31]

Kelly survived political and legal defeat and, by 1926, had a population of 50 people, stores, a hotel, a garage, a blacksmith shop, a livery stable, telephone service, and daily mail delivery to the post office. A school and Episcopal Church were also located in the village. The town even had taxi service, provided by Walt Spicer who owned the garage. A year later, there would no longer be a village of Kelly.[32]

Kelly's death began on June 23, 1925, when a section of the north slope of Sheep Mountain slid into the canyon, damming the Gros Ventre River. An estimated 50,000,000 cubic yards of sandstone sheared off an underlying layer of shale, creating a dam 225 feet high and one-half mile wide. An unusual amount of precipitation may have caused the slide. Waters of the Gros Ventre backed up and flooded several homesteads and the Horsetail Creek Ranger Station. On July 9, the *Courier* reported water seeping through the dam, and by July 16 the water level was five feet below the dam. Engineers inspected the dam and declared it safe.

Two years later, the Gros Ventre River ran full, fed by snowmelt and heavy rains. On the night of May 17, 1927, water spilled over the dam. Charles Dibble, a U.S. Forest Service ranger, warned people in the area, but no one seemed unduly alarmed. By 1:00 A.M., one bridge was gone. The next morning, the river had filled its channel. Dibble and several Kelly residents were knocking driftwood away from the village bridge when they saw heavier debris and a hayrack sweeping towards it. Becoming suspicious, Dibble and another man drove up the Gros Ventre Road to check the dam. Upstream from Kelly, they

encountered a wall of water roaring down the canyon. Dibble raced his Model T to a nearby house and asked the woman to raise the alarm downriver over the telephone. Speeding to Kelly, he warned the residents, most of whom evacuated the town and school. The Kneedy family did not believe Dibble, and all three drowned in the flood. The torrent of water started with a surge five to six feet high, followed by a wall as much as 50 feet high that swept boulders, trees, and buildings before it. Witnesses described the sound as a "terrific unexplainable roar and grinding of hissing and swishing water." The flood spread out in the Gros Ventre bottomlands, wiping out homesteads and the steel-truss Gros Ventre bridge. Wilson was flooded, and the approaches to the Wilson bridge washed out. Nine hours after demolishing Kelly, the high water surged past Hoback Junction into the Snake River Canyon.

The Kelly flood was Jackson Hole's greatest natural disaster; six people died in the flood; nearly 40 families lost their homes; state and county officials estimated property damage to be around $500,000. The village never recovered from the catastrophe. Only the school, church, and rectory survived the flood. Ray C. and Anna Kent bought up land in Kelly and eventually subdivided their property. By 1943, there were 14 residential lots. Kelly has evolved into a residential community comprised of year-round and seasonal homes.[33]

Other communities in Jackson Hole remained nothing more than post offices and sometimes schools, created to serve ranchers and homesteaders in a given locality. On occasion, postmasters operated a store or boarding house out of their residences.

South Park enjoys the distinction of having the first school in Jackson Hole. Sylvester Wilson allowed a room of his homestead cabin to be used as a classroom, and pioneers built the first schoolhouse on Ervin Wilson's property in 1896. The South Park Post Office was established on November 17, 1899, at the Francis M. Estes ranch, only to be discontinued on September 14, 1901. The Cheney Post Office replaced South Park on April 2, 1902, at the Selar Cheney Ranch. The Postal Service closed Cheney in 1917.[34]

Elk was one of the earliest post offices in the valley, created to serve homesteaders in the Buffalo

The Grovont Post Office was located at different farms along Mormon Row over the period of its existence. At the time of this photograph, it was located in the Chambers home. *Jackson Hole Historical Society and Museum*

Fork-Spread Creek area. In the early years, the post office moved from ranch to ranch, with each change in postmasters causing confusion over its location. It first opened at the Pierce Cunningham ranch; Maggie Cunningham was the first postmaster. After Maggie Cunningham gave up the post office in 1899, the Wolffs took it over for 13 years. Ada Seaton was postmaster for less than a year, followed by Lizzie Allen. The post office was located at the Elk Ranch from 1913 to 1916. The postmasters shifted regularly over the next 16 years: Gertrude Steingraber, 1916–1918; Grace L. Brown, 1918–1922; Joe Chapline, 1922–1927; Charlton Chapline, 1927–1928; Juanita Hogan, 1928–1930 at the Hogan Fox Farm (the existing Buffalo Dorm); Viola Budge, 1928–1930; and Carrie Eldridge, 1930–1932. On October 5, 1932, Eva Topping took over the post office. For more than 30 years, the Elk Post Office was situated at the Moosehead Ranch, until it closed in 1968. Joe Chapline operated or leased the Elk Store, a small general store during the 1920s.[35]

Another early community was Grovont, which served homesteaders in the flats east of Blacktail Butte. Grovont, a corruption of the French word Gros Ventre, was misspelled deliberately because the Postal Service liked post office names to be one word and easy to spell. Thus, they spelled Grovont as it was pronounced in French. Pioneer James Budge opened the post office at his homestead in 1899. His neighbor and close friend, James I. May, became postmaster in 1901. For the next 40 years,

the Grovont Post Office shifted from settler to settler in the Mormon Row area, as it has been referred to since the 1920s. Mary A. Budge served the longest, from 1903–1908 and 1934–1941, when the post office closed. When the Mays managed the post office, they served meals and rented rooms to travelers. As more homesteaders, many of them Mormons, preempted land east of Blacktail Butte, the need arose for a church and school. In the summer of 1917, local residents constructed a frame Latter Day Saints meeting house on one acre of land sold by Thomas and Bertha Perry. School was held in the basement of the church that year. By 1922, a separate school had been built on acreage south of the Grovont Church. Both the school and the church were removed in the 1970s. The church was moved to the Teton Village road north of Wilson, where it houses a pizza parlor today.[36]

Teton was a small post office created in 1906 to serve settlers on the west side of the Snake River north of Wilson. It was situated first on the Kaufman homestead, then the Lower Bar BC, and finally the JY from 1914, until it closed in 1925. During the 1920s, local residents supported a local school.[37]

On the east side of the Snake River was the community of Zenith. Designated a post office in 1902 on the Harry Smith ranch, it served homesteaders north of the Gros Ventre River and east of the Snake River. Mail carriers made deliveries two to three times a week. In the Wyoming State Archives, there is a black-and-white photograph of a group of children and a young woman. The label identifies them as the class at "Zenith School, 1902." By 1900, Zenith was one of several school districts in the valley; in the 1920s, the school was located on the Waterman Ranch.

Other post offices existed, most of them forgotten today. Antler lasted less than one year from March to December 1899. Located either at the site of old Moran or Whiteman's Lakeview Ranch, Cora Heigho served as postmaster of this obscure post office. The Brooks Post Office, 1905–1912, provided mail service to ranchers far up the Gros Ventre. Slide, 1916–1920, was located at Lower Slide Lake. Later post offices were associated more with tourism than ranching. The Hoback Post Office, described as a "resort," received and sent out mail once a week. It opened in 1921 and provided service until 1943.[38] The Postal Service established the Moose Post Office in April 1923 at William Grant's store, situated in the Huckleberry Springs area along the Moose-Wilson Road. The post office was moved to the local school near Menor's Ferry in 1929. At that time, Menor's Ferry became known as Moose.[39] The Moose area served a few homesteaders, dude ranchers such as the Estes, and others who catered to tourists, such as Maud Noble and the Dornans. At the end of 1923, Al Young relocated a sawmill in a marshy area near Moose, known as Sawmill Ponds today, where he produced lumber for developments in the area. In 1925, Moose area residents held a meeting to establish a school. Buster Estes served as treasurer for a fundraising drive. They built a small log school in the sagebrush flats west of the ferry in 1925. In the same year, the Episcopal Church constructed the Chapel of the Transfiguration just west of the Menor cabin. Church dignitaries dedicated the chapel on July 26. After the Snake River Land Company bought Maud Noble's property, they leased the store for use as the post office and for commercial purposes.[40]

The Jenny Lake Post Office was established specifically to serve tourists. It opened in 1926 and operated during the summers only, when visitors were present and facilities open. Housed first in a building owned by Homer Richards, it was moved to the Jenny Lake Store on the J. D. Kimmel property.[41]

Economically, agriculture and tourism formed the economic pillars of Jackson Hole and shaped the character of its communities. The valley never experienced large-scale consumptive industries like logging and mining. Commercial timber cutting in Jackson Hole remained a small-time activity, dominated by local mill operators who produced lumber for local use. Successful mining would have created entirely different communities as well as severe impacts on the environment.

Prospectors and geologists have explored Jackson Hole for minerals since the DeLacy expedition of 1863, but always with marginal results at best. The mysterious Mining Ditch, dug in the 1870s, demonstrates serious efforts to extract gold from the Snake River.[42] Prospectors sought gold in the valley well into the 1920s, but found only enough color to cause frustration. A few ventured up the rugged canyons seeking gold or possible paying veins of silver and lead, again with no success. Gold brought Albert Nelson and Billy Bierer to Jackson Hole in 1895, but they soon turned to homesteading. In 1894, Denver's *Rocky Mountain News* reported that a group of miners from Cripple Creek, Colorado, ventured into Jackson Hole to prospect for gold. Their leader, W. T. Sawyer, planned to return with approximately 100 people the next year. Sawyer filed a location notice for placer claims about one-half mile west of the present outlet of Jackson Lake in 1896.[43]

A few settlers panned for gold in the Snake and its tributaries for a living. They included such characters as Uncle Jack Davis and Johnny Counts, along with obscure prospectors such as Munger and John Condit. None of them became rich; Johnny Counts would wash 100 wheelbarrows of dirt per day, gleaning about a penny's worth of gold per load. Friends of Uncle Jack Davis found a mere $12 and about an equal value of amalgam in his cabin after his death. Placer mining proved a hard way to earn a living. Samuel and Noble Gregory "rocked" enough flour gold to pay for winter supplies at their respective ranches, but did not try to make a living at it. Holiday Menor had prospected and worked the mines in Montana, but gave up the life in Jackson Hole.[44]

Nevertheless, the gold bug bit speculators periodically. The Teton County records indicate three distinct periods of activity, when both settlers and outsiders filed placer claims along the upper Snake River and its tributaries; 1895–1896, 1902–1905, and 1931–1934. Few secured their claims by proving them up in accordance with the law, and those who claimed to do so may have lied because no one had to verify their testimony. Finally, there is no evidence that any of the claims were profitable. A prospector named Red Soper, working Deadman's Bar in 1916, reported good fishing at his claim rather than profitable mining.[45]

Prospectors continued to scout the country. In the first issue of the *Courier*, the editor wrote "Jackson has great possibilities as a mineral producer" according to miners familiar with the area. Copper bearing ore of 25 percent purity had been found in the Buffalo Fork area, prompting a Chicago company to raise $10,000 to finance a mine. Available evidence indicates that no mine was ever developed. E. C. "Doc" Steele directed the development of numerous placer claims owned by the Jackson Hole Mining Company, a local corporation. Doc Steele gave up the mining operation by 1911. He opened Jackson's first drugstore, then operated a saloon at Moran around 1913. In the Tetons, "high grade galena" had been discovered in the Fox Creek area at the head of Death Canyon and gold and silver ore had been found in the "western" hills. The ruins of a prospector's cabin exist on the Death Canyon Shelf and prospect pits and caves are extant in both Death and Avalanche Canyons. Along the Snake River in the southern end of the valley, the Hoffer brothers placer mined gold in paying quantities.[46]

Because of the lack of promising mineral strikes, corporate investments in mining were non-existent, with the possible exception of the Whetstone Mining Company. Captain Harris attempted to establish a large placer mine and mill on Whetstone Creek, a tributary of Pacific Creek. He built a giant sluice box consisting of four-inch planks bored full of pockets by a two-inch auger. As riverine soils washed down the boxes, the heavier gold should have filled the pockets but failed as pebbles, rather than gold, filled the holes. Harris filled his own pockets with stockholders' money and disappeared. Other companies purchased placer claims such as the Tertillata Gold Mining Company and Golden Bar Steam Dredging Company in 1895, but never developed their claims.

As late as 1932, a Chicago company set up a gold camp two miles south of the Elk Post Office during the speculation of the 1930s.[47] Like many other western regions, Jackson Hole has its own lost mine. In 1924, the *Courier* published a report about a prospector named John Hayball, who located a lode mine that produced high-grade gold ore. He interested two Idaho Falls men in the project, but died before revealing the site of the mine.[48]

In the north end of Jackson Hole, John Graul took up a claim in Webb Canyon in 1914. He painstakingly cut a tunnel into a basalt formation, but what he sought remains a mystery today. W. C. Lawrence, who had an asbestos claim in Berry Canyon, believed Graul sought platinum. Graul built a cabin, a tool shed, and cut a tunnel 193 feet in length. He returned to work the mine each season after the snow melted, until he was killed in a mining accident in Colorado in 1927.[49]

Coal became the only commercially viable resource mined in Jackson Hole. In the highlands east of the valley, an exposed coal field exists in the northern and eastern areas. Approximately 60 miles long, and by 9 to 18 miles wide, the field comprises more than 600 square miles of coal-bearing rocks. Because the coal is exposed in many areas, pioneers knew of its existence and attempted to establish mines. In September 1891, a group of settlers gathered to form the Inta Coal and Mining Company to raise capital and develop coal mines in the Gros Ventre valley. Aside from changing the name of the company to the Jackson Hole Coal Mining Company, there is no evidence that the locally inspired firm succeeded. The Reclamation Service developed the first mines in 1914 to provide a fuel source for the Jackson Lake Dam. The mines were located on Lava Creek, a tributary of the Buffalo Fork, and on Pilgrim Creek. In 1917, the service opened the Lava Creek mine to the public.

In 1920, developers reopened the Jake Jackson Coal Mine on Cache Creek. Located closer to Jackson, this coal sold for $12 per ton, less than half the cost of coal from the Lava Creek mine. As local demand for coal for heating and cooking increased during the 1920s and 1930s, other mines were developed. Dick Turpin had dug a tunnel in the Gros Ventre deposit in 1892, but no coal was mined and shipped out until a better road was built in 1924. Entrepreneurs such as John Nocker, Jess Luton, and Claude Shearer developed mines elsewhere such as Granite Creek and Slate Creek in the Hoback drainage, Ditch Creek, and Coal Mine Draw near Spread Creek. Because the cost of exporting coal was prohibitive, the Jackson Hole coal mines served a local market and, as a result, remained small operations. Nocker mined coal into the 1940s. All of the mines are abandoned today.[50]

Oil exploration came to the valley in the 1920s. On April 11, 1929, the *Courier* reported that two companies, Utah Oil and Midwest Oil, intended to drill two wells in the area during the summer. No subsequent reports indicate that the wells were sunk. Companies have drilled exploratory wells in the area since that time and, stimulated by the energy crisis of the late 1970s, oil exploration has been a significant and sometimes controversial activity in the region.[51]

Overall, the communities in Jackson Hole evolved over time. With the possible exception of Moran, there were no boomtowns similar to those that characterized the miners' frontier. Agriculture, particularly cattle ranching, formed the economic base. Most of the communities consisted of a post office, supplemented perhaps by a school and, less often, a church and store. Nevertheless, residents developed a surprising loyalty to their locality. The country school not only educated the children, but served as a social center for meetings, dances, and important life events such as weddings and funerals.

Of all the communities in Jackson Hole, Jackson emerged as the dominant town. Its location in the southern part of Jackson Hole amidst concentrations of settlers gave the village a significant advantage over other towns. The first post office, the first general store, and the first community building also gave Jackson a significant head start. Later entrepreneurs located the first newspaper and bank in Jackson. Politically, the town moved ahead of its rivals, incorporating in 1914 and becoming the seat of Teton County in 1921. Wilson never competed seriously with Jackson as a commercial center. Kelly developed in conjunction with the homestead boom north of the Gros Ventre River after 1913, but was wiped out

in the flood of 1927. Today, Kelly is a residential community of year-round and seasonal homes. Moran was the first community to rely primarily on tourism, especially hunters and fishermen, rather than agriculture. Although Ben Sheffield's Moran no longer exists, it set an early course for the valley as tourism surpassed ranching as the primary economic activity.

Notes

1. Robert V. Hine, *The American West; an Interpretive History*, (Boston: Little, Brown, 1973), pp. 252–267; and Billington, *Westward Expansion*, pp. 534–535 and 619–629.

2. Hine, *American West*, pp. 252–253; and Marcus Whiffen, *American Architecture Since 1780: A Guide to Styles* (Cambridge, MA: The M.I.T. Press, 1969), p. 87.

3. Hine, *American West*, p. 239.

4. Allen, *Early Jackson Hole*, p. 1.

5. K.C. Allan Collection, 7636, "Post Offices of Jackson Hole," University of Wyoming Archives, American Heritage Center; Mae Tuttle to Cora Barber, September 5, 1951, Jackson Hole Historical Society and Museum; reprinted in *Jackson Hole Guide*, December 5, 1974; and *Wyoming Tribune*, February 8, 1896 in Elizabeth Wied Hayden Collection, Subject File #5, Jackson Hole Historical Society and Museum.

6. Allan Collection, "Post Office, University of Wyoming Archives;" *Jackson Hole Guide*, December 2, 1965; Brown, *Souvenir History;* Hayden Collection, Subject File 5, Jackson Hole Historical Society and Museum; Hayden, *From Trapper to Tourist*, p. 50; and *Jackson Hole Guide*, December 14, 1972.

7. Brown, *Souvenir History*, p. 36; *Jackson Hole Guide*, October 14, 1965, and April 7, 1960; and Hayden Collection, Subject File 5, Jackson Hole Historical Society and Museum.

8. William Trester, "The Town of Jackson, June 1, 1907," photograph, Jackson Hole Historical Society and Museum. This is the earliest known photograph of the village of Jackson.

9. Hayden, *Trapper to Tourist*, p. 51; *Jackson's Hole Courier*, November 12, 1938; *Jackson Hole News*, November 1, 1978; and *Jackson Hole Guide*, October 9, 1952. Doctor Palmer's facility is sometimes referred to as an "insanitorium," although I could find no such word in dictionaries.

10. *Jackson's Hole Courier*, January 28, 1909, reprinted in *Jackson's Hole Courier*, January 29, 1948.

11. Ibid.; and *Jackson's Hole Courier,* April 30, 1914.

12. Brown, *Souvenir History,* pp. 11 and 36–37; and *Jackson's Hole Courier,* August 20, 1914.

13. Mumey, *Teton Mountains,* p. 307; and *Jackson's Hole Courier,* May 7, 1914.

14. Struthers Burt, *Diary,* p. 107.

15. Kemmerer *Camera,* April 18, 1918.

16. *Jackson's Hole Courier,* January 20, 1921, February 3, 1921, September 4, 1916 and March 23, 1944; and Brown, *Souvenir History,* p. 11.

17. *Jackson's Hole Courier,* January 6, 1921, June 16, 1921, April 11, 1918, May 2, 1918, June 6, 1918, and June 13, 1918.

18. Hayden Collection, Subject File 5, Jackson Hole Historical Society and Museum; *Jackson's Hole Courier,* August 18, 1948; interview with Martha Davis Riniker, transcript, File R, Jackson Hole Historical Society and Museum; and *Jackson Hole Guide,* September 23, 1965, reprint of Alice Winegar Diary.

19. Interview with Gretchen Huff Francis by Jo Ann Byrd, #16, "Last of Old West Series."

20. *Jackson's Hole Courier,* October 14, 1915, June 1, 1916, and May 16, 1915.

21. Saylor, *Jackson Hole,* pp. 143–146; and *Jackson's Hole Courier,* April 29, 1920, May 12, 1920, May 12, 1921, and May 26, 1921.

22. *Jackson's Hole Courier,* October 14, 1920, April 17, 1924, May 21, 1931, September 28, 1933, and July 17, 1941; and *Jackson Hole Guide,* January 25, 1973.

23. *Jackson's Hole Courier,* May 7, 1931, and April 28, 1932; and *Jackson Hole Guide,* December 29, 1966.

24. *Jackson's Hole Courier,* February 24, 1921.

25. Hayden, *Trapper to Tourist,* pp. 38–39; Brown, *Souvenir History,* pp. 33 and 35; *Jackson Hole News,* June 9, 1976; Allan Collection, "Post Offices," University of Wyoming; *Jackson's Hole Courier,* January 28, 1909; and interview with Walt Callahan by Jo Ann Byrd, #6, "Last of Old West Series." In 1976, the owners of the Wilson Hotel burned the building, citing prohibitive costs to restore the structure.

26. Office of Teton County Clerk and Recorder, Deed Record Book 1, p. 179; Deed Record Book 3, p. 95, A.R. and Nellie M. Kimball to Margaret Sheffield, Warranty Deed, April 12, 1915; Deed Record Book 3, p. 96, A. R. Kimball to B. D. Sheffield, Warranty Deed, April 12, 1915; Mixed Records Book 3, p. 337, Ed J. Smith to Charles P. Bartlett, Lease, November 16, 1900; Frank and Jennie Lovell to B. D. Sheffield, Warranty Deed, November 12, 1903; Lenore Diem, "The Research Station's Place

in History," University of Wyoming-NPS Research Center, Moran, WY, 1978, p. 5; Allen, *Early Jackson Hole,* p. 304; *Jackson Hole Guide,* March 2, 1972; and John Markham, "The Temporary Jackson Lake Dam."

27. "Dude Ranches Out West," [ca. 1927], Union Pacific Railroad, S.N. Leek Collection, 3138, University of Wyoming Archives, American Heritage Center; *Jackson Hole Guide,* March 2, 1972; and Teton County Records, Deed Record Book 4, 62, B. D. and Margaret Sheffield to the Snake River Land Company, Warranty Deed, July 9, 1929.

28. Rockefeller Archive Center, Harold P. Fabian Collection, IV3A7, Photograph, Collection Number 1047; Homestead Patent 708783, Norman Smith, 1918, and *Jackson's Hole Courier,* April 23, 1914, and September 3, 1914.

29. *Jackson's Hole Courier,* May 21, 1914, September 3, 1914, January 7, 1915 and January 6, 1921; Allen Collection "Post Offices;" and interview with Pearl McClary by Jo Anne Byrd, #25, "Last of Old West Series."

30. *Jackson's Hole Courier,* March 22, 1917, November 18, 1917, July 10, 1919, and October 20, 1921.

31. E. N. Moody, "Some Recollections of the Formation and Early History of Teton County," transcript, November 9, 1968, File H, acc. #305, Jackson Hole Historical Society and Museum; and *Jackson's Hole Courier,* May 12, 1921, February 3, 1921, April 28, 1921, June 16, 1921, June 30, 1921, July 14, 1921, February 1, 1923, and November 15, 1923.

32. *Jackson's Hole Courier,* May 20, 1926; interview with Jim Budge by Jo Anne Byrd, #5, "Last of Old West Series;" and *Jackson Hole Guide,* December 9, 1976.

33. Hayden, *Trapper to Tourist,* pp. 57–58; "Gros Ventre Slide Geological Area," pamphlet, U.S. Forest Service, U.S. Dept. of Agriculture, 1969; *Jackson's Hole Courier,* June 23, 1925, May 19, 1927, and May 26, 1927; *Jackson Hole Guide,* July 14, 1955, July 21, 1955, July 28, 1955, and August 11, 1955; *Jackson Hole News,* August 7, 1975; and *Jackson Hole Guide,* December 9, 1976, and August 12, 1971.

34. Brown, *Souvenir History,* p. 33; and Allen Collection, "Post Offices."

35. Brown, *Souvenir History,* 39; Allen Collection, "Post Offices;" and Teton County Records, Misc. Records Book 1, p. 481, Joseph Chapline to D. D. Eldridge, lease, September 17, 1927.

36. Allen Collection, "Post Offices;" Huidekoper, *Early Days,* p. 53; *Jackson's Hole Courier,* August 9, 1917, November 18, 1917, October 12, 1922, and June 11, 1925; and Teton County Records, Deed Record Book 2, p. 28,

Thomas W. and Bertha Perry to J. Wallace Moulton, Warranty Deed, December 12, 1919.

37. Allen Collection, "Post Offices;" Brown, *Souvenir History*, p. 39; *Jackson's Hole Courier*, June 11, 1925; and Huidekoper, *Early Days*, 82.

38. Allen Collection, "Post Offices;" and Brown, *Souvenir History*, p. 35.

39. Allen Collection, "Post Offices;" *Jackson's Hole Courier*, June 11, 1925, and December 26, 1922; and *Jackson Hole Guide*, June 2, 1973.

40. *Jackson's Hole Courier*, December 20, 1922, February 22, 1923, November 20, 1923, June 19, 1924, June 11, 1925, July 30, 1925, and August 25, 1932.

41. Allen Collection, "Post Offices."

42. Fritiof Fryxell, "The Story of Deadman's Bar," *Campfire Tales of Jackson Hole*, pp. 38–42.

43. *Jackson Hole Guide*, March 21, 1957; *Rocky Mountain News*, December 6, 1894; and Teton County Records, Mixed Records Book 1, p. 288, W. T. Sawyer, Location Notice, 3356, November 30, 1896.

44. Fritiof Fryxell, "Prospector of Jackson Hole," *Campfire Talks*, 47–51; *Jackson Hole Guide*, December 14, 1972; interview with Nobel Gregory, Jr. by Jo Ann Byrd, #13, "Last of Old West Series;" and Wyoming State Archives, Museums and Historical Department, Census of the United States, 1900, Jackson Precinct.

45. Teton County Records, Mixed Records; and *Jackson's Hole Courier*, February 10, 1916.

46. *Jackson's Hole Courier*, January 28, 1909.

47. Hayden, *Trapper to Tourist*, p. 30; and *Jackson's Hole Courier*, May 1, 1919 and September 29, 1932.

48. *Jackson's Hole Courier*, September 26, 1924.

49. Margaret Kelsey, "John Graul's Mystery Mine," pamphlet file, Grand Teton National Park, *Teton Magazine;* and interview with W. C. "Slim" Lawrence by John Daugherty, July 3, 1980.

50. R. W. "Jackson Hole Coal Field," *Geological Survey*, University of Wyoming; *Jackson's Hole Courier*, November 26, 1914, November 8, 1917, January 8, 1920, December 4, 1924, August 13, 1931, and May 26, 1932; Brown, *Souvenir History*, p. 25; and letter from Virginia Huidekoper, April 10, 1994.

51. *Jackson's Hole Courier*, April 11, 1929, and December 21, 1929.

CHAPTER 14

The Dude Wranglers

If you wish to sum up the dude business in a sentence, it consists in giving people homemade bedsteads but forty pound mattresses.

—Struthers Burt, *The Diary of a Dude Wrangler*

The Bar BC became one of the most famous dude ranches in the Rocky Mountain West. During the Bar BC's heyday in the 1920s, famous writers, artists, and Hollywood filmmakers got "westernized" at the ranch. *Jackson Hole Historical Society and Museum*

By the time Struthers Burt's autobiographical *The Diary of a Dude Wrangler* appeared in the *Saturday Evening Post* in 1924, dude ranching had "grown like a mushroom in wet weather."[1] As much as any other business, dude wrangling pioneered the modern tourist industry in the American West, particularly in the Rocky Mountain states of Montana and Wyoming. One historian rated the dude ranch "as the single most unique contribution of the Rocky Mountain West to the every-growing national vacation industry." In turn, the antecedents of dude ranching can be traced to other enterprises—first, and most important, cattle ranching, and second, guiding and outfitting sport hunters.[2]

Travelers first toured the American West in the era of the fur trapper to hunt and take in the scenery. Historian Francis Parkman wrote one of the first travel accounts, *The Oregon Trail*, published in 1849. After the Civil War, travel in the American West increased as itinerant trappers and settlers guided well-heeled tourists. In Jackson Hole, trappers and hunters like Beaver Dick Leigh often guided dudes, because they were familiar with the Teton country from their trapping and hunting forays. Western landscapes provided ideal settings for dude ranches. Indeed, Struthers Burt believed an attractive setting a prime requisite in choosing a dude ranch site.[3]

No place could top Jackson Hole for scenery. William Baillie-Grohman wrote the earliest known travel narrative of two trips into Jackson Hole, one made in the 1870s and one in 1880. He recorded this scene from a knoll near the Gros Ventre River:

At our feet lay the perfectly level expanse, about eight or ten miles broad and five-and-twenty in length. Traversing the basin lengthwise, we saw the curves of the Snake River—its waters of a beautiful beryl green, and . . . from a distance of five or six miles, of glassy smoothness—winding its way through groves of stately old cottonwood-trees. A month or two before, the Snake had inundated the whole Basin, and the grass that had sprung up retained its bright green tint, giving the whole picture the air of a splendid trimly-kept old park. Beyond the river the eye espied several little lakes, nestling in forest-girt seclusion under the beckling cliffs of the boldest-shaped mountain I am acquainted with, i.e. the Grand Teton Peak, rising in one great sweep. . . . It was the most sublime scenery I have ever seen.[4]

Abundant and diverse fauna and a cast of romantic figures such as Indians, trappers, and soldiers added another dimension to the appeal of the American West. The emergence of dude ranches coincided with America's elevation of the cowboy, arguably America's most eminent folk hero. Dude ranches evolved directly from working cattle ranches; their structures and physical layout were patterned after cattle ranches. Western dress mimicked cowboy garb.[5]

While the origins of dude ranching can be traced without difficulty, determining what constituted a dude ranch remains problematic. This has led to debate regarding the first dude ranches in Jackson Hole.[6] Even dude ranchers expressed uncertainty and failed to agree on a common definition. Their testimony in final proof papers demonstrates this uncertainty. One question on the Testimony of Claimant form asked, "is your present claim within the limits of an incorporated town or selected site of a city or town, or used in any way for a trade or business?" Struthers Burt on the Bar BC answered, "Yes, I am engaged in the summer tourist business." Buster Estes, the founder of the STS, responded "no," despite operating a dude ranch at the site. Tony Grace of the Danny Ranch testified in 1927, "have two cabins which I rent in summer." Harold Hammond, co-founder of the White Grass, answered in 1920 that "the claim is used some for summer tourists," while Peter Karppi of the Half Moon

Struthers Burt

Princeton-educated Struthers Burt was a popular writer whose book, *The Diary of a Dude Wrangler*, inspired a whole new generation of dude ranchers. Burt was originally opposed to the creation of a national park in Jackson Hole. However, by the 1920s, Burt used his power of the pen in national publications to lobby for the protection of the scenic qualities of Jackson Hole. *Jackson Hole Historical Society and Museum*

responded that "we handle summer boarders." Either they failed to recognize that dude ranching had become a distinct industry or gave obtuse responses in the belief that people, particularly General Land Office officials, were unfamiliar with dude ranches.[7]

By the early 1920s, however, dude ranchers were beginning to perceive their business as not only a distinct but unique institution. In *The Diary of a Dude Wrangler*, Struthers Burt reflected that "you come to the dude business slowly in actual life and you come to it usually by chance, just as I did." Burt, by this time dude ranching's most articulate spokesperson, described a dude ranch as simply an ordinary cattle ranch modified somewhat to care for dudes, but not a boarding house or hotel "much as it must seem like one or the other to the ignorant."[8]

The creation of the Dude Ranchers' Association in 1926 reflected the emergence of dude ranches as an institution and their tremendous growth during the 1920s. Association members grappled over the definition of a dude ranch. One goal of the first meeting was to "standardize practices," a reference to activities associated with dude ranching. Some suggested dropping the term "dude," believing it derogatory and undignified. The opinions of pioneer dude ranchers Dick Randall and the Eaton brothers prevailed, however, and the term dude was retained. In the northern Rockies, dude referred to "an outsider who paid for lodging, riding, hunting, or other services," and had no negative association with terms such as greenhorns or tenderfeet. The members voted unanimously to name their organization the Dude Ranchers' Association.[9]

The early membership represented three types of dude ranches. The first were working stock ranches situated in the high plains or foothills of the Rockies. Ranches set in the mountains formed the second group; often, these started as dude ranches rather than stock ranches. The final group consisted of hot springs resorts or spas, where swimming or bathing in waters known for their healing powers was the primary activity. This group later disappeared from the membership rolls.[10]

In 1933, an article appeared in *Dude Rancher Magazine* which defined a dude ranch as the following: They take paying guests; they evolved from old cattle ranches and many operate as both; they are "composed of little groups of cabins, corrals, and bunkhouses, all of which are familiar to the native westerner of the cattle country, they are rustic and unique;" and they present a way to "enjoy the outdoors under conditions of freedom and naturalness."[11]

In *Dude Ranching: A Complete History*, Lawrence Borne summarized the most important elements that have characterized dude ranches over the years. They were often the year-round home of the owner or owners. Setting was critical as virtually all were located in the western United States. They provided food, lodging, and horseback riding at one price, called the American plan. The ranch site and activities were situated in remote picturesque areas. Horseback riding constituted the most important recreational activity. Other pursuits included fishing, hiking, hunting, sightseeing and, on occasion, ranchwork. Dude ranchers accepted reservations only, and sometimes even required references from prospective guests. They refused walk-in traffic, an important distinction in determining genuine dude ranches in Jackson Hole. Finally, the atmosphere was a "key in-

gredient," though not readily apparent to observers and often intangible. Borne described a proper dude ranch atmosphere as "informal in manners and dress, people were on a first-name basis, hospitality was genuine, and guests did things together as part of a ranch family."[12]

Borne demonstrated that dude ranching "developed slowly from several divergent sources in different locales and varying circumstances."[13] However, the Eaton brothers—Howard, Willis, and Alden—generally receive credit for establishing the first dude ranch. In 1882, Howard Eaton homesteaded a parcel of land in the North Dakota badlands near the town of Medora. Joined by his brothers and financed by A. C. Huidekoper, Eaton formed the Custer Trail Ranch, a cattle outfit. Guests soon visited the ranch to hunt or experience western life. Bert Rumsey of New York was the first to pay room and board in 1882, though this violated traditional western hospitality. However, the boom-and-bust cycle of cattle ranching became apparent as the drought of 1886, followed by the killing winter of 1886–1887, hit the Eatons hard. Unlike many ranches, the Custer Trail Ranch survived the disaster of 1887, despite severe cattle losses. Meanwhile, the Eatons became aware of another economic drain, the high cost of boarding numerous guests each year. Economic reality drove the Eatons to charge guests $10 per week for room and board in 1891. In 1902, the Eatons sold the Custer Trail Ranch and relocated their dude ranch in the Bighorn Mountains of Wyoming. By this time wrangling dudes provided a solid income. Howard Eaton continued pack trips into Yellowstone National Park, pioneering a significant activity associated with dude ranching. The ranch continues to operate today.[14]

Although not as critical as cattle ranching, guiding hunters contributed to the evolution of dude ranching. Dick Randall, a pioneer dude wrangler, built the foundation of his well-known OTO Dude Ranch on outfitting and guiding hunters. He established a permanent hunting camp in 1888 and converted it to a dude ranch in 1898. Like the Eatons, Randall located his ranch in the Rockies, choosing a site in Montana near the north entrance to Yellowstone.[15]

Between 1900 and 1920, dude wranglers established ranches throughout the northern Rockies fol-

White Grass Dude Ranch interior. *Jackson Hole Historical Society and Museum*

lowing the example of the Eatons and Randall. An Englishman started the IXL Dude Ranch near the Eatons. After 1900, the Cody, Wyoming, area developed into a center for tourism and dude ranching. Billy Howell started the Holm Lodge, originally a stage stop between Cody and Yellowstone National Park. After visiting a homestead near Cody, Irving H. "Larry" Larom returned to purchase it in 1915, and with a partner named Winthrop Brooks, established the famous Valley Ranch. Dude rancher Charles M. Moore gradually found himself wrangling dudes, similar to Struthers Burt 's experience. At first, Moore established a boys' camp at his ranch near Dubois, Wyoming, where he conducted pack trips, taught outdoor skills, and a smattering of natural sciences. After World War I, he converted his camp to a full-fledged dude ranch. Both Larom and Moore became prominent dude ranchers, organizers and advocates of the business, and conservationists. Dude ranching came to Jackson Hole in the same period.[16]

People have disagreed over the first dude ranch in Jackson Hole. Questions over definition are the main cause of the dispute. It is generally accepted that Struthers Burt and Louis Joy became the first dude wranglers, when they built the JY in 1908. In 1932, the *Jackson's Hole Courier* "differed with

Mr. Burt" regarding his claim to being the valley's first dude-rancher. The article's author pointed out that Stephen Leek had guided dudes prior to 1900 and that Ben Sheffield had built the Teton Lodge at Moran in 1903. However, neither fit the characteristics of a dude ranch as defined by the Dude Ranchers' Association.[17]

Stephen Leek arrived in Jackson Hole in 1888, accompanied by his partner, an obscure man named Nick Gass. While camped on the west bank of the Snake River at its inlet to Jackson Lake, Leek met Elwood Hoffer, a hunting guide from Livingston, Montana, who was guiding a client. Hoffer may have inspired Leek to try his hand at outfitting. In 1889, Leek began serving as a hunting guide, as did pioneer Emile Wolff. In 1903, Ben Sheffield, also from Livingston, bought the Frank Lovell homestead at the outlet of Jackson Lake to serve as a headquarters for his outfitting business.

According to local tradition, John Carnes referred to his homestead on Flat Creek as his "dude ranch," although no evidence exists to indicate Carnes operated it as such. At an unknown date, homesteader Harvey Glidden tried to convert his Elka Ranch (also shown as Elko Ranch) to a dude outfit. Again, no evidence shows that Glidden succeeded. Some sources have described John Sargent's

Merymere and the nearby Lakeview Ranch, owned by Herb Whiteman and the Heighos, as dude ranches but this appears to be careless use of the term. Good evidence demonstrates that neither were dude ranches.

Using Borne's criteria, none of the previous examples qualify as dude ranches. Leek conducted his outfitting business from his South Park ranch and built a lodge at the north shore of Leigh Lake. He guided hunters, but never provided long-term room and board or horseback riding as a recreational activity. Sheffield's Teton Lodge manifested elements of a dude ranch, but accepted overnight or transient traffic, an unacceptable practice at an authentic dude ranch.[18]

The first bonafide dude ranches in Jackson Hole were the JY, the Bar BC, and the White Grass. Burt and Louis Joy began boarding dudes at the JY in 1908. Because of a poor relationship with Joy, Burt broke off the partnership and formed the Bar BC with Horace Carncross in 1912. A year later, wrangler Harold Hammond and one of the first Bar BC dudes, George Tucker Bispham, homesteaded adjacent 160-acre parcels and formed the White Grass Ranch. Planning to start a cattle ranch, they chose to wrangle dudes instead of cattle in 1919.

In 1914, war broke out in Europe, eventually engulfing many of the world's countries. Because the First World War cut off safe travel across the Atlantic and in Europe, Americans looked to their own country for vacations. Starved for holiday destinations, easterners discovered the West. The Bar BC expanded in these years. In 1912, Burt and Carncross scrambled in May and June to complete the construction of cabins and a main house for their first dudes. Six dudes spent the summer, but it was enough to encourage expansion of the ranch. In 1917, both partners borrowed $9,200 from the Philadelphia Trust Company, putting up the Bar BC as collateral security. A large amount of money for the time, it was used to expand the ranch. In July, Charles Fox, a local contractor, and a crew arrived at the Bar BC to "do some building." The war years launched the "golden age" of dude ranching, a period lasting from 1919 to 1929.[19]

Accordingly, dude ranches flourished in Jackson Hole in the 1920s. In addition to the growth in west-

Dude Ranches in Jackson's Hole

White Grass Ranch for Boys

The V. V. Ranch at head of Hoback Canyon

The Crescent Lazy H in Teton County

The Circle H Ranch

Dude ranch advertisement. *Jackson Hole Historical Society and Museum*

ern tourism, which generated demand for facilities, the dramatic slump in cattle prices led some ranchers to start taking in dudes. The Van Cleve family's Lazy K Bar in Montana was an example of this sort of development. By the mid-1920s, more than 60 dude ranches existed in the core states of Wyoming and Montana and were spreading to other states such as Colorado.[20]

Following the lead of the JY, Bar BC, and White Grass, aspiring dude wranglers started ranches in Jackson Hole. The Danny Ranch, the STS, the Half Moon, the Trail Ranch, the Double Diamond, the Castle Rock, the Circle H, the Flying V, the Red Rock, the Vi Bar Vi, the Triangle X, the Gros Ventre, and the Warbonnet were established. In addition, the Elbo, Flagg Ranch, the Cross and Crescent, the Flying Diamond, the Teton

Lodge, and the Jackson Lake Lodge were listed in a Union Pacific guide to dude ranches, though whether any of them qualified as dude ranches is doubtful.[21]

During this period, dude ranches in Jackson Hole established their character and influenced tourism in a significant way. More dude ranches than hotels existed in the valley, and facilities that could not be considered dude ranches were listed as such in brochures. Jackson Hole dude ranches were mountain ranches situated in the midst of spectacular mountain scenery. Few were working cattle ranches. Jack Woodman described his Flying V as a "producing horse and cattle ranch." Burt and Carncross intended to expand to cattle ranching, relegating the dude business to a secondary activity, but never achieved this aim. They bought the Anderson place on the Gros Ventre in 1916 intending to raise hay for nearly 100 head of saddle horses. Calling it the Lower Bar BC, they began raising cattle. Hammond and Bispham intended the White Grass to be a cattle ranch, but started taking in dudes in 1919. These were the exceptions, rather than the norm.[22]

The Union Pacific promoted the dude ranches in Jackson Hole. "Once reported to be the secluded refuge of outlaws and cattle rustlers," a Union Pacific brochure portrayed the valley as a fine hunting and fishing region and "one of the most beautiful scenically, in the country." The town of Jackson retained "much of its frontier atmosphere," yet was "equipped with all the essential conveniences of civilization." The "Old West" atmosphere, mountain scenery, and abundant fish and wildlife characterized the ambiance of dude ranches in Jackson Hole.[23]

Specific information about dudes is difficult to locate, but available sources indicate they were Easterners or from heavily populated centers in the Midwest. Owen Wister, Burt, and Carncross drew their clientele from Philadelphia and its surrounding environs, starting the so-called "Philadelphia connection" with Jackson Hole. Some early dudes at the Bar BC were former associates of Burt at Princeton University. The Double Diamond Boys' Ranch recruited its clients from the Philadelphia area. Guests had to be financially well-off to afford a holiday at dude ranches. Dudes tended to be more educated than

average Americans. The Bar BC attracted writers, possibly because both Struthers and Katharine Burt were established authors. When journalist Harry W. Frantz's typewriter was unloaded at the Bar BC, a cowboy laughed and remarked "that's the eighth typewriter on the ranch."[24] Burt found Bar BC guests to be a diverse group:

> We have entertained millionaires and poets and artists, business men of every description, spoiled little bobbed-hair flappers and large selfish women who have allowed their minds and bodies to grow fat; angels and those who weren't; people whose homes were in every part of the country from New York to San Francisco; Prohibitionists and Anti-Prohibitionists, Fundamentalists and Modernists, Reactionaries and Radicals, Futurists and Classicist, those who enjoy Ethel Dell and Frank Crane and those who read nothing but D. H. Lawrence and The Dial; the bow-legged and knock-kneed; the fortunate creatures with legs resembling Venus and Apollo—for, like the streetcar conductor, there is one thing at least every dude-wrangler knows, and that is the shape of the lower limbs of the men, women, and children on his place; Englishmen and Frenchmen and Canadians; and with a few exceptions this rule has held good.[25]

What drew affluent people to dude ranches? The cultural and natural setting has been alluded to already, but informality in dress and manners was another lure. The emergence of dude ranches coincided with a rebellion against convention. A growing middle class questioned and rejected dress codes enforced by most hotels, particularly in dining rooms. A Bar BC brochure suggested that men wear "ordinary clothes" for railway travel, but for the dude ranch listed the following items:

> felt hat, 2 neck handkerchiefs (silk or bandanna); 2 flannel shirts, 2 pair trousers (khaki and wool, long or short as preferred); ½ doz. heavy wool socks, ½ doz. suits woolen underwear; waist overalls, light mackinaw, waistcoat, with large pockets; coat or heavy sweater; 1 pair heavy boots, pair riding boots; 1 pair camp shoes, moccasins or rubber soled; heavy gloves or gauntlets.

Women received a similar list:

> Felt hat; neck handkerchief; riding suits (breeches, or divided skirts); raincoat for riding; heavy boots; field boots or riding boots; heavy sweater; heavy (wool-lined) coat; heavy wool stockings, etc.

In addition, lightweight clothing was suggested for warmer days. "In most cases any clothes will do, provided they are sufficiently old, and comfortable." The JY claimed proudly that it did not conform to "summer hotel conventionalities, ranch clothes being worn almost entirely." Dude wranglers, according to Burt, encouraged "Eastern damsels" to don western dress not to look like cowgirls, rather "because it is good for the souls and adds color" to the dude business. Some went to extremes, donning gaudy outfits they perceived to be cowboy dress, but appeared outlandish to experienced dudes and Westerners. One account described the spectacle of a dude dressed in lavender chaps, another in bright orange chaps. Even wranglers adopted more colorful apparel as western dress became more ornamental. Local residents coined a derogatory term for such dress—diamond-pointed. In the town of Jackson, stores carried western clothing such as cowboy hats, boots, belts, and denim jeans, then called waist overalls. Western dress became the preferred apparel of many dudes.[26]

Regarding living arrangements, dudes lived among the owners and wranglers. The Castle Rock Ranch proclaimed itself a "Home Away From Home." Indeed, dude ranches were very individualistic in that they manifested the personality of their owners or managers and attracted dudes of similar character, who regarded the ranch as a second home. It was impossible to assemble universally compatible dudes at larger dude ranches. Burt conceded that they need not "adore" each other, but learn to tolerate and be polite to each other. One writer recalled dining at a dude ranch in the valley, where the hostess sat at the head of the table and rang a cowbell for service. While the waitress served food, the hostess dished food to her plate before passing it on to the guests. The author speculated that this may have been a usual custom at dude ranches, "but appears so woefully unfitting with dude ranch technique." The custom was likely peculiar to this hostess.[27]

Dude ranches in the 1920s provided a western outdoor experience with few discomforts experienced by real cowpunchers. The trick was to balance simplicity with comfort or, as Struthers Burt portrayed the dude business, "giving people homemade bedsteads but forty pound mattresses." Food at dude ranches needed to be simple, yet wholesome and tasty. In the early years at the Bar BC, Nathaniel Burt recalled that canned food provided much of the fare, supplemented for a very short time by fresh produce from the vegetable garden. The first dude at the Bar BC in 1912 dined on canned fruits, coffee, beans, and carrots, while cabins were being completed. He did not complain, "but ate his bad food contentedly and slept on the ground, and made friends immediately." In 1911, Owen Wister brought his family to the JY at the foot of Phelps Lake. His daughter, Fanny Kemble Wister, recalled less than appetizing cuisine. "Food at the ranch was often scanty, being driven 104 miles by team over the mountains from St. Anthony, Idaho." Canned tomatoes were common, supplemented on occasion by fresh peas from Bill Menor, who Wister's daughter mistakenly believed raised the only vegetables in Jackson Hole. Meat consisted of elk and "Dried, smoked, salted bear meat (like dark brown leather)." At breakfast, she often found dead flies plastered between the flapjacks, like so many winged raisins.[28]

By the 1920s, the food had improved significantly, transportation had become more reliable, and many dude ranches in Jackson Hole prided themselves on their self-sufficiency. The Bar BC advertised its meals as tempting, supplemented by an "excellent garden" and dairy. Icehouses prevented food spoilage. H. H. Harrison's Circle H was a producing hay ranch, which also had a garden and dairy cows. Woodman's Flying V advertised daily supplies of milk, cream, eggs, and vegetables produced at the ranch. At the JY, the management produced fresh eggs, vegetables, milk, and meats. The Double Diamond and STS provided fresh vegetables and dairy products. Others bought these supplies. Wholesome food and outdoor life proved a great draw for dude ranches.[29]

Although a key attraction of a dude ranch experience was the opportunity to "rough it," ranchers made concessions to modern conveniences. Dudes lived most often in small single and double cabins set around a main house. The main house could include a dining room, kitchen, and sitting room, or it could anchor a complex of smaller buildings used for these functions. The JY had separate cabins for the living room and dining room. Dudes were seldom lodged in the main house. The Flying V was one exception, as the main lodge contained a few guest rooms. In Jackson Hole, dude ranch buildings were overwhelmingly rustic log structures. Roofs were dirt and pole in the early years, but board-covered, with rolled asphalt roofing became most common; later, wood shingle roofs the more common. Fireplaces were usually built of native quartzite cobble. As was the case at the Bar BC, dude ranchers obtained standard window and door frames ordered through catalogues or from sources in Idaho.

The dude ranch experience represented a compromise between western rustic ambience and comfort. Dude ranchers made concessions to the comfort of clients, but resisted providing what they considered luxuries. Two luxuries were indoor plumbing and electricity. Many dude ranches relied on kerosene lamps well into the 1930s, while others installed electricity—a notable improvement. Pit toilets were the standard sanitary facilities, while tin tubs filled with hot water hauled from a laundry or kitchen served as bathing facilities. Simplicity characterized the Bar BC's charm. Dudes "roughed it in comfort," as "all necessary comforts are provided, but luxuries are neither expected nor desired." As of 1927, the ranch supplied hot water and portable tubs for bathing. Buster and Frances Estes provided the same service each morning at the STS. Other dude ranches succumbed to pressure for comfort. The Crescent Lazy H boasted electric lights and a bathhouse with showers. Going a step further, the Elbo, new in 1927, offered the latest in indoor plumbing; each four-room cabin had hot water, a bath, and a toilet, while hot water, shower, and tub baths were available for each of the six one and two-room cabins. However, the Elbo resembled a "cabin camp," the predecessor of the modern motel more than a

dude ranch. Henry Stewart, the owner of the JY, compromised; dudes could wash themselves old-style by having a tub and hot water brought to their cabins, or use a central bathhouse with hot- and cold-running water. Thus, even as the dude ranch arrived as an institution, technological improvements such as indoor plumbing, electric power and, especially, the automobile, influenced peoples' expectations and altered the dude ranch.[30]

Dude ranches in Jackson Hole offered traditional activities. Horseback riding was the primary recreational activity, followed closely by pack trips, hunting, and fishing. Some dude ranches mentioned hiking, but its omission from most lists suggests that it was not all that popular with dudes. Phelps Lake provided an icy but convenient swimming hole for JY dudes, while the White Grass had a concrete-lined pool and the Bar BC a ditch-fed swimming hole. Bowing to the times, the Cross and Crescent Ranch, a small facility at Moran, advertised automobile tours of Yellowstone. But then, so did the venerable JY, offering dudes motor trips to Yellowstone and other scenic areas. They provided boats at some ranches, both for fishing and sightseeing. Only the JY mentioned mountain climbing as an activity, which was just emerging as a recreational sport in the 1920s.[31]

By its very nature, the dude business required tracts of undeveloped land, the more pristine the better. Ironically, dude wranglers introduced people to Jackson Hole who stayed on and increased development by homesteading public lands in the valley. For example, Owen Wister bought a homestead along the Snake River in 1912, after spending a season at the JY. Struthers Burt claimed responsibility for bringing a score of settlers into Jackson Hole. Some had worked at the Bar BC. Among them were Alfred and Frank Bessette, who came west to work at the Bar BC as a waiter and chef respectively. In 1914, Alfred Bessette homesteaded land south of Timbered Island. The following spring, his brother filed preemption papers on nearby acreage. Foreman and partner Joe LePage took over a relinquishment north of the Bar BC in 1924. Dudes also stayed. Bryant Mears homesteaded the Sun Star Ranch in 1915, now known as the 4 Lazy F. Tucker Bispham,

Costume parties, as well as literary discussion groups, provided the well-heeled clientle of the Bar BC with activities not normally associated with a "ranch." *Jackson Hole Historical Society and Museum*

an original Bar BC dude, teamed up with Harold Hammond in 1913 to form the White Grass. Bar BC dudes Eleanor Patterson, "the Countess of Flat Creek," and Lambert Cadwalader bought their own ranches, beginning the trend of affluent people buying ranches to realize their dream of owning a western ranch. Maud Noble was another Bar BC dude, who purchased Menor's Ferry in 1918. Dr. George Woodward established a camp at the outlet of Leigh Lake known as the Bar None or Wildmere. Much has been made of cowboy and dudene romances— perhaps too much. Yet it happened. Frances Mears, a young socialite from Pennsylvania, met wrangler Buster Estes at the Bar BC around 1918 and, much to her family's dismay, married him. In the early 1920s they established the STS, a small dude ranch near Menor's Ferry.[32]

Dude ranches in Jackson Hole contributed to the economy in a significant way. First, dudes brought money to spend in a cash-poor valley. During the 1920s, the only other important sources of cash were game animals and cattle. Further, the cattle business experienced a depression in these years, which magnified the importance of the dude ranching and tourist-related businesses. Dude ranches employed significant numbers—a larger dude ranch

hired as many as 20 to 25 employees, from cabin girls to wranglers. Walt Callahan, a top wrangler, worked at both the JY and the Bar BC. In 1917, the *Courier* reported homesteaders Jimmy Manges working at the White Grass, while Norm Bladon was employed at the JY. Mr. and Mrs. Ed Price were employed at the Bar BC. The expansion of dude ranches required builders providing another source of wages. In 1917, Charles Fox took a crew to the Bar BC to construct buildings. In 1920, Louis Joy remodeled the Wister cabin at the JY; nearby homesteader Charles Ilse helped with the project, while Frank Waterman hauled logs. Dude ranches also purchased produce from local farms and ranches. In late 1922, the Bar BC bought hay from Roy Nipper and Jake Johnson to feed livestock. John Moulton, who homesteaded on Mormon Row, turned to dairy farming in the 1920s, selling milk, cream, and butter to nearby dude ranches and tourist resorts.[33]

Wrangling dudes became a complex business. Some ranches remained small, such as the Danny Ranch and STS, while others such as the JY, Bar BC, and Crescent Lazy H grew into large outfits. Burt and Carncross learned "that a dude-ranch can be made profitable, because you can run it as an ordinary ranch" with little overhead. They built for 15 dudes in 1912, but found to their dismay that "overhead charges ate up the profits." They expanded the ranch to house 50 dudes in the decade between 1912 and 1922. Burt found they could wrangle 50 dudes with about the same outfit as it took to care for 30. To emphasize the point that dude ranching was a business, the Bar BC incorporated as Bar BC Ranches by 1922. It was the largest operation in the valley, with the upper ranch on the Snake boasting 45 buildings and housing 50 dudes. Located to the south, on the Snake River, was the JO, a boys' camp. On the lower Gros Ventre, Burt and Carncross operated the Lower Bar BC. In addition, they entered a partnership with Hammond and Bispham, and operated the White Grass under the Bar BC Ranches in the 1920s. The owners of the Half Moon, the Karppis and Anita Tarbell, filed articles of incorporation in 1928, issuing $30,000 worth of stock.[34]

Inventories indicated the complexity of the business. According to a 1932 inventory, the JY included more than 40 buildings, including a post office, library, and casino. Burt listed:

> eighty saddle-ponies, two work teams, ten cows, sixty saddles with their paraphernalia of bridles, blankets, and so on, complete camping outfits for about twenty people, a motor-bus, a smaller car, and an incredible amount of diversified supplies. We must be in a position to replace anything at a moment's notice. I cannot tell you how many sheets and blankets and quilts and things like that are stored away. These, I am glad to say, are in charge of a person delegated to keep track of them.[35]

An inventory of the Bear Paw Dude Ranch in 1949 took a full 26 pages and included everything from saddles and tack to furniture and linens, dishes, and kitchen utensils, to items such as a rubber boat, a moose head, and a "rawhide tomyhawk."[36]

Dude ranching made significant economic contributions to the West, but historians rely on general information rather than exact figures. Laurence Borne noted that the dearth of detailed statistics made it impossible to demonstrate conclusively the significance of dude ranching to the economy of a state or region. In March 1925, a *Jackson's Hole Courier* article, titled "Dude Ranches Grow Popular," reported that a total of 600 dudes vacationed in Jackson Hole in 1924. Jackson Hole dude ranches could house 394 guests in 1927. The Elbo, Flagg Ranch, Jackson Lake Lodge, Sheffield's Teton Lodge, and Leek's Camp could provide lodging for 325 guests. Assuming a ten-week season and 65 guests, Henry Stewart of the JY would earn $43,500, excluding extended pack trips. Assuming a monthly rate of $300, the popular Bar BC would gross $37,500 for a ten-week season. Tony Grace, owner of the Danny Ranch, charged a daily rate of $8, which included lodging, meals, and a saddle horse. Assuming 15 dudes stayed at the ranch for ten weeks, the gross income would total $8,400. At the Double Diamond boys' ranch, Joe Clark and Frank Williams charged a total fee of $800 for three months, including train fare from Philadelphia. A pack trip to Yellowstone cost $50 extra. The potential income of dude ranches suggests that the business contributed significantly to the local economy, especially in light of its growth in the 1920s.[37]

The stock market crash of October 29, 1929, crushed the optimistic future projected for dude ranching. Because of a banner season, 1929 became known as the "golden year" of dude ranching. Looking back during the depression, 1929 appeared even more gilded, especially in the spring of 1932, when a large number of businesses failed nationwide. These failures had a ripple effect on tourism and dude ranching, as people put off or cancelled vacations. Dude ranches experienced several fates in this gloomy period—failure, change of ownership, or survival. Those encumbered with large debts were especially vulnerable and some went bankrupt. Inability to pay property taxes drove others under. Some sold out, such as pioneers Dick and Dora Randall, who sold the OTO in 1934. Others weathered the depression and even thrived. Shrewd managers cut staff, activities, and overhead costs. For example, Larry Larom ended extended pack trips from his Valley Ranch west of Cody to Yellowstone and Jackson Hole.[38]

In spite of the depression, dude ranching fared better than many other businesses and industries. Wyoming citizens perceived them as a hedge against hard economic times that had crippled agriculture

and coal mining, both mainstays of the state's economy. The Great Depression forced stockmen to convert to dude ranching to bring in extra cash. The
Dude Ranchers' Association, formed in 1926,
thrived and remained active through the 1930s. Indeed, its promotional activities probably helped sus-
tain the industry. Railroads also provided valuable
publicity, especially by publishing booklets and brochures. In 1934, the University of Wyoming began
offering a degree in "recreational ranching," offering
evidence of the acceptance and stability of dude
ranching, even during harsh times.[39]

In Jackson Hole, the experience of dude ranchers mirrors events in the West. Union Pacific brochures indicate stability. About 1927, 20 dude
ranches and lodges were listed in the valley. Around
1930, 17 were listed. A subsequent booklet separated
dude ranches from other lodging facilities, recording
11 ranches and seven camps or lodges. Yet in 1932,
Dick Winger, an agent for the Snake River Land
Company, wrote an assessment of the dude ranches
in the valley, reporting only the Half Moon booked
full for the season and in sound financial shape.

When silver fox fur coats became fashionable in
the 1920s, some dude ranchers established fox farms
to provide extra income. Harold Hammond set up a
fox farm at the White Grass in 1925, selling pelts to
guests. John Hogan operated a small dude outfit in
"connection with the Snake River Fox Ranch" at the
confluence of the Snake River and Buffalo Fork.
Nathaniel Burt recalled the putrid odors that emanated from horse carcasses used to feed foxes at
Hogan's ranch. At the worst of the depression in
1932, the large main house at Jack Woodman's Flying V burned to the ground. Woodman did not re-
build, but sold out to mountaineers Paul Petzoldt
and Gustav Koven in 1935. The depression forced
Coulter Huyler to convert his summer retreat, the
Bear Paw, to a dude ranch in 1935.[40]

In 1927, the Snake River Land Company
formed to buy up lands for park purposes. Funded
by John D. Rockefeller Jr., company agents bought
out numerous important dude ranches and resorts.
They purchased the Elbo, the Danny Ranch, the
Triangle X, Hogan's fox farm, and pioneer dude
ranches, the JY and Bar BC. John S. Turner contin-

ued to operate the Triangle X through a series of
short-term leases, while Burt and Irving Corse
secured a lifetime estate in exchange for the sale of
their ranch. This buy-out reduced the level of dude
ranching in Jackson Hole.[41]

Jackson Hole dude ranches influenced the history of this valley tremendously and, in a larger context, this area became a major dude ranching center
in the West. Three early dude ranches pioneered the
business and led the way for a second wave of dude
ranches in the golden age of the 1920s. A third wave
grew out of the Great Depression of the 1930s. Each
ranch exhibited distinctive characteristics, usually the
stamp of its owners, yet each shared common traits
that shaped the business as a whole.

The first dude ranch was the JY. At the outlet of
Phelps Lake, Louis Joy filed a cash entry on 119
acres in October 1906, taking over a homestead entry filed first by David Spalding in 1903 or 1904. In
1903, Joy had filed a separate desert land entry on
159.75 acres. To prove up on the entry, he cut two
main ditches with laterals, and raised oats, barley,
and timothy on 23 acres. It is doubtful that Joy intended to farm or raise cattle, for Struthers Burt described the ranch as timbered land "absolutely useless
for ranching purposes." Rather, Joy set up a dude outfit. He received patents to the two parcels in 1907
and 1908.[42]

Dudes began coming to the JY in 1908 according to most sources. About this time, Struthers Burt
approached Joy to buy a half-interest in the ranch.
Having no cash, he secured a five-year option. Burt
and Joy formed a partnership common to the dude
business, merger of Easterner and Westerner. Burt
was a Philadelphian educated at Princeton, while Joy,
though born in the East, "had emigrated to a big
Spanish-American ranch in the Southwest" at the
age of 18. Since about 1886, he had worked as a
cowboy, foreman, forest ranger, cook, guide, and
sometime professional gambler. For the next three
years, Burt learned the craft of wrangling dudes.[43]
They began modestly, building two small cabins to
house five of Burt's Princeton associates; the next season they expanded their operation to 15 dudes. The
next year Burt and Joy took in no fewer than 40
dudes, turning some away.[44]

In 1911, Owen Wister brought his family to the JY for three months. Fanny Kemble Wister described the experience in the preface of *Owen Wister Out West; His Journals and Letters.* The four Wister children stayed in a small sleeping cabin. Bunks consisted of wooden frames filled with pine boughs and covered with gray blankets. "Every morning a bucket of hot water was brought to the cabin door by a filthy old man who, we thought, had something permanently wrong with his jaw." This man was the roustabout, an indispensable character who hauled hot water and wood to cabins, filled kerosene lamps on demand, and emptied slops from chamberpots if he could be persuaded to do so. Wister learned later that the lumpy jaw turned out to be a wad of tobacco "kept in his mouth in the same place for months." Presumably, he bit off a fresh chew occasionally. This may have been the same roustabout who attacked Horace Carncross with an ax. Fanny Wister was more impressed with the old wrangler who "filled us with awe and admiration." The children "hung around him as much as possible, for we knew he was the real thing." The cook was a cockney English woman, who had converted to Mormonism and emigrated to the United States. She left an indelible impression on Wister's daughter, who recalled vividly the cook's "terrible noisy rages" vented at her young daughter—"I'll knock your blooming 'ead against the blooming wall."[45]

Yet, when the season ended, Fanny Wister hated to return to the East. "What—sleep in a real bed again and see trolley cars? How frightful! No more smell of sagebrush, no more Snake River, no more Grand Teton. Why did we have to go back?" In her own way, she summed up the appeal of a dude ranch experience.[46]

In three seasons, the JY outfit had expanded its capacity from five to 40 dudes, demonstrating the potential of the business. In 1911, Struthers Burt fell out with Louis Joy and decided to start his own dude ranch. Burt formed a partnership with Horace Carncross and created the Bar BC in 1912.[47] Meanwhile, Joy continued to operate the JY.

Henry S. A. Stewart of Pittsburgh became enthralled with dude wrangling and leased the JY from Joy in 1916. Four years later, Stewart purchased the

ranch along with additional lands and raised cattle on the property.[48] Two personalities associated with the JY were Shadwick (also Chadwick) Hobbs and Dave Spalding. In 1924, Spalding, the original entryman on the JY, died at the age of 92. He had remained at the ranch after relinquishing his claim to Joy and was buried on the premises. During this period Shad Hobbs, a top wrangler, worked as the foreman at the ranch.[49]

Stewart continued to expand the ranch. In 1927, the JY was the largest dude ranch in the valley, housing 65 guests. Rates were $65 a week, which included food, lodging, and the use of boats and saddle horses. Popular activities included swimming, boating, mountain climbing, fishing, horseback riding, hunting, and camping. Stewart bought a separate ranch to provide fresh vegetables, eggs, milk, and meat and boasted that the ranch had managed to keep the same cook for a decade. For bathing, the ranch provided hot water and tubs or a central bathhouse. Stewart built a "unique" waterwheel to furnish power for the laundry house. In a concession to the times, the JY offered motor tours of scenic areas and rented automobiles to guests. Stewart also ran a store, selling licenses, camping clothes, candy, tobacco, cigarettes, and medicine, an unusual practice for a dude ranch.[50] Around 1930, Stewart reduced the capacity of the ranch to 60 guests but raised the rates to $75 per week.[51]

In 1932, Stewart sold the ranch to the Snake River Land Company for $49,064.03. A company inventory listed 38 buildings at the dude ranch with additional buildings on the "homestead" and the "farm." The more significant buildings included a new casino, a lodge, a new "living room" cabin, 50 × 25 feet, a dining room, a library, a two-story post office, a bathhouse, a large bunkhouse, and 20 dude cabins. The homestead complex consisted of a main cabin, foreman's cabin, barn, granary, and several outbuildings. The farmstead included a large chicken house, log pen, vegetable cellar, chicken house and incubator house, and a variety of barns and stables. The inventory indicates that the JY was a complex, self-sufficient operation. The 1932 sale ended dude ranching at the JY. Soon thereafter, the Rockefeller family began using the ranch for a private summer retreat.[52]

The Bar BC, an offshoot of the JY, was established by Struthers Burt and Dr. Horace Carncross. Burt severed his association with the JY after the 1911 season. Over a period of time, Burt perceived Joy "as a sort of financial Blue Beard who inveigled others into intimate business relations and then, when he had derived all the benefit he could from them, got rid of them with infinite subtlety." Burt believed Joy had no intention of making good on the option to buy a half interest in the JY and used Burt's eastern connections to bring dudes to the ranch. In the fall of 1911, Burt set out to find a suitable location for a dude ranch, fired "by a good old-fashioned hatred" for his former partner, possessing "infinitesimal capital" —$2,000—most of it borrowed. His new partner, Dr. Carncross, accompanied him.[53]

During their last two months at the JY, Burt and Carncross would saddle up and ride until evening, inspecting the countryside. Existing ranches were unsuitable, so they decided to take up homesteads and began to survey available public land. After considerable argument, "always with infinite mutual respect and forbearance," they settled on terraced lands along the Snake River east of Timbered Island. The partners considered a number of factors related to stock ranching, among them soils, terrain, prevailing winds, timber for winter shelter of livestock, building material, and firewood, grazing range, and water sources. In addition, scenic beauty, isolation or at least the feeling of it, the availability of fishing and hunting, and points of interest were considered in selecting a site. They even studied sites for a "river wind" to reduce mosquito problems.[54]

Burt and Carncross intended to run the Bar BC as a dude ranch, then hoped to expand into cattle ranching after the dude business was established. Becoming dude wranglers exclusively was not the goal of either man. Carncross was 41 years old in 1912 and well established as a physician. Burt's dream was to be a writer, but rather than reside in New York City, declare himself a writer and hold down a subsidiary job until he established himself, he chose to become a western rancher while he developed his reputation as an author. At the JY, Burt thought the

outfit would be devoted primarily to cattle ranching, but found himself wrangling dudes. Looking back in 1922, he wrote "for sixteen years I have been starting other things, only to find myself always in the dude business."[55]

To open by summer, Burt and Carncross boarded in Jackson and attended to a myriad of details over the winter of 1911–1912. They ordered supplies, ranging from building materials and tack to food staples and building logs. They recruited help for the following season such as teamsters, ranch hands, and builders. These tasks completed, they returned east to secure commitments from 15 dudes.[56]

On May 12, 1912, Burt and Carncross established residence on adjacent tracts through the Homestead Act of 1862. Burt staked out a claim on 154.03 acres, while Carncross took up 158.63 acres. The 1862 law required five years of continuous occupation, and farming the land for five years. On Carncross's acreage, improvements included nine log cabins, 320 rods of fences, and 25 acres of oats cultivated by the end of 1916. On Burt's property, by the same year, they constructed a frame laundry building (25 × 12 feet), nine cabins of various sizes, and seven 12 × 14-foot cabins. Other improvements consisted of a 20-foot well, 21 acres of grain, and 800 rods of fence. In addition, each partner filed a desert land entry in 1913, adding a total of 252.72 acres to the ranch. By 1917, the Bar BC comprised more than 600 acres and the home ranch consisted of 26 buildings, capable of accommodating as many as 25 dudes. Burt recorded those first hectic days in 1912, when he and Carncross set up camp at the ranch and scrambled to build a functional outfit. "In short, we had to build a small town in the wilderness, complete and self-sustaining in every detail."[57]

Burt and Carncross put most of their profits back into the ranch. In 1916, they purchased a ranch along the Gros Ventre River near Spring Gulch from John C. Anderson to raise hay and cattle. This ranch became known as the Lower Bar BC. A year later, each partner borrowed $4,600 from the Philadelphia Trust Company, securing it with the ranch. In the summer of 1917, the *Courier* reported that Charles Fox and a crew had left Jackson to "do some building" at the Bar BC. The operation paid well enough that the men were able to pay 15 percent interest per annum and pay off the loan in 1924.[58]

By 1922, the Bar BC had expanded to 45 buildings. In addition to single and double sleeping cabins, a main house consisted of two dining rooms, a kitchen, two sitting rooms, and two smaller rooms. Other buildings included a blacksmith shop, garage, saddle shed, granary, camp store house, three storage sheds, root cellar, office, ice house, outfit dining room, five bunkhouses, store, laundry, dance hall, and four houses for the owner and foreman. The cattle ranch and a boys' camp added 50 more buildings. There were four partners, three foremen, and around 45 employees. The Bar BC had emerged as a small empire in the valley.[59]

To control the increasingly complex operation, Burt and Carncross formed the Bar BC Ranches. Incorporated under the laws of the State of Delaware, the Burts and Carncross transferred all property to the corporation. New partners joined them, Irving Corse and Joe LePage. Corse came to the Bar BC after the First World War, working his way up from driver to foreman, and finally to full partnership. Joe LePage, a Canadian by birth, migrated west and became a cowboy. He made his way to Jackson Hole from Montana in 1917. A top wrangler, he became a foreman and a partner in a short time.[60] From 1924 through 1928, the White Grass was affiliated with the Bar BC Ranches. In 1924, Bispham and Hammond sold out to the Bar BC Ranches and became partners. They bought back the ranch in 1928.[61]

The Bar BC became a social center and a major employer in the valley. The comings and goings of people affiliated with the ranch were reported regularly in the *Courier*. In September 1914, the *Courier* noted the visit of Bar BC "tourists" to Jackson. Even during the winter, residents at the Bar BC hosted social activities such as a dance in February 1916. Felicia Gizycka recalled vividly her arrival at the Bar BC with her mother Eleanor "Cissy" Patterson in 1916. From Victor, they bounced over the pass in a crude ranch wagon. They reached the ranch after dark, soaked by a drenching rainstorm to find the Burts and Carncross hosting a costume party. Katherine Burt introduced herself to Cissy Patterson, saying, "Hello, I'm a cave woman." Gizyka's mother

was determined to leave the next day, but did not. They spent the summer at the ranch.[62]

Many well-known wranglers worked at the Bar BC at one time or another. Cal Carrington was the foreman until lured away by Cissy Patterson in 1917. Joe LePage became foreman and partner until his death in 1929. Bill Howard began his association with the Bar BC in 1922 and took over the foreman's job after LePage's death. A few wrangled dudes at the Bar BC, then moved on to start their own dude ranches, such as Hammond of the White Grass and Frank Williams of the Double Diamond. Some secured work guiding hunting parties from the Bar BC. One was George Ross, who worked at the ranch for 18 years and reputedly received a tip of $1,300 on one occasion—such a stupendous amount for the times it is difficult to believe. Other Bar BC alumni were Billy Stilson, Walt Callahan, Bill Jump, Jim Budge, and Fred Deyo.[63]

The arrival of dudes each summer created an interesting blend of East and West. The dudes at the Bar BC were affluent, often well educated individuals. The first Bar BC dudes knew Burt through their associations in Philadelphia or Princeton. Among them were Sydney Biddle, Tucker Bispham, Adolph Borie, Abram Poole, David Adler, and George Porter. Nathaniel Burt recalled that "it was this blend of wildness and sophistication, of remoteness and civilization that gave Jackson Hole and especially the Bar BC a special quality."[64]

By the late 1920s, the Bar BC was one of the best known western dude ranches. The unknown contributor to the 1927 Union Pacific brochure believed simplicity characterized the ranch best. "All necessary comforts are provided, but luxuries are neither expected nor desired." Fifty dudes could be accommodated in 32 rooms. The rates were $300 to $310 per month. Like many other dude ranches, the Bar BC management required references from prospective guests. At the end of July 1925, 35 dudes were at the Bar BC and, in 1928, more improvements were built at the ranch.[65]

In the late 1920s, the character of the ranch began to change. Writing was Struthers Burt's first love, and by this time both he and Katherine Burt were popular authors. Burt eased out of active management to devote his efforts to writing. In 1929, he purchased two homesteads along the south side of Pacific Creek and established the Three Rivers Ranch. He formed an association of partners who built cabins on the land as a summer retreat. It was patterned after a dude ranch, except that there were no paying guests. Even a contributor to the *Courier* sensed the changing times in reporting the arrival of Burt at the Bar BC in July 1927. It seemed like "old times" with Burt at the ranch. Further, the Bar BC held a few bitter memories for the Burts. In 1918, Burt's sister, Jean Burt, swallowed three antiseptic tablets and died one day later. Then, early in 1928, Horace Carncross died at his home in Whitemarsh, Pennsylvania. The death of Carncross ended a close partnership of two men of "opposing qualities." Several months later, Joe LePage died of influenza and pneumonia. Alone at his ranch above the Bar BC, he had grown so sick that he tied a note to the collar of a horse and set it loose to be found by neighbors. Help arrived and transported LePage to Jackson's small hospital, but too late. Bispham and Hammond had bought back the White Grass in 1928, severing their business connections with the Bar BC. This left Burt and Irving Corse as active partners.[66]

In the late 1920s, significant events were taking place that would impact the future of Jackson Hole. Influenced by his experience at wrangling dudes and living in the West, Struthers Burt became a fierce advocate of conservation. Along with a few others in Jackson Hole, he grew very concerned with developments that threatened the frontier and wilderness character of the Teton country. In particular, water reclamation projects and commercial developments associated with the automobile aroused his ire. He was a vocal opponent of Wyoming State Engineer Frank Emerson's proposal to build a dam at the outlet of Jenny Lake, the pristine mountain lake at the foot of the Teton Range. When Burt and Carncross filed their homestead entries in 1912, they were virtually alone. Jimmy Manges had a homestead a mile and a half to the west, while Bill Menor operated his ferry two miles to the south. During and after World War I, new settlers arrived in the area. When Chester Goss and Scott developed the Elbo, Burt wrote

to Horace Albright "this speedway down here, the El-Bo Ranch and the south end of Timber Island, not to mention Jenny's Lake, has about sickened me with this neck of the woods."[67] He established contacts with Horace Albright, the superintendent of Yellowstone by 1922, after the two had clashed over the proposed Yellowstone extension of 1919. Burt participated in the July 26, 1923, meeting at the Maud Noble cabin, where Albright formed an alliance with local conservationists to devise a way of saving Jackson Hole from commercial exploitation. For the next six years, Burt found time, in the midst of operating a dude ranch and writing, to work for the creation of a Grand Teton National Park. He and other advocates were rewarded when Congress set aside a 96,000-acre park in 1929.

Meanwhile, agents of John D. Rockefeller Jr. had created the Snake River Land Company in 1927, a Utah corporation formed to purchase lands in the valley. In 1929, the company proposed buying the Bar BC. This came as a complete surprise to Burt, who understood that his dude ranch would not be included in the purchase schedule. To Kenneth Chorley, he wrote, "out of a clear sky this whole thing was sprung on us a little over a month ago." After considerable negotiation over the price and the terms of a lifetime lease, plus the buyout of Horace Carncross' sole heir, Corse and Burt sold the ranch in 1930.[68]

After retiring from active management of the Bar BC, the Burts fell out with Irving Corse. In 1935, Burt wrote Harold Fabian requesting a copy of the Bar BC corporation's charter and by-laws. He confided to Fabian that "I want to get hold of a copy and, as I am not on the best of terms just at present with Irv [Corse]," was reluctant to ask Corse for the documents. In 1937, Corse bought out the Burts' interest in the dude ranch. The Bar BC lease was modified in 1938: The Burts and Corse's first wife, Angela, were dropped as designated lessees and Corse's new bride, Margaretta Sharpless Corse, added to it. According to Nathaniel Burt, his parents feuded with the Corses and the Pavenstedts, who were two percent shareholders, over management matters and profit sharing.[69]

Under the management of Corse and Bill Howard, the fortunes of the Bar BC declined slowly but relentlessly. Corse believed "that a Real Western Ranch should be as rundown as possible." The buildings at the ranch deteriorated. Also, fires took a toll. In the summer of 1939, fire destroyed a portion of the main house, the kitchen, and a commissary. Corse replaced the burned section of the lodge with a new wing. In the 1940s, fire destroyed a laundry house, the ruins of which are visible today. Then, in late 1959, fire burned one of the main residences, a 42 × 18-foot log cabin. Meanwhile, buildings were added. In 1934, Corse bought the LePage residence from the Snake River Land Company, dismantling, moving, and reassembling the cabin at the ranch. In 1938, he leased it to a family named Crocker. Three years later, he allowed a family named Harrison to build a cabin on the property, issuing a sublease for the cabin sites. At the south end of the ranch, Corse cleared an airstrip and constructed a small frame hangar. All of these changes eroded the distinct character of the Bar BC.[70]

The Corses operated the Bar BC as a dude ranch until the Second World War. Because of severe labor shortages, they suspended the operation. Corse left the valley to work for the navy as a flight instructor at the University of Wyoming. In 1942, Bill Howard sold his interest in the ranch and left the valley. After the war, Corse, stricken with arthritis and emphysema, was too ill to manage the Bar BC. He died in 1953.[71]

In 1950, Margaretta Corse issued a sublease to T. H. and Margaretta (Peggy) Frew Conderman to run a dude ranch operation through 1959. This was an unhappy arrangement. Mrs. Conderman later divorced her husband and married John Cook, who took over the lease. Mrs. Corse resumed management of the ranch, renting cabins and campsites through the summer of 1985. Poor health forced her to cease operations in 1986 and she died in 1988.[72]

The Bar BC was the second dude ranch in Jackson Hole. As such, it was one of the pioneer dude ranches in the cradle of dude ranching—Montana and Wyoming—and, under the guidance of Burt and Carncross, became the best known dude ranch

in the valley during the 1920s golden age of dude ranching.

The White Grass was the third and last of the pioneer dude ranches in Jackson Hole. In September 1913, Harold Hammond took up 160 acres of meadow and forest land at the foot of Buck Mountain. Two years later, George Tucker Bispham took up residence on 160 acres adjacent to Hammond's homestead. Easterner and Westerner—dude and wrangler—formed a partnership, bringing together one element Struthers Burt believed necessary for a successful dude outfit. At first, Hammond and Bispham intended to start a cattle ranch; taking in dudes was a secondary pursuit if done at all. According to Hammond's stepson Frank Galey, they did not start taking in dudes until 1919, the first summer after the Great War. However, the *Jackson's Hole Courier* in 1916 reported that Francis Biddle was a guest of the ranch and that Alexander Cadwalader was expected later in the season.[73]

A lack of capital and the First World War hindered their efforts to improve the ranch. For example, Hammond was absent from May 1 to October 1, 1914, "working four miles" from the White Grass, probably at the Bar BC. When the United States entered the war in 1917, Hammond enlisted in the army and was absent for nearly two years. Bispham seems to have been less active in managing the outfit, although he stayed at the ranch while Hammond served in the army. By 1919, the partners were determined to wrangle dudes, henceforth raising cattle became a secondary activity. Hammond reported the following improvements in his final entry papers, filed in July 1920: Buildings consisted of a 28 × 48-foot log house, a 30 × 50-foot log barn, a 16 × 48-foot storehouse, and a 14 × 28-foot bunkhouse. Harry Clissold, owner of the Trail Ranch, constructed the main lodge and some of the cabins. Other developments included three corrals, 120 panels of eight-pole fence, and 800 rods of buck-and-pole fence. Beginning in 1915, Hammond cultivated land, starting with 16 acres and expanding to 80 acres by 1920. He raised oats, barley, alfalfa, and timothy, harvesting it as hay. A one-mile ditch irrigated the fields. In 1922, Bispham filed his final proof papers. Improvements included three log houses, one being 26 × 36 feet, and 640 rods of buck-and-four-pole fence. Bispham had a total of 25 acres plowed and cultivated.[74]

Hammond testified that "his claim is used some for summer tourists," but the combined improvements of Bispham and Hammond suggest a small-scale operation. Indeed, they may have experienced some financial difficulties, for in 1924 both men and their wives sold the White Grass to the Bar BC ranches. Both were partners in the corporation and Hammond continued to manage the White Grass. Further, in the same year, Hammond established a fox farm, raising silver fox for their pelts. In early 1925, Hammond joined Lars Anderson of Cincinnati to set up the operation. At the end of the year, six pairs of silver fox arrived at the White Grass. In 1927, Hammond, Anderson, and Irving Corse filed articles of incorporation for the White Grass Silver Black Fox Ranch, Inc. Four hundred shares were issued at $25 each. The White Grass also continued to run a few head of cattle.[75]

Associated with the Bar BC empire, the White Grass appeared to prosper. Operating the ranch as a boys' camp in 1927, they had 16 guests. The White Grass could accommodate about 25 dudes during this period. A concrete-lined swimming pool was an unusual amenity. The rates were $11 per day for stays less than one month, reduced to $10 per day for a month or longer. Like the Bar BC, the White Grass required personal references from prospective guests.[76]

In 1928, Hammond and Bispham bought back their homesteads from the Bar BC Corporation, severing their ties with that outfit. Bispham ended his partnership in December, when he sold his land and improvements to Hammond for $12,500. Bispham built a new cabin at the White Grass where he and his wife spent several summers. Later they moved up to Burt's Three Rivers, where they built a cabin and joined this association. After Helen Bispham was thrown and dragged by her horse at Three Rivers in 1935, the Bisphams returned to the White Grass according to one source. Tucker Bispham died in 1949, never returning to Jackson Hole after 1935 according to his obituary.[77]

Meanwhile, Hammond expanded the capacity and amenities at the White Grass despite the Great Depression. In 1930, the ranch had 18 cabins in addition to the main house, outbuildings, and swimming pool. By the 1930s, the ranch could accommodate 35 dudes. In 1935, Hammond constructed a large log shower house, which provided showers and indoor plumbing and served as a laundry. A year later, private baths were added to many of the cabins. According to Frank Galey, the ranch's last owner, several long-time dudes rebelled at these conveniences. They continued to use outdoor privies and insisted on bathing in tin tubs with hot water delivered by the roustabout. During these years several wings were added to the main house, more than doubling its size. The front porch was closed off and wooden steps added. In recent years, modern sliding glass doors were added to one wing, marring its rustic character.[78]

Born in 1891 in Blackfoot, Idaho, Harold Hammond had come to Jackson Hole in 1901 to live with a sister. In 1910, he worked for the Reclamation Service at the Jackson Lake Dam, supervising the stock and stable. He then worked at the Bar BC as a wrangler before homesteading at the White Grass in 1913. After the war and while struggling to establish a dude ranch, Hammond married Marie Ireland in 1922. Several years later, she died. In 1936, Hammond married a longtime dudene named Marion Galey. She first came to Jackson Hole in 1919. A friend of Burt and Bispham, she spent the summer at the Bar BC. A young widow, she was accompanied by her two-year-old son, Frank. Smitten with Jackson Hole, she moved to the White Grass and stayed on through Christmas. Mrs. Galey may have been the first paying dude at the White Grass. Frank Galey believed that his mother may have fallen for Hammond as early as this period. The Galeys continued to spend time at the White Grass and after Mrs. Hammond's death, she married Hammond. Up to that time, Frank Galey had acquired a working knowledge of the dude business as a guest; in 1936, he started working as a hand for $30 a month. The Hammonds were married only a short time, when health problems began to beleaguer Hammond. After wintering in Arizona, he died in the summer of 1939. Marion Hammond and Frank Galey took over the operation.[79]

The Second World War hamstrung operations, nearly forcing the White Grass to close because of serious labor and supply shortages. Frank Galey enlisted in the service, and the ranch was left to caretakers. Galey returned in 1946 to find the ranch in disrepair. Because materials were still in short supply, they could only patch up cabins with makeshift materials. Galey bought a portion of the ranch in partnership with Norman Mellor.

This began the modern era of the White Grass. In 1966, Galey closed the silver fox farm, which had operated since 1925. He and his bride, Inge Galey, expanded the outfit's capacity from 30 to 55 dudes, and the ranch was booked full until it closed after the 1985 season. Galey bought out his mother and Mellors in the 1950s. In 1956, he sold all but a few acres of the White Grass to the National Park Service for $165,000 and a life estate. Frank Galey died of a heart attack in the midst of the 1985 season, ending the run of the longest operating dude ranch in the valley from 1919 through 1985.[80]

After World War I, dude ranching exploded in Jackson Hole. The growth of tourism and depressed agricultural prices following the war persuaded ranchers and entrepreneurs to take up dude wrangling. In addition, the success of the JY and Bar BC in the early years encouraged rapid growth of the business in the 1920s.

The STS was one of the most prominent of the second wave of dude ranches in Teton County. A good example of a small family dude ranch, its atmosphere reflected the character of its owners, Buster and Frances Mears Estes. Their marriage was perhaps the most famous of the wrangler-dude romances in the valley. Frances Mears, a Bar BC dudene from Philadelphia, Pennsylvania, first came to the valley in 1914, traveling over Teton Pass in a "white-top" wagon. At the Bar BC, she met Buster Estes, a wrangler at the ranch. Their romance blossomed and they married in spite of the objections of Mears's family. Her parents apparently disowned her, beginning an estrangement that lasted for several years.[81]

From Holiday Menor, Estes learned of a 76-acre tract along the Snake River that remained open to

settlement and promptly filed preemption papers. The Estes built a cabin in November and December 1922 and moved in January 1923. Starting with $50 and a milk cow, they built up a small but prosperous dude ranch. In the spring of 1923, their cow gave birth to a calf, which they traded to one of the Woodwards, a local family, in exchange for help in adding a roof and fireplace to their cabin. The Estes began a modest operation. Aside from their main house, they had only one cabin and one tent to house dudes. To earn cash, Estes worked at the sawmill located at Sawmill Ponds. Frances Estes sold food to tourist traffic, which increased steadily in the 1920s. They offered fresh eggs, milk, bread, tea, coffee, cake and cookies to walk-in traffic, advertising in the *Jackson's Hole Courier*. In 1924, they advertised ice cream, lemonade, and chicken dinners or suppers to order. Although this was not a typical dude ranch practice, the Estes did it to make ends meet and build up the ranch. Bill Woodward added the large fireplace to the lodge in 1925. When Buster Estes filed final proof papers in 1927, the ranch consisted of the following improvements: the five-room main house (14 × 46 feet with a 14 × 30-foot wing), a log garage (12 × 20 feet), a log cabin (12 × 14 feet), two frame cabins (12 × 10 feet), and a barn (14 × 30 feet). The entire tract was fenced with post, pole, and wire. Estes plowed and planted eight acres to oats and barley in 1923, but failed to harvest a crop. In succeeding years, they were content to raise a garden.[82]

In 1927, the STS was included in the Union Pacific brochure "Dude Ranches Out West." Riding, hiking, hunting, fishing, and camping were the listed activities. Able to accommodate ten guests, amenities included portable tubs and hot water each morning, along with ice, spring water, fresh vegetables, eggs, and milk. Around 1930, the Estes promoted their dude outfit as "the only small ranch left in this country." They charged $55 per week per person, cheaper than the $70 charged at the White Grass or the $70 to $105 charged at the Bar BC. Mardy Murie recollected that the Estes expanded their capacity to 24 dudes and were nearly always full. Indeed, the local paper periodically announced the arrival of dudes at the ranch, indicating success. By the 1930s, they had added up to ten cabins, two bunkhouses, a chicken house, and a laundry and bath.[83]

The depression hit the Estes hard. During the 1930s, they lowered their rates drastically to $20 per week. This included room and board but, in a break from traditional dude ranching practices, did not include saddlehorses. Horses cost $3 per day or $15 per week. In 1935, the Estes leased a 200-square-foot lot to Stella Woodbury, a dude from Kansas City, Missouri, for use as a cabin site. Two years later, the Nelson brothers built a large log house that is the current Murie residence. They may have granted the lease to bring in extra revenue. Around 1940, the Estes constructed a new log residence. They had been in the new home only a short time when the United States entered World War II. Closing the dude operation, they moved to Salt Lake City and worked in war industries to support the war effort. After the war, the Estes determined to quit the dude business. At this time, the Murie family—Olaus and Mardy Murie, and Adolph and Louise Murie—approached the Estes about purchasing a portion of or the whole ranch. The parties signed an agreement for a warranty deed in 1945; the Muries made a down payment with the balance due in 1950. The Murie family has owned and lived at the ranch since 1945. They never operated it as a dude ranch, making a handshake agreement to that effect with the Estes.[84]

The Double Diamond was another prominent dude ranch in the 1920s. Like the owners of the STS and White Grass, the partners of the Double Diamond were Easterner and Westerner, Frank Williams and Joseph Clark. Born in Colorado in 1883, Frank Williams moved to Jackson Hole in 1900 with his parents Otho and Josephine Williams and five siblings. As a young man he worked as a cowboy, wrangling cows in the Timbered Island area in 1908 and 1909. Later, Williams gained experience wrangling dudes at the Bar BC.

Joseph Clark was a dude from Philadelphia, who stayed first at the Bar BC and later at Dr. Woodward's Bar None on Leigh Lake. Years later, Clark passed his bar exam and became a prominent Philadelphia attorney. He represented Pennsylvania in the United States Senate from 1957 to 1969. Clark met

Williams while staying at the Bar None, and the two men agreed to start a dude ranch together.[85]

While working as a cowboy in the Timbered Island area, Williams had camped at the base of the bench east of Taggart and Bradley Lakes. The site left a strong impression on him as a prime location for a dude ranch. Much of the suitable land in the area belonged to Jimmy Manges, so Clark and Williams offered to buy a portion of his homestead. Manges sold 40 acres in 1926. Emma Williams, the wife of Frank, filed a desert entry on a minute tract consisting of 12.97 acres in 1924. She irrigated eight acres with a ditch and four laterals, drawing water from Bradley Creek. They raised timothy and clover for hay and a small garden.[86]

Clark and the Williams wasted no time in constructing buildings for the 1924 season. For unknown reasons, they decided to operate a boys' ranch. Perhaps they believed there would be less competition if they specialized in a different clientele. On May 1, 1924, the *Courier* announced the new partnership of Clark and Williams, calling their venture a "tourist resort." The two entrepreneurs assembled building materials and recruited 15 to 20 boys for the first season. One year later, they hosted 27 boys. The Double Diamond succeeded immediately.[87]

In July 1927, the Double Diamond expected 20 dudes. The boys were housed in tents on frames over flooring, centered around two wide log buildings that served as a kitchen and dining room. The ranch accommodated 25 boys of high school and college age. The main house was described as an extra large recreation hall and dining lodge. Forty-two saddle horses were kept at the ranch. The season ran from June 15 to September 15. The Union Pacific brochures of 1927 described the Double Diamond as follows:

> This ranch draws its patronage almost entirely from Philadelphia territory, and charges $800 for the season, including transportation from Philadelphia in the custody of counselors who remain with the boys throughout the entire trip; a side trip to Yellowstone is also offered at $50 additional, with refund if the trip is not made. The ranch has its own fresh vegetables, milk and cream. References are required and given.[88]

By the early 1930s, Clark and Williams had expanded the capacity of the Double Diamond to 35 boys. Possibly because of the depression, they reduced the price from $800 to $700 for the season. Nonetheless, increasing the capacity from 25 to 35 dudes increased their potential gross revenue by $4,500.[89]

During the depression, several changes occurred at the ranch. First, Joe Clark dropped out of active management as his law practice and political ambitions took more of his time. By the late 1930s, Clark was no longer listed as a contact for reservations. In 1946, Harry and Nola Brown bought his interest in the ranch. Clark, in turn, purchased one acre for a summer cabin. Second, the Double Diamond ceased operating as a boys' ranch and began catering to dudes of all ages. Since tents were inadequate for adults, who expected modern conveniences, they housed them in log cabins. However, this reduced the Double Diamond's capacity to 20 guests. Finally, to provide more flexibility for guests, they charged weekly rates ranging from $25 to $35 rather than a rate for the full season. Dudes also reduced the time of their stay in this era; most Double Diamond guests stayed from three to six weeks.[90]

Frank Williams continued to operate the ranch through World War II. In 1950, the ranch had eight guest cabins capable of housing 28 people. A tract appraisal, prepared in 1961, listed 18 buildings on the property. Most were log structures with wood sheathing and rolled asphalt roofing. All but two had indoor plumbing. The buildings were constructed around 1943; the barn and shed were all that remained of the original buildings.[91]

After Frank Williams died in 1964, his heirs sold the Double Diamond to the National Park Service for $315,000. Harry and Nola Brown acquired a lease to operate the property from 1964 through 1969. In 1970, the ranch was turned over once again to the National Park Service. The American Alpine Club has leased the property since 1970 using it as a hostel for mountaineers. In 1985, a wildfire swept through the ranch and burned eight buildings, more than half of the structures on the site.[92]

Not far from the Double Diamond was the Half Moon. The July-August issue of *Midwest Review* de-

scribed it as a "new venture" for girls located near the Moose Post Office on Cottonwood Creek. "It is directly under the famed Tetons and brand new rustic log buildings have been erected and the rugged beauty of the surroundings make it an ideal resort for girls." Mr. and Mrs. Peter Karppi took up residence on the 160-acre tract in the summer of 1923. Over the next five years, they built a four-room log building (30 × 22 feet), 12 cabins (14 × 15 feet), a log barn (18 × 20 feet), an icehouse, a well, and corrals and buck-and-pole fence. Karppi plowed and planted 20 acres of alfalfa, timothy, barley, and wheat. The crop was harvested, but used for grazing. In response to the question about using the property for business, Karppi wrote that "we handle summer boarders."[93]

Anita Tarbell became a partner in the operation by 1928, when the owners formed a corporation and issued stock. Tarbell worked at the ranch from 1928 until 1944. The ranch was an active dude operation from 1927 to 1962. Betty Anderson, an employee and later a co-director of the ranch, recalled that the teenage girls were usually from wealthy families who lived in urban areas in the East and Midwest. The Half Moon charged a flat rate of $500 to $600 for a two-month season, which included room, board, and a saddle horse. Pack trips were offered to backcountry areas.[94]

By the early 1960s, 27 buildings comprised the ranch: a dining hall, the owners residence, a lodge, an ice house, a rest room and shower house, a wash house, a saddle house, a loafing shed, and 15 cabins. Anita Tarbell had acquired controlling interest in the ranch in 1930. Tarbell died in July 1960 and left the ranch to Charles Guss. He sold it to the National Park Service in 1967 in exchange for a lease that he surrendered in 1972. The park removed the buildings soon after acquisition.[95]

One of the most short-lived dude ranches was the Danny Ranch, owned by Tony S. Grace. He established residence on a 160-acre homestead east of String Lake in October 1922. Grace built up a small dude ranch that consisted of a three-room log house (30 × 30 feet), two large guest cabins, store room, ice house, and barn. He cleared and cultivated 20 acres with little success. By 1927, he was content to seed the ground and allow his stock to graze on the crop. Grace wrote in his final proof papers that he rented the two cabins during the summer. About the same year Grace added two more cabins, raising the total capacity to 15 guests. The rates were $8 per day, which included room, meals, and use of a saddle horse. Grace also used the ranch as a headquarters for conducting hunting trips in the fall. The Danny Ranch was one of the smallest Jackson Hole dude ranches.

In 1930, Grace and his wife, Viola, sold the Danny Ranch to the Snake River Land Company for $24,000. After leasing the property for residential use, the Teton Lodge Company renovated it as a dude ranch. In 1934, the buildings were in poor condition, and the main house burned in 1935. In the late 1930s, however, the Jenny Lake Ranch was advertised in the Union Pacific brochure "Dude Ranches Out West." It consisted of the central lodge and dining room surrounded by one and two-room cabins capable of housing 65 dudes. Grace's gutted residence formed the nucleus of a much larger main lodge, which remains in use. Jenny Lake Lodge is operated by the Grand Teton Lodge Company today.[96]

On the eastern side of Jackson Hole where Ditch Creek enters the valley from the Mount Leidy Highlands was the old Flying V Dude Ranch. In 1928, Jack and Dollye Woodman bought the 160-acre homestead of Ransom Adams. They may have leased the property from him prior to that year as there are several references to the Flying V in the *Jackson's Hole Courier* prior to 1928. Jack Woodman described himself as a "university man, a bonded guide of wide experience, and a former U.S. Forest Ranger." Dollye Woodman was a daughter of the pioneer Budges and a registered nurse.

Accommodations at the ranch included a large 11-room main lodge, heated cabins, and floored tents for sleeping quarters. Because it had functioned originally as a working cattle ranch, Woodman promoted the Flying V as a "producing horse and cattle ranch, providing daily supplies of milk, cream, eggs and vegetables." The main lodge was one of the more impressive among dude ranches in the valley. It was a two-story, cross-shaped building with a gambrel roof covered with wood shingles. The front fa-

cade had two gable-roofed dormers on each side of the main wing.[97]

In December 1932, fire, possibly started by a banked woodstove, destroyed the lodge. The fire severely burned Florence Jones McPherson, who died several days later. She was the daughter of pioneer Joe Jones. In addition to the loss of life, this incident dealt a severe setback to the Flying V, happening in the worst period of the depression.

The rates at the Flying V were comparable to the more well known dude ranches, such as the JY and Bar BC. In the late 1920s and 1930s, the Woodmans charged both a flat rate of $550 for a two-month season, and a regular rate of $70 per week. Because of the depressed economy and the loss of the main lodge, Woodman decided to sell the dude ranch. In 1935, he signed an agreement for a deed with Gustav Koven and Paul Petzoldt to sell the ranch for $5,000. Koven made a down payment of $2,500 and agreed to pay the balance by April 2, 1936, at eight-percent interest. They conveyed the deed to Koven in 1935.[98]

Koven and Petzoldt were mountaineers, who hoped to set up a profitable dude ranch, hunting camp, and climbing headquarters at the Flying V. Few buildings existed on the property in 1935, suggesting that Woodman's operation had not been particularly successful. Paul Petzoldt recalled only a two-room guest cabin and a few outbuildings on the site. Over the next two seasons, Petzoldt helped construct three cabins, burned a dilapidated barn, and gathered logs and excavated a cellar for a new main lodge.[99]

Meanwhile, Koven formed a corporation, following the example of other dude ranchers. In 1936, he surrendered his ownership to the Flying V Ranch, Inc., a New Jersey corporation. About this time, the partners changed the name of the property to the Ramshorn. Petzoldt recalled that he suggested the name because he felt it would be more attractive to prospective dudes. A more cogent reason may have been to avoid confusion over brands, for Jack Woodman had sold his cattle, along with the Flying V brand, to the Chambers family. Thus, Koven and Petzoldt could not use the Flying V brand to iden-tify their livestock, and continued use of the name would have been confusing. Petzholdt and Koven broke off their partnership by 1937.

Koven continued to improve the ranch. The Woodward brothers constructed the new main lodge in 1937. Most of the present buildings were added in this period. Available information indicates that Koven was not active in operating the dude ranch. The Ramshorn is not listed in either the Union Pacific's "Dude Ranches Out West" published in the 1930s or the dude ranch index in the 1938 edition of Burt's *The Diary of a Dude Wrangler*. Koven leased the property for several years. Local guides Tom and Bill Jump rented the ranch, and used it as a headquarters for their hunting outfit. In 1946, Koven sold the Ramshorn to a partnership that included Greer Sugden, David Alleman, and Robert Irwin. None were local residents. Over the next five years, a succession of partners bailed out of the association, until only Sugden remained. He sold the ranch to Alvin Adams in 1951. The Sugden partnership and Adams intended to operate the Ramshorn as a dude ranch during the summer, a hunting camp in the fall, and a ski resort in the winter, hoping to squeeze revenue out of the ranch for most of the year. The only significant event occurred when the Prime Minister of Pakistan stayed at the Ramshorn as Adams's guest.[100]

However, Adams had no sooner acquired the ranch than he expressed an interest in selling it. Several reasons may have prompted this decision. As a vice-president of Pan American Airlines, Adams found himself too busy to devote time to the Ramshorn; further, the cost of maintaining the ranch proved expensive, more than Adams expected or wished to pay. After several attempts to sell the property and prolonged negotiations with the National Park Service, Adams sold the Ramshorn to the federal government in 1956 for $68,000. In 1958, the park issued a concession permit for the Ramshorn to Katie Starratt, who had managed the Old Elbo as a dude ranch since the 1940s. She took the name and brand to the Ramshorn, rechristening it the Elbo. Starratt operated the new Elbo as a modest but successful dude ranch. After Katie Starratt died in 1974, the National Park Service issued a special use permit to the Grand Teton Environ-

mental Education Center to operate the Teton Science School at the ranch.[101]

In early 1927, the *Jackson's Hole Courier* reported that Jack Turner was building a new dude ranch on Spread Creek in the upper end of the valley. John S. and Maytie Turner were Utahans, who vacationed periodically in Jackson Hole and became attached to the country. Their favorite campsite was situated in the forest above the Bill Jump and Jack Fee homesteads. In 1926, Jump was in the hospital, unable to care for his homestead. Seeing an opportunity, John Turner sold his land in Utah and bought the 160-acre property from Jump for $1,000. The Turners hoped to farm the land, raising potatoes, but gave up because of the short, unreliable growing season. Instead, they decided to raise cattle and build a few guest cabins for hunters. With this modest beginning, the Turners created the Triangle X Dude Ranch. Two years later, they bought the adjacent Jack Fee homestead from R. E. Miller for $3,655. The ranch totaled 320 acres at this time. About 1928, the ranch consisted of a large rustic headquarters and six dude cabins capable of housing 20 dudes. The rates were $5 per day.[102]

During this period, the family built up the ranch, despite indications of economic trouble. When the Snake River Land Company began purchasing land in 1928, the Triangle X was included in the purchase schedule. In 1929, John Turner and Harold Fabian, a company vice president, began negotiations. Fabian suggested to Tony Grace of the Danny Ranch that he sell his property "and concentrate the joint efforts of himself and Turner on building up the Turner place." Fabian expressed the willingness of the company to lease the Triangle X and any additional land the two dude ranchers thought necessary for a "successful operation." Grace lost interest in the partnership when one of the Turner daughters, Marian, married, his real motive for joining the Triangle X. John Turner wrote to Fabian that Grace "got sore" over the marriage. A month later, Tony Grace informed Fabian that he decided not to enter into a partnership with Turner. In July 1929, John and Maytie Turner sold to the Snake River Land Company for $20,000. The company leased the property to Turner in 1930 "to occupy and use as a cattle ranch, farm and dude ranch." The rental charge was one-third of all crops grown. A year later, the company and Turner agreed to alter the lease; the company charged ten percent of gross receipts as a rental fee.[103]

The elder Turner and his sons operated the property as a dude ranch through 1935. They charged $50 per week for room, board, and exclusive use of a saddle horse. In 1936, John S. "Dad" Turner and his wife left the ranch and moved to Turpin Meadows on the Buffalo Fork, buying the old Neal place. They started the Turpin Meadow Lodge, running it as a dude camp and hunting camp until 1952, when they sold the property. Meanwhile, the eldest son, John C. Turner, secured a lease to the Triangle X in 1936 from the Snake River Land Company and later from its successor, the Jackson Hole Preserve. After the Triangle X was incorporated into the new Grand Teton National Park in 1950, John C. Turner and Louise Turner (later Berschy) secured a concession permit to operate the ranch in 1953. Today, John C. Turner's sons continue to run the ranch, the only concessioner-operated dude ranch in the National Park System. With the closing of the White Grass in 1985, the Triangle X enjoys the distinction of being the longest-operating dude ranch in Jackson Hole.[104]

The Circle H Ranch was a small dude ranch situated west of the Snake River, not far from the White Grass. In the 1920s, H. H. and Ethyl Harrison started a small dude ranch on land homesteaded by Louis Joy and Billy Grant. About 1927, the Circle H had seven guest cabins and a "pleasant central lodge, containing dining and recreation rooms . . . tastefully furnished and ornamented with trophies of the hunt." The Circle H was a working hay ranch with its "own horses, dairy cows, and garden, insuring abundant fresh milk and vegetables on the table." It housed 14 dudes. Rates were $12 per day for room, board, and a saddle horse.[105]

It was a short-lived operation, for the Harrisons sold the ranch to John C. Dilworth in 1928 for $20,000. Dilworth did not operate the Circle H as a dude ranch. In 1945, Harry Barker Sr., bought the Circle H, revived the dude ranch and turned it into a successful enterprise. In 1966, Harry Jr. and

Margaret Barker sold the Circle H to the National Park Service in exchange for a 30-year or lifetime estate.[106]

In 1924, a young woman named Eva Sanford rode in a Model T over the graveled Togwotee Pass road into Jackson Hole, escorted by her parents. From Douglas, Wyoming, Sanford came to the valley to teach at Elk, the small country school located between Spread Creek and the Buffalo Fork. She taught at Elk for three years, boarding with the Cunninghams and the Harolds. In 1927, she learned of an available tract of public land located south of Spread Creek. Seizing the opportunity, she filed entry papers in May and established residence in November. In that same year, Sanford married Fred Topping, a middle-aged widower. Together, they built up a hunting lodge and dude ranch at their homestead.[107]

Topping had built a good reputation as a cowhand and hunting guide. Born in Quebec in 1883, he came west at the age of 24. He and his partner, George Greenwood, had settled in Wyoming in 1910. Working at Lander and, later, Pinedale, Topping came to Jackson Hole in 1912, bringing horses over Union Pass for the Frontier Days rodeo. Liking the area, he took up a homestead in the Spread Creek area in 1913. Topping developed a hunting guide business, working through both the White Grass and Sheffield's at Moran. In 1916, he married Doris Coffin, who died of influenza during the 1918 epidemic. He sold his homestead to Rudy Harold that year.[108]

In 1927, newlyweds Fred and Eva Topping moved into an existing residence on her 120 acres, which indicates that the parcel had been relinquished by a previous entrant. They cultivated 19 acres, grazed 20 head of cattle and horses, and started a fox and mink farm. However, because Executive Order 4685 had withdrawn public lands from settlement they experienced some difficulty in securing a patent. The entry was protested and investigated in 1930. The General Land Office examiner found the following improvements: four log cabins of various dimensions, three small chicken coops (possibly the fox farm), a log barn, a cow barn, a log garage, a partially constructed cabin, and more than

two miles of buck-and-pole fence. The General
Land Office concluded the Toppings had complied
with the homestead laws and approved the entry.
Eva Topping secured a patent in 1931.[109]

During the depression, Topping worked at various dude ranches as a guide, while Eva Topping kept
up the homestead. The dude business started as an
afterthought, when hunters camped on the property.
Soon Eva Topping began providing meals for a fee.
By 1937, they had decided to go into the dude business full time. The Union Pacific listed the ranch in
its brochure. Called the Moosehead, it was listed under "Camps–Guides–Lodges–Resorts" rather than
dude ranches, because it was not an "operating stock
or grain ranch." Accommodations consisted of a:
"dining room and kitchen in one building; a ranch
lobby; separate sleeping cabins of one and two
rooms. Hot and cold tub and shower baths. Mrs.
Topping is hostess and her garden and poultry department are show places. Ranch has its own dairy."
Activities included horseback riding, fishing, and
hunting trips, while the rates were $35 per week for
room, board, and a saddle horse. Room and board
cost $25 per week. The Toppings continued to ex-
pand the ranch until there were accommodations for
40 guests.[110]

In 1932, Eva Topping became the postmistress
of the Elk Post Office, which moved to the
Moosehead. The post office was located here until
its closure in 1967. At the end of that year, the Toppings sold to John Mettler, who continues to operate
the Moosehead as a dude ranch.[111]

The Bear Paw, founded by Coulter Huyler, was
another dude ranch dating from the 1930s. Huyler
was a dude from Connecticut, who first came to
Jackson Hole to hunt in 1925 or 1926. Taken with
the valley, he began looking to buy a summer retreat.
South of the JY, the homestead of Eliza Seaton
caught his eye. Huyler purchased the property in
1927 and, for the next decade, used it as a private
retreat for family and friends.[112]

In 1935 or 1936, Huyler started a small exclusive dude ranch that housed 16 guests. According to
his son, Jack Huyler, the depression forced Coulter
Huyler to make this decision. The accommodations
consisted of a main cabin, three double cabins with

baths, and two large one-room cabins. Influenced by
the standardization of lodging in the 1930s, Huyler
furnished the cabins with twin Simmons beds. He
placed the ranch in charge of Mr. and Mrs. Jack
Neal, both westerners. Neal was an experienced wrangler and guide, while his wife was a trained nurse. Activities included horseback riding, fishing, swimming,
mountain climbing, camping, motoring, and big
game hunting in season. The rates were $77 per week
with references and reservations necessary.[113]

The Bear Paw continued to operate during the
Second World War. Margaret Murie helped manage the ranch for two seasons, which she described
so well in *Wapiti Wilderness*. In this period, as many
as 40 dudes stayed at the ranch. Murie recalled
that the Huylers maintained the highest standards
of fine, simple, western life for their guests. In
1949, they sold the Bear Paw to the Jackson Hole
Preserve.[114]

Not far from the JY was the R Lazy S. In 1912,
Owen Wister, the author of *The Virginian*, bought
the homestead of Elsie James, intending to use the
property as a private retreat. The Wister family
stayed at the JY for four weeks while they constructed a primitive two-story cabin at the homestead. In mid-summer, they moved in, even though
the cabin was unfinished. Cots and furniture built of
packing crates served Wister, his wife, five children,
a German governess, and a houseman named Lloyd
Cook. They lived in the house for six to eight weeks.
It was the only time Wister resided on the property
for, in 1913, Wister's wife died giving birth. Stricken
with grief, Wister never returned to Jackson Hole.
The house stood empty for the next several years, until Wister sold to the Roeslers and Chauncey Spears
in 1920.[115]

Although considered a dude ranch according to
local tradition, the R Lazy S was not operated as
one in those years. In 1928, Chauncey Spears added
40 acres to the ranch through a timber and stone
entry. Roeslers and Spears sold to Robert
McConaughy in 1929, who started the dude ranch
operation. McConaughy sold the ranch to the Jackson Hole Preserve in 1947, but continued to lease it
until 1972, seven years after Rockefeller had donated
the property to the United States. The buildings

were removed after 1972. The McConaughys shifted their operation to the Aspen Ranch north of Wilson, Wyoming.[116]

Another property known as a dude ranch, but never advertised or promoted as such, was the Trail Ranch. Located one mile north of the White Grass, the ranch consisted of two homesteads totaling 260 acres. Harry C. Clissold homesteaded 160 acres in a meadow in the midst of lodgepole forest in 1916. Clissold testified that he built a log cabin (20 × 20 feet), barn, milk house, and ice house. In 1919, he plowed 20 acres and planted timothy and alsike clover. Harvesting only seven to eight tons of hay, Clissold converted the field to pasture. In September 1922, Clifford Ward and his wife filed an entry on 100 acres next to Clissold's parcel. Ward constructed a log house and a shed and cleared two acres for a garden.[117]

Clissold sold his ranch to J. Steven Conover Jr., in 1929 and moved to Jackson. Conover operated it as a dude ranch, hosting ten guests at rates of $55 per week per person. Conover sold to the Snake River Land Company in 1939. A man named Wesley leased the property from the company and the National Park Service until 1971. The park allowed the buildings to deteriorate until 1984, then demolished the remainder.[118]

The Four Lazy F, located one mile north of Moose, is a good example of a family retreat patterned after a western dude ranch. A Philadelphia dude named Bryant Mears filed an entry on the land in 1914 and took up residence in the winter of 1915. Improvements consisted of two log cabins, a small barn, a well, a ditch, fencing, and 18 acres cleared and cultivated. In 1916, he planted eight acres of oats and barley and harvested 14 tons of hay. One year later, he planted 18 acres of winter wheat, but harvested none of it. Mears had little time to develop what was then called the Sun Star Ranch for he was absent for long periods of time, first to marry in 1916–1917, then to serve in the army from 1917–1919. In 1927, Edward Mears sold the ranch to William Frew, a wealthy dude from Pittsburgh.

The Frews invested a considerable amount of money to build the ranch, patterning it after dude ranches. They named the ranch the Four Lazy F, the

brand for the Four Lazy Frews. The family used it as a retreat rather than an active dude ranch. In 1967, Emily Frew Oliver sold the ranch to the United States, retaining a life estate. For a number of years, the Frews and Olivers have accepted paying guests, but at the family's invitation only.[119]

Tourist enterprises existed that were called dude ranches, though such usage requires a loose definition. The Elbo Ranch, Leek's Camp, and Ben Sheffield's outfit at Moran were not dude ranches, even though they shared some similarities with dude ranches. The 1927 Union Pacific brochure listed both the Elbo and Leek's Camp as dude ranches. The Elbo and Leek's were listed under this heading based on the definition of a dude ranch "as home operating stock or grain ranches with accommodations for guests on advance reservations."[120]

The Elbo was the brainchild of Chester Goss, a California resident. Goss initiated his plan by purchasing 115 acres from James Manges in April 1926. The following May and June, he purchased the homesteads of Frank Bessette and Alfred Bessette. In addition, Goss homesteaded 11.6 acres adjacent to the western boundary of the Manges homestead. Possessing more than 423 acres, Goss and his partners, J. M. Goss and James G. "Gibb" Scott, began building tourist accommodations.[121]

In May 1926, the *Jackson's Hole Courier* reported that a store and cabins were being constructed and plans underway to build a racetrack and ball diamond. In July, the Elbo opened for business. Accommodations consisted of four-room cabins with hot water, baths, and toilets and one and two-room cabins with hot water, shower, and tubs for every six rooms. Goss built a store and gas station along the road to cater to tourist traffic, but the completed rodeo grounds located south of Timbered Island was the most conspicuous development. The Elbo rodeo grounds included a large grandstand, a one-half mile racetrack, a parking area, and concession stands under the grandstand. He also built small "tourist cabins" to cater to overnight traffic. Goss patterned the Elbo after western dude ranches, by raising breeding horses, requiring reservations, providing room, board, and use of saddle horses to dudes, and constructing rustic log cabins. However, cottage cabins, rodeo grounds, and a roadside store and gas station were not characteristic of bonafide dude ranches. Goss even installed a large sign at the Elbo, proclaiming it the "home of the Hollywood cowboy." While patterned after dude ranches, the Elbo was not in practice a dude ranch.[122]

In 1929, Goss sold the Elbo to the Snake River Land Company for $64,000. The company allowed the National Park Service to use some of the buildings for employee housing in the 1920s and 1930s. In 1942, Harry Espenscheid leased the property and operated a dude ranch. Katie Starratt leased the ranch from the late 1940s until 1958, when the Park Service moved her to the Ramshorn. The remaining buildings were removed in the early 1970s.[123]

Stephen Leek and his sons, Holly and Lester, developed Leek's Camp at Jackson Lake in 1927. It was an expansion of a hunting camp approved by the Forest Service in 1925. Unlike the majority of dude ranches and resorts, Leek's Camp depended on public lands for its existence. Leek secured a special use permit to 1.44 acres of forest land "for the purpose of maintaining a resort for the accommodation of tourists including hotel accommodations, store and gas station." Working vigorously, the Leek family had the camp ready to operate in the summer of 1927.[124]

As the permit suggests, the Leeks intended the operation to be a resort rather than a dude ranch. However, they set up a boys' camp, patterned after dude ranches. *The Midwest Review* reported the establishment of the Teton Camp for Boys and Leek's Camp in its July-August 1927 edition. According to the report, Leek was building "a series of lodges and cabins to accommodate parties of boys and dudes." Partners in the venture were the Leeks, Dillon Wallace, Arthur G. Timm, Dr. Thomas S. Dedrick, and Willis Howie. The article listed boating, fishing, hunting, pack and hiking trips as activities. In addition, the Leeks and Dillon Wallace set up a wildlife studies program for the boys. While the camp promised to be one of the "great popular resorts," it was not a dude ranch. By this time, the camp had a new central lodge and dining room, surrounded by cabins and tent cabins. Hunting and fishing were emphasized as the brochure boasted excellent trout fishing

with catches weighing 10 to 20 pounds. The rates were $5 per day for meals, cabin, and a boat. Between June 15 and August 17, Dillon Wallace conducted a boys camp for youths aged 14 through 19. Reservations were limited to 25 boys, and the cost, including transportation from Rock Springs, was $610."[125]

By 1934, Leek had turned the operation over to his sons. After Lester Leek died in that year, Holly Leek operated the lodge as a hunting and fishing camp. The Park Service issued Leek permits after the creation of Jackson Hole National Monument in 1943. After the war, Holly Leek sold his permit to Dr. N. E. Morad, who formed a corporation called Leek's Lodge, Inc. Morad ran the camp until 1965, when he sold the permit to Keith Wright. The new owner failed to pay off the loan, and the concession reverted to Morad. The permit went through two more owners until the National Park Service bought the permit in 1975 and, two years later, turned the operation over to Signal Mountain Lodge. Leek's Lodge was listed in the National Register of Historic Places in 1975 because of its architectural significance and association with pioneer and conservationist Stephen Leek. Most of the remaining buildings were removed.[126]

Sheffield's Teton Lodge at Moran and the Jackson Lake Lodge (Amoretti Inn) resembled dude ranches, but were early resorts that tapped increasing tourist traffic to Yellowstone. Moran was an ideal location for accommodations, situated between Jackson and the south entrance of Yellowstone, and near the junction of the road to Dubois and Lander to the east. Flagg Ranch, built by Ed Sheffield, was located just south of Yellowstone on the highway.

In the Moran area, two small resorts were started in the 1920s, both patterned after dude ranches, the Cross and Crescent, and the Flying Diamond. M. R. Grimmesey built the Cross and Crescent dude outfit on land leased at Moran. A small operation, the Cross and Crescent consisted of a lodge and three cabins capable of housing seven dudes. Services included room, meals, saddle horses and guided pack, hunting, boating, and auto trips. A short-lived enterprise, the Cross and Crescent seems to have operated in the late 1920s. The Flying Dia-

The Episcopal Church dedicated the Chapel of the Transfiguration near Moose in 1925. It was well attended by guests of nearby dude ranches. *Jackson Hole Historical Society and Museum*

mond was the registered brand of John W. Hogan, who operated the small dude ranch in conjunction with the Snake River Fox Ranch, known locally as Hogan's fox farm. Hogan purchased the property from homesteader William T. Carter in 1924. Around 1926, Hogan built the log lodge, which serves today as Park Service housing. In addition, he built three cabins to house up to 12 guests. The rates were $6 per day for room and board, and another $3 per day for a saddle horse. Hogan also outfitted pack trips and provided licensed guides for hunters.[127]

Outside of the present boundaries of Grand Teton National Park, a number of prominent dude ranches were established. Located south of Wilson, Wyoming, along Fish Creek was the Crescent H. Founded by Edward Brown in the 1920s, it could house 50 dudes. In 1927, Brown built a large lodge and dining room (40 × 60 feet), along with "commodious" log cabins. Brown also managed the Warbonnet, a boys' ranch associated with the Crescent Lazy H. The Red Rock Ranch, situated up the Gros Ventre valley along Crystal Creek, was originally a cattle ranch. W. P Redmond, a Jackson Hole pioneer, started a dude operation in the 1920s. The outfit was small, accommodating 20 guests in log cabins and tent houses. The Red Rock remains a working cattle and dude ranch today, having weathered a number of owners, lessees, and hard times. At Kelly, Wyoming, the Teton Valley Ranch continues to operate as a

boys ranch. Founded by David and Cornelia Abercrombie in 1927, it was originally known as the Gros Ventre Ranch, then the A Lazy D. The Wilson family purchased the ranch and converted it to a boys ranch around 1935. Other dude ranches included the Brooks Lake Lodge east of Togwotee Pass, the Skyline Ranch on the Snake River south of Moose, the Aspen Ranch north of Wilson, the Teton Pass Ranch west of Wilson, Elizabeth Woolsey's Trail Creek Ranch at the foot of Teton Pass, and the V₁ Bar V₁ located on the Hoback near Bondurant.[128]

During the Second World War, dude ranchers adapted to survive. They reduced ranch size to lower costs, rationed resources, and adjusted to the labor shortages caused by the war. In some cases, dudes themselves provided labor. Demand for foodstuffs made it attractive to raise cattle again; thus, many dude ranches began raising cattle and other foods to contribute to the war effort. Further, the Dude Ranchers' Association promoted dude ranches as retreats for weary soldiers and civilians involved in the war effort.[129] The owners of the Bear Paw, the Huylers, solved their labor shortage by persuading Mardy Murie to accept the job of housekeeper. Her daughter worked as a waitress, while her youngest son performed odd chores. Volunteer work for the Red Cross and at St. John's Hospital had failed to take Mardy's mind off of her oldest son and others who served in the military, so she entered the work force like so many other women during the war. In *Wapiti Wilderness,* she recalled the effort to keep the ranch going despite wartime shortages.[130]

In general, dude ranching has changed significantly and declined since 1945. The automobile emerged in the 1920s as a force of change, radically altering American society in ways no other technological advance in this century has duplicated. Cars were the first of many challenges dude ranchers confronted. Since the golden age of dude ranching, the western landscape has changed significantly. Developments to accommodate a larger population, notably urban centers, suburbs, increased industry, and highways have altered the landscape so important to the dude ranch setting.

The expectations of dudes have also changed over the years. Rising demand for modern conveniences evolved as dude ranching developed. By the 1930s, many Jackson Hole dude wranglers provided modern bathrooms and electric lights. In his preface to the 1938 edition of *The Diary of a Dude Wrangler,* Struthers Burt noted that dude ranching had changed as had Americans. In 1914, "we weren't one quarter as bathtub conscious, as twin-bed conscious, and as food conscious as we are today. The wise dude-wrangler has met this increased consciousness." He further noted that dudes enjoyed fresh fruit such as cantaloupe every day; in his day "you speedily forgot what a melon looked like." Dude ranches followed the trend to standardize amenities. For example, early automobile cottage camps advertised conveniences such as "Beauty-rest" mattresses; in the late 1930s Cornelia Abercrombie listed Simmons Beautyrest mattresses on each bed at the A Lazy D. The rustic simplicity of the first dude ranches could not survive the evolving expectations of guests.[131]

Further, Americans' tastes and demands in recreation have changed significantly. In general, rather than participate in vigorous outdoor activities, people have become more sedentary. As a result, horseback riding has declined as an activity. Trips tend to be shorter, and only the adventurous are interested in pack trips today. In contrast, cocktail lounges and modern pools have become typical at dude or guest ranches. In the 1970s and 1980s, the White Grass sported a game room in the loft of the barn, replete

with a pool table, juke box, and pinball machine. The popularity of motorized recreation has exploded in the last 30 years. Today, the Triangle X offers snowmobiling for winter guests. Rafting the Snake River was unheard of in the 1920s; today dude ranches offer float trips. In the early years, dudes were more self-reliant in choosing activities. Over time, dudes, like most tourists, have come to expect to be entertained.

Other factors influenced the decline of dude ranching. In Jackson Hole, the value of land has made it almost impossible for cattle and dude ranchers to resist selling out to developers. The properties have been either subdivided or converted to elaborate resorts. In some cases, the family dude ranch has succumbed because of the reluctance of children to take over the operation. Taxes and government policies and regulations have been, at best, neutral and at times hindered dude ranch operations.[132]

Today dude ranching remains a small yet stable part of the tourist industry in Jackson Hole. Some ranches have retained distinct characteristics and preserve the dude ranch legacy begun by the JY, Bar BC, and White Grass. Historically, dude ranching left a strong mark on the valley and, from a broader perspective, Jackson Hole was an important center for western dude ranching.

Notes

1. Struthers Burt, *Diary,* p. 48.

2. *Jackson's Hole Courier,* April 3, 1924, and September 15, 1932; University of Wyoming Archives, American Heritage Center, Charles Roundy Collection, 3550, Box 1; and Lawrence R. Borne, *Dude Ranching: A Complete History* (Albuquerque, NM: University of New Mexico Press, 1983), p. 27.

3. Edith M. Schultz Thompson and William Leigh Thompson, *Beaver Dick, the Honor and the Heartbreak: An Historical Biography of Richard Leigh* (Laramie, WY: Jelm Mountain Press, 1982); and Borne, *Dude Ranching,* pp. 9–10.

3. Saylor, *Jackson Hole,* p. 116.

4. William A. Baillie-Grohman, *Camps in the Rockies* (New York: Charles Scribner's Sons, 1882), pp. 208–209.

5. Freeman Tilden, *Following the Frontier with F. Jay Haynes, Pioneer Photographer of the West* (New York: Alfred A. Knopf, 1964), pp. 115–139; Owen Wister, *Owen Wister Out West: His Journals and Letters,* ed. Fanny Kemble Wister (Chicago: University of Chicago Press, 1958), pp. 52–58; and Borne, *Dude Ranching,* pp. 94–95.

6. Borne, *Dude Ranching,* p. 19.

7. Homestead Patents: 578666, M.S. Burt, 1916; 799046, Harold Hammond, 1920; 1014042, Buster Estes, 1927; 1037758, Peter Karppi, Jr., 1928; 1010872, Tony Grace, 1927.

8. Struthers Burt, *Diary,* pp. 48–53.

9. Borne, *Dude Ranching,* pp. 49–50.

10. Ibid., p. 51.

11. Roundy Collection, 3550, Box 1, University of Wyoming Archives.

12. Borne, *Dude Ranching,* p. 4.

13. Ibid., p. 9.

14. Ibid., pp. 19–22, 29–30.

15. Ibid., p. 27.

16. Ibid., pp. 31–37.

17. *Jackson's Hole Courier,* January 19, 1932.

18. Ibid.; Roundy Collection 3550, Box 2, University of Wyoming Archives; Brown, *Souvenir History,* p. 9; and Homestead Patents, Desert Land Entry 187, Lander, Harvey Glidden, 1901; Homestead Certificate 1245, Evanston, A. A. Adams Kiskadden, 1907; and 138274, Kiskadden, 1907.

19. Borne, *Dude Ranching,* pp. 39–40; Struthers Burt, *Diary,* p. 90; Nathaniel Burt, *Jackson Hole Journal,* p. 7; Office of the Clerk and Recorder, Teton County, Mortgage Record Book, pp. 103–104, Maxwell S. and Katherine N. Burt and Horace Carncross to Philadelphia Trust Co., May 1, 1917; and *Jackson's Hole Courier,* July 24, 1917.

20. Borne, *Dude Ranching,* p. 46.

21. "Dude Ranches Out West," ca. 1927.

22. Ibid.; Nathaniel Burt, *Jackson Hole Journal,* p. 52; and interview with Frank Galey by John Daugherty, February 3, 1984.

23. "Dude Ranches Out West," ca. 1927.

24. Nathaniel Burt, *Jackson Hole Journal,* p. 7; El Paso *Times,* August 19, 1923, Horace Albright Papers, 1923–1927, Yellowstone National Park Archives; Borne, *Dude Ranching,* pp. 304; "Dude Ranches Out West," ca. 1927, p. 9; and Struthers Burt, *Diary,* p. 50. Lawrence Borne found a dearth of information regarding the composition of dudes.

25. Struthers Burt, *Diary,* p. 148.

26. Warren James Belasco, *Americans on the Road: From Autocamp to Motel, 1910–1945* (Cambridge: MIT Press, 1981), p. 48; "Dude Ranches Out West" ca. 1927; "The Bar BC Ranch, Rates, Outfit, Etc.," pamphlet, Bosler Family collection 5850, Box 5, File 16, University of Wyoming Archives; and Borne, *Dude Ranching,* p. 112.

27. Struthers Burt, *Diary,* p. 55; "Dude Ranches Out West," ca. 1927; and Nellie Van Derveer, "Wyoming Folklore and Customs, Teton County," Dude Ranches, WPA Subject File 1448, State of Wyoming, Archives, Museums, and Historical Department.

28. Wister, *Wister Out West,* pp. xv–xvi; *Jackson Hole Guide,* September 9, 1978; and Struthers Burt, *Diary,* pp. 130–131.

29. "Dude Ranches Out West," ca. 1927.

30. Ibid.

31. Ibid.

32. Wister, *Wister Out West,* pp. xv–xvi; Struthers Burt, *Diary,* p. 4; *Jackson Hole Guide,* February 23, 1967; Homestead Patents: 799048, Frank Bessette, 1920; 824385, Alfred Bessette, 1921; and 1035980, Joe LePage, 1928; *Jackson's Hole Courier,* July 30, 1925; and *Jackson Hole Guide,* December 3, 1970.

33. Struthers Burt, *Diary,* pp. 180–181; interview with Walt Callahan by Jo Ann Byrd; #6, in "Last of Old West;" and *Jackson's Hole Courier,* July 12, 1917, May 31, 1917, July 1, 1920, July 26, 1917, and November 2, 1922.

34. Struthers Burt, *Diary,* pp. 91–92; "Dude Ranches Out West," ca. 1927; and *Jackson's Hole Courier,* November 29, 1928.

35. Struthers Burt, *Diary,* p. 91.

36. Harold P. Fabian Papers, Rockefeller Archive Center, Box 61, File 574, Real Estate-Huyler, 1943–1949, Inventory, Bearpaw Ranch.

37. "Dude Ranches Out West" ca. 1927; and *Jackson's Hole Courier,* March 5, 1925.

38. Borne, *Dude Ranching,* pp. 59–69, 80–81.

39. Larson, *History of Wyoming,* pp. 423–425, 443–446; and Borne, *Dude Ranching,* pp. 59–69, 80–81.

40. "Dude Ranches Out West," ca. 1927; Kenneth Chorley Papers, Rockefeller Archive Center, IVA3A, Box 21, File 176, "Dude Ranches Out West," pamphlet, ca. 1930, Union Pacific Railroad; "Dude Ranches Out West," ca. 1937, Union Pacific Railroad, Wyoming State Archives; Fabian Papers, Rockefeller Archive Center, Box 16, File 144, Hammond, 1929–1939; Nathaniel Burt, *Jackson Hole Journal,* p. 97; and Teton County Records, Mixed Records, Book 3, p. 389, John F. Woodman to Gustav Koven and Paul Petzoldt, Agreement for Deed, October 2, 1935.

41. Fabian Papers, Rockefeller Archive Center, Box 17, File 153, Elbo Ranch, 1932; Box 20, File 205, Elbo Ranch, 1929–1932; Box 22, File 244, Grace, 1928–1936; Box 22, File 232, Turner, 1929–1941; Box 21, File 229, Hogan, 1929–1935; Box 19, Files 183–184, JY Ranch, 1901–1945; Box 20, File 187, Bar BC, 1929–1940.

42. Homestead Patents: Homestead Cert. 560, Evanston, Louis Joy, 1906; Desert Land Cert. 748, Evanston, Joy, 1905; and *Jackson's Hole Courier,* June 2, 1932.

43. Struthers Burt, *Diary,* pp. 42–43 and 65.

44. Ibid., p. 64.

45. Wister, *Wister Out West,* pp. xiv-xvii; and Struthers Burt, *Diary,* p. 79.

46. Wister, *Wister Out West,* p. xvii.

47. Struthers Burt, *Diary,* pp. 78–102.

48. Teton County Records, Mixed Records, Book 1, p. 257, JY to H. S. A. Stewart, Lease, November 17, 1916.

49. *Jackson's Hole Courier,* September 25, 1924, and November 13, 1924.

50. "Dude Ranches Out West," ca. 1927; and "Tourism in Jackson Hole," *Midwest Review* 8 (July-August 1927):32–34.

51. "Dude Ranches Out West," ca. 1930, pp. 15–16.

52. Fabian Papers, Rockefeller Archive Center, Box 19, Files 183–184, JY Ranch, 1901–1945; *Jackson's Hole Courier,* June 2, 1932.

53. Struthers Burt, *Diary,* pp. 65 and 86–87.

54. Ibid., pp. 93–96.

55. Nathaniel Burt, *Jackson Hole Journal,* p. 7; and Struthers Burt, *Diary,* pp. 15 and 48.

56. Struthers Burt, *Diary,* p. 97.

57. Homestead Patents: 577944, Horace Carncross, 1916; 578666, Maxwell S. Burt, 1916; 584624, Burt 1916; and 584625, Carncross, 1916; and Struthers Burt, *Diary,* p. 88.

58. *Jackson's Hole Courier,* December 7, 1916, and July 26, 1917; and Teton County Records, Mortgage Records Book 3, p. 103, M. S. and Katherine Burt to Philadelphia Trust Co., mortgage, May 1, 1917; Book 3, p. 106, Horace Carncross to Philadelphia Trust Co., mortgage, May 1, 1917; see Mortgage Release Book 1, pp. 88–89.

59. Struthers Burt, *Diary,* pp. 90–91.

60. Teton County Records, Deed Records, Book 1, p. 307, Warranty Deed, Struthers and Katherine Burt and Horace Carncross to Bar BC Ranches, Inc., December 5, 1921; *Jackson's Hole Courier,* October 12, 1953 and January 10, 1929; "The Bar BC Ranch, Rates, Outfit, Etc.," Bosler Family Collection, 5850, University of Wyoming Archives; and *Jackson Hole Guide,* August 16, 1964.

61. Teton County Records, Deed Record Book A, p. 99, Warranty Deed, George Tucker Bispham to Bar BC Ranches, June 10, 1924; Deed Record Book A, p. 74, Harold and Marie Hammond to Bar BC Ranches, Warranty Deed, April 21, 1924; see Deed Record Book 3, pp. 536–537.

62. *Jackson's Hole Courier,* May 10, 1917, September 3, 1914, February 24, 1916; May 3, 1917, February 10, 1916; and Felicia Gizycka, "Jackson Hole, 1916–1965: A Reminiscence," *Vogue* (April 1, 1965):203.

63. Gizycka, "Jackson Hole, 1916–1965," p.203; *Jackson's Hole Courier,* January 10, 1929, January 27, 1949, and May 1, 1941; *Jackson Hole News,* July 30, 1970; Interview with Walt Callahan, #6, in "Last of Old West."

64. Nathaniel Burt, *Jackson Hole Journal,* pp. 7–9.

65. "Dude Ranches Out West, ca. 1927; and *Jackson's Hole Courier,* July 30, 1925, and June 14, 1928.

66. *Jackson's Hole Courier,* July 4, 1918, July 14, 1927, March 8, 1928, and January 10, 1929.

67. Struthers Burt to Horace Albright, July 18, 1927, Albright Papers, 1923–1927, Yellowstone Archives.

68. Chorley Papers, Rockefeller Archive Center, Box 16, File 133, Bar BC Ranch, 1929–1942. Struthers Burt to Kenneth Chorley, March 4, 1929; Fabian Papers, Rockefeller Archive Center, Box 20, File 187, Bar BC, 1929–1940.

69. Fabian Papers, Rockefeller Archive Center, Box 20, File 187, Bar BC 1924–1940, Struthers Burt to Harold Fabian, January 3, 1935; Chorley Papers, Rockefeller Archive Center, Box 16, File 133, Bar BC Ranch, 1929–1942, S. Burt to K. Chorley, September 20, 1937; and Nathaniel Burt, *Jackson Hole Journal,* pp. 78–79.

70. Fabian Papers, Rockefeller Archive Center, Box 20, File 187, Bar BC, 1929–1940, Bar BC Ranches to Frank W. Crocker, sub-lease, May 26, 1938; Bar BC Ranches to E. Webster Harrison, sub-lease, May 7, 1941; *Jackson's Hole Courier,* July 27, 1939, and November 7, 1959; and Federal Records Center, Denver, CO, Grand Teton National Park, 217320 Individual Fire Report, November 7, 1959.

71. *Jackson's Hole Courier,* October 12, 1953; and *Jackson Hole Guide,* August 6, 1964.

72. Corse, Tract 04-130, Bar BC Ranches Inc., to T. H. and Margaretta F. Conderman, Lease, September 30, 1950, Land Files, Grand Teton National Park.

73. Homestead Patents: 799046, Harold Hammond, 1920; 902573, G. Tucker Bispham, 1922; interview with Frank Galey by Jo Ann Byrd, #12, in "Last of Old West Series," *Jackson Hole Guide,* April 30, 1981; and *Jackson's Hole Courier,* June 8, 1916, and July 17, 1930.

74. Homestead Patents: 799046, Hammond, 1920; 902573, Bispham, 1922; and *Jackson Hole Guide,* July 19, 1973, and September 24, 1964.

75. Teton County Records, Deed Record Book A, p. 99, George Tucker Bispham to Bar BC Ranches Inc., Warranty Deed, June 10, 1924; Deed Record Book A, p. 74, Harold and Marie Hammond to Bar BC Ranches Inc., Warranty Deed, April 21, 1924; and *Jackson's Hole Courier,* February 26, 1925, December 3, 1925, April 7, 1927, and April 28, 1927.

76. *Jackson's Hole Courier,* July 7, 1927; and "Dude Ranches Out West," ca. 1927.

77. Teton County Records, Deed Record Book 3, p. 536, Bar BC Ranches to Harold Hammond, Warranty Deed, November 15, 1928; Deed Record Book 3, p. 537, Bar BC to G. T. Bispham, Warranty Deed, November 16, 1928; Deed Record Book 3, p. 557, G. T. Bispham to H. Hammond, Warranty Deed, December 19, 1928; *Jackson's Hole Courier,* November 1, 1928, and April 14, 1949; and Nathaniel Burt, *Jackson Hole Journal,* pp. 118–119.

78. *Jackson's Hole Courier,* July 17, 1930; "Dude Ranches Out West," ca. 1937; *Jackson Hole Guide,* August 8, 1973; and interview with Frank Galey by Jo Ann Byrd, #12, "Last of Old West Series."

79. Interview with Frank Galey, #12, "Last of Old West;" *Jackson Hole Guide,* September 24, 1964, and August 8, 1973; and *Jackson's Hole Courier,* July 20, 1939.

80. Ibid.; Teton County Records, Deed Record Book 11, p. 10, Frank Galey to the United States of America, Warranty Deed, December 17, 1956. There is some question whether the ranch operated at all during the war.

81. *Jackson Hole Guide,* June 11, 1964; interview with Margaret Murie by John Daugherty, February 13, 1984, tape, Grand Teton National Park; and *Jackson Hole News,* January 17, 1979.

82. Interview with Margaret Murie; *Jackson's Hole Courier,* July 27, 1922, August 7, 1924, and October 15, 1925; Homestead Patent 1014042, Buster Estes, 1927; and *Jackson Hole Guide,* June 11, 1964.

83. "Dude Ranches Out West," ca. 1927; "Dude Ranches Out West," ca. 1930; and *Jackson's Hole Courier,* July 7, 1927.

84. "Dude Ranches Out West," ca. 1937; Interview with Margaret Murie; Teton County Records, Mixed Records Book 6, p. 29, Buster and Frances Estes to Stella Woodbury, Lease, August 12, 1935; Deed Record Book 9, p. 89, Buster and Frances Estes to Adolph Murie, et al., Agreement for deed, August 22, 1945; Warranty Deed Record Book 8, p. 628, Buster and Frances Estes to Adolph Murie, et al., Warranty Deed, July 25, 1950; and Murie, *Wapiti Wilderness,* pp. 266–269.

85. *Jackson Hole Guide,* October 1, 1964, and February 20, 1964.

86. *Jackson Hole Guide,* October 1, 1964; and Teton County Records, Misc. Records Book 1, p. 307, James M. Manges to Frank Williams and Joseph Clark, Agreement for Deed, April 6, 1926; Deed Record Book 3, p. 447, James M. Manges to Double Diamond Ranch, Warranty Deed, August 30, 1926; and Homestead Patent, 1003939, Emma Williams, 1926.

87. *Jackson's Hole Courier,* May 1, 1924, June 26, 1924, and July 16, 1925.

88. *Jackson's Hole Courier,* July 7, 1927; interview with Harry Brown by Jo Ann Byrd, #3, "Last of Old West Series;" and "Dude Ranches Out West," ca. 1930.

89. "Dude Ranches Out West," ca. 1930.

90. Interview with Harry Brown, #3, "Last of Old West;" and Teton County Records, Deed Record Book 6, p. 417, Double Diamond Ranch to Joseph Clark, Warranty Deed, May 21, 1946.

91. Lodges and Dude Ranches, memorandum, February 27, 1951, Grand Teton National Park, Federal Records Center, Denver, Colorado; and Williams, Tract 05–122, Land Files, Grand Teton National Park.

92. Williams, Tract 05–122, Land Files, Grand Teton National Park.

93. "Tourism in Jackson Hole," *Midwest Review:* 35; Homestead Patent 1037758, Peter Karppi Jr., 1928.

94. *Jackson's Hole Courier,* November 29, 1928; Roundy Collection, 3550, interview with Betty Anderson, Tape #2, University of Wyoming Archive.

95. Half Moon Ranch, Tract 05–123, Land Files, Grand Teton National Park.

96. Homestead Patent 1010872, Tony Grace, 1927; "Dude Ranches Out West," ca. 1937; Fabian Papers, Rockefeller Archive Center, Box 22, File 244, Grace, 1929–1936; and University of Wyoming Archives, Fryxell Collection, 1638, Alexander Sprunt to F.M. Fryxell, April 2, 1934.

97. "Dude Ranches Out West," ca. 1927; Teton County Records, Deed Record Book 3, p. 496, Ransom Adams to John F. Woodman, September 17, 1928; and Photograph of Main Lodge, Flying V, courtesy of Don and Gladys Kent.

98. "Dude Ranches Out West," ca. 1927; "Dude Ranches Out West," ca. 1930; Teton County Records, Mixed Records Book 3, p. 389, John Woodman to Gustav Koven and Paul Petzoldt, Agreement for Deed, October 2, 1935; Deed Record Book 5, p. 275, Jack and Zina Woodman to Gustav Koven, Warranty Deed, October 2, 1935; and *Jackson's Hole Courier,* December 22, 1932, December 29, 1932, and November 21, 1935.

99. Telephone Interview with Paul Petzoldt by John Daugherty, December 10, 1982.

100. Teton County Records, Warranty Deed Record Book 9, p. 278, Greer Sugden to Alvin Adams, Warranty Deed, May 14, 1951; interview with P. Petzoldt; and Superintendent's Monthly Report, October 1954, Grand Teton National Park, Box 743799, Federal Records Center, Denver, CO.

101. Adams, Tract 06–108, Land Files, Grand Teton National Park; and *Jackson Hole Guide,* October 12, 1963.

102. University of Wyoming Archives, Roundy Collection, 3550, interview with Louise Turner by C. Roundy, tape; interview with Louise Turner Bertschy by Jo Ann Byrd, #1, "Last of Old West Series;" *Jackson's Hole Courier,* March 3, 1927; Teton County Records, Deed Record Book A, p. 377, William Jump to John S. Turner, Warranty Deed, July 6, 1926; Deed Record Book 2, p. 509, R. E. and Grace Miller to John S. Turner, Warranty Deed, April 19, 1928; and "Dude Ranches Out West," ca. 1927.

103. Fabian Papers, Rockefeller Archive Center, Box 22, File 232, Turner, 1929–1941.

104. Triangle X, Concession Files, Grand Teton National Park.

105. "Dude Ranches Out West," ca. 1927; Jackson Hole Platbook, Harold and Josephine Fabian Collection, Grand Teton National Park.

106. *Jackson Hole Guide,* September 18, 1969; and Barker, Tract 02–104, Land Files, Grand Teton National Park.

107. Interview with Eva Topping Briggs by Jo Ann Byrd, #2, "Last of Old West Series;" and Homestead Patent 1052322, Eva Topping, 1931. Mrs. Briggs recalled taking up residence on the property in 1925, while she testified to a date of 1927 in her final proof papers.

108. *Jackson Hole Guide,* March 5, 1970; and Teton County Records, Deed Record Book 3, p. 118, Fred and Doris Topping to Rudolph Harold, Warranty Deed, October 29, 1918.

109. Homestead Patent 1052322, Topping, 1931, Robert W. Dyer, G. L. O. Examiner, to Commissioner, G. L. O., February 18, 1931.

110. Interview with Eva Briggs, #2, "Last of Old West," and *Jackson Hole Guide,* March 5, 1970.

111. University of Wyoming Archives, K. C. Allan collection, 7636, Teton County Post Offices; Teton County Records, Deed Record Book 14, p. 407, Fred J. Topping to John Wyckoff Mettler, Jr., Warranty Deed, December 8, 1967; and "Big Wyoming Accommodations," leaflet, Wyoming Travel Commission, ca. 1981.

112. *Jackson Hole Guide,* September 3, 1964, and September 8, 1955.

113. "Dude Ranches Out West," ca. 1957; and *Jackson Hole Guide,* September 3, 1964.

114. Murie, *Wapiti Wilderness,* pp. 257–278; and *Jackson Hole Guide,* September 3, 1964.

115. Wister, *Wister Out West,* p. xiii; Franny K. Wister Stokes to Ray H. Mattison, October 2, 1962, Grand Teton National Park; Teton County Records, Deed Record Book 2, p. 26, Elsie M. James to Owen Wister, warranty deed, December 18, 1911.

116. Homestead Patents 1019746, Chauncey Spears, 1928; *Jackson Hole Guide,* September 17, 1964; and *Jackson Hole News,* December 7, 1973.

117. Homestead Patents: 908182, Harry Clissold, 1922; and 977162, Clifford Ward, 1925; and *Jackson Hole Guide,* July 19, 1973.

118. *Jackson Hole Guide,* July 19, 1973 and January 28, 1971; and *Jackson Hole News,* November 2, 1977; and "Dude Ranches Out West," ca. 1927.

119. Homestead Patent 805788, Mears, 1920; *Jackson's Hole Courier,* August 9, 1917, and October 6, 1949; and Teton County Records, Deed Record Book 2, p. 295, Bryant F Mears to Edward B. Mears, Warranty Deed, April 1, 1921; Deed Record Book A, p. 541, E. Mears to William and Margaretta Frew, Warranty Deed, February 9, 1927; Deed Record Book 14, p. 351, Emily Oliver to the United States of America, Warranty Deed, August 4, 1967.

120. "Dude Ranches Out West," ca. 1927; and "Dude Ranches," ca. 1937.

121. Teton County Records, Misc. Records Book 1, p. 280, James M. Manges to C. A. Goss, Agreement for Deed, April 1, 1926; Deed Record Book 4, p. 114, James M. Manges to C. A. Goss, Warranty Deed, May 16, 1929; Deed Record Book A, p. 355, Frank and Gertrude Bessette to C. A. Goss, Warranty Deed, June 7, 1926; Deed Record Book 4, p. 136, Alfred and Ella Bessette to C. A. Goss, Warranty Deed, May 1, 1926.

122. "Dude Ranches Out West," ca. 1927; *Jackson's Hole Courier,* May 6, 1927, July 7, 1927, and July 14, 1927; and "Before and After Pictures of Jackson Hole National Monument," Department of the Interior, National Park Service, 1945.

123. Teton County Records, Deed Records Book 4, p. 119, Chester A. and Jessie Goss to the Snake River Land Company, Warranty Deed, August 8, 1929; *Jackson's Hole Courier,* December 4, 1941; and Elbo Ranch, Concession Files, Grand Teton National Park.

124. Jean Carlton Parker, "Leek's Lodge: Historic Structures Report" (Denver, CO: National Park Service, 1978), pp. 20–21.

125. "Tourism in Jackson Hole," *Midwest Review:* 35; "Dude Ranches Out West," ca. 1927; and University of Wyoming Archives, S. N. Leek Collection, 3138, "Teton Camp for Boys," pamphlet; "Dude Ranches Out West," ca. 1930.

126. Parker, "Leek's Lodge," pp. 38–45.

127. "Dude Ranches Out West," ca. 1927; and Teton County Records, Deed Record Book A, p. 155, William T. and Esther Carter to John W. Hogan, Warranty Deed, November 1, 1924.

128. "Dude Ranches Out West," ca. 1927; "Dude Ranches Out West," ca. 1930; "Dude Ranches Out West," ca. 1937; *Jackson's Hole Courier,* April 14, 1927; and "Tour-ism in Jackson Hole," *Midwest Review;* and *Jackson Hole Guide,* September 18, 1969.

129. Borne, *Dude Ranching,* pp. 173–177.

130. Murie, *Wapiti Wilderness,* pp. 256–263.

131. Borne, *Dude Ranching,* pp. 180–189; Struthers Burt, *Diary,* preface to 1938 ed., pp. xii-xiii; Belasco, *Americans on the Road,* pp. 140–141; and "Dude Ranches Out West," ca. 1937.

132. Borne, *Dude Ranching,* pp. 189–190. Based on the use of limited sources and misinterpretation of data, Borne overestimates the impact of government policies on dude ranching.

CHAPTER 15

Tourists

Tourism is a state of mind. The pleasure trip is an act of being in the world tied to pleasurable sensations. It offers necessary relaxation from everyday routines and escape from the common-place.

—John A. Jakle, *The Tourist*

Tourists, enroute to Yellowstone, break for lunch. Their horses graze nearby. *National Park Service*

The *Jackson's Hole Courier,* on July 8, 1920, reported that five to 15 tourist cars per day churned up dust as they passed through the small cow town of Jackson. No fewer than five bands of "gypsies" or "tin-can" tourists had been seen camped along the route to Yellowstone. Jackson Hole, the *Courier* predicted, could expect ever-increasing tourism in the future.[1] Like the rest of the nation, the valley was witnessing a revolution brought on by the automobile. This revolution would transform Jackson and the valley from an agricultural community dependent on cattle ranching to an economy centered around tourism.

In the nineteenth century, nature—whether wilderness, rural settings, or natural "curiosities"—prompted people to travel. One region of the United States, the American West, attracted more attention than any other for several reasons. First, the West

possessed a special scenic appeal of contrast and scale. Deserts spread before shimmering snow-capped mountains offered vivid contrasts. As for scale, western landscapes dwarfed those known to most visitors, from jagged alpine peaks thrust into the sky to prairies rolling endlessly into the horizon. Second, romantic characters peopled the West. The cowboy symbolized the western frontier and became for many the stereotype of a westerner. Native Americans added a romantic appeal of their own to the West. Third, domestic animals and wildlife populated the Western landscape, adding another distinct element. Many traveled west primarily to hunt and fish, lured by the stories of abundant game. Set in the heart of the Rocky Mountains, Jackson Hole and the Teton Range attracted tourists.

The antecedents of tourism date from the era of the fur trapper, when travelers made their way west

Smith Hotel at Moran/Oxbow Bend, c. 1900. As the number of travelers through the valley increased, people such as Edward "Cap" Smith built hotels to accommodate them. *Collection of the Jackson Hole Historical Society and Museum*

primarily in search of wilderness and its inhabitants. Europeans such as William Drummond Stewart and Prince Maximillian were the most prominent examples. Touring the West with Stewart and the prince were two talented artists, Alfred Jacob Miller and Karl Bodmer, who left invaluable records of the landscape, wildlife, and Native Americans.

In the late nineteenth century, westerners began guiding wealthy Easterners and Europeans into the Jackson Hole region. Beaver Dick Leigh, an itinerant trapper, was one of the well-known guides. William A. Baillie-Grohman wrote an early account of a tour into Jackson Hole. Hearing stories about the area, he determined to visit it, having "Teton Basin [Jackson Hole] on the brain." Following the course of the Gros Ventre River, his guides led him to a site along the Snake River that "without exception was the most strikingly beautiful camp of my various trips." His small group gloried at the scene—the Grand Teton and other peaks in the distance, the tree-lined river before them. Baillie-Grohman considered it "the most striking landscape the eye of a painter ever dreamt of." Even two "unimpressionable western characters" admired the scene.[3] However, "young Henry—a hopelessly matter-of-fact being—turned sublimity into ridicule, by his 'Darn the mountains! Look at those beaver dams yonder.'" Like other travelers, Baillie-Grohman found that many western frontiersmen, caught up in making a living, failed to appreciate the grandeur of landscape

about them. The chagrined nobleman concluded that if young Henry were conducted into Olympus, "the only feeling that would move him would be expressed in a terse 'Doggarn it, if I ain't forgotten the traps and pison'."[4]

In 1883, the Teton country received considerable publicity when President Chester A. Arthur made an extended tour of northwestern Wyoming. Accompanied by friends in politics and the military, a large entourage consisting of 75 cavalrymen, 175 pack animals, and packers and guides, trailed down the Gros Ventre into Jackson Hole. At least four camps were made in Jackson Hole as the presidential party made their way to Yellowstone.[5]

A year later, homesteaders arrived in Jackson Hole. In a short time, ranchers and homesteaders took up outfitting and guiding, for dudes provided hard cash in a cash-starved valley. Occasionally, diaries or accounts of hunting trips surface, such as the account of John K. Mitchell and John B. Coleman, that indicate the importance of outfitting. Coleman came west to hunt in the fall of 1905. He hired James S. Simpson of Grovont to guide him. Wyoming laws required out-of-state hunters to hire guides. A $50 license entitled an out-of-state hunter to two deer, two antelope, two elk, and one bighorn sheep. Coleman suffered from an unspecified illness when he arrived, weighing only 138 pounds; "I came out weighing 162 pounds, the most I ever weighed in my life." The environment and outdoor life appar-

Early tourist facilities ranged from tents to simple log cabins, which made turn-of-the-century trips to a national park an adventure. This photo is by Ben Sheffield, who was an early guide and lodging camp owner. *Grand Teton National Park*

ently restored his health, a motive that drew many tourists to the West.[6]

The guide business proved lucrative enough for Ben Sheffield, an outfitter from Livingston, Montana, to build a lodge and camp at Moran. Stephen Leek became one of the valley's first guides. Leek continued to guide into the 1920s, "the only old settler who persists in following a pack horse into the mountains each season." Joe

Jones described Leek as "a good man in the hills with a pack outfit, but used to be much inclined to feed his dudes raw meat. In other words he imagined they were out to exemplify the crude lives of the early explorers [sic] and took pains to see they were not disapointed [sic]." In addition to hunting and fishing, a need to confront wilderness and relive the frontier experience lured dudes blinded by romantic notions west.[7]

These men are probably setting up a fishing or hunting camp, given the absence of women and the amount of equipment. *Grand Teton National Park*

If well-to-do visitors were willing to pay good money to rough it in the wilderness every fall, why not extend the season and provide a vacation opportunity for families? As noted in the previous chapter, dude ranchers pioneered the modern tourist industry in Jackson Hole. Louis Joy, Struthers Burt, Horace Carncross, and Harold Hammond established the first true dude ranches in Jackson Hole between 1907 and 1919: the JY, the Bar BC, and the White Grass. The dude ranch epitomized an idealized western experience, of which a wilderness setting was the most critical element.[8]

The conservation movement contributed significantly to tourism in the West. Yellowstone National Park was created in 1872, and as conservationists wielded more influence, laws such as the Forest Reserve Act of 1891 were passed, and general public land policy shifted from one of disposal to reservation. As railroads linked the continent, more tourists journeyed west. The Northern Pacific linked Lake Superior with Portland, Oregon, in 1887. The line passed north of Yellowstone, offering access. The Yellowstone tour became a popular vacation for people seeking a western experience. A few made their way to Jackson Hole. Reuben G. Thwaites left an account of a tour through Yellowstone into the Teton country in 1903. Traveling in two wagons, a "hack" and a chuck wagon, Thwaites set out with his family and guides. At the thumb of Yellowstone Lake, they decided to travel to Jackson Lake. "The guides demurred strongly, giving several excuses, one of which was that Jackson Hole had not long before been a resort for outlaws. We won the argument, and started south." They traveled over a very poor road, reaching Jackson Lake on July 12. Unlike Yellowstone, they encountered few travelers in this area. They camped near Sargent's place and rented a rowboat from him the next day, crossing Jackson Lake to the base of Mount Moran.[9]

When Henry Ford began mass production of the Model T in 1909, he launched a new era. In 1900, there were only 8,000 registered cars in the United States, and the machines remained a fad. Cars were unreliable and horrible roads made auto touring an adventure and, at times, a nightmare. They were a novelty in Jackson Hole and had little practical value. In 1902, the Interior Department

and army prohibited automobiles in Yellowstone primarily for safety reasons. In 1915, Secretary of the Interior Franklin K. Lane reversed this policy and opened the park to auto traffic, after tests proved that automobiles could negotiate the roads and grades.[10]

In this period, touring became a major element of Americans' love affair with automobiles. By 1910, the number of registered cars in America burgeoned to 458,000 vehicles. Middle-class Americans took to the roads, rejecting traditional vacations offered by railroads, resorts, and hotels. Historian Warren Belasco has described the period of auto touring between 1910 and 1920 as the "anarchist stage." Families rebelled against the regimented schedules of railroads and the rigid formality of traditional hotels. This mode of travel conferred freedom as road "Gypsies" toured wherever their cars could take them and camped along roadsides. Riding over rugged wagon tracks in a car evoked romantic images of stagecoaches and covered wagons. Tourists rode in vehicles that exposed them to the landscape and elements, eating dust. Nevertheless, trains rather than automobiles continued to symbolize the modern age; railroads dominated travel, carrying one billion passengers per year in 1910.[11]

Between the wars, from 1919 to 1941, the automobile changed the landscape of America and behavior of Americans perhaps as no other technological advance in the twentieth century has done. In 1920, 8,000,000 registered cars cruised the United States; by 1930, this number more than doubled to 23,000,000 cars. The patterns of modern tourism were set in this period—"tin can" auto campers evolved into modern tourists. During this era, the automobile replaced the train as the primary mode of transportation. Touring became routine rather than a novelty. As Henry Ford produced cars more cheaply, the average American could afford a vehicle. People considered to be of the lower classes began taking vacations. Dramatic improvements transformed the nation's roads in these years. More car owners generated political pressure for better roads, and state and local governments allocated money for road projects. Congress passed the Federal Aid Road Act of 1916, which provided $75,000,000 for highway construction. The Bureau of Public Roads was

Dude ranchers referred to automobile travelers as "tin can" tourists. Automobile travel drastically changed the way Americans took vacations. The ability to travel independently and stay just one night in a variety of locations created a whole new lodging industry of motor courts and other roadside service facilities.
Harrison Crandall photo, Jackson Hole Historical Society and Museum

created in 1918. The Federal Highway Act of 1921 provided for an interstate system of highways. Between 1921 and 1940, the mileage of paved highways in the United States more than quadrupled.

Along these improved roads and highways, a new landscape emerged. Gas stations, cafes, and cottage camps mushroomed along with the inevitable billboards to advertise them. In the early years, these roadside establishments were owned and operated by individuals rather than corporations. Cottage camps or cabin courts were the predecessors of modern motels, which emerged after 1945.[12] As time passed, increased speeds, more comfortable cars, and a growing sameness of the roadside scene "dulled the travelers awareness." Making time, or "speed and distance became a North American obsession in travel." Faced with limited funds and time, tourists tended to set schedules, cramming as many attractions as possible into vacations. Average miles driven per day increased steadily from 125 miles in 1916 to 400 miles in 1936. Ironically, the car, which symbolized a new freedom, became a prison, and "motoring emerged as a means to get somewhere rather than an end in itself."[13]

In Wyoming, the 1920s were bad years economically. Hard times hit the livestock business and coal

and oil industry, three mainstays in the state's economy. Tourism boomed in these years, and some Wyoming citizens saw it as the state's salvation. Municipal campgrounds and cottage camps sprang up in communities throughout the state. In spite of tough financial times, Wyoming raised money to match federal grants and, by 1939, most important roads had been graveled and oiled.[14]

After the First World War, roads improved rapidly in Jackson Hole. The Forest Service, Park Service, and state rebuilt and upgraded access highways into Jackson Hole. The Forest Service constructed a major road through the Hoback between 1918 and 1922. In 1918, the Bureau of Public Roads completed a new road over Teton Pass. The National Park Service contributed in part to the upgrading of the old military road over Togwotee Pass, completed in 1922. In the 1920s, the Bureau of Public Roads built a highway from Jackson to Menor's Ferry and erected a steel truss bridge across the Snake River at the ferry. Even before the bridge, autos crossing on the ferry had become routine.

Along the road to Jenny Lake, businesses blossomed to cater to the automobile traffic. Maud Noble opened a tea room in her cabin at Menor's Ferry. Tea rooms became common sites along American highways in the 1920s. Because of its location along the highway, a cluster of tourist facilities emerged at Moose. After the Snake River Land Company bought out Maud Noble and other landowners in the area, the Teton Investment Company leased a small store and gas station to various individuals, who also operated the Moose Post Office. When the highway was realigned in 1957, the National Park Service removed the store. On the east side of the Snake River, Evelyn Dornan and her son Jack Dornan developed tourist facilities on a small 20-acre homestead, which continues to be operated by the family as a private inholding today.[15]

Near the confluence of Taggart and Cottonwood Creeks, Chester Goss of California bought 115 acres from Jimmy Manges in 1926. With partners J. M. Goss and James Scott, Goss built a tourist facility called the Elbo Ranch. They built guest cabins for long-term dudes that included indoor plumbing; they also constructed a store and gas station to cater to the auto traffic along the scenic road. Near the ranch, Goss constructed rodeo grounds, an unsightly development that consisted of grandstands, a one-half mile racetrack, a parking lot, and concession stands. Most important, they built a collection of cottage cabins for overnight traffic. Goss put up the first billboard along the road, but dismantled it at Horace Albright's request. The Snake River Land Company bought the property in 1929.[16]

Jimmy Manges retired from homesteading in 1926. After selling out to Goss and selling 40 acres to Joe Clark and Frank Williams of the Double Diamond, Manges moved to a small 4.96-acre parcel at the north end of his homestead and built a cabin for residential use. He worked as a laborer and, in the fall, hired out as a cook for hunting guides. His X Quarter Circle X became a guest camp, more by accident than design. First, he allowed a family who had been camped on the sagebrush flats to build a small cabin on the premises. As tourism increased in the 1930s, he allowed auto campers and mountaineers to camp on the premises. Eventually, he built a tent camp and, later, crude cabins. Some long-term guests built their own cabins. About 1933 or 1934, several foremen for the Civilian Conservation Corps sought housing for their families. They built cabins and turned them over to Manges at the end of their tour

in exchange for a site. Originally, Manges took overnight traffic. As time passed, some guests returned each year, staying for several weeks or the summer. Manges's nephew Irwin Lesher and Lesher's wife, Marvel, began helping with the operation in the 1940s, which had expanded to more than 20 small cabins. Marvel Lesher recalled persuading Manges to raise his prices, which were absurdly low, and provide amenities such as clean linen. The Leshers managed the camp while Jimmy Manges retired to spend his days fishing. After his death in 1960, the Leshers continued the operation until 1980 when Marvel Lesher sold to the United States.

The X Quarter Circle X is difficult to classify. It was not a dude ranch. It resembled a cottage court more than any other type of tourist accommodation, yet guests returned year after year while overnight guests declined. It was not a resort, the accommodations being "rustic," to use a polite term. Location explains the appeal of Manges's camp. Situated at the base of the Grand Teton, the X Quarter Circle X offered a convenient base camp for mountaineers and unrivaled scenery for those who did not mind primitive conditions.[17]

East of the Manges property is a group of cabins known as the Highlands. Harry F. Sensenbach homesteaded the tract in December 1914. Aided by his wife and two sons, he attempted to raise barley and oats, but it became clear that this was not a suitable area for farming. In addition to heavy snows, drought wiped out his crop three years in a row. Improvements consisted of a four-room log house (25 × 25 feet), barn, chicken house, and storeroom. Sometime in the 1920s, Dad and Ma Sensenbach converted their house to a restaurant and added a few rental cabins. They may also have sold bootleg liquor and beer. In 1927, they sold all but 45 acres to Elena Gibo. After prohibition ended in 1933, the Sensenbachs' place became a well-known beer parlor and eating establishment. They sold out in 1944 to Maxine Heffner who, in turn, sold to Charles Byron Jenkins in 1946. Jenkins formed the Highlands Corporation, doubling the number of cabins on the property and adding on to the main lodge. In 1972, he sold out to the United States. The National Park Service converted the buildings to seasonal park housing.[18]

The old Jenny Lake Store was one of many tourist businesses that once lined the Teton Park Road from Moose to Jenny Lake. The sight of burgeoning and unsightly developments prompted John D. Rockefeller Jr. to initiate his program of land acquisition that eventually led to the expanded Grand Teton National Park. *Jackson Hole Historical Society and Museum*

A number of developments centered around the south end of Jenny Lake. As early as 1924, Charles Wort rented boats on Jenny Lake through a permit with the Forest Service. In the same year, Homer Richards filed a stock-raising entry east of South Jenny Lake junction. According to his final proof papers, Richards had constructed a small frame house, a partially complete log residence (37 × 20 feet), and seven cabins. To comply with the law, he grazed 18 horses on the property. Richards, a barber by trade, ran a barbershop, a gas station, and rented cabins to tourists. He and his family lived in town during the winters and resided at Jenny Lake in the summer. In 1929, Richards sold to the Snake River Land Company for $25,000. He used the stake to build one of the earliest cabin courts in Jackson, the Ideal Motel.[19]

The Jenny Lake Post Office opened on Richards's property in August 1926. Mrs. A. W. Gabbey was the first postmaster. By 1926, Jenny Lake had a dance hall, operated by Mr. and Mrs. Cliff Ward. Set alongside the road, it was an unsightly building. After the Snake River Land Company purchased the site, the dance hall was dismantled and rebuilt north of Jackson. The company also removed Richards's cabins.[20]

Rockefeller's agents bought all of the properties at the south end of Jenny Lake, except for one, a ten-acre parcel west of the road near Lupine Meadows. J. D. and Lura Kimmel bought ten acres from Sam Smith in 1929. Kimmel built two cabins west of Cottonwood Creek and spent his summers on the property. In 1937, he built a large two-story store for a

couple named Novotny, who had bought out the Gabbey's store and gas station. In the same year, he began constructing an auto court, completed in 1938. G. M. and Ann Novotny, along with Nell Roach, leased the development, known as the Jenny Lake Store and "Kimmel Kabins." The store also housed the post office. In 1944, the Kimmels sold their important holdings to Rockefeller in exchange for a life estate and the right to lease the property. After Lura Kimmel died in 1962, the development reverted to the United States. The park removed the large store and buildings next to the road and converted the cabin court to seasonal quarters.[21]

The building known as the Jenny Lake Visitor Center today was the Harrison Crandall Studio. Crandall, a professional photographer, became one of the park's and valley's most important publicists, selling thousands of post cards and photographs. His camera captured the scenery, people at play, and rustic dude ranch settings. His photographs are often idealistic depictions, but nonetheless comprise a remarkable photographic record.

In 1921, Harrison Crandall quit his job with the Biological Survey, bought a Model T and drove to Jackson Hole from Idaho. He returned with his bride Hildegarde and an Eastman Kodak 3A in 1922. At the suggestion of storekeeper Charlie Fesler, they wintered at Moran in 1922–1923. The young couple decided to homestead in the flats east of String Lake in 1924. In June they built a tent house at their homestead. Since the land was uncultivable, they leased the range for 40 head of horses and filed a stock-raising entry. They built a residence the first year and began selling pictures. Hildegarde Crandall recalled that they washed prints in glass frames at String Lake. In his final proof papers, Crandall wrote, "I make and sell pictures" in response to the question about using the property for a trade.

They experienced lean years at first. To make it at their remote tract, the Crandalls built a dance hall, which doubled as a studio. The String Lakes Pavillion was 70-feet-long with a plank floor, walls four-feet-high, and canvas sides. During the week, Hildegarde baked pies and other foods for a midnight supper, charging 50 cents per plate. The dance hall was a success, for the *Courier* reported that 250 people from all over the valley attended the first Saturday night dance. The Crandall orchestra provided music. Another dance was attended by an estimated 150 couples. Around 1926, Crandall tore down the pavillion and used the logs to build the studio. By 1927, Crandall opened it for business. Set in a grove of pines, the log studio with its distinctive cupola was one of the finest rustic buildings in the valley according to the *Courier.*

In 1929, the Crandalls sold out to the Snake River Land Company. Harrison Crandall secured one of the first concession permits in Grand Teton National Park and relocated the studio to its present site. Here, Crandall became the early park's greatest publicist; he was to the Teton Range and Jackson Hole what the Hayneses were to Yellowstone. He also painted in later years, and a number of his paintings survive in the valley. He retired in 1959 and turned his studio over to the park.[22]

Not far from the first site of the Crandall Studio is the Jenny Lake Lodge. Originally a small dude ranch owned by Tony Grace, the buildings were not in good condition when the Snake River Land Company purchased them. Harold Fabian felt that Grace's Danny Ranch and the Triangle X were ideal locations for dude ranches, but Grace declined to continue his outfit or join John S. Turner of the Triangle X, and the buildings deteriorated. Around 1933, the Teton Investment Company began upgrading the property. A fire destroyed most of the main lodge in 1935. Nevertheless, by the late 1930s, the company operated the Jenny Lake Lodge as a dude ranch. The lodge was described as follows:

> Central lodge and dining room with a number of one and two-room rustic log cabins, well furnished and thoroughly comfortable, accommodate 65 persons. All cabins have hot and cold running water and some have bath and toilet. Central bath facilities available without charge to those in cabins without bath. Excellent food is served in the central dining room overlooking the Teton mountains. Individual service featured.

The lodge continues to operate today as an exclusive resort.[23]

East of the Jenny Lake Lodge, A. W. and Lida Gabbey homesteaded in 1927. They rented housekeeping cabins at the Square G by 1931, but most developments occurred in the 1930s and 1940s. Although the Square G has been called a dude ranch, it seems to have been more akin to the Elbo. The cabins were housekeeping units, for guests cared for themselves. And for three years the ranch had no water; it was hauled in from String Lake. Gabbey contracted with a wrangler from Thermopolis who brought in saddle horses. In 1951, the Jackson Hole Preserve bought the property. The cabins were removed in 1956, with several relocated to Colter Bay.[24]

Signal Mountain Lodge is located on the eastern shore of Jackson Lake about one mile south of the Jackson Lake Dam. The resort began as a fishing camp started by Ole Warner in the 1920s through a Forest Service permit. Warner built 11 cabins and several outbuildings. (These were razed by 1963). According to one source, Charles Wort later secured a permit to the camp from the Department of the Interior. This is curious, because the Forest Service administered the land, except for the Bureau of Reclamation withdrawal area. In 1931, John A. Warner and Maggie Warner made a trust agreement with Charles Wort. In a complicated transaction, Wort took over the buildings and permit. In exchange, he paid off the Warners' $6,240.65 debt, and they agreed to manage Warners' Camp. Wort died in 1933 and his estate assigned the lodge to Clarence W. Harris in 1940.

Hunting allowed the tourist season to extend well into fall. This Ben Sheffield photo displays quite a collection of trophies for these men. *Jackson Hole Historical Society and Museum*

Wort's lodge and fishing camp emerged as a major development between 1928 and 1940, a remarkable feat because it occurred during the Great Depression. By 1937, 32 structures had been built on the site, which consisted of a small log lodge, store and gas station, and numerous guest cabins. In 1940, Wort's Camp was renamed Signal Mountain Lodge. Between 1940 and 1962, 22 buildings were added. Since that time, the lodge and numerous buildings have been replaced with frame structures. Less than a quarter of the buildings predate 1940. Interestingly, neither Wort's Camp nor Signal Mountain Lodge appeared under the category of lodges in the dude ranch guides. Today, the lodge is operated as a concession in the park.[25]

Sheffield's Moran was located at the outlet of Jackson Lake, and was an important stop for food and lodging. In 1916, Sheffield's lodge burned, a loss that included the post office. About 1922, he built a new lodge. By 1927, Moran was a lively community consisting of store, a garage, campgrounds, corrals, and rustic cabins set around a spacious main lodge. In 1928, Sheffield sold to the Snake River Land Company. Because of a shortage of accommodations in the area, but mostly to prevent new developments in the vicinity that might hinder the company's buyout program, they formed a separate corporation to operate the tourist village. Except for the main lodge, built in 1922, many of the 40 buildings and sanitation systems required major repairs. The Snake River Land Company advanced the Teton Lodge Company $35,000 to upgrade and expand facilities at Moran. Under Sheffield, around 1927, the Teton Lodge could accommodate 125 guests. The Teton Lodge Company, later the Teton Investment Company, expanded the capacity to 200 guests. In 1935, disaster struck again, when fire destroyed the main lodge. The National Park Service and the Grand Teton Lodge Company removed the entire village of Moran around 1955, moving many of the cabins to Colter Bay.[26]

In 1924, Eugene Amoretti of Lander, Wyoming, conceived a grand plan to build two lodges and seven camps in the area, combinations of resorts and dude ranches. His Amoretti Hotel and Camp Company built the Jackson Lake Lodge around 1922. The first modern lodge in the valley, some cabins had hot and cold running water, baths, and toilets. The lodge also rented tent cabins during the summer. It could accommodate 125 guests. Saddle horses were available, and hunting trips could be arranged in the fall. Dude wranglers J. S. Simpson and Toots Kennedy conducted a summer camp for high school and college-age women around 1928. The Snake River Land Company bought the lodge in 1930, and the predecessors of the Grand Teton

Lodge Company operated it until the 22 remaining cabins were removed after 1953 to make way for the new Jackson Lake Lodge.[27]

Leek's Lodge was located north of Colter Bay along the east shore of Jackson Lake. As noted in the previous chapter, the Forest Service issued Stephen Leek a special use permit to operate a hunting camp in 1925. A year later, he built several tent cabins on the site. In 1927, the Forest Service issued Leek a permit to establish "a resort for the accommodation of tourists including hotel accommodations, store, and gas station." By October 1927, Leek had built the main lodge. He operated the lodge as a hunting camp headquarters and boys' camp. In 1946, Dr. N. E. Morad bought the lease. By this time, a number of guest cabins had been built around the lodge. After 1950, the lodge became a concession in the park. After several owners, Signal Mountain Lodge acquired the permit in 1977. Most of the cabins were removed around 1972. The main lodge building was removed in 1998.[28]

Between 1910 and 1920, Ed Sheffield, the brother of Ben Sheffield, opened Flagg Ranch, a stopover for dudes traveling form Livingston, Montana, to Sheffield's Teton Lodge at Moran. In 1927, the *Midwest Review* described Flagg Ranch as "splendid accommodations for the tourist," consisting of a large main lodge surrounded by cabins and tent houses. In "Dude Ranches Out West," the entry for Flagg Ranch provided the following information:

FLAG [sic] RANCH is 23 miles from Moran on the Jackson Road, two and one-half miles south of Yellowstone's southern entrance, and a 50-mile stage ride from Ashton, Idaho, the nearest Union Pacific point. There is good trout fishing in the immediate neighborhood. Licenses, tackle, camping supplies, tobacco and incidentals may be procured at the ranch. Meals are $1 each; lodging, $1 per night. Accommodations and service are limited, but 25 persons can be reasonably provided for upon sufficiently advanced notice. The main log building has 15 rooms. On account of the ranch's isolation, it is best to inquire well in advance concerning rate and reservations. Address Flag [sic] Ranch, Moran, Wyoming.[29]

By 1939, the modern tourist industry, primed by the automobile, had altered Jackson Hole. In the town of Jackson, three cabin courts and three hotels catered to tourists, while lodges and camps were scattered throughout the valley. Gas stations dotted the landscape. In the 1950s, the National Park Service removed Moran and smaller properties such as the Square G, but replaced them with large-scale developments at Colter Bay and a new Jackson Lake Lodge. In 1945, Harold Fabian wrote, "Jackson is no longer the pioneer cow town where I first spent an October night in Mrs. Crabtree's Hotel. It has gone western in true Hollywood style."[30]

A trend related to dude ranching and tourism gathered momentum in the 1920s. In 1927, Struthers Burt warned Horace Albright that "each summer more and more rich easterners are buying places on this side of the river." The scenery and western character of the valley held a special appeal to those who had the leisure and could afford a 160-acre ranch. Tourists had started to become summer residents.

In 1926, W. Lewis Johnson purchased John Sargent's ranch, the only private land in the northern end of Jackson Hole. A retired executive for the Hoover Vacuum Company, Johnson visited the area in 1923 and left smitten with the rugged scenery. He bought Sargent's for a second home. In 1927, he had a large lodge constructed south of Sargent's old lodge. Constructed by local contractor Charlie Fox in 1930, the building was a two-story log residence with a breeze-way connecting it to the barn. Johnson died in 1931.

In 1936, Alfred C. and Madeleine Berolzheimer bought the Johnson property. The family changed their name to Berol at a later date. Alfred was a member of the family who owned the Eagle Pencil Company. He worked his way up through the company ranks to the presidency before his death in 1974. In 1937, work began on a new lodge for the Berols, which was completed in 1938. Craftsmen built custom-made pine furnishings for the house. In addition to hunting and horseback riding, Berol had a passion for target shooting. Consequently, he built a rifle range, pistol range, and trap shoot. The ranch acquired its name, AMK, from the initials of Alfred, Madeleine, and their son, Kenneth. In 1976, Berol's heirs sold to the National Park Service for more than

$3,000,000 and a life estate. Today, the buildings house the University of Wyoming Research Center.[31]

In 1927, Edward B. Mears sold the Bryant Mears homestead north of the Bill Menor homestead to William and Margaretta Frew, both Pennsylvania dudes. Naming the new ranch, the Four Lazy F (Four Lazy Frews) the family built a lodge and cabins patterned after a dude ranch both in spatial setting and building designs. In 1967, Emily F. Oliver sold the ranch to the National Park Service for monetary considerations and a life estate.[32]

Aside from John D. Rockefeller Jr., the largest private landowner in the area was Stanley Resor, the president of the advertising firm, J. Walter Thompson Company. Determined to become a gentleman rancher, he acquired large holdings west of the Snake River north and south of Wilson and went into the cattle business.[33]

Two other retreats are the Aspen Ridge Ranch and the Hunter Hereford Ranch, both located north of Ditch Creek in the east end of the park. In 1942, John C. and Eleanor K. Talbot bought the Stahn homestead and converted it to a summer home, which became known as the Aspen Ridge Ranch. They added two large log wings to the homestead residence, more than doubling the size of the building. Most of the buildings, the barn, garage, cabin, and irrigator's house were added between 1942 and 1956. They sold the property to the United States in 1956 in exchange for cash and a life estate.[34]

East of the Aspen Ridge Ranch, William and Eileen Hunter retired from the automobile sales business and bought the Jim Williams homestead in 1944. They decided to raise cattle as a retirement activity, rather than for a living. Architect E. F. Piers of Ogden, Utah, designed new buildings for the ranch. The Hunters had a 2,700-square-foot log residence built on a hill above the ranch buildings. A housekeeper's cabin, guest cabin, and woodshed were constructed near the residence. Down the hill, workers constructed several new outbuildings around the homestead cabin, bunkhouse, and woodshed. New buildings included a large log barn with attached feeding shelter, a garage and shop, an equipment shed, a hay shed, horse barn, and chicken house. One curiosity is a log frame structure with a stone fireplace that was a prop for the movie *Spencer's*

Mountain, made in 1962. The Nelson brothers, well-known log craftsmen, constructed the log residence in 1947 and probably the other buildings from that period. Bill Hunter died in 1951, and Eileen Hunter sold to the park in exchange for a life estate in 1957.[35]

The Forest Service made land available to individuals who wished to construct summer cabins for recreational use. Applicants usually sought lands along watercourses and lakes. Jackson Lake and the lakes along the base of the Teton Range were primary targets for such developments. Using the Executive Order of 1918 prohibiting any reservations on developments on the proposed 600,000-acre Yellowstone extension, the National Park Service used its review power to restrict residential leases, much to the anger of Forest Service officials. In the Senate hearings, the supervisor of Teton National Forest, A. C. McCain, introduced a development plan for the forest which proposed 3,000 summer home leases and resorts on national forest and adjacent lands. The Forest Service estimated the value of these developments to exceed $8,000,000. McCain testified that the park controversy held up 111 applications for special leases, many of them summer homes.

The Park Service agreed to leasing in some areas. Little is known about the Stevens cabin at Taggart Lake, but it may have been built through a Forest Service permit. Located within the boundaries of the 1929 park, it was removed around 1930. On the east shore of Spaulding Bay on Jackson Lake, the Forest Service issued six leases in the 1920s and 1930s. Among the lessees were Smalley, C. H. Brown, and Van Vleck. All associated buildings were removed by 1980, except for the Brown cabin. The Park Service bought the C. H. Brown place in 1975. Because of political pressure, the park issued a permit to Harry and Robert Brown to continue use of the property. Both have since passed away, and the buildings were removed in the late 1980s.[36]

The most notable residence initially under a Forest Service lease is the Brinkerhoff, located on Jackson Lake near Catholic Bay. The Forest Service originally issued a lease for a summer residence to Ben Sheffield in 1930. After Sheffield's home burned in the 1940s, Zachery K. Brinkerhoff and Z. K. Brinkerhoff Jr., purchased the permit in 1947 from R. E.

McConaughy. The Brinkerhoffs owned Brinkerhoff Drilling, an oil development company. Jan Wilking, a Casper architect, designed an elaborate log residence for the Brinkerhoffs, much grander than most summer cottages. Scotty Slotten and four log craftsmen of Swedish descent from the Wind River Valley constructed the building. Thomas Molesworth of Cody, Wyoming, made the lodge's rustic furnishings. The fireplace consists of rock collected in the Wind River Canyon. The Petter Iron and Ornamental Works of Dallas manufactured the fireplace screens and hardware. In 1955, the Brinkerhoffs sold the lodge and permit to the National Park Service. Today the lodge is used as a retreat for dignitaries.[37]

Tourism dominates the economy of Teton County today. The modern tourist industry began with the early hunting-guide business and dude ranching, best symbolized by the horse, but the automobile reshaped it, radically changing how Americans spend their leisure time. Thousands of vehicles pass through the town of Jackson today, a number that dwarfs the 5 to 15 cars per day rate in 1915.

Notes

1. *Jackson's Hole Courier*, July 8, 1920.

2. John A. Jakle, *The Tourist*, (Lincoln, NE: University of Nebraska Press, 1985), pp. 53, 225–244.

3. Thompson, *Beaver Dick;* Baillie-Grohman, *Camps in the Rockies*, pp. 208–211; and Marshall Sprague, *A Gallery of Dudes* (Boston: Little, Brown and Company, 1966).

4. Ibid., pp. 205–232.

5. Tilden, *F. Jay Haynes*, pp. 115–139.

6. *Jackson Hole Guide*, July 22, July 29, and August 5, 1965. These issues contained a reprint of the John K. Mitchell Diary; and John B. Coleman, "Hunting Big Game in Jackson Hole," Wyoming State Archives, Museums, and Historical Department, Wyoming-Jackson Hole, Folder 5 (W994-jk).

7. *Jackson's Hole Courier*, July 26, 1917; Jackson Hole Historical Society and Museum, Book 3, p. 55, "Leeks Cabin at Leigh Lake"; and Joe Jones to Horace Albright, January 11, 1924, Horace Albright Papers, 1923–1927, Yellowstone National Park Archives.

8. See chapter on dude ranching.

9. Ruben Gold Thwaites, "Through Yellowstone and the Tetons-1903," *National Parks Magazine* 36 (March 1962):8–11.

10. Haines, *The Yellowstone Story*, 2:264–267; and Jakle, *The Tourist*, pp. 120–121.

11. Belasco, *Americans on the Road*, pp. 7–39; and Jakle, *The Tourist*, pp. 120–121.

12. Jakle, *The Tourist*, pp. 70, 120–121, 126–127; and Belasco, *Americans on the Road*, pp. 129–173.

13. Jakle, *The Tourist*, pp. 146–149.

14. Larson, *History of Wyoming*, pp. 423–425, 411–413.

15. See chapter on the transportation frontier; *Jackson's Hole Courier*, July 12, 1917; interview with Fran Carmichael, #7, by Jo Ann Byrd in "Last of Old West Series," 1984, Teton County Library; interview with Ellen Dornan, #10, by Jo Ann Byrd in "Last of Old West Series;" and Homestead Patent 799739, Evelyn M. Dornan, 1925.

16. "Dude Ranches Out West," ca. 1927; *Jackson's Hole Courier*, May 6, July 7, and July 14, 1927; and "Before and After Pictures, Jackson Hole National Monument," 1945, Grand Teton National Park Library.

17. Lesher Tract, 05–119, Land Files, Grand Teton National Park; *Jackson Hole Guide*, August 18, 1960, and May 25, 1972; and interview with Marvel Lesher by John Daugherty, September 2, 1982, Grand Teton National Park.

18. Homestead Patent 801007, H. Sensenbach, 1920; *Jackson's Hole Courier*, August 11, 1949; The Highlands Tract, 05–120, Land Files, Grand Teton National Park; and interview with Bob Krannenberg, #19, by Joanne Bird in "Last of Old West."

19. Homestead Patent 1021747, Homer Richards, 1928; interview with Homer Richards, #34, by Joanne Bird, "Last of Old West Series;" and *Jackson Hole Guide*, June 20, 1957.

20. *Jackson's Hole Courier*, August 19, 1926, October 4, 1926, and March 26, 1931.

21. Ann Novotny to Mrs. Robert Irvine, October 1, 1973, Local History, Pamphlet File, Grand Teton National Park Library; and *Jackson Hole Guide*, May 30, 1963.

22. *Jackson's Hole Courier*, June 5, 1924, and July 21, 1927; *Jackson Hole Guide*, June 20, 1957, October 6, 1966, and December 17, 1970; interview with Hildegard Crandall by Jo Ann Byrd, #9, "Last of Old West Series;" Homestead Patents 1023025, Harrison Crandall, 1928; and letter from Virginia Huidekoper, April 10, 1994.

23. "Dude Ranches Out West," ca. 1927 (contains a small photograph of Grace's lodge); "Dude Ranches Out West," Union Pacific Railroad, ca. 1938, Subject File: Dude Ranches F, Wyoming State Archives; and Rockefeller Archive Center, Harold P. Fabian Papers, IV3A7, Box

22, File 244, Grace Parcel, 1928–1936, Harold Fabian to Vanderbilt Webb, December 19, 1935.

24. Homestead Patent 1057117, A.W. Gabbey, 1931; interview with Bob Krannenberg, by Jo Ann Byrd #19; and *Jackson Hole Guide*, May 26, 1983.

25. Appraisal Report, Signal Mountain Lodge, March 1, 1963, Concession Files, Grand Teton National Park; Office of the County Clerk and Recorder, Teton County, Mixed Records, Book 3, p. 571, Trust Agreement, John A. and Maggie Warner to Charles J. Wort, September 23, 1931; *Jackson's Hole Courier*, September 7, 1933 and September 17, 1936; and Signal Mountain Site Plan, December 1, 1962, Concession Files, Grand Teton National Park.

26. "Tourism in Jackson Hole," *Midwest Review* 8 (July-August 1927): 34–35; Fabian Papers, Rockefeller Archives Center, Box 23, File 261, Sheffield, 1928–1931, Site Map of Moran; Box 27, File 308, Reports-Moran 1929–1930; "Dude Ranches Out West," ca. 1927; and "Dude Ranches Out West," ca. 1938.

27. *Jackson's Hole Courier*, April 24, and May 8, 1924; Fabian Papers, Rockefeller Archive Center, Box 26, File 291, History of the Companies, November 9, 1953; "Tourism in Jackson Hole," *Midwest Review* 8, p. 35; and "Dude Ranches Out West," ca. 1927.

28. "Dude Ranches Out West," ca. 1927; and Jean Carlton Parker, "Historic Structure Report: Leeks Lodge," National Park Service, 1978, pp. 17–49.

29. Markham, "The Ashton-Moran Freight Road," Map.

30. Nellie Van Derveer, "Sports and Recreation," WPA Subject File 1325, Wyoming State Archives; and Fabian Papers, Rockefeller Archive Center, Box 47, File 458, Report on Jackson Hole Project, Harold Fabian to John D. Rockefeller Jr., September 26, 1945.

31. Struthers Burt to Horace Albright, October 14, 1927, Albright Papers, 1923–1927, Yellowstone Archives; and Kenneth L. and Lenore Diem, *A Tale of Dough Gods, Bear Grease, Cantaloupe, and Sucker Oil* (Laramie, WY: University of Wyoming, 1986). According to Virginia Huidekoper, the Berolz-heimers changed their name in the 1940s and sent announcements notifying people of the change. Letter from Huidekoper, April 10, 1994.

32. Teton County Clerk, Deed Records, Book A, p. 541, Warranty Deed, Edward Mears to William and Margaretta Frew, February 9, 1927; and Nathaniel Burt, *Jackson Hole Journal*, pp. 69–70.

33. "Hearings on H.R. 2241," 1943, pp. 180–185.

34. Interview with Mrs. Eleanor Talbot by John Daugherty, August 1983; and Talbot Tract, 06–107, Land Files, Grand Teton National Park.

35. Hunter Tract, 05–126, Land Files, Grand Teton National Park; interview with Eileen Hunter by John Daugherty, September 1983; and Fryxell Collection, 1638, Box D, File 5, Albert Nelson to Fritiof Fryxell, October 24, 1947.

36. "Hearing on S. Res. 226," 1933, pp. 407–416; Righter, *Crucible for Conservation*, p. 32; *Jackson's Hole Courier*, August 11, 1932; Superintendent's Monthly Report, June 1955, Federal Records Center, Denver, CO; and Brown Tract, 10–106, Land Files, Grand Teton National Park.

37. The Brinkerhoff, List of Classified Structures Report, HS0133, Grand Teton National Park.

CHAPTER 16

Park of the Matterhorns

By Reynold G. Jackson

During the years following his 1872 expedition to the remote and wild Yellowstone region of Wyoming, Ferdinand Vandeveer Hayden presented a series of lectures to organized groups and to the public at large. These lectures were illustrated with stunning slide images by photographer William Henry Jackson. Prominent among the dazzling array of pictures were the first views of the Teton mountain range, now, of course, one of the most recognizable and well-known national park regions in the United States. The American public was amazed by the dramatic scenery, and the fact that such landforms existed within the country. Imaginations were stirred by visions of needle-like pinnacles and snow-covered, sharply-defined summits. Images of the Teton Range are now so prevalent that the rugged peaks have almost become the symbolic representation of what mountains should look like. Indeed, when we try to picture in our mind the classic mountain image, the craggy peaks of the Tetons almost immediately appear.

The Tetons have played a pivotal role in the historic development of climbing and mountaineering in this country. Phrases such as "the home of American mountaineering" and "the center of United States alpinism" have long been used to describe the region and its relative importance in the evolution of

American climbing.[1] There are several reasons for this. At first, exploration of a previously unknown area of the country was sufficient cause for one to endure the hardships involved in traveling to the isolated Tetons. During the last century this relative isolation has, of course, changed, with highways leading virtually to the foot of the peaks. Once the range became easily accessible, mountaineers from all over began to arrive, pulled by the irresistible draw of the high peaks. Today, the summit of the Grand Teton is little more than three horizontal miles from the nearest approach road. Additionally, every peak between Death Canyon on the south and Moran Canyon on the north can be climbed in one day from a campsite at Jenny Lake, which is the center of mountaineering activity. And the climbing challenges are tremendous!

Sooner or later, virtually everyone who has done any mountain climbing in the United States visits the Tetons and ascends one or more of the high peaks. There is perhaps no climbing area in the country that can match the Tetons for general mountaineering of an alpine nature with excellent rock and moderate snow. This combination of characteristics · provides an excellent training ground for the novice, as well as the vast majority of climbers who simply seek enjoyable and challenging routes. There are also extremely difficult mixed alpine climbs that provide a testing ground for those who aspire to travel to the other great ranges of the world. From the large Himalayan expeditions of the past, to the modern alpine-style ascents of today, Teton climbers have played a key role in pioneering new routes throughout the world.

The Grand Teton has become one of the most popular peaks in the country, ranking as one of the finest mountaineering objectives in the United States. This reputation is certainly deserved. This complex mountain offers a wide variety of challenging routes on its many faces and ridges. Today one has a choice of some 80 routes and variations to the summit, with 15 more available on the adjacent Enclosure. Enjoyable ridge scrambling, high-angle rock walls, moderate snowfields, glaciers, and steep ice chutes are all to be found on this varied peak. This collection of outstanding alpine routes sets the Grand Teton apart from and above the lesser peaks of the range. The Teton Range has seen more climbing than perhaps any other range of equal size in the entire continent.

From the summit of the Grand, almost every other peak in the range can be seen. The most prominent peak from this viewpoint is Teewinot Mountain, its sharp pinnacles silhouetted against the flat plains of Jackson Hole. The Wind River Range forms the eastern horizon and one can easily pick out flat-topped Gannett Peak, the highest in Wyoming. To the north, one can see well into Yellowstone National Park and beyond, to Pilot, Index, and Granite Peaks. The rolling hills and cultivated fields of Idaho complete the vista to the west.

The climbing history of the Teton Range is lengthy and convoluted, and only a very brief outline can be given within these pages. The goal of this chapter is to provide an overview of Teton mountaineering history, as complete as possible, from its origins in the middle of the nineteenth century to the present day. In a broader sense, this history is woven intricately into the more complex evolution of climbing in the United States. By taking a look at some of the climbers who passed through the Tetons over the years, we can see not only how they affected Teton climbing history, but how they helped shape mountaineering in this country and throughout the world.

Grand Teton: Structure and Nomenclature

Since much of the mountaineering history of the Teton Range is that of the Grand Teton itself, it is necessary to try and understand the complex structure of this amazing peak. On the south, the Grand Teton is bounded by the Lower Saddle (11,600+), which separates it from the Middle Teton. Ferocious winds howl across this broad saddle from which most of the summit climbs of the Grand Teton are launched. The much sharper Gunsight Notch (12,160+) on the north isolates the Grand from its neighbor, Mount Owen. Teton Glacier lies at the foot of the steep and renowned North Face, which is bounded on the east by the pinnacled East Ridge and on the west by the North Ridge. Glacier Gulch forms the major drainage below Teton Glacier. The slabby southeast face of the mountain harbors both the East Ridge snowfield and the Otterbody Snowfield, named for its remarkable resemblance to the animal. Below the steep rock of the southeast face is Teepe Glacier, technically not an actual glacier but merely a prominent snowfield in Garnet Canyon, just south of the East Ridge.

Teepe Pillar and Glencoe Spire, two major pinnacles towering above the north fork of Garnet Canyon, are separated from the upper portion of the mountain by Black Dike, which cuts across the southern portion of the Grand Teton at about 12,000 feet. The three major ridges on the south—Exum, Petzoldt, and Underhill—named for pioneer Teton mountaineers of the 1930s, all rise above this obvious dike. From the Lower Saddle, two large couloirs or gullies extend upward for 1,500 feet to the Upper Saddle (13,160+), which lies at the base of the cliff band that guards the summit of the peak. The Upper Saddle separates the Enclosure, or western spur (13,280+) of the mountain, from the main summit (13,770). The Enclosure itself is supported by a southwest ridge, which extends down into Dartmouth Basin and a very long northwest ridge, with origins in Cascade Canyon, 5,600 feet below. The impressive northern aspect of the Enclosure rises vertically above the upper south end of Valhalla Canyon and is separated from the Grand Teton by the well-

Mt. Owen and the Grand Teton from the west. Photograph taken from near the summit of Table Mountain.
William Henry Jackson, U.S. Geological Survey

known Black Ice Couloir, which terminates at the Upper Saddle. The west wall of the Grand extends from the Black Ice Couloir north to the north ridge that reaches from the Grandstand, above Gunsight Notch, up to the summit.

Trappers, Explorers, and Surveyors

The origin of mountaineering in the United States is linked to the early exploration of the North American continent. As European settlers pushed gradually westward across the low-lying hills and then the Great Plains, they were presented with no real physical barrier until they reached the Rocky

Mountains. Lieutenant Zebulon Pike's party, which began its exploratory journey westward near St. Louis in 1806, were the first adventurers to attempt an ascent of a high peak when they reached the area now known as the Front Range of Colorado. They ended up climbing what amounted to a minor summit and, as Pike put it, could see his "Grand Peak [later known as Pike's Peak] at a distance of 15 or 16 miles from us."[2]

The next exploration of this region was led by Major Stephen Long of the U.S. Topographical Engineers, during the summer of 1820. One of the objectives was to ascertain the height of Pike's Peak. Edwin James, the botanist of the expedition, led a climbing party to the summit of the peak, which was the first known major ascent in North America. Captain Benjamin Bonneville's curiosity about the interior of the Wind River Range in Wyoming led to the next stage in the development of mountaineering. In September 1833, rather than detour around the range, Bonneville decided to explore the possibility of a direct route through the mountains from east to west. Finding the way rougher than expected, he climbed one of the highest peaks in order to scan the surroundings and find a possible way through. We may now only speculate as to which peak Bonneville's group climbed, but it could have been one of the high mountains in the vicinity of Gannett Peak, Wyoming's highest (13,875). Lieutenant John C. Fremont, led by renowned guide Kit Carson, was the next explorer to visit the Wind River Range in 1842. His group climbed what they believed was the highest peak in the range and, quite possibly, the highest in the Rocky Mountains, unfurling the Stars and Stripes on the summit. Again, it is unknown as to which peak was actually climbed, but speculation centers on either Fremont Peak or Mount Woodrow Wilson.

The next peaks to attract the attention of mountaineers were the volcanoes of the Pacific Northwest. In 1853, Thomas Dryer climbed Mount Saint Helens. Climbing parties reached the crater rim of Mount Rainier in 1852, 1855, and 1857. In 1870, the first documented ascent was made when Hazard Stevens and Philemon Van Trump finally reached the summit. Edmund Coleman, who had climbed Mount Baker in 1868, dropped out during the approach.

After much lobbying by geologist Josiah Dwight Whitney, the California legislature established its Geological Survey in 1860. Whitney became its chief, and his ambitious plan was to accomplish a complete inspection of the state. Among various scientific objectives, Whitney became curious as to which mountain was the highest in the state and if it was, perhaps, the highest in the country. He and his assistant, William Brewer, climbed Mount Shasta in the northern part of the state with this idea in mind. In 1864, a portion of the Geological Survey journeyed to the High Sierra. Among the group was Clarence R. King, who later became the first director of the U.S. Geological Survey. (The race for this highly esteemed directorship was hotly contested between King, Ferdinand Hayden, and Major John Wesley Powell.) Climbing what they believed was the highest peak, which they named Mount Tyndall, King's group observed a yet higher summit to the south, applying the name of their chief: Whitney. The loftiest peak in the continental United States was finally climbed in 1873 by three local men from the Owens Valley.

The Grand Teton was well known to travelers in the early nineteenth century as an important landmark of the headwaters of the Columbia River. The Tetons were a focal point for the fur-trapping business that prospered in the beaver-rich rivers and streams that surrounded the range. Fur trappers were the first Europeans to explore much of the wild area of western America, and their stories and exploits have now become legendary. The Grand, Middle and South Tetons were the famous "Trois Tetons" (roughly translated, three breasts), well-known landmarks to the few individuals who journeyed through this section of the United States during the first half of the nineteenth century. There has been much written elsewhere about these hardy mountain men. They were more interested in the abundant game in the valleys, and thus had little time for mountain climbing and exploration. This chapter will, therefore, only deal with those who were directly involved with climbing, and about whom there exists a written record.

One such individual was an expatriate Brit by the name of Richard "Beaver Dick" Leigh who came to the Rockies in 1849, and who made his home in Teton Basin from 1863–1899. Leigh spent most of his time trapping in the canyons on the west side of the range, but there is some indication that his explorations penetrated into the very heart of the mountains. As Leigh noted in a letter to the editor of the *Rocky Mountain News:*

> . . . as I know no liveng man as ever crossed from the East to the west side of the range althow I believe it can be done in one plas only without going to the conant trale north of the Trale creek pass south and that it over the sadle betwene grand teton and the one on the south of it altho myself and John Lunphara of Bitterroad vally tryet in 58 but it was too much for us. . .3

This passage places Leigh and his companion in Garnet Canyon, later regarded as the hub of Teton climbing, sometime during the year 1858.

Beaver Dick Leigh is the well-known guide for many of the expeditions to both sides of the Tetons during the latter half of the nineteenth century. This included the 1872 Hayden Survey expedition, during which the first recorded attempt to ascend the Grand Teton occurred. Leigh may have been Nathaniel P Langford's source for an 1873 article in *Scribner's Monthly,* in which Langford reported that a mountain man named Michaud had attempted the ascent of the Grand Teton in 1843, 29 years earlier:

> About the year 1843 an old trapper named Michaud provided himself with ropes ladders etc. but failed to reach the top, though he made the most strenuous efforts.[4]

The identity of Michaud remains uncertain. He may have been Michaud LeClaire, who served as a messenger for the Hudson's Bay Company, carrying dispatches from Fort Hall (near present-day Pocatello, Idaho) to Montreal, Canada. The ledger books of the Columbia River Fishing and Trading Company for 1837 also include a page for a Mitchael LaClair but whether this is the person to whom Langford was referring to may never be known for certain.[5]

Beginning in 1867, Dr. Ferdinand V. Hayden began a series of exploratory ventures into relatively unknown areas of the American West for the purpose of surveying their natural resources. Hayden was successful in obtaining appropriations from the U.S. Congress for these explorations and his parties were comprised of a number of naturalists, scientists and their assistants. The published annual reports of the surveys met with great popular approval, so much so that the congressional appropriations steadily grew. The 1872 Hayden Survey Expedition (properly the U.S. Geological Survey of the Territories) marks the beginning of recorded exploration of the Teton Range. This was the second of the famous "Hayden Surveys," as they have come to be known, to explore the Yellowstone region, and Congress allotted $75,000 for the expedition.

Ferdinand V. Hayden had the distinct knack of convincing extremely talented individuals to join him on these daring, exploratory ventures. One such individual was William Henry Jackson, who at that time was just beginning his career as a photographer. Through the use of the relatively new medium of photography, Hayden wished to convince others in Washington D.C. that certain choice areas of the West should be established as natural preserves that would be protected from exploitation and preserved for future generations. While the idea that Yellowstone, the world's first national park, did not originate with Hayden, he is now recognized as having been the first to promote the concept in public.[6]

We are mainly concerned here, however, with that segment of the 1872 Hayden expedition known as the Snake River Division, which fell under the capable leadership of James Stevenson, Hayden's right-hand man and long-time friend. The main objectives of the Snake River Division were to explore, map, and report on the Teton Range and the country to the east and west. One of the party's guests was Yellowstone's newly-named first superintendent, Nathaniel Pitt Langford, who had lectured, written articles, and lobbied tirelessly to have the park established. The Snake River Division traveled north from Ogden, Utah, by horseback along the old stagecoach route to Fort Hall. Converting to a pack train at this point, they then ventured east and established a base camp at the mouth of Teton Creek on the west side of the range on July 23, 1872. This base camp was occupied for nine days until August 2.

On July 27, a party of six including William H. Jackson, Charles Campbell, Philo Beveridge, Alexander Sibley, and perhaps John M. Coulter, explored the north fork of Teton Canyon for the first time. They also made the first ascent of Table Mountain, where just below the summit Jackson exposed his now-famous negatives, and gave the world its first glimpse of these mighty peaks. Meanwhile, 14 other members of the expedition attempted an ascent of the Grand Teton, leaving camp on July 28 and establishing a high camp in the south fork of Teton Canyon. Two of the 14, Nathaniel Langford and James Stevenson, claimed to have reached the summit via an ice cliff from the Upper Saddle on July 29, 1872. Three other members of the expedition reached the Lower Saddle. Frank Bradley, a geologist, stopped at the saddle to wait for the mercurial barometer carried by Rush Taggart, assistant geologist; while two 17-year-old boys, Sidford Hamp and Charles Spencer, continued some distance above the Lower Saddle but, in all probability, stopped short of the Upper Saddle. There is no question that Langford and Stevenson reached the Upper Saddle and the Enclosure, as they were the first to describe the archeological structure located at that lofty site. Langford mentioned this structure in an article that later appeared in *Scribner's Monthly*. His first description of the site was given to a reporter from the *Helena Herald* the day after the expedition was finished, and is probably the most accurate:

> The top of the Teton, and for 300 feet below, is composed entirely of blocks of granite, piled up promiscuously, and weighing from 20 to 500 pounds. On the apex these granite slabs have been placed on end, forming a breastwork about three feet high, enclosing a space six or seven feet in diameter; and while on the surrounding rocks there is not a particle of dust or sand, the bottom of the enclosure is covered with a bed of minute particles of granite not larger than the grains of common sand, that the elements have worn off from these vertical blocks until it is nearly a foot in depth. This attrition must have been going on for hundreds and, perhaps, thousands of years, and it is the opinion of Mr. Langford that centuries have elapsed since the granite slabs were placed in the position in which they were found.[7]

The Enclosure on the summit of the western spur of the Grand Teton. *Jackson Hole Historical Society and Museum*

Hence we see the origin of the name of the "Enclosure," which now refers not just to the structure, but to the entire western spur of the great peak. Who actually built the Enclosure? It is possible, of course, that it was the mysterious Michaud during the course of his attempt. It is more likely, however, that American Indians constructed it long before 1843, possibly as a vision quest site.

Much of the controversy that was to later erupt after the 1898 Rocky Mountain Club ascent of Grand Teton centers on whether or not Langford and Stevenson went beyond the Enclosure to the summit of the Grand. An interesting illustration that appears in Langford's article, entitled "Looking off from the summit of Mount Hayden," was made by famed landscape artist Thomas Moran from a sketch by William Henry Jackson.[8] Behind the two figures on the "summit," rises what very well could be the higher, true apex of the Grand Teton. Additionally, in many of the newspaper articles that appeared immediately following the 1872 climb, such as Langford's, the man-made structure (Enclosure) was erroneously reported to be on the actual summit of the peak. These errors subsequently led to confusion and, therefore, considerable doubt as to the validity of the Langford and Stevenson climb.

The question of whether or not Langford and Stevenson actually continued up to the summit from the vicinity of the Upper Saddle remains the basis of the famous and continuing controversy over who made the first ascent of the Grand Teton. In 1898, when William O. Owen and party reached the summit, they found no evidence of prior human passage. No cairn had been erected, and nothing had been left behind. Also, no photographic evidence exists from the 1872 climb. Of course, Langford and Stevenson may not have had enough time to do much of anything except to find their way safely down off the peak. It may be safe to say that we will never know if they actually made the climb, but it is clear to this author that a concise, objective presentation of the facts concerning their attempt has yet to be made.

On August 13, 1872, the two divisions of the Hayden Survey finally reunited in the Lower Geyser Basin of Yellowstone National Park. On August 16, the entire expedition assembled, listened to remarks by their intrepid leader Hayden, and were immortalized in several photographs taken by Jackson. Nathaniel Langford then came forward with a surprising proposition. He proposed that the great peak that had been climbed by he and Stevenson be known as Mount Hayden. The proposal was met with cheers and Hayden not only accepted, but stated that he considered it the highest honor of his life. However, the name never took hold, and the toponymy reverted back to the trappers' somewhat crude "Grand Teton."

Another attempt of the Grand Teton was made by members of the Hayden Survey party in 1877. In July of that year, Thomas Cooper, Stephen Kubel, Peter Pollack, and Louis McKean reached the Lower Saddle from the west and continued toward the Upper Saddle for several hundred feet. At this point, Pollack and McKean apparently stopped while Cooper and Kubel continued a considerable distance further. The various accounts of this climb differ, and it is not certain whether they reached the Upper Saddle and the Enclosure.

In 1878, sheer chance prevented a successful ascent of the Grand Teton by a third Hayden Survey party. James Eccles, a member of the Alpine Club (London), together with his Chamonix, France guide Michel Payot, accompanied the Hayden expedition to the Teton–Yellowstone region; they were slated to attempt the peak with triangulator A. D. Wilson, and his assistant, Harry Yount, (and perhaps also A. C. Ladd) on August 20. Eccles and Payot were detained at the last minute by a necessary search for two mules that strayed from their camp in the Hoback, and they were unable to join Wilson. If they had, it seems probable that they would have reached the summit since Payot was a professional guide and Eccles an experienced mountaineer. The previous summer, on July 31, 1877, Eccles and Payot had climbed a technically difficult route on the south face of Mont Blanc in the French Alps. That they were now in the Tetons is significant from the standpoint of having a guide-client type of climbing party for the first time planning an ascent of the Grand Teton, a precursor to the thousands of guided parties who now climb the peak each summer. As it was, Wilson's party got as far as the Enclosure, where he took a series of readings with his heavy surveying instruments. By extraordinary chance, 97 years later in 1975, a metal matchbox with "A. D. Wilson," inscribed in his own handwriting, was discovered by Leigh N. Ortenburger in a crack in the rocks at the summit of the Enclosure. Not only was Wilson the most experienced climber in the Survey at that time, but he may well have been the best climber in the United States in the 1870s. He had climbed many of the higher peaks of the United States, including Mount Rainier, and was very disappointed at not having reached the summit of the Grand.

In 1880, while passing through Jackson Hole during a hunting expedition, a well-to-do, itinerant Englishman and member of the Alpine Club, William Baillie-Grohman, explored the environs of the Grand Teton and reached the Lower Saddle in a haphazard attempt from a low camp. From his journal entries it seems reasonable to assume that Garnet Canyon had been explored for the second time in recorded history.[9]

CONTROVERSY

The second unsubstantiated ascent of the Grand Teton was by Captain Charles Kieffer, Private Logan Newell, and a third man, probably Private John Rhyan, about September 10, 1893. The only evidence for this ascent is a letter from Kieffer to William O. Owen on April 3, 1899, in which Kieffer describes his climb.[10] Kieffer's military records show that he was stationed at Fort Yellowstone during the summer of 1893 and, hence, presumably did have the opportunity to make the ascent. If Kieffer's drawing, which accompanies his letter, is to be taken literally, it shows his route to have been the Exum Ridge! (This technically difficult route was named for Glenn Exum's remarkable solo ascent in 1931.) Kieffer's letter also indicated that he returned in 1895, but failed because "the gradual snow field . . . had fallen and left a steep jump off that we could not climb."

In 1891, William O. Owen made the first of several attempts to climb the Grand Teton. With his wife, Emma Matilda, Mathew B. Dawson, and wife Jennie Dawson, Owen apparently reached a point somewhere between the Lower and Upper Saddles via the couloir from Dartmouth Basin. Owen returned in 1897 with Frank Petersen and made several unsuccessful attempts from different directions, one in the couloir descending to Teepe Glacier from above the Second Tower. He was nearly killed during a glissade on the glacier below, a precursor to the most common type of climbing accident today.

Finally, on August 11, 1898, a party of six sponsored by the Rocky Mountain Club (formerly the Rocky Mountain Climbers Club, or R.M.C.C., established in 1896 in Denver, Colorado) started toward the Grand Teton from a camp in the cirque north of Shadow Peak. At the Lower Saddle, Thomas Cooper, veteran of the 1877 attempt, decided not to continue; and Hugh McDerment elected to go no further at the Upper Saddle. The remaining four, Franklin Spalding, William O. Owen, Frank Petersen, and John Shive continued to the summit with Spalding largely responsible for leading and finding the route.

The Rocky Mountain Club climb was the first documented ascent of the Grand Teton. Two days later, Spalding, Petersen, and Shive returned to the summit to build a cairn and leave their names chiseled in the summit boulder while Owen obtained photographs from the Enclosure. The site of Owen's camp in the cirque between Shadow Peak and Nez Perce, along with a cache of 27 very heavy eyebolt "pitons" discarded in 1898, was discovered by Leigh Ortenburger in August 1969. One of these pitons, quite solidly placed, can be found even today in a boulder at this 1898 campsite. On July 6, 1984, the only piton actually placed by Owen on the Grand Teton was found by Rich Perch and Dan Burgette in the lower end of the Stettner Couloir. Others had been found abandoned on the rocks in 1934 on the upper Owen-Spalding Route and in 1948 at the start of the Pownall-Gilkey Route.

The now famous controversy between Owen and Langford broke out immediately after Owen's publication of a full-page article in the *New York Herald* shortly after the 1898 ascent, in which he claimed to have been part of the first group to ascend the Grand Teton. The outdoor magazine, *Forest and Stream,* then became the primary forum in which the controversy played out before a national audience. In a series of letters to the editor and in various statements and affidavits, Owen waged verbal war with Langford. The debate continues to the pre-

John Shive, Franklin Spalding, and Frank Petersen on the summit of the Grand Teton on the first certain ascent, 1898. *William O. Owen*

sent day, and may be the greatest of all American mountaineering controversies. Since historical "proof" is extremely unlikely to be forthcoming for either side of the argument, it may be best to just say that in 1872 Langford and Stevenson *may* have climbed the Grand Teton; in 1893 Kieffer, Newell, and Rhyan may have climbed it; and in 1898 Spalding, Owen, Petersen, and Shive definitely *did* succeed in reaching the summit.

Ten days after the ascent of the Grand Teton in 1898, the Bannon topographic party ascended Buck Mountain and saw the banner left by the Owen party on the summit of the Grand Teton. This topographic party also climbed several of the easy peaks along the divide during their work, which culminated in the U.S. Geological Survey (USGS) Grand Teton quadrangle map. Although the 1898 ascent of the Grand Teton received considerable publicity, it had little influence in attracting other mountaineer-

PEAKS & HISTORIC MOUNTAINEERING SITES & THE TETON RANGE

1. The Wall

This relatively minor summit was probably the first Teton peak to be climbed. In 1872, James Stevenson and Nathaniel P. Langford reached the top of a peak on the divide, which may have been this summit. The Bannon topographic party also may have climbed this peak in 1898.

2. Table Mountain

The first ascent of Table Mountain was around July 27, 1872, by William Henry Jackson, Charles Campbell, Philo J. Beveridge, Alexander Sibley and, perhaps, John Coulter. William Henry Jackson took the first photographs of the Teton Range from this peak.

3. Icefloe Lake

Icefloe Lake was the first high alpine lake in the Teton Range to be reached in a documented climb. Several members of the Snake River Division of the Hayden Survey visited the lake on July 29, 1872.

4. Dartmouth Basin

This large alpine basin immediately west of the Lower Saddle received its first documented visit on July 29, 1872, by members of the 1872 Hayden Survey on their way up to the Lower Saddle.

5. Lower Saddle (11,600+ ft.)

Located between the Grand and Middle Tetons, the Lower Saddle is often the scene of ferocious winds that prevail from the west. The first documented climb of the Lower Saddle was on July 29, 1872.

6. The Enclosure

The name "Enclosure" now applies to the entire western spur of the Grand Teton. Originally, this name described only the circular man-made structure on the summit of this subpeak.

7. Grand Teton (13,770 ft.)

The debate over who was the first to climb the Grand Teton may be the greatest American mountaineering controversy. Nathaniel Langford and James Stevenson claimed to have climbed the Grand in 1872, but the first documented climb was made in 1898 by William Owen, Frank Petersen, John Shive, and Franklin Spalding.

8. Garnet Canyon

Garnet Canyon is the "epicenter" of Teton mountaineering. Richard "Beaver Dick" Leigh may have explored this canyon as early as 1858.

9. Garnet Canyon, Petzoldt Caves

Paul Petzoldt used this area as a campsite during the early days of mountain guiding in Grand Teton National Park.

10. Garnet Canyon Trail

Glacier Trail and the 1.1 mile spur trail to the "Platforms" area of Garnet Canyon were among the first trails constructed in Grand Teton National Park.

11. Shadow Peak Cirque

From a camp at the eastern edge of this cirque, William Owen and his fellow climbers launched their successful ascent of the Grand Teton in 1898.

12. Glacier Trail

Like Garnet Canyon Trail, the Glacier Trail was one of the first trails constructed in Grand Teton National Park.

13. Amphitheater Lake

This lake served as a base camp for many historic first ascents on the north side of the Grand Teton. A memorial plaque honoring Theodore Teepe, who was killed in 1925 while descending Teepe Glacier, is affixed to a boulder on the eastern shore of the lake.

14. Valhalla Canyon

Jack Durrance and Henry Coulter entered this canyon on their historic first ascent of the west face of the Grand in 1940.

(legend continues on page 278)

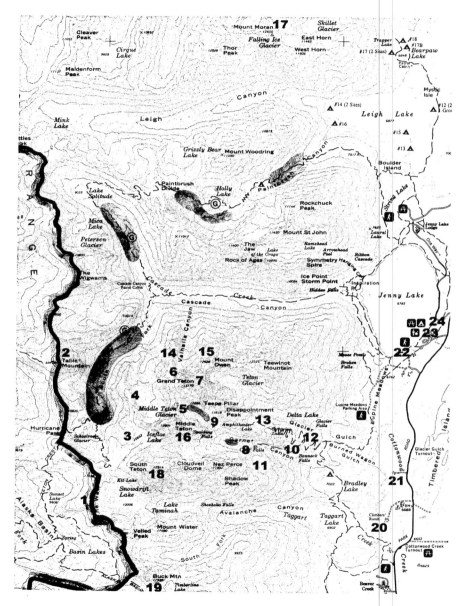

Cleaver Peak
Cirque Lake
Maidenform Peak
17 Mount Moran
Skillet Glacier
Falling Ice Glacier
Thor Peak
East Horn
West Horn
Trapper Lake
A #18
A #17B
A #17 (2 Sites)
A Bearpaw Lake
Patrol Cabin

Mystic Isle

Canyon
A #14 (2 Sites)
Leigh
Leigh Lake
A #12 (2 Groups

Mink Lake
A #16
A #15
A #13

Grizzly Bear Lake
Mount Woodring
Paintbrush Canyon
Boulder Island

Lake Solitude
Paintbrush Divide
Holly Lake
G
Rockchuck Peak
String Lake

Mica Lake
G
Mount St John
Jenny Lake Lodge
Laurel Lake

Petersen Glacier
Cascade Canyon Patrol Cabin
The Jaw
Lake of the Crags
Rock of Ages
Ramshead Lake
Arrowhead Pool
Symmetry Spire
Ribbon Cascade

The Wigwams
Cascade
Creek
Ice Point
Storm Point
Inspiration Pt.
Hidden Falls
Jenny Lake

Cascade
Canyon
Moose Ponds

2 Table Mountain
14 **15** Mount Owen
Teewinot Mountain
Broken Falls

6
Grand Teton
7
Teton Glacier
Alpine Meadows Parking Area

4
Middle Teton Glacier
5 Teepe Pillar
Disappointment Peak
13 Delta Lake
Glacier Falls
Lupine Meadows Parking Area

3
Icefloe Lake
Middle Teton
16
9 Amphitheater Lake
12
Gulch
Burned Wagon Gulch

Hurricane Pass
Schoolroom Glacier
Spalding Falls
Garnet **8** Falls
Canyon
10
Bannock Falls
Glacier Gulch Turnout

South Teton
18
Cloudveil Dome
Nez Perce
11
Bradley Lake
21

Kit Lake
Snowdrift Lake
Shadow Peak
Climbers' Ranch

Sunset Lake
Lake Taminah
Shoshoko Falls
Avalanche
Canyon
Taggart
Taggart Lake
20
Cottonwood Creek Turnout

Spring
Mount Wister
Veiled Peak
South
Fork
Beaver Creek

Basin Lakes
Buck Mtn
Timberline Lake
19

Alaska Basin

PEAKS & HISTORIC MOUNTAINEERING SITES & THE TETON RANGE (continued)

15. Mount Owen
This peak is named for William O. Owen, organizer of the 1898 ascent of the Grand Teton. Robert Underhill, Fritiof Fryxell, Kenneth Henderson, and Phil Smith made the first documented climb of Mount Owen on July 16, 1930.

16. Middle Teton
The first ascent of the Middle Teton, the third highest of the Teton peaks, was made by Albert Russell Ellingwood on August 29, 1923, via the steep southern couloir that now bears his name.

17. Mount Moran
Named for artist Thomas Moran, Mount Moran is the most complex and massive mountain in the range. LeGrand Haven Hardy, Ben C. Rich, and Bennet McNulty made the first ascent on July 27, 1922.

18. South Teton
South Teton is the fifth highest peak in the range. Its first ascent was on August 29, 1923 (the same day as the first ascent of the Middle Teton) by Albert Ellingwood and Eleanor Davis.

19. Buck Mountain
Topographer T. M. Bannon and his recorder, George A. Buck, ascended Buck Mountain ten days after the Owen-Spalding party climbed the Grand Teton

in 1898. On the summit, they built a large cairn known as "Buck Station."

20. American Alpine Club/Grand Teton Climbers' Ranch
Originally the Double Diamond dude ranch, this ranch has been leased by the American Alpine Club since 1970 and serves as a hostel for moutaineers.

21. Lucas-Fabian Homestead
Homestead of Geraldine Lucas, the first local woman to ascend the Grand Teton. The first woman to climb the Grand was Eleanor Davis.

22. Civilian Conservation Corps (CCC) Camp
Built by the CCC, the "C-Camp" became home and general hang-out for the numerous climbers who passed through Grand Teton National Park.

23. Jenny Lake Ranger Station
The park's first visitor center, the Jenny Lake Ranger Station has been the focal point of mountain climbing in the Teton Range since the park's establishment.

24. Jenny Lake Boulders
A popular climbing area, these boulders were chronicled in the humorous *Guide to the Jenny Lake Boulders*, written in 1958 by John Gill and Yvon Chouinard.

Mountaineering Map of Grand Teton adapted from the "Shaded Hiking Relief Map," Earthwalk Press.

ing visits. During the summer of 1912, Professor Eliot Blackwelder, while studying the geology of the sedimentary strata, mostly on the west slope of the Tetons, made a few ascents of peaks on and west of the divide.

The ascent of the north summit of Mount Moran in 1919 by LeRoy Jeffers was accorded more publicity than perhaps any other single Teton ascent. This ascent was due, in part, to an article that appeared in a 1918 issue of *Scientific American* containing this challenging statement: "The summit has never been attained and probably never will, as the last 3,000 feet of the mountain are sheer perpendicular walls of rock."[11] The Jeffers climb then provided the competitive motivation for a party of three that included Dr. L. H. Hardy, Ben C. Rich, and Bennet McNulty to make the first ascent of the higher south or main summit. The party beat Jeffers by ten days when he returned to make what he disappointingly discovered to be the second ascent in 1922.

GENTLEMEN CLIMBERS/
LADY ALPINISTS

The summit of the Grand Teton was not visited again for 25 years. This lack of attention is truly astonishing since wide notice was given to the 1898 ascent, and there was much climbing activity in the United States and Canada during the intervening quarter century. The Teton Range was still relatively isolated, however, from any major population center and, therefore, was left alone and remained largely unexplored. The next phase of activity began on August 25, 1923, when three students from Montana State College made a remarkable climb of the Grand Teton. Quin Blackburn, the leader (who later served in the Antarctic with Byrd), David DeLap, and Andy DePirro made the third documented ascent (the Owen party climbed the peak twice) and descent via the Owen-Spalding Route in a single day without ropes or any technical climbing equipment!

The trio of Montanans had passed an encampment of eight other mountaineers, who were there at the invitation of Horace Albright, then the superintendent of Yellowstone National Park. Albright had contacted several climbing clubs with the express purpose of attracting the attention of mountaineers to the unlimited climbing potential of the region. This, he hoped, would then generate publicity about the Teton range—an area that Albright passionately felt should be protected and preserved as a national park. The group that was camping in Bradley (Garnet) Canyon included Albert Russell Ellingwood and Eleanor Davis (Ehrman), who were both members of the Colorado Mountain Club.[12] Ellingwood, a professor of political and social science, had learned to rock climb in the English Lake District while attending Oxford University. He was easily one of the strongest climbers of the day and had made the first ascent in 1920 of Lizard Head in Colorado, the most technically difficult climb in the United States at the time.

The group's climb of the Grand Teton on August 27, 1923, completed two days after the group from Montana, marked the first ascent of the peak by a woman. Davis, a physical education instructor at Colorado College, where Ellingwood also taught,

PHOTO. BY W. O. OWEN,
AUGUST, 1898.

Upper west face of the Grand Teton, showing the Owen-Spalding route, with figure waving the American flag near summit. *William O. Owen*

was a strong climber and a vice president of the Colorado Mountain Club. This early climb by a woman is very significant. Strong female climbers were rarely seen in the predominantly male-dominated sport of mountaineering. Yet, here we see in the Tetons a tradition that has continued to the present day, namely, noteworthy alpine achievements by women who could hold their own in the sport. It is also interesting to note that, for the first time, mountaineers were traveling to the Tetons from their home ranges, pursuing climbing in their leisure time as a recreational activity and as a component of adventure travel.

Albert R. Ellingwood on the first ascent of the northeast ridge of Mt. Moran. *Carl Blaurock*

On August 29, Ellingwood, accompanied once again by Davis and E. W. Harnden, approached Middle Teton by way of the previously unexplored south fork of Bradley (Garnet) Canyon. Intent upon making the mountain's first ascent, Ellingwood did so via the steep couloir that now bears his name. His companions waited a short distance below the summit while a brief storm slammed into the peak. After the storm cleared and, after descending to the high saddle between the Middle and South Tetons, Ellingwood and the indomitable Davis then went on to make the first ascent of the northwest couloir of South Teton. All in all, this was an incredibly productive trip by the visiting Colorado mountaineers. Ellingwood returned the following year with fellow Colorado Mountain Club member Carl Blaurock,

climbed the Grand Teton once again, and then pioneered the northeast ridge route to the top of Mount Moran. Photographs taken by Blaurock during the ascent show Ellingwood climbing in his trademark leather gauntlet gloves.

MOUNTAIN GUIDING ARRIVES IN THE TETONS

Guided climbing in the Teton Range traces its origins to Paul Petzoldt and the year 1924. Paul Petzoldt began his lengthy career as a world-class climber and professional mountain guide with four ascents of the Grand Teton made in 1924. On one of these climbs, Petzoldt guided some Jackson Hole locals up the Grand, including 59-year-old Geraldine Lucas, a retired schoolteacher and Jackson Hole homesteader, who was the second woman to reach the summit. On another climb, William O. Owen, a day shy of his 65th birthday, got to the summit a second time, thanks to Petzoldt's quickly developing expertise. On August 4, 1925, after the first successful ascent of the Grand Teton that year, the first known mountaineering fatality in the range occurred when Theodore Teepe was killed while descending the large snowfield/glacier on the upper eastern face of the peak. This feature has been referred to as Teepe Glacier ever since. Petzoldt was instrumental in the recovery of Teepe's body.

The summers of 1925 and 1926 saw the first climbs of Phil Smith and Fritiof Fryxell who, during the next decade, made much of the climbing history of the range. Fryxell's excellent account of Teton climbing history up to 1931 appears in his book, *The Teton Peaks and Their Ascents*. Smith made the first ascents of Disappointment Peak and Mount Wister in 1925 and 1928. Horace Albright's dream of a Grand Teton National Park became reality on February 26, 1929, and Fryxell and Smith became the first members of the ranger staff. Fryxell had this to say about the park's establishment: "The peaks—these are the climax and, after all, the *raison de'etre* of this park. For the Grand Teton National Park is preeminently the national park of mountain peaks—'the Park of Matterhorns'."[13]

Guided by Paul Petzoldt, 59-year-old Geraldine Lucas, a retired school teacher and local homesteader, reached the summit of the Grand Teton in 1924. One year earlier, Eleanor Davis became the first woman to climb the Grand Teton. *Jackson Hole Historical Society and Museum*

The Golden Age

Fryxell and Smith seized the moment and began systematically exploring the range, making many first ascents, and placing summit registers on the prominent peaks. A complete record of the climbing history of the range is available, beginning in 1898, due largely to the fact that Fryxell painstakingly transcribed these summit registers to a card file. Fryxell and Smith also initiated the practice, in force up through 1993, of requiring climbers to check in with park authorities as a safety measure and to report all

new routes and unusual climbs. In 1929 and 1930, they made first ascents of Teewinot Mountain, Nez Perce Peak, Mount St. John, and Symmetry Spire. Fryxell, climbing solo, made the first ascents of Rockchuck Peak and Mount Hunt. With others he climbed Mount Woodring (Peak 11,585) and Bivouac Peak for the first time.

Many of the climbers who had made important first ascents and who were key players in the development of Teton climbing up to this point were members of the various mountaineering and outing clubs that were scattered throughout the country. The Rocky Mountain Climbers Club (1896), the American Alpine Club (1902), and the Alpine Club of Canada (1906) were among the first of these organizations. Universities such as Harvard, Yale, Dartmouth, and others all had mountaineering clubs that were formed in the 1920s. These clubs produced many strong climbers, and provided a framework for the organization of climbs and expeditions. A healthy spirit of competition existed between groups and, year after year, they began to come to the fabled Teton Range.

In 1929, the first climb of the Grand Teton by a route other than the Owen-Spalding Route of 1898 was made by Robert Underhill and Kenneth Henderson, both with previous climbing experience in the Alps. Underhill and Henderson, both members of the Appalachian Mountain Club, successfully ascended the East Ridge. Ellingwood and others had attempted this formidable route, but Underhill and Henderson found the key to getting around the Molar Tooth, a needle-like gendarme part way up. During the previous year, Underhill had climbed both the Peuterey Ridge and the Brenva Spur on Mt. Blanc in the French Alps. Besides being proficient alpinists, both he and Henderson were also technical rock climbers who learned their craft at New Hampshire's Cannon Mountain and other now well-known New England areas. In 1930, with Fryxell and Smith, they climbed the summit knob of Mount Owen, which had balked three attempts in 1927 and one in 1928. Underhill and Henderson also climbed the spectacular Teepe Pillar in 1930. Underhill's travels took him across the United States, and he may well have been the person most responsible for the development of roped climbing in this country at

Left to right: Robert Underhill, William O. Owen, Fritiof Fryxell, and Glen Exum, 1931. *Jackson Hole Historical Society and Museum*

that time. His article, "On the Use and Management of the Rope in Rock Work," was requested by Francis Farquar, editor of the *Sierra Club Bulletin*. Underhill was invited to the Sierra to share his revolutionary techniques and provide instructional training. A landmark climb, the East Face of Mount Whitney, was climbed by Underhill and the strongest climbers in California at the time. This select group included Norman Clyde, sometimes referred to as the "dean" of the Sierra Club climbers, Glen Dawson and Jules Eichorn.[14]

The summer of 1931 was very important in the history of Teton mountaineering. On July 15, 1931, Glenn Exum, while working as Petzoldt's assistant guide and at Paul's suggestion, made his famous solo ascent of the ridge on the Grand Teton that now bears his name. On the same day, Underhill and ranger Phil Smith pioneered the easternmost of the three great ridges on the Grand's southern flank.

Underhill also teamed up with Petzoldt for the first ascent of the East Ridge of Mount Moran. Underhill and Fryxell, in quick succession, then climbed the East Ridge of Nez Perce, the North Ridge of the Middle Teton, and the North Ridge of the Grand Teton.

It is this final climb that has become the touchstone for generations of Teton climbers. At the time of its first ascent, the North Ridge of the Grand Teton was regarded as the most difficult alpine climb in the United States. Even today, it has a reputation as *the* classic climb in the range. Previously dismissed as unclimbable by all who examined it, Underhill and Fryxell secretly believed that it was worth a try, especially after Underhill's solo reconnaissance of the route in 1930. Leaving their campsite at Amphitheater Lake at 5:30 A.M., the two climbers proceeded up and across Teton Glacier and arrived at the top of the Grandstand at 9:55 A.M. The serious climbing then began, and they soon found themselves beneath the infamous "Chockstone Chimney." Fryxell describes the crux of the climb:

Five feet out on the sheer west wall of the chimney we both found toe-room, and I climbed to Underhill's shoulders, then to his head. I could touch the chockstone but nowhere find the slightest hold. When exhausted by futile efforts I lowered myself to Underhill's side and we resorted to pitons. Underhill drove a first piton at the limit of his reach, and, from my shoulders, a second one three feet higher. A ring was snapped into each. After we were both roped securely to these, Underhill mounted to my shoulders and, using the upper ring, launched an offensive. But because of the absence of holds he likewise failed and dropped back to my shoulders. When rested he tried a second time, with the same result. At the third attempt he found a foothold well out to the right and, somehow, pushed himself over onto the chockstone— a magnificent exhibition of rock climbing.[15]

What Fryxell does not mention is his final, hoarse whisper to Underhill, "Stand on the piton!" Underhill was a major player who greatly influenced the development of technical climbing in North America. One sees in the above quote the reluctance with which these climbers used pitons. The use of pitons was still regarded unfavorably by the older generation. Underhill was visionary in that he firmly believed that pitons would test new limits of a climber's skill, and open a whole new realm of climbing possibilities.

That same summer, Fryxell made the first climbs of Cloudveil Dome, East Horn, Storm Point, and Ice Point. Hans Wittich climbed the Dike Route on Mount Moran and the Wittich Crack on the Grand Teton. During the next three years, the following major first ascents were completed, chiefly as a result of the efforts of Fryxell and Smith: Rendezvous Peak, Rolling Thunder, Eagles Rest, Doane Peak, Ranger Peak, Veiled Peak, and Prospectors Peak. Fred and Irene Ayres made their first visit to the park in 1932 and subsequently accomplished many first ascents, notably Rock of Ages and other pinnacles around Hanging Canyon, the West Horn, and Traverse Peak.

After 1935, interest shifted to the making of new routes. Throughout the 1930s, Petzoldt was guiding during the summers and made many important new climbs, such as the first ascents of Thor Peak, the North Face, West Couloir of Buck Mountain, the West Ridge of Mount Moran, and the Koven Route, West Ledges, and Northeast Snowfields of Mount Owen. The pioneering first winter ascent of the Grand Teton was made by Paul Petzoldt, his brother Eldon, and Fred Brown on December 17, 1935. They skied to the Caves in Garnet Canyon on the first day, and then spent two days ferrying loads to the Lower Saddle. From there, they proceeded to the summit via the Owen-Spalding Route. The group experienced a pleasant temperature inversion that allowed them to be in shirtsleeves on the summit while the valley below was locked in a frigid −20°F deep freeze.

In the same decade, T. F. Murphy, the chief of the party assigned by the U. S. Geological Survey to map Grand Teton National Park, ascended a great number of vantage points in order to determine elevations and sketch the topography. During the summers of 1934 and 1935, he climbed most of the peaks south of Buck Mountain, almost all the peaks of the divide, a few of the peaks west of Mount Moran, and many of the peaks bordering Webb Canyon. A climb-

er visiting one of these lonesome peaks may still find a cairn that was probably built by Murphy and his assistants, Mike Yokel Jr., and Robert E. Brislawn.

Jack Durrance, Alpinist and Rock Climber

On August 25, 1936, during his first summer in the Tetons, Jack Durrance teamed with Paul and Eldon Petzoldt to make the first climb on the North Face of the Grand Teton—the most famous north face in the United States. Durrance had come to the Tetons to work for Petzoldt's burgeoning guiding business. Previously, he had spent eight years in Germany, attending high school in Garmisch and working in Munich. There, he came in touch with mountaineers climbing at the highest standards in the Alps, including the Schmid brothers, who had made the stunning first ascent of the North Face of the Matterhorn.

For their ascent of the North Face, the trio had left the valley very early in the morning in order to sneak by another group who were camped at Amphitheater Lake. This strong group included Fritz Wiessner, Bill House, and Betty Woolsey, and rumor had it that they were in the Tetons to attempt the same climb. Earlier that same summer, Wiessner and House had made the impressive first ascent of the south face of Mount Waddington in British Columbia, which was the most difficult climb in North America. Woolsey had rock climbed back east, and was captain of the U.S. Women's Olympic Ski Team from 1937 to 1940. After being scooped on the Grand's North Face, Wiessner satisfied himself by completing the first free ascent of Underhill's North Ridge Route a few days later. This was a magnificent achievement, quite possibly the country's first climb at the 5.8 level of difficulty. Wiessner, an expatriate from Germany, was an outstanding rock technician and alpinist. Both Durrance and Wiessner were brilliant climbers who greatly influenced the American climbing scene; their paths crossed once again in the Himalaya on the legendary K2 expedition of 1939.

Jack Durrance was a passionate rock climber whose favorite routes were the ridges. With Henry Coulter and other Dartmouth climbers, he made many new routes: the East Ridge of Disappointment Peak, the Durrance Ridge of Symmetry Spire, the North Face of Nez Perce, the Southwest Ridge and Northwest Ridge of Mount Owen, the lower half of the Exum Ridge, the Southwest Ridge of the Enclosure and the West Face of the Grand Teton. The West Face had been considered by Underhill and Fryxell to be the last remaining problem on the Grand. It required the skill and experience of the next generation, however, to make the first successful ascent.

On August 14, 1940, Durrance and Coulter climbed up into the pristine cirque on the northwest side of the peak that they named Valhalla Canyon. In Jack Durrance's words, they had taken "everything we owned," including two light sleeping bags, a large, rubberized-cloth bivouac sack, and a Primus stove and pot. Their technical arsenal included "a short ice axe, ten rock pitons imported from Europe and a 120 foot, linen climbing rope from the Plymouth Cordage Company."[16] Climbing in high-topped, smooth-soled sneakers, they also included, in case the rock was wet, Durrance's felt-soled kletter-shoe and Coulter's rope-soled sandals. Legend has it that as Durrance was beginning the crux final pitch of the climb, he turned to Coulter, wondering if the belay was on, and was met with a loud snore. Durrance unleashed an abusive tirade and Coulter, by now wide awake, assured his friend that he could indeed safely proceed. This was a landmark climb and, even today, the West Face of the Grand Teton, a route that is seldom done, has a well-deserved reputation of being one of the most classic and difficult alpine climbs in the range.

Many of Durrance's routes are now considered classics and, at the time they were pioneered, represented the highest caliber of American rock climbing. Jack Durrance was a pivotal figure in the climbing scene in the Tetons and the United States. With Durrance, we see the transition from the "gentleman climber" to the totally committed climber and alpinist. The American climbing scene was about to change, but it would have to wait until the world was not preoccupied with war. In the final development of new routes before World War II, Petzoldt in 1940 and 1941 led the now popular Chicago Mountaineering Club and North Ridge Routes on Mount Moran, and the Petzoldt Ridge on the Grand Teton.

World War II

Climbing in the Tetons ground to a halt during the war years. Many of the climbers were in the service, some enlisting in the Tenth Mountain Infantry Division that was formed in July 1943. The first element of the Division was formed at Fort Lewis, Washington, and the soldiers trained on the slopes of Mount Rainier. Camp Hale, Colorado, later became the primary training center. Several of the climbers and mountaineers who were to later make significant contributions to American climbing served with this famous group. Men such as Paul Petzoldt and David Brower acted as instructors, imparting their knowledge and expertise to the troops. A significant wartime advancement was the development and later availability of specialized equipment, in the form of surplus, such as nylon climbing rope, ring angle pitons, and aluminum carabiners. The war also brought climbers from different areas together for the first time, which allowed for much information sharing.[17]

Grand Teton, North Wall

Between 1936–1940, the number of climbers who successfully ascended the Teton peaks each year was in the 200–400 range. The years following World War II brought an enormous increase in the number of climbers visiting Grand Teton National Park, with a corresponding rise in the investigation of new routes and old routes that had been climbed only once. New walls, ridges, and couloirs, purposely avoided by the pre-war climber as being too difficult, were now sought out and explored for the first time with a competence matched rarely by earlier climbers. Several ascents now considered classics were successfully completed. The most important new routes and first ascents of this period include: the North-Northwest Ridge of Buck Mountain, the West Chimney of the North Face of Mount Wister, the direct South Ridge of Nez Perce, the North Face of Cloudveil Dome, the Southeast Ridge of the Middle Teton, the West Face of the Exum Ridge, the Red Sentinel, the Southwest Ridge of Disappointment Peak, the North Face and Northwest Ridge of Teewinot Mountain, the North Face and North Ridge of Mount Owen, the Southwest Ridge of Storm Point, the direct Jensen Ridge of Symmetry Spire, the East Face of Thor Peak, the South Face I of Bivouac Peak, and the direct finish on the North Face of the Grand Teton. Nearly all of these were pioneered by a small group of active mountaineers including William Buckingham, Donald Decker, Richard Emerson, Art Gilkey, Paul Kenworthy, Robert Merriam, Leigh Ortenburger, Richard Pownall, and Willi Unsoeld. Many of these men served prestigiously either as climbing guides or seasonal climbing rangers.

The direct finish on the North Face of the Grand represents the major achievement of the time period. Climbers have a peculiar fascination for cold, icy, and foreboding north faces. The great north faces of the Alps, best represented by that of the Eiger, were long considered the ultimate alpine objective, wrought with danger from falling rock and ice. Since the time of the ascent by the Petzoldt brothers and Jack Durrance, the North Face of the Grand had taken on this mystique. Pre-war climbers had avoided the uppermost section, or "headwall." It was the challenge of the headwall, the Direttissima north face, that now beckoned to the next generation. By the time climbing guides Dick Pownall and Art Gilkey teamed up with Ray Garner in August 1949 to attempt the climb, the North Face had become the stuff of legend. Pownall brilliantly led the now-famous "Pendulum Pitch," tensioning across a blank section and gaining access to the highest of the four upward-sweeping ledges that are found on the face. After 17 hours, the best climbers of the day found themselves on the summit.

In 1953, the final portion of the North Face was unlocked by climbing guides Leigh Ortenburger and Willi Unsoeld and climbing ranger Richard Emerson. Because of the face's fearsome reputation, prospective climbers had to overcome an enormous amount of inner fear to even attempt the climb. During the ascent, Emerson, a master rock technician who had learned his craft in the Tenth Mountain Division, led the "Pendulum Pitch" free, as well as the delicate friction traverse into the "V". The classic direct North Face of the Grand Teton had been climbed. Both Emerson and Unsoeld participated in the 1963 American Mount Everest Expedition. During that trip, Unsoeld teamed up with Thomas F. Hornbein and together they made the first ascent of the West Ridge Route, one of great mountaineering feats in the history of the sport. Leigh Ortenburger, besides being the primary climbing historian of the Teton Range, became America's foremost Andean mountaineer. Durrance's west face route received its second ascent during the summer of 1953 by Ortenburger and Mike Brewer. Ortenburger and Emerson, as well as Don Decker, also pioneered the direct south buttress of Mount Moran. Durrance's climbs had been equaled and surpassed, and a new generation was making its mark.

The second postwar decade, from 1955 to 1964, saw a rapid advance in climbing ambition, courage, competence, and equipment. In step with rock-climbing progress throughout the United States, new routes were pioneered that required a high level of technical skill in free climbing and pitoncraft. The use of expansion bolts as a means by which blank faces could be ascended saw its debut during this period although, surprisingly, rock-drilling equipment had been used as early as 1898 during the Owen ascent of the Grand. The first bolts used in the United States were those placed by David Brower and his team, who had successfully climbed Shiprock in New Mexico in 1939. There is a great proliferation of bolts in some areas of the country today, especially since the advent of portable, motorized hand drills. Fortunately, there are, even now, few bolts in Teton rock. Direct aid or artificial climbing, which was a rarity in the Tetons prior to 1958, became an accepted practice and was required on many of the most difficult new routes.

Rock Climbing in the 1960s, The Yosemite Influence

By 1960, the number of climbers in the Tetons had grown to 2,300. The most significant climbs of this era were made by Fred Beckey, William Buckingham, Yvon Chouinard, Barry Corbet, William Cropper, John Dietschy, David Dingman, David Dornan, John Gill, James Langford, Peter Lev, Frederick Medrick, Leigh Ortenburger, Irene Ortenburger, Richard Pownall, Al Read, Royal Robbins, Pete Sinclair, Herb Swedlund, Willi Unsoeld, and Ken Weeks. In many instances the new climbs, often variations rather than routes, were made on smaller faces and ridges. With a new emphasis on rock climbing rather than general mountaineering, three important areas—the south ridges of Mount Moran, the South Ridges of Disappointment Peak, and the buttresses in Death Canyon—were extensively developed, although the routes in general do not lead to any summit. The easier sedimentary peaks of the north and south ends of the range, which remained untouched by previous climbers, were explored by Arthur J. Reyman, John C. Reed Jr., Robert Stagner, and Leigh and Irene Ortenburger. A partial list of the more important climbs of this era includes: the Raven, the Snaz, the Pillar of Death in Death Canyon, the Wedge on Buck Mountain, the direct North Face of Mount Wister, the Big Bluff of Nez Perce, the Robbins-Fitschen and Taylor Routes on the Middle Teton, the Northwest Chimney and the Medrick-Ortenburger on the North Face of the Grand Teton, the Black Ice Couloir on the Enclosure, the North Face and Northeast Face of Teepe Pillar, the North Face of Red Sentinel, the several north face and south ridge routes of Disappointment Peak, the Northwest Face of Teewinot, the Serendipity Arête and Crescent Arête of Mount Owen, the three east face routes on Table Mountain, the East Face of Yosemite Peak, the South Face of Ayres' Crag 5, the direct South Face of Symmetry Spire, the several ridge and buttress routes and the North Face of Mount Moran.

The deliberate search for difficult rock climbs, new in the Tetons, became the goal of many climbers. Through and into the 1950s, the range had been

regarded as primarily a mecca for alpinists. Now, the type of climber who passed through the Tetons may have just been to Yosemite, the Bugaboos, or the Shawangunks. Climbers who had learned their craft at one of these areas brought with them to this, the most accessible of alpine ranges, a level of rock climbing skill not seen in preceding generations. Home for many of the climbers of this era was the abandoned Civilian Conservation Corps (CCC) camp, located at the south end of Jenny Lake and originally known as Camp NP-4.[18] This camp was built in 1934 and occupied through 1942, as part of President Franklin D. Roosevelt's New Deal, one of many programs designed to lift the nation out of the worst depression in its history. By some estimates, up to 500 CCC workers built trails, backcountry cabins, and removed inundated trees from around the shore of Jackson Lake, whose surface area increased 50 percent by the dam constructed in 1916. The Park Service eventually established a more official climbers' campground at the site of the old CCC camp, with a camping limit of 30 days, as opposed to the then usual ten. The "C-Camp," as it was called, became home and general hangout for the numerous climbers who passed through on their way to and from the other climbing destinations across the country.

Among the CCC camp's occupants in 1957 were Southern Californians Yvon Chouinard and Kenneth Weeks, who had started climbing during nest-raiding excursions as falconers. Chouinard is now looked upon as being one of the most influential figures in modern American and world mountaineering. His talent and expertise encompassed all of the various climbing disciplines from rock and ice craft to bouldering and aid climbing. Chouinard's ice tools and pitons, products of the Great Pacific Iron Works Company, revolutionized rock and ice climbing techniques everywhere. Among his many first ascents in the Tetons, he is, perhaps, most remembered for opening up several routes in Death Canyon, including the Snaz and the Raven Crack. He also co-authored the tongue-in-cheek *Guide to the Jenny Lake Boulders* with America's most notable bouldering specialist, mathematician John Gill. Also during the summer of 1957, the first ascent of the classic Irene's Arête was accomplished by John Dietschy and Irene Beardsley. Beardsley continued to knock off cutting-edge alpine climbs, including the first all-female ascent of the North Face of the Grand Teton with Sue Swedlund in 1965. Later, while managing to pursue a career as a physicist and mother, this remarkable individual became the first woman to climb the fearsome Annapurna I, an 8,000-meter peak in Nepal.

Royal Robbins and Joe Fitschen were active in the Tetons during this period. Robbins was one of the strongest rock climbers in the world, as evidenced by such legendary climbs as the first continuous ascent of the Nose, and the first ascents of the Salathe and North America Wall routes on El Capitan in Yosemite. Since the Tetons were the crossroads of American mountaineering at the time, the passage of individuals such as these through the climbers' camp brought new ideas, expertise, and an era of intense competition. A few days after the first ascent of the awesome Northwest Chimney Route on the Grand Teton by Leigh and Irene Ortenburger and Dave Dornan, the route saw its second ascent by Robbins, Chouinard, and Fitschen. The Californians upped the ante by free climbing a pitch that the others had used direct aid on, and by finishing with the crux pitches of Durrance's West Face. As a result, the Teton regulars were stirred up and, inevitably, change would come once again to the home of American climbing.

Another Yosemite climber who traveled to the fabled Teton Range during this era was Herb Swedlund, who began as an Exum guide in 1961. Swedlund had a strong background in rock climbing, exemplified by his success with Warren Harding and Glen Denny on the southwest face of Mount Conness in the high Sierra a few years before. On July 29, 1961, Swedlund, partnered by Ray Jacquot, made the first ascent of the Black Ice Couloir on the Grand Teton, perhaps *the* classic ice route in the United States. Generations of climbers had peered into the depths of the couloir from the Upper Saddle and simply shaken their heads, dismissing the gully as too dangerous to be considered seriously as a climbing route. It had repulsed several attempts by the leading ice specialists of the day, including Yvon Chouinard. After the first successful ascent by Swedlund and Jacquot, it joined the ranks of other legendary climbs—those that were often discussed but seldom repeated.

Swedlund had climbed the elegant South Buttress Right on Mount Moran four days earlier with local climber David Dornan, thus completing the first ascents of the finest rock and ice routes in the entire range in a week-long *tour-de-force*.

The years from 1965 to 1975 saw a continuation of the search for new routes. New snow routes on Cloudveil Dome (Zorro Snowfield), Moran (Sickle Couloir), and the South Teton (Southeast Couloir) proved notable. Ice climbing was sought and found in the infamous Run-Don't-Walk Couloir on Owen, and the Hidden Couloir of Thor Peak. New mixed rock-and-ice climbs of major proportions were discovered or pieced together on the northwest flank of the Grand Teton, such as the combined Black Ice Couloir-West Face and the Lowe Route on the formidable north face of the Enclosure. This last climb marks the first time that climbers ventured onto what was the final, unexplored region of the Grand Teton. Following the only weakness in the huge wall, George Lowe and Mike Lowe were faced with difficult aid and free climbing in an immense chimney system.

Winter Alpinism

Beginning in 1965, with the first winter ascent of Mount Owen, a small group of committed and talented climbers from the Salt Lake area began a systematic series of other pioneering winter climbs in the Teton Range. The knowledge and experience gained from such ascents established this group as the new powers in the range. From February 28 to March 2, 1968, the North Face of the Grand Teton was climbed in one alpine-style push by Rick Horn, George Lowe, and Greg and Mike Lowe. This extraordinary ascent shattered the psychological barriers for winter climbing and encouraged similar challenges during the next few years. The first winter ascent of the West Face of the Grand Teton by George Lowe and Jeff Lowe in 1972 is perhaps the finest example of this kind of extreme alpine winter ascent. Both of these climbers went on to make other cutting-edge climbs throughout the world, with George among those to make the first ascent of the East Face of Mount Everest and Jeff becoming America's foremost ice specialist.

After 1965 and continuing well into the 1970s, the major emphasis once again centered on rock climbing. New faces were found: South Face of Spalding Peak; Middle, Briggs-Higbee Pillar on the North Face of Middle Teton; West Face of the Enclosure; Owen, Northwest Face; Crooked Thumb, direct North Face; Moran, West Buttress and North Buttress; and Bivouac, South Face routes II and III. Untrodden ridges were also climbed: Prospectors, upper North Ridge; Wister, Northwest Arête; and Second Tower, South Ridge. The small pinnacle of the Red Sentinel yielded two new and difficult routes. A new pinnacle, McCain's Pillar, provided a difficult ascent. Some of the better climbs were but variations on previous routes, such as Garnet Traverse on the direct South Ridge of Nez Perce; the Direct Buttress on the Northwest Ridge of Teewinot; and the Italian Cracks on the Grand Teton. Other innovative climbs included the South Buttress Central of Moran and the Southeast Chimney and Simpleton's Pillar on the Grand Teton. There were only a few new climbs in Death Canyon (Escape from Death, Widowmaker, Doomsday Dihedral) on Moran's No Escape Buttress, and on the Glacier Gulch Arêtes. A significant technical advance was made with the first free ascent of the South Buttress Right in 1973 by Steve Wunsch and Art Higbee, using a bypass of the main aid pitch. The major contributors of these climbs were Roger Briggs, Peter Cleveland, Jim Ericson, Art Higbee, John Hudson, Dave Ingalls, Ray Jacquot, Peter Koedt, Juris Krisjansons, George, Dave, Mike, and Jeff Lowe, Leigh Ortenburger, Rick Reese, Don Storjohann, Ted Wilson and Steve Wunsch.

The Modern Era

The period through 1993 has seen important developments, many in novel directions. The existing Teton extremes of the climbing spectrum—both mixed alpine climbing and pure rock climbing—were explored and extended. The year 1977 saw the beginning of both types, with the new High Route on the north face of the Enclosure and new severe rock routes in Death Canyon (Yellow Jauntice) and on No Escape Buttress of Moran (No Survivors). The

south face arena of Cloudveil Dome was opened that year (Cut Loose, Armed Robbery) and extended the following year (Silver Lining, Contemporary Comfort). But the explosion in rock climbing came with the frantic activity of 1978 and 1979, when seven new, very high standard routes were made on the same Death Canyon buttress that houses the now classic Snaz (Lot's Slot, Vas Deferens, Fallen Angel, Cottonmouth, August 11th Start, Caveat Emptor, Shattered). These remain today as some of the most difficult rock routes in the Tetons.

After the closing of the C-Camp in 1966, the Jenny Lake campground became the gathering place for climbers during the next few years, until the opening of the Grand Teton Climbers' Ranch around 1970 (previously the Double Diamond Dude Ranch). A certain degree of conflict arose during this interim period between the typical, vacationing park visitors and the more raucous climber-types, who were quite often in the Tetons for more extended periods of time. These conflicts were the source of considerable consternation to the Jenny Lake rangers who were tasked with keeping law and order in this region of the park.[19] One early inhabitant of the Climbers' Ranch was Mike Munger, an exceptional rock climber and alpinist from Boulder, Colorado. Munger emerged as the most powerful rock climber of the late 1970s and early 1980s. In the summer of 1977, Munger began a systematic exploration of the range, opening up many of the routes in Death Canyon mentioned above. He and others were also responsible for free climbing a number of existing aid climbs such as The Open Book on Grunt Arête in Garnet Canyon, now considered a classic rock climb in the range.

A number of additional rock-climbing routes were discovered in Stewart Draw on Buck Mountain (Peaches), in Leigh Canyon on No Escape Buttress (Direct Avoidance, Spreadeagle, Gin and Tonic), on buttresses and a pinnacle in Avalanche Canyon (Blind Man's Bluff, Abandoned Pinnacle), and on buttresses in Hanging Canyon (the three "bird" Arêtes: Avocet, Ostrich, and Peregrine). A major objective, the free ascent of the original South Buttress Right on Moran, was finally achieved on August 2, 1978, by Buck Tilley and Jim Mullin. The proximity to Jenny Lake of the southwest ridge of Storm Point has resulted in several new variations on generally good rock in the vicinity of Guides' Wall. The most recent new climbs in Death Canyon (Aerial Boundaries, 1985; Sunshine Daydream, 1987) are two of the finer routes among the many in that area.

The Grand Teton yielded five more routes or variations on its broad eastern expanse: Horton East Face, Beyer East Face I and II, Keith-Eddy East Face, Otterbody Chimneys. The golden rock of the direct East Ridge of Teewinot was also first climbed. A second major area for long routes of first-class climbing was extended on the huge diagonal west face of the south ridge of Mount Moran. To complement the Western Buttress (1969) the new West Dihedrals and Revolutionary Crest were added.

Perhaps the major accomplishment of recent times has been the emergence of the new, mixed, and very difficult routes on the north and west sides of the Grand Teton. In 1979, the Route Canal was established. In 1980, the prolific alpinist Steve Shea established two difficult ice lines on the north face of the Grand. In 1981, two important climbs, Loki's Tower and the Visionquest Couloir, were completed. Alberich's Alley was added in 1982 to the other classic ice lines on the west sides of the Grand and Enclosure. The first ascent of Emotional Rescue, a route put up on the golden rock of the Enclosure buttress, occurred during the summer of 1985. The set was extended in 1991 with the impressive and improbable Lookin' For Trouble on the north face of the Enclosure. These alpine climbs, when added to the existing routes—North Ridge, West Face, Black Ice Couloir, Northwest Chimney, Lowe Route, and High Route—provide an alpine climbing arena unmatched in the United States.

The return of truly alpine conditions to the Tetons brought on by generally poor weather during the summer of 1993 directed attention toward untraveled, ephemeral ice lines and major mixed climbs. The north chimney of Cloudveil Dome (Nimbus) was finally climbed, and the south-facing chute on the Second Tower was linked with the upper East Ridge of the Grand. The High Route on the Enclosure was done largely as a thin ice climb, and the Goodro-Shane Route on the north face of the Grand repeated in difficult late fall conditions.

Many climbers contributed to these most recent advances in Teton mountaineering and rock climbing, notably Jim Beyer, Dan Burgette, Yvon Chouinard, Jim Donini, Charlie Fowler, Paul Gagner, Keith Hadley, Paul Horton, Renny Jackson, Ron Johnson, Tom Kimbrough, Stephen Koch, Alex Lowe, Jeff Lowe, Greg Miles, George Montopoli, Mike Munger, Leigh Ortenburger, Steve Rickert, Steve Shea, Jim Springer, Mike Stern, Jack Tackle, Buck Tilley, Tom Turiano, Mark Whiton, Jim Woodmencey and Steven Wunsch.

CONCLUSION

The Teton Range occupies a special place in the history of American climbing. Many of those who have passed through here have been intimately involved with the evolution of mountaineering in the other great ranges of the earth. Throughout the world and here in the United States, climbing has exploded as a recreational activity. Approximately 10,000 climbers visited Grand Teton National Park in 1991 and attempted an ascent of one of the 800 routes available on some 200 peaks in the range. Park managers struggle with the management and preservation of extremely crowded, high-altitude regions such as the Lower Saddle, through which thousands of climbers pass on their way up the Grand Teton each year. In the past, the bulk of the activity occurred during the summer months. With the popularity of backcountry skiing, ski mountaineering, and climbing, winter use in the interior portions of the range has also significantly increased. Exploration of the range has also extended into some of the more extreme areas of the sport of climbing. The Grand Teton has been descended now on skis by at least three different routes. Climbers have skied and snowboarded the Black Ice Couloir. The direct North Face of the Grand Teton has been climbed in a single day from the valley, solo, and in the winter. As we enter the next millennium, what the future may have in store with regard to climbing is anyone's guess. Undoubtedly, mountaineers will forever be drawn to the Teton Range and the long, classic alpine routes leading to the summits of the peaks.

GLOSSARY & TERMS

AID CLIMBING: Climbing that involves the use of various types of paraphernalia (pitons, nuts, camming devices, etc.) to support body weight to accomplish upward progress. AID CLIMBING is distinguished from FREE CLIMBING.

ALPINE CLIMBING: Climbing routes in the mountains that may require a mixture of rock, snow, and ice climbing techniques. This type of climbing can also be referred to as MIXED CLIMBING. An ALPINIST is a practitioner of the sport of mountaineering who is well-schooled in all of these various techniques that may be required during an ascent of a high peak.

BELAY: To feed a rope either in or out (depending upon whether the climber is leading or following) in such a manner as to be able to hold a fall. This may be accomplished either by passing the rope around one's body or by passing it through some sort of friction device. The belayer is secured to the mountain by way of "bomb-proof" anchors.

BOLT: A device that is placed into a previously drilled hole in the rock. Bolts are of various types including the expansion type that exerts outward pressure on the interior of the drilled hole. Bolts are used to accomplish upward progress on blank stretches of rock, protection during free climbing, and in belay anchors. The use of portable drilling equipment recently has caused a proliferation of bolts in certain climbing areas of the country.

CAIRN: Rocks that are stacked that act as a marker on a mountain summit or that indicate a hiking or scrambling route through a section of terrain.

CARABINER: A metal snap-link that is used to attach the climbing rope to the various types of climbing equipment that are in use today including pitons, cams, bolts, etc.

COULOIR: A steep gully or chute. Couloirs form as drainage paths and often channel various types of debris including water, rock, ice, avalanches, etc.

CRUX: The most difficult portion of a climb. This term can be used to refer to the most difficult pitch or the most difficult single move or moves on a particular climb.

DIFFICULTY RATINGS: A classification system in which the difficulty of a particular climb is assigned a specific grade. For rock climbing in the United States, the Yosemite Decimal System is used and currently this scale extends from 5.0 to 5.14.

FREE CLIMBING: Climbing in which upward progress is unsupported by the various types of equipment available to the climber. This equipment is placed only to safeguard the climber through the belay in the event of a fall.

KLETTERSCHUE: A German term referring to tight-fitting rock climbing boots.

PITCH: The distance between one belay position and the next. Some climbs are multi-pitch.

PITON: A metal device that is usually driven into a crack in the rock with a hammer tapering at one end and having an eye through which a carabiner is clipped on the other. Pitons come in many different sizes.

ROCK CLIMBING: Climbing that primarily consists in upward travel on rock. A great variety of technical equipment has been developed for this type of climbing, including "sticky rubber" soles for shoes and many different types and sizes of protection devices.

Notes

General references: Lorraine and Orrin H. Bonney, *The Grand Controversy* (New York, NY: The AAC Press, 1992); Bob Godfrey, Chelton, and Dudley, *Climb! Rock Climbing in Colorado* (Boulder, CO: Published for the American Alpine Club by Alpine House Publishing, 1977); Chris Jones, *Climbing in North America* (Berkeley, Los Angeles, London: Published for the American Alpine Club by the University of California Press, 1976); Leigh N. Ortenburger, and Reynold G. Jackson, *A Climber's Guide to the Teton Range* (Seattle, WA: The Mountaineers, 1996); and Alfred Runte, *National Parks, The American Experience* (Lincoln, NE: University of Nebraska Press, 1979).

1. Chris Jones, *Climbing in North America* (Berkeley, Los Angeles, London: University of California Press for the American Alpine Club, 1976).

2. Z. M. Pike, *The Journals of Zebulon Montgomery Pike*, ed. Donald Jackson (Norman, OK: University of Oklahoma, 1958).

3. Richard [Beaver Dick] Leigh, Letter to Mr. Editor, (Denver) *Rocky Mountain News*, probably late December 1894.*

4. Nathaniel P. Langford, handwritten manuscript, the first version of his subsequent article in *Scribner's Monthly*, Yellowstone National Park library, Wyoming.*

5. Fort Hall Ledger Book, 1837, Columbia River Fishing and Trading Company, Manuscript 938, p. 136, Oregon Historical Society, Portland, Oregon.*

6. Mike Foster, *The Life of Ferdinand Vandeveer Hayden.* (Niwot, CO: Roberts Rinehart Publishers, 1994), p. 235.

7. Nathaniel P. Langford, "Dr. Hayden's Geological Survey," *Helena Daily Herald*, September 9, 1872, p. 1, c. 2.*

8. Nathaniel P. Langford, "The Ascent of Mount Hayden," *Scribner's Monthly* 6 (2) (June 1873): 146.

9. Baillie-Grohman, *Camps in the Rockies.*

10. The Kieffer letter was first uncovered in the Owen papers at the Western History Research Center, University of Wyoming, Laramie, by Leigh N. Ortenburger in the spring of 1959.*

11. "The Jackson Hole Country of Wyoming," *Scientific American*, March 30, 1918, p. 272.

12. At a meeting held June 3, 1931, the United States Geographic Board gave official status to 61 place names in Grand Teton National Park, which had previously been approved by the National Park Service. Garnet Canyon was originally named for the geologist on the 1872 Hayden Survey, Frank Bradley, who was one of the members of the expedition that made it to the Lower Saddle.

13. Fritiof M. Fryxell, "The Grand Tetons: Our National Park of Matterhorns," *American Forests and Forest Life 35* (August 1929): 455.

14. Jones, *Climbing in North America*, p. 127.

15. Fritiof M. Fryxell, *The Teton Peaks and Their Ascents* (Grand Teton National Park, WY: The Crandall Studios, 1932), pp. 56–57.

16. Interview of Jack Durrance and Henry Coulter by Renny Jackson, September 23, 1988.

17. Interview of Gerald B. Cullinane, member of 87th Mountain Infantry Regiment, F Company, 10th Mountain Division, by Renny Jackson, December 6, 1997.

18. Daugherty, John, "A Place Called Jackson Hole: A History," draft, Grand Teton National Park, National Park Service.

19. Pete Sinclair, *We Aspired: The Last Innocent Americans* (Logan, UT: Utah State University Press, 1993).

*Notes marked with this symbol were taken from an as yet unpublished manuscript by Leigh N. Ortenburger on the history of the Teton Range in the nineteenth century, and based on research done by that author. Ortenburger is considered by many to be *the* climbing historian of the range.

CHAPTER

Conservationists

. . . we believe the entire Jacksons Hole should be set aside as a recreation area . . . .

—1925 Petition, signed by 97 Jackson Hole landowners.

The two reasons which have moved me to consider this project are: 1st, The marvelous scenic beauty of the Teton Mountains and the Lakes at their feet, which are seen at their best from the Jackson Hole Valley; and 2nd, The fact that this valley is the natural and necessary feeding place for the game which inhabits Yellowstone Park and the surrounding region.

—John D. Rockefeller Jr., *A Contribution to the Heritage of Every American: The Conservation Activities of John D. Rockefeller Jr., 1957*

Establishment of the National Elk Refuge in Jackson Hole became necessary as homesteaders took up the prime land in the valley, which had previously been winter range for elk. *Jackson Hole Historical Society and Museum*

When[1] John Holland and John Carnes settled in Jackson Hole in 1884, they followed a tradition ingrained in the American character by 300 years of history. The worth of natural resources correlated directly to their utility to people. Americans exploited resources wantonly with little regard for future needs or their intrinsic value. Ironically, abundant natural resources reinforced these values and patterns of use. Americans deceived themselves into believing these resources inexhaustible. The continent's natural wealth underpinned America's astounding industrialization and growth in the late nineteenth century, generating the "myth of super-abundance," a widely shared view in the Gilded Age.[1]

Disturbing examples countered this fallacy. Commercial loggers had deforested many areas in the upper Midwest, leaving bared lands and damaged watersheds. The decimation of the North American bison, more commonly known as the buffalo, provided another startling example. Once numbering more than 60,000,000 fewer than 1,000 bison were known to exist in the United States and Canada following the great slaughters of the 1870s and 1880s. No sooner had the bison been almost exterminated than ranchers introduced cattle on the vacated lands, turning their livestock loose to graze on the open range. This resulted in serious depletion of the grasslands.[2]

Perceptive individuals were appalled by these events and pushed for reform. The conservation movement was born in the late nineteenth century, galvanized by the wasteful use of resources. This movement coincided with the rising importance of science and technology in American society and was, in fact, "a scientific movement," led by people educated in hydrology, forestry, and geology. Conservation's "essence was rational planning to promote efficient development and use of all natural resources." Rather than prevent the development and use of natural resources, conservationists believed that scientific practices applied to resource exploitation would open new opportunities. The utilitarian conservationists' viewpoint influenced federal policy in the late nineteenth century and achieved dominance during the administration of President Theodore Roosevelt.[3]

Utilitarian conservation emerged from the movement to develop water reserves in the West by building dams and irrigation systems. This culminated in the Carey Act of 1894, a failed attempt to promote water development through private and public partnership. The Reclamation Act of 1902 created a federal bureau and provided authority for federal financing of water projects. Concerned over the depletion of forest watersheds and forests through intensive lumbering, Congress passed an amendment known as the Forest Reserve Act in 1891, which gave the president the authority to withdraw forest lands from the public domain. These laws shaped the history of the West in a profound way. The Reclamation Service launched four projects in 1903; by 1910, 24 projects were in progress. Through the Forest Reserve Act alone, 13,000,000 acres of land were set aside by President Benjamin Harrison.[4]

Another faction of the conservation movement favored withholding lands from commercial use, or at least limiting such use; this group became known as preservationists. Their spokesman in the late nineteenth century was John Muir who, through books and articles, publicized the need and validity of setting aside preserves for recreational and aesthetic purposes. After 1900, preservationists and utilitarians clashed dramatically over the proposal to build a dam in the Hetch Hetchy Valley in Yosemite National Park. The dam's purpose was to store water for domestic use in San Francisco. The fight elevated conservation issues to a national level, and although the dam was built, Americans for the first time entertained serious doubts about the benefits of development as opposed to preservation of wildlands.[5]

The emergence of the conservation movement coincided with frontier settlement in the 1890s. In general, western citizens opposed conservation practices, because they usually involved prohibiting or re-

stricting activities on public lands. Americans had been used to a federal policy devoted to handing over the public domain to the private sector; westerners viewed with suspicion and hostility policies reserving lands. Yet conservation has a long history in the Jackson Hole region, preceding settlement by 12 years. In 1872, Congress established Yellowstone National Park, a 2,000,000-acre preserve "reserved and withdrawn from settlement, occupancy, or sale . . . and dedicated and set apart as a public park or pleasuring ground for the benefit and enjoyment of the people. . . ." This law represented a radical departure from previous land laws passed by Congress.[6]

The first homesteaders had been in Jackson Hole a mere seven years when Congress passed the Forest Reserve Act of 1891. Even though the law failed to define the function of the new reserves and provide for their protection, it did withdraw selected lands from settlement or other transfer to private ownership. Consequently, some scholars consider the 1891 law among the most significant pieces of conservation legislation in American history. President Harrison, exercising his new authority, issued a proclamation that established the Yellowstone Timber Reserve. Comprised of more than 1,000,000 acres of forest land situated around Yellowstone National Park, the southern part of the reserve included a portion of Jackson Hole.[7]

Congress passed the Forest Management Act of 1897 to administer the forest reserves. The law empowered the Secretary of the Interior "to regulate the occupancy and use" of the forests. General Land Office employees administered the reserves initially. They were experts in public land law, not forest or range management. Nevertheless, the division launched management activities later followed by the Forest Service such as fire suppression and prevention, timber sales, grazing permits, tree planting, and even timber management plans.[8]

Meanwhile, President Grover Cleveland created 13 new forests, among them the Teton Forest Reserve in 1897. The new 829,410-acre forest included the northern section of Jackson Hole. In 1898 or 1899, Charles "Pap" Deloney, the valley's pioneer merchant, was appointed the first supervisor of the forest. Forest Superintendent A. D. Chamberlin gave Deloney classic instructions: "As I have no rangers in that portion of the reserve there is nothing for you to do as far as I am concerned but go up there and take it." The reserve received an appropriation in 1898 and Deloney set to work. In 1900 the Forty-Mile Fire burned in the Hoback area through the summer. For the first time, the Forestry Division hired crews to suppress a wildfire in the Jackson Hole area. A heavy snowfall finally extinguished the fire in the fall, although a telegram to Washington reported "through our heroic efforts the fire has been put out." Deloney resigned in 1902, turning the duties over to W. Armor Thompson, a local settler.[9]

Events demonstrated that forest personnel needed to become more professional and active in the field. Artist and Cody rancher A. A. Anderson grew increasingly alarmed over the squandering of resources such as overgrazing, poaching, and forest fires, some allegedly started by sheep grazers. Anderson traveled to Washington, D.C., to lobby for an expanded Yellowstone reserve, along with sufficient funding to manage it. President Roosevelt agreed and issued an order creating the Yellowstone Forest Reserve in 1902. Anderson was appointed special forest superintendent of the gigantic reserve, which encompassed 8,329,000 acres. He divided it into four divisions, the Shoshone, Absaroka, Wind River, and Teton. Robert E. Miller was appointed supervisor of the Teton Division. In 1905, Congress transferred all forest reserves from the Interior Department to the Department of Agriculture and changed the name of the Bureau of Forestry to the Forest Service. Three years later in 1908, President Roosevelt issued another executive order carving seven national forests out of the Yellowstone reserve. This order established the forests in the region as they generally exist today. Comprising nearly 2,000,000 acres, the new Teton National Forest included most of the mountains and forests around Jackson Hole.[10]

Anderson created an organization to manage the Yellowstone reserve. Division heads such as Miller reported directly to Anderson and, in turn, rangers reported to the division supervisors. Recruiting a staff posed a significant problem. The first rangers were hired primarily for their skills as wranglers, packers, and outdoorsmen rather than professional skills in range management or forestry. Desired technical skills included land surveying and timber measure-

ment. In a real sense, forest rangers or "government men" represented a new breed of frontiersman—the resource manager. These individuals brought the theories of conservation into practice in the field. Forest Service employee C. N. Woods recalled administering a Civil Service exam in 1908, probably in Jackson Hole:

> There were no definite educational requirements. Some passed the examination who had never completed the eighth grade in school. If one could read and write and knew a little arithmetic, and if he could ride and pack a horse, run a compass line, and do the simplest surveying, he stood a good chance of passing the examination. Practical experience was the principal requirement. A knowledge of woods work and of the handling of livestock on the ranges, helped.

Professional foresters were scarce in the early years. For example, in 1905, American universities had produced only 115 foresters, most of whom joined the Forest Service.[11]

Special Forest Supervisor Anderson launched several major projects. First, he initiated a boundary survey. Ten men, using 35 saddle and pack animals, performed the survey in three months, no mean feat considering the rugged terrain and size of the 13,000-square mile reserve. Second, he continued to direct the establishment of a permit system for grazing and timbering. W. C. Deloney had issued the first grazing permits in 1901, arousing the ire of local settlers accustomed to free run of the range. It is unclear if there was a fee. By 1906, when complete records were kept for the first time, the Forest Service charged ten cents per head for cattle up to 100 head and 20 cents per head for numbers in excess of 100. Horses cost 20 cents. The first recorded timber permits were issued in 1904. Ben Sheffield purchased 1,920 poles, 30 cords of wood, and 32,400 board measures of saw timber at a cost of $49.50 on June 7. A week later, Ed Blair purchased 100,000 board measure of timber for his mill near Wilson. In addition, the Forest Service sold native hay to Louis Joy and Ben Sheffield.[12]

The new permit systems met resistance, especially from ranchers. When the Forest Service mailed out instructions for permits in 1901, they

Game warden Charlie Peterson in
the doorway of a "tusker's" cabin,
ca. 1920. Poaching patrol was a
daily routine for rangers in the
early twentieth century. Elks Club
members used elk teeth for cere-
monial jewelry, which made poaching a profitable enterprise. *Jackson
Hole Historical Society and Museum*

"aroused quite a protest from settlers." After a season, however, Jackson Hole ranchers accepted the
system and even seemed to support it, for they circulated a petition in the fall of 1901 urging an expansion of the existing reserve.[13]

Cattlemen supported the new grazing restrictions because, in their view, the system would keep
sheep out of the reserve. Local ranchers resented the
intrusion of "tramp sheep" in their area, because they
believed sheep destroyed the range, and sheep ranchers often ranged their sheep far from their home
ranch. When Anderson received reports of 60,000
sheep from Utah trespassing on the reserve, he assembled 65 rangers on Horse Creek near Jackson
Lake, all "armed and well mounted," to drive them
off the forest. Because 40 armed sheep herders
guarded the herds, violence was a real possibility.
Anderson's company confronted them and served
sheep owners with injunctions prohibiting them
from trailing or grazing sheep on forest lands. This
confrontation ended peacefully, while Anderson succeeded in enforcing the authority of the Forest Service. Violence erupted in the Green River Valley
when cattle ranchers slaughtered 800 sheep and
burned a herder's camp. Smaller ranchers opposed
grazing permits originally because they feared that
large cattlemen would squeeze them out. Their fears
failed to materialize, for of 56 permits issued in

1906, only four exceeded 300 head, while the overwhelming majority of permittees owned fewer than
100 head of cattle.[14]

The new bureau joined forces with state game
wardens and local lawmen to drive tuskers and poachers out of Jackson Hole. Elk and beaver were particular targets of poachers. Tuskers killed elk for their eyeteeth, which were used for jewelry. In particular, the
Benevolent and Protective Order of Elks mounted
eyeteeth on watch fobs as an unofficial badge. Appalled at the slaughter, the Elks Club became a potent force in protecting the animal, and stopped using
elk teeth as a badge. Prices ranged from $10 to $25
per pair, but contemporary accounts record prices as
high as $100. These prices tempted a number of peo-
ple to become tuskers. "Poacher" patrol became a routine duty of the forest ranger. It proved hazardous
duty. Once, an unknown sniper took a shot at ranger
Al Austin. On another occasion, south of Yellowstone
National Park, Anderson blundered into three tuskers
he had previously ordered out of the reserve. Putting
on a "bold front," he gave them a week to pack their
camp and move out. He expected to be shot as he
left, but nothing happened. "I was playing in luck,"
he recalled. In September 1907, Rudolph Rosencrans
spent 12 days traveling and serving as a witness
against tuskers Binkley and Purdy at their trial at
Fort Yellowstone.[15]

It was a long and often bitter struggle to create the Grand Teton National Park we know today. Shown here is the 1929 dedication of the original Grand Teton National Park. Horace Albright, director of the National Park Service, is speaking to the crowd. *Grand Teton National Park*

The Forest Service made improvements that benefited the residents of Jackson Hole and defused resentment. For example, by 1909 the Forest Service had built telephone lines that connected isolated areas of the valley with Jackson and Victor, Idaho. Rangers also improved transportation links in the valley, cutting trails in the forest and building bridges. In 1904, C. N. Woods, John Alsop, and Rudolph Rosencrans built a bridge on the Buffalo Fork near its confluence with the Snake. In 1908, Rosencrans repaired the same bridge during the winter.[16]

Settlers in Jackson Hole also accepted the Forest Service because local residents filled the ranks of the organization. Bobby Miller, first the division supervisor, and then supervisor of the Teton National Forest from 1908 to 1918, was among the first homesteaders in the valley and a lifelong resident. In a real sense, the Forest Service, though a federal bureaucracy, was part of the community. Even "government men" from outside the country assimilated quickly.

Supervisor Miller directed local policy and operations during the important formative years. A. C. McCain took over as supervisor in 1918 and served until 1936. McCain directed the Teton National Forest through a tumultuous period that included the controversy over the creation of a Grand Teton National Park, the Great Depression, and the implementation of New Deal programs such as the Civilian Conservation Corps in 1933.

To administer the reserve, employees constructed ranger stations, patrol cabins, and fire lookouts. The first cabin was built in the fall of 1899 on the shores of Jenny Lake. The cabin existed as late as 1922, but was removed sometime after that date. By 1908, forest ranger Al Austin had built the Stewart Ranger Station at Beaver Creek. After the creation of Grand Teton National Park in 1929, the building was used alternately as the park headquarters and a residence. The Park Service built major additions in 1938. The building is used as office space today and is the oldest known Forest Service building in the park. The Arizona Guard Station was another early Forest Service building located on Arizona Creek near Jackson Lake. Built in 1919 according to park records, the rustic cabin was relocated to the Lizard Creek Campground in the 1960s where it is used as a camp-tender's station today.[17]

Fire suppression was a significant job of the Forest Service. To help fulfill this responsibility, the Forest Service built fire lookouts on high locations and staffed them during the fire season (usually June through September). In the 1930s, the Forest Service built fire lookouts at six locations, among them Blacktail Butte and Signal Mountain. In 1940, they built a 79-foot steel lookout tower on the knoll west of Spaulding Bay, along with a small quarters at its base. The Blacktail Butte Lookout was a simple frame building with windows on three sides. The Signal Mountain Lookout was an attractive building

Spaulding Bay fire lookout, built c. 1940. Fire suppression was a goal of early wilderness management. However, the fuels build-up that this suppression created would have a devastating effect by the 1980s, when fires raged out of control throughout northwest Wyoming. *Grand Teton National Park.*

made with stone walls and sliding easement sash on all four sides. Both lookouts had a pyramid-shaped roof covered with wood shingles. All three had been removed by the mid-1960s.[18] Two complexes associated with early Forest Service administration remain extant in the Teton National Forest; one is the Rosencrans' Blackrock Ranger Station, and the other is the Huckleberry Mountain Lookout tower. Both are listed in the National Register of Historic Places.[19]

The Reclamation Service followed the Forest Service into Jackson Hole. Through the Reclamation Act of 1902, the federal government became involved in water development projects in the West. Reclamation Service surveyors entered Jackson Hole in the fall of 1902 seeking suitable sites for water storage. They evaluated Jackson Lake and other large lakes. Engineers returned and completed a temporary log crib dam at the outlet of Jackson Lake by 1907. After this dam failed in 1910, the Service launched an even larger project, building the present

concrete dam over the winter in 1910–1911. By 1916, the concrete structure had been built up and an earthen dike extended to the north. The dam and dike raised the water level of Jackson Lake 39 feet, impounding 847,000 acre feet of water. The dam was part of the Minidoka Project, a large-scale water reclamation program designed to irrigate arid lands in Idaho. As documented in a previous chapter, the construction of the dam influenced the history of Jackson Hole in several ways, but most important, it remains the largest water reclamation project in the valley's history and left a profound environmental impact.[20]

Elk generated the first local support for conservation. When homesteaders arrived in Jackson Hole in the 1880s, an estimated 25,000 animals comprised the Jackson Hole elk herd. Whether or not the first pioneers adopted a conservation ethic toward the herd is questionable, for sources suggest a wasteful attitude toward wildlife. Mrs. Mae Tuttle, the former Mary White, recalled anything but a conservationist's ethic: "There was so much game wasted in those days . . . it makes me shudder to think of the times we have shot down a fat elk and taken only the hams and the loins and left the rest to the coyotes." She also recalled an occasion when settlers gathered along the Snake River to participate in a fishing contest sponsored by a manufacturer of fishing line. "Do you remember Mr. White caught two gunnysacks full of trout? . . . Most of the fish were wasted though everybody ate all they could."[21] Further, as settlers preempted lands that made up elk migratory routes and winter range, conflicts developed. As a result, elk raided haystacks during the winter. Ranchers tried different tricks to frighten off the elk, but offenders were sometimes shot, albeit as a last resort.

The Wyoming territorial government implemented game protection laws as early as 1869, but there was little effective enforcement. Despite a law prohibiting the killing of game animals for anything except food, "game hogs" and hide hunters raped the territory. Laws protecting wildlife were enacted by the state of Wyoming after 1900, but again with little effect. The state appointed a state game warden in 1899 to enforce hunting laws.[22]

The first well-known effort to enforce hunting laws provoked the so-called "Indian Scare of 1895."

The incident resulted from a long-simmering dispute over Native American hunting rights in Wyoming. The Fort Bridger Treaty of 1868 guaranteed members of the Shoshone and Bannock tribes hunting rights on public lands in Wyoming, rights exercised by the tribes. Settlers perceived that the Indians threatened their livelihood, for by 1895, "perhaps two dozen families . . . had come to depend on guiding for their support." Moreover, elk was a mainstay in the diet of most homesteaders. Not only did settlers resent Indians hunting in violation of state laws, but rumors circulated that they slaughtered elk for their hides. During the summer of 1895, Constable William Manning led several posses after hunting parties from Fort Hall, Idaho. On July 11, a posse arrested a group of Bannocks, including women and children, at Battle Mountain in the Hoback Canyon. Accounts of what happened next are unclear, but the Indians may have panicked in fear of being massacred, and broke for the forest. Manning's posse killed one Bannock and wounded one other.

Panic swept through the valley as settlers forted up at the ranches of Pierce Cunningham, R. E. Miller, and Erv Wilson. Alarming reports reached the outside world of massacred settlers in Jackson Hole. All were false. The only casualties were Sylvester Wilson, who died of a heart attack, a calf killed during the night, mistaken for a warrior bent on retaliation, and "Old Capt. Smith," who was wounded. Mae Tuttle"always believed that the idiot shot himself." The incident precipitated a case that went to the Supreme Court. *John H. Ward vs. Race Horse* affirmed the rights of states to regulate hunting and wildlife, which proved to be a landmark case. Economic self-interest, fueled by racial animosity, motivated the settlers' actions.[23]

Contemporary sources demonstrate that state hunting laws were not applied uniformly, nor enforced in some cases. In 1897, Col. S. B. M. Young, the acting superintendent of Yellowstone, complained to the Secretary of the Interior about the slaughter of elk in Jackson Hole. Young considered state protection inadequate and recommended extending the authority of the military into Jackson Hole to protect the elk herd. A. A. Anderson reached similar conclusions. He recalled the occasion when he caught a young man red-handed for killing

deer out of season. Though young, the poacher was no fool. He requested a trial by his peers and, after deliberating, a six-man jury concluded that, "he did it, but we won't find him guilty this time."[24]

In 1902, *Outdoor Life* published letters critical of lax wildlife protection in Wyoming and, in particular, Jackson Hole. A letter from William L. Simpson of Lander, Wyoming, appeared in the January issue, titled "Game Conditions in Wyoming." Simpson witnessed incidents in the fall of 1901 that left him "unutterably surprised at the conditions confronting the wild game of the state. . . . At Jackson's Lake, I personally observed elk teeth trafficked in violation of the law, and in the presence of a deputy game warden." He complained that game protection was a farce in western Wyoming and laid the blame on unqualified wardens directed by Albert Nelson, the Wyoming state game warden at the time. In December of that year, the magazine published a letter written by Harvey H. Glidden, the owner of the Elka Ranch in Jackson Hole. Glidden leveled serious allegations against forest rangers, game wardens, and justices of the peace, accusing them of incompetence, corruption, and violating game laws. Holding these positions were prominent citizens, among them Pierce Cunningham, Webster LaPlante, Albert Nelson, and D. C. Nowlin. He singled out Capt. Edward Smith as a notorious poacher and illegal trader in trophies, whose violations wardens ignored. "It is commonly known Old Cap shed more elks' blood than would float any house and barn in the valley if all were put in a tank." Referring to Constable Manning as "Old Hungry Bill," Glidden perceived that ". . . bumptious Bill has been sucking the public teat for many seasons past, giving nothing but evil for the good money he has received. . . ." As a result of lax enforcement and tusking, Glidden wrote that "elk teeth are the coin of the realm, all over Jackson's Valley and vicinity, for the purchase of supplies of all kinds, particularly whiskey."[25]

The venom in Glidden's letter casts suspicion on his objectivity. His allegations are difficult to reconcile with the good reputations of Cunningham and Nelson. Perhaps personal or political feuds, forgotten today, motivated Glidden. He did express hope that the elections in 1902 would bring change. Taken alone, the letter should be ignored; yet taken in context with the observations of Mae Tuttle, William L. Simpson, A. A. Anderson, and Col. Young, it cannot be ignored. Together, they indicate that typical frontier attitudes prevailed in the valley.

By 1902, tuskers were entrenched in Jackson Hole and had slaughtered elk for about five years. About 1906, a group of more than 20 conservation-minded citizens formed a vigilance committee to oust tuskers from the valley. At a meeting in the town of Jackson, Otho Williams warned that anyone not willing to hold the end of a rope should leave. They elected three representatives to deliver fair warning to William Binkley and Charles Purdy, both notorious tuskers, and their henchmen. William Seebohm, Bill Menor, and Charles Harvey confronted Binkley at his ranch (today part of the Teton Valley Ranch) and passed on the message to clear out, if he and his partners valued their lives. The tuskers heeded the warning. This extra-legal act marked the beginning of change.[26]

The winter of 1908–1909 marked a turning point, when human impacts on wildlife habitat wreaked havoc on the Jackson Hole elk. After 1900, more settlers entered the valley, preempting the elks' winter range or blocking migratory routes. Exterminating natural predators such as the wolf eliminated one form of population control, aggravating the problem. In 1908–1909, several factors combined to cause a massive die-off: the elk population had increased, the winter was especially severe, and much winter range had been settled. Some ranchers donated hay once the extent of the disaster became apparent, but several thousand elk perished. Appalled at the disaster, local settlers clamored for action on the part of the state and even the federal government.

Stephen Leek, in particular, led the effort to save the elk herd from future disasters. He took glass-plate photographs of starving and dead elk, which he used for lectures, articles, and tours to publicize the dilemma. In 1909, the state of Wyoming allocated $5,000 for winter feed, and Congress followed by providing $20,000 in 1911. Yet, without adequate winter range, a healthy elk herd appeared remote. Congress acted again in 1912, authorizing the creation of a national elk refuge. The government carved the nucleus of the refuge out of 1,000 acres of public land and 1,760 acres of purchased private land in the

Flat Creek area north of the village of Jackson. R. E. Miller sold his ranch in 1914, a key acquisition in the new reserve, and Guy Germann followed in 1916, selling 250 acres. The Izaak Walton League donated purchased lands and, later, John D. Rockefeller Jr. added parcels. Today, the National Elk Refuge comprises over 24,000 acres.

The establishment of the elk refuge represented a significant achievement for conservation, and it owed its existence to the support of local citizens. The elk brought many pioneers such as Leek and Miller into the conservationist camp. Even more important, most citizens supported the government buy-out of homesteads for the refuge, signaling a dramatic change in beliefs. It was now acceptable for government to reserve public land in the name of resource conservation.[27]

The stage was set for the entry of the National Park Service. In 1929, an act of Congress created Grand Teton National Park. In 1943, President Franklin D. Roosevelt issued a proclamation through the Antiquities Act of 1906 establishing the Jackson Hole National Monument. In 1950, Congress enacted new legislation merging the park and monument. These are simple facts that fail to illuminate a struggle that spanned 50 years. Contrast this with the time span taken to create Yellowstone, a mere two years from idea to establishment. The story of Grand Teton National Park is the story of strong personalities, often pitted against each other—John D. Rockefeller Jr., Bill Simpson, Struthers Burt, Robert E. Miller, Harold Fabian, Clifford Hansen, Dick Winger, A. W. Gabbey, and Horace Albright. Further, the history of this park is the story of conflicts between institutions and ideologies. Conflicts occurred, or were perceived, between utilitarian conservationists and preservationists, the Forest Service and the National Park Service, national interests and state and local concerns, the wealthy and the common man, East and West.[28]

The effort began with the creation of a new bureau—the National Park Service. During the summer of 1916, Stephen T. Mather, the future director of the new bureau, conducted a promotional tour of Yellowstone in support of the pending legislation. During this trip, Mather and his assistant, Horace Albright, drove a party to Jackson Hole. Awestruck by the mountain scenery, Mather and Albright determined that the Teton Range and Jackson Hole should become part of the park system. On August 25, 1916, Congress approved the enabling legislation to create the National Park Service.[29]

The idea of a national park in Jackson Hole was not new. In 1897, Colonel S. B. M. Young proposed extending the authority of the military to cover the migratory routes of elk in Jackson Hole. This proposal did not include the mountains. A year later, Charles D. Walcott, head of the U. S. Geological Survey, made a similar proposal, except that the Teton Range should be included to protect them. In addition, he suggested the creation of a "Teton National Park." Neither the Interior Department nor Congress acted on either suggestion. This changed when Albright and Mather established the new bureau.[30]

Albright and Mather affirmed their commitment to adding the Teton Range in 1917, when Albright prepared the first annual report to Secretary of the Interior Lane. Adding part of the Tetons, Jackson Lake, and the headwaters of the Yellowstone River to Yellowstone National Park was one of seven "urgent needs facing the Park Service." Later in the year, Albright wrote a draft document proposing policy objectives for the new organization. He distributed the draft for comments, then submitted a final to Mather for approval. Mather supported it, and Secretary Lane signed it as a letter to Mather on May 13, 1918. Albright described it as "a landmark for those early years and became our basic creed." Regarding expansion of the park system, "you should study existing national parks with the idea of improving them by the addition of adjacent areas. . . . The addition of the Teton Mountains to the Yellowstone National Park, for instance, will supply Yellowstone's greatest need, which is an uplift of glacier-bearing peaks." Working with the Wyoming congressional delegation, Mather and Albright drew up a bill to expand the boundaries of Yellowstone into the Teton country. Wyoming Congressman Frank Mondell introduced H.R. 116651 in April 1918. To protect the extension area pending legislation, President Woodrow Wilson issued a proclamation prohibiting any sort of entry or disposal of public land without Park Service approval.[31]

Mondell introduced a revised bill in the House of Representatives in February 1919. The House approved the bill unanimously, but in the Senate, John Nugent of Idaho killed it, responding to pressure from Idaho sheep ranchers, who feared losing grazing permits. As historian Bob Righter noted, "an opportunity had been lost. Never again would park extension be so non-controversial." This failure allowed opposition in Jackson Hole time to organize against the Yellowstone extension. Four groups in particular opposed the extension—local Forest Service employees, ranchers, dude ranchers, and Jackson businessmen.[32]

On July 10, 1919, Horace Albright assumed his duties as the new superintendent of Yellowstone National Park. Not only did he guide activities in Yellowstone for a decade, but being near Jackson Hole allowed him the opportunity to promote the park idea. At first, this advantage backfired. On August 25, 1919, Albright traveled to Jackson Hole with Governor Robert Carey of Wyoming to participate in a meeting with local residents about the proposed Yellowstone extension. Albright made "a serious tactical mistake in not carefully checking the attitudes of the citizens before going to the meeting."[33] Persuaded by Governor Carey and dude rancher Howard Eaton, Albright entered the meeting blissfully ignorant. He believed that he could gain support for the park by proposing to build modern roads, a ploy that had worked elsewhere. He was wrong, later recalling that it was "about the most disagreeable evening of my life."[34]

In a meeting packed with opponents, Albright was argued and shouted down. Ranchers opposed any extension because it would reduce grazing allotments. Dude ranchers, notably Burt and Carncross of the Bar BC, opposed the plan because they did not want improved roads and hotels. Further, they expressed the general resentment against monopolies exercised by concessioners in Yellowstone, and against the regulations imposed by the army, which had administered the park. Jackson Hole residents also vented their dislike of railroads, which puzzled Albright, but which reflected that era's widespread backlash against the railroad companies. Worst of all, "the cattlemen succeeded in winning Governor Carey over to their side of the case." A supporter of the expansion when he entered the meeting room, the governor wrote Albright later that he opposed any extension at all, although he left the door open for further discussions.[35]

Other events in 1919 proved timely for park supporters. During that year, a plan surfaced to construct a dam at the outlet of Jenny Lake. Damming the flow of Cottonwood Creek would have raised the water level of Jenny Lake 20 feet and Leigh Lake ten feet. Many Jackson Hole residents were appalled at the proposal, particularly dude ranchers. Opponents of the project objected to the commercial spoilation of the pristine mountain lakes. The Jackson Lake Dam had left a monumental eyesore along the shores of the lake because the Reclamation Service failed to cut down trees in the inundated area. As a result, the water flooded several thousand acres of forest, killing the trees. The dead and fallen trees made an unsightly mess. Struthers Burt called Jackson Lake "an example so good that it is constantly being used as an object-lesson by the enemies of stupid spoilation."

In addition to spoiled scenery, the dam aroused opposition for other reasons. In 1921, the *Courier* published an editorial titled "Remember Jackson's Lake," which specified reasons for opposing dams on Jenny Lake and other lakes in the valley. Also, "using the Snake River for a ditch," benefitted only Idaho farmers and damaged property in Jackson Hole. The editorial recalled the 1917 flood that washed out the approaches to the Snake River bridge. Local residents blamed the Reclamation Service for releasing too much water in this incident.[36]

While the Forest Service acquiesced to the proposed dam on Jenny Lake and approved dams at the outlet of Emma Matilda and Two Ocean Lakes, the National Park Service blocked the projects. Based on correspondence and reports, historian Robert Righter characterized the Park Service as "downright pugnacious" on the issue. Horace Albright, using the veto power granted by the 1918 executive order, provided the spine. The Park Service stand against dams in Jackson Hole was an important turning point. Opponents of the projects, contrasting the position taken by the Forest Service with the Park Service, came to view, albeit over time, a national park in Jackson Hole favorably. Valley residents such as Joe

Jones, among the first to support the park, and Struthers Burt began to correspond with Albright. Thus began an alliance between Albright and important local figures.[37]

Meanwhile, Albright lobbied hard for an extension of Yellowstone's boundaries into Jackson Hole. He corresponded with people having political influence, as well as with renowned authors. Whenever possible, he brought influential visitors to Jackson Hole to promote his vision for a park. Albright made a special effort to get to know people in Jackson Hole, seeking allies and taking the measure of opponents. Homesteader and Jackson businessman Joe Jones gave Albright important information in these years. At the 1919 meeting it became apparent that Struthers Burt could be an articulate and formidable opponent of extension. Albright believed Burt's and Carncross's motives were based on self-interest—they wanted to keep the public out of Jackson Hole to protect the wilderness setting of their dude ranch. But the dude ranchers and Park Service found common interests in protecting the valley from commercialization. By 1920, Burt and Albright were exchanging letters and, on September 26 of that year, Albright visited Burt at the Bar BC.[38]

National Park Service and local interests merged at the well known meeting at Maud Noble's cabin on July 26, 1923. Albright was invited to the meeting. Present were Joe Jones, Dick Winger, Struthers Burt, Jack Eynon, Horace Carncross, and Maud Noble. The group considered ways to preserve the valley from commercial exploitation. They devised what has come to be known as the Jackson Hole Plan. Although the plan varied somewhat, depending on the source of information, the group decided to do two things. First, seek private funds to purchase private lands in Jackson Hole. To that end, the group decided to raise travel money to send a small delegation east to solicit funds. Second, create a reserve or recreation area that would preserve the "Old West" character of the valley, or "a museum on the hoof"

Specifically, lands were to be purchased north of the village of Jackson. Rustic log architecture would prevail, and Jackson would be preserved as a frontier town. Ranching would continue in Spring Gulch and in areas south of Jackson. Indigenous wildlife such as antelope would be reintroduced, wildlife range protected, and the wilderness character of the valley protected.

The participants did not support a national park or an extension of Yellowstone's boundaries, "because they wanted the traditional hunting, grazing, and dude-ranching activities to continue." Though the plan fell short of his dream, Albright generally supported it, seeing it as a way to protect the valley from commercialization. Further, this meeting set the course of events that led to the involvement of John D. Rockefeller Jr. Yet a national park seemed best suited to the central aim of the so-called Jackson Hole Plan. Joe Jones had supported a park extension as early as 1909, and Burt seems to have embraced the idea by 1923. In a letter to Albright dated September 11, 1923, Burt wrote exuberantly:

> For God's sake let's put this thing over—It is the biggest idea of its kind since the actual inception of Yellowstone itself—a *natural history museum on the hoof;* the only thing of its kind in the world. A park that of itself would finance all the other parks in the country; And a monument to the men who would help it along, with the Grand Teton as their headstone— that's big enough to fire any man's imagination.[39]

During the 1920s, two events occurred that cleared the way for the establishment of Grand Teton National Park. The President's Committee on Outdoor Recreation created the Coordinating Commission on National Parks and Forests to evaluate proposed park extensions and resolve boundary disputes between the Park Service and Forest Service. The Teton Range and Jackson Hole were among a number of areas studied by the commission. In October 1925, they issued a report and recommendations. They recommended the creation of a separate park to include the main portion of the Teton Range, about 100,000 acres, but believed the bulk of the proposed 600,000-acre Yellowstone extension of 1918–1919 should remain national forest.[40]

Two years later, a sub-committee of the Senate Public Lands toured Yellowstone to study the proposed boundary changes. On July 22, 1928, the sub-committee conducted a meeting in the upstairs hall of the Clubhouse in Jackson. Seventy-seven people attended the meeting. A show of hands, save one, favored the park. Pioneer William Manning disapproved of any legislation that would remove land from the tax rolls of Teton County. After being reassured that the park would include only national forest land, he withdrew his objection. That evening at the JY, a small group of opponents approached Senator John B. Kendrick to request another meeting. The senator agreed reluctantly. The small delegation included William C. Deloney, state representative, R. C. Lundy, state senator, and pioneer Stephen Leek. After expressing objections to the park proposal, they conceded it would be established and agreed to support it if an amendment was added to prohibit the construction of new roads and hotels in the new park.[41]

The Coordinating Commission's recommendation and the 1928 hearings provided the momentum for the introduction of a bill to establish Grand Teton National Park. On February 26, 1929, President Calvin Coolidge signed the bill, creating a 96,000-acre park that included the Teton Range and the scenic alpine lakes at the base of the range. Though less than proponents hoped for, it represented a significant victory.[42]

Controversy dogged the new park. Later, a story surfaced that Albright promised that no further extension would be considered if a park bill was approved. In a 1933 letter to Wilford Neilson, Albright denied making such a commitment. "What doubtless happened was that I agreed that there should be no more Yellowstone park extension agitation. . . ." Nevertheless, antagonists have perpetuated this story for years as an example of Horace Albright's perfidy.[43]

Meanwhile, to implement the Jackson Hole Plan, Burt and Albright raised $2,000 to locate a wealthy benefactor. Jack Eynon and Dick Winger traveled east in 1924 to visit well-heeled Jackson Hole dudes. Eynon met with members of the influential Hanna family, who expressed interest in the plan, but in the end offered no help. Although Eynon and Winger "could not have worked harder nor more conscientiously," they failed. Without financial support, the plan appeared dead.

John D. Rockefeller Jr. entered the picture in this period. In 1924, he brought his three sons west to visit Glacier, Mesa Verde, and Yellowstone Na-

Mr. and Mrs. John D. Rockefeller Jr. on a boat ride on Jenny Lake, 1931. The Rockefellers were so moved by the beauty of the valley that they provided the financial support for a plan to buy up private lands and donate them to the National Park Service. *Jackson Hole Historical Society and Museum*

tional Parks. The Park Service made their travel arrangements. Wanting to mix with the public without undue attention, Rockefeller traveled under his middle name—Davison. Albright and his counterparts at Glacier and Mesa Verde were instructed not to discuss park business with Mr. Davison. Although Albright obeyed, he scheduled a visit to Jackson Lake. He told Rockefeller about "a small hill above Jackson Lake that offered a fine view of the lake and the Teton Range," where Rockefeller enjoyed a picnic amidst the rugged scenery. The site was Lunch Tree Hill.

In 1926, the Rockefeller family returned to Yellowstone for a 12-day vacation. The party included John D., Mrs. Abby Rockefeller, and sons Laurence, Winthrop, and David. Albright arranged their lodging and itinerary. Unrestricted this time, Albright conducted the family through Yellowstone and Jackson Hole. They arrived at the Jackson Lake Lodge (Amoretti Inn) about noon. They hiked up Lunch Tree Hill near the lodge and ate box lunches on the summit, watching evening descend over the mountains.

The next day, the Rockefeller party drove down the road from Moran to Jenny Lake. Rockefeller asked why telephone lines were placed west of the road, detracting from the view of the Teton Range. Never one to lose an opportunity, Albright explained that the Forest Service built the line, despite his suggestion that the lines be placed east of the road.

Near Jenny Lake they passed a "wobegone-looking old dancehall, some dilapidated cabins, a burned-out gasoline station, a few big billboards" and other eyesores such as a "bootleg joint." Albright recalled that Mrs. Rockefeller grew increasingly upset. Both Mr. and Mrs. Rockefeller expressed dismay over the unsightly commercial developments in this area and asked if there was some way to stop them. Albright explained that virtually all buildings were on private property, thus would have to be bought out. Somewhere enroute to the JY, Rockefeller asked Albright to submit a map and list of the offending properties, as well as estimated costs to buy them. Elated, Albright promised to do so.

The group stopped at the Bar BC to visit the Burts, then drove on to the JY, owned by Henry Stewart. After lunch, they returned to Yellowstone via an old wagon road that took them past Menor's Ferry and the Bar BC. At "a high point along this bluff from which one can view the entire valley in all directions," the entourage stopped to enjoy the scenery. "As we stood on this little 'rise' and absorbed the beauty of the scene spread before us, I told Mr. and Mrs. Rockefeller of the meeting at Miss Noble's cabin three years earlier and the plan to protect and preserve for the future this sublime valley." Neither offered any response nor did Albright pursue the subject any further.

The location of this high point has been a source of debate, because some historic significance has been attached to Albright's disclosure of the Jackson Hole Plan. First, the site has been confused with Lunch Tree Hill, which it was not. Second, Albright's recollections do not provide a precise site. In his 1933 letter to Neilson, written closest in time to the 1926 trip, Albright described their route as an old wagon track overlooking the Snake. Not only did it offer a good view of the Teton Range, but Antelope Flats and the lands around Blacktail Butte were "still bathed in sunshine." In an interview conducted in 1967, Albright recollected the following:

> I took them back up to near Menors Ferry and then on a road, I don't remember where it went but it went up around where the Oliver [4 Lazy F] place is and beyond the Bar B-C. I fooled along the river, showing it [to] them. Then to a point well above the Bar B-C. I think to Hedricks Point or near what's called Hedricks Point.

Based on this description, Hedricks Point was the site. The problem is that this location is situated on the east side of the Snake River. To get there, Albright would have had to cross Menor's Ferry and then take the maintained county road to Hedricks Point. In no source or interview does he mention crossing the Snake. It is likely from his description that the Rockefeller party traveled north along the old wagon road *west* of the Snake River to a point near Burned Ridge.[44]

At any rate, the Rockefeller visit proved to be a turning point in the history of Jackson Hole. Albright contacted Dick Winger, who assembled maps, a list of properties, and property values in the Jenny Lake area. In the winter of 1926–1927, Albright traveled to New York and delivered the material to Rockefeller. After perusing the maps and list, Rockefeller said, "Mr. Albright, this isn't what I wanted from you." Confused, Albright reviewed their discussion that day. It became clear that Albright misunderstood Rockefeller. Rather than limit his program to the Jenny Lake area, the millionaire philanthropist was only interested in the "ideal proposal," a buy out of all private lands north of Jackson and Spring Gulch. Elated, Albright requested more maps and cost estimates from Winger.[45]

After reviewing the new proposals, Rockefeller turned the project over to an aide, Colonel Arthur Woods. Albright, acting on the advice of Burt and Winger, outlined a general strategy for the program. Rockefeller would purchase the property and eventually donate it to the National Park Service. But first, and most important, Albright recommended secrecy—if news of Rockefeller's involvement and the purpose of the program leaked out, land prices would inflate and opponents would work hard to thwart the program. He suggested that a hunting-and-recreation company be formed to buy the land. Albright recommended that Woods hire the Salt Lake City law firm of Fabian & Clendenin to run the company.[46]

Rockefeller's agents formed the Snake River Land Company, a Utah corporation, in the summer of 1927. Kenneth Chorley, Rockefeller's chief agent at Colonial Williamsburg, orchestrated its organization with Woods and remained active over the years. They chose Vanderbilt Webb, a New York attorney, to serve as president of the company, Harold P Fabian of the Salt Lake firm as vice president, and Robert E. Miller as field agent in Jackson Hole. Miller seemed a curious choice, because he was known to oppose park extension. On the other hand, as Albright conceded, he was a pioneer and "knew Jackson Hole lands through long experience as a banker in Jackson."[47]

The company launched an ambitious program, seeking to buy more than 30,000 acres for around $1,000,000. Although the company incorporated in 1927 and had engaged Miller by May of that year, the first purchases were not made until 1928. In April, the *Courier* reported that the Snake River Land Company had purchased 7,000 acres, all situated east of the Snake River. Miller remained secretive, stating only that the game herds attracted the money and that the land would remain in private hands. People have speculated over the years that Miller may have known the true intent of the scheme and of Rockefeller's involvement. No documented information has ever affirmed these rumors. It is difficult to conceive that so bitter an opponent of the Yellowstone extension would have worked knowingly for the Jackson Hole Plan. Miller maintained that he had no knowledge of the ultimate goal of the Snake River Land Company. In the 1933 Senate hearings, he testified that Vanderbilt Webb assured him that the company had no connection with park expansion in Jackson Hole.[48]

Papers related to the Snake River Land Company indicate that the principal characters expected to buy the targeted lands and turn them over to the Park Service within several years. Burt believed that income from leases would defray annual expenses, such as property taxes, during the interim. No one anticipated that 20 years of bitter controversy would pass before the settlement of 1950, and no one could have predicted the direction the Snake River Land Company and its successor, the Jackson Hole Preserve, would take in these years.

Further, the intense hostility aroused by the company's activities surprised Rockefeller and company officers. Hostility on a local and even state level stemmed from several sources. First, some opposed the extension of a park into Jackson Hole, period. Second, activities of the company generated opposition. Third, perceptions of the company's motives, regardless of their inaccuracy, influenced local attitudes as much as the company's actions. Finally, the Snake River Land Company was a business. Its officials managed it as such. Kenneth Chorley recognized years later that "good public relations . . . were not the forte of the Jackson Hole Preserve" nor its predecessor, the Snake River Land Company.[49]

The first crisis occurred within two years, and were centered on the activities of R. E. Miller, the company's purchasing agent. Webb, Chorley, and Fabian grew concerned at the slow pace of the purchase program. This was not necessarily Miller's fault, as Webb and Chorley were too optimistic about the time needed to buy lands. More specifically, Miller concentrated on buying out properties east of the river. This was contrary to the priority of buying up lands west of the river, along the critical scenic corridor between Menor's Ferry and Jenny Lake. Webb, Chorley, and Fabian suspected that Miller bought properties with mortgages held by his Jackson State Bank. In 1929, Fabian reported that Miller held just over $88,000 in mortgages for properties on the purchase schedule. This was not extraordinary because, being the only bank in Jackson Hole, Miller was bound to hold a number of mortgages.

Furthermore, as a banker, Miller had made some enemies, earning him the nickname "Old Twelve-Percent." Personal antagonism on the part of some locals toward Miller hindered the program. Miller's contract with the Snake River Land Company also encouraged him to drive a sharp bargain; by achieving lower total prices, he stood to gain significant bonuses. Finally, Miller failed to communicate regularly with Fabian, Webb, and Chorley. Exasperated, they eased Miller out and replaced him with Dick Winger and Mrs. H. H. Harrison; Miller's contract expired at the end of 1929.[50] Nevertheless, the company made significant strides prior to 1930. The Ferrins, who controlled several thousand acres, including the Elk Ranch, were bought out. The company also bought the resort and land of Ben Sheffield at Moran for $100,000 early in 1929, a very important acquisition.[51]

Miller's successor, Dick Winger, soon ran into trouble. Webb and Chorley, always accountable to Rockefeller, expressed dissatisfaction with Winger's progress. For reasons that remain uncertain, Chorley always had reservations about Winger. Fabian shared those feelings at first, but concluded that "he is the one man whom I have been able to tie to there with absolute confidence." Albright supported Winger fully, admiring his "fine mind and world of courage." Fabian found him a sensitive, yet pugnacious man. As such, Winger had made enemies in Jackson Hole, among them R. E. Miller. Winger's running battles with Miller and other opponents, such as Roy Van Vleck, Bill Simpson, and A. C. McCain, certainly influenced the controversy. At any rate, Winger remained the company agent. He was paid a commission at first and later an annual salary of $3,600, until he left the company in 1946.[52]

During this time, it is difficult to gauge the level of support versus opposition to the park, for the views of valley residents fluctuated, and vocal minorities can raise a noise far out of proportion to their numbers. In general, opinions seemed to have swung from opposition in 1919 to support in the 1920s. In 1926, Struthers Burt estimated that 40 percent of Jackson Hole 's populace favored the Yellowstone extension. A year later, Burt believed 80 percent. Early support peaked in 1929 with the establishment of Grand Teton National Park. Opposition increased in

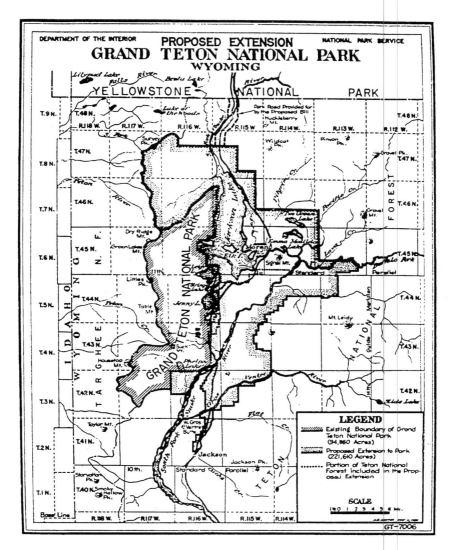

Proposed Extension, Grand Teton National Park, 1938. *National Park Service*

the 1930s with the exposure concerning Rockefeller's involvement with the Snake River Land Company.

One myth has persisted over the years that landholders opposed selling their homesteads and ranches, but sold out of economic necessity or were coerced to sell. While the economy was a factor, little evidence exists to hint at coercion. The agricultural depression of the 1920s laid ranchers low and influenced their decision to sell. This was a significant factor. In July 1919, Joe Markham, William C. Thompson, George H. Whiteman, and H. C. McKinstry wrote a letter to Albright in which they went on "record as being in favor" of the extension since Albright had addressed their concerns. In a subsequent letter, Markham advised the superintendent that most people in the northern end of the valley would support the extension if certain privileges could be preserved, such as the right to carry firearms and exterminate wolves and coyotes.[53]

As depressed cattle prices impacted ranchers and the valley's economy, gloom characterized the mood of people. In 1920, Albright met pioneer rancher Bill Crawford. Over lunch, Crawford informed Albright that he and all the other ranchers opposed any extension unless their ranches were bought out. "He said nobody would make a living on these properties, that the climate was too cold, the soil too barren, and that people were destroying the lives of themselves and their families by trying to ranch in this country." Crawford hoped the government or private parties could finance such a scheme. In 1921, J. D. "Si" Ferrin and Bill Kelly discussed a similar plan with Albright.[54]

Albright's papers from the early 1920s contain numerous letters concerning the economic dilemma of ranchers in Jackson Hole. In late 1923, he informed Hal Evarts that "practically every ranchman in Jackson Hole is broke and in debt up to his ears. There is no hope of these poor people getting out of debt." Separate observations tend to confirm Albright's assessments. In 1924, George Ryter composed a 113-page letter to Mrs. Rose Crabtree, while wintering as the caretaker at Cissie Patterson's Flat Creek Ranch. Discussing conditions in the valley, Ryter believed "many ranchers would be glad to go." More than a few owed taxes going back several years. If the Jackson Hole Plan failed to materialize,

he believed most ranches would "pass into the hands of the few. Perhaps moonshine-booze/hilarity will make us forget our troubles."[55]

Hard times seem to have peaked in 1925. In that year, ranchers circulated a petition supporting a buyout of private lands in response to anti-park agitation in Jackson Hole. Si Ferrin and Pierce Cunningham reputedly authored most of the petition and circulated it for signatures. The authors expressed concern that opponents of the Yellowstone extension had deliberately misrepresented facts, which had been repeated in editorials throughout the Wyoming press. The authors also stated that the Yellowstone extension involved little more than a transfer of public land from one federal agency to another, and numerous public documents presented facts regarding the extension. The petition went further, proposing "that the entire Jackson Hole should be set aside as a recreational area, or should be administered as a recreational area, through whatever agency, state or national, is considered best fit to do it." Based on hard experience at ranching, signers believed "that this region will find its highest use as a playground. . . . The destiny of Jackson's Hole is as a playground, typical of the west, for the education and enjoyment of the Nation, as a whole." They not only pledged themselves to cooperating to further the project, "but we will at any time . . . sell our ranches at what we consider a fair price." What is remarkable about this petition is that 97 landowners endorsed it; and many were Jackson Hole's first pioneers and had a reputation for being park opponents. These people owned more than 27,000 acres, much of it in the area encompassed by the Jackson Hole Plan. The 1925 petition indicates that significant support existed for the plan. It is clear that economics were an important motive.[56]

As the Snake River Land Company officers began organizing in 1927, supporters urged haste. Burt, believing 1927 might be a good year for ranchers, feared some might be less willing to sell, developing "a crimp in their backs as usual." Burt also observed that "each summer more and more rich Easterners are buying places on this side of the river and this means more and more land the Government will not be able to control." In October, he repeated the urgency of purchasing parcels as soon as possible. Jackson Hole was no longer in a dejected state of mind. "The Kelly flood has been forgotten, the cattlemen, for the first time in years, expected to make money, and the recent buying up of numerous ranches by rich men had whetted the appetite of every one."[57] Still, available documents indicate that a significant number of ranchers were ready to sell, although their motives were complex. A few like Tony Grace were willing to sell for altruistic reasons; others such as Si Ferrin wished to sell for personal financial reasons.[58]

Another charge leveled against the Snake River Land Company concerned prices paid for land. Stories have persisted over the years that the company paid less than fair market value. In a letter to Wilford Neilson dated April 6, 1933, Harold Fabian revealed total purchases up to that time. The Snake River Land Company had paid a total of $1,400,310.04 for 35,310.396 acres of land. This included payments to homestead applicants in exchange for relinquishing claims to the United States. The company paid an average of $39.66 per acre, or $6,345.60 for 160 acres that usually contained improvements.[59] These figures compare favorably with other real estate transactions during this period.

Several variables determined the appraisals made by Dick Winger and R. E. Miller. Buildings, fences, the condition of improvements, ditches, cultivated land, irrigated land, pasture, wasteland—all were factors in determining fair market value. No appraisal records survived in the company files kept by Fabian and Chorley. Individual appraisal records probably remained with Winger and Miller. Prices for individual properties differed according to these variables, along with their condition. For example, Roy Nipper received $4,000, or $25 per acre, for a dryland farm and ranch buildings in poor condition. His neighbor, Norm Smith, received more than $12,000 for a well-kept homestead and irrigated acreage. Also, the fact that the Smith property was located near Menor's Ferry may have given it some strategic importance.[60]

A significant cause of bitterness on the part of some landowners revolved around higher prices paid for properties in "scenic areas" as opposed to viable agricultural lands. Company agents considered land west of the Snake River the most scenic, and the most threatened. As such, the company offered higher prices for this land. Ranchers and farmers on Mormon Row could not comprehend why land worthless for agriculture should be worth so much more than their well-kept farms. For example, the Snake River Land Company targeted 1,545 acres in the township that included Jenny Lake. They estimated the cost to be $174,376, or $112.82 per acre. But more than 6,000 acres in the Mormon Row-Antelope Flats area was projected to cost $247,867.62. Strictly hay meadows and pasture, this land averaged $40.88 per acre. Although the company adopted a policy of not disclosing prices, people had no such policy. More was probably known about prices the company paid than Fabian, Webb, and Chorley could have imagined. Frank McBride sold his 480-acre ranch for $12,000 in April 1928. Two years later, he learned that some neighbors had received $40 per acre, while he had received $25. McBride wrote a letter to the company, not angry or especially bitter, asking for an additional $15 an acre, "beaing [sic] that the Co. is all well-to-do people." He had been forced to sell, because the Jackson State Bank threatened to foreclose on a $1,000 mortgage dating from 1918. Being a businessman, Fabian, of course, denied the request.[61]

In an interview years later, Harold Fabian recalled that John D. Rockefeller Jr., "had always said that he would rather pay more than less." Yet, the Snake River Land Company operated in a businesslike manner. Estimates were made, price schedules drawn up, and budgets allotted. Webb, Chorley, Fabian, and Winger managed Rockefeller's money carefully. None liked to feel they got the wrong end of a sharp bargain. They were expected to work within budgets, and Winger had to secure approval to make offers higher than the scheduled amount. For example, Fabian gave Winger the authority to offer Joe Jones $10,000 for his homestead, well over the projected $7,300 price. However, Fabian instructed Winger to use the $3,400 saved on the purchase of the Herb Whiteman place at Moran. After Mary Cowles accepted an offer of $35 per acre for 468 acres on the Buffalo Fork, Fabian informed Winger that the offer was no longer good as the land was worth no more than $17.50 per acre. In this case, hard negotiating backfired. Cowles sold to the Cockrells, who started a cattle outfit on the property that continues to operate today. In 1929, the owner of the JY and park supporter Henry Stewart asked Fabian to re-convey title of 160 acres to Harold Brown and his wife. According to Stewart, the couple sold under duress, as Mrs. Brown had been ill and required surgery. Members of the Dupont family, friends of the Browns, determined to help them out and pay their bills. Fabian reported Stewart as being very adamant, believing the Browns sold for too little money. He hoped the company would re-convey title or, in lieu of that, pay a higher price for the land. Fabian passed the request on to Chorley, but wrote "Mr. Miller says to forget it and I agree with him." The company refused Stewart's request, but did give the Browns a short-term lease to enable them to continue operating the Moose Post Office at the property. In 1929, Struthers Burt complained to Kenneth Chorley about Miller's high handedness toward some landowners, suggesting that local resentment had increased as a consequence.[62]

In general, the company treated landowners fairly, both in prices paid and in other matters. In 1935, Winger had property lines surveyed. A survey of the Gottfried Feuz property showed his fences being several hundred feet off of the actual property lines. Feuz was "about sick" over the mistake, but Winger assured him the company had no intention of ordering him to move fences and buildings. Some locals were poor neighbors to the company. In the same letter, Winger reported serious incidents of vandalism and theft at the Elk Ranch. A horse had been shot, fences broken down, boards stolen from ditch headgates, and a long list of tools and gasoline stolen. "Midnight salvage crews" stole virtually anything on unoccupied company properties.[63]

Another cause of resentment stemmed from the company's practice of removing structures and improvements. The purpose of the buyout was to remove unsightly development and restore the natural landscape. Further, by eliminating improvements, the company reduced property taxes. Dr. F. M. Fryxell recalled watching buildings being moved tortoise-like down the Jenny Lake Road in the late 1920s and early 1930s. When the company tore down a barn on the old Manges homestead, Jimmy Manges vowed never to construct a solid building again on the X Quarter Circle X. He kept his vow. In some

cases, improvements were sold; in other instances, buildings were burned, such as the Nipper property. By 1936, a geographer reported "a large part of the settlement has now been removed from this territory, removed so completely that only when viewed from the air or from the summit of one of the buttes can the faint traces of occupance be discerned." Based on homestead records, the company removed as many as 200 or more buildings in this period.[64]

Sentimental value is impossible to appraise. The dramatic change in the landscape aggravated the emotional trauma some settlers experienced in selling. Some had poured years of sweat into their homesteads, raised families, and lived through the usual assortment of life crises such as illness or the death of a family member. No wonder people found it a gut-wrenching experience. These emotions fueled ill feelings toward the Snake River Land Company and Rockefeller.[65]

Friends of the Jackson Hole Plan and park extension sometimes received more consideration than others in terms of prices paid for their land. Jack Eynon held out for $12,000 for his 160-acre ranch, considerably more than the appraised value. He justified the price based on his "hard and constant" work for the project. Webb, Chorley, and Fabian deliberated over the price for some time, aware of the problem of inflating prices and vulnerability to charges of favoritism. In the end, they paid Eynon's asking price, which was $7,200 above appraised value. Joe Jones, among the first park advocates, received $10,000 for his parcel, more than its appraised value. John and Maytie Turner were paid $20,000 for 320 acres. Although the homestead was in excellent condition, the price was very high compared to other land in the Spread Creek area. Winger himself filed a timber and stone entry for which he received $10,000, clearly more than its real value. In the end, Fabian, Chorley, and Webb may have agreed to pay these prices rather than risk losing valuable allies.[66]

After the company began buying land in 1928, Miller, Winger, and Fabian grew concerned about speculators buying land and holding out for higher prices. H. C. Ericcson was an attorney from Kansas, who filed a 640-acre stock-raising entry in July 1926 near Deadman's Bar. He began purchasing other tracts in the valley, clearly engaging in land speculation. In March 1930, Ericcson wrote to Fabian informing him that he secured an option to buy 323 acres from Charles "Beaver Tooth" Neal for $13,460, or $41.67 per acre. Ericcson offered to sell it to the company for $50 per acre, a modest profit of $2,690. In lieu of that, Ericcson proposed to "establish adequate accommodations for the general traveling public."[67]

Before initiating the Jackson Hole Plan, Rockefeller's agents also had to eliminate more than 20,000 acres of public domain available for settlement. Kenneth Chorley conferred with Secretary of the Interior Hubert Work and Chief Forester W. B. Greeley to explain the company's project, and discuss the problem that public land available for settlement would cause the company. Out of this meeting came the executive order of July 7, 1927. President Coolidge withdrew thousands of acres from settlement, ostensibly to protect elk habitat. This executive order, coupled with five additional orders withdrawing smaller tracts, ended the homesteaders' frontier in Jackson Hole. More important for the company, it prevented speculators from appropriating public lands.[68]

Both the Park Service and company agents corresponded with the General Land Office, challenging the validity of pending homestead entries. General Land Office agents generally favored entrants when interpreting the legal requirements to secure title to public land. The Park Service and Snake River Land Company encouraged land office agents to investigate entries closely. In 1929, Chorley complained to Secretary of the Interior Ray Lyman Wilbur about a number of timber and stone entries considered "bogus." He cited entries made by Dick Winger's wife, Marta Winger, Wilford Neilson, a supporter of the Jackson Hole Plan, and Dr. Charles W. Huff. In 1931, Fabian asked Winger to determine if Fred and Eva Topping had resided on their entry (the Moosehead). Winger promptly replied, "There can be no possible objection to the issuance of the patent as the Toppings have continuously lived there" and exceeded requirements for final proof. The main exception occurred when the Government Land Office denied A. W. Gabbey's claim to a stock-raising entry in response from pressure from Albright and the Park Service.[69]

As the purchase program progressed, Albright recommended the company adopt Struthers Burt's recommendation that purchased properties be operated to defray operating expenses and property taxes. From the outset, leases became very important. Believing the Triangle X to be an ideal location for a dude ranch, the company leased it back to John "Dad" Turner in 1930. By 1931, income from hay production and leases and rentals made up two-thirds of the company's income. As the controversy over the extension of a park into Jackson Hole dragged on into the 1940s, leases became more extensive and entrenched. Management became more complex. In 1941, Winger complained about problems in harvesting hay. Aside from being rained out, Winger found the crews to he "undependable, untrustworthy, and incompetent. At least, one third of my crew gets drunk every night—locals as well as floaters."[70]

The Snake River Land Company also found itself in the tourist business. A myth has persisted over the years that Rockefeller bought lands in Jackson Hole to enter the tourist business and monopolize it. Nothing could be further from the truth. When the company acquired Sheffield's Teton Lodge at Moran, they decided to continue operating it for two reasons. First, virtually no accommodations existed between Jackson and the great old lodges in Yellowstone. Travel was slower on poor roads in much slower vehicles, making Moran a logical stop. Second, company agents feared that closing Moran would hurt the land acquisition program. They reasoned "if the operation at Moran is stopped other places will spring up and flourish and give us no end of trouble." Operating tourist facilities took Rockefeller and his agents in unexpected directions. To run the operation at Moran, Fabian orchestrated the formation of the Teton Lodge Company and the Teton Transportation Company. These later merged to form the Teton Investment Company.

Moran required a considerable investment to improve and repair guest cabins, bathrooms, and the lodge. The Snake River Land Company advanced the Teton Lodge Company $35,000 to repair the tourist village. By 1933, the land company had invested $173,712.01 in Moran and the Jackson Lake Lodge. In return, the company received $28,707.36,

The Congressional Appropriation Committee visited Jackson Hole in 1931, and posed for a photograph by Jackson Lake Lodge. Harold Fabian, the local administrator of the Rockefeller-financed Snake River Land Company, is in the top row, second from left. *Grand Teton National Park*

which included $15,000 repaid on the $35,000 advance. Rockefeller owned none of the Teton Investment Company. Profit proved no motive for the land-holding company's venture into the tourist business.[71]

In his letter of February 16, 1927, to Rockefeller, Albright suggested that a company be formed ostensibly to buy land for a recreation and hunting club. Albright stressed that the ultimate goal of turning the land over to the Park Service should be kept secret to avoid opposition. Further, Rockefeller should work through agents to avoid being associated with the project, thus raising prices and suspicions. However, Rockefeller's association could have been discovered at the time the Snake River Land Company was formed. On August 23, the *Courier* reported President Coolidge's executive order withdrawing 23,617 acres from settlement to promote elk conservation. Chorley was mentioned as being involved in the withdrawal. A little detective work would have revealed Chorley's employer. In April 1928, the editor of the *Courier* reported the first purchases of the Snake River Land Company. Bringing up Chorley's name in connection with the 1927 withdrawal, the editor suspected that all were connected. In June 1929, Albright received a letter from Walter B. Sheppard, an occasional visitor to Jackson, concerning the future of Jackson Hole. In the letter, Sheppard asked, "How far will Mr. Rockefeller go?" Alarmed,

Albright passed the letter on to Chorley. In August, the *Courier* reported that the Snake River Land Company intended to turn the land west of the Snake River over to the Park Service. Because people were getting dangerously close to the truth, the company issued a press release on April 6, 1930. Revealed were Rockefeller's involvement, the role of Albright and the National Park Service, and the objective of the Snake River Land Company.[72]

The revelation galvanized opposition. William Simpson, Roy Van Vleck, and R. E. Miller spearheaded the anti-park forces. A. C. McCain, the forest supervisor, opposed the program as much as he dared. The local Lions Club served as a gathering place for opponents. After the *Jackson's Hole Courier* came out in favor of the park plan, opponents established an anti-park paper, the *Grand Teton*, described as a "vindictive, spunky, devil-may-care, master-of-insults newspaper." Choreographed by the "Three Musketeers"—Winger's reference to Simpson, Van Vleck, and Miller—opponents of the Jackson Hole Plan agitated until the Senate passed a resolution to investigate the activities of the National Park Service, the Snake River Land Company, and the Teton Investment Company. This resulted in Senate subcommittee hearings in August 1933.[73]

The Snake River Land Company suspended buying land pending the hearings. By that time, they had acquired more than 35,000 acres and spent more than $1,400,000. In retrospect, it was a remarkable accomplishment. But the company's internal correspondence indicates that Webb and Chorley grew increasingly impatient with the slow progress of the program after 1929. In 1930, Chorley wrote to Webb "extremely concerned due to a lack of progress last fall and winter." He perceived Winger's performance in acquiring six properties in six months as too slow. "This situation must change. I have assured Mr. Rockefeller that we should be able to practically clean up the situation by the end of this year." Chorley asked Webb to take the matter up with Fabian.[74]

Several developments influenced the company program after 1929. As noted earlier, Dick Winger replaced Miller as purchasing agent in 1929. And, as the company leased and disposed of properties, other activities conflicted with real estate negotiations. For example, in 1930, Chorley wrote to Albright expressing concern about the slow-moving pace of land acquisition. "Confidentially between ourselves, I am inclined to think that Harold [Fabian] has become so immersed in other activities, especially the Teton Lodge Company, the acquisition of the Jackson Lake Lodge, the reconstruction of Moran, the entertainment of the Fox Film people . . . that he has temporarily lost sight of the fundamental purpose; namely, the acquisition of property." Indeed, responding to Webb and Chorley's concern about Winger, Fabian expressed disappointment in his "complete absorption in the work he is doing for the Fox people." Fabian blamed himself for giving Winger "too much rope" by letting him organize housing at Moran and supervising camps and supplies for the Fox Film Company, while they filmed "The Big Trail." [75]

Chorley had "very distinct misgivings with regard to Winger," while Fabian and Albright were strong advocates. In a 1931 letter, Fabian reminded Webb and Chorley that Winger bailed them out in 1929 "when Miller flopped on us." Fabian, in a series of letters, pointed out that Winger worked against serious obstacles. The revelation of the company's plan and financier aroused opposition, and people tended to hold out for higher prices. Further, in 1929, the company deleted Mormon Row farms and ranches from the project at the behest of Governor Frank Emerson, who had been led to believe the landowners opposed the sale. This occurred after

Winger optioned many of the properties. After some Mormon Row residents complained, the lands were returned to the schedules, but the damage had been done. Fabian noted that "remaining parcels were the tough nuts to crack." The tough nuts included holdouts such as Geraldine Lucas, Pete Karppi of the Half Moon, Henry Gunther, and the Wolff family.

Finally, some worked against Winger to stymie the project, or out of personal spite toward him. Fabian knew "that Miller with all his influence and canniness has been and still is fighting Winger as hard as he can." In May 1931, Winger learned from Dr. Charles Huff that Miller advised Geraldine Lucas to hold out for $100,000. The previous winter, Winger had learned from settler Joe Heniger that Dr. Huff had been counseling Mormon Row settlers to keep their prices high. Heniger believed Huff acted to secure a higher price for his land.[76]

As the controversy continued, the company and its successor, the Jackson Hole Preserve, continued to purchase land, eliminating the "tough nuts" as opportunities presented themselves. One of the most important purchases occurred in 1944, when Fabian acquired the Lucas property. Geraldine Lucas had died in 1938 and willed the ranch to her son, Russell Lucas. He promptly sold the estate to J. D. Kimmel, who intended to subdivide the land for residential lots. Fabian and Kimmel became acquainted and fast friends in the intervening years.

In 1944, Kimmel invited Harold and Josephine Fabian for a drive up the Gros Ventre River valley. Josephine Fabian recalled vividly the following conversation: "Fabian, I can ruin your whole damn project," said Kimmel. Fabian replied, "I know you can Uncle Kimmel." Knots must have twisted Harold Fabian's stomach at the thought of a subdivision at the foot of the Teton Range. After a few minutes of silence, Kimmel said ". . . but I ain't a goin' to." Kimmel proposed to sell the Lucas place and his holdings at Jenny Lake—tourist cabins, gas station, store—for what he paid in exchange for a lease. True to his word, Kimmel sold out in 1944. The sale brought critical parcels under federal ownership.[77]

Meanwhile, events important to park extension occurred in 1933. First, Horace Albright, who had served as director of the National Park Service since 1929, resigned to accept a lucrative offer to serve as

Wyoming Senators John B. Kendrick and Robert Carey with Superintendent Woodring, 1931.
Grand Teton National Park

president of the United States Potash Company. Nevertheless, he remained active in conservation issues, the Park Service and, especially, the park extension in Jackson Hole.

Second, the Senate Subcommittee on Public Lands and Surveys convened its hearings on August 7, which lasted through August 10. Company agents and the Park Service prepared well for the hearings. Most important, Albright, Fabian, and J. H. Rayburn, president of the Teton Investment Company, prepared histories of their activities. The histories were presented in the form of letters to Wilford Neilson, the editor of the *Courier,* who published them in the spring of 1933. The letters were compiled into a booklet and published as "Mr. John D. Rockefeller Jr.'s Proposed Gift of Land for the National Park System in Wyoming." The hearings attracted a lot of publicity, in part because of Wyoming Senator Robert Carey's sensational allegations of illegal tactics employed by the Snake River Land Company, such as burning fences and homes. Carey asserted that events in Jackson Hole had elements similar to the Teapot Dome scandal. However, by the conclusion of the hearings, it was apparent that the allegations against the National Park Service and the Snake River Land Company had no foundation.

The only questionable practice concerned Park Service pressure on the General Land Office to scrutinize pending homestead entries. The Park

Service believed many of the entries were "fraudulent and not in good faith," and asked the General Land Office to inspect certain entries to assure compliance with the law and cancel any fraudulent or improper applications. Inspectors evaluated 56 pending entries in Jackson Hole; they approved 47 in favor of the settlers and rejected only nine entries, most of which were abandoned and, therefore, rightly cancelled. One exception concerned the stock-raising entry of Albert W. Gabbey, near String Lake. The General Land Office disapproved his entry, stating that the land was not classifiable as stock-raising. Yet, other stock-raising entries in the area had been approved, notably the entry of Harrison Crandall adjacent to Gabbey's claim. Eventually, Gabbey secured title to his stock-raising claim in 1940, on the grounds that the law had been applied inconsistently.

Other complaints surfaced such as charges of manipulating the location of the Moose Post Office to further the land purchase program, but the hearings exonerated the National Park Service and Snake River Land Company. Further hearings were cancelled, and press accounts derided the whole event. *The Denver Post* characterized the affair as less than "a tempest in a teapot. . . . It was not even a 'squall in a thimble.'"[78]

The 1933 hearings opened the door to a settlement. Indicative that the park extension was no longer such a contentious issue, Bill Simpson resigned as editor of the *Grand Teton* and the paper shut down in 1934. In June of that year, Senator Robert Carey introduced a bill in the Senate to expand the boundaries of Grand Teton National Park. Among other compromises, the bill proposed to reimburse Teton County for the loss of taxes incurred by the extension. The federal government was to pay an annual sum to the county for 20 years after the purchase of property. A federal organization, the Bureau of the Budget, hamstrung the bill at the 11th hour. Reluctant to establish a precedent of paying counties in lieu of taxes for federal lands, the bureau added an amendment requiring compensation from sources other than the Treasury Department. The bill died in the House of Representatives.[79] In 1935, Carey introduced another bill (S. 2972), which in no way resembled the 1934 bill. For one thing, Jackson Lake was excluded, along with other land. Further, the issue of reimbursing the county for lost taxes had not been resolved. This bill died in committee after the Park Service withdrew support.[80]

The tax issue remained the most serious hurdle in the 1930s. Teton County officials and citizens refused to give up revenue, especially in a tax-poor county. And, during this period, opposition to the park extension seemed to gain strength again. Objections to a park in Jackson Hole surfaced from unexpected quarters. The National Parks Association, a preservationist organization, opposed including Jackson Lake. The association believed it was a bad precedent to consider conveying national park status to a dam and reservoir. The sagebrush flats east of the river also did not meet national park standards in association members' judgment. Fear of setting these precedents threatened to kill the grand plan.[81]

The National Park Service seized the initiative again in 1937–1938. The bureau prepared a 16-page pamphlet titled "A Report by the National Park Service on the Proposal to Extend the Boundaries of Grand Teton National Park, Wyoming." The document outlined the history of park extension and extolled the benefits of tourism, but most important included a bill to extend the boundaries of Grand Teton National Park.

The reaction in Jackson Hole was swift and harsh. New leaders emerged to direct anti-park activities. The new editor of the *Courier,* Charles

Kratzer, wrote weekly editorials railing against the plan, while Felix Buchenroth, Peter Hansen, A. C. McCain, and Millward Simpson organized opposition. They orchestrated a meeting with Governor Leslie Miller, at which 162 of 165 voted against the plan. Politically, the issue grew hotter, prompting the Wyoming congressional delegation to call for hearings.[82]

A Senate Subcommittee convened hearings in Jackson on August 8, 1938. The Jackson Hole Committee prepared their anti-expansion case very well. They beat the Park Service and Snake River Land Company to the punch, arranging food, entertainment, and lodging. Millward Simpson, an implacable foe, conducted the hearings. Simpson assembled an impressive array of statements, petitions, and witnesses against the park extension. He even presented a letter written by Struthers Burt to Congressman Frank Mondell in 1919, detailing his opposition to the old Yellowstone extension. Burt, of course, had become one of the strongest proponents of the plan! The Jackson Hole Committee gave the pro-park faction an old-fashioned beating. The result: the Wyoming delegation would not support expansion legislation, and Congress would not pass a bill against the Wyoming solons' wishes.[83]

It seemed a national park embracing Jackson Hole would remain a dream. On October 27, 1938, Horace Albright composed a short letter to Harold Fabian. Regarding Jackson Hole, he wrote:

> When you get a chance write me again telling me how things are going, and give us any suggestions that you have as to what we should do in the Jackson Hole country. In a talk with J.D.R. Jr. I detected a note of discouragement. In fact, he asked whether we thought we could get fifty cents on the dollar if we sold the land. If he ever loses interest in this project it is gone for good. This is confidential, of course.

In 1942, John D. Rockefeller Jr.'s growing discouragement and impatience culminated in his well-known November 26 letter to Secretary of the Interior Harold L. Ickes. Rockefeller concluded, reluctantly, that if the federal government did not want the gift of land or could not "arrange to accept it on the general terms long discussed . . . it will be my thought to make some other disposition of it or to sell it in the market to any satisfactory buyers." The National Park Service and Secretary Ickes determined to persuade President Franklin Delano Roosevelt to create a national monument out of public lands in Jackson Hole. Through the Antiquities Act of 1906, the chief executive could "declare by public proclamation historic landmarks, historic and prehistoric structures, and other objects of historic or scientific interest" located on public lands to be national monuments. It offered a way to circumvent the stumbling block of Congress, which would not act against the Wyoming delegation. On March 5, 1943, Ickes presented a memorandum on the subject to the president, along with a proclamation to create Jackson Hole National Monument. Understanding that the proclamation might be unpopular, Roosevelt nevertheless signed it on March 15. Jackson Hole National Monument was now a fact, a 221,000-acre addition to the national park system.[84]

Generally, it has been interpreted that Rockefeller was serious about divesting himself of the Jackson Hole lands. Harold Fabian recalled hearing Rockefeller state, in Chorley's office on one occasion, "if the Government won't accept it as a park, then I'm going to put the whole place up for sale." Further, it has been accepted that his letter generated the concept of a national monument. Available documents indicate otherwise. The idea of a national monument had surfaced in the late 1930s. By early 1939, the National Park Service had prepared a draft proclamation, which Rockefeller agents rejected as a poorly prepared document and too controversial. Robert Righter, after examining evidence and interviewing principal characters, believes that Rockefeller "was not prepared to abandon the Jackson Hole project" and the November 27 letter was sent to provoke action. Indeed, Rockefeller indicated his determination to see the project through. After Rockefeller's 1931 visit to Jackson Hole, Superintendent Sam Woodring wrote the following in his monthly report: "Mr. Rockefeller is thoroughly convinced of the ultimate need of enlarging this park, and stated that he intended for the Snake River Land Company, his agent to carry out the extension plan even though its completion might require many more years."[85]

The anti-park forces mobilized opposition. They did not seem to have known of the national monument option and the proclamation caught them by surprise. Since it occurred during the midst of World War II, opponents likened Roosevelt's action to the Japanese attack on Pearl Harbor or the German *Anschluss* in Austria. Opponents criticized the monument as a blatant violation of states' rights. Despite specific policy statements assuring the protection of private property, the regional press, the *Courier* and the "Committee for the survival of Teton County" circulated information that private landowners in the monument would be condemned and displaced. This was incorrect. Governor Lester Hunt wrote a letter to President Roosevelt that specified state objections to the monument. Opponents believed the monument would destroy the local economy and county, as taxable land would be removed from the rolls. Ickes endorsed a policy statement, written in late March, that addressed fears of Wyoming citizens, but to no avail. Local groups published pamphlets and documents filled with misinformation. One must conclude that much of it was deliberate.[86] On May 2, 1943, a group of ranchers, heavily armed, gathered near the monument and trailed some 500 cattle across it, possibly hoping for a confrontation. The Park Service ignored the stunt, and little would have come of it but for the participation of Wallace Beery, the famous Hollywood actor. The drive focused national attention on the monument. Many were unaware that ranchers had a right to trail cattle across the monument. Moreover, Governor Hunt raised the issue at a governor's conference, and the Wyoming delegation rallied their colleagues in Congress. Considering that the nation was engaged in a world war, the monument drew much attention in Congress.[87]

As the controversy grew more vocal and bitter, Wyoming Congressman Frank Barrett introduced a bill to abolish the Jackson Hole National Monument. In the spring of 1943, the House Committee on Public Lands conducted hearings on the monument. In August, a Senate Committee visited the valley and, at a hearing in Jackson, sentiment overwhelmingly was against the monument. Barrett's bill passed both the House and Senate but, as expected, President Roosevelt exercised a pocket veto to kill it.[88]

Opponents took the issue to the courtroom. The state of Wyoming filed suit against the National Park Service, seeking to overturn the proclamation. Judge Blake T. Kennedy heard testimony from August 21–24 at the Twelfth District Court in Sheridan, Wyoming, and issued a ruling on February 10, 1945. In the *State of Wyoming vs. Paul R. Franke* (superintendent of Grand Teton National Park), Kennedy found for the defendant, the Park Service, although he refused to rule on the merits of Jackson Hole as a national monument. Instead, he found the issue "to be a controversy between the Legislative and Executive Branches of the Government in which, under the evidence presented here, the Court cannot interfere."[89]

Jackson Hole National Monument survived these onslaughts, although like a storm-battered ship. For example, amendments attached to Department of Interior appropriations prohibited the National Park Service from spending money to administer the monument. Also, the proclamation transferred 130,000 acres of land from the Teton National Forest to the National Park Service. It was an uneasy transition, because local and regional Forest Service administrators opposed the monument. The Park Service took over U.S. Forest Service ranger stations. The Forest Service removed all fixtures from the Jackson Lake and Kelly Ranger Stations, essentially gutting them. "Movable" equipment, as local Forest Service officials interpreted their instructions, included plumbing, bathroom fixtures, doors, cupboards, drawers, cabinets, and hardware. At the Jackson Lake Ranger Station, the Forest Service removed an underground water tank, which required cutting a four-foot-square hole in the floor. At Kelly, a kitchen range, hot water tank, pipes, and a built-in dinette and hutch were removed. As of 1945, both buildings were in poor condition. Forest Supervisor Kozoil was transferred, allegedly for these actions. Two years later, Grand Teton Superintendent Franke reported that local gossip circulated that Kozoil's promotion and transfer was a reward for this "active opposition" to the monument. Franke recalled another incident that occurred during the congressional investigation of August 1943, "which greatly aided our cause." About August 15, someone placed a live

skunk in the Jackson Lake Ranger Station, which died in the building. Franke placed no blame, but an investigation indicated the culprit had a key to the building. "We made no statement of any kind, but a leak occurred somewhere, and the public placed blame on the Forest Service," believing they did it to prevent the congressmen from viewing the gutted building. However, Franke praised recent cooperation between the two agencies and urged Washington to let local offices resolve their differences quietly.[90]

Local supporters of the national monument also faced tough times. It took courage to openly support the extension. Olaus Murie, who emerged as a rational and articulate spokesman for the park in these years, recalled that: "card parties, dinner parties had their embarrassments if certain ones on 'the other side' were present. In some inexplicable way an atmosphere was created in which one felt inhibited from even mentioning the subject. There was no such thing as getting together and talking it over." In 1948, Harold Fabian received a fourth-hand report that two businesses, Lumley's and Fred's Market, had been threatened with a boycott for their pro-park support.[91]

After the war, the time seemed ripe for compromise, although Congressman Barrett continued anti-park agitation. Between 1945 and 1947, he introduced three bills in Congress to destroy the monument, directly or indirectly. Two bills never left committees, and Barrett's H.R. 1330 died on the floor of the House. Hearings held on the last resolution indicated changing attitudes, as more than half of the statements favored the monument. In Jackson Hole, a local poll showed a shift; while 182 people still opposed the monument, 142 supported it, and a whopping 234 offered no opinion!

The rhetoric and misinformation distributed by park and monument opponents haunted them. Dire predictions, such as Governor Hunt's fear that "a large community will be disrupted and many people compelled to start anew in some other place," failed to materialize. Further, after the war, it became apparent that tourism pointed the way to the future. Roosevelt's prediction "that the resumption of tourist travel will result in a great deal more money flowing

The staff of the newly created Grand Teton National Park, 1929. Left to right: Fritiof Fryxell, Superintendent Samuel Woodring, Julia Woodring, Edward Bruce, and Phil Smith.
Grand Teton National Park

to Teton County and the State of Wyoming" was proving more realistic than the predictions of doom.[92]

In 1949, interested parties gathered in the Senate Appropriation Committee chambers and hammered out a compromise. The agreement resulted in the creation of a new Grand Teton National Park on September 14, 1950. The new park included most of the 1929 park and Jackson Hole National Monument. The law contained three significant concessions. Section Four protected existing grazing rights and stock driveways. Section Five allowed the federal government to reimburse the county for lost tax revenues, eliminating the most vexing stumbling block to compromise. Section Six provided for a controlled reduction of elk within the park boundaries, though this has been a contentious issue over the years. On December 16, 1949, with a solution apparent, John D. Rockefeller Jr., conveyed a gift of 32,117 acres to the United States government and its citizens.[93]

The new Grand Teton National Park of 1950 represented the culmination of 50 years work, often marred by bitter controversy. A small group of individuals had determined that it was in the national interest to preserve the Teton Range and much of Jackson Hole as a part of the National Park System and, eventually, they prevailed.

During this entire time, while the political controversy simmered and occasionally boiled over, the National Park Service endeavored to administer the park, beginning with the 96,000-acre Grand Teton National Park of 1929. First, the National Park Service had to establish a presence. Albright selected Samuel Woodring, the chief ranger of Yellowstone, to serve as the first superintendent. The first budget totalled $11,750. Edward Bruce became the first permanent ranger, and Julia Woodring, the superintendent's wife, worked as clerk. The two first seasonal rangers were Phil Smith and Fritiof Fryxell. Avid mountaineers, they completed many of the first ascents of the peaks in the Teton Range and picked a number of names for topographic features in the area, especially peaks.[94]

The staff resided and worked out of the old Elbo Ranch until they moved headquarters to the Stewart Ranger Station and developed an administrative and maintenance area. The superintendent's residence, rustic log houses, garages, and three maintenance buildings were constructed between 1934 and 1937 with New Deal funding and Civilian Conservation Corps (CCC) labor. The CCC added wings onto the Stewart Ranger Station in 1939, which served as park headquarters. Known as Beaver

Landscape architect Thomas C. Vint (far left), head of the National Park Service Design Bureau, on a visit to Grand Teton soon after the park was created. Superintendent and Mrs. Sam Woodring are on the far right.
Grand Teton National Park

Creek, this area remained the headquarters until the fall of 1958, when operations were shifted to the new buildings at Moose.[95]

In 1930, the park received funds to improve roads, trails, and campgrounds at Jenny and String Lakes. Comfort stations with running water were to be built at the campgrounds. The Park Service allocated $66,800 for administration and developments in 1930. Woodring, using staff or contractors, built the patrol cabin at Moran Bay and one of the comfort stations at Jenny Lake, along with a water and sewer system in 1930. In addition, Woodring hired local workers to dismantle the Lee Manges cabin at Windy Point and move it to Jenny Lake. The Snake River Land Company had donated it to the park. By May, it had been reassembled for use as a temporary museum and office. The Jenny Lake Ranger Station served as the park's first visitor center and is used as a ranger station today.[96]

Between 1930 and 1932, the National Park Service constructed the Leigh Lake patrol cabin, which may have been built of logs salvaged from Stephen Leek's "clubhouse" at the north end of Leigh Lake. The String Lake comfort station was built in this period. It may have been moved to its present site after 1932. In 1932, a snowshoe cabin was built in Death Canyon for packers and the trail crew. One year later, a second comfort station was built at Jenny

Lake.[97] Park Service architects designed buildings and structures specifically to conform to the landscape, launching a golden age of rustic log architecture, dubbed in recent years "parkitecture."

In 1931, the park received $74,427. In addition, $108,000 was spent on approach roads in Jackson Hole to both Yellowstone and Grand Teton National Parks. Concerned over the eyesore caused by dead trees along Jackson Lake, the Park Service and Bureau of Reclamation each put up $50,000 to begin a cleanup.[98]

During this period, the park issued permits to its first concessioners. Most were centered at Jenny Lake. A. C. Lyon conducted a saddle and packhorse outfit, Charles Wort rented boats for use on Jenny Lake, and Karl Kent operated the Jenny Lake Inn, known locally as the "Nest." Kent's operation was removed around 1931 or 1932. In 1931, photographer Harrison Crandall moved his rustic log studio from his former homestead near String Lake to Jenny Lake. Through a concession permit, he operated a photographic studio until the 1950s. The Teton Transportation Company, running bus service from the rail terminus at Victor, secured a permit to travel to Moran via the Jenny Lake Road. Other vintage concession buildings at Jenny Lake include the Wort boathouse and Kenneth Reimer's cabin, built about 1936.[99]

Civilian Conservation Corps (CCC) Camp NP-4 at Jenny Lake operated from 1934 through 1942. Crews worked throughout the park, building roads, trails, houses, and other infrastructure. The two large buildings to the left still stand at the south end of Jenny Lake. *Grand Teton National Park*

The road from Menor's Ferry, past Jenny Lake, to Moran was a main highway through the valley, especially after the Bureau of Public Roads improved it and completed the bridge at Menor's Ferry in 1927. Grand Teton National Park widened, graded, and oiled portions of this road during these years and built at least seven vistas on the road along Jenny and Leigh Lakes. For example, in 1932, the park improved 12 miles of road in the park, including six miles oiled along the lakeshore and two miles oiled outside the north entrance. The most infamous road was the Leigh Lake Road. Woodring decided to build a road along the east shore of Leigh Lake to Bearpaw Lake. His superiors approved, for surveys began in September 1930. The road was built to the end of Leigh Lake about 1932. However, this road violated the 1929 enabling legislation, which prohibited the construction of new roads in the small park. Consequently, Secretary of the Interior Harold Ickes ordered its removal. By 1940, it was gone, angering a number of local people.[100]

Constructing trails was the highest of Superintendent Woodring's priorities. He envisioned a series of high standard trails for horse use. This did not sit well with either Phil Smith or Doc Fryxell, who believed primitive hiking trails more appropriate. Trails already existed, but were poorly developed and main-

tained. Indians and trappers had used trails in the Berry Creek drainage over Conant and Jackass Passes. Struthers Burt frequently rode a horse trail into Death Canyon. At the head of Death Canyon, a sheep drift crossed Fox Creek Pass and cut through a portion of the park. In 1921, the Forest Service improved the trail in Death Canyon, providing a route to the summit of the range. Crews packed a compressor into the canyon to drill holes for blasting. The Forest Service cut the Pemble Trail from south of Phelps Lake to Beaver Creek after the turn of the century.[101]

Inspecting trails in 1929, Woodring found them in fair condition, but believed they required "a great deal of maintenance" to meet Yellowstone standards. Horseback riders trekked regularly up to the Teton Glacier on a steep and hazardous trail. Woodring made the trip and scouted a new route. He noted, "There are wonderful possibilities for one of the best trail systems in the country at a reasonable cost." In the fall of 1929, a party of park employees and dude ranchers packed over the proposed Skyline Trail, scouting a route.[102]

The following spring, the park initiated work on the south loop of the Jenny Lake Trail, scouted and flagged by Fryxell. Another was to be built along the west shore of String Lake and connect with the now

The superintendent's residence under construction by the CCC. The National Park Service Design Bureau in San Francisco designed the park's rustic buildings, which were carefully crafted to complement the natural setting. *Grand Teton National Park*

obliterated Leigh Canyon Trail at the outlet of Leigh Lake. The park planned a new trail to Amphitheater Lake and Teton Glacier. By the end of September, the Jenny Lake Trail had been completed, a quarter-mile trail connecting with the String Lake Trail. Also built was a 104-foot bridge across the String Lake outlet. In addition, more than four miles of switchbacks had been graded to Teton Glacier. Forest Service trails in the Bradley-Taggart Lakes area had been upgraded and realigned in some places. A log bridge, 96 feet in length, had been built near Bradley Lake.[103]

By the end of July 1931, the park had built or reconstructed 60 miles of trails and built dozens of bridges. The Valley Trail extended 20 miles from Phelps Lake to Leigh Lake. The Jenny Lake Trail had become very popular since its construction. In July 1931, a crew finished the 81-foot bridge at Taggart Creek. As many as 90 men were employed on trail work in 1931. This involved a considerable amount of rock work, requiring the use of compressors and explosives.[104] By the end of 1932, 50 miles of new trail, four-feet-wide, had been constructed over three seasons. In June 1933, crews connected the Cascade Canyon and Death Canyon Trails, completing a loop known as the Skyline Trail. By 1935, Grand Teton National Park

had a well-developed trail system, totaling 90 miles.[105]

Grand Teton National Park was established just prior to the onset of the Great Depression. Despite tight budgets, the National Park Service managed to complete an extensive trail system, roads and a number of buildings, before Franklin D. Roosevelt launched the New Deal. This program provided new funds and an important source of labor, the Civilian Conservation Corps. The CCC was one of many programs intended to lift the nation out of the depression. Young men between the ages of 17 and 25 enlisted to perform conservation work on public land. Civilian Conservation Corps crews attacked projects that required intensive labor. Camps were set up at several locations in the valley, at Leigh Lake, Lizard Point, and "Hot Springs" near Colter Bay. In 1934, Camp NP-4, the most prominent camp, was built at the south end of Jenny Lake. CCC crews manned this camp through 1942.

Civilian Conservation Corps laborers worked on a variety of projects. The Superintendent's Report for August 1936 listed the following: landscaping headquarters; improvement and development of a campground at Jenny Lake; construction of fireplaces; construction of barriers at Jenny Lake camp-

When the Bureau of Reclamation built Jackson Lake Dam, the shoreline trees were flooded and killed. One of the biggest undertakings by the CCC was to clear the thousands of acres of downed trees ringing the lake. *Grand Teton National Park*

Olaus and Mardy Murie at their home near Moose. Both were respected wildlife authors who gained national prominence as leaders in the wilderness movement. *Jackson Hole Historical Society and Museum*

ground; construction of table and bench combinations at Jenny Lake; construction of permanent employees' dwellings headquarters; extension of water system; Jackson Lake shore cleanup; trail construction at Phelps Lake-Granite Canyon and Teton Glacier-Garnet Canyon; telephone line construction at the headquarters at Death Canyon; maintenance and lakeshore cleanup; and general trail maintenance.

Without doubt, the most significant accomplishment of the Civilian Conservation Corps in Jackson Hole was the cleanup of dead and downed trees along the shores of Jackson Lake. Contractors worked on the project in 1931 and 1932. The CCC finished the job of cleaning up the bulk of 7,000 acres between 1933 and 1937. In September 1936, the superintendent of Grand Teton National Park reported that CCC crews were finishing the last 85 acres. "By next summer, Jackson Lake will present to the tourist a clean, natural beach," it was reported. Soon after, the United States entered the war in 1941, and the CCC program ended. The camps were dismantled. Several buildings from Jenny Lake, intended to be a temporary measure, were moved to other locations and remain in use today.[106]

During the struggle to add Jackson Hole to the park, the modern environmental movement emerged, led by people such as Aldo Leopold, Robert Marshall, Sigurd Olson, Howard Zahniser, and David Brower. In 1927, the *Jackson's Hole Courier* announced the arrival of a young biologist-naturalist named Olaus Murie. He had arrived fresh from Alaska, where the Biological Survey had employed him. The bureau instructed Murie "to make a complete study of the famous elk herd in Jackson Hole." His wife, Margaret (Mardy), and two babies followed him into the valley. Through his experience in Alaska and Jackson Hole, he moved from scientist to conservationist. In 1945, disenchanted with the lack of challenging projects and policies of the Biological Survey, Murie was ready for change. Offered the post as director of the Wilderness Society, he accepted, after an agreement was reached that he could work half time at half salary. But more important, he could direct the society's affairs from his ranch at Moose, Wyoming. Olaus and Mardy Murie had pooled their resources with his brother Adolph and Louise Murie to purchase the STS Dude Ranch.

From here, assisted by Mardy, Olaus Murie directed the Wilderness Society through a number of significant environmental battles until his death in 1963. Over the years, innumerable politicians and environmentalists have visited the ranch to formulate policy and discuss issues. Two Wilderness Society Council meetings were held at the ranch in 1949 and 1955. Living at the ranch, the Muries organized conservation lobbying efforts and political activities. He worked tirelessly for the establishment of an Arctic Wildlife Refuge and was a leader in the effort to stop the proposed Echo Park Dam in Dinosaur National Monument. He lobbied hard for years in behalf of national wilderness legislation, but died one year before the passage of the Wilderness Act of 1964. Murie attained national stature, helping set the course of the modern conservation movement. He was one of "a small coterie of trained leaders" whose studies, ability as a spokesman, and writings "earn him a prominent position in the ranks of American preservationists." Since 1963, Mardy Murie has stepped into the breach as a leader in the modern conservation movement. She continues to be active in environmental affairs today.[107]

It is a giant step from the Murie place to the first hints in 1897 at an extension of Yellowstone's boundaries into the Teton country. Conservation, represented by federal agencies such as the Forest Service and Park Service and the philanthropy of John D. Rockefeller Jr., is arguably Jackson Hole's most important historic theme, because of its impact on the character of this valley. For those who fought for conservation, Struthers Burt suggested the most suitable tribute, a national park as "a monument to the men who would help it along, with the Grand Teton as their headstone—that's big enough to fire any man's imagination."[108]

Notes

1. Righter, *Crucible for Conservation*, pp. 17–18.

2. Hays, *Conservation*, pp. 27–28 and 49–51; and Park, *The World of the Bison*, pp. 37–51.

3. Hays, *Conservation*, pp. 1–3.

4. Ibid., pp. 5–48; and Roderick Nash, *Wilderness and the American Mind* (New Haven: Yale University Press, 1967), pp. 133–134.

5. Nash, *Wilderness*, pp. 122–140 and 181.

6. John Ise, *Our National Park Policy: A Critical History* (Baltimore: John Hopkins Press, 1961), pp. 15–20; and Haines, *The Yellowstone Story*, p. 471.

7. Righter, *Crucible for Conservation*, p. 20.

8. Hays, *Conservation*, pp. 37–38.

9. *Jackson's Hole Courier*, February 17, 1949; Esther B. Allan, "History of Teton National Forest," pp. 109–110; and *Jackson Hole Guide*, October 7, 1965.

10. *Jackson's Hole Courier*, February 17, 1949; A. A. Anderson, *Experiences and Impressions* (New York: MacMillan Co., 1933), pp. 90–95; Harold Steen, *The U.S. Forest Service: A History* (Seattle: University of Washington Press, 1976); and Allan, "History of Teton National Forest," p. 143.

11. Anderson, *Experiences*, p. 95; Allan, "History of Teton National Forest," pp. 113–114; and C.N. Woods, excerpts from "Thirty-Seven Years in the Forest Service," no date, no publisher, in Pamphlet File, Grand Teton National Park.

12. Anderson, *Experiences*, pp. 94–95; and *Jackson's Hole Courier*, February 7, 1949.

13. *Jackson's Hole Courier*, February 17, 1949.

14. Ibid., and Anderson, *Experiences*, pp. 100–104.

15. Anderson, *Experiences*, pp. 108–113; Jack Ward Thomas and Dale E. Toweill, eds., *Elk of North America: Ecology and Management* (Harrisburg, PA: Stackpole Books, 1982), pp. 540–544; "Diary of Rudolph Rosencrans," K. C. Allan Collection, 7636, University of Wyoming Archives. American Heritage Center; and Al Austin, "Biography," no date, acc. no. 1037, Jackson Hole Historical Society and Museum, Jackson, Wyoming.

16. *Jackson's Hole Courier*, January 28, 1909 (reprinted in *Jackson's Hole Courier*, January 29, 1948); Woods, "Thirty-Seven Years;" "Diary of R. Rosencrans," K. C. Allan Collection, University of Wyoming Archives.

17. *Jackson's Hole Courier*, February 17, 1949; Allan, "History of Teton National Forest," pp. 165–166; Elizabeth Wied Hayden Collection, Subject File, #5, Jackson Hole Historical Society and Museum; *Jackson's Hole Courier*, October 10, 1922; and Grand Teton National Park, Building Maintenance Files.

18. Grand Teton National Park, Building Maintenance Files.

19. *Jackson Hole News*, January 9, 1980.

20. U.S. Reclamation Service, "Reconnaissance, Jackson Lake, 1902," Survey Books, 4 vols., and "Jackson Lake Reservoir Highline Traverse, Lowline Traverse, and Section Ties, 1909" Survey Books, 8 vols. (volume 1 of both surveys were missing), State of Wyoming, Archives, Museums and Historical Department; and John Markham, "The Temporary Jackson Lake Dam."

21. Mae Tuttle to Mrs. Cora Barber, September 5, 1951, acc. 65, Jackson Hole Historical Society and Museum Files.

22. Larson, *History of Wyoming*, pp. 75, 215–216, and 385.

23. Hayden, *From Trapper to Tourist*, pp. 40–42; Saylor, *Jackson Hole*, pp. 138–142; and Tuttle letter, September 5, 1951, Jackson Hole Historical Society and Museum.

24. Saylor, *Jackson Hole*, p. 159; and Anderson, *Experiences*, pp. 113–114.

25. William L. Simpson, "Game Conditions in Wyoming," *Outdoor Life* 9(1902); and Harvey H. Glidden, "The Wyoming Game Situation," *Outdoor Life* 10(1902).

26. Hayden, *Trapper to Tourist*, pp. 53–54; Al Austin, "Biography," Jackson Hole Historical Society and Museum; and Hayden Collection, William Seebohm letter, Subject File, #5, Jackson Hole Historical Society and Museum.

27. Hayden, *Trapper to Tourist*, pp. 53–54; Righter, *Crucible for Conservation*, pp. 8–9; and *Jackson's Hole Courier*, March 9, 1916.

28. Righter, *Crucible for Conservation*. Histories of Jackson Hole included sections about the creation of Grand Teton National Park, but none offered a complete story. Moreover, errors were common. Robert Righter recognized a good story untold, and researched and wrote a manuscript in the 1970s, which was published in 1982.

29. "Mr. John D. Rockefeller Jr.'s, Proposed Gift of Land for the National Park System in Wyoming," no publisher, no date, p. 4; and Horace M. Albright, as told to Robert Cahn, *The Birth of the National Park Service: The Founding Years, 1913–1933* (Salt Lake City, UT: Howe Brothers, 1985), pp. 39–40.

30. Righter, *Crucible for Conservation*, pp. 22–23.

31. Albright, *The Birth of the National Park Service*, pp. 65–74; and Righter, *Crucible for Conservation*, pp. 28–29.

32. Righter, *Crucible for Conservation*.

33. Albright, *Birth of the National Park Service*, pp. 94–99.

34. Yellowstone National Park Archives, Horace M. Albright Papers, 1919–1922, Horace Albright to Stephen T. Mather, October 21, 1919.

35. Ibid., *Jackson's Hole Courier*, October 16, 1919; and Righter, *Crucible for Conservation*, pp. 30–31.

36. Righter, *Crucible for Conservation*, pp. 32–33; Struthers Burt, *Diary*, p. 121; and *Jackson's Hole Courier*, January 6, 1921, and January 13, 1921.

37. Righter, *Crucible for Conservation*, pp. 32–33; see Albright correspondence for 1921 in his papers from 1919–1922 in Yellowstone Archives.

38. Horace Albright to Stephen T. Mather, October 16, 1919, and September 23, 1920, HMA Papers, 1919–1922, Yellowstone Archives.

39. "John D. Rockefeller Jr.'s Gift," pp. 15–17; Erwin Thompson, *Maud Noble Cabin: Historic Structures Report*, History Section (Washington D.C.: National Park Service, 1970), pp. 11–27; Righter, *Crucible for Conservation*, pp. 33–34; Albright, *Birth of the National Park Service*, p. 154; and Struthers Burt to Horace Albright, September 11, 1923, HMA Papers, 1923–1927, Yellowstone Archives.

40. Righter, *Crucible for Conservation*, pp. 35–37; Albright, *Birth of the National Park Service*, p. 189; and "John D. Rockefeller Jr.'s Gift," pp. 19–20.

41. U.S. Congress, Senate, "Hearings Before the Committee on Public Lands and Pursuant to S. 237," 70th Cong., 2nd sess., Part 2.

42. Leo H. Dietrich, et al., *Jackson Hole National Monument, Wyoming: A Compendium of Important Papers Covering Negotiation in the Establishment and Administration of the National Monument*, 4 vols. (Washington, D.C.: Dept. of the Interior, ca. 1945, 1950), 2, Part 1, No. 7; and Righter, *Crucible for Conservation*, pp. 40–41.

43. Righter, *Crucible for Conservation*, p. 40; and "John D. Rockefeller Jr.'s, Gift," p. 32.

44. "John D. Rockefeller Jr.'s Gift," pp. 16 and 23–24; "Interview with Mr. Horace Albright by Assistant Superintendent of Grand Teton National Park Haraden and Chief Naturalist Dilley at Jackson Lake Lodge, September 12, 1967," Grand Teton National Park Library, pp. 33–34; Righter, *Crucible for Conservation*, p. 46; Albright, *Birth of the National Park Service*, p. 164; and Marian Schenck to John Daugherty, September 4, 1986, personal correspondence.

45. "John D. Rockefeller Jr.'s. Gift,"p. 25; and "Albright interview," 1967, p. 41.

46. Horace Albright to John D. Rockefeller, Jr., February 26, 1927, HMA Papers 1923–1927, Yellowstone Archives.

47. "John D. Rockefeller Jr.'s. Gift,"p. 27; and Righter, *Crucible for Conservation*, pp. 49–51.

48. *Jackson's Hole Courier*, April 12, 1928; and "Hearing on S. Res. 226," 1933, pp. 36–40.

49. Righter, *Crucible for Conservation*, pp. 52 and 130.

50. Rockefeller Archive Center, Harold P. Fabian Papers, 1V3A7, Box 1, File 4, Financial Reports, 1929–1932,

1942; Righter, *Crucible for Conservation,* p. 51; and "John D. Rockefeller Jr.'s Gift," p. 59.

51. Fabian Papers, RAC, Box 23, Files, Sheffield, Parcel 109, 1928–1931; Box 21, Files 220–221, Ferrin, Parcel 70, 1927–1938; Box 21, File 218, Ferrin Parcel 68, 1919–1930; Box 24, File 268, Ferrin, Parcel 115, 1928; Box 24, File 271, Ferrin, Parcel 118, 1929.

52. Fabian Papers, RAC, Box 5, File 34, Correspondence-Richard Winger; Contract, March 8, 1930; Horace Albright to Harold Fabian, November 13, 1929; H. Fabian to Vanderbilt Webb, July 17, 1931; H. Fabian to Kenneth Chorley, August 10, 1931.

53. Joe Markham to Horace Albright, July 29, 1919 and Markham to Albright, August 9, 1919, in Albright Papers, 1919–1922, Yellowstone Archives.

54. "John D. Rockefeller Jr.'s Gift," pp. 11–12.

55. Horace Albright to Hal Evarts, September 25, 1923, Albright Papers, Yellowstone Archives; and George Ryter to Rose Crabtree, March 25, 1924, MS 872, Wyoming State Archives. This is a voluminous 113-page letter, written over the winter of 1923–1924.

56. "Hearing on S. Res. 226," 1933, pp. 266–268; and *Jackson Hole Guide,* October 6, 1955.

57. Struthers Burt to Horace Albright, July 18, 1927, and Burt to Albright, October 14, 1927, Albright Papers, Yellowstone Archives.

58. Ibid.

59 "John D. Rockefeller Jr.'s Gift," p. 78.

60. Fabian Papers, Rockefeller Archive Center, Box 17, File 165, Nipper, 1928, Box 20, File 198, Smith, 1930–1932.

61. Ibid., Box 16, File 127, Plans, Ca. 1934, Box 18, File 173, McBride, 1928, Frank McBride to Snake River Land Company, November 12, 1930.

62. Ibid., Box 53, File 501, transcript, interview with Harold P. Fabian by Ed Edwin, July 11, 1966; Box 18, File 175, Jones, 1929–1930, Harold Fabian to Dick Winger, July 30, 1930; Box 20, File 209, Brown, 1929–1930, Fabian to Kenneth Chorley, August 5, 1929, Fabian to Joe Allen, October 28, 1929; and Righter, *Crucible for Conservation,* p. 60.

63. Fabian Papers, Rockefeller Archive Center, Box 16, File 135, Feud 1933–1935, Dick Winger to Harold Fabian, November 1, 1935; Box 7, File 44, Elbo Ranch, 1929–1934, Sam T. Woodring to Harold Fabian, May 14, 1931.

64. Superintendent's Monthly Report, July 1930, Grand Teton National Park; *Jackson's Hole Courier,* May 7, 1931, and June 4, 1931; interview with Marvel Lesher by John Daugherty, September 2, 1982; interview with Dr. F. M.

Fryxell by John Daugherty, September 14, 1983, Grand Teton National Park; and Preston James, "Regional Planning in the Jackson Hole Country," *The Geographical Review,* 26 (July 1936):449.

65. Fabian Papers, Rockefeller Archive Center, Box 16, File 141, Harthoorn, 1931–1933; Box 58, File 543, May 1950.

66. Ibid., Box 22, File 235, Eynon, 1930–1931; Box 18, File 175, Jones, 1929–1930; Box 22, File 232, Turner, 1929–1936; Box 22, File 240, Winger, 1929–1931; and Righter, *Crucible for Conservation,* p. 60.

67. Fabian Papers, Rockefeller Archive Center, Box 21, File 227, Ericsson, 1929–1930; Box 22, File 230, Ericsson, 1929–1931; Box 22 File 239, Ericsson, 1928–1931; Box 16, File 131, Neil, 1928–1930, H. C. Ericsson to Harold Fabian, March 5, 1930.

68. "Hearing on S. Res. 226," 1933, pp. 76–79.

69. Fabian Papers, Rockefeller Archive Center, Box 16, File 126, Pending Entries, Eva S. Topping, 1930–1931; Box 16, File 123, Pending Entries, 1928–1933; "Hearing on S. Res. 226," 1933, pp. 302–330; and Righter, *Crucible for Conservation,* p. 83.

70. Fabian Papers, Rockefeller Archive Center, Box 7, File 51, Elk Ranch, 1939–1941, Dick Winger to Harold Fabian, August 8, 1941; Box 16, File 128, and Permits, 1936–1941; Box 58, Files 544–551, Leases 1946–1949.

71. Ibid., Box 32, File 363, "Chronology of Events," March 6, 1929-October 18, 1932; Righter, *Crucible for Conservation,* pp. 57–59; and "John D. Rockefeller Jr.'s Gift," pp. 56–57 and 81–91.

72. Horace Albright to John D. Rockefeller Jr., February 16, 1927, Albright Papers, 1923–1927, Yellowstone Archives; *Jackson's Hole Courier,* August 23, 1927, and April 12, 1928; Rockefeller Archive Center, Kenneth Chorley Papers, IV 3A3, Box 29, File 258, Miscellany A-Z, Walter B. Sheppard to Horace Albright, June 6, 1929; *Jackson's Hole Courier,* August 15, 1929; and Righter, *Crucible for Conservation,* pp. 64–65.

73. Righter, *Crucible for Conservation,* pp. 66–78.

74. Fabian Papers, Rockefeller Archive Center, Box 5, File 634, Correspondence, Richard Winger, 1930–1933, Kenneth Chorley to Vanderbilt Webb, June 13, 1930.

75. Chorley Papers, Rockefeller Archive Center, Box 26, File 223, Real Estate, Agent, Winger, 1930–1935, 1941–1943, Kenneth Chorley to Horace Albright, June 17, 1930, Harold Fabian to Vanderbilt Webb, June 17, 1930.

76. Righter, *Crucible for Conservation,* 64; and Fabian Papers, Rockefeller Archive Center, Box 5, File 34, Correspondence, Winger, Harold Fabian to Vanderbilt Webb,

July 17, 1931; Box 6, File 35, Schedules, Dick Winger to Harold Fabian, May 4, 1931; Box 5, File 34, Correspondence, Winger, H. Fabian to Kenneth Chorley, August 10, 1931, and D. Winger to H. Fabian, November 19, 1930.

77. Josephine Fabian, "The Lucas Place, 1914–1975," unpublished ms., ca. 1978, Grand Teton National Park; and Fabian Papers, Rockefeller Archive Center, Box 59, File 562, Kimmel Purchase, 1946–1947.

78. Albright, *Birth of the National Park Service,* 304–305; "Hearing on S. Res. 226," 1933, pp. 222 and 30–330; and Righter, *Crucible for Conservation,* pp. 76–84.

79. Dieterich, *Jackson Hole Compendium,* 2:Part 1, Nos. 8–9; and Righter, *Crucible for Conservation,* pp. 85–87.

80. Dieterich, *Jackson Hole Compendium,* 2:Part 1, No. 10.

81. Righter, *Crucible for Conservation,* pp. 88–92.

82. Dieterich, *Jackson Hole Compendium,* 2:Part 1, No. 1; and Righter, *Crucible for Conservation,* pp. 92–96.

83. Righter, *Crucible for Conservation* pp. 96–97; and "Hearing on S. Res. 250," 1938.

84. Dieterich, *Jackson Hole Compendium,* 2:Part 2, Nos. 13 and 14; and Righter, *Crucible for Conservation,* p. 110.

85. *Jackson Hole Guide,* October 12, 1972; Righter, *Crucible for Conservation,* pp. 106–110; and Superintendent's Monthly Report, October 1931, Grand Teton National Park

86. Righter, *Crucible for Conservation,* pp. 111–113; and Dieterich, *Jackson Hole Compendium,* 2:Part 2, Nos. 17 and 18.

87. Righter, *Crucible for Conservation,* pp. 114–115; and Ise, *National Park Policy,* pp. 498–504.

88. "Hearing on H.R. 2241," 1943; and Righter, *Crucible for Conservation,* pp. 116–118.

89. Dieterich, *Jackson Hole Compendium,* 2:Part 3, No. 42; and *State of Wyoming vs. Paul R. Franke,* Judge's Memorandum, February 10, 1945.

90. Righter, *Crucible for Conservation,* pp. 121–123; Superintendent Paul R. Franke to Assistant Director Arthur Demaray, June 30, 1945, Jackson Hole National Monument, Federal Records Center, Denver, CO.

91. Murie, *Wapiti Wilderness,* p. 121; Fabian Papers, Rockefeller Archive Center, Box 42, File 425, Supt. of Properties, 1948, Guy Robertson to Harold Fabian, March 6, 1948.

92. Righter, *Crucible for Conservation,* pp. 123–127 and 142–151; and Dieterich, *Jackson Hole Compendium,* 2:Part 2, No. 17. President Roosevelt made this prediction in a letter to Governor Lester Hunt, dated April 29, 1943.

93. Dieterich, *Jackson Hole Compendium,* 2:Part 4, Nos. 56–60.

94. "John D. Rockefeller Jr.'s Gift," pp. 38–39.

95. "Hearing on S. Res. 250," 1938, pp. 420–421; Superintendent's Monthly Reports, August 1929 and November 1931; *Jackson's Hole Courier,* July 13, 1931; Building Maintenance Records, Grand Teton National Park; Superintendent's Annual Report for 1932, Grand Teton National Park; and Superintendent's Monthly Report, November 1958, Federal Records Center, Denver, CO.

96. *Jackson's Hole Courier,* January 30, 1930; Superintendent's Monthly Reports, April, May, June, July, August, 1930, Grand Teton National Park; and "John D. Rockefeller Jr.'s Gift," pp. 38–39.

97. Superintendent's Annual Report, 1932; Superintendent's Monthly Report, Special Memorandum to the Director, June 29, 1932.

98. "John D. Rockefeller Jr.'s Gift," pp. 38–39.

99. Superintendent's Monthly Report, March 1930; Superintendent's Monthly Report, Special Memorandum, June 26, 1931; and Superintendent's Monthly Rept., July 1936, Grand Teton National Park

100. Superintendent's Annual Report for 1932; Superintendent's Monthly Report, September 1930, Grand Teton National Park; and A. W. Gabbey to Fritioff Fryxell, January 15, 1941, Fryxell Collection, 1438, D-Box 4, Correspondence, University of Wyoming Archives.

101. Fryxell Interview, September 14, 1983, Grand Teton National Park; Struthers Burt, *Diary,* pp. 73–75; and *Jackson Hole News,* November 2, 1977.

102. Superintendent's Monthly Reports, June, September, and October 1929, Grand Teton National Park.

103. *Jackson's Hole Courier,* May 29, 1930; Superintendent's Monthly Reports, September and October 1931, Grand Teton National Park

104. Superintendent's Monthly Reports, July and August 1931, Grand Teton National Park

105. Superintendent's Monthly Report, August 1932, Special Memorandum, August 15, 1932, and Superintendent's Monthly Report, June 1933, Special Report, June 29, 1933, Grand Teton National Park; and Grand Teton National Park brochures, 1935 and 1941.

106. Superintendent's Monthly Reports, August 1936 and September 1936, Press Memorandum; Photograph Files, Grand Teton National Park; and Building Maintenance Files, Grand Teton National Park.

107. Nash, *Wilderness,* p. 200; interview with Margaret Murie by John Daugherty, February 13, 1984, Moose,

Wyoming; Frank Graham Jr., "Mardy Murie and Her Sunrise of Promise," *Audobon* 82 (May 1980):106–127; Gregory D. Kendrick, "An Environmental Spokesman: Olaus J. Murie and a Democratic Defense of Wilderness,"

Annals of Wyoming, 5D(Fall 1978):213–302; and Murie, *Wapiti Wilderness.*

108. Struthers Burt to Horace Albright, September 11, 1923, HMA Papers, 1923–1927, Yellowstone Archives.

Picturing Jackson Hole and Grand Teton National Park

By William H. Goetzmann

This essay is concerned with the various ways in which Jackson Hole and Grand Teton National Park have been pictured by cartographers, artists, photographers, film makers, and television. Add to this dreamers and the present author's point of view, especially since almost all the pictures and films and vistas do represent unique points of view—including those of a visitor today who is concerned with the historical setting (memories) as well as shifting media and representations of this staggeringly beautiful place that is nonetheless haunted by its past.

❧

The Teton Mountains that tower over Jackson Hole are among the most familiar landmarks in the American West. They have been photographed perhaps more than any other mountains in that vast region. Ansel Adams's striking view of the Snake River winding towards the majestic snow-covered peaks, made in 1942 for the Interior Department, is an image of grandeur that stands as the climax vision of the Grand Teton National Park, if not the whole Rocky Mountain West.

Now, in the late twentieth century, more people have seen this iconic picture than marveled at William H. Jackson's nineteenth-century photograph of the Mount of the Holy Cross in western Colorado. To a religious Victorian age, Jackson's 1873 photograph of a remote mountain face on which a huge cross made of snow hung glistening in the sun was the ultimate symbol of America's holy mission in the West. Thomas Moran's highly romantic painting of the Mount of the Holy Cross seemed to make it almost an American cathedral that far overshadowed anything from Medieval Europe. America's Manifest Destiny was reified, confirmed, christened, and blessed by the Almighty.

Ansel Adams's mighty view of the Tetons, on the other hand, as an icon for the twentieth century, says something else. It may denote a tourist and sportsman's destination but it does not stand for a mission of conquest. It denotes the pristine grandeur of nature—the towering beauty of all outdoors untouched by human presence, though we know, of course, that some human, some photographer, has framed, conceived and captured the scene. It needs

The Tetons—Snake River by Ansel Adams, 1942. *National Archives*

no beckoning cross, however. Indeed, Adams's view of the forests, the curling river, and the mountain peaks begs that they be left alone the way they were a million years ago.[1]

We know now that that has not been the case. Image makers from accomplished painters to snapshot photographers have come to Grand Teton National Park to capture not only its natural beauty, but also glimpses of its history, the dude ranch era, and its colorful life. Jackson Hole, the lively town of Jackson, once a gambling mecca for cowboys and movie stars, and even the Tetons themselves, have become a fantastic tourist destination—not yet as overrun as Yosemite, Yellowstone, and the Grand Canyon. Indeed, since the struggle to create and expand the National Park was finally consummated by Horace Albright of the Park Service, John D. Rockefeller II,

Franklin Delano Roosevelt and Congress in 1943, a different course has been taken.[2] Snake River Valley farms and ranch houses have been torn down or, like Dr. Horace Carncross's and Struthers Burt's famous Bar BC dude ranch, have been left abandoned. Today the cabins where famous literati gathered to fish and hunt and commune with nature, and the dance hall complete with an illegal whiskey still and bar where they gathered to play, is now a ruin, slowly being invaded by a bend of the Snake River. It is still the subject of tourists with cameras who, in their minds, appreciate its authentic rusticity and glamorous past.

Mormon Row, part of which still stands out on a meadow in the shadow of Blacktail Butte, is testimony of the difficult Mormon trek over Teton Pass in 1893. It is dominated now by a barn, tin-roofed in

The Mount of the Holy Cross by William Henry Jackson, 1873. *U.S. Geological Survey, William Henry Jackson #1276*

fairly recent times, while the rest of the row, including a few houses, is slowly falling to pieces. Moulton Barn, on the other hand, also part of the Mormon settlement, still stands intact in all of its rustic glory with the Tetons rising behind it. There are also outbuildings and a sagging corral. The Mormons, like earlier settlers, ranched and had large hayfields spread out along Ditch Creek. Not far from it, to the west, near present day Moose, Wyoming, is the site of Menor's Ferry over which some of the Mormons crossed the Snake River. Nothing now marks John Holland's and John Carnes' Flat Creek Ranch, the first homesteaders in the valley in 1884.[3] It is now part of the Elk Refuge. We can visit the Cunningham cabin on Spread Creek where a posse from Jackson gunned down George Spenser and young Mike Burnett, thinking them to be cattle rustlers. But, John D. Sargent's ten-room log lodge, Merymere, on the shores of Jackson Lake is gone. A photograph of John Sargent sitting contentedly by his fireplace remains. But the mysterious lodge, where Sargent (a relative of John Singer Sargent) believing his wife to be having an affair, drowned her "lover" and probably killed his wife by breaking both her hips, is gone. Later, for pay, he married a second wife who liked to play the violin while naked in a tree on the main trail to Yellowstone. But legendary Merymere

(a name that would be cherished in Britain) is no more. Perhaps the tree is still there, but Merymere is gone, along with Sargent who, sitting in his favorite rocker before the fireplace, blew his brains out with a rifle when his exhibitionist wife was taken away and his support disappeared.[4]

Much history has been neglected or removed from Jackson Hole in favor of a return to nature where the preservation of the great elk herd seems primary, and where the buffalo still roam while visitors still hope to see antelope on Antelope Flats and moose feeding near glacier-made ponds. As one looks down from Signal Mountain, the whole valley seems empty with only the forest and the river and vast green meadows over which the Tetons and the National Park Service stand guard.

Despite the fact that the valley of the Tetons was never a crossroad of the West—to the mountain men the Green River or even Pierre's Hole to the west of the Tetons seemed more inviting for their rendezvous and to many a tourist it was a stop on the road to Yellowstone Park—it has been pictured many times.

Start with the maps since they are a picture of a part of the earth. William Clark's great manuscript map of 1810 shows John Colter's 1807 route from Manuel Lisa's fort on the Big Horn through what is

John Dudley Sargent, sitting by
the fireplace at his Merymere
lodge. *Jackson Hole Historical
Society and Museum*

now Jackson Hole to Pierre's Hole.[5] The Tetons are
not on this map. However, in Clark's map of 1814
that accompanied Nicholas Biddle and Paul Allen's
*History of the Expedition Under the Command of Cap-
tains Lewis and Clark* published in Philadelphia in
1814, Colter's route past Lake Biddle (Jackson
Lake?) and into the Jackson Hole region is shown,
together with three clearly delineated mountain
peaks overlooking the lake to the West. According to
one authority, a party from the Northwest Company
came far south through Yellowstone and into Jackson
Hole where a French engagé named the mountains
Les Tetons.[6] If this happened, the news of the Tetons
does not appear on Chevalier Lapie's map of 1821,
widely published in *Nouvelle Annales des Voyages* in
Paris, though he seems aware of Wilson Price Hunt's
travels through the Wind River Valley and Union
Pass, as well as Robert Stuart's return through Jackson Hole and South Pass. Indeed Lapie's map was
published along with an abridgement of Wilson
Price Hunt's westward route and Robert Stuart's
"traveling memoranda" of his return eastward via
Jackson Hole, the Wind River Mountains and what
came to be known as "the South Pass"—the route of
American migration to Oregon and California. Perhaps Lapie's omission was due to American Fur
Company mogul, John Jacob Astor himself who,
while insisting that the news of the expedition be

first published in the prestigious *Nouvelles Annales de
Voyages,* by no means wished to provide explicit directions to his competitors in the fur trade including
the British Northwest Company.

One really had to wait until English cartographer Aaron Arrowsmith's Hudson's Bay Company
published his map of "British North America"
(1834) to see the Tetons on a widely distributed
map. By then, though Jackson Hole was well known
to fur trappers, including the Americans David Jackson and Jedediah Smith, Arrowsmith misplaces it on
his map. The next public cartographic exposure appeared on Captain Benjamin Bonneville's map of
1837 where the Tetons are placed somewhat north of
Jackson Hole. Captain Washington Hood of the
Corps of Topographical Engineers located the Tetons on his official *Map of the United States Territory
of Oregon* published in 1838 obviously aimed to establish American claims vis-a-vis Britain to the
Northwest region.

Earlier in 1836 the mountain man Warren Ferris
had drawn a map clearly showing the location of
Jackson Lake and the Tetons. This map did not
come to light for over 100 years, nor did a similar
map drawn by Jim Bridger. Still another map that locates, however carelessly, Jackson Hole and the Tetons is the celebrated Frémont-Gibbs-Smith map of
1831. This was a version of Lt. John C. Frémont's

1845 map of his circumnavigation of the West, possessed by George Gibbs of Fort Vancouver on which Gibbs placed all the geographical data known by the great mountain man explorer Jedediah Smith with whom, in 1831, he spent many weeks. This map, which so excited cartographic historian Carl I. Wheat and mountain man historian Dale L. Morgan, surfaced as late as 1954, though the information must also have appeared as early as 1831 as told also to Samuel Parkman who was readying Smith's journals and maps for publication just before the legendary explorer was murdered by Comanches on the Cimarron River while on the way to Santa Fe.

For a long period of time, Jackson Hole and the mighty Tetons were neglected except by a few settlers, ranchers and elk's tooth poachers who lived in sod-roofed dugouts. Because Elks Clubs spread rapidly over the United States the front teeth of the noble beasts were in high demand for club members' watch chains. Luckily by 1900 the Elks Clubs did not require that a man possess such a tooth to be a member and the dwindling elk herds were saved.

In 1859 Capt. William F. Raynolds, guided by the legendary mountain man Jim Bridger, and assisted by a party of scientific men including Ferdinand V. Hayden, set off from Ft. Pierre on the Missouri to explore the Upper Missouri and Upper Yellowstone country for a system of wagon roads reaching as far north as the Mullan Road at Fort Benton and as far south as Fort Laramie. Needless to say, he failed in this ambitious mission even while leading his snow-bound and starving men including Bridger over the Continental Divide. He did succeed, however, in exploring and scientifically mapping the Jackson Hole area while Hayden made the first geological report on the Tetons and surrounding regions. His cartographer, J. H. Snowden, made six original maps. Blocked by snow, Raynolds never reached the wonders of Yellowstone. Instead he had to listen to Bridger tell him over and over about the geysers and paint pots in what must have been an exquisite form of torture, especially since Raynolds knew full well that if he could reach and explore the Yellowstone geyser basins, he would become famous. But it was not to be. Sketches of the Teton Basin by the artists of the expedition, J. D. Hutton and Antoine Schonborn, are possibly among the sketches at

Yale. In 1871 Schonborn was to see and sketch the Yellowstone with Ferdinand V. Hayden's expedition. Schonborn committed suicide in Omaha, Nebraska, after the 1871 expedition to Yellowstone.[7]

In 1870, Lt. Gustavus Doane, a cavalryman, escorted a party of Montana businessmen and politicians into Yellowstone that included N. P Langford, Henry D. Washburn and Cornelius Hedges. They explored its wonders and determined to make it a national wilderness park.[8] They sent articles and sketches to *Scribner's Magazine* that were turned into surprisingly accurate illustrations by the artist Thomas Moran who had not yet seen Yellowstone and its marvels. Because the party entered from the north at Fort Ellis, Montana, Jackson Hole did not figure in their itinerary. Perhaps they did not even know of it.

The most important early map of the Jackson Hole area was made by Gustavus Bechler on Professor Ferdinand V. Hayden's second expedition into Yellowstone in 1872.[9] In 1871, Hayden, head of the United States Geological Survey of the Territories, sponsored by the Department of the Interior, had led an extensive exploring expedition into the Yellowstone region, taking with him the artist Thomas Moran and the photographer William H. Jackson. Moran's sketches and Jackson's photographs, together with the intense lobbying of N. P Langford and the railroad tourist interests of Jay Cooke, convinced Congress to make Yellowstone the nation's first national wilderness park.

Hayden's expedition of 1872 was most relevant for Jackson Hole. The professor and his men, now famous, explored and mapped the Jackson Valley and the Tetons. James Stevenson, Hayden's primary assistant, led that wing of the expedition. Stevenson and N. P Langford climbed to the top of Grand Teton Peak. It was a claim that was first disputed by William O. Owen, who climbed the peak in 1898, and has disputed ever since. In fact, due to Owen's relentless lobbying, in 1926 the legislature of Wyoming proclaimed him the first to ascend to the crest of the Grand Teton.[10] Most importantly however, Bechler's map represented the most extensive and careful delineation of the region made to date. It was a climax view, and Hayden's party named most of the features of the region, including Jenny Lake, a memorial to the heroic Indian wife of mountain man "Beaver Dick" Leigh, an early settler in the region. One of the Tetons was named Mount Moran after the spectacular artist who had accompanied the 1871 expedition to Yellowstone.

In the summer of 1873, Captain William A. Jones also explored in Jackson Hole and produced another carefully-drawn overall map together with 49 specific geological and geographic maps, plus a spectacularly colored overall geologic map by Theodore Comstock.[11] This was the first thorough scientific study and view of the geologic history of Jackson Hole, which is so complex and interesting, with the great fault bloc Teton Range thrust upwards over a lower plate, and then the massive eroded valley formed by ancient glaciers, leaving boulders, moraines and drumlins and the winding Snake River, ever-shifting, its former banks forming hillocks that trace its ancient course. Comstock's study and vivid map opened a whole new area of "picturing" Jackson Hole. It began to resurrect its ancient history. .

There have, of course, been many subsequent cartographic images of what is now Grand Teton National Park, especially important maps that delineated the increasing extent of the park including John D. Rockefeller Jr.'s enormous contribution. During the struggle to enlarge the park from its 1929 founding to its 1943 final boundaries that created the adjoining Jackson Hole National Monument, maps were naturally crucial, especially to Rockefeller's Snake River Land Company that was secretly buying out the valley's ranch properties.[12]

Cartographically picturing the region will probably never really end. Standard United States Geological Survey (U.S.G.S.) topographical maps are today being replaced by detailed Landsat space satellite maps made under the auspices of the United States Geological Survey and the National Aeronautics and Space Agency.

～§◎◎～

For most people, pictures mean paintings, drawings and photographs. So many of these have been made over the years, especially by tourists, that only the highlights can be considered here. It is likely that

J. D. Hutton and perhaps Antoine Schonborn, the artists who accompanied Capt. William F. Raynolds's expedition into the valley in 1860, were the first artists to sketch Jackson Hole.

William H. Jackson, in 1872, was the first to photograph the Tetons. He did so from a base camp in Pierre's Hole on the west side of the mountains. For eight days Jackson and his assistants struggled with heavy cameras and stubborn mules to climb high enough to make an unobstructed and spectacular view of the central Tetons. He succeeded finally, but still from afar, with lesser peaks and valleys, including that of Glacier Creek intervening. On the ninth day Jackson finally found himself face to face with the west side of the Grand Teton peak, 13,747 feet high. He himself was variously out on a ledge on Table Mountain on the Idaho side and then in a cleft between two major outcroppings. Jackson was well aware of the adventure in photographing the Tetons. He had one of his assistants make a wet plate photograph of him with another assistant, his camera and his small portable darkroom tent way out on the edge of a high precipice with the three Tetons looming in the background miles away. Jackson, in the fashion of Eadweard Muybridge, was often into self-dramatization, but this photo is one of his classics. Later Jackson would enter Jackson Hole proper on the east side of the Tetons and make numerous photographs from what have become familiar tourist vantage points.[13] Some of these he would turn into post cards, later sold by the Detroit Publishing Company. One of his better views from east of the Tetons is a long-range flat panoramic view across the Snake River that captures virtually the whole mountain range in the picture. It prefigures Ansel Adams's stunning view but with far less drama. This photograph was probably made in 1878 when Jackson joined Hayden's last field survey that took him and a photographic division through Jackson Hole. The party, led by Hayden himself, was accompanied by William H. Holmes, one of the great topographic artists of his time. The 1878 expedition entered via Hoback Canyon to the south. From Hoback Canyon, Jackson proceeded northward through Jackson Hole, following the Snake River into Yellowstone. Jackson wrote very little about Jackson Hole and the Tetons in his autobiography so he must not have

Panoramic View of the Great Teton Range, Looking East by William Henry Jackson, 1872. Note figure standing on the peak in the middle-right foreground *U.S. Geological Survey, William Henry Jackson #410*

been as impressed by its beauty as he was by the fireworks at Yellowstone. Perhaps, after seven years of photographing landscapes, he was jaded. Many of Jackson's photographs can be found in the picture archives of the U.S.G.S. in Denver. Jackson was fortunate that his Yellowstone and Jackson Hole photos and camera survived. As early as 1871, Capt. J. W. Barlow, leading a military expedition into Yellowstone, took along Thomas J. Hines as a photographer. Hines's photographs arrived in Chicago just in time to be destroyed in the great fire of that year.[14]

Another of the West's great photographers was F. Jay Haynes of Fargo, North Dakota. Haynes, along with Jackson, was perhaps the most enterpris-

ing of all western photographers. He worked under contract with the Northern Pacific Railroad for many years, photographing the building of the road as well as the scenery and towns along its transcontinental route. As a major part of his equipment he had his own railroad car studio—"Haynes Palace Studio." He first entered Yellowstone in 1881, only three years after Hayden had mapped it and Jackson had made his final photos of the scenery. Immediately Haynes saw the tourist possibilities of Yellowstone and applied to the Secretary of the Interior for an exclusive photographer's concession in the park. With annual persistence he got his exclusive concession in 1884 and land upon which to build two sub-

The Three Tetons by William
Henry Jackson, 1872. *U.S. Geological Survey, William Henry Jackson
#162*

stantial studio buildings—one at Old Faithful and
one at Mammoth Hot Springs.

But even as he was applying for the concession
at Yellowstone, Haynes explored Jackson Hole for
other photographic possibilities. In fact, he became
the official photographer for President Chester A.
Arthur's excursion to Yellowstone and Jackson Hole
in 1883. Haynes took a memorable group photograph of President Arthur flanked by General Philip
Sheridan and Secretary of War Robert Lincoln. The
red-faced, mutton-chopped Arthur is seated, wearing
a tam like some feudal Scottish chieftain. The excursion permitted no reporters or women, and at each
of his three camps in Jackson Hole—Gros Ventre
River Canyon, on the Gros Ventre near Blacktail
Butte, and along a bend of the Snake River just below the fork of the Buffalo River—a bar tent was

prominent. When the explorers weren't fishing, Arthur's favorite sport, they were drinking in a sort of
Bohemian Grove, male-bonding camp in Jackson
Hole. On one occasion, when the Indian guides
staged a war dance for the President, one of the
drunken dancers nearly "whacked Great Chester on
the head!" Haynes, of course, photographed the
dance that must have been a high point on what one
author has called "The Bottle Trail."[15]

Indeed, Haynes took a number of splendid photographs on the trip. The Tetons, of course, dominated many of his pictures that also often feature Indian scouts astride horses on a strong foreground of
meadow, gravel or sand bars. One photo is certainly
a harbinger of modernism. It featured bands of light
and dark horizontally across the picture, making the
Teton Valley scene almost abstract. The foreground

President Chester A. Arthur, seated center, toured Yellowstone and Jackson Hole in 1883. F. Jay Haynes was the official photographer for the presidential excursion.
F. Jay Haynes, National Park Service

is a light gravel bar, then the dark Gros Ventre River, then another thinner streak of light gravel, then a bank of dark trees and, finally, a distant view of the Tetons as the focal point of the picture. New York's avant garde Photo-Secessionists would have liked it, even though it was a bit in advance of their own art photographs.

Several other of Haynes's pictures remind one of Edward Curtis's early Alaska work (1899).[16] One camp scene features the pith-helmeted president looking out across the Snake River from his camp in the evening—a sunset glow just beyond the distant Tetons. Another is a tight shot of an Indian guide framed by two trees with the Tetons merely a backdrop in the distance. Still another sequence of photos appear to be self portraits and experimental shots. The first shows a black cowboy hunter holding a mule in a broad field before the overwhelming presence of the Tetons. Haynes is sprawled on the ground. Then in a stereoscope repetition of the scene, the mule has vanished. Clearly, in many of his surviving photographs, Haynes was not only trying for artistry, but also challenging the overwhelming presence of the Tetons by using interesting dark and light foregrounds that often included, but did not necessarily need, human figures even for scale. The enterprising Haynes is often thought of as a buck-

ster, a mere post card photographer, but his scenes of Jackson Hole and the valley testify to his conscious attempts at artistry.

Perhaps the central figure in Jackson Hole photography was Harrison "Hank" Crandall. Originally from Newton, Kansas, Hank Crandall was first inspired to be a Teton Valley photographer by a William H. Jackson photo of the Tetons that he saw in a grade school geography book.[17] Crandall was a generation later than Jackson, but Jackson lived so long he became Crandall's contemporary and actually visited him at Jenny Lake in 1929 at the dedication of Grand Teton National Park. Crandall was also a generation younger than Haynes. He came to Jackson Hole, after service in World War I, in 1921. The following year, he brought his wife Hildegarde, some camping equipment, and a 3A Special Edition Eastman Kodak camera to Jackson Hole in a Ford Model T that bumped over roads that had "not yet been built." He made friends with the storekeeper at Moran, spent the winter as his renter, and the following spring staked out a homestead claim east of String Lake, near what is now Jenny Lake Lodge. Crandall built a log cabin and began his career as a photographer and landscape artist. When Grand Teton National Park was established in 1929, Hank sold his cabin and moved the substantial studio and showroom that he had built to the Jenny Lake area, where it still stands. He was a family man, however, and with the birth of two daughters he was persuaded to move to Boise, Idaho, for their education. Jackson Hole had only primitive schooling. He came back to Jackson Hole every spring and summer to continue his painting and photographic business which, like Haynes's at Yellowstone, was made a park concession at the behest of Horace B. Albright, then Director of the National Park Service. Crandall made scenic photos of the Tetons that he sold as park mementos or as post cards. He did a good business during the dude ranch era of the twenties and thirties, during which time writers like Owen Wister, who wrote *The Virginian* (ca. 1902), stayed at the Bar BC Ranch.

As early as 1921, Crandall was selling pictures to dudes as fast as he could make them. All through the twenties he sold countless photos of dudes in cowboy outfits—or cowgirl outfits. Celebrities like Cissy Patterson Gizycka, heiress to the *Chicago Tribune* fortune, a Polish countess on the loose and the wildest woman in Jackson Hole, had her picture taken by Crandall while at the Bar BC Dude Ranch, although her paramour, Cal Carrington, the foreman at the ranch, allegedly a former horsethief, probably avoided Crandall's lens.[18]

Crandall's photos were exuberant and theatrical, far from the brooding darkness of his contemporary, Ansel Adams. One of his best photos is a self-portrait showing him far up among the snowy crags of the Tetons. Another, in color, showed a mountain climber dangling from a rope below a mountain ledge. He liked to see the Tetons and his subjects stand out against blue skies. He also produced documentary photos for motion picture company location scouts, frequently using his panoramic camera that produced 7 × 17-inch negatives. But, because ranching, cowboys and dudes were at every hand, he photographed them more often than the Tetons. At the same time, he painted delicate pictures of the valley's wildflowers and made them into collector's item post cards. And when he had time he did paint his beloved Tetons. His work went all the way to the East Coast, appearing in magazines and calendars and in John D. Rockefeller's dressing room. In 1931, Rockefeller wrote Crandall, "The beautiful colored picture

Harrison Crandall is Grand Teton National Park's best-known photographer. His former studio now serves as the visitor center at Jenny Lake. *National Park Service*

you gave us when we were here last has been framed and hangs in my dressing room. It gives us constant delight." The affable Hank Crandall, who liked to photograph pretty cowgirls and handsome cowboys, was a romantic in the Roaring Twenties way out West.[19]

Ansel Adams, born in 1902 in San Francisco, provided a contrast with virtually everyone else who photographed in Jackson Hole. Very much the art photographer from the beginning, he came to know Alfred Stieglitz, Paul Strand, Edward Weston, Imogen Cunningham, Mabel Dodge Luhan, Georgia O'Keeffe, and Beaumont and Nancy Newhall of the Museum of Modern Art. In 1920, dazzled by Yosemite, he decided to become a professional photographer and a pillar of the Sierra Club. He even married Virginia Best in Yosemite in 1928.[20] Photographing Yosemite had a long tradition from C. L. Wead's first efforts to those of Carleton Watkins and

Below Zero-Bison by Thomas Mangelsen. Mangelsen, a wildlife photographer who has traveled throughout the world, has done some of his finest work in Jackson Hole. *Thomas D. Mangelsen*

Eadweard Muybridge. Adams was certainly challenged by their work as he began his career photographing Yosemite and the high Sierras. He also admired the matter-of-fact work of the early survey photographer, Timothy O'Sullivan, who was deliberately not an art photographer.

Ansel Adams became an institution as a photographer. He had over 500 exhibitions, his own gallery in San Francisco, and a studio in Yosemite. He traveled all over the West, making his extraordinary photographs. He even developed the "Zone Method" of controlling light and dark in his black-and-white pictures.[21] This was followed by several other books and films on photographic techniques as Adams seemed to "scientize" photography while developing techniques that almost mechanically lent high drama to his pictures.

This chapter started with a description of Adams's striking but dark picture of the Snake River and the Tetons in a rainstorm—a picture that became an American icon. He made many other photos in Jackson Hole, probably in 1942 when Secretary of the Interior Harold Ickes commissioned him to photograph all the national parks. A look at a series of Adams's pictures reveals not a man with dudes or tourists in mind, but a person with an inner feeling and a tremendous ambition to control his

scenes like Renaissance artists. He photographed a spare, slanted view of the Tetons and Jackson Lake at sunrise. It could be a Japanese print. He did Mount Moran with bands of light-colored aspens and dark pines dominating one half of the picture. Mount Moran is seen almost as a three-dimensional backdrop, indicating that Adams was respectful of the mountain but not dominated by it. There were other pictures of Mount Moran, some in which the storm-clouded sky dominated three-fourths of the picture, making the Tetons recede to a far less commanding position. Like all the other photographers who had visited the valley, he was challenged by the Tetons. In one photo, *Tetons and Jackson Lake, Driftwood*, the driftwood seems like a mountain from which he views the Tetons and their reflection far across a lake. Edward Curtis had used this technique on his trip with E. H. Harriman to Alaska in 1899.[22] Many of Adams's pictures feature water or stands of trees rather than the mountain. He is in *control* of nature just as is his organization, the Sierra Club. In one of his best pictures, Adams really ignores his subject, Mormon Row, and entitles his picture incorrectly *Ranch and Mount Leidy, Jackson Hole*. He is facing east, away from the Tetons. Adams is now passing out of fashion in the march of the "New Topographers" like Lewis Baltz, Robert

Adams and Len Jenshel who photographed the West as a deteriorating suburban wasteland—in Peter Blake's term "God's own junkyard"—or Peter Goin, Richard Misrach and Patrick Nagatani, who delight in photographing atomic testing sites in Utah and Nevada. They see the west as Death Valley, a total Zabriski Point. Or, like Mark Klett in his re-photographic project, they trace the changes man and time have wrought on, say, O'Sullivan's familiar photographed landmarks of the nineteenth century.[23] None of these new topographers have worked in Jackson Hole, probably because, as much as possible, with the exception of Jackson itself, Teton Village and the Rockefeller Lodge, traces of human activity have been extensively effaced, though some farms and ranches remain, dotting the valley. Man is not prominent in nature.

Three modern photographers have also done striking work in the Tetons. One, currently operating out of Omaha and Jackson, Thomas D. Mangelsen, is a wildlife photographer. Though he has traveled to Arctic regions and Africa making color photos of animals and their exotic locales, some of his best works have been of wildlife in Jackson Hole. One that stands out profoundly is a picture of two lonely buffalo on a windswept rocky plain with the temperature far below zero. Seen through a filter in a chilling blue atmosphere, they stand outlined against the snow-covered Tetons almost obscured by clouds of blowing snow off of which the dim winter sun is reflecting. Mangelsen has done other chromatic photos of the Tetons themselves but his trademark is a sensitivity to animal life, and where they fit in their particular ecosystem. Many of these appear in his book *Images of Nature: The Photographs of Thomas D. Mangelsen.*[24]

Perhaps the premier color photographer of the national parks is David Muench. His photographs of Grand Teton National Park are spectacular. They appear in his book, *National Parks of America,* together with a text by a former Secretary of the Interior, Stewart Udall and his brother, James Udall. By the late twentieth century, when environmental issues are at the political center stage, it is almost mandatory for Interior Secretaries to commission art photographs of America's wilderness areas as a subtle form of po-

litical propaganda. Muench's photographs, however, are special—perhaps the best western photographs ever made. In his *National Parks of America,* Muench includes four stunning views of Grand Teton National Park. The most spectacular perhaps is *January Dawn: Teton Range,* rose red as taken through a filtered lens. Two pictures feature Lake Solitude, one with a misty "snowmelt design" that not only reflects the Tetons in the hidden lake but also appears to cast a halo around them. The fourth picture, *Moonset, Grand Tetons,* features a daylight moon over the pinkish Tetons which makes them look deliberately artificial. Muench's photographs have appeared in such magazines as *National Geographic, New York Times, Wilderness, Outdoor Photographer, Photographic, Life, Sierra* and the *Smithsonian Magazine.* Recently he has been working with his son Marc Muench whose landscape photographs follow in his father's footsteps but also sometimes include human figures.[25]

Still other photographers of note are Ed Riddell and Jim Olson whose stunning scenes in both black and white and color illustrate a reprint of the legendary geologist of Jackson Hole, Fritiof Fryxell's little classic, *The Tetons: Interpretations of a Mountain Landscape.* Olson's views are from the tops of the Tetons or close up among the peaks, thus offering relatively unusual points of view affording panoramas of the valley or the intimate high up views of the mountain climber, for the Tetons are very often the destination of such adventurers. Riddell's views are moody with storms and sunsets in the manner of Ansel Adams.[26]

Another contemporary photographer, Frederic C. Joy, immigrated to Jackson Hole from Utah in 1958 to continue the family tradition of scenic photography started by his grandfather, who was married to the gorgeous Miss Utah of his day and termed by a disgruntled Struthers Burt, a former partner, a "Bluebeard" in 1911. Frederic C. Joy, his grandson, does not have Miss Utah in tow, but he has made what are among the most refreshing color photographs of the Teton region. Much of his work is reminiscent of Eliot Porter's pictures of the Glen Canyon of the Colorado.[27] These are close-up abstractions of erosions of the Tetons by glacial meltwater unlike those of any other photographer in the area. Besides these abstractions, Joy celebrates the fields of flowers and golden aspens that lie before the Tetons, as well as historical landmarks like the Bar BC Ranch, its red-roofed saddle barn in the foreground before a background of autumn trees and the Tetons in the distance.

But what of the millions of people with Nikons and Kodaks who take pictures in the park—of the Tetons, the wildlife, themselves? Robert Bednar, a recent student of mine, has argued that all of these pictures, such as those of the Moulton Barn, the most photographed barn in the West, do not represent reality but the hyper-real.[28] They represent, according to Bednar, the photography of the already expected. In the poet Ezra Pound's terms they are "shades of a shade," "daguerreotypes of a likeness,"[29] pictures of pictures already made a thousand times. As such, Bednar sees them as artificial simulations and, therefore, a dead end as to reality and contact with nature itself. Could this be true of Jackson Hole with its iconic Tetons? Is it all a cliché?

The historian Carl Becker once wrote an essay entitled "Everyman his own historian." I wonder if the millions of snapshots aren't really discoveries, re-exploration of a part of the earth thought to have been discovered, mapped and pictured by mountain men, explorers, surveyors and professional photographers? Hand-held camera visitors to the Teton Valley are likewise explorers. They may pit themselves consciously against, or in imitation of, previous photographers, but with new equipment, new technology and different, even ironic, outlooks, they really are making the age-old landscape—new. It is a struggle to make something new—except babies.

⚜

The number of artists, professional and amateur, who have painted in Jackson Hole is incalculable. Some names are unfamiliar: Jenny Mabey, John Fery, Charles Chapman, a prolific artist and influential teacher, Ulysses Dow Tenney, Quita Pownall, Charles Partridge Adams, a prominent Denver artist who painted the Tetons on one occasion, but roughly 800 paintings of Colorado. Others like Gilbert

Munger of the Federal Lithographic Bureau who made the chromolithographs for Clarence King's *Systemic Geology* (a key U.S. 40th Parallel Survey volume) are barely known even to scholars. A few, such as J. D. Hutton and Antoine Schonborn, who accompanied Capt. Raynolds in 1860, made some pencil sketches and watercolors that have survived at Yale.[30]

Harrison Crandall, who found some time in the 1920s to paint beautiful panoramic views of the Teton Valley, will ultimately be remembered for his careful color renditions of 32 different species of wildflowers to be found in the valley. His work in this respect was more than a hobby, it was of prime importance to the United States Biological Survey. These delicate paintings represent an ecological cross section of the valley, circa 1920–40.[31]

That grandiose painter of the scenic West, Albert Bierstadt, traveled west on a wagon road trip to the Wind River Mountains with Frederick West Lander in 1859–60. Then he made a visit to Yellowstone Park in 1881, part of a three-month journey through the West. As a result, at least six paintings of the Tetons and Jackson Hole are attributed to him. They have titles like *Teton Range, Moose, Wyoming*, when there wasn't a Moose, Wyoming, at the time, and *Rainbow on Jenny Lake, Teton Range, Wyoming*, a garish and sentimental work possibly derived from stereographs taken by his brother Charles, a Niagara Falls photographer who made stereo pictures throughout the West. Other views, entitled *Grand Tetons, In the Tetons* and *Landscape with Waterfall, Study for Scenery in Grand Tetons* seem inaccurate. Certainly none capture the stunning majesty of the Tetons, which, if he had actually seen them, might well have soared to five or ten miles high. According to the best authorities, Bierstadt invented his Tetons, Jenny Lake and its rainbow, and Moose, Wyoming.[32]

The other "grand" painter of the Tetons was Thomas Moran. Between August 21 and August 29, 1879, escorted by Capt. Augustus Bainbridge, some troopers of the 14th Infantry and some Indian scouts, he made an excursion from Fort Hall, Idaho, along Teton Creek west of the Tetons, hoping to cross over into the Snake River Valley. He never made it, despite being guided by local Indians. On

The Three Tetons by Thomas Moran, 1895. Moran's painting of the Tetons from the Idaho side now hangs in the Oval Office of the White House, facing the president. *The White House*

August 23 he wrote in his diary while still west of the Snake River Range, "The Tetons are now plainly visible but not well defined owing to the mistiness of the atmosphere. They loom grandly above all the other mountains."[33] He was at least 22 miles away. By the 25th he could note in his diary, "The Tetons have loomed up grandly against the sky. From this point it is perhaps the finest pictorial range in the United States or even N. America." Later in the day he wrote, "This afternoon we made sketches of the Teton Range but the distance, 20 miles, is rather too far to distinguish the details, especially as it is very smoky from fires in the mountains on each side of the peaks." The next day he came upon Beaver Dick Leigh and his wife Jenny. They were trapping beaver. On the 27th it rained. They started their return on the 28th; on the 29th of August, Moran's notebook diary ends. The wonder is that Moran was able to produce at least four decent sketches of the Tetons. One sepia-colored watercolor is known to have been done on the 26th. It views the distant Tetons across a vast plain and over an intervening mountain range. Another watercolor, *The Tetons* is painted from a point very near the place where William H. Jackson had made his photograph on a ledge high up on Table Mountain. It is a dramatic, snow-covered storm scene rendered by Moran in blue and white. It is possible that this sketch was, in fact, influenced by Jackson's photograph. Later, possibly in 1890, when he was participating in the U.S. Indian census, Peter Moran, Thomas's brother, also painted a substantial multi-colored watercolor 12 × 18-inch view, *Grand Tetons View,* that now hangs in the Roswell Museum, Roswell, New Mexico.[34] More recently, a number of Moran pencil sketches have been on display at the Natural Wildlife Museum just outside of Jackson, Wyoming. They are from the collection of the Grand Teton National Park Visitor Center near Moose, Wyoming.

It is unfortunate that neither Bierstadt nor the Morans really got into Jackson Hole and thus we have no grand "Big Picture" by any of them of the face of the Grand Tetons. An 1895 oil painting by Moran of the Tetons, from the Idaho side, does hang in the Oval Office of the White House, facing the president. There are three other oil paintings of the Tetons by Moran: *The Teton Range* (1897), *The Teton Range* (1899), and the recently discovered *Solitude* (1899). The latter appears to have first been a depiction of the Rocky Mountains that Moran converted to a Teton picture by simply painting the three Tetons in white above the Rockies' horizon line. *Solitude* and the other Teton paintings were clearly based on the field sketches, though the foreground, a rushing river and part of Lake Solitude, resembles the foreground of his painting of the Mount of the

Grand Tetons View by Peter Moran. Peter Moran (who was Thomas Moran's brother) probably created this watercolor painting in 1890, when he participated in the U.S. Indian census. *Permanent Collection, Roswell Museum and Art Center*

Holy Cross. As Moran got older his western scenes became more standard and dependent on much earlier work. Both Bierstadt and Moran missed the chance of a lifetime, though Moran, on his return trip from Pierre's Hole west of the Tetons eventually made numerous sketches of the majestic cliffs of the Green River from which he made many salable paintings. Family lore has it that his daughter used to say, "whenever we needed money, papa painted another Green River."

Because these two famous grand landscapists of the nineteenth and early twentieth centuries never entered the Valley of the Tetons, they missed one of the great subjects for the landscape artist—one that with its many colored foliage and majestic peaks would have been almost perfect for their talents and romantic spirit. By contrast, perhaps in compensation, we do have one grand panoramic drawing of the Teton Valley by the West's foremost topographic artist, William H. Holmes, most famous for his breathtaking scientific renditions of the Grand Canyon to accompany Capt. Clarence Dutton's *Tertiary History of the Grand Canyon District* (1881). Holmes's wonderful panorama of Teton Valley appears in the portfolio *Maps and Panoramas* that accompanied F. V. Hayden's last *Report of the United States Geologi-*

cal and Geographical Survey of the Territories (1878).[35] Holmes would later become the Director of the Bureau of American Ethnology, though he was also a significant artist and an expert on structural geology. His observations made John Wesley Powell's *Report on the Geology of the Eastern Portion of the Unita Mountains* (1876) a classic, and he painted a splendid view of a laccolith formation or giant dome that constitutes the basic formations of both Yellowstone and the Grand Canyon. Holmes's panoramas of the Tetons and the Wind River Mountains should be prominently displayed at the Grand Teton National Park Visitor Center. Their stark but quintessentially accurate views provide a welcome alternative to the romantic paintings by lesser artists of the valley, even those of that often celebrated painter, William Robinson Leigh, a colorist who painted the Tetons in 1911 and who was clearly influenced by other Moran paintings. Leigh accompanied a Cody, Wyoming, taxidermist on his Teton expeditions.[36]

Holmes's panoramas also stand in contrast to the popular work of Conrad Schwiering, who for many years was "The Painter on the Square" in Jackson. Honored by the National Cowboy Hall of Fame's Trustees Gold Medal "for your outstanding contribution to Western Art," Schwiering, a pupil of Charles

William H. Holmes was one of the great topographic artists of his time. A member of the 1878 Hayden expedition, Holmes created this panoramic view of *The Teton Range from Upper Grosventre Butte. U.S. Geological Survey (Maps and Panoramas, Twelfth Annual Report of the United States Geological and Geographical Survey of the Territories, 1878).*

Chapman, mentioned at the outset of this section, is an impressionist who has probably painted more than 500 Jackson Hole and Teton Mountain scenes.[37] He never tired of painting the Tetons because, due to changing light values and seasons, the mountains are "never static." Indeed, if one spends enough time studying the Tetons, they come to remind one of Japan's sacred Mount Fujiyama; they change colors from the time the mists rise in the morning until the evening sun sets upon them. Japanese artists never tire of painting Mount Fuji, while painters like Schwiering have to explain their fascination with the Tetons. From his gallery at the Wort Hotel in the center of Jackson, especially during its gambling heyday, Schwiering sold his paintings to countless celebrities and movie stars as well as tourists, just as Hank Crandall sold many a painting to the dudes of the twenties and thirties. As recently as August 29, 1997, modernist cowboy artist, Bill Schenck, opened his "The Teton Series" at the Martin Harris Gallery in Jackson. Schenck, who specializes in irony, painted Donald Duck against a stage-painted Tetons background, suggesting a theme of post-modern unreality.

· Perhaps the dean of all so-called "cowboy artists" was John Clymer who, recently deceased, was a long-time resident of Teton Village. Clymer's later works were history paintings, and one who is knowledgeable of his work cannot cross the bridge over the Snake River on the road to Wilson without noticing the familiar Snake River sandbar upon which

Clymer placed a series of stages of composition (one sketch after another, adding more detail each time) of his painting of the mountain men heading up the "Platte River" [sic] to illustrate to students just how he went about composing his western history paintings. He was a generous man and history painters like Tom Lovell and Kenneth Riley are in his debt as are movie makers of a certain era.[38]

Donald Buys the Rubber Snake Ranch by Bill Schenck. Schenck, who specializes in irony, painted Donald Duck against a stage-painted Tetons background. *Bill Schenck*

≈◈≈

Hollywood and the motion picture, as well as the television industry, provided still another picturing of Jackson Hole. Because of the gleaming snow-covered freshness of the Tetons, countless television commercials have been filmed in the region. One of the most notable was an Old Milwaukee beer commercial. The film makers sent out a casting call for "authentic-looking Jackson Hole fishermen." As one newspaperman put it, "Looking for fishermen in Jackson Hole is like looking for criminals in the state pen."[39] Hundreds of locals immediately auditioned. None of them looked just right. The director, weary of screening virtually the whole male population, finally found the right outdoorsman. Dan Woodward at the Jackson National Fish Hatchery would be, as the paper put it, "the leading man." The two other "stars" were Breck O'Neill, a stuntman and his downstairs neighbor, Todd Link. Clearly, the real thing wouldn't do.

This theme of pseudo-authenticity was carried forward on many interesting levels. The big scene (a 30-second clip) was shot at sunset at Oxbow Bend of the Snake River. It purported to be dawn in the commercial. Then, because Jackson Hole fish were not photogenic enough, the film company imported 50 huge yellowbelly cutthroat trout from the Star Valley Trout Ranch in Afton, Wyoming. They were kept in live boxes at a second site on Pacific Creek. The fish were not fed for several days. A large number of them died, and as the report recounted, "the rest were too stressed out to move." So Dale Best, the Fish Hatchery biologist, was ordered to stitch a thin but strong monofilament to the upper lips of several huge fish that had survived. The cameras were lowered underwater and then, just at the right moment, the fish were yanked above the water surface as if by one of the three fishermen. The fish were dubbed "heroes" by the company. An ordinary trout was attached to Woodward's fly and lifted by him into his net. Woodward "caught" several this way and then the big yellowbellied microfilamented "hero" fish attached to his line, leaped its high dance above the sparkling waters. The artificially dirtied-up rustic-looking fisherman celebrated with, what else, an ice tub full of Old Milwaukee beer at "dawn." As the reporter concluded, "It doesn't get any better than this." It was art. Today it would be called a "neo-constructivist temporary wildlife experience." This artistic experience was shown whenever possible at NFL football game breaks. It only cost about $250,000 to make.

The hazards of filming commercials became apparent during the filming of a Mountain Dew commercial. One tourist complained to the local

The Cowboy and the Lady, filmed in 1922, was Jackson Hole's first feature film. The movie, which starred Hollywood ingenue Mary Miles Minter, was shot on the old Pederson Ranch on the south side of the Gros Ventre River north of Jackson. *Jackson Hole Historical Society and Museum*

The 1940 movie *Wyoming*, some of which was filmed on the shores of Jackson Lake. *Jackson Hole Historical Society and Museum*

newspaper that clearing the brush from the shore destroyed the ecosystem and that his female friend, cruising before the cameras in a canvas kayak, had hit the camera platform, turned over and ripped her boat.[40]

More recently, during the 1997 Major League All Star baseball game, a Chevrolet rolled onto the TV screen, the driver's side door opened and the whole Teton Range flowed out—"like a rock." Other commercials filmed in Jackson Hole include ones for Jeep, Toyota, Levis, Maxwell House Coffee, and Ski Doo.

As far as dedicated research can tell, filming in Jackson Hole began in 1921 when the valley was only just opened to dudes. The silent film was entitled *Nanette of the North,* a play on Robert Flaherty's popular documentary *Nanook of the North.* The original footage of *Nanette* perished in a fire in Jackson. It was reshot in Alaska.

Soon after, in 1922, the controversial Hollywood ingenue, Mary Miles Minter showed up as the heroine of *The Cowboy and the Lady,* Jackson Hole's first feature film. It was shot on the old Pederson Ranch on the south side of the Gros Ventre River north of Jackson. That same year, whether before or after her visit to the valley is not precisely known, the famous director-actor Desmond Taylor was found shot to death. Purportedly her lover, Mary had sent him mis-

sives on butterfly stationery that read: "Dearest—I love you—I love you—I love you—xxxxxxxxxx X yours always! Mary." Mary and the actress Mabel Normand (a movie cowgirl from the 101 Ranch) were the prime suspects. Mary, who looked like Mary Pickford and who was on her way to stardom, suddenly found her career ended. Latter day research indicates that Taylor was probably a homosexual and that Mary's mother, Charlotte Shelby, shot him in a jealous rage. Mary married her milkman and lived along with Charlotte in obscurity in Santa Monica. She died on August 5, 1954. *The Cowboy and the Lady* was her last big film as the star.[41]

In 1930 John Wayne made his movie debut in Raoul Walsh's *The Big Trail* filmed in Grand Teton National Park. Wayne played a mountain man and Marguerite Churchill was his citified co-star who initially fears him, then rushes to his arms. Then, after a·lapse of ten years, Wallace Beery appeared as the lead in *Wyoming.* Six years later he appeared as the gruff but lovable co-star of little Margaret O'Brien in *Bad Bascomb* in 1946, much of it filmed at Teton Pass and near Signal Mountain. Beery, who, like Mary Miles Minter, was born on April Fool's Day, began his work in the movies as Sweedie, a Swedish maid. As a female impersonator he made at least eight Sweedie films including *Sweedie's Hopeless Love.* They were not westerns. In 1916 he married Gloria

During the shooting of the 1946 movie *Bad Bascomb*, many cast members stayed at area dude ranches. *Bad Bascomb* tells the story of the Mormon trek into Jackson Hole. *Jackson Hole Historical Society and Museum*

Swanson. They were divorced in 1918, long before Beery made his gruff hero films in Jackson Hole.[42]

Bad Bascomb told the story of the Mormon trek into Jackson Hole where they came over Teton Pass in a rough crossing. To keep their wagons from rolling out of control downhill, the Mormons reversed the wheels, putting the large wheels on the downslope side and the smaller wheels on the up slope. Ropes tied to the wagons let them down the steep slope slowly, and logs placed at intervals below the front wheels enabled them to negotiate the descent, though some wagons crashed. Hollywood duplicated this descent mode exactly, though several spectacular crash scenes were filmed along Spread Creek to the west of the valley. Beery liked Jackson Hole so much he built a cabin on Jackson Lake below Signal Mountain. During the shooting of the picture many of the cast bunked in the scattered dude ranches. Beery, of course, played a bad man with a heart of gold continually fighting off romantic advances by Marjorie Main. After helping the Mormons fight off an Indian attack, in the end, rather than marry Marjorie Main, Beery goes back to town and is hanged for his evil deeds.

Even though it was the era of the television western, it was 1952 before another major film was

Wallace Beery, star of *Wyoming* and *Bad Bascomb*, liked Jackson Hole so much that he built a cabin on the shores of Jackson Lake below Signal Mountain. *Jackson Hole Historical Society and Museum*

The Big Sky, released in 1952, was adapted from A.B. Guthrie's novel. Portions of *The Big Sky* were filmed at Menor's Ferry. One of the make-believe keelboats used in the movie has been restored by the Montana Historical Society. *Jackson Hole Historical Society and Museum*

made in Jackson Hole. This was *The Big Sky*, an adaptation of Pulitzer Prize-winning A. B. Guthrie's splendid novel based on the first script that the noted Montana novelist ever wrote. Howard Hawks had purchased the rights to Guthrie's novel, perhaps the best ever written about the mountain men. RKO produced it. The somewhat oddly chosen stars for the movie were an unknown, Dewey Martin, as the hero Boone Caudill, Kirk Douglas as his red-headed friend Jim Deakins, whom Boone Caudill kills when his Indian wife, played by Elizabeth Threatt, produces a red-haired baby.[43]

The real stars of the film are the two exact replicas of the old Missouri River keelboat of the 1820s that the mountain men poled and tugged by ropes up 2,000 miles of the Big Muddy, contending with logs, brush, poison ivy, snakes, wolves and hostile Indians. The best feature of *The Big Sky* keelboats is their silent motors that make such labor in the movie make believe. One of these boats, that originally cost $28,000 in 1952, has been recently restored by the Montana Historical Society. Much of the film features the keelboat on the Snake River as it came out of Jackson Lake. Menor's historic ferry crossing was another place the boat was filmed. The crew camped in a large tent village near Moran, Wyoming.

An anthropologist from the American Museum of Natural History, reviewing *The Big Sky* found it grossly inaccurate. The keelboat was satisfactory, but birchbark canoes on the Upper Missouri? No. The tipis were furnished with southern Arizona bric-a-brac such as Apache baskets, the Blackfeet (actual tribe members) "are portrayed with the same magnificent disregard for fact that we have learned to expect in the average grade-B horse opera," he ejaculated. Teal Eye, the female lead "slinks about in a costume that recalls Minnehaha in a school pageant." The New York anthropologist and some later Indian commentators made the point that to Hollywood all Indians were alike. He concluded "perhaps it is too much to expect that the purveyors of what passes for history in most movies should be aware of them" [the special culture and dress of the Blackfeet].[44] The critic had nothing to say of the casting and acting. He should have. Can the film be remade today?

At the same time, another of Guthrie's scripts was coming to life—*Shane*. This interpretation of a New Haven, Connecticut, reporter's novel is perhaps the best loved of all the films made in Jackson Hole. Directed by George Stevens, this film, like the unfortunate *The Big Sky*, aimed to get away from the gunfighter-saloon-girl town western or even the cowboy extravaganza. Realism was said to be the keynote. It

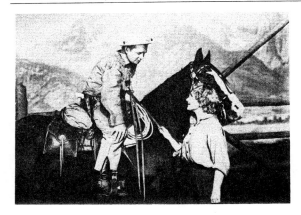

Alan Ladd and Jean Arthur in *Shane*, which was made in 1953 and is one of the most popular movies filmed in Jackson Hole. *Jackson Hole Historical Society and Museum*

was indeed the first film with loud realistic gun shots that startled audiences. *Shane* is the story of settlers just like those who came into Jackson Hole in the late nineteenth century and the mysterious "Knight Errant" gunman who defends them. Van Heflin starred as hard-working honest Joe Starratt, the settler; Jean Arthur, no glamour girl, played his wife; Ben Johnson, always authentic, played the town bully; Jack Palance played the gunfighter; and Alan Ladd played the mythical samurai who defends the homesteaders, Shane. Brandon de Wilde as the child, Joey Starratt, almost stole the show. One can still hear him calling "Shane, Shane, Shane," as the wounded Alan Ladd rides out of their lives and into the Tetons. While realistic, *Shane* had much of the mythical about it to which the slow-moving reptilian gunfighter Jack Palance contributed a great deal, as did the paradise scenery of the Tetons and Jackson Hole itself.

Most visitors to the park want to see the *Shane* sets and locations. Alas, the rude town with its saloon and general store is now long gone from Antelope Flats. A slowly crumbling homestead cabin, the Luther Taylor Homestead with a Teton Mountain background, still remains. So does Mormon Row and Schwabacher's Landing where the homesteaders crossed the river to reach the town. The Ernie Wright Cabin near Kelly Warm Springs was also

used as the Starratt Homestead, though a complete interior of the cabin was built inside the unfinished Jackson Hole High School. Teton Valley Ranch, on the Gros Ventre, also figured in the film. It is to some a significant question as to whether some of the *Shane* cabins should be restored, though the local authority on the subject of their location has not committed himself.[45] Restoration of early settlers' cabins and dude ranches sometimes runs counter to the philosophy of Grand Teton National Park, though one notes on the U.S.G.S. and the National Geographical Society official topographical maps that not far from Jackson, near Miller Springs, is the historic Miller Cabin, where Teton Jackson, the notorious outlaw, holed up.[46]

Spencer's Mountain, made in 1963, also caused a stir. It starred Henry Fonda who was variously termed "a great guy, very down to earth" and a bad interview. Maureen O'Hara, James McArthur and Mimsy Farmer were also in the film about a boy, oddly named Clayboy, growing into manhood in a poor homesteader family, grateful for the chance to go off to college where he will be with blonde beauty Mimsy Farmer, his first love. It is a story of family sacrifice that became a TV series, *The Waltons.*

Spencer's Mountain was filmed primarily near Triangle X Ranch, not far from the Cunningham

The town set for *Shane* once stood on Antelope Flats. *Jackson Hole Historical Society and Museum*

Cabin. As one writer put it for the Jackson Hole *Gazette,* "The hill behind Triangle X Ranch may have had another name once, but the Turners of the Triangle X Ranch call it "Spencer's Mountain."[47] From it one could look far across the flats and Jenny Lake to the Tetons in the distance. Actually the Triangle X was the same location where *Jubal,* starring Glenn Ford and Ernest Borgnine, was made in 1956. Fonda, between takes for *Spencer's Mountain,* went fishing only to get a hook in his eyelid. So great was the Jackson Hole hysteria about *Spencer's Mountain* that someone wrote that "Henry Fonda milked a cow in the Moulton Barn!"

In 1969, the Hunter Hereford Ranch was the setting for *The Wild Country,* released in 1971. The movie starred Steve Forrest, Vera Miles, Ron Howard and Buck Taylor. It is the story of a pioneer family that moves west from Pittsburgh, homesteads and, as in *Shane,* is forced to fight the cattlemen. On the Hunter Hereford Ranch the town of Kelly, washed away in a flood in 1927, was reconstructed and the old Moulton Cabin was moved to the Twin Creek Ranch to serve as the family homestead. To-day the Hunter Hereford Ranch still stands in good condition, one side of the barn altered by the film-makers to look antique. The hay shed and stud barn were also remodeled to serve as movie props. Hollywood added Greek Revival windows to the north side of the hay shed so that it could serve as a movie-set church. The cabin and stable still stand, used to store equipment, and a lone buffalo calls the ranch home.

As of 1993 there had been a number of more or less significant films made or partially made in Jackson Hole, including Sylvester Stallone's *Rocky IV,* the video releases for *Dances With Wolves, Lakota Moon* (an all-Indian film pilot made in 1991 but never released), Clint Eastwood's *Any Which Way You Can, The Wrong Guys* and parts of James Michener's *Centennial.* Much of *Dream West,* a TV series starring Richard Chamberlain as Lt. John C. Frémont, who never saw Jackson Hole but did climb a high peak in the Wind River Mountains that he named for himself, was made in the valley. Another TV series of the 1960s, *The Monroes,* was the story of five or-phaned children, the oldest of whom is played by the fresh and beautiful Barbara Hershey. She was the star, along with her Great Pyrenees dog, Snow. How-ever, in the atmosphere of the sixties, the series was too wholesome. It had a short run. Another whole-some production of the nineties, however, *A River Runs Through It,* was partially filmed in Jackson Hole. The famous falls sequence was filmed on Fall Creek, not the Yellowstone.

One film made in and around Jackson Hole in 1979 that curiously has not received enough praise is

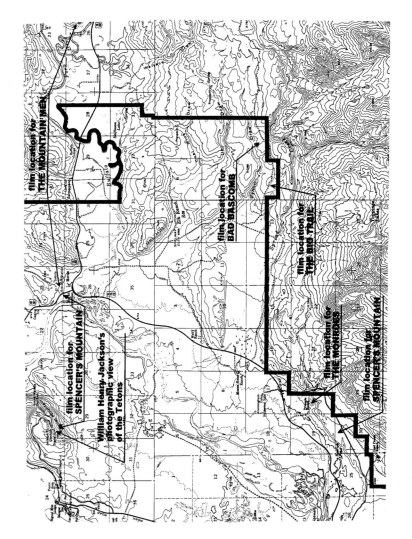

film location for
THE MOUNTAIN MEN

film location for
BAD BASCOMB

film location for
THE BIG TRAIL

film location for,
SPENCER'S MOUNTAIN

William Henry Jackson's
photographic view
of the Tetons

film location for
THE MOLLISONS

film location for
SPENCER'S MOUNTAIN

Photograph and film locations in the Jackson area, part 1. *U.S. Geological Survey*

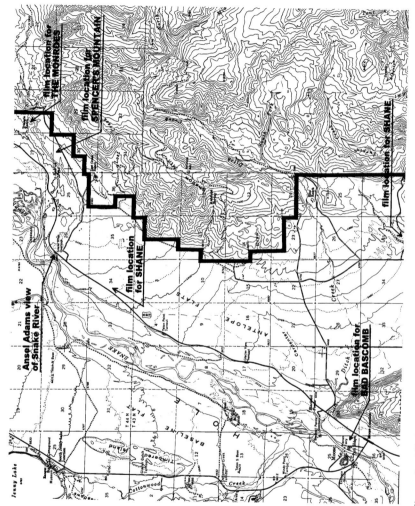

film location for
THE MONRDES

film location for
SPENCER'S MOUNTAIN

film location for SHANE

film location
for SHANE

Ansel Adams view
of Snake River

Film location for
BAD BASCOMB

Jenny Lake

Photograph and film locations in the Jackson area, part 2. *U.S. Geological Survey*

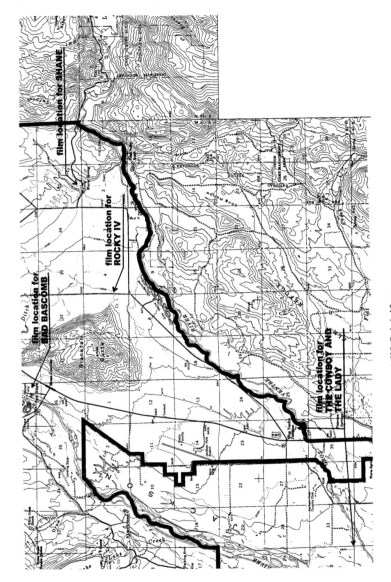

film location for SHANE

film location for ROCKY IV

film location for BAD BASCOMB

film location for THE COWBOY AND THE LADY

Photograph and film locations in the Jackson area, part 3. *U.S. Geological Survey*

Charleton Heston's *The Mountain Men,* which also starred the late Brian Keith. This picture, perhaps the best one ever filmed in Jackson Hole, made by far the best use of its scenic possibilities, from the opening credits which feature the Tetons and Jackson Lake, to many locations along the Snake River, as well as the higher fields near Triangle X Ranch east of the river. Some spectacular sequences were filmed in Yellowstone's geyser basins, others at the foot of the Togwotee Pass in five feet of snow. It is also an authentic film that recreates an uproarious mountain man rendezvous on the Triangle X Ranch. This scene, filmed over a two-week period, required the construction of 80 tipis, rows of tents for fur traders, wagons, a corral, fire sites and extraordinary costuming for a large number of people. Many of the 500 "mountain men" who participated in the rendezvous scene were recruited from mountain man re-enactment clubs all over the country. The Indians were recruited from the Wind River Reservation, Fort Hall, Idaho, and Ogalalla, Nebraska. The script was written by Charleton Heston's son, Frazer, himself an expert on mountain man history. Many of the scenes bring the history paintings of John Clymer, Tom Lovell, Kenneth Riley and Frank McCarthy to life.[48]

Perhaps it was too authentic, too historical for audiences of the 1970s and since, though James Michener's *Centennial,* partially filmed in Jackson Hole, holds up well today. Now, however, many prefer their history as pseudo-authentic documentaries like Ken Burns's recent TV series, *The West,* partly filmed in Jackson Hole and loaded with politically correct messages and talking heads as well as many gaffes such as *photographs* of Coronado and the leaders of the 1680 Pueblo Revolt.

One wonders, has the documentary with expert authenticators as talking heads taken the place of historically-oriented feature films? What of the Old West and its history where, in 1928, Owen Wister, the prolific author Struthers Burt, and Ernest Hemingway, completing a draft of his very modernist book, *A Farewell to Arms,* could still fish the Snake and appreciate rustic living on Burt's Three Rivers Ranch, with its jerry-built dude cabins with sod roofs and homemade furniture? Then it was a dude-ranch paradise in which even the fastidious publisher

Alfred A. Knopf reveled. It was where Wallace Stegner and Bernard DeVoto tried to blend the Old West with the new. Have Jackson Hole's human inhabitants either turned banal, contemporary or disappeared? Is Jackson Hole *too* scenic, *too* identifiable for modern film makers who prefer road films, urban dramas where the Mafia reigns, stories of serial killers, or Stephen Spielberg's special effects movies? Are we tuned toward the vast universe of *Contact,* in which case Jackson Hole is too small, its historic past too brief.[49] In addition, the park's relentless return to a pristine, non-human ecosystem seems the wave of the future as few of the picture makers now look back. The tourists and environmentalists are mostly into nature and its destruction by "rapacious" alien humans, not the settlers' era portrayed in *Shane* and *Spencer's Mountain.* For Jackson Hole and its temporary historical denizens substitute Zabriski Point in Death Valley and the Nevada Atomic Test Sites as we follow the avant garde picture makers of a West that is no longer ours.

Postscript

The National Park Service's "nature only" policy has largely effaced Jackson Hole's historic dimension. Famous dude ranches, as well as the barns and cabins used in film making, are being left to molder away. This has caused some controversy. Struthers Burt sold his ranch, the Bar BC, and Nathaniel Burt sold the Three Rivers Ranch at cost to the Rockefeller Snake River Land Company, and they thus became part of the Grand Teton National Park. Both Burts, strong advocates of the Rockefeller expansion of the park, felt it was their patriotic duty. As they and others lived on at the Three Rivers Ranch as lessees under the terms of sale, neither father nor son envisioned the destruction of the ranches. They believed them to be historic sites, not only because famous people like the publisher Alfred Knopf, who served on the National Park Service Advisory Board, had stayed there, but also because of the distinctive vernacular architecture of the ranch buildings.[50] Nathaniel Burt felt, and Roy Graham Associates, a restoration architectural firm who made an assess-

The Moulton Barn, with the majestic Teton Range in the background, is popular with photographers. The barn is located on Mormon Row.
Roger Whitacre

ment in 1994, felt that the Bar BC Ranch buildings of Burt's first dude ranch were part of the landscape. Listed on the National Register of Historic Places, they should be properly cared for and, if necessary, restored though at some, possibly donor, expense.[51] An offer of funding for restoration purposes with respect to the Three Rivers Ranch was offered by Burt's son, Nathaniel.[52] His offer was rejected. Some buildings were moved, and the rest, owned by the National Park Service, were demolished. In an era where American history is being severely distorted for political purposes, it does seem important that some vestiges of the past remain—some evidence of the staying power of the pioneer past and the romantic cowboy past—even into the mid-twentieth century. The buildings and the furniture of the Bar BC, which is still standing, were made on the ranch; the stone chimneys were constructed with stones from the Snake River by an amateur local builder. It represents a time before the pre-fabricated age and, to an historian and even a tourist, the Bar BC Ranch, while not a work of art, is a work of interest—a sight to be seen and interpreted, as are some of the remaining structures from the era of motion picture making. To many people the Old West *is* the West and Jackson Hole, with its colorful setting and his-

tory, should probably be more interesting than one's hometown hike-and-bike trail or a ski resort. Keeping in touch with the past is keeping in touch with nature in *all* its varied forms.

Notes

1. On June 11, 1942, Ansel Adams wrote to Nancy Newhall that he was heading to Billings, Montana, "then to Yellowstone, then to Glacier, then on west to Rainier and Crater Lake, then home." He was on a Harold Ickes-inspired National Parks assignment. Adams apparently changed his itinerary to include Jackson Hole, the Tetons and the Snake River Valley. Just at that time, however, Franklin Delano Roosevelt and the National Park Service were in a furious battle with the ranchers at Jackson Hole over young John D. Rockefeller Jr.'s secret purchases of land with the Snake River Land Company as a front. Rockefeller intended to give his huge parcel of Teton Valley to the National Park Service. The cattlemen, Wyoming congressmen and senators, local politicians and the U.S. Forest Service all objected. The movie actor and valley resident, Wallace Beery, led an armed posse and a herd of cattle across park land. Fortunately, the National Park Service ignored the opera bouffé gesture and no shootouts occurred.

With this heated conflict brewing, it appears that Ansel Adams detoured from Yellowstone into Jackson

Hole and made his photograph *The Tetons and the Snake River, Grand Teton National Park* that included much land that Rockefeller intended to give for park expansion. Taken in a rainstorm, it was a majestic photograph that clearly touted the vast emptiness of unspoiled nature. Was it also meant as one of Interior Secretary Ickes's public appeal weapons in the war with the ranchers and the Forest Service over which he had no control? This would explain Adams's change of itinerary. See Ansel Adams, *Letters and Images 1916–1984* (Boston: Little, Brown and Co., 1988), p. 135; and Betts, *Along the Ramparts,* Chapter 18; for Beery's action, see p. 209. Also see Righter, *Crucible for Conservation,* passim, especially pp. 114–115.

Ansel Adams himself said "I do not recall that I ever intentionally made a photograph for environmentally significant purposes"—this despite the fact that his photographs appeared regularly in Sierra Club books and calendars. Quoted in Robert Bednar, "Postmodern Vistas, Landscapes, Photography, and Tourism in the Contemporary American West," unpublished dissertation, University of Texas, Austin, American Civilization Program, 1997, pp. 145–146.

2. Righter, *Crucible for Conservation,* pp. 126–152; and author's personal inspection of the Bar BC Ranch, June 25, 1997.

3. Betts, *Along the Ramparts,* p. 147.

4. Ibid, p. 152. For the Spencer and Burnett killings, see Frank Calkins, *Jackson Hole* (New York: Alfred A. Knopf, 1973), pp. 122–123.

5. For examples of the maps mentioned here, see Carl I. Wheat, *Mapping the Transmississippi West, 1540–1861,* 5 vols. (San Francisco: The Institute of Historical Cartography, 1958), vol. 2. For Lewis and Clark, opposite p. 56, for Chevelier Lapie, pp. 73–76, Aaron Arrowsmith, opposite p. 148, Capt. B. L. E. Bonneville, opposite p. 158, Capt. Washington Hood, opposite p. 160, Warren Ferris, opposite p. 156, Fremont, Gibbs Smith, opposite p. 128, but also see pp. 119–139. For Jim Bridger's map, see Goetzmann, *Exploration and Empire,* p. 119. The original map is at the Wyoming Heritage Center, Laramie, Wyoming.

6. Betts, *Along the Ramparts,* p. 59.

7. *Report on the Exploration of the Yellowstone River, by Brevet Brigadier General, W. F. Raynolds* (40th Congress 1st Session, Senate Executive Document No. 77, 1868). Also see Mary C. Withington, *A Catalogue of Manuscripts in the Collection of Western Americana Founded by William Robertson Coe, Yale University Library* (New Haven: Yale University Press, 1952) entry 393, pp. 214–217, in which she states that Yale has three watercolors, six pen and ink sketches, three pencil sketches, 41 photographs of paintings and sketches, and six photographs from the Raynolds expedition. For Schonborn's suicide, see Goetzmann, p.

503. J. D. Hutton did make two pencil sketches of the Tetons that are at Yale. Three early photo reproductions of sketches of the Snake River and the Tetons by Schonborn and one pen and ink drawing by Raynolds are in the Western Americana Collection of the Beinecke Library at Yale.

8. Haines, *The Yellowstone Story,* pp. 106–140. Two of Moran's *Scribner's* drawings appear on p. 136. Also see Bonney, *Battle Drums and Geysers,* passim, for a more complete account and analysis of Lt. Doane's expeditions. For the 1870 expedition see pp. 171–373. On the spot sketches by Walter Trumball, Private Charles Moore and Thomas Moran's site unseen *Scribner's* versions appear on pp. 251–253, 271–273, 275, 279 (compare with photo p. 278 and oil painting pp. 280, 346, 351, see photo pp. 352–353) 354, 356, 406, 425, see maps opposite p. 198 and opposite p. 294.

9. Ferdinand V. Hayden, *Sixth Annual Report of the United States Geological Survey of the Territories, Embracing Portions of Montana, Idaho, Wyoming, and Utah,* (Washington: Government Printing Office, 1873), opposite p. 255.

10. Betts, *Along the Ramparts,* pp. 121–123.

11. Capt. William A. Jones, *Report upon a Reconnaissance of Northwestern Wyoming, including Yellowstone National Park, Made in the Summer of 1873* (Washington: Government Printing Office, 1875), cartographic appendix.

12. Betts, *Along the Ramparts,* ch. 18. Also see footnote 1 supra.

13. Clarence S. Jackson, *Picture Maker of the Old West,* pp. 159–171.

14. Goetzmann, *Exploration and Empire,* pp. 408–409. Also see J. W. Barlow, *Report of a Reconnaissance of the Basin of the Upper Yellowstone in 1871* (42nd Congress, 2nd Session, Senate Executive Document 66, 1872).

15. Montana Historical Society, *F. Jay Haynes, Photographer* (Helena: Montana Historical Society Press, 1981), pp. 11–13; Betts, *Along the Ramparts,* pp. 139–145; and for the pictures described, see Merrill G. Burlingame Special Collections 1878–1988, H-1044, H-1045, H-1236, H-1241, H-1242, H-1042, Montana Historical Society, Helena, Montana.

16. For Edward Curtis see William H. Goetzmann and Kay Sloan, *Looking Far North, the Harriman Expedition to Alaska, 1899* (New York: Viking Press, 1982), pp. 79, 185–191.

17. Jackson Hole Historical Society, Harrison Crandall, typescript, May, 1991, Obit, *Jackson Hole Guide,* Dec. 17, 1970; and Elizabeth Flood, "Harrison Crandall, photographer"; picture file, William H. Jackson at Grand Teton National Park dedication, 1929, 58.2207.01, QFL, Jackson Hole Historical Society and Museum, Jackson, Wyoming.

18. See Paul F Healy, *Cissy, A Biography of Eleanor M. "Cissy" Patterson* (Garden City, NY: Doubleday & Co., 1966), p. 57. Also see Alice Albright Hoge, *Cissy Patterson* (New York: Random House, 1966) pp. 55–67.

19. See footnote 17 supra.

20. Ansel Adams, *An Autobiography* (Boston: New York Graphic Society and Little Brown and Company, 1985), passim. Also see Jonathan Spaulding, *Ansel Adams and the American Landscape, a Biography* (Berkeley: University of California Press, 1995), passim.

21. Spaulding, *Ansel Adams*, pp. 171–172.

22. Goetzmann and Sloan, *Looking Far North*, pp. 79; 185–191.

23. Peter Goin, *Nuclear Landscapes* (Baltimore: Johns Hopkins University Press, 1991), passim; Patrick Nagatani, *Nuclear Enchantment* (Albuquerque: University of New Mexico Press, 1991), passim; Richard Misrach, *Bravo 20: The Bombing of the American West* (Baltimore: Johns Hopkins University Press, 1990), passim; Mark Klett, *Second View: The Rephotographic Survey Project* (Albuquerque, University of New Mexico Press, 1984), passim; and Rick Dingus, *The Photographic Artifacts of Timothy O'Sullivan* (Albuquerque, University of New Mexico Press, 1982), passim, but see especially pp. 28–29.

24. Thomas D. Mangelsen and Charles Craighead, *Images of Nature: The Photographs of Thomas D. Mangelsen* (New York: Hugh Lauther Levin Associates, 1989), passim.

25. David Muench, *National Parks of America*, text by Stewart L. Udall and James R. Udall (Portland, Oregon: Graphic Arts Center Publishing Co., no date), pp. 82–86.

26. Fryxell, *Interpretations of a Mountain Landscape.* Photographs opposite pp. vii, 6, 7, 14, 15, 30, 31, 46, 47, 62, 63.

27. Frederic Joy, *Light Reflections.* (Jackson, WY: no publisher, no date), passim. Also see Eliot Porter, *The West* (New York: Little, Brown Books, 1988), pp. 65, 66, 68, 69, 70.

28. Robert M. Bednar, supra footnote 1, p. 19 ff. It should be said that DiLillo's barn in *White Noise* is set in the Midwest, but the identical situation applies to the Moulton Barn.

29. Ezra Pound, *The Cantos of Ezra Pound* (New York: New Directions Books, 1943, 1937, 1940, 1948), "New Cantos" (following p. 150) p. 20.

30. See footnote 7 supra.

31. See footnote 17 supra, but also see Nancy Cooper and Quita Pownell, *32 Rocky Mountain Wildflowers* (Laramie, WY, no date), Original painted photographs.

32. National Inventory of American Paintings. A telephone conversation on August 4, 1997, with Dr. Nancy

Anderson, Associate Curator of American Art at the National Gallery of Art and co-author with Linda Ferber of *Albert Bierstadt: Art and Enterprise* (New York: The Brooklyn Museum and Hudson Hills Press, 1990). Dr. Anderson, one of the major Bierstadt scholars, consulted her exhibition files on Bierstadt and together with Linda Ferber concluded that Bierstadt had never seen the Teton views that he painted, hence these are among his weakest works.

33. Thomas Moran, Field Notebook, Aug. 22–29, 1879 (MS Catalogue No. 1753, accession no. 114, History File, Grand Teton National Park Headquarters, Moose, Wyoming). This notebook was transcribed and published by park geologist Fritiof Fryxell. Also see "Thomas Moran's Journey to the Tetons in 1879," *Augustana Historical Society Publications* (Rock Island, IL: Augustana Historical Society Publications), No. 2, 1932, pp. 7–12.

34. The most accessible reproductions of Moran's Teton watercolor sketches are in Peter Hassrick, *Water Color Sketches of Thomas Moran, Yellowstone and Grand Teton National Parks* (Yellowstone and Grand Teton Natural History Associations, 1991), and Carol Clark, *Thomas Moran: Watercolors of the American West* (Austin, TX: Amon Carter Museum and University of Texas Press, 1980), see especially pp. 54–56, 97. For Peter Moran's watercolor of the Tetons, made in 1879, see Patricia Trenton and Peter Hassrick, *The Rocky Mountains: a Vision for Artists in the Nineteenth Century* (Cody, WY: Buffalo Bill Historical Center and Norman: University of Oklahoma Press, 1983), p. 288. For dating Peter Moran's painting, see Robert P. Porter and Carroll D. Wright, *Report on Indians Taxed and Indians Not Taxed in the United States* (except Alaska) in the *Eleventh Census 1890* (Washington, D.C.: Government Printing Office, 1894), pp. 628–630. For Moran's late oil paintings of the Tetons, see Nancy K. Anderson, *Thomas Moran*, catalogue, with contributions by Thomas P. Bruhn, Joni L. Kinsey, and Anne Morand, to accompany Thomas Moran Exhibition at the National Gallery of Art, September 24, 1997 (Washington, D.C., National Gallery of Art and New Haven and London: Yale University Press, 1997), pp. 150, 154, 155, 157.

35. Ferdinand V. Hayden, *Twelfth Annual Report of the United States Geological and Geographical Survey of the Territories* (Washington, DC: Government Printing Office, 1878), see especially Atlas Folio Number 7. Also, see William H. Goetzmann, *William H. Holmes, Panoramic Art* (Fort Worth, TX: Amon Carter Museum, 1977).

36. D. Duane Cummins, *William Robinson Leigh, Western Artist* (Norman: University of Oklahoma Press and Tulsa, OK: Thomas Gilcrease Institute of American History and Art, 1980), p. 92.

37. Dean Fenton Krakel, *Conrad Schwiering, Painting on the Square* (Oklahoma City: Powder River Book Co., National Cowboy Hall of Fame, 1981), passim, see especially pp. 12–14.

38. For Clymer's "Platte River" drawing and painting see Mary Carroll Nelson, *Masters of Western Art* (New York: Watson-Guptill Publications, 1982), pp. 46–51.

39. "Selling suds, Madison Avenue uses Jackson Hole to hook beer drinkers," *Jackson Hole News*, Sept. 24, 1986, cover and p. 37. Brad Johnson, a sometime star of movie westerns, was part of the fishermen's ensemble, where he was "discovered" by movie makers. He was not mentioned in the *Jackson Hole News*.

40. Jean Heller, "Film Company's use of river, forest land here criticized," *Jackson Hole Guide*, Sept. 1986.

41. Sidney D. Kirkpatrick, *A Cast of Killers* (New York: E. P. Dutton, 1986), passim, see especially pp. 28, 230–31, 249. Also see "Western Film Classics," *Teton Magazine*, 1994, p. 6, for location of *The Cowboy and the Lady*. Photo no. 315 of the Pederson Ranch and photo of Mary Miles Minter with cowboys in film files in Jackson Hole Historical Society.

42. Ephraim Katz, *The Film Encyclopedia* (New York: Harper and Row, 1979), p. 98.

43. *Great Falls Tribune*, August 19, 1931.

44. Elizabeth Downs, editor, "The Screen: Authentic comments on films in the field of nature, geography and exploration," *Natural History:* Oct. 1952, p. 384.

45. Personal tour with Grand Teton National Park architect Michael C. Johnson, June 26, 1997, and consultation with Wyoming film expert Walt Frazier, June 25,1997, Jackson, Wyoming, to whom special thanks are due.

46. Calkins, *Jackson Hole*, p. 114.

47. "Return to Spencer's Mountain," *Jackson Hole Guide*, April 5, 1995, for locations and assessment of Henry Fonda and fish hook story. Another less flattering assessment by Marilou McCarthy, "Shoot Out at Jackson Hole," *Chicago Tribune Magazine*, July 21, 1963, see especially subsection three, "The Trouble with Henry." Several accounts mentioned the fact that Fonda was always accompanied by a striking brunette female companion. See Movie Files, Jackson Hole Historical Society and Museum. Jackson, Wyoming.

48. Emory J. Anderson, "Reels roll in Jackson Hole" publication unidentified in Movie Files, Jackson Hole Historical Society and Museum.

49. In 1919 Struthers Burt published *John O'May and Other Stories* with Charles Scribner's Sons in New York and shortly after the literary tradition in Jackson Hole centered on Struthers Burt and family. In 1920, he won the O'Henry Memorial Prize for his story "Each in his Gen-eration." He also published *Chance Encounters*, a collection of short stories with Charles Scribner's Sons in 1921, *The Interpreter's House* in 1924 and *The Diary of a Dude Wrangler* that same year, both with Scribner's. The latter is one of the classic works on the subject. In 1927, just before the meeting with Hemingway, he had published *The Delectable Mountains* with Scribner's. Later that year, he would publish a collection of essays. Burt's stories appeared in most of the major magazines. He became a well-known popular writer and commentator. His wife, Katherine, published five novels in three years, mostly about Wyoming and especially about life in Jackson Hole in the winter. Her first novel, *The Branding Iron* (1919) was made into a silent movie, as were two others. Katherine Burt afterwards spent a great deal of time in emerging Hollywood. This brought Hollywood guests to their dude ranch, the Bar BC, and later to their new Three Rivers dude ranch.

Wister, already famous for *The Virginian*, took his family to the JY Ranch in 1911. By 1912 he had his own cabin on 160 acres along the Snake River. (This cabin has now been moved to Big Horn, Wyoming, the setting of *The Virginian*). Almost as soon as it was built, he became tired of it in 1913. As he put it in a letter to John Jay Chapman, "Strangely and rather sadly, my longing for Wyoming and roughing it is gone." Quoted in Darwin Payne, *Owen Wister: Chronicler of the West, Gentleman of the East* (Dallas: Southern Methodist University Press, 1985), p. 281.

Other writers who were in the Bar BC set were Gracie Lewis, the ex-wife of Sinclair Lewis, Stuart Cloete, a South African, Irwin Edman, Sally Carrigher, Margaret Muric and Josephine Fabian. Most of their books were about Teton Valley. Nathaniel Burt, Struther's literary son, called Carrigher's book a "classic." It was also made into a documentary film. See also Struthers Burt, *The Diary of a Dude Wrangler*; Nathaniel Burt, *Jackson Hole Journal*; Raymond C. Phillips, Jr., *Struthers Burt* (Idaho: Boise State University, 1983); and Carlos Baker, *Ernest Hemingway, A Life Story* (New York: Charles Scribner's Sons, 1969), p. 196.

50. Nathaniel Burt, Memorandum re: Three Rivers Ranch to the National Park Service, date unknown, Archives, National Park Service, Denver, Colorado.

51. Roy Eugene Graham Associates, "Bar BC Ranch Grand Teton National Park, Wyoming, Historic Structures Report," July 1, 1994, Archives, National Park Service, Denver, Colorado.

52. Nathaniel Burt Memorandum in footnote 50 supra.

/

CHAPTER **19**

Conclusion

Everyone in Jackson Hole is an environmentalist—until their ox is being gored.

—Anonymous, 1980

Welcome to Jackson Hole, where men remain boys and women work three jobs.

—Unnamed Local Pundit, 1990

This history is as much a story of place—Jackson Hole—as it is of people. Traditionally, historians perceived the history of the American West as a process whereby successive waves of frontiersmen moved west to tame the wilderness. Frederick Jackson Turner's frontier hypothesis, first proposed in 1893, was the genesis of this view. Turner's theory imposed the view that the significant history of the West ended with the closure of the frontier in 1890. With the passing of time, historians found this approach insufficient to explaining Western history, particularly in the twentieth century. As historian Patricia Limerick observed, "Turner's frontier was a process, not a place."[1] Thinking of Western history as a story of place, rather than a process, offers new perspectives and makes developments in the West since 1900 much more comprehensible.

Viewing the history of Jackson Hole as a "place" raises a second point; the most persistent theme binding this story together is the interaction between humans and the environment. Beginning with prehistoric people, successive groups have passed through this valley. Each perceived and used the land and re-

sources differently. Native Americans and their prehistoric ancestors prized the roots and seeds of many native plants that grow here. Hunters and gatherers, they depended exclusively and directly on natural resources for their survival. Few in number, Indians had a light impact on the land. The first Euro-Americans, fur trappers, quickly drove the beaver to commercial extinction in Jackson Hole. Unlike later ranchers and farmers, grubbing sage and turning over virgin soil held little appeal for mountain men.

The arrival of settlers ushered in a new era. For the first time, people took up permanent residence in the valley. They perceived resources differently than trappers or Indians, initiating changes that reshaped the valley's landscape. Unlike prehistoric people, settlers made little use of edible plants, instead relying on transportation links to haul in food staples as demonstrated by trash piles of tin cans revealed by snow melting under the spring sun. Opposing perceptions of resources and appropriate uses formed the essential conflict between nineteenth-century developers and conservationists. Few places illustrate this story so well as Jackson Hole. Federal laws cre-

359

ated reserves, principally national parks and national forests, which halted settlement and development on much of the public domain. Private philanthropy joined the fray when John D. Rockefeller Jr., donated the money to buy back private lands and return them to the public domain. His initiative did not just stop the clock, it turned the clock back.

History is fundamentally the study of continuity and change. The clash between preservationists and developers persists today in the West, demonstrating the continuity with our past. It is wrong to presume that many of today's issues in the West are new. They are rooted in the past. However, historians Michael P. Malone and Richard W. Etulain caution that "the overriding feature of modern western history is a persistent barrage of change."[2] Four developments were critical in shaping the history of this valley.

First, the fur trade was very important to Jackson Hole. Mountain men were the first Euro-Americans to breach the mountain barriers encompassing this valley, opening the door for later migrations. Situated in the heart of prime trapping country, near the headwaters of the majority of the West's great rivers, Jackson Hole became the crossroads of the fur trade in the northern Rockies. Further, it was mountain men who guided explorers and trappers west.

The arrival of John Holland and John Carnes in 1884 marked the beginning of dramatic changes. Settlers introduced domestic plants and animals, displacing some native species. The impact of overgrazing is evident in the valley. Native animals perceived as threats were killed off, most notably the gray wolf. Homesteaders cut ditches to irrigate fields, which drastically affected water resources. The Jackson Lake dam memorializes government sponsorship of massive reclamation projects.

The rise of the conservation movement occurred concurrently with the settlement of the frontier. The creation of federal reserves withdrew millions of acres from the public domain, preventing their transfer to private ownership, and enabling government to introduce conservation practices and regulation to reduce wasteful consumption of resources. The enabling legislation for Yellowstone National Park, and the Forest Reserve Act of 1891 endure as the most significant laws in the history of the conservation movement. The fact that more than 96 percent of the land in Teton County is public land administered by federal agencies has been decisive in shaping this valley's history.

The last major development occurred when tourism blossomed, displacing cattle ranching as the dominant economic activity in Jackson Hole. This event caused significant changes in perceptions regarding the highest value and use of resources.

Two other influences, technology and population growth, fostered significant change in this valley. Technological improvements in transportation, notably the internal combustion engine, reduced the geographic isolation of Jackson Hole, an element that lent it a special charm at one time. The advent of the automobile led to modern highways, often through seemingly impenetrable routes like the Snake River Canyon. Improved snow removal equipment enables road crews to keep passes and highways open year round today, a difficult task 40 years ago, impossible 75 years ago. Today, a modern airport allows people to ride modern planes in comfort, their only inconveniences lost luggage or bad coffee.

In 1900, fewer than 700 people lived in Jackson Hole; today more than 11,000 people live in Teton County. In 1929, about 10,000 visitors came to the newly-created Grand Teton National Park; today roughly 2,500,000 visitors tour the park annually. Increases in both the permanent and migratory population have elevated the pressure on resources significantly.

Less tangible than technology or population, but no less pervasive in the history of the Teton country, are myths. Sooner or later, Limerick observed, "when professional scholars investigate the past, friction is almost inevitable."[3] In the course of my research, I found information that refuted local myths about people and events. However, conflicts between history and myth are not bad. James Robertson, in his book *American Myth, American Reality* found that myths serve a valuable purpose by providing "good, 'workable' ways" for people to understand confusing and contradictory events and complex people and their behavior. For scholars, myths provide important clues about peoples' perceptions and make good history better.[4]

For example, according to local legend, Jackson Hole's preeminent poacher, "Beaver Tooth" Neal, was never caught or convicted for his illegal activities. A number of tales portray Neal as a crafty individual, who consistently outwitted game wardens, usually characterized as dim-witted buffoons. In reality, Neal had a lengthy record of convictions. In 1909, Pierce Cunningham, as justice of the peace, fined Neal $50 plus court costs after Forest Service rangers caught him in the act of poaching and arrested him. In 1914, Neal's neighbors, Jack Shive and Nate Smith, traveled to Kemmerer, Wyoming, to testify against Neal regarding poaching charges. Nineteen years later, in 1933, a court sentenced Neal to 90 days in jail and fined him $100 for illegal possession of 11 untagged beaver pelts. The *Jackson's Hole Courier* noted that Neal had for two decades "occupied a prominent place in the Justice Court's records."[5] The Neal myth illustrates two important points from a historian's perspective. First, some in Jackson Hole regarded poachers as folk heroes, despite the harm they wreak on wildlife. Second, anti-government sentiment, the underpinning of the Neal myth, runs strong in the Teton country.

A more significant conflict with local myths occurs over the activities of the National Park Service and Snake River Land Company in connection with park extension efforts in the 1930s. John D. Rockefeller Jr., and Horace Albright were special targets for vilification. Even though Senate sub-committee hearings proved all charges baseless, save the A. W. Gabbey incident, rumors still persist about strong-arm tactics used in the land purchase program. With the exception of one first-hand account, I found no evidence of perfidy. Also, despite irrefutable evidence to the contrary, some continue to believe the Rockefeller family bought resorts and dude ranches to monopolize the tourist industry. While myths, used judiciously, augment history, they make an accurate reconstruction of events more difficult.

The lack of sources or incomplete or contradictory sources also make the historian's task difficult. These are common problems in all fields of history, but are especially prevalent in local history. For example, few ranchers kept records that provide exact dates of construction of buildings. Hence, in many

cases, research can only establish a period of construction for structures on a property. The story of Bill Blackburn's fiddle illustrates the difficulty of researching local history.

Bill Blackburn was a pioneer in the valley and one of its characters. Wilford Nielson, an attorney and editor of the *Jackson's Hole Courier,* told this story about Blackburn. A man of strong opinions, Blackburn once engaged Nielson and others in the newspaper office in a debate over the traits that gave violins their musical quality. Blackburn firmly believed that age was the most critical factor. To prove his point, he left the *Courier* office, gathered all the violins he could lay his hands on, and returned. He tested each violin and compared their dates of manufacture. His bore the inscription "Anno 1711," therefore played the sweetest music.

After Blackburn left to locate other violins, Nielson wrote "Anno 1709" on brown wrapping paper and secured it to one of the violins. Feigning surprise, Nielson showed his discovery to Blackburn when he returned. Blackburn took one look and grunted, "yours is 1709 and mine is 1711. Mine is just two years older." Nielson had to concede defeat.[6] This story inspired me to create a file titled "Blackburn's Fiddle;" this file became the repository for suspect information, inconsistent dates or information, and riddles of Jackson Hole history that appear to have no solution.

This study establishes the historic contexts pertinent to Grand Teton National Park. Not all have representative resources that fit them, nor do all properties within a context warrant nomination to the National Register of Historic Places. In addition, some subjects are classified as elements of a larger context. The following are significant contexts: Fur Trade; Explorers and Scientists; Homesteading (Pre-1900, Post-1900, and Farming); Irrigation/Reclamation; Cattle Ranchers; Dude Ranching; Commerce/Communities; Conservation (Forest Service, Park Service, Snake River Land Company); and Tourism. Several properties fitting these contexts stand out. Their absence would have made a difference in the history of Jackson Hole.

The Murie Ranch is significant because of its association with Olaus and Margaret Murie. For 17

ated reserves, princ
forests, which halte
much of the public
joined the fray whe⊓
nated the money to
turn them to the pul
not just stop the cloc

History is fundan
and change. The clash
developers persists tod⌐
the continuity with our
that many of today's iss
are rooted in the past. I₋
Malone and Richard W.
overriding feature of mo
sistent barrage of change.
critical in shaping the hi⸀

First, the fur trade wa
son Hole. Mountain men ᵛ
cans to breach the mountaⁱ
this valley, opening the doo
Situated in the heart of prim
the headwaters of the majorit
rivers, Jackson Hole became t⸀
trade in the northern Rockies.
tain men who guided explorers

The arrival of John Holland
1884 marked the beginning of d⸀
tlers introduced domestic plants
ing some native species. The impa⸀
evident in the valley. Native animal⸀
threats were killed off, most notably
Homesteaders cut ditches to irrigate t⸀
drastically affected water resources. Th⸀
Lake dam memorializes government spo⸀
massive reclamation projects.

The rise of the conservation movement
concurrently with the settlement of the fronti⸀
creation of federal reserves withdrew millions o⊓
acres from the public domain, preventing their tr⸀
fer to private ownership, and enabling government
introduce conservation practices and regulation to reduce wasteful consumption of resources. The enabling legislation for Yellowstone National Park, and   t⸀
the Forest Reserve Act of 1891 endure as the most   cl⸀⸀
significant laws in the history of the conservation   tory ⸀

ld West character,
kson Hole—th
kson exhibits

le named
because
a lot of
n it." A
upport
been m
when th
what
'degard
ty near
he Snak
ors car
ride th
Lake. t
ought
g mor dis-
ect o re
he en-
vant e
de ed
ych.
n sin-
ite o
c ev
t
d
y

of the "crabgrass frontier," historian Kenneth T. Jack-
label for suburbanization. Homes are designed
with garages stuck prominently on the front façade,
as subdivisions consume agricultural land in the valley. Developers coin names like "Buck Meadows,"
then proceed to pave over those meadows with asphalt, preempting more mule deer range. Drive-up
windows have become a prominent feature of businesses, strip development best describes Broadway,
Jackson's "main drag," and shopping centers, suburbia's marketplace, have erupted with their trademark
behemoth parking lors. Even Grand Teton National
Park has not escaped the suburban influence with
two government housing areas at Moose and Colter
Bay that are tract developments.[10] This process will
continue in Jackson Hole so long as private land is
available.

In recent years, cities have experienced a phenomenon called gentrification, a process whereby affluent people buy up residences and businesses in decayed urban neighborhoods and renovate them.
Gentrification escalates property taxes and rent, driving out lower income people. A similar trend is occurring in Jackson Hole today. People with higher incomes are buying land and residences as second
homes. This has driven real estate values to a plateau
that makes home ownership difficult for people earning low to moderate incomes. Concurrently, rental
housing costs have increased significantly. Like suburbanization, the second home trend is "a manifestation of such fundamental characteristics of American
society as conspicuous consumption, a reliance upon
the private automobile, upward mobility, the separation of family into nuclear units, the widening division between work and leisure, and a tendency toward racial and economic exclusiveness."[11]

Finally, thanks to advanced communications and
improved transportation, people relocate here and
either commute by airplane to work, or use computer
technology to work out of their homes. This development will increase for the foreseeable future.

If the future remains difficult to predict, does the
history of a place called Jackson Hole teach us anything? Its most fundamental and persistent theme is
the interaction between humans and the environment. This valley's history teaches us how dependent
we, and our civilization, are on the environment and

years, Murie directed the activities of the Wilderness Society, confronting numerous environmental issues of national importance. Murie was an important spokesman and leader of the modern environmental movement. After his death in 1963, Mardy Murie continued promoting environmental causes. The Murie's youngest son, Donald Murie, expressed his feelings about his father in a letter to his mother. While driving to the ranch from the town of Jackson, he observed trumpeter swans, a few early elk on the refuge, and a red-tailed hawk suspended in the sky. "I was very suddenly hit by an overwhelming feeling that great as my loss was, theirs was even greater. They had lost an important interpreter and ambassador, an influential lobbyist in the human court."[7]

Listed in the National Register of Historic Places, Menor's Ferry represents the transportation frontier. From 1894 through 1926, the ferry served as a major link in Jackson Hole's transportation system. Nearby is the Maud Noble cabin, a part of Menor's Ferry, significant for one event, the 1923 meeting of citizens concerned over the commercialization of the valley. While the meeting has been debunked by some in recent years, it was important because local conservationists and Horace Albright decided on a course of action to protect Jackson Hole.

Beaver Creek is significant for its associations with early park administration and, even though altered, the old administration building for its association with the early Forest Service. The rustic log buildings served as the first headquarters from 1930 to 1958. The log buildings also possess architectural significance, representing the best of WPA-CCC construction.

Along the Snake River is the Bar BC. The second dude ranch in Jackson Hole, it is the most important for several reasons, among them its association with Struthers Burt, an author, conservationist, and pioneer dude rancher. It was among the earliest dude ranches in the West and operated until the 1940s. Burt's *Diary of a Dude Wrangler* helped assure the Bar BC's place in history. This ranch represents a way of life and a context extremely important to this valley's history and identity today.

At Jenny Lake, two buildings are especially important. One is the Crandall Studio. Harrison Crandall established himself as the park's greatest publicist, taking thousands of pictures sold as postcards and large framed prints. The Jenny Lake Ranger Station, moved in 1930 from the Lee Manges place, was the park's first ranger station and museum.

Finally, there is the Pierce Cunningham cabin. A crude structure, it may be the oldest homestead cabin surviving in the valley. Listed in the National Register, it is preserved and interpreted by the park today. Pierce Cunningham was one of the valley's outstanding citizens, serving as a justice of the peace and later, county commissioner. Also a rancher, he raised cattle for years, then turned to sheep ranching for a time. The cabin was saved originally because it was the scene of the shootout where a posse gunned down two alleged rustlers.

When historians reach the end of their research and hitch it to the present, the temptation to speculate on the future, though dangerous, is irresistible. For example, years ago, forecasters predicted that the work week of Americans would decrease, allowing more leisure. This has not happened for most Americans, because of economic and social change. Recent studies indicate that Americans work longer each week than in the past. In addition, more women have entered the workforce, either by personal choice or economic necessity. This has resulted in less leisure time for many Americans. Working couples struggle to schedule vacations together. Less leisure time has resulted in shorter, but more frequent, family outings.

Several observations can be made about Jackson Hole today that will most likely remain true in the future. It is a community grappling for an identity, which is reflected in ongoing debates over land-use planning, zoning, and development. Teton County claims the distinction of having the highest cost of living in Wyoming. Conversely, because low paying jobs in the tourist industry comprise the bulk of employment, the county has the lowest average wage in the state. People working two to three part-time jobs is not uncommon. It has the staunchest environmental base in Wyoming. Yet it is environmentalism tinged with self-interest. I have often heard individuals protest forcefully against commercial extraction of resources in the national forest, yet remain blind to impacts caused by recreational uses that they favor.

While the valley promotes its Old West character, using slogans like "Welcome to Jackson Hole—the last of the Old West," the town of Jackson exhibits a blend of Colorado ski resort and national park gateway community. Its western heritage is the product of marketing, not history or reality.

The truest and most realistic frontier people are still going strong—real estate speculators. Historian Patricia Limerick observed, "if Hollywood wanted to capture the emotional center of Western history, its movies would be about real estate," and its heroes, surveyors, realtors, and lawyers. From the treaty that divided the Northwest Territory between Great Britain and the United States to surveyors plotting lots in the town of Jackson, the history of the American West has always been, at its most basic level, about property.[8] Prior to 1900, a wealthy dude named Moser hoped "to buy the whole valley because he felt this valley would one day be worth a lot of money and he could make a cleaning on it." And could the signers of the 1925 petition supporting a "museum on the hoof" in Jackson Hole been motivated in part by real estate speculation when they qualified their offer to sell their land "at what we consider a fair price?" Harrison and Hildegard Crandall considered subdividing their property near String Lake, before deciding to sell to the Snake River Land Company. Around 1940, rumors circulated that J. D. Kimmel planned to subdivide the Geraldine Lucas property south of Jenny Lake. Set in the heart of land that park supporters sought to protect, one observer believed that "nothing more disastrous would happen to the proposed project of preserving the valley."[9]

The conquest of land continues today, the competition heated and stakes high, with the advantage to the bearer of the biggest bank account, moderated only by the ebb and flow of boom-and-bust cycles. Rather than present an Old West shootout on summer evenings at the Jackson square, a real estate closing or even a foreclosure would capture a more prevalent western experience.

In 1970, the United States became the first nation in the world where suburbanites outnumbered urban and rural residents. Suburbanization has reshaped the character of Jackson Hole. Molded by the automobile, the valley exhibits all the elements

of the "crabgrass frontier," historian Kenneth T. Jackson's label for suburbanization. Homes are designed with garages stuck prominently on the front fagade, as subdivisions consume agricultural land in the valley. Developers coin names like "Buck Meadows," then proceed to pave over those meadows with asphalt, preempting more mule deer range. Drive-up windows have become a prominent feature of businesses; strip development best describes Broadway, Jackson's "main drag;" and shopping centers, suburbia's marketplace, have erupted with their trademark behemoth parking lots. Even Grand Teton National Park has not escaped the suburban influence with two government housing areas at Moose and Colter Bay that are tract developments.[10] This process will continue in Jackson Hole so long as private land is available.

In recent years, cities have experienced a phenomenon called gentrification, a process whereby affluent people buy up residences and businesses in decayed urban neighborhoods and renovate them. Gentrification escalates property taxes and rent, driving out lower income people. A similar trend is occurring in Jackson Hole today. People with higher incomes are buying land and residences as second homes. This has driven real estate values to a plateau that makes home ownership difficult for people earning low to moderate incomes. Concurrently, rental housing costs have increased significantly. Like suburbanization, the second home trend is "a manifestation of such fundamental characteristics of American society as conspicuous consumption, a reliance upon the private automobile, upward mobility, the separation of family into nuclear units, the widening division between work and leisure, and a tendency toward racial and economic exclusiveness."[11]

Finally, thanks to advanced communications and improved transportation, people relocate here and either commute by airplane to work, or use computer technology to work out of their homes. This development will increase for the foreseeable future.

If the future remains difficult to predict, does the history of a place called Jackson Hole teach us anything? Its most fundamental and persistent theme is the interaction between humans and the environment. This valley's history teaches us how dependent we, and our civilization, are on the environment and its resources. Pressure on natural resources continues as the valley's population increases, perhaps more from visitors than year-round residents. Conflicts over resources will intensify, particularly between environmentalists and developers. How much private land should be set aside for scenic easements? Should public money be used to buy easements? How many board feet of lumber should be harvested annually from national forests? How much development is needed to provide for the public enjoyment of Grand Teton National Park ? When all available private land in Jackson Hole is developed, how much pressure will be exerted to gain access to public lands and what form will it take—land exchanges, boundary adjustments, leases, outright de-authorization? These questions are rooted in the past and will preoccupy the people of Jackson Hole in the future.

The history of this valley teaches us to be less anthropocentric in our outlook. Living before the Teton Range reinforces the concept that humankind is not the center of the universe and brings people closer to the natural world. Earth history is much longer than human history by a long shot. Four and one-half billion years of earth history should teach us that this planet and its ecosystems got along fine without humans and could do so again.

The Teton country has many moods that stimulate the senses, but one must pay attention. Fresh, clean air carrying the scent of evergreen or willow is here for the taking. Wind strumming the leaves of quaking aspen, and the unforgettable bugling of elk in the fall, remind us of our wild past, not so long ago. In the long night of winter, a snowfall can envelop the park in a silence so profound that it becomes a presence. It is a silence that most of packed humanity does not know exists. On a hot, summer day, dipping your feet in the snow-fed rush of Cascade Creek feels fine briefly, before the icy water begins to numb your feet. Bluish-black huckleberries come into their prime in summer and have a sharp, sweet taste all their own. Evening sunsets wash the

granites and snowfields of the Teton Range in colors that neither cameras nor artists' paints can capture with exactitude. Nor do words duplicate the alpen glow that teases the eye with pale yellow, changes to gold, then to auburn, and finally a deep rose, before retreating in darkness. The clear night sky of the Tetons reveals a host of new stars, a night sky from our ancient past, not diminished by urban lights. All of these things make the Teton country a special place and, like other wild places that remain today, teach us to hope.

Notes

1. Patricia N. Limerick, *The Legacy of Conquest: The Unbroken Past of the American West* (New York: W. W. Norton & Co., 1987), pp. 17–32.

2. Michael P. Malone and Richard W. Etulain, *The American West: A Twentieth Century History* (Lincoln: University of Nebraska Press, 1989), p. 8.

3. Limerick, *Legacy of Conquest*, p. 323.

4. James Oliver Robertson, *American Myth, American Reality* (New York: Hill and Wang, 1980), pp. xv–xvii.

5. *Jackson's Hole Courier*, January 28, 1909; reprinted in *Jackson's Hole Courier*, January 29, 1949; and *Jackson's Hole Courier*, May 17, 1914 and July 6, 1933.

6. *Jackson's Hole Courier*, July 6, 1950.

7. Donald Murie to Margaret E. Murie, April 17, 1982, personal correspondence.

8. Limerick, *Legacy of Conquest*, pp. 55–57.

9. *Jackson Hole Guide*, April 5, 1956; "Hearing on S. Res. 226," 1933, pp. 266–268; interview with Hildegard Crandall by Jo Ann Byrd #9, "Last of the Old West Series;" and Sanford Hill, landscape architect, to Regional Director Howard Baker, Special Memorandum, 1940, Grand Teton National Park files.

10. Kenneth T. Jackson, *Crabgrass Frontier: The Suburbanization of the United States* (New York: Oxford University Press, 1985), pp. 283–284.

11. Ibid., p. 4.

Epilogue

In 1927, a series of events occurred—some distinct and others related—that set a new pattern for the future of Jackson Hole. John D. Rockefeller Jr., financed the Snake River Land Company to buy private lands for the purpose of returning them to the public domain. President Calvin Coolidge issued a series of executive orders that withdrew thousands of acres from homestead entry. The Bureau of Public Roads completed a new highway from Jackson Lake to Menor's Ferry, where they constructed a steel truss bridge. And water breached the natural dam on the Gros Ventre River, causing the worst flood in the valley's recorded history.

One summer, I stole a few moments to watch a rancher bale hay. Traditionally, Jackson Hole ranchers stored hay in huge stacks that resembled oversized loaves of bread. This day, a tractor pulled a baling machine over rows of mown hay, producing neat, rectangular blocks at predictable intervals. As the fragrance of fresh-cut grass drifted in a slight breeze, it struck me that the baling machine was much like 1927, when events reshaped the course of history in this valley. Whether in a stack or baled, hay remains hay, but it is very different in appearance. So too was a new pattern created for Jackson Hole, one that would ironically become apparent only with the passing of time.

Appendix

The following pages have maps showing the resources within Grand Teton National Park that have been either listed or determined eligible to the National Register of Historic Places. All maps are reproduced courtesy of the U.S. Geological Survey.

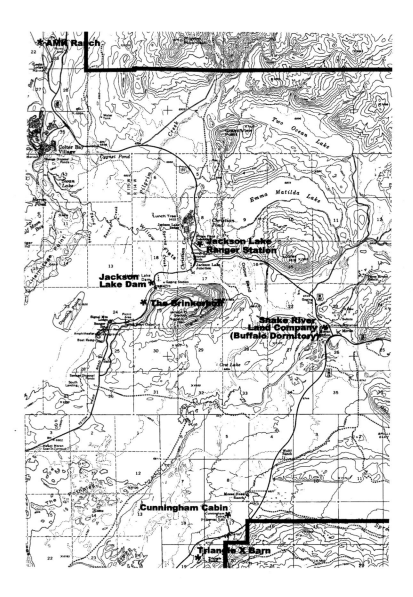

AMK Ranch

Colter Bay Village

Jackson Lake Ranger Station

Jackson Lake Dam

The Brinkerhoff

Snake River Land Company (Buffalo Dormitory)

Cunningham Cabin

Triangle X Barn

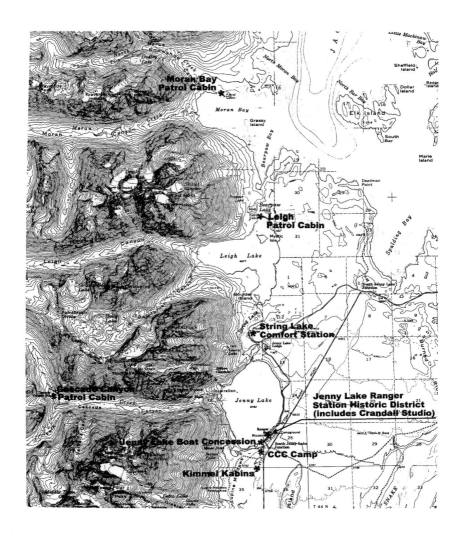

Moran Bay
Patrol Cabin

Leigh
Patrol Cabin

String Lake
Comfort Station

Cascade Canyon
Patrol Cabin

Jenny Lake Ranger
Station Historic District
(includes Crandall Studio)

Jenny Lake Boat Concession

CCC Camp

Kimmel Kabins

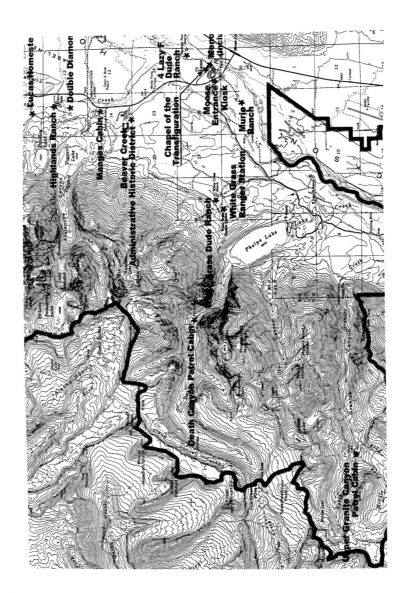

Lucas Homeste

Double Diamon

4 Lazy F Dude Ranch *

Mayo Ranch

Highlands Ranch *

Ranges Cabin *

Moose Entrance Kiosk

Chapel of the Transfiguration *

Murie Ranch *

Beaver Creek Administrative Historic District *

White Grass Ranger Station *

White Grass Dude Ranch *

Creek

Creek

Phelps Lake

Death Canyon Patrol Cabin *

per Granite Canyon Patrol Cabin *

370

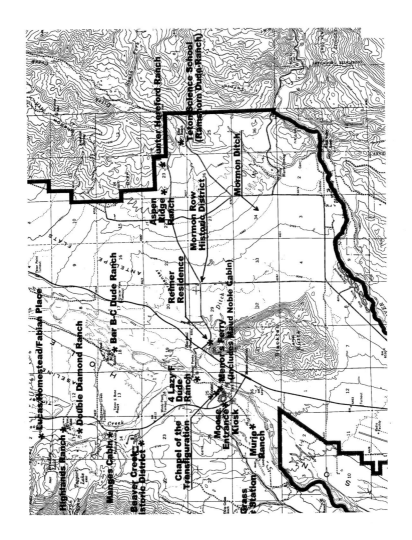

Highlands Ranch ★
Lucas Homestead/Fabian Place ★
Double Diamond Ranch ★
Manges Cabin ★
Beaver Creek Historic District ★
Chapel of the Transfiguration ★
4 Lazy F Dude Ranch ★
Bar B-C Dude Ranch ★
Renner Residence
Aspen Ridge Ranch ★
Hunter/Hereford Ranch ★
Teton Science School (Elbo/Horn Dude Ranch) ★
Mormon Row Historic District
Mormon Ditch
Moose Entrance
Kiosk
Menor's Ferry (includes Maud Noble Cabin) ★
Murie Ranch ★
Grass Station ★

371

Note on the Sources

Two general histories of the American West provided background information for this study, Ray Allen Billington's *Westward Expansion: A History of the American Frontier* and Frederick Merk's *History of the Western Movement*. Both are excellent sources. After I completed the first draft manuscript, two books were published that provided new ways to see the history of the American West. Patricia N. Limerick's *The Legacy of Conquest: The Unbroken Past of the American West* offers the best fresh look at the American West. In her book, Limerick stresses the continuity of themes and issues in the West. Michael P Malone's and Richard W. Etulain's *The American West: A Twentieth Century History*, published in 1989, is must reading for people interested in the history and current issues of this region.

For a general text on Wyoming history, T. A. Larson's *History of Wyoming* is the best source. Numerous histories and memoirs have been written about Jackson Hole. David J. Saylor's *Jackson Hole, Wyoming: In the Shadow of the Tetons* remains the best general history of this area. Robert B. Betts' *Along the Ramparts of the Tetons*, not only is a good source, but is entertaining reading. Though criticized for its lack of footnotes, *From Trapper to Tourist in Jackson Hole* by Elizabeth Wied Hayden remains an excellent history. Noley Mumey's *The Teton Mountains* is a dated but still useful history. It should be used with caution, however. Forgotten by many is a booklet titled *A Souvenir History of Jackson Hole*, written by teacher Roland Brown Jr. and his seventh and eighth grade students in 1924. There are some errors, but this book proved useful in several instances. It also reveals insights about how people of this period viewed their past. For a good pictorial history of Jackson Hole, see Virginia Huidekoper's *The Early Days in Jackson Hole*.

Concerning more specialized subjects, Merrill Mattes wrote the definitive history of the fur trade in this area, titled "Jackson Hole, Crossroads of the Western Fur Trade," which appeared in two segments in the *Pacific Northwest Quarterly*. I used Mattes' work extensively to write the chapter on the fur trappers. Robert Righter's *Crucible for Conservation: The Creation of Grand Teton National Park*, published in 1983, is the best history documenting the struggle to establish a park in this valley. I relied heavily on this book in summarizing the park story in the conservation chapter.

Archival sources provided much of the primary material for this work. Homestead records, housed in the National Archives facility at Suitland, Maryland, proved essential in reconstructing settlement in the park area. The Harold P Fabian papers at the Rockefeller Archive Center revealed a wealth of information concerning the activities of the Snake River Land Company and politics related to park expansion. I also found Horace M. Albright's papers, housed at the Yellowstone Archives, especially useful to understanding the tumultuous decade of the 1920s in this valley. The American Heritage Center at the University of Wyoming contains the papers of numerous people associated with Jackson Hole. The Wyoming State Archives hold numerous manuscripts pertinent to this area. In particular, the state curates reports prepared under the auspices of the Works Progress Administration. A woman named Nellie Van DerVeer wrote numerous essays under this program. Her work provided useful information, but contained some errors and was inexplicably vague in some cases. In Denver, park records stored at the Federal Records Center and materials at the Denver Public Library, particularly the Murie Papers, were useful.

Several facilities in Jackson Hole provided important materials. Documents in park files were important sources, though they are not indexed or filed in an organized way. The county records were very important in documenting homesteading and property ownership in the park. The Jackson Hole Historical Society and Museum maintains a large collection of papers and photographs. Especially important is a subject index to local newspapers and the center's collections, which made my research much easier. Old copies and microfilm copies of the *Jackson's Hole Courier*, the *Jackson Hole Guide*, and the *Jackson Hole News* are available in the Teton County Library. The *Courier* provided considerable information for this study.

Bibliography

Books

Adams, Ansel. *An Autobiography.* Boston: New York Graphic Society and Little Brown and Company, 1985.

Adams, Ansel. *Letters and Images 1916–1984.* Boston: Little, Brown and Co., 1988.

Albright, Horace M. *The Birth of the National Park Service: The Founding Years, 1913–1933.* As told to Robert Cahn. Salt Lake City: Howe Brothers, 1982.

Albright, Horace M., et al. *Mr. John D. Rockefeller's Proposed Gift of Land for the National Park System in Wyoming.* No publisher, 1933.

Allen, Marion V. *Early Jackson Hole.* Redding, CA: Press Room Printing, 1981.

Alter, J. Cecil. *James Bridger, Trapper, Frontiersman, Scout, and Guide, Historical Narrative.* Salt Lake City: Shepard Book Company, 1925.

Anderson, A. A. *Experiences and Impressions.* New York: MacMillan Company, 1933.

Anderson, Nancy K. *Thomas Moran.* Catalogue, with contributions by Thomas P. Bruhn, Joni L. Kinsey, and Anne Morand, to accompany Thomas Moran Exhibition at the National Gallery of Art, September 24, 1997. Washington, D.C., National Gallery of Art and, New Haven and London: Yale University Press, 1997.

Baillie-Grohmann, William A. *Camps in the Rockies.* New York: Charles Scribner's Sons, 1882.

Bartlett, Richard A. *Great Surveys of the American West.* Norman: University of Oklahoma Press, 1962.

Bedford, Henry F., and Trevor Colbourn. *The Americans; A Brief History.* Edited by John Morton Blum. New York: Harcourt Brace Javanovich, ca. 1976.

Belasco, Warren James. *Americans on the Road: From Autocamp to Motel, 1910–1945.* Cambridge, MA: The MIT Press, 1981.

Betts, Robert B. *Along the Ramparts of the Tetons: The Saga of Jackson Hole, Wyoming.* Boulder: Colorado Associated University Press, 1978.

Billington, Ray Allen. *Westward Expansion: A History of the American Frontier.* With the Collaboration of James Blaine Hedges. Fourth editon, revised. New York: MacMillan, 1974.

Bonney, Orrin H., and Lorraine J. Bonney. *Battledrums and Geysers: The Life and Journals of Lt. Gustavus Cheney Doane.* Chicago: Sage Books, 1970.

Bonney, Orrin H., and Lorraine J. Bonney. *Bonney's Guide to Grand Teton National Park and Jackson's Hole.* Houston: By the author, 1972.

Borne, Lawrence W. *Dude Ranching: A Complete History.* Albuquerque: University of New Mexico Press, 1983.

Brown, Roland W., Jr., ed. *A Souvenir History of Jackson Hole.* Salt Lake City: 1924,

Burt, Nathaniel. *Jackson Hole Journal.* Norman: University of Oklahoma Press, 1983.

Burt, Struthers. *The Diary of a Dude Wrangler.* New York: Charles Scribner's Sons, 1924.

Calkins, Frank. *Jackson Hole.* New York: Alfred A. Knopf, 1973.

Campfire Tales of Jackson Hole. Moose, WY: Grand Teton Natural History Association, 1970.

Chittenden, Hiram Martin. *The American Fur Trade of the Far West: A History of the Pioneer Trading Posts and Early Fur Companies of the Missouri Valley and the Rocky Mountains and of the Overland Commerce with Santa Fe.* Two volumes. Stanford, CA: Academic Reprints, 1954.

Chittenden, Hiram Martin. *The Yellowstone National Park Historical and Descriptive.* Fifth Edition. Cincinnati: Robert Clarke, 1905.

Clark, Carol. *Thomas Moran: Watercolors of the American West.* Austin, TX: Amon Carter Museum and University of Texas Press, 1980.

Clark, Ella. *Indian Legends From the Northern Rockies.* Norman: University of Oklahoma Press, 1966.

Clark, Tim W. *Ecology of Jackson Hole, Wyoming, A Primer.* Salt Lake City: Paragon Press, 1981.

Cooper, Nancy and Quita Pownell. *32 Rocky Mountain Wildflowers.* Laramie, WY: no publisher, no date.

Crowder, David. *Rexburg, Idaho.* Caldwell, ID: Caxton Printers, 1983.

Cummins, D. Duane. *William Robinson Leigh, Western Artist.* Norman: University of Oklahoma Press, and Tulsa, OK: Thomas Gilcrease Institute of American History and Art, 1980.

Dale, Harrison Clifford. *The Ashley-Smith Explorations and the Discovery of a Central Route to the Pacific, 1822–1829.* Revised edition. Glendale, CA: The Arthur H. Clark Company, 1941.

DeVoto, Bernard. *Across the Wide Missouri.* New York: Houghton Mifflin Company, 1947.

Diem, Lenore. *The Research Stations Place in History.* Laramie: University of Wyoming Research Center, 1978.

Diem, Lenore. *A Tale of Dough Gods, Bear Grease, Cantaloupe, and Sucker Oil.* Laramie: University of Wyoming, 1986.

Dingus, Rick. *The Photographic Artifacts of Timothy O'Sullivan.* Albuquerque: University of New Mexico Press, 1982.

Driggs, Howard W. *History of Teton Valley.* Edited by Louis J. Clements and Harold S. Forbush. Rexburg, ID: Eastern Idaho Publishing Company, 1970.

Dykes, Jeff C. *The West of the Texas Kid, 1881–1910: The Recollections of Thomas E. Crawford.* Norman: University of Oklahoma Press, 1962.

F. Jay Haynes, Photographer. Helena: Montana Historical Society Press, 1981.

Fagan, Brian M. *World Prehistory: A Brief Introduction.* Boston: Little Brown & Co., 1979.

Ferris, Warren A. *Life in the Rockies.* Edited by Paul C. Phillips. Denver: Old West Publishing Company, 1940.

Foster, Mike. *The Life of Ferdinand Vandeveer Hayden.* Niwot, CO: Roberts Rinehart Publishers, 1994.

Fremont, John Charles. *The Expedition of John Charles Fremont.* Edited by Donald Jackson and Mary Lee Spence. Two volumes. Urbana: University of Illinois Press, 1970.

Frison, George C. *Prehistoric Hunters of the High Plains.* Second Edition. New York: Academic Press, 1991.

Frison, George C. "The Foothills-Mountains and the Open Plains: The Dichotomy in Paleoindian Subsistence Strategies Between Two Ecosystems." *Ice Age Hunters of the Rockies.* Edited by Dennis Stanford and Jane S. Day. Niwot, CO: Denver Museum of Natural History and Denver Press, 1992.

Fryxell, Fritiof M. *The Teton Peaks and Their Ascents.* Grand Teton National Park, WY: The Crandall Studios, 1932.

Fryxell, Fritiof M. *The Tetons, Interpretations of a Mountain Landscape.* Berkeley: University of California Press, 1938.

Gillette, Bertha Chambers. *Homesteading with the Elk: A Story of Frontier Life in Jackson Hole.* Idaho Falls: Mer-Jons Publishing Company, 1967.

Goetzmann, William H. *Exploration and Empire: The Explorer and Scientist in the Winning of the West.* New York: Alfred A. Knopf, 1966; and New York: Vintage Books, 1972.

Goetzmann, William H. *William H. Holmes, Panoramic Art.* Fort Worth, TX: Amon Carter Museum, 1977.

Goetzmann, William H. and Kay Sloan. *Looking Far North, the Harriman Expedition to Alaska, 1899.* New York: Viking Press, 1982.

Goetzmann, William H. and William N. Goetzmann. *The West of the Imagination.* New York: W.W. Norton & Company Ltd., 1986.

Goin, Peter. *Nuclear Landscapes.* Baltimore: Johns Hopkins University Press, 1991.

Hafen, LeRoy R., ed. *The Mountain Men and the Fur Trade of the Far West.* Ten volumes. Glendale, CA: The Arthur H. Clark Company, 1965–1972.

Haines, Aubry L. *The Yellowstone Story: A History of our First National Park.* Two volumes. Yellowstone National Park, WY: Yellowstone Library and Museum Association in cooperation with Colorado Associated University Press, 1977.

Harris, Burton. *John Colter, His Years in the Rockies.* Basin, WY: Big Horn Book Company, 1977.

Hassrick, Peter. *Water Color Sketches of Thomas Moran, Yellowstone and Grand Teton National Parks.* Yellowstone and Grand Teton Natural History Associations, 1991.

Hayden, Elizabeth Wied. *From Trapper to Tourist in Jackson Hole.* Fourth edition, revised. Moose, WY: Grand Teton Natural History Association, 1957, 1981.

Hays, Samuel P. *Conservation and the Gospel of Efficiency: The Progressive Conservation Movement, 1890–1920.* Cambridge: Harvard University Press, 1959.

Healy, Paul F. *Cissy, A Biography of Eleanor M. "Cissy" Patterson.* Garden City, NY: Doubleday & Co., 1966.

Hine, Robert V. *The American West; an Interpretive History.* Boston: Little, Brown, 1973.

Hoge, Alice Albright. *Cissy Patterson.* New York: Random House, 1966.

Hough, Donald. *The Cocktail Hour in Jackson Hole.* New York: W. W. Norton and Company, 1951.

Huidekoper, Virginia. *The Early Days in Jackson Hole.* Boulder: Colorado Associated University Press, 1978.

Hultkrantz, Åke. *Belief and Worship in Native North America.* New York: Syracuse University Press, 1979.

Hunt, Charles Butler. *Natural Regions of the United States and Canada*. San Francisco: W. H. Freeman, 1974.

Irving, Washington. *Astoria*. Two volumes. Philadelphia: Lea and Blanchard, 1836. Reprint. Philadelphia: J. B. Lippincott, 1961.

Irving, Washington. *Adventures of Captain Bonneville*. Two volumes. New York: G. P. Putnam's Sons, 1837.

Ise, John. *Our National Park Policy: A Critical History*. Baltimore: Johns Hopkins Press, 1961.

Jackson, Kenneth T. *Crabgrass Frontier: The Suburbanization of the United States*. New York: Oxford University Press, 1985.

Jackson, Clarence S. *Picture Maker of the Old West: William H. Jackson*. New York: Charles Scribner's Sons, 1947.

Jackson, William H. *The Pioneer Photographer: Rocky Mountain Adventures with a Camera*. In collaboration with Howard R. Driggs. New York: World Book Company, 1929.

Jackson, William H. *Time Exposure: The Autobiography of William H. Jackson*. New York: G. P. Putnam's Sons, 1940.

Jakle, John A. *The Tourist*. Lincoln: University of Nebraska Press, 1985.

Jones, Chris. *Climbing in North America*. Berkeley, Los Angeles, London: University of California Press for the American Alpine Club, 1976.

Joy, Frederic. *Light Reflections*. Jackson, WY: no publisher, no date.

Katz, Ephraim. *The Film Encyclopedia*. New York: Harper and Row, 1979.

Kirkpatrick, Sidney D. *A Cast of Killers*. New York: E. P. Dutton, 1986.

Klett, Mark. *Second View: The Rephotographic Survey Project*. Albuquerque, University of New Mexico Press, 1984.

Krakel, Dean Fenton. *Conrad Schwiering, Painting on the Square*. Oklahoma City: Powder River Book Co., National Cowboy Hall of Fame, 1981.

Larson, T. A. *History of Wyoming*. Lincoln: University of Nebraska Press, 1965.

Lawrence, Paul. *John Colter: A New Look at an Old Mystery*. Jackson, WY: Pioneer Press, 1978.

Lewis, Meriwether. *The Expedition of Lewis and Clark*. Edited by William H. Goetzmann and Archibald Hanna. Three volumes. Reprint, 1814 edition, unabridged. Philadelphia: J. B. Lippincott Company, 1961.

Limerick, Patricia N. *The Legacy of Conquest: The Unbroken Past of the American West*. New York: W. W. Norton and Company, 1987.

Love, John D., and John C. Reed, Jr. *Creation of the Teton Landscape: the Geologic Story of Grand Teton National Park*. First edition, revised. Moose, WY: Grand Teton Natural History Association, 1971.

Malone, Michael P., and Richard W. Etulain. *The American West: A Twentieth-Century History*. Lincoln: University of Nebraska Press, 1989.

Mangelsen, Thomas D. and Charles Craighead. *Images of Nature: The Photographs of Thomas D. Mangelsen*. New York: Hugh Lauther Levin Associates, 1989.

McNeill, William C. *Mythhistory and Other Essays*. Chicago: University of Chicago Press, 1986.

Merk, Frederick. *History of the Western Movement*. New York: Alfred A. Knopf, 1978.

Misrach, Richard. *Bravo 20: The Bombing of the American West*. Baltimore: Johns Hopkins University Press, 1990.

Morgan, Dale. *Jedediah Smith and the Opening of the West*. New York: Bobs-Merrill Company, 1953.

Muench, David. *National Parks of America*. Text by Stewart L. Udall and James R. Udall. Portland, OR: Graphic Arts Center Publishing Co., no date.

Mumey, Nolie. *The Teton Mountains: Their History and Tradition*. Denver: Artcraft Press, 1947.

Murie, Margaret, and Olaus Murie. *Wapiti Wilderness*. New York: Alfred A. Knopf, 1966.

Murie, Olaus J. *The Elk of North America*. Harrisburg, PA: The Stackpole Company, Washington, D.C.: The Wildlife Institute, 1951.

Nagatani, Patrick. *Nuclear Enchantment*. Albuquerque: University of New Mexico Press, 1991.

Nash, Roderick. *Wilderness and the American Mind*. New Haven: Yale University Press, 1967.

Nelson, Mary Carroll. *Masters of Western Art*. New York: Watson-Guptill Publications, 1982.

Olson, Linda L., and Tim Bywater. *A Guide to Exploring Grand Teton National Park*. Salt Lake City: RNM Press, 1991.

Park, Edward. *The World of the Bison*. New York: J.B. Lippincott Company, 1969.

Parker, Reverend Samuel. *Journal of an Exploring Tour Beyond the Rocky Mountains*. Fourth edition. New York: Huntington and Savage, 1844.

Paul, Elliot H. *Desperate Scenery*. New York: Random House, 1954.

Payne, Darwin. *Owen Wister: Chronicler of the West, Gentleman of the East*. Dallas: Southern Methodist University Press, 1985.

Phillips, Paul Chrisler. *The Fur Trade*. With concluding chapters by J. W. Smurr. Two volumes. Norman: University of Oklahoma Press, 1961.

Pike, Z. M. *The Journals of Zebulon Montgomery Pike*. Edited by Donald Jackson. Norman: University of Oklahoma, 1958.

Porter, Eliot. *The West*. New York: Little, Brown Books, 1988.

Porter, Robert P., and Carroll D. Wright. *Report on Indians Taxed and Indians Not Taxed in the United States* (except Alaska) in the *Eleventh Census 1890.* Washington, D.C.: Government Printing Office, 1894.

Pound, Ezra. *The Cantos of Ezra Pound.* New York: New Directions Books, 1943, 1937, 1940, and 1948.

Raynes, Bert and Meg. *Birds of Jackson Hole, A Checklist.* Moose, WY: Grand Teton Natural History Association, no date.

Righter, Robert W. *Crucible for Conservation: The Creation of Grand Teton National Park.* Boulder: Colorado Associated University Press, 1983.

Robbins, Roy M. *Our Landed Heritage: The Public Domain.* Lincoln: University of Nebraska Press, 1962.

Robertson, James Oliver. *American Myth, American Reality.* New York: Hill and Wang, 1980.

Rollins, Philip Ashton, ed. *The Discovery of the Oregon Trail; Robert Stuart's Narratives.* New York: Charles Scribner's Sons, 1935.

Ross, Alexander. *The Fur Hunters of the Far West.* Edited by Kenneth A. Spaulding. Reprint, 1855 edition. Norman: University of Oklahoma Press, 1956.

Russell, Osborne. *Journal of a Trapper.* Edited by Aubrey L. Haines. Lincoln: University of Nebraska Press, 1965.

Saylor, David J. *Jackson Hole, Wyoming: In the Shadow of the Tetons.* Norman: University of Oklahoma Press, 1970.

Sinclair, Pete. *We Aspired: The Last Innocent Americans.* Logan: Utah State University Press, 1993.

Sprague, Marshall. *A Gallery of Dudes.* Boston: Little, Brown, and Company, 1966.

Spaulding, Jonathan. *Ansel Adams and the American Landscape, a Biography.* Berkeley: University of California Press, 1995.

Steen, Harold. *The U.S. Forest Service: A History.* Seattle: University of Washington Press, 1976.

Thomas, Jack Ward, and Dale E. Toeill, eds. *Elk of North America: Ecology and Management.* Harrisburg, PA: Stackpole Books, 1982.

Thompson, Edith M. S., and William Leigh Thompson. *Beaver Dick, the Honor and the Heartbreak: An Historical Biography of Richard Leigh.* Laramie, WY: Jelm Mountain Press, 1982.

Tilden, Freeman. *Following the Frontier with F. Jay Haynes; Pioneer Photographer of the West.* New York: Alfred A. Knopf, 1964.

Trenholm, Virginia, and Maurine Carley. *The Shoshonis: Sentinels of the Rockies.* Norman: University of Oklahoma Press, 1964.

Trenton, Patricia, and Peter Hassrick. *The Rocky Mountains: a Vision for Artists in the Nineteenth Century.* Cody, WY: Buffalo Bill Historical Center, and Norman: University of Oklahoma Press, 1983.

Turner, Christy G. II. "New World Origins: New Research from the Americas and the Soviet Union." *Ice Age Hunters of the Rockies.* Edited by Dennis Stanford

and Jane S. Day. Niwot, CO: Denver Museum of Natural History and Denver Press, 1992.

Victor, Frances Fuller. *The River of the West; Life and Adventure in the Rocky Mountains and Oregon.* Hartford: Columbian Book Company, 1870.

Vinton, Stallo. *John Colter, Discoverer of Yellowstone Park.* New York: Edward Eberstadt, 1926.

Walker, Deward Jr. "Protection of American Indian Sacred Geography." *Handbook of American Indian Religious Freedom.* Edited by Christopher Vecsey. New York: Crossroads Publishing, 1992.

Wheat, Carl I. *Mapping the Transmississippi West, 1540–1861.* Five volumes. San Francisco: The Institute of Historical Cartography, 1958.

Whiffen, Marcus. *American Architecture Since 1780: A Guide to Styles.* Cambridge: The M.I.T. Press, 1969.

Wildlife of Grand Teton. Moose, WY: Grand Teton Natural History Association, no date.

Wilson, E. N. *The White Indian Boy: The Story of Uncle Nick Among the Shoshones.* With Howard R. Driggs. Revised edition. Yonkers-on-Hudson, NY: World Book Co., 1919.

Wister, Owen. *Owen Wister Out West: His Journals and Letters.* Edited by Fanny Kemble Wister. Chicago: University of Chicago Press, 1958.

Wister, Owen. *The Virginian: A Horseman of the Plains.* New York: The MacMillan Company, 1902.

Withington, Mary C. *A Catalogue of Manuscripts in the Collection of Western Americana Founded by William Robertson Coe, Yale University Library.* New Haven: Yale University Press, 1952.

Wright, Gary. *The People of the High Country: Jackson Hole Before the Settlers.* New York: Peter Lang, 1984.

Wormington, H. M. *Ancient Man in North America.* Seventh Edition. Denver: Denver Museum of Natural History, 1957.

Young, F. G., ed. "The Correspondence and Journals of Captain Nathaniel J. Wyeth, 1831–1836." *Sources of the History of Oregon.* Volume 1. Eugene, OR: University Press, 1899.

Magazine Articles

Bonney, Orin, and Lorraine Bonney. "Shootout at the Cowboy Bar." *Teton* 14 (1981).

DeLacy, Walter W. "A Trip Up the South Snake River in 1863." *Contributions to the Historical Society of Montana* 1(1876).

Downs, Elizabeth. "The Screen: Authentic Comments on Films in the Field of Nature, Geography and Exploration." *Natural History,* October 1952.

Fryxell, Fritiof "The Grand Tetons: Our National Park of Matterhorns." *American Forests and Forest Life* 35 (August 1929).

Glidden, Harvey H. "The Wyoming Game Situation." *Outdoor Life* 10 (1902).

Graham, Frank Jr. "Mardy Murie and Her Sunrise of Promise." *Audubon* 82 (May 1980).

Gizycka, Felicia. "Jackson Hole, 1916–1965: A Reminiscence." *Vogue* (April 1, 1965).

Hoebel, Adamson. "Bands and Distributions of the Eastern Shoshone." *American Anthropologist* 40, No. 3, 1938.

Hultkrantz, Åke. "The Shoshones in the Rocky Mountain Area." *Annals of Wyoming.* Volume 33, April 1961.

"The Jackson Hole Country of Wyoming." *Scientific American,* March 30, 1918.

James, Preston. "Regional Planning in the Jackson Hole Country." *The Geographical Review* 26 (July 1936).

Jenkins, Stephen H., and Peter E. Busher. "North American Beaver." *Mammalian Species.* No. 120, June 8, 1979.

Judge, Frances. "Carrie and the Tetons." *Montana* (Summer 1968).

Judge, Frances. "Second Life." *Atlantic Monthly* 192 (November 1952).

Judge, Frances. "Vital Laughter." *Atlantic Monthly* (July 1954).

Kelsey, Margaret. "John Graul's Mystery Mine." *Teton Magazine* 7 (1974–1975).

Kendrick, Gregory D. "An Environmental Spokesman: Olaus J. Murie and a Democratic Defense of Wilderness." *Annals of Wyoming* 50 (Fall 1978).

Langford, Nathaniel P. "The Ascent of Mount Hayden." *Scribner's Monthly* 4 (June 1873).

Mattes, Merrill J. "Jackson Hole, Crossroads of the Western Fur Trade, 1807–1829." *Pacific Northwest Quarterly* 37 (1946).

Mattes, Merrill J. "Jackson Hole, Crossroads of the Western Fur Trade 1830–1840." *Pacific Northwest Quarterly* 39 (1948).

Shimkin, D. B. "Wind River Shoshone Ethnogeograhy." *University of California Anthropological Records.* Volume 5, Number. 4 (1947).

Simpson, William L. "Game Conditions in Wyoming." *Outdoor Life* 9 (1902).

Steward, Julian. "Some Observations of Shoshonean Distributions." *American Anthropolgist.* Vol. 41 (1938).

Steward, Julian. "Culture Element Distributions XXIII: Northern Gosiute Shoshoni." *University of California Anthropological Records.* Volume 4, Number 2 (1945).

"Thomas Moran's Journey to the Tetons in 1879," *Augustana Historical Society Publications,* Rock Island, IL: Augustana Historical Society Publications, No. 2 (1932): 7–12.

Thwaites, Ruben Gold. "Through Yellowstone and the Tetons-1903." *National Parks Magazine* 36 (March 1962).

"Tourism in Jackson Hole." *Midwest Review* 8 (July-August 1927).

Wright, Gary. "The Shoshonean Migration Problem." *Plains Anthropologist.* Vol. 23, No. 80 (1978).

Wright, Gary, Susan Bender, and Stuart Reeve. "High Country Adaptations." *Plains Anthropologist.* Vol. 25, No. 89 (1980):181–197.

Newspapers

Chicago Tribune
The Denver Post
Great Falls (MT) *Tribune*
Helena (MT) *Daily Herald*
Jackson's Hole Courier
Jackson Hole Guide
Jackson Hole News
Kemmerer (WY) *Camera*
(Denver) *Rocky Mountain News*

Published Government Documents

Barmore, William J., et al. *Natural Resources Management Plan, Grand Teton National Park.* Moose, WY: National Park Service, 1986.

Barlow, J. W. *Report of a Reconnaissance of the Basin of the Upper Yellowstone in 1871.* Washington, D.C.: 42nd Congress, 2nd Session, Senate Executive Document 66, 1872.

Barnowsky, Cathy W. "Late-Quaterery Vegetational and Climatic History of Grand Teton National Park and Vicinity." *Jackson Lake Archeological Project: The 1987 and 1988 Field Work.* Lincoln, NE: National Park Service, Midwest Archeological Center, 1991.

Connor, Melissa A., and Kenneth P. Cannon, Stephan E. Matz, Denise C. Carlevato, and Colleen Winchell. *Jackson Lake Archeological Project: The 1987–1988 Field Work.* Lincoln, NE: National Park Service, Midwest Archeological Center, 1991.

Connor, Melissa A., and Kenneth L. Pierce, Scott Lundstrom, and John M. Good. *Final Report on the Jackson Lake Archeological Project, Grand Teton National Park, Wyoming.* Lincoln, NE: National Park Service, Midwest Archeological Center, 1998.

Deaver, Sherri. *American Indian Religious Freedom Act (AIRFA) Background Data.* Billings, MT: Bureau of Land Management, 1986.

Dietrich, Leo H., et al. *Jackson Hole National Monument, Wyoming: A Compendium of Important Papers Covering Negotiation in the Establishment and Administration of the National Monument.* Four volumes. Washington, D.C.: Department of the Interior, ca. 1945–1950.

Dirks, Richard A. and Martner, Brooks E. *The Climate of Yellowstone and Grand Teton National Parks.* U.S. Department of the Interior: National Park Service, Occasional Paper Number 6, 1982.

Graham (Roy Eugene) Associates. "Bar BC Ranch Grand Teton National Park, Wyoming, Historic Structures Report." July 1, 1994.

"Gros Ventre Slide Geological Area." Pamphlet. U.S. Forest Service.

Hayden, F. V. *Sixth Annual Report of the U.S. Geological Survey of the Territories . . . for 1872.* Washington, D.C.: Government Printing Office, 1873.

Hayden, F. V. *Eleventh Annual Report of the United States Geological and Geographical Survey . . . for the Year 1877.* Washington, D.C.: Government Printing Office, 1879.

Hayden, F. V. *Twelfth Annual Report of the United States Geological and Geographical Survey . . . for the Year 1878.* Washington, D.C.: Government Printing Office, 1883.

Jones, William A. *Report upon a Reconnaissance of Northwestern Wyoming, including Yellowstone National Park, Made in the Summer of 1873.* Washington, D.C.: Government Printing Office, 1875.

Loendorf, Lawrence L. *Tracks Through Time: Prehistory of the Pinon Canyon Maneuver Site Southeastern Colorado.* Lincoln, NE: National Park Service, Midwest Archeological Center, 1995.

National Park Service. *Grand Teton National Park - Wyoming.* Washington, D.C.: Government Printing Office, 1935.

National Park Service. *Grand Teton National Park - Wyoming.* Washington, D.C.: Government Printing Office, 1936.

National Park Service. *Grand Teton National Park - Wyoming.* Washington, D.C.: Government Printing Office, 1941.

Parker, Jean Carlton. *Leek's Lodge: Historic Structures Report.* Denver: National Park Service, 1978.

Raynolds, William F. *Report on the Exploration of the Yellowstone River, by Brevet Brigadier General, W. F. Raynolds.* Washington D.C.: 40th Congress 1st Session, Senate Executive Document No. 77, 1868.

Reeve, Stuart. "Lizard Creek Sites (48TE700 and 48TE701): The Prehistoric Root Gathering Economy of Northern Grand Teton National Park, Northwest Wyoming." Lincoln, NE: National Park Service, Midwest Archeological Center, 1983.

Thompson, Erwin. *Maud Noble Cabin: Historic Structures Report.* Washington, D.C.: National Park Service, 1970.

U.S. Congress. House. Committee on Public Lands. "A Bill to Abolish the Jackson Hole National Monument . . .; Hearings on H.R. 2241." 78th Congress, 1st session, 1943.

U.S. Congress. Senate. "Hearings Before the Committee on Public Lands Pursuant to S. 237." 70th Congress, 2d session. Part 2, 1928.

U.S. Congress. Senate. "An Investigation of Proposed Enlargement of the Yellowstone and Grand Teton National Parks: Hearing on S. Res. 226." 72d Congress, 2nd session, 1934.

U.S. Congress. Senate. Subcommittee of Committee on Public Lands and Surveys. "A Resolution to Investigate the Questions of Enlarging Grand Teton National Park in Wyoming: Hearing on S. Res. 250." 75th Congress, 3rd session, 1938.

Young, Jack F. *Soil Survey of Teton County, Wyoming, Grand Teton National Park Area.* U.S. Department of Agriculture: Soil Conservation Service, 1982.

Unpublished Papers, Letters and Manuscripts

Allan, Esther B. "History of Teton National Forest." Unpublished manuscript. U.S. Forest Service, 1973.

Allan, K. C. "Alphabetical List of Jackson Hole Post Offices." K. C. Allan Collection, 7636. University of Wyoming, American Heritage Center.

Anderson, Emory J. "Reels Roll in Jackson Hole." Movie Files, Jackson Hole Historical Society and Museum.

Austin, Al. "Biography." No date. Acc. 1037. Jackson Hole Historical Society and Museum.

"The Bar BC Ranch, Rates, Outfit, Etc." Pamphlet in the Bosler Family Collection, 5850. University of Wyoming, American Heritage Center.

Bednar, Robert. "Postmodern Vistas, Landscapes, Photography, and Tourism in the Contemporary American West." Dissertation. University of Texas, Austin American Civilization Program, 1997.

"Big Wyoming Accommodations." Leaflet. Wyoming Travel Commission, ca. 1981.

"Buffalo Fork Canal Application for a Permit to Divert and Appropriate Water in the State of Wyoming." May 7, 1909. Water Resources Files, Grand Teton National Park.

"Calves Prices." File MM. Jackson Hole Historical Society and Museum.

Census of the United States, 1900, Wyoming, Uinta County, Enumeration District 65, Jackson Precinct, Elec. Dist. 15, Schedule 1, - Population, 9 sheets. State of Wyoming Archives, Museums, and Historical Department.

Coleman, John B. "Hunting Big Game in Jackson Hole." Jackson Hole, Folder 5 (W994-jk). Wyoming State Archives, Museums, and Historical Department.

Connor, Melissa A., and Raymond Kunselman. "Mobility, Settlement Patterns, and Obsidian Source Variation in Jackson Hole Wyoming." Paper Presented at the Second Biennial Rocky Mountain Anthropological Conference, 1995.

Daugherty, John. "Historical Overview of the Teton Science School." Unpublished manuscript. Grand Teton National Park, 1983.

Davis, A. N. G.L.O. Commissioner, Homestead Entry Ledger. Courtesy of Noble Gregory, Jr.

Doane, G. C. "Expedition of 1876–1877." Transcript of unpublished manuscript. Grand Teton National Park Library.

"Docket 9, Snake River Land Company, Protestant vs. Utah-Idaho Sugar Company." Water Resources Files, Grand Teton National Park.

"Dude Ranches Out West." Union Pacific Railroad, Pamphlet ca. 1927. Stephen Leek Collection, 3138, University of Wyoming-American Heritage Center.

"Dude Ranches Out West." Union Pacific Railroad, Pamphlet ca. 1930. Kenneth Chorley Papers, IV A3A, Box 21, File 176, Rockefeller Archive Center.

"Dude Ranches Out West." Union Pacific Railroad, ca. 1937. Wyoming State Archives, Museums, and Historical Department.

Fabian, Josephine. "The Lucas Place, 1914–1975." Unpublished manuscript. Grand Teton National Park.

Ferrin, Merrit. "The Elk Ranch." Transcript. Acc. 1455. Jackson Hole Historical Society and Museum.

"Fort Hall Ledger Book, 1837." Columbia River Fishing and Trading Company. Oregon Historical Society, Portland, Oregon.

"Jackson Hole, Wyoming Cattle Brands." File 13, Brands. Acc. 481. Jackson Hole Historical Society and Museum.

"Jackson Lake Dam." Determination of Eligibility, National Register of Historic Places. Wyoming State Archives, Museums, and Historical Department.

Langford, Nathaniel P. Handwritten manuscript of the first version of subsequent article in *Scribner's Monthly.* Library, Yellowstone National Park.

Love, Charles M. "An Archaeological Survey of the Jackson Hole Region, Wyoming. M.A. Thesis. Department of Anthropology, University of Wyoming, 1972.

Markham, John. "The Ashton-Moran Freight Road, 1910–1927." Unpublished manuscript. Pamphlet File. Grand Teton National Park Library.

Markham, John. "Biography of Mr. Joseph James Markham." Unpublished manuscript. Biographical Files. Wyoming State Archives, Museums, and Historical Department.

Markham, John. "Cattle Drives." Unpublished manuscript. Wyoming State Archives, Museums, and Historical Department.

Markham, John. "The Hatchet and Elk Ranches." Unpublished manuscript. State of Wyoming Archives, Museums, and Historical Department.

Markham, John. "The Temporary Jackson Lake Dam." Unpublished manuscript. Wyoming State Archives, Museums, and Historical Department.

McBride, Maggie. "My Diary, 1896." Unpublished manuscript. Jackson Hole Historical Society and Museum Files.

McKeel, William L. "An Interdisciplinary Overview of the Water Resources of Grand Teton National Park." Unpublished thesis. Laramie: University of Wyoming, 1972.

McKinstry, Linda. "Memoir." Unpublished manuscript. Subject file, Wyoming-Jackson Hole (W994-JH). University of Wyoming-American Heritage Center.

Merkel, William L. "Water Rights in Grand Teton National Park with a Tabulation of Adjudicated Water Rights." Unpublished manuscript. No date. Grand Teton National Park.

Moody, E. N. "Some Recollections of the Formation and Early History of Teton County." Transcript of speech. November 9, 1968. File H. Acc. 305. Jackson Hole Historical Society and Museum.

Moran, Thomas. Field Notebook, Aug. 22–29, 1879. MS Catalogue No. 1753, accession no. 114, History File, Grand Teton National Park Headquarters, Moose, Wyoming.

Murie, Donald. Letter to Margaret E. Murie, April 17, 1982.

Rosencrans, Rudolph. "Diary." K. C. Allan Collection, 7636. University of Wyoming-American Heritage Center.

Ryter, George. Letter to Rose Crabtree. March 25, 1924. Ms. 872. Wyoming State Archives Museums, and Historical Department.

Schenck, Marian. Letter to John Daugherty, September 4, 1986.

Schoen, James R. "High Altitude Site Locations in the Bridger, Gros Ventre and Teton Wilderness." Paper presented at the Third Biennial Rocky Mountain Anthropological Conference, September 18–21, 1995, Bozeman, Montana.

"Spread Creek Canal Application for a Permit to Divert and Appropriate Water in the State of Wyoming."

December 23, 1912. Water Resources Files, Grand Teton National Park.

Tuttle, Mae. Letter to Mrs. Cora Barber. September 5, 1951. Jackson Hole Historical Society and Museum.

"Twin Lakes Reservoir and Supply Ditch." Water Resources Files, Grand Teton National Park.

U.S. Reclamation Service. "Jackson Lake Reservoir Highline Traverse, Lowline Traverse, and Section Ties, 1909." Survey Books. 8 Vols. Grand Teton National Park Collections.

U.S. Reclamation Service. "Reconnaissance Books." Volumes 2–4, 1902. Grand Teton National Park Collections.

Van DerVeer, Nellie. "An Old Time Christmas in Jackson Hole." WPA Subject File 1321. Wyoming State Archives, Museums, and Historical Department.

Van DerVeer, Nellie. "Sports and Recreation." WPA Subject File 1325. Wyoming State Archives, Museums, and Historical Department.

Van DerVeer, Nellie. "Teton County - Agriculture and Industry." Unpublished manuscript. WPA File 1327. Wyoming State Archives, Museums, and Historical Department.

Van DerVeer, Nellie. "Teton County - General." WPA Subject File 1336. Wyoming State Archives, Museums, and Historical Department.

Van DerVeer, Nellie. "Teton County - Historical Lore." Unpublished manuscript. Subject File 1321. Wyoming State Archives, Museums, and Historical Department.

Van DerVeer, Nellie. "Teton County - Pioneer Stories." Unpublished manuscript. WPA Subject File 1328. Wyoming State Archives, Museums, and Historical Department.

Van DerVeer, Nellie. "Teton County - Towns." WPA Subject File 1322. Wyoming State Archives, Museums, and Historical Department.

Van DerVeer, Nellie. "Wyoming Folklore and Customs, Teton County - Dude Ranches." WPA Subject File 1448. Wyoming State Archives, Museums, and Historical Department.

Woods, C. N. "Thirty-seven Years in the Forest Service." No date. No publisher. Pamphlet File, Grand Teton National Park.

Wright, Agnes Spring. "Early Settlement in Jackson Hole." File W994;K. No date. University of Wyoming, American Heritage Center.

Oral History

Byrd, Jo Ann. "Last of Old West Series." Teton County Library, Jackson, Wyoming. Typed Transcripts: Louise Turner Bertschy, #1; Eva Topping Briggs, #2; Harry Brown, #3; Phylis Brown, #4; Jim Budge, #5; Walt Callahan, #6; Fran Carmichael, #7; Ada Clark, #8; Ellen Dornan, #10; Frank Galey, #12; Noble Gregory, #13; Lamar Crandall Hardeman, #15; Gretchen Huff Francis, #16; Don and Gladys Kent, #18; Bob Krannenberg, #19; Pearl McClary, #25; Clark Moulton, #27; Almer Nelson, #30; Charlie Peterson, #31; Parthenia Stinnett, #38; Bill Tanner, #39; and Joella Taylor, #40.

Coulter, Henry. Interview by Renny Jackson, September 23, 1988.

Cullinane, Gerlald B. Member of 87th Mountain Infantry Regiment, F Company, 10th Mountain Division. Interview by Renny Jackson, December 6, 1997.

Dilley, William. Interview by Horace Albright, September 12, 1967. Transcript. Grand Teton National Park.

Durrance, Jack. Interview by Renny Jackson, September 23, 1988.

Frazier, Walt. Interview by William H. Goetzmann, June 25,1997.

Fryxell, F.M. Interview by John Daugherty, September 14, 1983. Tape. Grand Teton National Park.

Galey, Frank. Interview by John Daugherty, February 3, 1984. Notes.

Haraden, Robert. Interview by Horace Albright, September 12, 1967. Transcript. Grand Teton National Park.

Jump, Ethel. Interview. Transcript 1966, Jackson Hole Historical Society and Museum.

Lawrence, W. C. "Slim." Interview by John Daugherty, July 3, 1980. Notes.

Lesher, Marvell. Interview by John Daugherty, September 2, 1982. Tape. Grand Teton National Park.

Murie, Margaret. Interview by John Daugherty, February 13, 1984. Tape. Grand Teton National Park Library.

Petzoldt, Paul. Interview by John Daugherty, December 10, 1982.

Riniker, Martha Davis. Interview. Transcript. File R. Jackson Hole Historical Society and Museum.

Talbot, Eleanor. Interview by John Daugherty, August 1983. Notes.

Grand Teton National Park Records and Files

Building Maintenance Files
Collections Accessions Files
Concessions Files
Land Files
Library Collections
Museum Collections
Superintendent's Annual Reports, 1929–1935

Superintendent's Monthly Reports, November 1929–January 1932, January 1936-June 1937
Superintendent's Monthly Reports, December 1953–December 1959. Box 74399, Federal Records Center, Denver, Colorado
Water Resources Files

Collections

Albright (Horace M.) Papers, 1923–1929. Yellowstone Archives. Yellowstone National Park.
Allan (Karl C. "Sunny") Collection, 7636. University of Wyoming-American Heritage Center.
Barry (J. Neilson) Collection. Grand Teton National Park Library.
Burlingame (Merrill G.). Special Collections 1878–1988, H-1044, H-1045, H-1236, H-1241, H-1242, H-1042. Montana Historical Society, Helena, Montana
Burt (Nathaniel) Collection, 665. University of Wyoming-American Heritage Center.
Chorley (Kenneth) Papers, IV 3A3. Rockefeller Archive Center, Pocantico Hills, New York.
Fabian (Harold P.) Papers. IV 3A7. Rockefeller Archive Center, Pocantico Hills, New York.
Fabian (Harold and Josephine) Collection. Grand Teton National Park.
Fryxell (Fritiof) Collection, 1638. University of Wyoming-American Heritage Center.
Hayden (Elizabeth Wied) Collection. Jackson Hole Historical Society and Museum.
Leek (Stephen N.) Collection, 3138. University of Wyoming-American Heritage Center.
Markham (John) Papers, 934. Jackson Hole Historical Society and Museum.
Mattes (Merril J.) Collection, 120. University of Wyoming-American Heritage Center.
Murie (Adolph) Collection, 8004. University of Wyoming-American Heritage Center.
Murie (Olaus and Margaret) Collection, 1221. University of Wyoming-American Heritage Center.
National Archives, Record Group 49, "Records of the Bureau of Land Management." Homestead Patents.
Records. Office of the Teton County Clerk and Recorder. Jackson, Wyoming.
Roundy (Charles) Collection, 3550. University of Wyoming-American Heritage Center.

Photographs

"Before and After Pictures of Jackson Hole National Monument." Department of the Interior, National Park Service, 1945.
Bicentennial Photograph Collection. Jackson Hole Historical Society and Museum. Teton County Library.
Main Lodge, Flying V Ranch. Photograph. Courtesy of Don and Gladys Kent.
Menor's Ferry Photograph Collection. Harold and Josephine Fabian Collection. Grand Teton National Park.
National Archives.
Photograph Files, Grand Teton National Park.
Photograph Files, Jackson Hole Historical Society and Museum.
Stimson, J. E. Photograph Collection. Wyoming State Archives, Museums, and Historical Department.
U.S. Geological Survey Library.

Maps

Carlisle, C. C. "Map of Teton Irrigation Project." June 23–July 6, 1912 and October 29–November 4, 1912. Grand Teton National Park Water Resources Files.
Jackson Hole Platbook, Snake River Land Company. Harold and Josephine Fabian Collection. Grand Teton National Park Library.
Note: The following maps can be found in the Jackson Hole Platbook or the Office of the Teton County Clerk and Recorder.
Blout and Artist. Township lines, Subdivisions, and Meanders. Township 44 North, Range 114 West, 6th Principal Meridian. Surveyed June 30–July 19, 1902.
Blout and Artist. Township Lines, Subdivisions, and Meanders. Township 45 North, Range 114 West, 6th Principal Meridian. Surveyed June 25–July 6, 1893.
Blout and Artist. Resurvey Township Lines, Subdivision, and Meanders. Township 45 North, Range 113 West, 6th Principal Meridian. Surveyed July 21–August 20, 1902.
Owen, W. O. East and South Township Lines. Township 43 North, Range 116 West, 6th Principal Meridian. Surveyed October 9, 1892, June 9, 1893.
Owen, W. O. East Boundary Township Line. Blout and Artist. Resurvey 11th std parallel. Davis, A.D. Resurvey East and South Boundary, Meanders and Subdivisions. Township 44 North, Range 116 West, 6th Principal Meridian. Surveyed June 15, 1893. Septem-

ber 24, 1902. September 14–18, 1916. October 7–16, 1916.

Owen, W. O. Township Lines and Subdivisions. Township 41 North, Range 116 West, 6th Principal Meridian. Surveyed October 6–19, 1892.

Owen, W. O. Township Lines and Subdivisions. Township 42 North, Range 116 West, 6th Principal Meridian. Surveyed May 23–30, 1893.

Owen, W. O. Township Lines and Subdivisions. Township 42 North, Range 115 West, 6th Principal Meridian. Surveyed June 1–5, 1893.

Owen, W. O. Township Lines, Subdivisions, and Meanders. Township 43 North, Range 115 West, 6th Principal Meridian. Surveyed June 10–15, 1893.

Owen, W. O. Township Lines and Subdivisions. Township 44 North, Range 115 West, 6th Principal Meridian. Surveyed June 17–24, 1893.

U.S. Geological Survey. *Grand Teton Quadrangle.* 1901.

U.S. Geological Survey. *Gros Ventre Quadrangle.* 1910. Reprinted 1949.

U.S. Geological Survey. *Mt. Leidy Quadrangle.* 1902.

U.S. Geological Survey. *Shoshone Quadrangle.* 1907. Reprint, 1911.

Index

Made in United States
North Haven, CT
07 March 2023

33683870R00233